AKBAR

Also by Ira Mukhoty

Daughters of the Sun: Empresses, Queens and Begums of the Mughal Empire
Heroines: Powerful Indian Women of Myth and History

AKBAR
THE GREAT MUGHAL

IRA MUKHOTY

ALEPH BOOK COMPANY
An independent publishing firm
promoted by Rupa Publications India

First published in India in 2020
by Aleph Book Company
7/16 Ansari Road, Daryaganj
New Delhi 110 002

Copyright © Ira Mukhoty 2020
The Image Credits on pp. 477–80 constitute an extension of the copyright page.

All rights reserved.

The author has asserted her moral rights.

The views and opinions expressed in this book are the author's own and the facts are as reported by her, which have been verified to the extent possible, and the publisher is not in any way liable for the same.

The publisher has used its best endeavours to ensure that URLs for external websites referred to in this book are correct and active at the time of going to press. However, the publisher has no responsibility for the websites and can make no guarantee that a site will remain live or that the content is or will remain appropriate.

No part of this publication may be reproduced, transmitted, or stored in a retrieval system, in any form or by any means, without permission in writing from Aleph Book Company.

ISBN: 978-93-89836-04-2

3 5 7 9 10 8 6 4 2

Printed at Thomson Press India Ltd, Faridabad

This book is sold subject to the condition that it shall not, by way of trade or otherwise, be lent, resold, hired out, or otherwise circulated without the publisher's prior consent in any form of binding or cover other than that in which it is published.

For Mohit

CONTENTS

Cast of Characters	xi
Select Chronology of Major Events	xx
Introduction	xxv

Part 1: The Prince and His Regents (1526–1561)

A Conqueror and a Refugee Prince	3
Bride in the Desert	16
The Afghan, the Hindu, and the Timurid	31
While the Padshah Hunted	42
Timurid Matriarchs and their Colossal Dreams	51

Part 2: The Young Padshah (1561–1569)

Of One Dancing Girl and Then Two More	63
Men of the Sword and the Pen	70
A Sufi Shrine, a Rajput Princess, and a Notorious Murder	75
My Soul Was Seized with Exceeding Sorrow	82
Books for a Padshah	90
Durgavati, Rani of the Gonds	95
Uzbek Clansmen and a King in the North	99
Legends of Rajasthan	115

Part 3: The World is a Bridge (1569–1578)

The Making of a Complicated Harem	127
The Firangis and the Salt Sea	138
The Gilded Princes	154
City of Dreams	164
Duhu Deen Ko Sahib	171
Lord of the Storm	177
The Man Who Set the World on Fire	183
The Haramsara and the Hajj	195
The Saffron Fields	202
A Light Divine	210

Part 4: The Year of the Lion (1579–1585)

Padshah-i Islam	225
The Truth Is an Inhabitant of Every Place	232
Allahu Akbar	242
The Slow March to Kabul	252
The Lion of God	266
Universal Civility	278
The Book of War	287
A Shirazi Visitor from the Deccan	299
Other Worshippers of God	306
Akbar and Birbal	314

Part 5: Paradise on Earth (1585–1598)

A Rajput in the Snow	323
The Dar al-Sultanat	335
The Memory-Keepers	343
The Garden of Perpetual Spring	352
Shri Maharajadhiraja Maharaja of the Mughal Empire	361
Poison in Paradise	370
Mirza Aziz Koka in Mecca	378
The Road to the Deccan	386
The Prince, the Painter, and the Priests	399
From Bibi to Sultan	406

Part 6: Crouching Lion, Rising Sun (1598–1605)

The Last Campaign	413
Frontier Lands	421
The Art of Rebellion	427
An Assassination	439
An Englishman at the Mughal Court	449
Death of an Emperor	458
Rising Son	465
Acknowledgements	475
Image Credits	477
Notes	481
Bibliography	523
Index	533

AKBAR'S EMPIRE

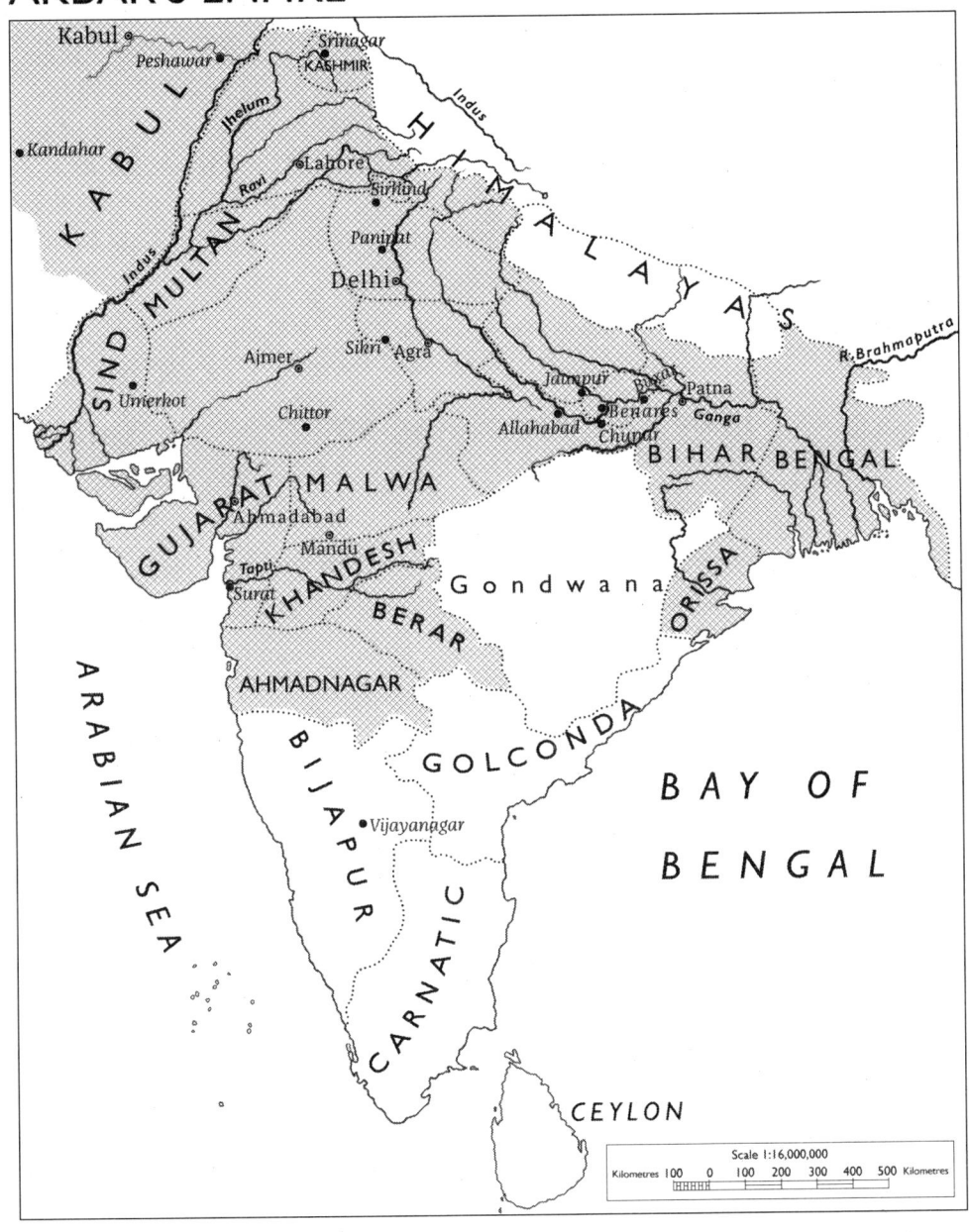

This map has been prepared in adherence to the 'Guidelines for acquiring and producing Geospatial Data and Geospatial Data Services including Maps' published vide DST F.No.SM/25/02/2020 (Part-I) dated 15th February, 2021.

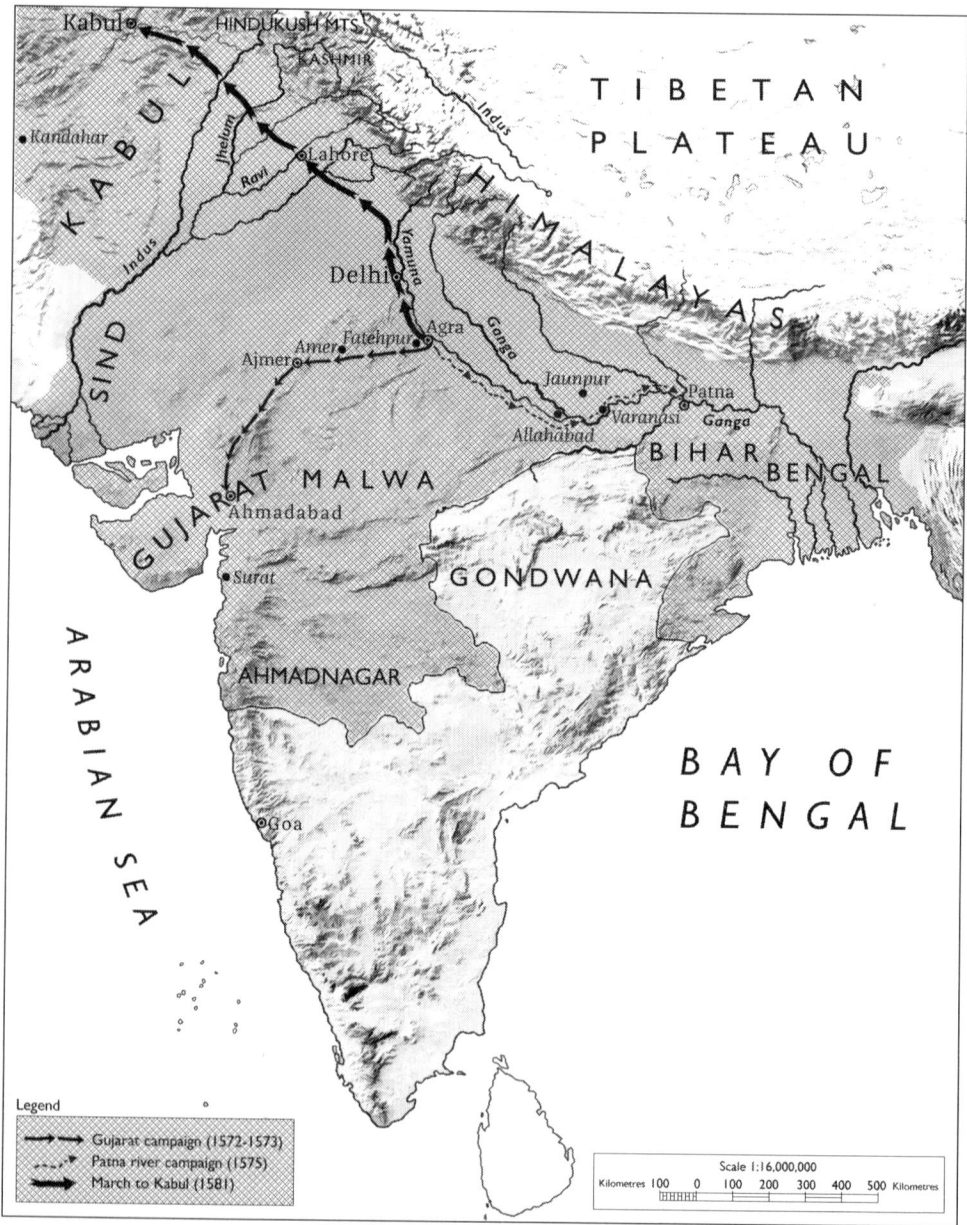

CAST OF CHARACTERS

MUGHAL FOREBEARS

Chenghiz Khan (1162–1227): Also known as Genghis Khan, founder of the Mongol Empire, which became the largest contiguous empire in the world.

Timur (1336–1405): Also known as Tamarlane, Timur-i Lang (Timur the Lame). Founder of the Timurid Empire in and around Central Asia. He was the great-great-great-grandfather of Babur.

THE MUGHALS

Babur (1483–1530): Founder and first Padshah of the Mughal Empire, Akbar's grandfather. A direct descendant of Timur.

Bairam Khan (1501–1561): Persian nobleman from the time of Humayun. Was wakil-e-saltanat and khankhanan during Akbar's reign. Talented general who worked tirelessly to protect the empire when Akbar became Padshah at the age of thirteen. As Akbar began to take more interest in the running of his empire, he began to chafe under Bairam Khan's guardianship and had him dismissed in 1560. He was assassinated en route to Mecca.

Munim Khan (d. 1575): Chaghatai nobleman from the time of Humayun. Ataliq of Akbar. Influential after the defeat of Bairam Khan, and was made khankhanan for a while. Defeated Daud Khan Afghan, and later died in Bengal.

Humayun (1508–1556): Son of Babur, second of the Great Mughals of India, Akbar's father. Had to fight his three brothers, Kamran, Askari, and Hindal, as well as Sher Shah Sur, when he became Padshah of Hindustan. Lost the empire inherited from Babur, the founder of the Mughal Empire, and went into exile to Persia. Eventually reclaimed India but died within six months of returning to power, falling down the stairs of his library.

Bega Begum (1511–1582): Senior wife of Humayun, known as Haji Begum after she completed the hajj. Remained in Delhi after the death of Humayun and supervised the building of Humayun's tomb.

Gulbadan (1523–1603): Daughter of Babur and sister of Humayun. Accompanied Akbar to Hindustan and lived a long and adventurous life, performing a women-only hajj that lasted seven years. Greatly loved and admired by Akbar. Was asked by Akbar to write an account of her brother's life. This account was the first one by a Mughal woman and gave an unprecedented look into the Mughal harem.

Hamida Banu Begum (1527–1604): Persian wife of Humayun and mother of Akbar. Very influential, especially once Akbar became Padshah at the age of thirteen. Was given the title Maryam Makani.

Maham Anaga (d. 1562): Akbar's milk mother, Adham Khan's mother. Participated in the fall from power of Bairam Khan. Was considered effective 'ruler' of Hindustan between 1560 and her death in 1562.

Adham Khan (1531–1562): Milk brother of Akbar, son of Maham Anaga. Resented the curtailing of his powers by Akbar. Was killed on Akbar's orders for having murdered Shamsuddin Ataka Khan.

Salima Sultan Begum (1539–1612): Granddaughter of Babur and wife of Bairam Khan. Akbar married her after Bairam Khan was killed. Influential, erudite, and a keen collector of books. Greatly respected by her stepson Salim.

Mirza Muhammad Hakim (1553–1585): Son of Humayun and Mahchuchak Begum, half-brother of Akbar. Held the appanage of Kabul. Tried to declare himself the legitimate Timurid heir of Humayun in the 1580s, with the support of the rebellious Uzbeks. Positioned himself as an orthodox Sunni ruler as opposed to Akbar's eclectic religious views. Was defeated by Akbar in 1582 and died of alcoholism in 1585.

Shamsuddin Muhammad Ataka Khan Ghaznavi (d. 1562): Foster father of Akbar and husband of Jiji Anaga. Held the high post of khankhanan. Part of the large Ataka Khail. Became powerful after the fall of Bairam Khan. Was murdered by Adham Khan.

Jiji Anaga (d. 1600): Milk mother of Akbar, mother of Aziz Koka, wife of Shamsuddin Ataka. Her large and influential family were collectively known as the Ataka Khail.

Mirza Aziz Koka (1542–1624): Milk brother of Akbar, titled khan azam or azam khan. Favourite of Akbar's due to the Padshah's love for his mother, Jiji Anaga. An orthodox Muslim man, initially critical of Akbar's religious policies. Went to Mecca because he was angry with Akbar but returned chastised and became a disciple of Akbar's sulh kul. Survived into Jahangir's reign.

Abdur Rahim (1556–1627): Son of Bairam Khan and his Mewati wife. Distinguished courtier and khankhanan at Akbar's court, ataliq to Salim, accomplished poet, and a great patron of poetry and literature. Was sent to the Deccan on campaigns with Murad, then Daniyal. Akbar gave him the title 'Mirza Khan'.

Salim (1569–1627): Akbar's eldest son, called Shaikhu Baba by his father. Initially the chosen heir, and favoured by Akbar. Always had the support of the powerful women of the Mughal harem such as Salima Sultan Begum, Hamida Banu, and Gulbadan. Gradually started gathering his own coterie of disaffected noblemen as Akbar began favouring his other sons and grandsons. Rebelled in 1600 and set up an independent court at Allahabad. Forgiven by Akbar, he became Padshah Jahangir upon the death of his father in 1605.

Murad (1570–1599): Akbar's son. Sent to the Deccan to subdue Ahmadnagar. Died of alcoholism.

Daniyal (1572–1605): Akbar's son, died of alcoholism.

Khusrau (1587–1622): Salim and Man Bai's son. Supported by an alliance of Aziz Koka and Man Singh to oppose Salim's claim to the throne.

Khurram (1592–1666): Salim and Jagat Gosain's son. Akbar's favourite grandson. The future Padshah Shah Jahan.

THE RAJPUTS

Raja Bharmal Kachhwaha (1498–1574): Ruler of Amer, father of Harkha Bai. Arguably changed the fortunes of the Kachhwahas by marrying a daughter to Akbar. Officer at the Mughal court.

Raja Bhagwant Das (1527–1589): Son of Raja Bharmal. Became a high mansabdar and was appointed guardian of the harem at the end of his life.

Harkha Bai Kachhwaha (1542–1623): Akbar's first Rajput wife, mother of Salim, daughter of Raja Bharmal, and aunt of Raja Man Singh. Brought Rajput traditions into the Mughal harem. Survived Akbar and was known by her title Maryam uz Zamani.

Kuar (later Raja) Man Singh (1550–1614): Son of Bhagwant Das. A favourite of Akbar's, who called him farzand (son). Became one of the highest noblemen of the empire, with a mansab of 7,000. Defeated Rana Pratap at the Battle of Haldighati. Instrumental in subduing Bengal, Orissa, and Bihar. Great patron of architecture—built the Govardhan Temple in Mathura and Rohtas Fort in Bihar.

Man Bai (1570–1604): Daughter of Bhagwant Das. Named Shah Begum after her marriage to Prince Salim. Khusrau's mother.

COURTIERS

Tansen (1500–1586): Musician from Gwalior who was called to Akbar's court. Akbar's favourite musician, composer of many lyrics in Brajbhasha.

Shaikh Mubarak (1505-1593): Father of Abu'l Fazl and Faizi. A man of great learning and religiosity. Initially an orthodox theologian, he later became attracted to Sufism and the ideas of the Mahdavis. Joined Akbar's court in 1573 and was instrumental in introducing the Padshah to the ideas of scholar and philosopher Ibn Arabi, amongst others.

Raja Birbal (1528–1586): Hindu courtier and great favourite of Akbar. Often distinguished by personal marks of favour by Akbar. A talented poet, he held the title Kavi Rai. Died during the Yusufzai campaign in 1586, and was deeply mourned by the Padshah. The only Hindu to become a disciple of Akbar's sulh kul.

Abd al-Qadir Badauni (1540–1605): Mughal courtier and orthodox Sunni Muslim, Badauni was highly disapproving of Akbar's religious policies and wrote a covert, critical biography of Akbar's reign. He was also the most prolific translator of Akbar's ateliers, participating in the translation of various works from Sanskrit to Persian, including the Mahabharat and the Ramayan.

Abu'l Fazl (1551–1602): Son of Shaikh Mubarak, Abu'l Fazl was a brilliant scholar educated primarily by his father. He joined Akbar's court in 1574 and participated in the ibadat khana discussions where he used his great learning to humiliate the ulema. He wrote the *Akbarnama* and the *Ain-i Akbari*, in which he detailed his ideas, including the Ibn Arabi notion of the ruler as a perfect man. His influence on Akbar was resented by many, including by Akbar's son, Salim, who had him assassinated by Bir Singh Deo.

Abu'l Faiz (1547–1595): Son of Shaikh Mubarak and elder brother of Abu'l Fazl. Known by his pen name Faizi. A Persian poet and a scholar, he became poet laureate of Akbar's court in 1588, and was appointed tutor to Akbar's sons.

Raja Todar Mal (d. 1589): Supremely talented Hindu finance minister. Brought in many changes to the revenue collection of the state, making it more efficient and profitable.

Fath Allah Shirazi: A learned Shia scholar from Iran, who first served at the court of Ali Adil Shah of Bijapur before joining Akbar's court. An erudite and knowledgeable man, he was a great favourite of Akbar's and was instrumental in introducing financial reforms in revenue collection alongside Raja Todar Mal. He was named joint wazir along with the raja.

OPPONENTS AND REBELS

Abdullah Khan Uzbek: Uzbek clansman, rebelled against Akbar.

Ali Quli Khan Uzbek and **Bahadur Khan Uzbek:** Brothers who came to Hindustan in the train of Humayun. Rebelled against Akbar and were defeated.

Bahadur Shah: Ruler of Khandesh from the Faruqui dynasty. Refused to submit to the Mughal forces when they advanced on Khandesh. Resisted at Asirgarh fortress where he was besieged for almost a year by Akbar's forces. Surrendered to Akbar in 1600 and died in captivity.

Baz Bahadur: Sultan of Malwa, Sur dynasty. Well known as a connoisseur of music and poetry. Paramour of Roopmati. Was defeated by the Mughals, and later incorporated into the empire.

Bir Singh Deo: Younger son of Raja Madhukar Bundela of Orchha. Rebelled against the naming of his elder brother to the gaddi of Orchha upon the death of his father. Sought Prince Salim's help, who in turn asked him to assassinate Abu'l Fazl. Salim made Bir Singh Deo Raja of Orchha after he became Padshah Jahangir.

Chand Sultan: Born into the Nizam Shahi dynasty of Ahmadnagar, Chand Sultan married the sultan of Bijapur, Ali Adil Shah. After the death of her husband, ruled as regent of Bijapur before returning to Ahmadnagar, to rule as regent in her hometown. She tried to create an alliance to face the Mughal forces but was eventually murdered by her own disaffected noblemen.

Rani Durgavati: Queen of Gondwana. Ruled as regent for her minor son for many years. Defeated by the Mughals in battle and committed suicide.

Hemu: Styled Raja Vikramaditya, prime minister of Adil Shah Sur. Mounted a feisty challenge for the throne of Delhi. Captured after the Second Battle of Panipat. Killed by Bairam Khan and possibly Akbar.

Rana Pratap: Ruler of Mewar. Was defeated by Mughal forces led by Kuar Man Singh at the Battle of Haldighati. Resisted the Mughals till the end of his life.

JESUITS

Anthony Monserrate and **Rudolf Acquaviva:** Part of the First Jesuit Mission. They tried for many years to convert Akbar to Christianity, and finally left disappointed. They left behind their observations on Akbar and the Mughal court and influenced the art of Hindustan.

THE CLERGY (ULEMA)

Maulana Abdullah Sultanpuri: Shaikh al-Islam, makhdum ul-mulk. Humiliated during the ibadat khana discussions. Supported Mirza Hakim's rebellion and was banished to Mecca by Akbar.

Shaikh Abd un-Nabi: Sadr us-sudur. Akbar was initially in thrall to the sadr, later disenchanted by his mediocrity. He supported Mirza Hakim's rebellion and was banished to Mecca by Akbar.

Shaikh Mustafa Gujarati: A Mahdavi whose dairah was plundered during the Gujarat campaign. He was taken to Ahmedabad where he was tortured and questioned by the Mughal courtiers.

SOME IMPORTANT PAINTERS

Abd al-Samad: Persian miniature artist who came to Hindustan at Humayun's behest. Was made master of the mint by Akbar and oversaw the creation of the *Hamzanama*.

Abu'l Hasan: Son of Aqa Riza, favourite artist of Padshah Jahangir.

Aqa Riza: Persian artist. Joined Akbar's atelier, then Salim's rebel court where he was responsible for the Persianate style of the early years of Salim's patronage.

Basawan: Hindu painter in Akbar's atelier.

Daswant: Palanquin-bearer, then painter at Akbar's court. Committed suicide.

Farrukh Beg: Persian painter. First with Mirza Hakim at Kabul, then Akbar, then Bijapur, at the court of Ibrahim Adil Shah II, then with Jahangir.

Govardhan: Painter at Akbar and Jahangir's court. Distinctive palette of gold, dusty whites.

Manohar: Son of Basawan, painter at the courts of Akbar and later Jahangir.

Mansur: Painter at Akbar's and Jahangir's courts. Jahangir's favourite animalier.

Mir Sayyid Ali: Persian miniature artist who came to Hindustan at Humayun's behest.

Mohammad Sharif: Son of Abd al-Samad; sent by Akbar to Salim as an ambassador but joined Salim's rebel court.

Akbar's Marital Links with the Ataka Khail

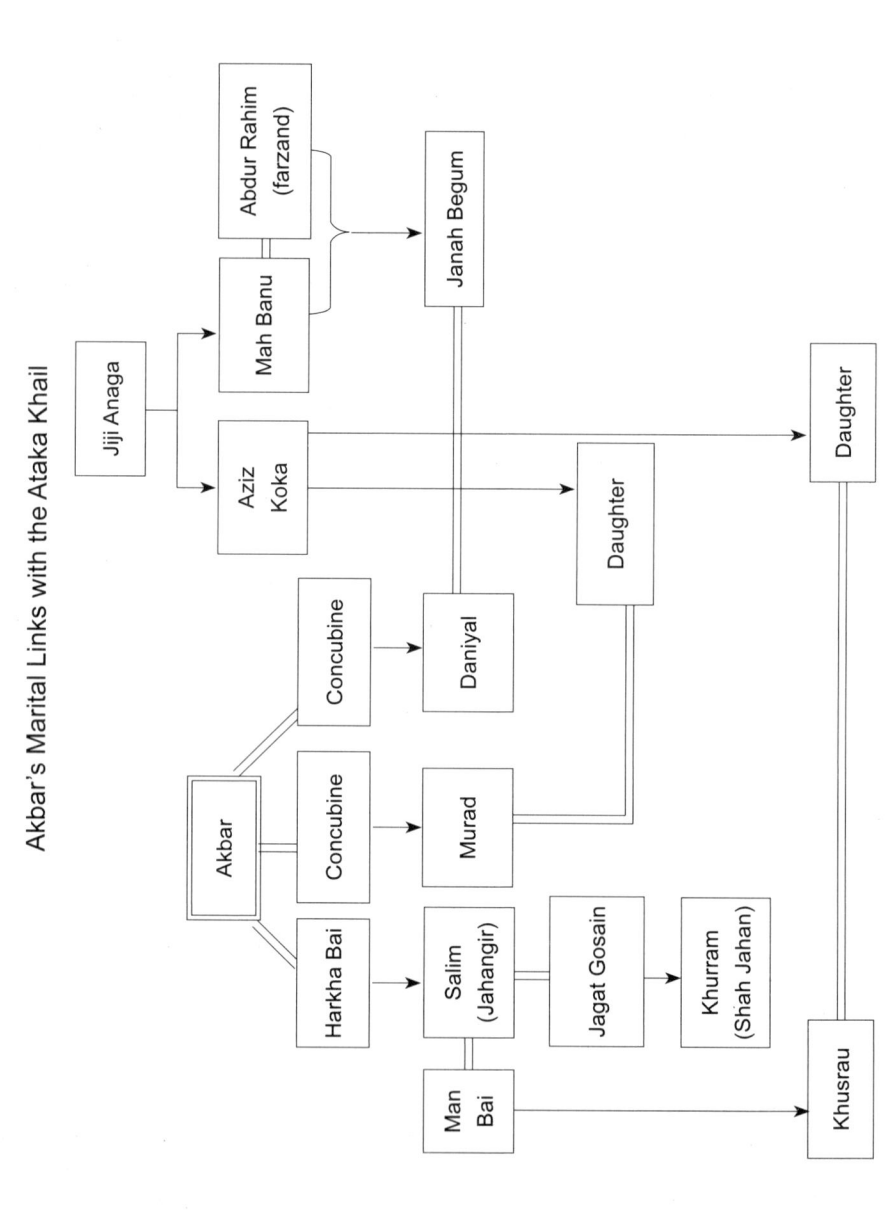

Some of Akbar's and Salim's Rajput Alliances

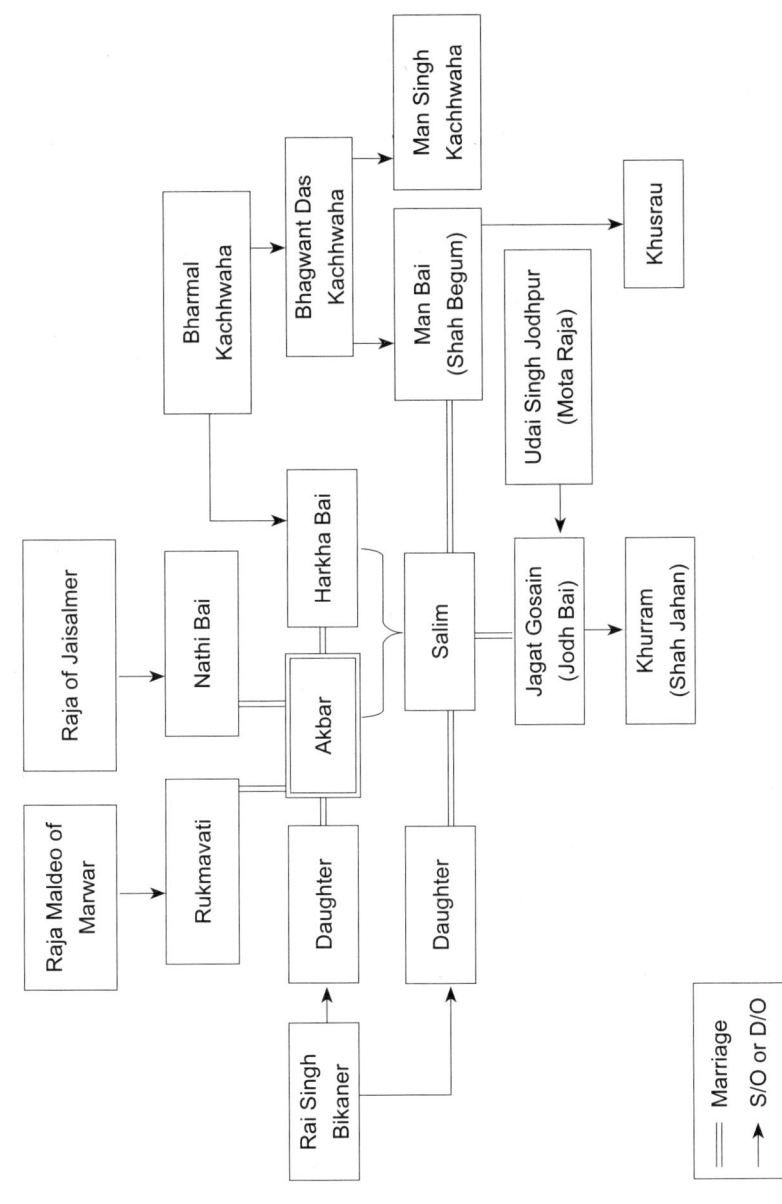

SELECT CHRONOLOGY OF MAJOR EVENTS

1504: Babur conquers Kabul and establishes his capital there.

1526: First Battle of Panipat. Babur defeats the Lodis. Ibrahim Lodi is killed in battle.

1530: Babur dies after appointing his eldest son, Humayun, as his heir. Humayun ascends the throne.

1539: Battle of Chausa between Humayun and Sher Shah Sur. The Sur army emerges victorious over the Mughals.

1540: Sher Shah Sur establishes the Sur Empire.

1541: Humayun marries Hamida Banu Begum.

15 October 1542: Hamida Banu gives birth to Akbar, future Padshah of Hindustan, at Umerkot, in the palace of Rana Prasad. His milk mothers include Maham Anaga and Jiji Anaga.

July 1543: Humayun marches towards Kandahar, loses Hindustan. Flees to Safavid Persia with Hamida Banu Begum (Maryam Makani).

1543–44: Akbar is left behind in Kandahar in the care of Askari's wife, Sultanam Begum.

1544: Humayun marches back towards Kandahar. Akbar is sent back to Kabul, where he is reunited with the elderly Khanzada Begum, elder sister of Babur.

1545: Sher Shah Sur dies.

1553: Kamran is captured and blinded. He dies three years later in Mecca.

1553: Muhammad Hakim, or Mirza Hakim, is born to Humayun's new wife, Mah-chuchak Begum. A few months later, Akbar is given a new ataliq, Munim Khan.

23 July 1555: Sikandar Shah is defeated at the Battle of Sirhind and Humayun reconquers Hindustan.

January 1556: Death of Humayun.

14 February 1556: The thirteen-year-old Akbar is proclaimed Padshah

Ghazi of Hindustan.

October 1556: Hemu, a Sur general, takes over Delhi.

November 1556: Second Battle of Panipat between Hemu and the forces of Akbar. The Afghan army is defeated and Hemu is beheaded by Bairam Khan. Mughal forces enter Delhi and Agra.

1558: Royal begums arrive in India from Kabul.

1560: Akbar dismisses Bairam Khan.

1560: Mughal forces, under the command of Adham Khan, Maham Anaga's son, defeat the forces of Baz Bahadur and capture Malwa with immense brutality.

January 1562: Akbar visits the dargah of Khwaja Muinuddin Chishti in Ajmer.

1562: Akbar uses Chingizid yassa law in order to marry into the shaikhzada families. Assassination attempt on Akbar by a freed slave from Ajmer. Arrow strikes Akbar on the shoulder.

1562: Akbar abolishes the jiziya tax.

1562: Akbar commissions the *Hamzanama* which is finally completed in 1577.

1562: Akbar is married to Harkha Bai, daughter of Raja Bharmal of the Kachhwaha Rajputs in Amer, later known as Maryam uz Zamani (popularly but mistakenly known as Jodha Bai). Akbar meets twelve-year-old Man Singh for the first time.

February 1568: After a brutal four-month siege of Chittor, Akbar declares it a sarkar of the Mughal Empire and places it in the charge of Asaf Khan.

December 1568: The fort of Ranthambore is besieged by the Mughal forces and conquered. The Baghela Rajputs, Rathores of Bikaner, and the Bhatis of Jaisalmer also submit to the Padshah and become part of the Mughal Empire.

31 August 1569: A son is born to Harkha Bai and Akbar names the child Salim. The future Padshah Jahangir.

January 1570: Akbar sets off on foot from Agra to fulfil a vow he had made to walk to the Ajmer shrine.

November 1570: Rao Kalyanmal of Bikaner and his heir, Kuar Rai

Singh, are brought into the Mughal fold. The Har Raj of Jaisalmer submits to Akbar.

1571: Akbar relocates to Fatehpur Sikri.

1572: Annexation of Gujarat, the first campaign. Ahmedabad is taken without a fight from Itimad Khan Gujarati.

1572: Rana Pratap ascends the gaddi of Mewar.

23 December 1572: The mirzas are defeated at Sarnal.

January 1573: Surat is besieged by the Mughal forces. Akbar convinces the Portuguese to allow the imperial boats to use the ports for pilgrim journeys.

3 June 1573: Akbar returns to Agra after his triumphs.

23 August 1573: Second campaign to Gujarat, after Ikhtiyar ul-Mulk and Muhammad Husain Mirza besiege Mirza Aziz Koka, son of Jiji Anaga and Akbar's foster brother, in Ahmedabad.

June 1574: The Padshah travels along the rivers Yamuna and Ganga to assist Munim Khan in defeating Daud Khan Karrani, the rebellious Sultan of Bengal.

1574: Siege of Patna. The city falls to Mughal forces and Daud Khan flees.

1575: The royal women's hajj commences.

1575: Daud Khan surrenders after the Battle of Tukaroi.

1575: Declaration to send a caravan to hajj every year.

1576: Daud Khan Karrani is beheaded.

1576: The Battle of Gogunda or Haldighati between Rana Pratap and the forces of the Mughal Empire led by Man Singh. The Mughal army wins but the rana escapes.

1578: Jesuits from Europe, including Rudolf Aquaviva, arrive in Goa.

1578: Akbar invites scholars and thinkers outside the Islamic fold to his ibadat khana.

1579: After the announcement of a mazhar, Akbar is proclaimed the Padshah-i Islam or Mujaddid of the Age. The phrase 'Allahu Akbar' is included in a verse by Faizi, a poet of the Mughal court and brother of Abu'l Fazl.

1582: Mirza Hakim is defeated. He dies of alcohol poisoning three years later.

1582: Raja Todar Mal is made the imperial diwan.

1582: The Persian translation of the Mahabharat, *Razmnama: The Book of War,* commences. It is completed eighteen months later.

1585: Yusuf Shah Chak, Sultan of Kashmir, is defeated at Baramullah.

1586: Yusufzai Disaster, in which more than 8,000 Mughal soldiers, including Birbal, are killed.

1586: The Marwar Rathores send a daughter, Rajkumari Mani Bai (also known as Jagat Gosain), the daughter of Rao Udai Singh, to be married to Prince Salim. Akbar gives her the title Taj Bibi though she was popularly known as Jodh Bai.

1586: Akbar leaves Fatehpur Sikri for Attock Fort and the north-west frontier, then moves his capital to Lahore.

1587: Akbar issues an order permitting widows to remarry.

1589: Abu'l Fazl begins work on the *Akbarnama*.

1595: Peace treaty between Chand Sultan and the Mughals negotiated by Abu'l Fazl.

1596: The Mughal Empire grows to an unprecedented scale.

1598: Akbar leaves Lahore for the Deccan.

1598: Defeat of the rebellious Uzbeks after the death of Abdullah Khan Uzbek.

1599: Ahmadnagar is besieged. Chand Sultan is murdered by rivals from within her domain and the Mughals capture the city and the fort.

1600-1604: Salim openly revolts against his father.

January 1601: Ten-month siege of Asirgarh, the Faruqui stronghold, ends.

August 1602: Abu'l Fazl is assassinated by Bir Singh Deo on the orders of Prince Salim.

27 October 1605: Death of Akbar, ten days after his sixty-third birthday. His body is buried at a mausoleum in Sikandra, Agra. Salim becomes Padshah Jahangir.

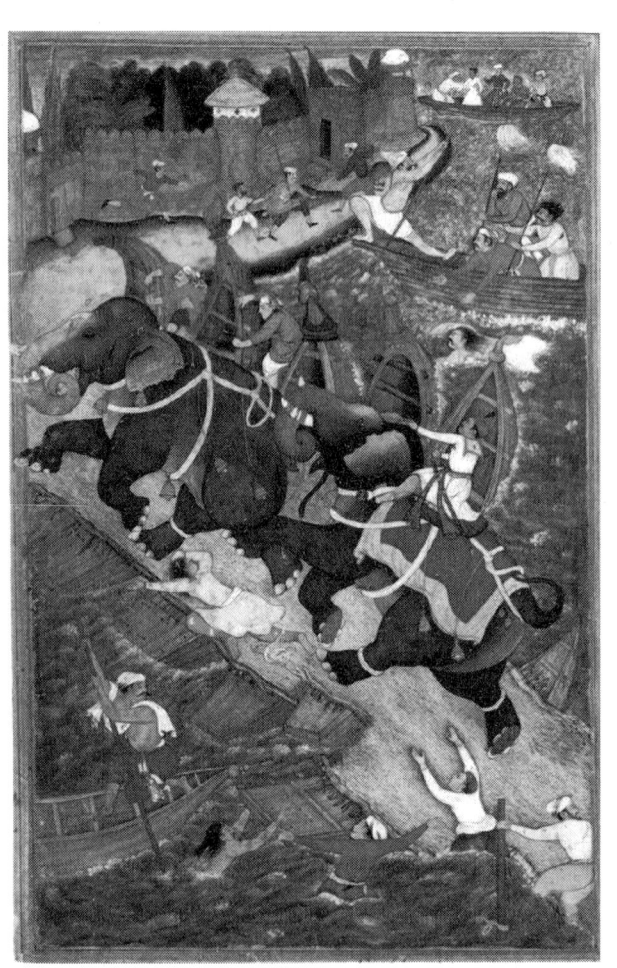

INTRODUCTION

In the frigid mid-winter of 1544, two children were sent north from Kandahar to Kabul, 500 kilometres away. While the snow fell silently and relentlessly on the desolate landscape, the small party stumbled on through the mountain passes and ravines, their horses' steaming breaths loud in the night. There were a number of women in the party including Maham Anaga and Jiji Anaga, and they tried to comfort the children, two-year-old Mirak, and his four-year-old sister, Baca. But their passage was terrifying in the slate-black dark, filled with dangers, the shifting snow, the howling winds, and the djinns they knew skulked beside crossroads and caves. The journey was all the more frightening, for they were hostages, and they feared for their lives. From time to time, they would halt at the stark homes of local Hazara chieftains and the men, their voluminous turbans grown monstrously huge in the flickering candlelight, would gather around the frightened children, who were travelling in disguise because of the threat to their lives. The child Mirak howled in terror at the endless night till a lamp was brought to him, providing meagre comfort. The 'lights of joy', we are assured, 'showed themselves in his cheeks'. Eventually, the two hostages arrived in Kabul, where they had been summoned by their uncle Kamran. For these were no ordinary children, but the daughter and son of Humayun, once Padshah of Hindustan—Bakshi Banu Begum, and Abu'l-Fath Jalal-ud-din Muhammad Akbar, known simply as Akbar.

Though Abu'l Fazl* with retrospective confidence would claim that Kamran grew contrite and abashed when he beheld the 'lustrous forehead' of the child Akbar, the truth was a great deal more prosaic. Humayun had lost the empire he had inherited in Hindustan† from

---

*Akbar's courtier and author of the biography of the emperor, the *Akbarnama*.
†The word Hindustan had been in use in Persia since the third century BCE to refer to the land lying beyond the river Sindh, or Indus (pronounced Hind). The Mughals, therefore, referred to the land they came to rule as Hindustan (Hind-Stan), as a geographic and ethnic term, not a religious one. In this book, I have used the word Hindustan since it is the one the Mughals used, rather than India, used by the ancient Greek (Indike) and Latin (India) writers.

his father, Babur, and had had to abandon Akbar almost as soon as the child was born, besieged by his own brothers as well as local chieftains, and one especially inexorable foe, Sher Shah Sur. For Humayun was not the only claimant to the fledgling Mughal Empire that Babur had founded. His brothers, Kamran, Askari, and Hindal, all considered themselves equally worthy contenders and challenged him for the throne as soon as Babur died. Kamran, especially, was ambitious, driven, and ruthless, and when he discovered Humayun's weakness—a certain predictable tendency to leave a campaign half-finished—he resolved to use all means possible to hustle his elder brother out of his birthright in Hindustan. One of these means was the kidnapping of Humayun's only son, Akbar, and his sister. The taking of royal hostages was an accepted strategy in these wars of succession, a way of exerting very effective pressure on rivals to the throne and containing their ambitions. The unfortunate children of unsuccessful claimants were often imprisoned for life, miserable shadows of their fathers' lost ambitions.

In 1544, when Humayun rode back into Hindustan after exile in Persia, his two young children were summoned by Kamran to his court in Kabul where it was hoped their presence would deter an attack by their father. This terrifying, headlong rush in the swirling snow, his fate uncertain, was very likely one of the first memories Akbar would have.

The historical record does not tell us whether the terrified toddler in the snowy wastes of Afghanistan would have any inkling that, in a little over ten years, he would be emperor of Hindustan and that, in the course of a nearly fifty-year reign, he would create one of the most magnificent empires in history. What is known is that when Akbar—whose name itself means 'Great'* and is therefore in no further need of the descriptor—became emperor at the age of only thirteen upon the unexpected death of his father, Humayun, there were very few signs of the remarkable legacy he would ultimately bequeath to the land that would come to be known as India.

In fact, Akbar was a distracted, undisciplined, and rambunctious child and youth who, in the parlance of the twenty-first century, may have suffered from attention-deficit disorder. So unruly and

---

*In Arabic.

self-willed was Akbar that no tutor was able to hold his attention and he grew up effectively unschooled and practically illiterate. This would remain one of the great mysteries of Akbar's life, for he would eventually be known for his reverence for learning, penmanship, books, and scholarship, and would patronize some of the most extraordinary works of writing, translation, and illustration ever undertaken in the country. Scholars have theorized that Akbar's illiteracy may have stemmed from dyslexia but, whatever the cause, Akbar's unconventional childhood, especially for a prince, meant that he developed a certain way of relating to the world around him, a tendency to experience reality in a visceral, malleable manner which he would later rely on to judge ideas and men. No new thought, or new courtier, would be blindly accepted, no matter the weight of their reputation nor, indeed, the lack of it. Every novel idea and weighty personage was coldly and carefully analysed, as Akbar sought to 'see' into the very heart of truth.

Instead of spending his childhood as befitted a Timurid prince, practising calligraphy and learning astronomy, mathematics, history, and philosophy, Akbar spent those years in the company of his beloved animals and their keepers, and his foster family. He raced pigeons, and ran alongside camels and dogs, and hunted cheetahs, lions, tigers, and deer. And, most importantly, Akbar tested his physical strength and courage against wild bull elephants, learning to ride and tame them when they were at the very height of their ferocious ill-temper. In fact, he would test himself almost to the point of insanity, putting himself in harm's way so consistently and so provocatively that it would appear that only extraordinary luck and a divine will kept him alive.

Akbar was to use this vast physical courage all his life, as he threw himself into battle from the age of twenty, to create an empire that would encompass most of the subcontinent up to the Deccan as well as present-day Afghanistan, Pakistan, and Bangladesh. The only other Indian empire[*] to bring more of the subcontinent under its control was the Mauryan Empire,[†] and its greatest emperor, Ashoka, would

---

[*]Akbar is regarded by scholars as an Indian ruler despite the Central Asian origins of the Mughal dynasty because he was born, ruled, and died in the Indian subcontinent.
[†]Historians are agreed that the Mauryan and Mughal empires were the two largest Indian

be the only ruler in Indian history to be ranked in the same league as the Mughal Padshah by many. Although a detailed comparative study of the two is beyond the scope of this book, the Muslim emperor and the Buddhist emperor who ruled eighteen centuries before him had some traits in common and we will touch upon these briefly later in the book. Because so much of history writing is Eurocentric, the history of Asia and India can sometimes become entirely the story of colonization, of the inevitable spread of European technology and modernity to a region which was seen as backward and somehow lacking in civilizational greatness. What can become obscured is that at the end of the sixteenth century, arguably the greatest empire on earth was the Mughal. That, indeed, the three great empires at the time—the Turkic* Ottomans, the Persian Safavids, and the Timurid Mughals (that made up the Dar al-Islam†)—were Islamicate. Each of these was more magnificent than anything the world had seen before. And, of the three, it was the Mughals, led by Akbar, who would create the greatest wealth. In 1615, as quoted by historian Richard M. Eaton, 'one observer estimated the Mughals' annual revenue at 120 million silver coins, compared to forty-five million for the Ottoman Empire and just fifteen million for neighbouring Iran'.

This empire was created through the military genius of Akbar, and settled by his psychologically acute understanding of human nature. As he began to expand his domain, he disregarded all the old rules of warfare that had been used in the country and used speed, fury, and firepower in such a manner that it appeared as though he was able to bend the very forces of nature to his will. In battle after battle, in Malwa, Gujarat, and Rajasthan, he crossed deserts, forded rivers, and led men across the country at such speed and in such harsh conditions that these feats were deemed almost miraculous, his enemies left literally awestruck. Nor were these simply acts of physical bravado. They were carefully planned tactics, showing a fierce intelligence and a willingness to constantly evolve. Combined with this tactical

---

empires in the subcontinent. However, it should be noted that it is difficult to calculate their areas since there were no cartographic boundaries during those periods.
*The terms Turkic, Turk, Turki all refer to the people who spoke various dialects of Turkish (Turki). The region they occupied ranged from the Oxus River, Central Asia, up to the western frontiers of China. See Richard Eaton, *India in the Persianate Age.*
†Land of Islam.

skill and physical endurance, Akbar also used the relatively new gunpowder technology in innovative and previously unknown ways. Understanding the need for speed and manoeuvrability in battle, Akbar improved upon the basic musket and cannon so that artillery became portable and effective even in the harshest environments. Akbar devised ingenious rockets, and created swivel guns which could be fitted onto camels and elephants. He improved siege-craft and developed lightweight cannon that could be easily pulled into battle, as well as super-heavy cannon that could be effective against the most redoubtable fortresses. These advances and techniques, combined with the ferocity and effectiveness of Mughal mounted archers, increased accuracy and firepower to such an extent that it made the Indian battlefield the most dangerous place on earth at the time.

Once some spectacular victories had been won, Akbar was quick to use his position of strength to subdue his opponents without resorting to violence, since the cost in lives to both sides could be so high. He organized intimidating ring hunts called qumarghas, which were so effective a demonstration of his soldiers' lethal skill that opponents quickly became more circumspect. He crossed the country ceaselessly, his enormous travelling camp an eloquent testimony to the increasing wealth and power of the empire. He gave opposing generals face-saving alternatives, was willing to resort to bribery when advisable, and constantly demonstrated to the most determined enemies that it was more profitable to be part of the Mughal Empire than opposed to it.

A chance encounter with a rather unprepossessing raja when Akbar was twenty years old changed the future course of the Padshah's life, and the very fabric of the Mughal Empire. Raja Bharmal of Amer offered a daughter in marriage to Akbar in 1562 in exchange for the Padshah's support against his own warring brothers. In marrying Harkha Bai, Akbar gained not just a bride, but the loyalty of her entire clan, and he would then go on to devise a unique way to incorporate non-Muslim courtiers into the Mughal administration by making them respected and equal participants in the fate of the empire. Muslim monarchs had married Hindu brides before but the women had almost always had to convert to Islam, whereas Akbar allowed his brides—and there would be many Rajput and Hindu brides over the next decades—the complete freedom to exercise their own religion. The Rajput rajas and the other Hindu rulers who submitted to Akbar were slowly incorporated into the Mughal imperial service and many would attain places of the highest honour.

And it was not only Hindu rulers but a great many diverse elements that were included in Akbar's imperial nobility. Thus in addition to the Rajputs and other Hindus there were shaikhzadas,* the Sayyids of Barahas,† Sufi shaikhs, Shia Persians and many more, all stakeholders in the prosperity of the empire. A pragmatic and calculated outcome of these measures was that no one particular clan or faction was allowed overweening power over the others, as had happened in the beginning of Akbar's reign with the Uzbeks, and his foster brother Adham Khan's family. All courtiers were incorporated into the Mughal mansabdari system, the efficient land revenue extraction infrastructure devised by Akbar and Raja Todar Mal, improving upon the framework left behind by Sher Shah Sur. In this system, a unified military–administrative network was put in place, replicated throughout the empire, and based on the ultimate authority of the Padshah himself.

Akbar's genius lay in recognizing men of talent, whatever their background, and promoting them to exactly the office that suited their particular skills. Wrought through decades of learning to gauge the motivations of men and women, Akbar developed an uncanny ability to judge talent in men. From the untrained potential he spotted in Daswant, the painter, to the financial acumen of Raja Todar Mal, the military genius of Kuar Man Singh, the literary aptitude of Abd al-Qadir Badauni‡, the administrative skill of Fath Allah Shirazi and many more, Akbar promoted men through the courage of his own conviction, even when it caused resentment and opposition. He promoted Hindus against the advice of Muslim advisers, and Shias against the inclination of the orthodox Sunnis,

---

*Indian Muslims.
†A clan of Indian Muslims, considered brave warriors but with a reputation till then of being brusque and rough-mannered.
‡A courtier at Akbar's court, he disapproved of Akbar's religious policies and wrote a covert, critical account of his reign. He was the most prolific translator of Akbar's ateliers.

and stood up to the petty bickering of the ulema, all to the glory of the Mughal Empire which, by the end of the sixteenth century, saw a hundred metric tons of silver flowing into the country from European powers buying manufactured products as well as natural resources. The unimaginable wealth and the quality of the goods of the Mughal Empire drew merchants and travellers from around the world. Rembrandt would be influenced by the luminous paintings of the Mughal court, the world would get its first translation of the Mahabharat into Persian through the *Razmnama*, and the West would discover the Upanishads through the translations of Dara Shukoh, Akbar's great-grandson.

As each new region was incorporated into the Mughal Empire, it added a sliver of local colour to the court culture which became, by the end of the sixteenth century, a cauldron of different rituals, textures, and nuances. Over time, this became the dominant feature in various sub-imperial courts. Everywhere in the empire, rulers and governors incorporated elements into the way they ruled, through marriages, political alliances, and cultural exchanges.

The different parts of the country were physically connected through the building of roads, dak chaukis, and sarais, and were linguistically connected by Persian, which became the administrative language of the empire even in the smallest of towns. In this fashion, Mughal culture became infused with the taste and texture of Hindustan to create a distinctive hybrid culture that embodied the various strands of the subcontinent as also the ancestral lands of the Mughals. And so, delicately flavoured Central Asian dishes fused with local cooking techniques and spices to create a distinct cuisine, today bastardized in countless 'Mughlai' restaurants across the globe. Mongol lutes and flutes met the Hindustani veena and raags and Dhrupad music became the rage in the sixteenth century. Brajbhasha phrases sneaked into imperial vocabulary and Persian idioms were adopted by Rajasthani court poets. The clothes in the Rajput courts, the weapons in the battlefields, the nuances of language, the blending of styles in architecture and painting all formed a new Mughal culture so variously layered that even today, it would be impossible to cleave this identity into its separate parts.

In 1578, at the age of thirty-six, Akbar experienced a spiritual epiphany during a qumargha hunt. This brought about a distinct change in the way he ruled his empire. Although he continued to wage war to expand his empire, he also greatly increased his focus on what we would now call governance. He worked to improve the lot of his subjects and also tried hard to find a solution to the grievances that arose from the conflicting religious views within the empire. He established religious and philosophical discussions as soon as he returned to his capital in Fatehpur Sikri in a hall called the ibadat khana (house of worship) in which religious thinkers were invited to participate in discussions and debates. Akbar invited Sunnis and Shias, Hindus, Christians, Jains, millennial Mahdavis, and many others, to what was perhaps the world's first site of interfaith debates on such a large scale. Akbar's astonishing conclusions from these fevered and sometimes furious discussions was that blind superstitions and irrational beliefs led to violence, and that all beliefs should be gauged through the pure lens of reason. He urged people to learn about others' religions, so as to dispel intolerant prejudices against each other and develop, instead, a sense of empathy. This, Akbar was convinced, would lead to a spirit of universal peace and active tolerance, which he called sulh kul. All religions, he believed, were either equally true or equally untrue and so deserved equal respect and protection.

Today, in a world fatally fractured along religious lines, it seems inconceivable that in the sixteenth century an emperor worked so hard to promote religious harmony and reverence for all faiths. This atmosphere of easy-going acceptance of a variety of faiths, customs, and beliefs in Mughal Hindustan under Akbar was quite opposed to the violent intolerance of neighbouring Safavid Persia or, indeed, the raging religious wars in Europe. As Persia in the late sixteenth century began to persecute all non-Shiite factions including Sunnis and Sufis, the subcontinent was seen as a land of capacious acceptance.

Akbar kept himself closely informed of happenings overseas and was curious about other countries and monarchies and sent embassies to the Safavid and Uzbek monarchs, to the Portuguese at Goa, and even contemplated sending an embassy to Philippe II of Spain and Portugal. This curiosity remained a keystone of Akbar's character, and it allowed him to continuously seek innovative solutions to the world around him. Apart from the many improvements he made to muskets, rockets, and other military technology, Akbar was also a pioneer in ship-building, construction methods, metallurgy, alchemy, and a great deal more. The Mughal Empire was a place of enormous innovation, invention, and opulence. Military historian Andrew de la Garza has shown that Timurid rulers like Akbar were at the heart of the 'Timurid Renaissance' in the fifteenth and early sixteenth centuries, during which great advances were made in the arts, literature, architecture, engineering, and the sciences, far surpassing the achievements of other empires at the time.

From an early age, Akbar displayed a spirit of compassion and empathy which, combined with his courage and self-belief, allowed him to make audacious and brave decisions. He abolished the jiziya and the pilgrimage tax on non-Muslims, to the horror of conservative Muslims. He prohibited the slaughter of cows and peacocks, in deference to Hindu sentiments. He instituted patronage for Hindu and Jain temples. He ended slavery in the empire and set the example by freeing all the bandas* in his household. He tried to discourage the practice of sati, while trying not to offend Hindu sentiments, and personally rode out to prevent royal Rajput women from being forced to commit sati as soon as he heard of such instances. He set up food kitchens and inns for the poor, and tried to distribute wealth to the needy to permanently eradicate poverty. And against the tenets of both Hinduism and Islam, he tried to elevate the position of women, recognizing their essential vulnerability within both these religious systems. Aside from discouraging sati, Akbar raised the minimum marriageable age of boys and girls, advocated monogamy, and criticized the Muslim laws of inheritance that favoured boys. In the sixteenth century, and for an Islamic monarch, this remains a unique achievement.

One of the reasons that Akbar was so willing to look beyond Islam for truths and validation was that, as relatively recent converts to Islam, the Mughals were less tenacious in their allegiance to religion alone. They carried with them many other symbols of their legitimacy. They comfortably inhabited the pre-Islamic pagan practices and elements of Chenghiz (Genghis) Khan's yassa laws as well since their ancestor,

---

*Slave-boys.

Timur, could lay claim to a Chingizid heritage, for he had married women from that illustrious clan. It should be pointed out though that the Mughals were much more attached to their Timurid past than to their Chingizid one, striving for the perfection of Samarkand and its refined culture of elegant gardens, buildings, art, poetry, and music. In strictly Islamic states at that time, the rulers were bound by the sharia and were meant to submit to the ulema, the Muslim clerics. These clerics would have expected the clear prohibition by the ruler of all things forbidden by the sharia and a jihad against followers of other religions. The jiziya tax imposed on all non-Muslim subjects would have been considered essential in further debasing non-believers and shackling their ability to live a luxurious life. However, in a country like India this sort of strict adherence to the sharia would have been politically catastrophic. The Sultans of Delhi (thirteenth to sixteenth century) had pragmatically ignored many of the injunctions of the sharia but none of the dynasties preceding the Mughals had been able to successfully establish themselves for a significant period of time. But the Mughals, and most especially Akbar, were positively cavalier in their attitude towards the ulema and the sharia and much more willing to find innovative ways in which to integrate their non-Muslim subjects into the empire. Akbar dispensed with the jiziya early on in his reign, and it would remain abolished almost continuously for a further hundred years.

◆

Given the range and breadth of his achievements, and his indisputable claim to be regarded as one of India's greatest monarchs, and one of the very greatest in world history, it is surprising that few full length biographies have been written about Akbar in modern times. There are a great many scholarly works, certainly, about aspects of his life and reign, and a trove of primary material, but this has not resulted in comprehensive studies of his life and reign. The scholarly works have often delved deeply into particular aspects of Mughal rule, but there are no recent accessible accounts of many of the Mughal emperors, not to mention of the most remarkable of them all. This is perhaps unsurprising, for most great Indian monarchs remain in dusty obscurity lit up palely only in the light of scholarly texts.

Where the Mughals are concerned, moreover, modern writings have been heavily influenced by ideology—as we can see in the nationalist writings of the early twentieth century, and the Marxist analyses of mid-twentieth-century scholars. More recently, popular narratives of suspect scholarship have veered sharply towards the identification of the Mughal Empire with the infamous notion of one thousand years of oppression of Hindus.

Be that as it may, in recent years, there has been a very welcome spike in interest in historical writing, both fiction and non-fiction. Perhaps as a nation, as we attempt to come to terms with our complex heritage, we are taking a close look at the past, to understand it as well as our present. It is therefore essential that we are able to go beyond infantilizing binaries that present Akbar as the 'good' Muslim ruler to oppose Aurangzeb's 'bad' ruler image, and past the even more lamentable excoriating of all Muslim rulers. We must reassess these constructs, deconstruct the various legacies we have inherited from our colonial past and arrive at an objective understanding of our history and key figures who people it. This is especially true of larger-than-life personalities like Akbar.

This book is divided into six parts, each of which is further subdivided into several chapters. Each part is dedicated to a significant phase in Akbar's life. Part 1 (1526–1561) of the book traces the arrival of the Mughals into India from Central Asia, the establishing of the Mughal Empire by Babur in 1526, and the peregrinations of Humayun, the second Padshah of Hindustan. These are the years in which Humayun lays the foundation of the great Mughal miniature painting tradition, first in Kabul and then in Delhi, and elaborates symbols of kingship that would endure for centuries, while the young Akbar resolutely resists all his father's efforts to educate him. After Humayun's sudden death, Akbar becomes Padshah under the able regency first of Bairam Khan and then Maham Anaga. Akbar at this stage remains uninvolved in the running of the empire, satisfied to let affairs of state lie in the capable hands of his regents while he immerses himself in hunting.

In Part 2 (1561–1569), we find Akbar suddenly galvanized into action and finally assuming his role of Padshah Ghazi of Hindustan, first in Delhi and then in Agra. This is a time dominated by the

Turki–Chaghatai nobility, with a small but increasing influx of Persian merchants, soldiers, and artists. At this time, Akbar gives enormous impetus to the development of Mughal miniatures by commissioning the *Hamzanama* (*The Adventures of Amir Hamza*), the largest artistic endeavour undertaken by a Padshah. We see here a youthful Akbar slowly discovering the latent, almost untameable power he has within himself, and finding ways to focus his blistering energy. The court continues to evolve, incorporating many new Rajput elements through Akbar's Rajput wives and their relatives as Rajasthan is folded into the Mughal Empire after two determined and bloody sieges: Chittor and Ranthambore.

In Part 3 (1569–1578), the capital shifts to Fatehpur Sikri where Akbar builds his red sandstone dream city on a hillock inhabited by a Sufi saint. As a fitting testament to Akbar's unique vision, the different buildings and structures Akbar built in Fatehpur Sikri continue to baffle scholars even today, though historian Syed Ali Nadeem Rezavi has brought many new elements to light.

Part 4 (1579–1585) focuses on the court at Fatehpur Sikri as Akbar starts his philosophical discussions in the ibadat khana. The composition of the nobility changes as Akbar consciously balances the Turki–Chaghatai noblemen with Rajput and Persian officers. Many Hindu elements are incorporated into Mughal etiquette, and the translation of the Mahabharat into Persian is undertaken. Akbar also neutralizes the last remaining challenge from a Timurid prince, his half-brother Mirza Hakim. Now Akbar is free to create a new Hindustani identity composed of many different elements and beliefs.

In Part 5 (1585–1598) the court relocates once again, this time to Lahore, to stabilize the volatile situation in the north-western frontier of the empire. Kashmir is incorporated into the Mughal Empire and Akbar travels to Srinagar three times. He commissions great works of history, including the enormous *Akbarnama* and *Ain-i Akbari* by Abu'l Fazl, as he starts on his grand project to anchor his life and his lineage in the fabric of Hindustan's memory. As Akbar's three sons grow up, the atmosphere at court becomes charged with jealousies and rivalries as each prince begins to attract noblemen to his cause. The works of art created at this time are more sober, meditative, and exquisite. Mughal artists begin experimenting with European ideas of space and perspective as the Jesuits bring European art to the Mughal court.

In Part 6 (1598–1605), Akbar leaves Lahore as the Mughals make inroads into the Deccan. His capital moves back to Agra. There is a slackening of ambition as the Padshah becomes more and more caught up in a battle of wills with his sons, especially Salim. Salim rebels by establishing a parallel court at Allahabad and creates his own taswir khana (atelier), consciously distancing himself from his father's preferred Hindustani style and patronizing a more Persian style. These last years of Akbar's life are dominated by these rebellions from his sons and the catastrophic consequences of their decisions.

◆

Despite his many superhuman achievements Akbar remains endearingly human, almost surprisingly so. Too often when we imagine Akbar, it is as a somewhat one-dimensional, bloodless cut-out. Many see him as a perfect man, a 'great' ruler, and an exemplary human being. He is also seen, sometimes, as something of a simplistic caricature through tenacious myths that have an enduring hold on our collective memory. The Akbar–Birbal stories, for example, are not 'true' in the sense that we remember them. Through the work of scholar C. M. Naim, the Akbar–Birbal stories have been understood to be a form of resistance, a sort of wilful but gentle pushback by the powerless against the inevitability of Mughal might.

But Akbar's journey, like that of all human beings, was complicated and uneven. He had an explosive anger that he struggled to contain, not always with success. He occasionally used surprisingly robust expletives in Hindi, which his biographer Abu'l Fazl very fortuitously chose not to expunge from the records. He cried often, and openly, upon the death of beloved courtiers and family members, and even became outright maudlin when listening to poignant songs and ballads. He struggled with bouts of melancholia, which some travellers attributed to epilepsy, a disease which appeared to run in the Mughal family. Nor was he ashamed to admit to that most human of traits: errors in judgement. From initially admiring the fortitude in women who committed sati, he became deeply critical of Hindu men who demanded such a deplorable act from their wives as a show of loyalty. From being very respectful in his youth to the orthodox ulema, he became critical, and then judgemental, of their corrupt and petty ways.

Perhaps one of the most fascinating aspects of Akbar's life and personality was his deep bond of love, affection and respect, with the multitude of women who accompanied him on his journeys. Oftentimes the influence and achievements of Mughal women is extricated from the sweep of history and the cascade of time altogether, and relegated to a separate chapter. This presents the role of women as a static, unchanging phenomenon, unaffected by other historical events. By giving Mughal women their due, and showing how important they were to Akbar throughout his life, I hope I have been able to provide an accurate portrait of their lives and the crucial roles they played in Hindustan at the time. In the early years of Mughal rule, the Timurid women led unfettered lives; they accompanied Humayun in his wanderings and rode into Hindustan on horseback. These women were thinly veiled, participated in the public life of the Padshah, and their advice was constantly sought, as it was in the time of Babur. Hamida Banu, Salima Sultan, and Gulbadan were particularly respected and accomplished women.

As the purdah became less porous through the interaction of the zenana with the Rajput women that Akbar married, these women nonetheless retained their independence of thought and even action. The work of historian Ruby Lal has shown that there were interesting ways in which these women managed to 'escape' the purdah, and I have written of these episodes in this book. There were subtler ways of resistance too, and Akbar always had to be supremely wary of displeasing these powerful matriarchs when he was experimenting with his religious ideas, punishing the ulema, or reining in a favoured prince. The contours of Akbar's wives remain more shadowy, but not yet indistinct. Abu'l Fazl was fierce in his censorship of these women and there were other writers, like Badauni, who railed against the influence that the Padshah's 'Hindu wives' had on his food habits, his clothes and his very thoughts. There are the equally petulant writings of the Jesuits, who blamed Akbar's women for his resistance to the charms of conversion. There are also the farmans of these women, their patronage of temples, the influence they exercised on behalf of priests and clerics. Through these fragile sources a picture can yet be gleaned. And there are extraordinary women present amongst Akbar's adversaries too, such as Rani Durgavati and Chand Sultan. As always, I find that to acknowledge the influence and power of women in a man's life never diminishes the man, quite the contrary.

The discovery of the evolution of the personality of Akbar through these many phases of his life was one of the truly surprising discoveries in the writing of this biography. As he interacted with the multitudes around him and their different truths, Akbar borrowed from their various symbols and beliefs. At different stages of his life, Akbar was a staunch Muslim ruler, a Timurid prince, a Sufi divine, a Hindustani raja, and a mujaddid (reformer) of the second Islamic millennium. To be able to inhabit these many roles, Akbar was buoyed and surrounded by a legion of men and women, who marked time to the cadence of his journey, and shaped him in ways big and small. This book is also a record of those men and women, the great, teeming, noisome mass of humanity and creatures that were so essential to the moulding of Akbar even as he maintained within himself an enigmatic, entirely unknowable, and still core. Similarly, the culture that the Mughals created did not magically appear from the darkness, perfect and luminous in every respect as Abu'l Fazl would have us believe. It came about through trial, experiment, chance, canny calculation, and careful balance. It is these negotiations that I have attempted to trace for, largely anchored by the legacy of Akbar, they would result in an empire of magnificence that would endure a further 200 years after his passing.

Akbar was defined by restlessness, extraordinary courage, curiosity, strength, and intelligence. His shaping of the empire of the Mughals took it to heights it had never scaled before and would never rise to again. It is this swirling, luminous tapestry of action, adventure, ideas, and battles that I have tried to recreate here, a world now almost completely effaced, for all empires must fall. Except, sometimes, at dawn, in the charcoal shadows of the Red Fort, or in the husky alaap of a Dhrupad raag, or in the whispered sweep of a patterned kameez as a woman walks by, for a little while longer, a certain Mughal fragrance lingers.

PART 1

THE PRINCE
AND HIS REGENTS
{1526–1561}

~

A CONQUEROR AND A REFUGEE PRINCE

In 1404, an elderly European man stood uncertainly before one of the most splendid courts in the world, set within a garden outside Samarkand. He was balding, with a russet beard and fine, deep-set eyes but, even in his best robes, he would have felt drab and inadequate at the high entrance to the garden he stood before, decorated in blue and gold glazed tiles, behind which soldiers on six elephants were waiting to receive him. When Ruy González de Clavio, ambassador of Henry III of Castile, was conducted by soldiers into the presence of the monarch, he saw before him an old man sitting cross-legged on silk carpets, a beautiful palace behind him. The monarch was dressed in silk robes and wore a high white hat surmounted by a gleaming ruby and studded with pearls and precious stones. In front of him was a sparkling fountain and red apples floated on its crystal waters. The monarch's face was deeply lined, the skin lying in folds like an empty leather water gourd, and his narrow eyes were almost sightless beneath exaggeratedly arched eyebrows. But his voice was strong as he greeted Ruy González and the other kneeling ambassadors and enquired about 'his son, the king of Spain', for this monarch was Timur Beg, or Timur-i-Lang,* the great Central Asian warlord who had conquered most of the Eastern Muslim world to create the largest empire in the world at the time.

Ruy González would return to Europe where he would write at length about his journey to Timur's court. He would write of gargantuan feasts, of roasted horse and sheep meat, carved and served with corn bread, of various dressed meats, and meatballs accompanied by rice, of melons, grapes, and nectarines, and a cooling drink made of cream and sugar. He described garden pavilions and tents called dilkusha, glorious in their rich, silken cloths and fluttering tassels, set amid the fragrant shade of fruit trees. He wrote of feasts held every day by the monarch or noblemen in tented camps by the river during which the royal women were present too, eating

---

*Also known as 'Timur the lame' due to an injury to his leg, and as Tamarlane.

and drinking with the men. Wine was served in addition to cream and sugar, 'for they do not consider that there is either pleasure or festivity without being drunk' and the most drunk amongst them all was celebrated by being hailed 'Bahadur', a 'valorous man'. Alongside the daily festivities, the affairs of state continued and all those who were found to have been derelict in their duties during Timur's long absences were hanged by the feet or beheaded.

Despite the opulence of the court described by Ruy González in 1404, Timur's beginnings, in 1336, were rather more pedestrian. He was born an ethnic Turk from a nomadic tribe in present-day Uzbekistan, in a region which was slowly crumbling under the weight of its earlier glory as the empire created by the great Mongolian ruler Chenghiz Khan fragmented into small, warring principalities. But Timur was a warlord of genius—charismatic, relentless, and violent. Pragmatic about not being a descendant of Chenghiz Khan himself, Timur married Chingizid women and always referred to himself and his dynasty as guregen or gurkani (in-laws) in a suitably deferential acknowledgement of the power of the Great Mongol. Timur was careful never to style himself as anything grander than amir, or beg, and never claimed for himself the exalted title of khan.* There was, however, nothing submissive about Timur's ambitions and, using a combination of military brilliance, the threat of extreme violence, and the willingness to convert enemies into allies, Timur set out from his capital of Samarkand in 1370 to conquer as much of the known world as he possibly could. By 1404, when he returned to Samarkand, Timur had sacked Baghdad and Delhi, marched up to Moscow, overrun Tiflis, Aleppo, and Damascus, and had accepted offers of submission from the Sultan of Egypt and the co-emperor of the Byzantine Empire, and was even contemplating the conquest of China.

Timur was pragmatic in claiming symbols of legitimacy from all sources that were available to him since his conquered peoples included a wide range of cultures from Persianized Turks to urban Sunni Muslims. For Timur, Chenghiz Khan's yassa laws that regulated the public and martial life of nomadic warriors were as binding as

---

*Amir and beg could be compared to the title of 'lord', whereas 'khan' would have been used only for a monarch.

the charisma of the vibrant new religion—Islam. The sharia* of Islam was never as inflexible for Timur and his descendants, the Timurids, as it was for orthodox Muslims, and they found novel and accommodating ways to adjust to the needs of a heterogeneous group of subjects. Timur reached out to the legitimacy of the Sufis and adopted for himself an obscure pre-Islamic Persian title with supernatural implications—Sahib Qiran, Lord of the Auspicious Conjunction. Though meaningless to a modern reader, a Lord of Conjunction was a potent and sacred symbol of power in the medieval ages. It was given to a person whose sway over the material and divine world could only be explained by a 'conjunction of the two superior planets', namely Saturn and Jupiter, which could be calculated only through a thorough understanding of astrology. Astrology at the time was a deeply respected science throughout the world. Up until the scientific revolution of the seventeenth century, it was treated on a par with history, grammar, and the sciences, and was an essential part of an elite education.

In 1398, Timur set his sights on the fabled city of Delhi and turned his fearsome cavalry towards the Khyber Pass. The sultans of Delhi had long protected the north-west mountain passes from the plunder of Chenghiz Khan's armies, but by the fifteenth century, the might of the Tughlaqs of Delhi had shrunk considerably. Timur and the Tughlaq army clashed. Timur destroyed the Tughlaq army and plundered the city of Delhi, 'massacring a reported 80,000 inhabitants and so thoroughly ruining the built landscape that it took the city nearly a century to recover'. For Timur never intended to remain in Delhi. He dreamed of building a glorious capital in Samarkand filled with Persianate art and architecture and he returned in 1399 to do exactly that with the booty and treasure he had plundered. Dreams for an empire in Hindustan would be for his descendant, Zahir al-din Muhammad, better known as Babur.

After Timur died in 1405, parts of his sprawling empire continued to be ruled for another 100 years by a succession of his descendants, while northern Hindustan, shattered by the effects of Timur's plundering invasion, fragmented into a collection of independent

---

*The sharia is Islam's legal system deriving from the Koran, and the fatwas—the rulings of Islamic scholars.

provinces. According to historian Richard M. Eaton, this process had already begun before Timur's invasion due to the slow collapse of the Delhi Sultanate and, by 1400, 'the northern two-thirds of the subcontinent had become a patchwork quilt of independent kingdoms...' It was at this moment that a talented and ambitious warrior of impeccable lineage looked towards the once lustrous capital of Delhi for consolation and glory.

Babur was a man who had a promising pedigree for a Central Asian warlord in the early sixteenth century. A descendant of Timur from his father's side and a Chingizid from his mother's, Babur's was a destiny which was waiting to be forged. But this destiny would not unfurl itself in the storied city of Samarkand, or in his beloved homeland of Ferghana in Central Asia. These would be forever forfeit, to Babur's abiding grief, to a tribe whose time had come—the Uzbeks. 'For nearly 140 years the capital Samarkand had been in our family,' wrote Babur bitterly in his memoir, the *Baburnama*, 'then came the Uzbeks, the foreign foe from God knows where, and took over.' The Uzbeks were a Turki-speaking tribe like Babur's, but they were ethnically distinct and, under the leadership of Shaibani Khan Uzbek, they harried Mirza* Babur, only twelve years old when he lost his father, first from Samarkand, and then out of Ferghana altogether. 'Mischief and devastation,' lamented Babur, 'must always be expected from the Mughul horde.' Finally, in 1504, bolstered by his intrepid grandmother, Aisan Daulat Begum, his mother, Qutlugh Nigar Khanum, and '300 lightly armed men' Babur conquered Kabul. For twenty years in this crossroads city filled with a scattershot of languages and traders and merchants from different corners of the world, Babur tried to create a capital that would live up to his Timurid ambitions. He planted gardens, straightened streams, and welcomed exiled Timurid family members from across Timur's old empire, driven to Kabul by the relentless rise of Shaibani Khan Uzbek. All this Babur would accomplish with his tightly knit warband, described by historian Jos Gommans:

> Like many Chinggisid khans or Timurid mirzas, Babur had a warband of his own, consisting of both relatives and

---
*Title for a Timurid prince or nobleman.

retainers, who were linked to each other through marriage and companionship. The latter was sustained in recurrent social events ranging from hunts to drugs-and-drinking bouts.

Babur would always celebrate and revere his Timurid identity over his Chingizid one for his loathed foes, the Uzbeks, also claimed Chingizid blood. It would therefore be all the more galling for Babur's descendants that they would be called by the Persian word for Mongol—Mughal. After several unsuccessful attempts to reclaim Samarkand, Babur realized that he would have to abandon his homeland forever and, instead, decided to look eastwards. Bolstered by the new title of Padshah,* Babur conducted five raids on Hindustan during his years in Kabul. His campaigns were based on the fragile claim that, since Timur had conquered Delhi in an earlier age, the city was legitimately his. Finally, in 1525, Babur sent a goshawk to the Afghan Lodi ruler in Delhi, Ibrahim Lodi, with the request that he hand over Delhi to Babur for 'the country which from old had depended on the Turk'. Ibrahim Lodi refused. So, at the age of forty-two, accompanied by his thirteen-year-old son, Humayun, Babur marched on Delhi with 8,000 Timurid and Pashtun warriors.

At the First Battle of Panipat, in 1526, Babur secured a decisive victory over the much larger Lodi army, and Ibrahim Lodi himself was killed in battle. While the exact strength of the Lodi army is not known, Babur calculated it to be 100,000-strong with 1,000 elephants. Unlike Timur, for Babur this was no plundering raid. This was the longed-for country, rich in resources and manpower, where he could build an empire of magnificence to rival that of his illustrious ancestor, Timur. Having won the battle, therefore, Babur then protected the population of the city and secured the safety of Ibrahim Lodi's mother† before going to give thanks at the dargahs of the two great Sufi saints of Delhi, Qutbuddin Bakhtiyar Kaki and Nizamuddin Auliya. Babur and Humayun then moved south to Agra, deeper into the hinterland, and Agra would become Babur's capital city.

---

*Babur claimed the title of Shah, or Padshah, while his ancestors had not taken a title greater than amir.
†To Babur's great chagrin, Ibrahim Lodi's mother was unmoved by his largesse and tried to have him poisoned.

In 1527, Babur defeated Rana Sangha, the Sisodiya ruler, and his 80,000 cavalry, at Khanua. At the Battle of Panipat and the Battle of Khanua, Babur was able to face terrifying odds, armies ten times larger than his own and composed of fierce warriors armed with steel weapons and horses, because of his innovative use of a recent invention in warfare—gunpowder. The most deadly weapon in his arsenal at this time was the tufang, or matchlock musket, much easier to master than the composite bow. As we will see, under his grandson, Akbar, 'a new style of combat built around gunpowder, infantry and combined arms tactics replaced an old order based on the warhorse and elephant'. By the seventeenth century, the Mughal Empire would be using 'more than a million soldiers under arms and controlling nearly a quarter of the world's economic output'.

Entirely aware that though he was victorious, he was thoroughly outnumbered in Hindustan, Babur came to arrangements with the defeated Sisodiyas. As a result of these pragmatic understandings, of the 145 noblemen who served under Babur, only 52 can be identified as strictly 'Mughal', while as many as 33 were classified as Afghans or Indian shaikhzadas. Babur further noted that one of his Afghan officers supplied troops which consisted of only 250-300 Turanis* and 2,000 Hindustanis. This incorporation of Hindustani troops into his army at this early stage of the Mughal Empire reflects Babur's willingness to work around some of the injunctions of the sharia in the face of his parvenu status in Hindustan, where he was keen to adopt new symbols of legitimacy. Babur understood the challenges he was faced with in a heterogeneous country. Many considered the Mughals detrimental to all Hindustanis, Muslims and Hindus alike. Among the detractors were luminaries like the founder of Sikhism, Guru Nanak, who despaired that due to the coming of the Mughals, the Muslims were losing their 'five-time prayers' and the Hindus their 'hours of worship', and Babur would need to overcome that resistance.

The Afghans of the Lodi dynasty, meanwhile, melted into the countryside and removed themselves to Bihar and Bengal, where we will encounter them time and again, as they resisted integration into the upstart Mughal Empire. Over the next four years, Babur

---

*Turki-speaking Timurid–Chaghatai Sunnis.

consolidated his fledgling empire and extended it 'in a strip of territory stretching from eastern Afghanistan through central Punjab to the mid-Gangetic plain'. Scholars have shown that Babur may also have begun to centralize political and administrative authority at this point by separating a nobleman's personal income from the revenue he was assigned for the disbursing of salaries to retainers. He also divided his territories into two parts—khalisa, or crown lands, and jagirs*. Two-thirds of the land under cultivation was divided between Babur's military generals, who deposited a fixed amount of money as land revenue into the state treasury.

To create a Timurid homeland, Babur sent messages to displaced Timurid descendants who had been set adrift by the rise of the Uzbeks, inviting them to be part of his court. According to his daughter Gulbadan, Babur sent 'letters in all directions, urgently saying, "We shall take into full favour all who enter our service and especially such as served our father and grandfather and ancestors... Whoever there may be of the families of Sahib-Qiran (Timur) and Chingiz Khan, let them turn towards our court."' Ninety-six Timurid women answered this call, in addition to the noblemen, and a glimmer of Timurid culture was founded at Agra.

◆

There was a great deal that Babur would find alien in Hindustan, even more so when he compared it to what he felt he had lost in Ferghana. Yet Babur would write about this new land evocatively, showing an almost grim resolve to find solace in its stark beauty. For despite the dismaying lack of melons, good horses, elegant clothes, and tidy streams, Babur was canny enough to realize the vast resources that Hindustan had to offer. He noted with amazement the fertility of the soil of the Indo-Gangetic plains, which could produce two harvests a year. The most durable image of the countryside, today as it was more than 400 years ago, was the peasant in his fields, with his plough and oxen, an indistinct blur against the immensity of the landscape and the blazing sun high in the sky. For the traveller who first experienced the endless plains of northern Hindustan, the heat was a feral presence, constant and unabating. To travel in India,

---

*Land grant of the revenue of a village or district.

warned the Portuguese missionary and traveller, Father Sebastien Manrique in 1640, was to be 'heated by ague or by the heat which the titanic and glowing planet causes'.

But there were, indeed, two harvests, one in autumn and another in spring. In the autumn, crops such as millets, pulses (lobia, moth, and moong), sesame, and sugarcane were harvested. The spring crops were wheat, barley, chickpeas, and masoor. And there was rice, in Bengal, around Delhi, and in parts of what is now Haryana. Cash crops included cotton, sugarcane, indigo, and opium as well as black pepper and ginger in Kerala. Wells and ponds irrigated the fields, from which water was drawn using a so-called Persian wheel worked by oxen or a simple pulley and yoke using camels. Where irrigation was not available, peasants waited for thunderstorms and for the monsoon. Villagers kept cows and buffalo and sold dairy products such as milk, yoghurt, ghee, and meat in the town markets. And while most people lived in the countryside, an unexpectedly large number lived in the great towns and cities. Calculating the population of the country in the sixteenth century is difficult as there was nothing even approaching a census; by 1600 it was estimated at 100 million by W. H. Moreland, a nineteenth-century British historian of India, and 130–140 million by historian Shireen Moosvi,* accounting for 24 per cent of the world population. According to historian Irfan Habib, about 15 per cent of the population lived in cities, the larger ones teeming with 250,000 to 500,000 people.

Even though agriculture was the mainstay of the peasantry, a number of people were also engaged in the manufacturing sector, which exported goods to western Asia and Europe. The products were also consumed by the large domestic market in the towns. 'Cotton textiles (calico, dyed and printed), silk fabrics, indigo and damascened steel' were some of the prized products being manufactured in the country.

The villagers lived in simple, nearly bare huts, which were notoriously impermanent. Famine, war, pestilence, or migration for work could force villagers to leave their homes, a small bag of belongings balanced on their heads, while the huts were reclaimed

---

*This figure is considered inflated by other historians including Sanjay Subrahmanyam and Ashok V. Desai.

by the elements. Even in the cities, buildings often fell into genteel ruin once abandoned.

Though Babur would not see much of the rest of the country, Hindustan was a land of baffling variety, each region rich in its own culture and language. In the fifteenth century, there had been an explosion of vernacular languages, which grew alongside the great literary languages, Sanskrit and Persian; Bengali, Gujarati, Hindustani, Kannada, Kashmiri, Oriya, Punjabi, Sindhi, as well as scores of dialects were spoken by substantial portions of the population. Each region had its own microclimate, from the heat of the Gangetic plains and the plateau of the Deccan, to the cool mountains of Kashmir, and the lush torpor of the Deccan sultanates.

It was an empire largely comprising ploughs and bullocks and cultivated fields. Eaton has described the melange of societies that would meld together as the semi-nomadic Timurids settled into largely agricultural Hindustan to create their Mughal Empire:

> Central Asia's semi-pastoral culture was based on rearing livestock and mastering horse-based warfare, and it assessed wealth largely in terms of movable assets: sheep, horses, goats, camels. The Indian world Babur encountered, by contrast, was one of ploughs and bullocks, a sedentary and agrarian society that understood wealth mainly in terms of fixed resources: harvested grain, manufactured goods, precious metals. If the kingdom that Babur established in India was initially a transplant of Central Asia's semi-pastoral oasis culture, his descendants would root the state ever more deeply in India's agrarian economy, its socio-religious culture and its political life.

◆

But all these changes in the composition of society and the economy would make themselves felt in the future, for after four short years in Hindustan, Babur died in 1530 after appointing his eldest son, Humayun, as his heir. Problems would arise almost immediately for Humayun as his three brothers, Kamran, Askari, and Hindal, challenged his accession. The Timurids did not have a system of primogeniture* and instead followed a law of co-sovereignty in which all royal princes had an equal right to rule. Timurid mirzas, sons, and brothers of the ruler, were raised to become ferocious warriors and competitors, able rulers of tribes of men so that the strongest and most capable amongst them would become Padshah when the time came, and that was not necessarily the firstborn. To allow them the independence and the financial clout to form a power base, mirzas were granted lands, or appanages, which were theirs for life and from which they could generate revenue. Kamran had been given the important territories of Kandahar and Kabul, Askari had Multan, while Humayun himself controlled Badakhshan. Upon Babur's death, all his sons retained their fiefs while Badakhshan was now given to a Timurid cousin, Mirza Sulaiman. Kamran, ambitious and driven, and the most tempestuous of Humayun's brothers, immediately invaded the Punjab and thereby deprived his brother of half his empire at one go. Humayun, meanwhile, inherited the title of Padshah and Babur's limited lands in Hindustan, and the khutba† was read in his name in Delhi, Kabul, and Ghazni, demonstrating his righteous backing by the ulema.

Humayun's situation was made even more fraught by the presence of many warring parties. Disaffected Afghan nobles gathered in the east, in Bihar and Bengal, making the situation in those lands intermittently volatile. To the west, the ruler of the rich state of Gujarat, Sultan Bahadur, was also showing signs of belligerence, while to the south lay the independent kingdoms of Burhanpur, the Hindu state of Vijayanagar, and then the sultanates of the Deccan.

So while Humayun, in his nascent Mughal Empire in Hindustan, had to contend with many chieftains from within his lands who were unconvinced about his claim to the throne, of whom the Afghans were the most dangerous, he also had to manage his brothers' fierce ambitions and shifting loyalties. He had to do so, moreover, while remaining true to Babur's peremptory and irrevocable request to never spill the blood of a brother.

---

*The system whereby the first-born son of a ruler automatically inherited the throne upon the death of the monarch.
†Sermon delivered from a pulpit by a Muslim preacher during Friday prayers. A new monarch would have his name recited on the first day after his coronation ceremony.

As Humayun struggled to contain the fractious ambitions of his brothers while adhering to his impossible Timurid ideals, he sought a more intangible but potentially incandescent source of power. The Timurids had long been associated with Sufi orders but these were traditionally the Naqshbandi saints of Central Asia. Humayun sought to gain the support of Shattari Sufis—mystics from a highly respected Hindustani order of saints. Brothers Shaikh Ghawth and Shaikh Phul were actively courted by Humayun; they were 'not only immensely popular local saints but also experts in the Arabic, Persian and Sanskrit learned traditions'. In this way, Humayun was the first of the Mughals to use Hindustani intermediaries who were adept at both Persian and local forms of worship, and had indigenous knowledge of cosmological forces. Shaikh Phul, especially, had a formidable reputation as one who could control the planets themselves by invoking divine names and claimed for himself the not inconsiderable miracle of having been escorted by the angel Gabriel through the seven heavens to witness the glory of God. It was in this context that Humayun developed an elaborate court ritual involving dress codes and uniforms, and the use of auspicious names. One of the most visible accoutrements Humayun devised for himself and a few intimate courtiers was a distinctive raised headgear called the Taj-i Izzat, or Crown of Glory. It sent a subtle yet powerfully symbolic message about the sacred nature of Humayun's kingship, a sacrality he reinforced by his ability to read the planets and, as we shall see, his kinship with Ahmad of Jam, a twelfth-century mystic.

In 1538, when Humayun set off on an expedition to Bengal, his brother Hindal lured Shaikh Phul to Benares and had him murdered, in a wordless if bloody acknowledgement of the saint's powers over Humayun*. Sher Khan, ruler of Bihar, sensing weakness, barred Humayun's route and decimated the Mughal army at Chausa. He then took the title Sher Shah Sur, making his ambitions clear. The Padshah's three brothers also joined the fray against Humayun necessitating an escape that would eventually lead the Padshah out of Hindustan altogether. Seeking to travel through Kabul, he asked Kamran for permission which his brother insolently, yet predictably,

---

*At this stage all three brothers opposed Humayun though Hindal, youngest of the siblings, would soon come over to Humayun's camp.

refused. 'What was the good of my courtesy in showing kindness and brotherliness to the Mirza,' lamented the beleaguered Padshah, 'if he is now talking to me in this way?' Humayun's retainers and supporters slowly deserted him in his wanderings through the badlands of Hindustan—the eternally sparring kingdoms of the Punjab and Sind. His small retinue included the women of his harem, who shared the uncertain fortunes of their Padshah and whose vulnerability had been exposed at the battle of Chausa. Many women were lost at that battle, presumed drowned. Bega Begum, Humayun's most senior wife, was captured by the Afghans and her six-year-old daughter, Aqiqa, was lost.

While Humayun did apply himself for many years to defending the territories his father had left him, there was perhaps something in his very character that prevented him from successfully establishing himself in a violent and merciless world. An account left by his waterbearer Jauhar Aftabchi of the beleaguered Padshah is revealing:

> At Mandu, a deserter presented himself. The officers wanted to torture him to make him reveal where the enemy had hidden its treasure. Humayun replied: 'Since this man has come to me of his own free will, it would not be magnanimous to use force against him. If success can be achieved by means of kindness, why use harsh measures? Order a banquet to be prepared. Ply the man with wine, and then ask him where the treasure is hidden.'

Unfortunately, Humayun himself partook too readily of the pleasures he proposed to the prisoner, often disappearing after a hard-won battle for many weeks into his harem, where he 'unfurled the carpet of pleasure' and gave himself over to opium and wine. His father would have been entirely unimpressed by this behaviour—something he had witnessed in his own uncles in Herat, and blamed on an increasingly sedentary lifestyle. 'They were good at conversation, arranging parties and in social manners,' wrote Babur about these pleasure-loving uncles, 'but they were strangers to soldiering, strategy, equipment, bold fight and military encounter.'

In the darkest moment of his life, Humayun had a dream on the banks of the Ravi which must have offered consolation to the mystically minded Padshah, for he dreamed of a son. 'His blessed heart was cast down', Gulbadan, Humayun's sister, admitted in her family chronicle, and when he fell asleep, he 'saw in a dream a venerable man, dressed in green from head to foot and carrying a staff'. This ancient man identified himself as 'Ahmad of Jam', the twelfth-century mystic who was so exceptionally large that he was known as Zinda-Fil, or Colossal Elephant, and he promised Humayun an illustrious son for whom he proposed the name Jalal-ud-din Muhammad Akbar.

It was not only Humayun who experienced miraculous premonitions and extraordinary occurrences around Akbar's birth. Shamsuddin Ataka* Khan, his future wakil,† had a dream when he was only twenty-two in which 'he saw the moon come into his arms', a sign which was joyfully interpreted as an intimation of great good fortune to come. Akbar's mother, too, when she was pregnant with him, was said to glow with an effulgence so bright from her forehead that her brother, Khwaja Muazzam, said that 'the divine light so streamed from the shining brows that he had not strength to gaze steadily at it'. And Jiji Anaga, his future milk mother, had a vision, in which she said 'a great light approached me and entered my bosom. I felt as if the world-warming Sun had fallen into my breast'. Through this association with Akbar, 'I and my family,' she admitted candidly, 'became famous throughout the seven climes.'

If these luminous claims may appear disquieting to a modern reader, or overblown, they were not so in the sixteenth-century Islamic world. For the Mughals were very aware of the mystical claims of Timur, who was said to be a descendant of the mythical Alanqua herself, a princess of Moghulistan who was impregnated by a divine ray of sunshine and gave birth to three 'shining' sons. They understood, also, Timur's title of Lord of the Conjunction and all its potent symbolism. The Mughals of Hindustan, as proud descendants of Timur, would adopt the idea of the Auspicious Conjunction as a symbol of legitimacy and Humayun, of all the Great Mughals, was the most devoted to trying to understand the workings of the cold and pitiless stars.

---

*Akbar's foster father.
†A post equivalent to chief minister.

BRIDE IN THE DESERT

The desperate wanderings that Humayun was forced into through the betrayals of his brothers and the genius of Sher Shah Sur, however, brought about a chance encounter that would change the very shape of the Mughal Empire. In a town in Sind, Humayun met a young woman from a Persian family, Hamida Banu Begum, and decided to make her his wife.

Hamida Banu was only fourteen years old when she received the proposal from the much older wandering Padshah. She maintained a staunch, dignified resistance for forty days, during which Humayun's stepmother, Dildar Begum, gently encouraged the young girl to consider the proposal. Hamida Banu 'resisted and discussed and disagreed' but finally it was settled and Humayun 'took the astrolabe into his own blessed hand and, having chosen a propitious hour', the marriage was celebrated. The bride was, after all, from the family of Ahmad of Jam, just as Humayun had envisioned in a dream, and the planets, it seemed, were finally aligned for glory.

Nevertheless, the immediate future of Humayun's small party was decidedly more grim. They wandered the inhospitable lands of Jodhpur and Jaisalmer, whose local chieftains refused them help, and 'the country through which they fled being an entire sandy desert', we are told by the medieval historian Ferishta, 'the troops began to be in the utmost distress for water. Some ran mad, others fell down dead; nothing was heard but dreadful screams and lamentations.' Hamida Banu, now pregnant with her first child, rode alongside her husband, while their few remaining soldiers ran beside the horses. Horses were scarce at this point and when Humayun asked to borrow a horse from one of his noblemen, Tardi Beg, 'so ungenerous was this man and so low was royalty fallen, that he refused to comply with his request'. The historian William Erskine has a more generous assessment of Tardi Beg who, he believes, 'was a rough old soldier, who kept his own men and cattle in order, and resented any attempt to make him liable for the faults and negligence of others'. But, at last, on a foetid day in August, the party arrived at a small desert town Umerkot where the ruler of the town, Rana Prasad, gave them a gracious welcome.

After two months in Umerkot, Humayun rode away under a waxing moon towards Bhakkar* with the rana, while Hamida Banu was left behind in the fort with the rest of the harem under the charge of her brother, Khwaja Muazzam. The most senior woman of the household at this time was Khanzada Begum, eldest sister of Babur. Three days later, on the full moon night of 15 October 1542, Hamida Banu delivered a baby boy. 'The moon was in Leo,' wrote Gulbadan, 'it was of a very good omen that the birth was in a fixed Sign.' This brisk account of the birth of the future Shadow of God was not, however, expansive enough for Abu'l Fazl. In his chronicle of the Padshah's life, the *Akbarnama*, the event is much more precisely placed within a cosmological framework that concorded with the radiant destiny of this infant boy. As Hamida Banu laboured to deliver her child, wrote Abu'l Fazl, the astrologer, Maulana Chand, 'was perturbed as the moment was inauspicious. "In a short time, a glorious moment will arrive, such as does not happen once in a thousand years,"' he assured the doubtful women, and urged them to delay the labour. Fortuitously, at that very moment, a particularly homely-looking midwife walked into the room, so disgusting Hamida Banu that her labours were arrested. And so it happened that a commonplace hour was averted and Hamida Banu did indeed give birth to Akbar at Maulana Chand's 'glorious moment'. A runner was sent to convey the good news to Humayun who, according to much later accounts from Akbar's court, 'fell a'dancing, and from excess of exultation, revolved with a circular motion' because he had realized that the 'horoscope of this Light of Fortune was superior, in several respects and by sundry degrees, to that of his Majesty, the Lord of Conjunction (Timur)'. Humayun then broke a pod of musk and distributed it amongst his amirs saying; 'This is all the present I can afford to make you on the birth of my son, whose fame will, I trust, be one day expanded all over the worlds as the perfume of the musk now fills this apartment.'

In Umerkot, a veritable tribe of women was now appointed to suckle the infant. Jiji Anaga, wife of Shamsuddin Muhammad of

---

*In Punjab, present-day Pakistan.

Ghazni, was singled out for this important and highly coveted task. This was done in gratitude, for her husband had saved Humayun from drowning at the battle of Kanauj. These women were to supply not only their life-giving milk but also, it was believed, some of their virtuous qualities. But Jiji Anaga was not immediately able to suckle the newborn as she was herself pregnant with the future Mirza Aziz Koka, Akbar's milk brother. At least ten additional women were listed as having suckled Akbar, including one Hindu woman, Bibi Rupa. In charge of all these women was Maham Anaga, the superintendent of the milk nurses, who also had with her Adham Khan, her ten-year-old son. All these women and children would surround Akbar with fierce love and careful tenderness and many would walk alongside him, sharing his destiny, far into the future. Some had blazing careers at his court and one, Jiji Anaga, was so loved by Akbar that at her death, half a century later, his grief for her would be more extravagant than that for any other woman save his own mother.

A summons soon arrived from the eager Humayun who had pitched camp in a large garden in the town of Jun in Sind and, when Akbar was less than two months old, the Mughal party departed from Umerkot. Hamida Banu travelled with her baby in a litter, described by a later traveller as a 'takht revan', a wooden box with latticed sides, covered with hides and fixed upon two poles which were carried by mules. The party arrived in Jun on 20 December 1542, and Humayun's many hardships must have felt somewhat diminished when he took his son in his arms for the first time and kissed him on the forehead. The Mughal party remained in Jun for a few months, all the while losing supporters who left brazenly in a show of bad humour or skulked away in secrecy. Even more worrying was news that Kamran and Askari were jointly planning to conquer Kandahar, at that point held in Humayun's name by Hindal. Hindal, most amenable of Humayun's brothers, beloved of his sisters, was known to be easily influenced by his brothers. There was, however, occasion for rejoicing when one of Babur's soldiers from the Turkoman Qaraqoyunlu clan, Bairam Khan, came to join forces with Humayun. The Padshah, it was reported, was 'much rejoiced by the arrival of so celebrated a character'. And, indeed, the fortuitous reappearance of this talented general and shrewd strategist would ensure the future of the empire. But desperate now for the support of his brothers, Humayun turned to the one person he believed might still hold some sway over these recalcitrant siblings, his aunt and eldest kinswoman, Khanzada Begum. So, at the age of sixty-four, Khanzada Begum bravely made the journey north through almost a thousand miles of rough terrain, marauders, and enemies, to reason with her nephews in the name of her brother, the Padshah Babur.

By this time, the Governor of Sind had grown tired of his unwelcome guest and, in July 1543, the Mughal cortège headed towards Kandahar. 'The people of Hindustan,' muttered their disenchanted Padshah, 'have an extraordinary mode of evincing their fidelity', as his entourage continued to be depleted by occasional desertions. When a few months later, he heard that his brother Askari was galloping towards them with 2,000 soldiers, Humayun realized that Hindustan was now lost. Instead of heading to Kandahar, he decided to head for Persia, to seek asylum at the court of Shah Tahmasp.

Regarding the decision to leave Akbar behind in Hindustan, the accounts vary in the details. According to Gulbadan, who would have heard about the events from Hamida Banu herself, the imminent arrival of Askari precipitated such a frenzy that though Khwaja Muazzam and Bairam Khan were able to get Hamida Banu onto a horse to follow Humayun, 'there was not a chink of time in which to take the emperor Jalal-ud-din Muhammad Akbar'. According to Jauhar, who was present at the time, it was Humayun who found it 'requisite' to leave the young prince behind. According to Nizamuddin Ahmad, a court historian of Akbar's who was not present at the event, 'the weather was very hot, so he [Akbar] was left behind'—a somewhat startling declaration given the lateness of the year and the proximity to Kandahar. Abu'l Fazl himself sweepingly assured readers that Humayun would have realized that Akbar was 'under the protection of Divine love'. What is certain is that Humayun rode away to Persia with a very small cortège of some thirty or forty persons, which included only two women, one of whom was Hamida Banu. It seems surprising, given Akbar's tender age, that his mother did not remain with him. The accounts all agree that Humayun summoned Hamida Banu as soon as he realized he would have to ride away and she, as a young bride of only sixteen, may not have felt she had real choice in the matter. But that she may have had conflicted feelings, maybe even regret, about this decision seems to be reflected in the fact that she is the only one to have said, via Gulbadan, that there was such an urgency to leave that it was out of her control that Akbar got left behind.

Akbar had with him the remainder of the Mughal party, including the milk mothers who would always watch over him with such dedicated ferocity that they would even endanger their lives to ensure his safety. Askari arrived at the camp looking for Humayun, but he was told that 'he went hunting long ago'. So Askari ordered that the young Akbar be taken to Kandahar, where he was handed over to the care of Askari's wife, Sultanam Begum, who doted on him.

For the next year, he remained in Kandahar, surrounded by his milk mothers, kokas (milk brothers), and foster fathers. As the young child grew up realizing he was effectively a hostage of his uncles while his parents remained untraceable, it was not surprising that as a young man he would have an unassailable faith in these foster families and would speak of a 'river of milk', a precious bond that he would never betray. For many of these women, Turki was their native language and Akbar would have grown up hearing this language spoken around him in addition to courtly Persian and the Arabic of the Koran. Akbar remembered an incident decades later in which Maham Anaga reminded Askari of a Turki custom in which when a child first learns to walk, his father strikes the child with his turban, causing him to fall, thus warding off the evil eye. Askari agreed to perform this duty in lieu of his absent brother and Akbar reminisced that 'this striking and falling, are visibly before me'.

When Kamran heard in the winter of 1544 that Humayun was marching back towards Kandahar, he understood that the circumstances had irrevocably changed. Unlike the fugitive Padshah he had hounded out of Hindustan, this Humayun was now returning at the head of 14,000 horsemen with the blessings of the Shah of Persia himself. Included among the troops were noblemen of distinguished lineage, outstanding for their bravery, who would hold high positions later at Akbar's court such as the Uzbek chief, Haidar Sultan Shaibani, and his sons, Ali Quli Khan and Bahadur Khan. It was at this critical juncture that Askari panicked and when he received his brother Kamran's demand for Humayun's children, he hastily sent Akbar and his half-sister Bakshi Banu on their perilous journey to Kabul. There they were reunited with the elderly Khanzada Begum, who wept as she held the cherished boy in her arms and kissed his hands and feet. 'They are the very hands and feet of my brother the Emperor Babur,' sobbed the old woman, who still grieved for her beloved younger brother, dead fourteen years previously. 'He is like him altogether.' Also present in Kabul were Akbar's young aunt, Gulbadan, his stepmother, Bega Begum, who had been sent back by Sher Shah Sur, and several of Babur's widows. The children spent a few months in Kabul with Kamran and Akbar remembered another episode that dated back to this time. A kettledrum had been gifted to Kamran's son, Mirza Ibrahim, but the young Akbar wanted it too. Kamran thought it would be amusing to have the boys wrestle for the drum, no doubt counting on the strength of his older son to defeat Akbar and thereby humiliate his nephew, who was becoming an increasingly unwelcome presence. For there was no stronger reminder of the threat that Humayun posed than his son, Akbar and Kamran therefore did not look upon Akbar with favour and was hoping he would be shown his place by Mirza Ibrahim. To the utter discomfiture of Kamran, on this occasion, the two-and-a-half-year-old Akbar grabbed his older cousin by the waist, lifted him up, and threw him to the ground. When Akbar strode around beating the little kettledrum, to the amusement of his indulgent servants, Kamran, in a fit of petulance, ordered the child to be weaned immediately. While this may appear to us to be relatively old for a child to be weaned, it was quite the custom for children then to be suckled till the age of five. Moreover, Kamran would have been depriving the motherless Akbar of the comfort of his milk mothers. What was surprising, however, was the boisterous strength and confidence of the child Akbar, traits which would survive into adulthood, much magnified.

As Humayun marched back to reclaim his empire, he first seized Kandahar where he defeated Askari. Askari would eventually be exiled to Mecca, where he would die. Hindal, youngest of Humayun's brothers, came over to the Padshah's camp and Humayun finally marched towards Kabul and Kamran deserted the city. Heralded by drummers, Humayun rode into the city in November 1544 in the middle of the night and Akbar was finally reunited with his grateful father. 'Merely to look at him,' wrote Gulbadan about Humayun, 'eased the sorrow-stricken heart.' Another woman was added to the Mughal household when Humayun took a new wife, a woman named Mah-chuchak Begum, who would bear him four daughters and two sons over the next ten years. There were also two new additions Humayun brought back with him from Persia who would alter the artistic landscape of Hindustan forever.

Shah Tahmasp, though he had enjoyed a robust, libertine adolescence, had recently gone through a phase of tawba, or repentance. Though still only in his twenties, a young man with penetrating eyes and a luxurious auburn beard, he had banned alcohol, gambling, prostitution and, to Hindustani arts' eternal gratitude, painting, from his realm. So a short while after his arrival at Kabul, Humayun was able to send invitations to two Persian painters, Mir Sayyid Ali and Abd al-Samad, whom Shah Tahmasp would release from his own ateliers. According to legend, Mir Sayyid Ali had impressed the Mughal Padshah with the admittedly awe-inspiring skill of painting a polo match on a grain of rice, complete with goal posts and four horsemen. As art historian J. M. Rogers describes it, the employment of two expensive artists by Humayun when he was so reduced in circumstances, with his empire still only a dream, was a considerable act of faith and passion.

In the joyful Mughal household, meanwhile, celebrations continued for days, with prayers, and raucous gatherings, and games, music, and dance. Humayun sent for Hamida Banu, who had been left behind in Kandahar and wishing to see if Akbar would recognize his mother instructed all the women of the harem to dress in a similar manner. The women wore several layers of woollen robes, cinched loosely at the waist, long, loose sleeves, and high Turki caps. Akbar was brought in on a servant's shoulders and placed on a diwan. Then, to loud shouts and exclamations, the robust and ruddy little boy rushed into his waiting mother's grateful arms.

The province of Kabul had been described by Akbar's grandfather, Babur, when he had made it his capital in 1504. He described the fortress citadel as being 'situated in an exceptionally elevated place with wonderfully good air. It overlooks the large lake and three meadows...which when green make a beautiful sight.' He also wrote of a more dubious spot in an orchard by a canal where 'much debauchery is indulged in'. In 1545 the Mughal party may also have seen some of the trees Babur experimented with—a sour cherry sapling, sugarcane plants, banana trees, in addition to the local species—apricot, quince, pear, peach, and almond trees. A place of pilgrimage would have been Babur's last resting place—a grave open to the skies in his favourite garden, the Bagh-e-Babur, where he lies to this day.

A circumcision ceremony was now held for the young prince for which all the bazaars and halls and gardens were elaborately decorated. The circumcision ceremony was an important rite of passage for Mughal princes, signalling the end of their infancy and their inclusion in the public spectacle of Mughal imperial life. Neighbouring noblemen were invited and tent halls were set up in gardens under the cold sky, watched by slow-winged kites. Kabul's marketplaces and boulevards were all decorated as well and food and drink were consumed over days of festivities. The banquet would have included biryan (from a Persian word meaning frying or roasting), which was a special dish in which the meat of a Dashmandi sheep would have been cooked with ghee, saffron, cloves, pepper, and cumin seeds. There would have been various kinds of kebabs and perhaps even sanbusa (samosa), or qutab as it was called in Turki. There would almost certainly have been pilau, a Central Asian speciality cooked in oil from the fatty tails of sheep, as described by a mid-nineteenth century European traveller:

> A few spoonfuls of fat are melted...in a vessel, and as soon as it is quite hot, the meat, cut up into small pieces, is thrown in. When these are in part fried, water is poured upon it to the depth of about three fingers and it is left slowly boiling until the meat is soft; pepper and thinly sliced carrots are then added, and on top of these ingredients is put a layer of rice, after it has been freed from its mucilaginous parts. Some more water is added, and as soon as it has been absorbed by the rice the fire is lessened, and the pot, well-closed, is left over the red-hot coals, until the rice, meat, carrots are thoroughly cooked in the

steam. After half an hour the lid is opened, and the food served in such a way that the different layers lie separately in the dish, first the rice, floating in fat, then the carrots and the meat at the top, with which the meal is begun.

Rather than this hearty recipe, the pilau cooked would have been the more refined Persian variety, developed under the Abbasid caliphs of Baghdad. Food historian Lizzie Collingham writes that the highly aromatic dish was cooked using numerous additions: 'fruit pilaus, turmeric and saffron ones, chicken pilaus for special occasions; some varied by the addition of onion and garlic, or with raisin and almonds, and others varied by the color of the rice'. Since barley and wheat were the crops of Persia, and rice a luxury from India, this dish grew as a way in which to make this expensive main ingredient a centrepiece of the meal, not simply a side dish.

The women gathered in the gardens of Bega Begum, Humayun's first wife, resilient and outspoken and the most senior of the Mughal women as Khanzada Begum had recently died, and decorated the place in a 'new fashion' according to Gulbadan, possibly inspired by Hamida Banu's long sojourn in Persia. Even the food they now ate may have had a fragrance of the great banquets Hamida Banu and Humayun had enjoyed in Persia, where they had been feted with 'fine sherbets of lemon and rosewater, cooled with snow...preserves of watermelon, grapes and other fruits, with white bread'.

The decade that Humayun and Akbar would spend in Kabul was not a time of arid 'exile', which was often the narrative of nineteenth-century British historians like Mountstuart Elphinstone or H. M. Elliot. It was a time charmed by bracing creativity in which various subterranean streams of legitimacy and art were adopted to form the very beginning of Mughal art and culture. Art historian Laura E. Parodi has shown that the Kabul years were essential to the development of the Mughal school, and that this movement began very early in Humayun's reign. From 1545 onwards, Humayun established a fully-fledged kitab khana which employed Khurasani trained artists who, it is now believed, probably worked for Humayun from an even earlier time, predating his Persian interlude. There was another artist with Humayun in Kabul, Dust Muhammad of Herat, also intriguingly known as Dust-e Divana, or Dust the Fool. The chronicler Bayazid Bayat wrote about Dust Muhammad's 'fondness for wine, which he was unable to give up' but which he was now able to continue at Humayun's more indulgent court.

Amidst the brooding chinar trees and flushed pomegranate blossoms of Kabul, Dust Muhammad painted a masterpiece of refinement, allegory, and symbolism now believed to commemorate the feasts around Akbar's circumcision. In this extraordinary piece of work, there are rocks in the shape of an elephant, alluding to Humayun's dream of Ahmad of Jam, the Colossal Elephant. There are, unusually, large groups of women, identified as Hamida Banu, Gulbadan, Bega Begum, Gulbarg Begum, and Maham Anaga, and there are identifiable caves and rocks that place the event almost certainly at Khwaja Seh Yaran, outside Kabul. Indeed, in the use of symbolic accoutrements like headgear, clothes, colours etc., for particular persons and places, this painting represents one of the very first attempts at 'portraiture' in Mughal art. All these elements are clues to the tapestry of Akbar's later vision and the importance of the role of Mughal women, but they are also an acknowledgement, now forgotten, of the enormous debt Mughal art owed to Humayun.

Though the art continued, peace in Kabul was illusory for Kamran had not abdicated his claim. For the next few years, the tussle continued, and during one of Humayun's absences, Kamran took possession of Kabul and the Mughal household once again. At one point, when Kabul was being besieged by Humayun who was preparing for his great guns to be fired at the fort, in a cold-blooded and dastardly act, Kamran placed the young prince Akbar upon the battlements. According to the contemporary chronicler Nizamuddin Ahmad, Maham Anaga threw herself upon the child and clutched him to her bosom, placing herself between the guns and the prince. In the end, after months of skirmishing, Kamran was forced to flee and Humayun took back Kabul. Once peace was re-established, however cursory, the rituals of Mughal courtly life continued. One of the most important aspects of the upbringing of a Mughal prince was his education and this was now undertaken in the case of Akbar. But Akbar would prove to be a spectacularly indifferent student, giving rise to all manner of speculations and insinuations for centuries.

The official beginning of a Timurid mirza's education was the second event after his circumcision which marked the end of his infancy. A thorough education allowed a prince to rule wisely and be able to gauge men and help raise them to their full potential. According to the scholar Munis Faruqui, 'a well educated prince combined the best qualities of a man of the pen...and a man of the sword'. Humayun, an extremely literary man himself, and fully conversant with the solemnity of the occasion, chose the propitious hour for beginning this grave task after much consultation with 'acute astrologers and time-knowing astrolabe-conners'. But when that hour came around, viz. 20 November 1547, while the teacher Mullazada Mulla Asamudin Ibrahim was waiting, the 'scholar of God's school had attired himself for sport and had disappeared'. The unfortunate teacher was soon dismissed on the seemingly whimsical charge of being too fond of pigeon-flying, though he seems to have instructed his pupil rather too well in this respect, as kabootar-bazi was a sport that Akbar would enjoy to distraction. The next teacher assigned to the royal pupil was Maulana Bayazid but he fared no better than his predecessor and was similarly discharged. After this, it appears that tutors were not exactly rushing forward to take on the task because Abu'l Fazl admits that Humayun had to draw lots between three men and, finally, Maulana Abdul Qadir was chosen. Akbar, however, was at that time 'continually giving his attention to that wondrous creature the camel...He used to observe and contemplate,' wrote the indulgent Abu'l Fazl, 'the strange make and ways of camels, which were the biggest animals in that region and...made serious reflections on... their endurance and patience'. Patience would have certainly been required of the camels as Akbar led them around by a rope, raced them against horses, and fed them thorns. He also spent many hours watching pigeons fly, running alongside dogs, hunting deer and, as witnessed by one of his alarmed father's amirs, sleeping on the open ground. The impression of the young Akbar at this stage was of a robust, strong-willed, and easily distracted child filled with vital, restless energy and exulting in the wildness around him.

As a result of this unfettered, exuberant childhood spent avoiding his long-suffering tutors and running through the countryside in the raucous company of his kokas, Aziz, Zain, and Adham, Akbar grew up effectively illiterate. This was a perplexing reality in a man who would later own a fortune in manuscripts and who would orchestrate the largest translation and writing project undertaken at the time. It was certainly not for want of opportunity, for Aziz Koka, who was brought up alongside Akbar, grew up to be an erudite, literary, and extremely well-read man. Abu'l Fazl would explain the inconsistency through a miraculous, divine filter, comparing Akbar to the Prophet Muhammad, who was also illiterate. Akbar, too, would encourage parents to keep one of their children in a state of illiteracy, in imitation of the Prophet. That Akbar was a distracted, volatile child, who found it difficult to focus on the onerous task of a demanding Mughal education, is clear but there was one creative skill he was able to acquire, one that required as much concentration and physical immobility as learning grammar or history or religious studies, and that was painting. While he was in Kabul, Akbar learnt to paint from Abd al-Samad, and there is a rare miniature from the reign of Humayun which depicts this momentous event, when Akbar is shown presenting a painting he has made to his father. For this the young boy would have had to sit on his haunches, one leg folded under his body, his drawing board resting on his raised thigh, for hours at a time. So it would appear that Akbar was quite capable of sustained periods of applied work when it came to painting. His illiteracy, therefore, has been understood by modern scholars as being due to a dyslexic condition, which would appear to best explain why Akbar was able to paint and yet, in a court which valued writing and calligraphy so highly, was unable to write. In the sixteenth century, and at the mystically charged moment of the second Islamic millennium, this supposed illiteracy would not be deemed a failing but would be interpreted by Abu'l Fazl as further proof of the Padshah's grandeur, of his being quite beyond the limitations of ordinary mortals.

While Akbar was being initiated, albeit reluctantly, into a more formal and visible role as a Mughal mirza, life continued in its prosaic, everyday way in the harem, where he remained the cossetted and adored child of the women. At the age of six he suffered a bout of toothache, for which Bega Begum brought a remedy from her stores. Hamida Banu, however, was immediately vigilant, terrified of poison at a time when royal children's lives were extremely threatened. Bega Begum, sympathetic to Hamida Banu's fears, first swallowed some of the medicine herself before giving it to Akbar and so 'the minds of those present were set at rest...and also my pain soothed', remembered Akbar. Indeed, Akbar loved Bega Begum dearly and admitted later to Abu'l Fazl that 'the kindness and affection which she showed to me and my love for her are beyond expression. Everyone who did not know the real facts [that she was his stepmother], thought that she was my own mother.'

A certain calm may have prevailed in the harem, but this was not true of much of the rest of the Mughal court. Humayun had been involved in a series of deadly skirmishes with Kamran over control of Badakhshan and Kabul. It was during one such almost desultory raid that Hindal was killed, long after he had joined Humayun and was fighting for the Padshah. The harem was inconsolable and Gulbadan wrote about her grief over the death of this youngest son of Babur with almost unconsoled sorrow, fifty years later, when she said 'would to Heaven that merciless sword had touched my heart and eyes, or Saadat Yar, my son's, or Khizr Khwaja Khan's*! Alas! A hundred regrets! Alas! A thousand times alas!'

With the death of the first of his uncles, Akbar was suddenly catapulted into the much more incendiary world of Mughal politics at the age of nine. He inherited all of Hindal's entourage and his lands around Ghazni and this appanage was now his to govern entirely. He also inherited a more fragile and complicated thing, his nine-year-old cousin, Ruqaiya Begum. It was a Timurid custom for cousins to marry and, at this point, the young cousins were betrothed to one another. But perhaps Akbar, at this stage immersed in the world of his kokas, their roughhouse fights, the hunts and the pigeons, revolted at the idea of having to even consider this girl as a future bride. Much later in his life, Akbar would work hard to convince his subjects about the evils of child marriage and his vehemence seems to have arisen from a bleak and personal space. He would raise the marriageable age of boys to sixteen and girls to fourteen, and would forbid the marrying of one's cousin or close relative: 'The marriage of a young child is displeasing to the Almighty,' he would say, 'for the object [procreation] which is

---

*Gulbadan's husband.

intended is still remote, and there is proximate harm.' Nevertheless, his first wife would be Ruqaiya Begum who would long outlive Akbar and would never bear any children herself.

Meanwhile, Hindal's servants seem not to have been impressed by their new master's scholarly skills and his inclination for pigeon racing, for they complained to Humayun and this most erudite of Padshahs wrote his son a gentle rebuke, in the form of a poem:

> Sit not idle 'tis not the time for play
> 'tis the time for arts and for work.

His precious son's wilful refusal to learn to read must have worried Humayun to distraction. This was, after all, the Padshah who so valued books and manuscripts that he took his library with him to the battlefield. On one occasion, after his camp was plundered, he first enquired about the condition of his books. Art historian Kavita Singh writes that upon being told his library was safe, Humayun sighed and said, 'God be praised that things which cannot be replaced are safe. As for other things, they were a small matter.' He would have consoled himself, perhaps, with the arrival from the Safavid court of some extraordinary artists—the gold worker Wais, the bookbinder Maulana Fakhr and, finally, the painters Mir Sayyid Ali and Abd al-Samad.

A month after the death of Hindal, in the winter of 1551, Humayun sent the nine-year-old Akbar with his new entourage to take charge of his lands in Ghazni. Appointed to help Akbar was an ataliq, or guardian, Khwaja Jalal al-din Mahmud. If the milk mothers were crucial figures in a Mughal prince's life, watching over his physical safety, the ataliqs were equally important, appointed through various stages of a prince's childhood and early manhood. Depending on the age of the prince, these men helped him navigate the potential minefield of the Mughal nobility. They had to do this, moreover, while maintaining the delicate and sometimes conflicting balance between the prince's best interest and the Padshah's. According to Faruqui, the ataliq 'was ideally a figure of fierce authority, perhaps the most important such male figure in his life'. Akbar spent most of the next few months in Ghazni as a provincial governor, while Kamran continued to defy Humayun, plundering and ravaging the countryside. After living for a while disguised as a woman in a burqa, and after decades of resistance and violence, Kamran was finally captured in 1553 by a Gakkhar chieftain and sent to Humayun.

That Humayun was extremely conflicted over Kamran's fate is evident in Gulbadan's account of the episode. He gathered all the Mughal nobility and the soldiers together and asked them for their advice. 'Brotherly custom has nothing to do with ruling and reigning,' he was told. 'If you wish to act as a brother, abandon the throne.' In the end, it was decided to blind Kamran, effectively ending his challenge to rule. 'Though my head inclines to your words, my heart does not,' grieved Humayun, who had tried to reason with Kamran for many years. Finally the order to blind Kamran was given but the servants baulked, and 'disputed among themselves who was to perform the cruel act'. But the deed was done, at last, and Kamran was led back to his own camp where the water-bearer Jauhar, 'seeing the prince in such pain and distress, could no longer remain with him'. Kamran was sent to Mecca where he died four years later while his young son, Abu'l Qasim, was kept a prisoner.

In Kabul, meanwhile, a son was born to Humayun's new wife, Mah-chuchak Begum, and he was given the name Muhammad Hakim*. A few months later Akbar was given a new ataliq, Munim Khan, a Chaghatai nobleman who had been in Humayun's service since the time of his peregrinations in Sind. This was an honour which Munim Khan celebrated with a great banquet and the distribution of gifts. By 1554 Humayun was the last of the Timurid mirzas still able to stake a claim to the empire founded in Hindustan with such blistering haste by Babur. Sher Shah Sur had died in 1545 and when Humayun heard of the death of his son, Islam Shah, in November 1554, he must have felt that the stars, cold and uncaring, were at last turning favourable to him.

---

*Henceforth known as Mirza Hakim.

THE AFGHAN, THE HINDU, AND THE TIMURID

Humayun set off to reconquer Hindustan in a remarkably cavalier manner at the end of 1554. With only 3,000 men and his twelve-year-old heir, he boarded a raft made of timber at Jalalabad and 'pleasantly floated down the river to Pyshavir'. The harem had been left in Kabul, which was under the governorship of Munim Khan, with only Maham Anaga accompanying Akbar to Hindustan. After they had crossed the Indus, Humayun had Akbar bathed and brought before him and, under a crescent moon, he read some verses of the Koran and, at the end of each verse, breathed on the prince 'and was so delighted and happy, it might be said that he had then acquired all the good fortune of this world, and the blessings of the next'. Humayun was forty-six years old at this time, a slim, elegant man with a narrow face and a short, pointed beard. He would have been wearing his distinctive high turban, a long qaba (kurta-like gown), as was the fashion, with a sleeveless overcoat and furs. This moment with his father may have been one of the last abiding memories Akbar would have of Humayun. The Padshah so happy in the gathering dawn, the holy verses, and the gentle breath, with Akbar himself a conduit for Humayun's blessings. 'Alas that the Emperor Humayun died so early, and that I had no opportunity of showing him faithful service!' he said to Abu'l Fazl many decades later.

The retaking of Hindustan by Humayun was easy for a number of reasons. His own brothers were no longer a threat. The Afghan forces were dispersed and fragmented. Timur's long-ago invasion had fractured the cohesion of the Delhi Sultanate, seeding small chiefdoms headed by erstwhile Tughlaq governors in provinces far from Delhi. Sher Shah Sur's dynasty had been an unforeseen blaze of stability, but it had crumbled equally spectacularly following the rapid collapse of five successive Sur pretenders, bringing political chaos to the region around Delhi. Given all this, Humayun, greatly aided by his general Bairam Khan, who brought a further 5,000 troops from Kandahar, was able to regain his lands remarkably easily. The Punjab was captured and so was the great city of Lahore. Sikandar Shah's forces were twice defeated, and on 23 July 1555, Humayun entered Delhi.

Though Humayun brought only a small force with him into Hindustan, the composition of its nobility was unique. Of the fifty-one nobles listed as having joined his forces by 1555, twenty-seven were identified as Turani, often high-ranked, and sixteen were Shia Persians, or Iranis,* usually lower ranked. 'Before this,' writes historian Iqtidar Alam Khan, 'in no state ruled by a Muslim dynasty did Shi'as and Sunnis coexist in the nobility in such remarkable amity'.

As Humayun settled into Delhi, the young Akbar continued to be fascinated by the animals he discovered around him. He killed a nilgai with a sword and was enchanted by a cheetah which was presented to him by a nobleman who had captured it at the battle of Machhiwara†. The cheetah's keeper, Dundu, was given the title Fath Khan and Akbar spent many happy hours with this animal and his keeper. Humayun and Akbar also spent some time together painting under the guidance of the two great Persian master artists, Mir Sayyid Ali and Abd al-Samad. One of Akbar's tenacious memories of Humayun, vibrant even half a century later, would appear to be intimately linked to his love of paintings. 'My father esteemed much things like this,' he would say to a Jesuit priest about a beautiful image of the Virgin Mary in 1602, 'and if anyone had given it him, he would have granted him any boon he might have asked.' There is an exquisite miniature that survives from this early Mughal *taswir khana* that might depict these precise moments. In a painting filled with swirling movement entitled 'Prince Akbar presents a painting to his father Humayun', the miniature depicts that evanescent hour between end of day and beginning of night. The evening's entertainment is about to begin after a day spent hunting and a young Akbar presents a painting to his father, who eagerly bends forward. The image being presented is in fact *that very painting* and Kavita Singh postulates that Akbar might have contributed to it along with the master Abd al-Samad. Singh also points out that 'the range of colours used suggests that it was made

---
*Persian speaking, from the Persianate empire.
†Fought between the Mughals and Sikandar Shah Sur.

in a well-stocked studio, and the meticulous finish is the result of laborious and time-consuming processes of layering and burnishing the surface'. The library depicted in the miniature may even be the Sher Mandal, the two-storey pavilion in the Deenpanah* (Asylum of Faith), where Humayun housed his precious books and manuscripts.

Four months later, Humayun decided to send Akbar north as governor to the crucial and turbulent region of the Punjab. Since Munim Khan was still in Kabul, Akbar was now assigned a new ataliq, Bairam Khan, and the large contingent departed for the Punjab. En route they were joined by additional troops which included a master artilleryman under whose training Akbar 'became as much a master of this art as masters of a single art and craft are'.

In the Deenpanah, which had been taken over in the interim and added to by Sher Shah Sur, Humayun introduced a host of new inventions to his court. Drummers now announced the Padshah's arrival and, when Humayun rose to leave the court, muskets were fired. He wore garments according to a strict colour code he had created to align with the planets, and two-storey barges he had designed sailed on the Yamuna. Scholar A. Azfar Moin has shown that many of the mysterious and elaborate ceremonies that Humayun developed at his court to bolster his own claims to a sacred kingship for the Mughals in Hindustan were influenced by his time spent at the Persian Safavid court. Moin demonstrates that far from being the 'eccentric dilettante' of modern rhetoric, Humayun attempted to create a legitimate source of power by using Sufic symbols, equally appropriate in Hindustan's landscape as it had been in Persia's, and provided his successors with some powerful sacred symbolism. Humayun also introduced the system of mansab† for his officers in lieu of the earlier 'beg' and adopted some of Sher Shah Sur's important administrative measures as described by Eaton:

> These included...division of the kingdom's administration into fixed territorial units, or sarkars, subdivided in districts, or parganas. From Sher Shah's administration on, revenue and judicial officers were posted at both sarkar and pargana levels,

---

*Purana Qila, also known today as the Old Fort.
†A position, or rank.

thereby ensuring an orderly system of land-revenue assessment and collection. Further, to centralize his administration, Humayun designated as much revenue-producing land as possible as khalisa, or land administered directly by the state, rather than by nobles.

The system of assigning a mansab to an officer—linking the strength of the contingent expected of him to his revenue from assigned territories in a fixed ratio—had been accepted by both Babur and Humayun when they encountered it in Hindustan. As we will see later, Akbar would use this system to good effect.

Humayun seems to have had an intimation of his own end during the last months of his life. He became melancholic, spoke of dreams and auguries and, even more ominously, slowly reduced his consumption of opium. On the night of 24 January 1556 he went up to the roof of his library with his astrologer to watch Venus rising. On hearing the muezzin's call to prayer, Humayun hurried down the steep, shadowy steps of the library, tripped on his long fur robes, and fell down the stone stairs. Three days later, just six months after regaining his throne, the Padshah of Hindustan was dead.

When news reached Akbar at Kalanaur, almost 500 kilometres away from Delhi, that his father had died, he was inconsolable. He wept, we are told, and 'was upset beyond human imagination'. Maham Anaga and Shamsuddin Ataka Khan tried to console the young prince but their attempts only increased his sobs. Akbar was only thirteen years old when Humayun died and very unlike his father physically. He was of average height but broad in the shoulders and, at this age, had not even a wisp of a whisker. In Kabul, Humayun's other surviving son, Mirza Hakim, was just two years old. But despite Akbar's youth and sorrow, Bairam Khan could not afford to wait while the prince grieved. The death of Humayun had been hidden from the populace and the soldiery, given the precariousness of the nascent empire. In Kalanaur, therefore, on the banks of the Ravi, on a hastily constructed brick throne set in a garden, Akbar was proclaimed Padshah, third of the Mughals of Hindustan.

Akbar's grandiose title notwithstanding, Mughal claims to sovereignty in Hindustan were gossamer thin. The remarkable reign of the Pashtun Afghan Sur clan had come to an end but there were still individual Sur pretenders who sought to challenge the audacious claims of this young Mughal parvenu. Sikandar Shah Sur was still a dangerous presence in the Punjab while Adil Shah remained truculent in Bihar. Even the territories controlled by the Mughals were more in the form of garrison towns rather than substantial holdings. Moreover, the Surs had ruled peacefully for fifteen years, which was as long as the rule of Babur and Humayun combined. As historian Annemarie Schimmel has noted, 'Akbar's territories were hemmed in by rivals. To the north, Kashmir, Sind...were fully independent'. Kabul was nominally under Mirza Hakim, Bengal was an independent kingdom as were Malwa, Gujarat, and Orissa. This was also true of many of the Rajput clans. The Deccan sultanates held sway in the south while further away still Vijayanagar was a Hindu kingdom. The Portuguese held ports, including Goa. The Mughal Empire, paltry as it was at this time, consisted of 'seven or eight military zones, commanded by leading nobles from their headquarters at Kabul, Qandahar, Lahore, Multan, Delhi, Agra, Etawa, Kalpi, Kol and Sambhal'. These noblemen were entrusted with overcoming Afghan and other local resistance, and attempting to establish some form of regular administration. These high nobles were also assigned a jagir, or revenue assignment, which usually lay within the territory they commanded. This was not a perfect overlay, however, for the area commanded far exceeded the extent of the jagir.

Nor was the situation within the Mughal army free from misgivings. Many from within the soldiery were disenchanted with the plains of Hindustan and yearned to return to the green mountains of Kabul and so, 'to placate the self-sacrificing heroes who had recently entered India', a summons was sent to Kabul to bring the imperial harem and also 'the wives and families of the other attendants...as quickly as possible...so that the men would settle there...' The men may have won the battles, but the women and children were needed to create a haven and a place of comfort.

Since Akbar was a minor at the time, the Mughal Empire needed a regent, or wakil. Bairam Khan was deemed most suitable by the nobility and was appointed wakil-e-saltanat, with the title khankhanan, and Tardi Beg immediately handed over the custody of Mirza Kamran's second son, Abu'l Qasim, to Bairam Khan. Abu'l

Qasim was an important hostage because as a Timurid mirza himself, he could become the locus of potentially fractious noblemen. Of immediate concern was Sikandar Shah Sur, one of the Sur pretenders, who had indulged in the boldest posturing and so the imperial army, under Bairam Khan, decided to neutralize him first. Sikandar Shah retreated towards the Sivalik mountains; the army followed him and remained in the area, hunting and accepting the fealty of the zamindars who submitted to the Padshah. Then the imperial army moved back to Jalandhar in the Punjab, during the monsoon of 1556, when news arrived of another turbulent mirza. Mirza Sulaiman was the descendant of a Timurid prince who had submitted to Babur decades previously and who had been given the fief of Badakhshan when Humayun rode back to Hindustan. Now with Humayun dead, Mirza Sulaiman almost capriciously decided to lay claim to Kabul, which was then being controlled by Munim Khan. But in October, news arrived of a much more discordant uprising, one with dreams of empire, for Hemu, a general from Adil Shah's (a Sur descendant) army, had defeated the Mughal forces and had taken Delhi. As soon as he heard of the death of Humayun, while Akbar was still grieving in Kalanaur, Hemu had wasted no time at all. He had marched out of Chunar, the headquarters of Adil Shah, and had stormed and taken Agra. Gathering the enemies of the Mughals, who were legion, into his own army, Hemu then marched on Delhi itself.

Hemu, a Hindu of the Baniya caste, was an unlikely hero in an age of giants. He began life obscurely enough as a petty trader but caught the attention of Adil Shah, and slowly gained prestige through his shrewd intelligence, industry, and honesty. Abu'l Fazl was notoriously scathing of this first great adversary of Akbar's and railed that 'outwardly he had neither rank...nor race...nor beauty of form...nor noble qualities'. No doubt Abu'l Fazl was piqued by this man of obscure origins who had the ambition to challenge Akbar when he was at his most vulnerable. Abu'l Fazl fulminated that it was through 'evil speaking, plotting and calumny' that Hemu rose to become prime minister but there is little doubt that Hemu, while apparently a man of underwhelming physical stature, was one of considerable acumen and skill, and even Abu'l Fazl had to admit that 'ill-starred' though he was, Hemu had already won twenty-two battles against powerful amirs. Realizing that the young Mughal Padshah was far away, and that the city was under the nominal charge of Tardi Beg, Hemu seized his chance and marched towards Delhi.

Delhi, as well as the northern cities of Agra and Bayana, in addition to Gujarat, were reeling under the catastrophic effects of a famine and the consequent epidemics of two successive years between 1554 and 1556, leading to political chaos. 'Men of wealth and position had to close their houses,' wrote Badauni, sixteen years old at the time, 'and died by tens or twenties or even more in one place, getting neither grave nor shroud.' These dead included Hindus as well as Muslims and those who survived were reduced to living on 'the seeds of the Egyptian thorn, wild dry grass and cowhides'. 'The writer of these pages,' continued Badauni, 'with these guilty eyes of his saw man eating his fellow-man in those terrible days'. Brought on by drought and crop failure, these were 'two years [of] continual anarchy and terror...and lawless crowds attacked the cities of the Muslims'. Abu'l Fazl also wrote about the epidemics, noting the plague that spread as a result of the mounds of the dead and the marauding parties being formed to seize and eat solitary victims.

But as Hemu rode towards Delhi with his enormous army of 50,000 cavalry and 500 elephants, the soldiery and the animals continued to find rations, as did the Mughal army. 'While people were crying for bread and taking each other's lives,' wrote Badauni, 'the elephants of Himun's army...were fed solely upon rice, and oil, and sugar.' As soon as he was encamped in the plains of Tughlaqabad, Hemu unleashed his ferocious war elephants. Under the command of Tardi Beg, the Mughal amirs were undecided about whether to fight or flee and, irresolute and unconvinced, were roundly defeated by Hemu, who captured 100 of their elephants, 1,000 Arab horses, and an immense quantity of booty. Part of the reason for Mughal indecision seems to have been the removal of powerful Mughal amirs from the region by Bairam Khan himself, who had moved quickly to neutralize competitors after he became wakil-e-saltanat. Hemu now took the grandiose title of Raja Hemchandra Vikramaditya and Tardi Beg fled towards the Punjab where Bairam Khan was waiting for him, fury and murder in his heart.

That Tardi Beg and Bairam Khan were headed for a clash without the accommodating presence of Humayun had been clear for a long time. Of the small group of fifty-one nobles who had come to Hindustan with Humayun in 1555, almost all were foreign-born Muslims. More than half of those were high status chiefs from Central Asian Turki–Chaghatai or Uzbek lineages while a smaller group of sixteen noblemen were Persian Shias. Tardi Beg, the Turki-speaking brusque old Central Asian Sunni nobleman from the retinue of Padshah Babur himself, would have considered himself superior in every way to Bairam Khan. To Tardi Beg, the Shia Bairam Khan would probably always have remained Humayun's muhrdar, his seal bearer, and a negligible Persian parvenu. Early in Humayun's reign Bairam Khan had wanted to sit on the same carpet as Tardi Beg, who was Governor of Etawah at the time, and Tardi Beg had peremptorily refused. But Bairam Khan's stature had risen meteorically since then, with Humayun taking Bairam Khan to Persia, and appointing him ataliq to Akbar. Though Bairam Khan still addressed the older man as tugan, or elder brother, their standing had changed enormously. Bairam Khan meanwhile needed to act quickly to bring order within the ranks of the fiercely independent Central Asian noblemen who each, according to the scoffing Ferishta, 'esteemed himself at least equal to Keikobad and Keikaoos (the legendary Persian heroes)'. Tardi Beg wanted to continue the retreat, possibly all the way back to his stronghold of Kabul, and Bairam Khan needed to act decisively and unambiguously to show the nobility that there was a new kingmaker who would not tolerate defeat or disaffection. As to the exact sequence of events that led to Tardi Beg lying in a pool of blood in the Mughal camp, there are various interpretations, reflecting the disquiet felt upon the murder of this old warlord of Babur and Humayun.

According to Abu'l Fazl, there was ancient rivalry between the two men and Bairam Khan, seizing the opportunity of the embarrassing defeat of the Mughals, lured Tardi Beg into his own quarters through an invitation carried via Maulana Pir Muhammad Shirwani*. When Tardi Beg entered the tent, Bairam Khan excused himself on some pretext and Tardi Beg was immediately murdered by his attendants. The young Akbar, all accounts agree, was not present at the time of the killing. He was out hawking, as usual, in the 'delightful plains'

---

*The wakil-i mutlak, or administrator, of Bairam Khan's establishment.

of Sirhind with his sparrow hawks. 'When it was reported to him,' wrote Abu'l Fazl, 'no change in his countenance occurred, and he entrusted retribution to almighty God while observing destiny without a wrinkle of complaint on his brow.'

With Tardi Beg out of the way, Bairam Khan now ignored the army's advice to retreat and marched, along with Akbar, to Panipat to confront Hemu. Akbar would not participate in the battle himself, for Bairam Khan kept him at a safe remove, guarded by 3,000 horsemen. About the ancient battlefield of Panipat, a later historian wrote that it was a 'uniform yellow-gray waste of sterile earth. Everywhere empty silence reigns and it would almost seem as if this desert had been designed for the battlefield of nations.' But even without the whimsical imagery of a historian, Panipat would have been charged with sacred symbolism for the Mughal army as the scene of Babur's miraculous victory over Ibrahim Lodi in 1526. Bairam Khan now drew on the memory of that famous victory and gave a rousing speech to his assembled generals. The shoulder blade of a sheep was inspected for good omens and with the assurance that the stars were on their side, the Mughal army readied itself for battle.

Bairam Khan's forces began the day by capturing Hemu's artillery, which had been sent in advance under his generals Mubarak Khan and Bahadur Khan. But after initial jubilation, the Mughals turned to look over the 'sparse grasses and stunted thorn-bushes' of Panipat and saw a sight which must have struck them with scudding fear, battle-hardened warriors though they were, for this was something they had never seen before. It was a vision from a nightmare, or from hell itself. As the earth began to quake beneath their feet and the air was filled with swirling dust, screams, and wails, Hemu charged the Mughals with 1,500 war elephants, all trumpeting in rage and fury. The elephants wore armour and had daggers and spears attached to their lashing trunks and 30,000 'pugnacious Rajput and Afghan horsemen' galloped in front of them. Hemu led the charge himself, seated upon his elephant Hawai, as he screamed out his war cry, 'Band o Bastan'*! His left wing was led by his nephew Ramya while the great Afghan amirs of the Surs rode on elephants picked especially for their courage. As the mass of elephants, black clouds

---

*Give and Take!

glittering with armour and wicked knives, charged the Mughal army with horrifying speed, the Mughal forces were thrown into pandemonium and disarray. Riders struggled to control horses that had never confronted elephants and the Mughal amirs died in large numbers at the hands of their foe, 'their blood-dripping blades like hungry lions'. Screaming horses were lifted off the ground by the elephants and flung onto the earth, glossy with blood. The Mughal army numbered 10,000 soldiers but a scathing Abu'l Fazl deemed that only 5,000 were worthy of the designation. They swung their deadly scimitars and the archers wielded their composite bows* but had it not been for a chance arrow which struck Hemu through the eye in the heat of the battle, Bairam Khan's gamble to confront Hemu's army may have had a very different outcome.

Seeing their general slumped in his howdah on Hawai, Hemu's Afghan amirs and soldiers lost heart and the battle was won for the Mughals. Hemu was brought to the Mughal camp, limp and bloodied, but alive. Bairam Khan wanted Akbar to kill Hemu himself, thus eliminating a dangerous foe and earning the title ghazi, slayer of infidels. We will never be sure if Akbar obeyed or not, for according to Abu'l Fazl's writings, which were closely monitored by Akbar himself decades later, Akbar refused to kill a wounded enemy. But was the fourteen-year-old able to articulate this to his formidable ataliq who had just won a famous victory or were these, in fact, the compassionate thoughts of the fifty-year-old Padshah? Abu'l Fazl writes that he wishes that Akbar had 'unveiled' his true nature and not allowed Hemu to have been killed at all, since such a brave and worthy opponent could have been won over and made an honoured member of the Mughal court. In just a few years, diplomacy alongside martial strength would, in fact, become the keystone of Akbar's policy, allowing him to establish one of the largest empires ever seen in Hindustan. But at fourteen, Akbar was only beginning his extraordinary journey. In any event, Hemu was slain, with Akbar probably striking a blow, and his head was sent to Kabul as a grisly

---

*This Mongol bow was made of layers of wood and sinew, bound together using glue made from animals. The extreme recurve shape of the bow made it even more powerful than the English longbow and it is considered the most effective medieval weapon to have existed before the advent of the gun. A skilled user could fire over six shots per minute.

summons to the Mughal harem while his body was displayed in Delhi—a gruesome warning to those who would dream of empire.

An enormous amount of Hemu's treasures, which were hidden at Mewat, were now captured by the Mughal forces. His family was also captured and his elderly father was given the chance to convert to Islam and save his life. 'For eighty years I have been worshipping my God according to my religion,' protested the old man gallantly, 'how could I abandon it now?' Maulana Pir Mohammad Sherwani was unmoved and executed the old man and the treasure now fell into Mughal hands. The army marched rapidly from Panipat and Akbar finally entered Delhi for the first time as Padshah of Hindustan in 1556. The populace of Delhi, noblemen and traders, came to offer congratulations to the young Akbar who, meanwhile, had discovered what was to remain one of the enduring passions of his life—the elephants of Hindustan.

If camels were the largest creatures that Akbar had seen in Kabul he was now confronted in Hindustan with an animal that was truly worthy of awe. In trying to ride and subdue 'mast'* elephants, Akbar would challenge not only his own physical courage but also test his immortal self, and would repeatedly conjure up and call upon the blessing of God himself. Scores of curious onlookers as well as petitioners arrived every day to assess this fourteen-year-old Padshah. They watched in wonder as the youth hung on to the swaying animals, his bare feet digging deep into their flesh as he sat on their necks in sweating disarray. One day in Delhi when Akbar was riding a charging elephant his bemused well-wishers ran screaming from its path. However, one small group of observers, Rajputs from a clan in Rajasthan, did not move, preferring death to dishonour, and Akbar was impressed. He was told that they were led by one Raja Bharmal and while Akbar might have been pleased by the resolute courage of these men, history doesn't record Raja Bharmal's opinion of the young Padshah.

In Kabul, meanwhile, Hemu's head hung on the Iron Gate of the city and drums had joyfully heralded the news of Akbar's victory. Hamida Banu Begum, now a widow and queen mother, prepared to make the journey to Hindustan to meet her son, the newly proclaimed Padshah.

---

*Bull elephants in their annual cycle of testosterone-driven aggressive behaviour.

WHILE THE PADSHAH HUNTED

When the imperial caravan led by Munim Khan left Kabul for the plains of Hindustan, the circumstances of many of the women in it had sadly altered. Hamida Banu and Bega Begum were now widowed. Hamida Banu had left her native Sind as a feisty fourteen-year-old bride and now she was returning as queen mother of the empire, at the age of thirty-one. Gulbadan had lost all her beloved brothers, dead or exiled. Only Mah-chuchak Begum, along with her children, was to remain in Kabul. The caravan included many other single women—widows, unmarried women, divorcees—Timurid women who had answered Babur's long-ago call to come to Hindustan. At Akbar's court, these Timurid women with their nostalgia for a lost world, their Turki language and their abiding memory of Timurid culture and etiquette would help the Padshah retain his link to the old ways of his ancestors.

In addition to these women were the families of all the soldiers in Hindustan and this large group made its winding way through the high mountain passes of Kabul into the fertile plains of Hindustan. The soldiers and nobility were all dressed in styles that were resolutely 'foreign': long coats and cloaks and caps all made from thick cloths and furs. At an earlier time, Babur had been notoriously disdainful of the 'peasants and people of low standing' in Hindustan who, according to his critical eye, 'go about naked. They tie on a thing called languta, a decency-clout which hangs two spans below the navel.' Babur would have been even more unimpressed had he known that kings, too, at non-Muslim courts before the fourteenth and fifteenth centuries did not wear upper garments except for a loosely draped unstitched cloth thrown around the shoulders. According to historian Balkrishan Shivram, before the influence of Islam, the 'body was viewed as an integral aspect of the person' and the untailored cloth served to emphasize the bare body. Islam, however, held that God provided clothing to cover man's essentially shameful nakedness. Not only was the body to be covered but clothing was to be modest and loose-fitting, reflected in a medieval Persian saying: 'neither men nor women should wear a tight robe beneath which their body is revealed'. This sartorial restriction, however, would change enormously in the coming decades. In the meantime, when the caravan halted at Jalalabad, news reached the travellers of the murder of Tardi Beg by Bairam Khan and they took careful stock of Bairam Khan's ambitions.

Munim Khan, who was leading the imperial caravan, was a Turki Chaghatai nobleman like Tardi Beg and an old favourite of the harem. Munim Khan and the women would have understood that this murder was an indication of the subtle game of realignment that had been played by Akbar's new ataliq. They would have heard of all the ways in which Bairam Khan had neutralized the Turani nobility in Hindustan—by imprisoning and executing the few who openly opposed him and distributing largesse to those who were more complaisant. Munim Khan judged it prudent not to confront Bairam Khan at the moment and turned back towards Kabul while the caravan, now under the guardianship of Shamsuddin Ataka Khan, continued on its slow march. Along the way, Hamida Banu suffered personal tragedy when her two young daughters died, as young children did with terrifying regularity at the time. Now the only child she had left was Akbar, and he was to become the lodestone of her life and the focus of her considerable talent and energies.

Meanwhile Akbar and the Mughal army had left Delhi as Sikandar Shah had once again gathered some disaffected Afghans and zamindars and was stirring rebellion in the Punjab. Following the defeat of Hemu, most of these Afghans just moved further east to Bihar and Bengal, ruminating resistance. Hunting along the way and 'indulging in recreation and pleasure', the Mughal forces chased Sikandar Shah back to his fortress at Mankot. As the siege of Mankot dragged on for months, Akbar was able to spend a great deal of time with his beloved elephants, even riding the mast bull elephants when they were charging each other. Decades later Akbar would remember the name of the first bull elephant he had controlled in this way—Jhalpa.

It was while the siege of Mankot was underway that news arrived of the imminent arrival of the caravan from Kabul. Maham Anaga was sent ahead to Lahore to greet the party and it was outside Mankot that Akbar was reunited once again with his mother, Hamida Banu, his aunts, and his milk mothers. The Mughal camp was suddenly filled with effervescence and clamour as the soldiery, 'who had grown homesick during the long drawn-out siege', met wives, and children, and kinsfolk after such a long absence in lands that were yet to feel like home.

While the siege of Mankot carried on, another marriage was arranged for the young Padshah who, as we have seen, was already married to Ruqaiya Begum. The bride-to-be was a granddaughter of Munim Khan and a daughter of Mirza Abdullah Moghul. It is clear that Bairam Khan was opposed to this marriage and, annoyed but unable to directly contradict Hamida Banu, he found excuses to keep delaying the inevitable 'until Nasir ul-mulk* informed him that to delay such affairs was extremely displeasing'. According to historian Iqtidar Alam Khan, this marriage had been decided by Hamida Banu and the ladies of the imperial harem in agreement with Munim Khan to block the dismayingly powerful influence of Bairam Khan upon Akbar, an influence clearly judged troubling. Bairam Khan found that he was increasingly thwarted in his designs in the next few months and tempers frayed, repeatedly.

Once the siege of Mankot was lifted, Sikandar Shah having finally surrendered in May 1557, the imperial party made its way towards Lahore. Rehabilitated, and then again dismissed, Sikandar Shah would die two years later, in Bengal. En route, Akbar enjoyed many elephant fights, this having become a veritable obsession. During one such fight, as the two elephants raged and crashed into each other, there was a loud commotion and amidst all the uproar Bairam Khan became convinced that Akbar was trying to have him trampled to death inside his tent. He sent a furious letter to Maham Anaga demanding 'of what sort of crime have trouble-makers accused me to cause such disfavour that he [Akbar] has set mad elephants upon me?' While Maham Anaga rushed to soothe Bairam Khan, Akbar, perhaps overwhelmed and conflicted by the atmosphere of suspicion and retribution at the camp, had grown 'sick of the sight of shortsighted people and flown into a rage'. Expressly forbidding anyone from following him, Akbar galloped away on a notoriously fiery Persian horse named Hayran,

---

*The title of a high-ranked officer.

while his retinue waited in abashed silence. After he had returned to camp, he gathered only his immediate entourage and the small party went ahead to Lahore without informing Bairam Khan.

That Akbar should have felt frustrated and overcome at this point is understandable. After the death of his father, he had placed his trust in his ataliq to secure his throne and to fight his battles. He had been content to indulge in hunting and in elephant fights encouraged, possibly, by a complicit Bairam Khan who could then consolidate not just the imperial power, but also his own ambitions. Now the harem had blindsided Bairam Khan, questioning his motives, and forming an unexpected barrier between the Padshah and his guardian. For Akbar had implicit and profound trust in these women. Not just in his mother, Hamida Banu, but also his aunt, Gulbadan, stepmother, Bega Begum, and his milk mothers, Maham Anaga and Jiji Anaga. Throughout his life he would show them extravagant devotion and would grant them their smallest wishes. He would never forsake a single one of them and would mourn them, long after they were gone. To have to reconcile the clashing desires of these two factions would have necessarily troubled and exasperated the young emperor.

When the Mughal camp arrived in Lahore a few days after Akbar, Bairam Khan renewed his accusations, this time attacking the Padshah's foster father, Shamsuddin Ataka Khan. 'Since from time to time I find His Majesty lacking in favour,' wrote Bairam Khan angrily, 'I must attribute it to your backbiting and slander. What have I done that you are inimical to me and, thirsty for my blood, you cause the emperor's temperament to deviate? Will you go so far that he will make an attempt on my life?' These were grave and calculated accusations and Ataka was unsettled enough to rally his relatives and appear before Bairam Khan to swear fealty to the powerful khankhanan. Ataka Khan, Akbar's devoted old foster father, was sent away to Bhira by Bairam Khan soon after thus eliminating another of the young Padshah's old retainers. In Lahore there was now further cause for Bairam Khan to be satisfied for he was reunited with his wife, a princess of Mewat,* and his infant son, Abdur Rahim.

---

*Humayun and Bairam Khan had married the daughters of Jamal Khan of Mewat, an important zamindar.

Within a few months, when the Mughal camp was stationed at Jalandhar on its way to Delhi, Bairam Khan reminded Akbar of a promise Humayun had made to wed him to the young Salima Sultan Begum, a granddaughter of Babur, and therefore a Timurid princess. The women of the harem, we are told, especially Maham Anaga, exerted themselves greatly and arranged for this marriage within a week. Akbar, through his biographer Abu'l Fazl, later expressed his scorn at the presumption on the part of Bairam Khan to wish to ally himself to the royal family itself. However, at the age of fifteen, Akbar was not strong enough yet to directly oppose the khankhanan. This was an exalted connection indeed for Bairam Khan and further exposed his soaring ambitions. That Maham Anaga was keen to placate the khankhanan implied that she felt uneasy under his suspicious scrutiny. The harem, and especially Maham Anaga, must have felt the need to maintain the fragile equilibrium between Akbar's happiness and Bairam Khan's ambitions. We will see, later in this chapter, how Maham Anaga is thought to have played a key role in the deposing of Bairam Khan but, for the moment, she was careful not to antagonize him.

The Mughal court continued its peregrinations, leaving for Delhi, 'dispensing justice and indulging in revelry' en route. Measures were slowly put in place to curtail Bairam Khan's power and all the ministers and amirs now met twice a week in the imperial audience hall where all important matters were first presented to Akbar, who then approved the decisions taken. Once in Delhi, however, the Padshah resumed his favourite activities and one day, while riding on a raging mast elephant called Lakhna, he was flung to the ground and nearly crushed to death. While his servants and attendants wailed and lamented, Akbar got back onto the elephant and brought him under control. Akbar, it would seem, was testing his strength and his courage beyond endurance and almost beyond reason.

After six months in Delhi, the Mughal court got ready to move to Agra by boat. Sikandar Shah had been neutralized and the Punjab somewhat secured. The remaining Afghan noblemen had, however, relocated to Bihar and Bengal. Delhi was too far north to deal with these affairs and so Agra, 240 kilometres further south, was chosen as the new capital. Boats and skiffs were decorated, their seats covered with fine fabrics, while banners snapped in the sudden breeze that had sprung up. All the important amirs had ordered boats to be decorated for their retinues, too, so as the court set sail on the wide and placid Yamuna it looked like 'the river itself had been decorated for a festival or tulips and lilies had poked their heads out from the water'. The Mughals fished and hunted along the way and the voyage was marked by celebrations and a clangorous din. Three weeks later, on 30 October 1558, the court reached Agra, 'the water and air of which put Baghdad with its Tigris and Cairo with its Nile to shame'. The city seems to have been much improved since the time, thirty years earlier, when Babur passed through and wrote in utter contempt that 'the grounds were so bad and unattractive that we traversed them with a hundred disgusts and repulsions'. Akbar now settled into the old Badalgarh* Fort while mansions and gardens were built on both banks of the Yamuna for the amirs and their attendants.

In Agra, Bairam Khan attempted a last, futile bid to educate the young Padshah as befitted a Timurid king, and brought to the court a Persian immigrant called Mir Abd al-Latif Qazwini to tutor him. Abu'l Fazl approvingly called him a man 'of great eloquence, and of excellent disposition, and so moderate in his religious sentiments, that each party used to revile him for his indifference'. Indeed Mir Abd al-Latif Qazwini enjoyed a certain notoriety for being 'accused in Persia of being a Sunni and in Hindustan of being a Shia'. Akbar studied the *Masnawi* of the Persian poet Maulana Rumi under his tutor and it is believed that a particular section of the poem most appealed to him. This was the section in which God told the Prophet Moses that he had been sent to unite mankind and not to divide it. While it is possible that the tutor may have communicated a love of Persian Sufi poetry to Akbar, the Padshah continued to resist all attempts to formally educate him.

By the next year, 1559, Bairam Khan, fifty-eight years old now, began to act in an increasingly erratic and blustery manner. He baulked at the tighter control over his actions, such as the twice-weekly meetings between the amirs and the Padshah, Akbar's growing independence, and what he would see as increasing interference from the harem and their loyalists. He banished the loyal Maulana Pir

---

*An ancient fort inhabited by many successive rulers, including Ibrahim Lodi.

Muhammad Shirwani and brought in Haji Muhammad Khan Sistani as his personal wakil. Shaikh Gadai, who had already been appointed sadr,* was now allocated more responsibilities. He also raised some of his patently unqualified servants to positions of eminence. The reaction to all these strategies was immediate and scathing. The nobility began openly to ridicule Bairam Khan and his appointees and a particularly appreciated jibe was one that denigrated the promotion of Haji Muhammad Khan Sistani when it claimed that 'a dog has assumed the status of a sweet seller'. It was further claimed, disastrously for Bairam Khan, that he was opposed to the Chaghatai nobility and was aiming to eliminate them. But the most abhorrent thing he could do, certainly in Akbar's estimation, was to attack the young Padshah's beloved elephant-keepers.

Twice in the course of the year, Bairam Khan had felt himself threatened by rampaging imperial elephants and both times he had had their keepers executed. These elephant-keepers were men that Akbar knew personally and intimately, just as he knew their charges by name. To have these brave and loyal men so summarily executed would have appeared to Akbar almost a personal affront. There were further reasons for Akbar's impatience with his khankhanan. According to Badauni, Akbar was not even allotted a sufficient privy purse and his own servants were kept in a niggardly fashion whereas Bairam Khan's servants were rich and had been generously promoted. A number of historians blamed the supposedly pernicious effect Maham Anaga was having on the relationship between the Padshah and his ataliq; she was accused of having too much ambition herself. Nizamuddin Ahmad grumbled in his *Tabaqat-i-Akbari* that 'at every opportunity they said to His Majesty…words which might produce disfavour in his mind [towards Bairam Khan] especially Adham Khan, who on account of his being the son of Maham Anka, had precedence over all who were specially favoured, and always in concert with his mother followed the path of envy.' However, Abu'l Fazl maintained that it was Akbar, instead, who discussed the matter with Maham Anaga, 'who was a marvel of sense, resource and loyalty'. As a result of this and other discussions at court, the Padshah decided that he

---

*Ministers who administered the religious department of government and controlled charitable grants.

would assume sovereignty and inflict suitable punishment on Bairam Khan.

In March 1560, having consulted with Maham Anaga, Akbar left Agra for Delhi on the pretext of visiting Hamida Banu who was at that time residing in Delhi. He was, instead, initiating a well-calculated coup against Bairam Khan. Akbar's entire foster family were clearly active participants since, in addition to Maham Anaga, her son and son-in-law also arrived in Delhi as did Ataka Khan from the Punjab. A farman* was also sent to Munim Khan in Kabul, where he had been waiting ever since Bairam Khan had murdered Tardi Beg. As news spread of Bairam Khan's fall from grace, the nobility and soldiers quickly displayed their loyalty by riding to Delhi so that the entire army was soon gathered there. An agitated Bairam Khan tried to send messengers to Akbar who refused to entertain them and, instead, sent a letter to his regent:

> For reassuring you, we had written that though there may arise a quarrel between father and son, yet neither can be indifferent to each other. Since you are our Khan Baba, the same relationship applies between us. In spite of this grief and hurt and improper and unworthy acts (from you) we hold you in our affection and favour and love you. We still call you and recognise you as 'Khan Baba' as in the past.

The balance of power, however, had changed irrevocably between Akbar and his 'Khan Baba' and the Padshah made it clear that Bairam Khan was to arrange his affairs and proceed to Mecca.† Bairam Khan left with a small retinue including his wives, his son, and Shaikh Gadai. As he did not head for Mecca immediately, his actions were interpreted as rebellious and Akbar sent Maulana Pir Mohammad Shirwani to pursue him. Humiliated and exasperated, Bairam Khan moved deeper into the Punjab. Akbar was disconcerted enough by the actions of Bairam Khan to send an army to confront him. There were even worrying rumours that Bairam Khan was planning to declare Kamran's son, Mirza Abu'l Qasim, Padshah in place of Akbar. While the army set off under Ataka Khan, Akbar himself made

---
*A royal decree.
†Sending a courtier to Mecca was the equivalent of an honourable banishment.

preparations to follow his troops into the Punjab. Bairam Khan's followers were routed by the imperial forces at Sultanpur, and the disgraced khankhanan finally sought refuge with the Hindu ruler Raja Ganesh of Talwara. Munim Khan, making his way south from Kabul, met with Akbar and his retinue at Machhiwara and then they all continued on to Sirhind.

At Sirhind, Munim Khan was given the title khankhanan and was appointed wakil. His new responsibilities would include control over financial as well as military and administrative affairs, as had been the case with Bairam Khan, and Akbar would also show him the same deference he had shown Bairam Khan, always addressing him as Khan Baba. At Talwara, meanwhile, Bairam Khan had taken stock of all that he had lost, and contemplated with sorrow his utter disgrace. He asked for Munim Khan to be sent to accept his surrender saying:

> I have taken refuge with the infidels urged by necessity. If you come and, seizing my hands take me out of the hills, I shall go with you.

He was then presented, weeping and debased, before Akbar who embraced his Khan Baba and made him sit on the takht beside him one last time and spoke to him kindly, with all his old affection. Akbar dismissed Bairam Khan with honour, bestowing a special robe on him and giving him 50,000 rupees in cash for his maintenance but this would be the last time that Akbar would meet his ataliq and Bairam Khan left the court, heading for Mecca, his dreams evaporated and exiled from the empire he had helped create.

TIMURID MATRIARCHS
AND THEIR COLOSSAL DREAMS

When the Mughal court moved to the new capital city at Agra on the last day of 1560, it had a new wakil-e-saltanat.* When the imperial camp reached the city, colourful tents and fluttering pavilions were set up inside the fortress of Badalgarh and Munim Khan was assigned Bairam Khan's old quarters. To celebrate this remarkable reversal in his fortunes, the new khankhanan held a grand banquet to which he invited Akbar. To have the Padshah himself grace one's home was considered a unique honour and an exceptional privilege and Munim Khan served Akbar himself, and offered him magnificent gifts. With his ethnic Turki background, Munim Khan may have included dishes at his banquet that reflected his lustrous heritage. Grains were an important part of Turki diet and kashk, a porridge made of crushed wheat and meat, may have been served in addition to more extravagant dishes such as murg mussalam, an elaborate item made by removing the bones of a whole chicken, marinating it in yoghurt and spices, stuffing it with rice, nuts, minced meat, and boiled eggs, and then baking it in clarified butter and yet more spices.

Akbar was making such visible signs of favour to Munim Khan because not everyone was satisfied with this choice and there were other contenders jostling for key positions. A cautious, careful man, whose nature appeared to be reflected in a perennially worried expression and a scraggly beard, there were others who were more ruthless than Munim Khan. Principal among them was Akbar's foster father, Ataka Khan, who wrote a long, complaining letter to the Padshah saying that though he had been awarded Bairam Khan's 'banner, drums and tuman tugh...a fur garment, a robe of victory, and insignia of pomp', he had hoped to gain Bairam Khan's title of

---

*The position of wakil was superior to the other four main offices of the Mughal Empire viz. the diwan or wazir (chief minister), the mir bakshi (minister of military affairs), the mir saman (minister of the imperial household including karkhanas, workshops) and the sadr (minister of religious matters).

khankhanan too. But Akbar was unmoved and propitiated him with the title azam khan.

Akbar at eighteen had grown into a young man of impressive physical strength. 'He was of medium stature but inclining to be tall,' wrote his son, Jahangir, in his memoir. 'His complexion was wheaten or nut coloured, rather dark than fair, his eyes and eyebrows dark black and the latter running across into each other; with a handsome person, he had a lion's strength which was indicated by an extraordinary breadth of chest.' His lion's strength would no doubt have been developed by the continuous hunts he engaged in and his confrontations with lethal animals. Akbar had recently witnessed the capturing of cheetahs, by digging pits in which the animals were trapped, and was excessively pleased. He noted, however, that the deep pits constructed to trap the animals were likely to injure them so he would later devise a system using a shallow pit with a trapdoor which could be shut so that cheetahs were caught unharmed. Whenever he was informed of a cheetah being thus caught, he would ride up to the pit, catch and blindfold the animal, and then spend weeks training it himself. But if Akbar was mesmerized by the countryside around him in Hindustan, the unending fields, the crouching cheetahs, and the corkscrew dances of the kabootars, he was also fascinated by the throngs of people who inhabited his empire. It became a habit for him at this time to lose himself in the laughing, heaving crowds that gathered at festivals and pilgrimage spots. One such incident, recounted to Abu'l Fazl, ended with the Padshah of Hindustan having to conduct a rather ignominious exit. He had gone one evening, incognito, to a large gathering outside Agra where 'both the good and the bad assemble[d]'. Akbar was enjoying the chaotic multitude, the flapping banners, and the candlelit shadows when, he later narrated, 'suddenly some ruffian recognised me.... When I became aware of this, I, without the least delay or hesitation, rolled my eyes and squinted and so made a wonderful change in my appearance.' What the bemused crowds made of their grimacing emperor is, sadly, not recorded but these incidents show a young Akbar trying to decipher his world beyond the familiar etiquette of the Mughal camp and court.

Other incidents did not have such a benign outcome, as recorded by a Persian merchant to the court, Rafiuddin Shirazi. Shirazi confirms Akbar's passionate love of hunting, and the large number of hunting animals he now kept in the shikhar khana, the hunting lodge, at Agra. These included dogs, cheetahs, hawks, and falcons. Akbar had designed a special hunting outfit, green with a yellow tint, like a medieval camouflage jacket. Akbar and his retinue wore these jackets when they went hunting with bow and arrow, or muskets, or sometimes just armed with swords. Akbar often chose to hunt alone, chasing his prey for hours at a time. It was during such an excursion that he found himself in a village 'whose inhabitants were of a rebellious bent'. Capturing the suspicious-looking lone young hunter in his dusty green jacket, they threw him into a cattle-pen, from which he was rescued only after the village was besieged by Maulana Pir Mohammad Shirwani and the imperial troops. On another occasion, Akbar found himself hungry and thirsty, as well as alone, at the end of a long hunt and walked into the shack of a bhatiyari (female innkeeper) and ate a meal. The meal would have been simple, perhaps consisting of 'rice boiled with green ginger, a little pepper and butter; bread made of a coarse grain...baked on a small round iron hearth; boiled lentils; and local fruit and vegetables'. Some fellow-travellers, unimpressed with the bedraggled aspect of the hunter, 'gave him a few lashes and told him to get out of the place'.

The young Padshah, it was noted, became exceedingly fond of cockfights at this time. Cockerels, bred to fight to the death, would duel each other in an enclosed pit. Every nobleman who came to perform the kornish, the salutation to the emperor, was urged to remember to bring a cock along. There was much amusement when Ataka Khan played a prank on the emperor by bringing a hen to fight with the royal cock.

The prosaic workings of empire also continued while the young Padshah found novel filters through which to understand his land and his people. The jagirs of noblemen were now increasingly seen as a fixed income, for which they were assigned a collection of villages, called a pargana.* These crucial assignments were the responsibility of the central diwan. This revenue assignment was meant to be quite

---

*Parganas were sometimes called mahals. A number of parganas together made up the sarkars, or districts, which were in turn organized within a subah, or governorship.

separate from the territories that the noblemen were required to administer. During these early years of Akbar's empire, the parganas that were assigned to a nobleman were largely contiguous, leading to a worrying concentration of land controlled by these powerful noblemen, with an even more troubling tendency for the jagirs assigned to particular clans of men to all be grouped together in areas of potential strife. This meant that there was also a very slow rotation of the assignment of these jagirs. Within a few years, in 1565, clan distribution would be dangerously concentrated as follows, as described by Iqtidar Alam Khan:

> Uzbeks in the Jaunpur region; Qaqshals in Kara-Manikpur; Jalairs in Lucknow and Awadh; Mirzas in Sambhal; and the Atka clan in the Punjab.

While these clans were anchoring themselves within their territories and Akbar was immersing himself in unconventional discoveries, others were pursuing a more scholarly existence. Shaikh Mubarak Nagauri, the learned theologian, scholar, and Mahdavi* sympathizer, had established his madrasa in Agra and was imparting to his two young sons, ten-year-old Abu'l Fazl and his elder brother Faizi, a rigorous and uncompromising education. The Mahdavi movement blazed through the sixteenth century with its emphasis on a direct experience of God and a forsaking of worldly desires. As the new Islamic millennium grew closer, there was a fervent belief that at the end of the first thousand years of Islam, a new Mahdi, or Imam, would be born into the world and he would 'restore the sinking faith to its pristine freshness'. This would be followed, it was believed, by the Day of Judgement and the end of the world, calculated at 1591. Shaikh Mubarak's particular stream of Mahdavi beliefs revolved around a Sufi-tinged belief in a series of mystical numbers. 'With his powerful knowledge and practice,' wrote Abu'l Fazl about his father, 'he did not allow me to associate with wayward, disreputable people, and he constantly guarded over me with advice to maintain inner purity, external cleanliness, an eloquent tongue and a pleasing manner of experience.' This was no ordinary childhood for Abu'l Fazl, who admitted that 'from the beginning I did not play hide-and-go-seek

---

*A millennial movement, brought about by the end of the first Islamic millennium.

like a child, for my mother and my father were my guardians'. Abu'l Fazl's childhood was also unusual for a more sinister reason. Shaikh Mubarak had been persecuted by the ulema of the Sur court for his freewheeling eclecticism and this led to the family being hounded from their home. Shaikh Mubarak had finally migrated to Gujarat, on the advice of a Sufi shaikh, Salim Chishti, and the family had to live in hiding for a while when some within the ulema even asked for Shaikh Mubarak to be executed.* For the sensitive and talented young sons of Shaikh Mubarak, these difficult years would forever be remembered and a careful tally made of the men who had sought their father's destruction.

There was another student at Shaikh Mubarak's madrasa, a twenty-year-old highly intelligent and spiritually minded young man called Abd al-Qadir Badauni. Badauni would later write of Shaikh Mubarak's orthodox Sunni piety, at this point of his life: 'In early life he observed many austerities...'[I]f any body was present while he was giving religious instruction wearing a golden ring, or silk clothing, or red hose, or red or yellow garments, he at once made him remove the item, and if anyone appeared with long breeches descending below the heel, he immediately had them torn to the proper length. If, while walking through the streets, he heard the noise of any singing he would start violently.'

At this stage, though Badauni received an orthodox religious education, he was also intensely interested in intellectual discourse and mysticism as well as history, Persian, Hindustani music, astronomy, and the law. At Shaikh Mubarak's madrasa, Badauni met Abu'l Fazl and Faizi, beginning a forty-year-long association that would bring him only bitterness and disappointment.

While Shaikh Mubarak's madrasa was fizzing with enquiry and arguments, and the Padshah was occupied with a more visceral experience of his kingdom, the management of state was largely carried out by Munim Khan and Maham Anaga. At the very start of the new dispensation, after the fall of Bairam Khan, it was Shahabuddin Ahmad Khan who consulted with his mother-in-law, Maham Anaga, and 'gave everyone who came to the threshold...hopes of rank and jagir...' All Maham Anaga's supporters were generously

---

*Some of those men, such as Abdullah Sultanpuri, then became part of Akbar's ulema.

rewarded and, when Munim Khan became wakil, Maham Anaga was prompt in showing him allegiance. Abu'l Fazl wrote later that no matter who held the title of wakil, the real business was transacted by Maham Anaga 'for this noble work, wisdom and courage was necessary, and in truth, Maham Anaga possessed these two qualities in perfection'.

There were other commentators who would not be so accepting of the visible role of a powerful woman. Writing about this episode in Akbar's reign, Badauni would gloomily quote from the *Nahj-ul Balaghat* to describe this new order of affairs, a veritable end-of-world scenario:

> A time will come on men, when none will become favourites but profligates, and none be thought witty but the obscene, and none thought weak but the just; when they shall account the alms a heavy imposition and the bond of relationship a reproach, and the service of God shall be a weariness unto them, and then the government shall be by the counsel of women, and the rule of boys, and the management of eunuchs.

Working alongside Maham Anaga was Munim Khan, and while Maham Anaga was considered a capable woman, Munim Khan was shackled by an overly conciliatory attitude, wishing to remain friendly with all the different clans that made up the nobility. He failed to take any measures to keep the privileges and independence of the nobility checked. On the contrary, it was whispered that he would not even submit a proposal to the young Padshah before first ensuring the noblemen approved of it. If this made of Munim Khan a popular wakil, it resulted in the imperial coffers running dry, for many dues to the state remained uncollected, and a growing number of noblemen quietly siphoned booty away for themselves. Things became so dire that on one occasion, when Akbar applied to Maham Anaga for a sum of money, she had to give him the seventeen rupees from her own purse as the state coffers were empty.

Akbar now reacted to this situation, transferring Munim Khan's jagir from Hisar Firoza* to Alwar. Though he would eventually transfer it back to Munim Khan, it was a sharp reminder that Akbar was

---

*Hisar Firoza was an important outpost along the edge of Rajasthan in the northwest.

Padshah and was now determined to personally administer the strategically important fort of Hisar, having finally understood the need to both curb the power of his nobles and improve the state's finances.

While Maham Anaga was involved in the administration of the empire, she also began work on the first great building project of the Mughals in Delhi, the Khair-ul-Manazil mosque and madrasa. Built right across from the Deenpanah Fort of Humayun, and next to Sher Shah Sur's great gate, the Lal Darwaaza, the Khair-ul-Manazil mosque was built to proclaim Maham Anaga's crackling ambitions. In building a grand mosque and madrasa, Maham Anaga claimed for herself an ancient role that Timurid women were required to perform—visible piety. It was, at that time, one of the finest mosques in Delhi and the madrasa was a rare example of early Mughal female patronage of an educational institution. This structure was not built as a tribute to a son, a father, or a husband. The inscription at the entrance proudly proclaimed the name of the benefactress, 'Maham Beg, the Protector of Chastity, erected this building for the virtuous'. This monument, largely forgotten today, is a reminder of the influence 500 years ago of a non-royal woman, the only woman who never left Akbar's side from the moment she became his milk mother, the resilient nature of this ancient bond, and the endurance of the Padshah's love and respect for Maham Anaga.

There was another building that was begun at around the same time, much more vaulting in its ambitions and explosive in the cascading effect it would have on Mughal architecture. And yet, given the importance of this monument, it is surprising that so much of it remains shrouded in mystery, especially the exact date of its construction and its patron. When Humayun died unexpectedly, at an awkward moment of vulnerability for the empire, his body was initially hastily buried within the Deenpanah Fort. Then, as Hemu threatened to march upon Delhi, Humayun's body was removed, in even greater haste, to Sirhind. Finally, once the convulsions of empire formation had subsided, sometime in the 1560s, construction was begun for a final resting place for Padshah Humayun. An enormous area, thrumming with political and religious significance, was chosen next to the Yamuna for what would become the first major mausoleum of the Mughals. For this was planned not just as a grave for Humayun but as a family cenotaph for the Mughals and would come to contain some 150 Mughal graves. The site was close to the old Deenpanah Fort but also to the holy burial ground and khanqah* of the towering thirteenth-century Sufi saint Hazrat Nizamuddin Auliya because it was considered a great blessing to be buried next to a Sufi saint. The Lodis, old enemies of Babur, were also buried in companionable proximity in what is now known as the Lodi Gardens. The architect for Humayun's tomb was a Persian, Mirak Mirza Ghiyas, who had returned to Hindustan in Humayun's train after his exile. Mirak Mirza Ghiyas had worked extensively not only in Herat and Bukhara but also in India before beginning work on Humayun's tomb.

A huge char-bagh, a paradisiacal garden tomb, with the mausoleum at its centre was designed on a monumental scale in red sandstone and white marble, unprecedented till then. According to tradition and oral records, the primary patron was Humayun's widow, Bega Begum. Bega Begum was the most senior of Humayun's wives, a Timurid cousin of Humayun's and, by Gulbadan's account, a fiercely independent woman who did not hesitate to speak her mind, even to her husband, the Padshah. Now that the turbulence of Akbar's early days were over, Bega Begum devoted herself to her pious duties and became the guardian of her husband's legacy. She left to perform the hajj soon after the construction of the tomb had begun. It is possible, therefore, that Bega Begum oversaw the beginning of the tomb, then left for the hajj and when she returned, she brought back 300 Arab masons and scholars and a new title for herself—Haji Begum.

When she returned to Hindustan, Haji Begum did not settle in Agra at Akbar's court. Unlike Hamida Banu, whose raison d'etre, as seen even in her support of Maham Anaga against Bairam Khan, would be to guard over Akbar's tenacious grip on the empire, Haji Begum relinquished all claims to imperial grandeur and politics upon the death of Humayun. Instead, with dignity and grace and 'in spite of the ties of love between her and H. M. [Akbar]', Abu'l Fazl tells us, 'she had taken up her residence in the neighbourhood of the tomb of [Humayun] and devoted herself to works of

---

*A khanqah was the place where a Sufi saint lived and from where he spread his teachings. It was considered a spiritually holy place.

charity'. A Jesuit traveller, Father Monserrate agreed that 'one of his wives had loved [Humayun] so faithfully that she had had a small house built by the tomb and watched there till the day of her death. Throughout her widowhood she devoted herself to prayer and to alms-giving.' Monserrate sighed that 'had she only been a Christian, hers would have been the life of a heroine'. After her return from Mecca, therefore, Haji Begum remained at the site of the construction of Humayun's tomb, where men hauled the red sandstone from quarries in Rajasthan and Hindustani craftsmen transformed a Persian vision from wood into stone. Abu'l Fazl, who naturally was not present at the time, only mentioned succinctly that the tomb was built by Akbar but then Abu'l Fazl, as we will see later, was never shy to claim all grand achievements on Akbar's behalf. Some scholars have argued that the scale of the building would necessarily imply an imperial patron but Mughal women, especially senior wives, were independently wealthy. Hamida Banu would leave a fortune upon her death and Haji Begum would live on in the Arab Sarai after the hajj, maintaining 500 women a day on her alms. Some of the money for the project may have come from Akbar, certainly, but its memory-keeper was Haji Begum, once Empress of Hindustan.

Bairam Khan, meanwhile, never did reach Mecca. He was murdered on the shores of the Sahasralinga Lake in Gujarat in an act of revenge by an Afghan youth whose father had been killed at the Battle of Machhiwara, commanded by Bairam Khan. When Akbar heard of this random act of violence, he immediately summoned Bairam Khan's widow, Salima Sultan Begum, his cousin and a Timurid princess, along with her stepson, Abdur Rahim, to his court. Akbar married Salima Sultan Begum and yet another powerful, influential Timurid woman joined the Mughal harem.

While the Timurid women were busy securing their immortal legacies Akbar, too, was about to show signs of the blistering force of nature he was to become. For five years, he had immersed himself in the feral countryside of Hindustan, and the pursuit of its cheetahs, tigers, antelope, and elephants, content to leave the affairs of his empire to capable allies. He had watched his clan-based, imperious, and prickly nobility grow dangerously assertive and territorial.

Finally, it was an act of wilful arrogance and presumption that caused Akbar to explode into action. The unlikely cause of Akbar's provocation involved a singer and aesthete and in the dynamics that led to his fall, it was Maham Anaga's family that paid the price, its power destroyed almost overnight.

PART 2

THE YOUNG PADSHAH
{1561–1569}

~

OF ONE DANCING GIRL
AND THEN TWO MORE

Miyan Bayazid Baz Bahadur Khan, Sultan of Malwa, was a man who, by all accounts, enjoyed a life of leisure. The son of a governor under Sher Shah Sur, Baz Bahadur had demonstrated rather admirable warrior qualities, and had set himself up as the sultan after killing all his brothers. But after a short interlude attending to administrative affairs he would 'enter the harem and after his meal...occupy himself with singing and music'. One of the courtesans he most famously enjoyed singing with, and writing Hindi poetry for, was Roopmati.*
According to a popular contemporary legend, Roopmati herself 'advised her lover to sacrifice pleasure and luxury for a season and bestir himself to set the affairs of his kingdom in order' when news arrived of the Mughals at their frontier. But 'too drunk to recognize day from night', according to Abu'l Fazl, 'he occupied himself with song and music'. The Mughals, for their part, justified the attack on the rich province of Malwa by claiming rather damningly that Baz Bahadur occupied himself with 'unlawful and vicious practices' and a Mughal force under Adham Khan was dispatched to Malwa in April 1561, 'to spread justice and be balm for the wounds of the oppressed'.

Despite much harrumphing by Abu'l Fazl about the 'tyranny and injustice Baz Bahadur had wrought upon the people of Malwa', Adham Khan had been sent to Malwa at least partly due to the presence of elephants in the region, a source of wealth in themselves, and the treasured prerogative of kings. After Timur's sack of Delhi, one of the governors of the crumbling Tughlaq dynasty had declared himself ruler of this rich, landlocked region in west-central Hindustan in the early fifteenth century. The fort of Mandu, set on a plateau, was greatly enhanced by successive rulers, and elephants were acquired from the forests in the east to compensate for a lack of war horses. The Khaljis eventually took over as sultans of Malwa in the mid-

---

*There is uncertainty about her actual position. Some sources claim she was a queen, others that she was a favoured dancing girl.

fifteenth century, continuing to invest in architecture in the province. By the time Akbar turned his attention to the region, a plenitude of war elephants and a distinctly Persianate culture were what Malwa had inherited and what Adham Khan had been sent in search of.

The Mughals won a quick battle and Baz Bahadur, rather disappointingly for a famous paramour, abandoned Roopmati and fled to Burhanpur. The Mughal takeover of Malwa was particularly harsh. All Baz Bahadur's retinue and wives were taken prisoner as were all his servants and sympathizers. There was to be no clemency for the prisoners, Hindu or Muslim. Adham Khan and Pir Mohammad Khan 'had the captives brought before them, and troop after troop of them put to death, so that their blood flowed river upon river'. Badauni, who appeared to have been present at this gruesome massacre, was horrified. He described the Sayyids and shaikhs pleading for their lives, clutching their Korans in their hands but Pir Muhammad Khan 'put them all to death and burnt them'. When others attempted to stop the murders he told them flippantly that 'in one single night all these captives have been taken, what can be done with them!' As for Roopmati, so far had her fame spread that Adham Khan wanted to see her for himself. Baz Bahadur, however, had left orders for his wives and dancing girls to be killed if ever they were captured. Other reports claimed Roopmati drank poison rather than betray her lover. In either event, Roopmati displayed rather more spirit than her paramour and never was captured by Adham Khan. But Adham Khan did obtain a great deal of buried treasure, elephants, dancing girls, harem girls, precious objects, and 'began to indulge in pleasure' whereas he should have sent everything immediately to the Padshah in Agra.

Instead, Adham Khan sent back to Agra victorious reports of the battle as well as a rather derisory gift of a few elephants. Akbar immediately realized what Adham Khan had done and, in the first instance of decisive action taken entirely independently, decided to confront him. Adham Khan was Akbar's elder koka and had enjoyed a considerable amount of imperial indulgence. But his behaviour in Malwa was a scandalous insult to the dignity of the Padshah and Akbar would no longer tolerate this. Moreover, Akbar had understood the need to check the capricious behaviour of noblemen seeking to assert their independence, and was now starting to take measures to reverse this. Leaving Munim Khan in charge of Agra, a furious Akbar rode out from the city with a small group of elite courtiers without informing any of the nobility. This small group travelled from Agra to Malwa through the rising heat of early summer in just sixteen days. Akbar knew that if he acted quickly, Maham Anaga would have no time to alert her recalcitrant son and warn him of the Padshah's displeasure. Indeed, when the imperial troops reached Sarangpur in present-day Madhya Pradesh, Adham Khan was caught completely unawares and he quailed when he understood the meaning behind this sudden, explosive arrival. When the harem along with Maham Anaga arrived the next day, she quickly brought her son back to his senses and arranged for a lavish banquet at which Adham Khan hurried to present to the Padshah 'everything he had taken from Baz Bahadur's estate, animate and inanimate', and immense treasure thus poured into the imperial coffers. Unfortunately, this was not the end of Adham Khan's presumptuous behaviour. He convinced some of his mother's servants to bring away two 'rare beauties' of Baz Bahadur's from within the imperial harem itself. These dancing girls were particularly valued because the courts of Malwa had long patronized music and dance, first under Sultan Ghiyasuddin Tughlaq, and then under Baz Bahadur, and the exquisite precision and grace of their technique were known and admired. When Maham Anaga realized what her son had done, she knew that this was an insolence Akbar would no longer tolerate. She had the two young women killed so that Akbar would never find out about Adham Khan's insane act of transgression. Akbar did not say anything further about the matter to Adham Khan but the Padshah was only biding his time. The world had changed while Adham Khan was in Malwa and no longer would the Padshah forgive those who acted against his imperial dignity, even if they were the favoured ones.

This violent episode of the murder of the dancers from Malwa also highlights a troubling and easily erased aspect of ancient and medieval history—the enslavement of women. Female slaves were an integral part of affluent households while even simpler homes like those of merchants and cultivators owned a few such slaves who were often acquired during raids on enemy clans and kingdoms. These women then spent their lives carrying out the endless domestic duties which were indispensable in a household such as cutting vegetables, grinding flour, sweeping, smearing the floor with cow dung, bringing in the firewood, transporting water, dealing with human waste, weeding, cutting grass and so on in a brutal cycle of exhaustion. Many were forced into concubinage with the men of the house. These women could be from varied backgrounds and Ibn Battuta, the fourteenth-century traveller from Morocco, writes of captives being cheap as 'they are dirty and do not know the civilized ways'. These plain women were more likely to be used for menial jobs while more accomplished women fetched a higher price and could be sold for concubinage. At the time of the Mughals, women slaves in the households of noblemen were called paristaran, or sahelis, and talented and beautiful sahelis were highly valued, leading to jealousies and intrigues exactly as happened in the case of Baz Bahadur's dancing girls.

After dealing with Adham Khan, the Mughal court made a more leisurely return to Agra, stopping to hunt and accept tributes from chieftains en route. Near Narwar, as the cortège was passing through a forest, a tigress with her cubs stepped on to the path in front of them. While his entourage froze with fear, Akbar walked up to the tigress and killed her with a single stroke of his sword, having in his arms the strength of 'the Lion of God'.

On returning to Agra, Akbar continued with his efforts to curb the powers of individual nobles. Accompanied by Munim Khan, he travelled eastwards towards the fiefs of two notoriously independent-minded brothers, Ali Quli Khan and Bahadur Khan, Uzbek clansmen who had travelled to Hindustan with Humayun. Akbar met with the brothers at a town called Kara, by the Ganga, where they submitted much tribute and a large number of elephants, who went by whimsical names such as Jag Mohan, Palta, and Dilshringar. When he returned to Agra, in August 1561, Akbar summoned Ataka Khan to court and, in a sign of a change of guard that would lead to a notorious murder, appointed his foster father wakil-e-saltanat in lieu of Munim Khan. Munim Khan's shambolic management of the state's finances could no longer be tolerated, nor could his complicit attitude towards Adham Khan. Adham Khan was recalled to the capital from Malwa, and 'Maham Anaga's heart which was distressed by the separation from her honoured son, was thereby comforted'. After observing his reckless behaviour in Malwa, Maham Anaga no doubt believed she would be able to watch over her errant son better in Agra.

Akbar's immediate and decisive reaction to Adham Khan's continued disobedience shows that he had understood the fatal flaw at the heart of the empire he had inherited. The nobility he had been bequeathed by Humayun contained a large majority of Turani officers. The high posts and honours had been commandeered by the Turanis, with the Persians, aside from Bairam Khan, contenting themselves with the role of scribes and minor officials. The Uzbek clan, the Ataka Khail* and Adham Khan's family, had all grown powerful and their clout would need to be curtailed. For the next ten years Akbar would work incessantly to dramatically change that situation, by raising Persians to high honours and by incorporating shaikhzadas and Rajputs into the nobility. The Turani element, dangerous and subversive, would be consistently undermined, the traditions and the culture they represented now a desultory reminder of a past that would no longer be considered relevant.

Nor was the old Turani nobility the only danger to the young Padshah and his empire. Indeed the entire kingdom was circled by warlords, pretenders, chieftains, and kings:

> Powerful Afghan chiefs held considerable territory from the central Ganges valley through Bihar to Bengal, and in Malwa. Rajput lineages dominated Rajasthan, while further south lay the rich and powerful state of Gujarat. For many disaffected parties uprooted by the return of Mughal power, the sultanate of Gujarat offered an attractive refuge and source of patronage.

In the next few years Akbar would confront all these dangers—Malwa, Gujarat, Rajasthan, Bihar, and Bengal. Akbar's empire, at this time, was made up of all the lands that Babur had once ruled, and that Humayun had lost:

> A broad band of land across the sweep of the Indo-Gangetic plain, from Afghanistan to the eastern border of modern Uttar

---

*The members of Jiji Anaga and Shamsuddin Ataka Khan's family were so large that they were collectively known as the Ataka Khail, or Ataka clan.

Pradesh. The empire was still relatively small, only about a third of what it would be at the end of Akbar's reign, though it was already the largest and the most powerful state in the subcontinent, as India was at this time fragmented into over twenty kingdoms.

But even as he was beginning to turn his attention towards taming the capricious and sometimes violent wills of his men, there were times when Akbar was still a reckless twenty-year-old, and opaque even to himself. One day in Agra, having had a few cups of wine, Akbar went to the polo field he had constructed outside the Agra Fort to watch his elephants fight. The elephant Hawai, possibly Hemu's captured beast, who was noted for its 'choler, passionateness, fierceness and wickedness', was in a particular fury that day. Akbar jumped onto the enormous elephant and goaded it to fight the elephant Ranbagh, the 'Tiger in Battle'. The elephants shook their massive heads and crashed into each other, to the utter consternation of the retinue and onlookers, who stood by wailing and pleading with the young Padshah. 'Although I was sober and the elephant was very easy to handle and responded well to my will,' was Akbar's surprising confession to his son Jahangir many years later, 'I pretended that I was dead drunk and the elephant was uncontrollable.' Hearing the commotion, Ataka Khan rushed out and threw his turban to the ground in horror, while the people raised their hands to the heavens and shouted out for divine help. Akbar saw his Ataka and irritatedly shouted at him: 'If you don't stop acting like that, I'll throw myself from this elephant right now.'

Akbar now found himself in a situation which was not easy to defuse because he could not admit to the onlookers that 'neither was I drunk nor was the elephant out of control'. As the spectators, now mute, watched in terror, the routed Ranbagh ran down towards the Yamuna, towards a bobbing bridge of boats. Ranbagh, followed by Hawai, lumbered onto the unsteady bridge and the skiffs swayed and creaked and finally collapsed, as the men holding onto the boats jumped away in alarm into the warm river. The elephants swam across the river and Ranbagh escaped into the forest and Akbar at last halted Hawai. Even Abu'l Fazl admitted that to the superficial observer it might seem as though Akbar 'must have some sort of imbalance in his mind' for it was unheard of for rulers to risk their lives in this way. But for Akbar, radiating an almost uncontrollable physical energy, these confrontations with his own mortality were a test, a challenge to the divine to either take him or spare his life 'for we cannot bear the burden of existence without divine pleasure'.

MEN OF THE SWORD AND THE PEN

The rather niggardly amount that Akbar was able to obtain from Maham Anaga in an emergency was only a minor incident but it was symptomatic of a much larger and potentially disastrous problem in this fledgling Mughal Empire—a severely depleted treasury. Land revenue had long been a source of wealth and income for the monarchs of Hindustan, the wealth of the rulers depending on their ability to profit from the agrarian productivity of India, while taxes on trade, manufacture, and other activity were a great deal less important to the overall revenue, most estimates putting them at less than 10 per cent of the total earnings. Akbar's predecessors had usually contented themselves with seizing the treasures of defeated opponents, as Babur had done with Ibrahim Lodi after the Battle of Panipat. Commanders of the victorious party were then appointed an appanage, or iqta, from which to extract revenue. These iqtas were often managed in a predatory manner by the commanders, and also had a tendency to become hereditary. Akbar now took stock of the financial debacle in the empire, which had arisen due to outdated land revenue information from Sher Shah Sur's reign being used to extract taxes. The situation had been further exacerbated by Bairam Khan's excessive largesse, as he had handed out huge cash incentives to bind men to his cause.

In the 1560s unhappy, therefore, with the inaccuracy of these estimates for tax based on land size, crop yield, and market price, which had continued from the time of Sher Shah Sur, Akbar directed his men to begin collecting data on the actual market prices and revenue rates of various crops in the provinces of Agra, Allahabad, Awadh, Delhi, Lahore, Multan, and Malwa. The officials were directed to be as fair and accountable as possible, as described by Abu'l Fazl:

> The collector was directed to be the friend of the agriculturist; to give remissions in order to stimulate cultivation...to grant every facility to the raiyat [farmer] and never to charge him on more than the actual area under tillage; to receive the assessment

direct from the cultivator and so avoid intermediaries; to recover arrears without undue force; and to submit a monthly statement describing the condition of the people, the state of public security, the range of market prices and rents, the conditions of the poor and all other contingencies.

As we have seen, the revenue system was based on the division of the empire into provinces, or subahs, which were administered by a governor, later known as the subedar. The governor controlled the largest body of troops in the area and was responsible for keeping the peace. The subahs were further divided into sarkars, or districts, which were the real administrative units of the land, and had a military commander, a faujdar, assigned to them. The revenue-collecting work in the sarkar was carried out by the amalguzar* while kotwals were appointed to all provincial capitals and cities, to maintain order. Some of the lands were owned outright by the state, and were called khalisa land.

The sarkars were made up of parganas, which grouped together the smallest measure of land, the village. Northern Hindustan consisted of tens of thousands of villages, gathered into parganas, from which tax was historically collected using the zamindars, who controlled revenue collection in each pargana. The zamindars were almost always Hindus, and themselves employed a number of cavalrymen and foot retainers, constituting an important semi-military class. 'Without the support of Hindu agrarian magnates and officials,' writes Iqtidar Alam Khan, 'it was now obviously becoming difficult to run a state system.' Attempts were made to constrain the autonomy of the zamindars, by making them officers of the Mughal state. The land revenue was collected not in crops, but in cash, the copper dam, and this monetized the rural economy.

Because the holders of iqta land had tended to become almost autonomous, extracting tribute from zamindars or farmers exceeding their official grants, Akbar would devise a much more efficient and centralized system in the coming decades for revenue extraction. After more accurate figures on the productivity of land were gathered, a temporary assignment of land revenue from a particular territory,

---

*A revenue officer.

known as a jagir, would be parcelled out to each officer. Later still, as we will see, an integrated decimal hierarchy for top officer administrators—the mansab (rank) system—would be created.

The mansabdars were to supervise the collection of the land revenue and all officers, royal or not, minor or grand, were incorporated into the same imperial service. There was no distinction between military and civil affairs and all officers were given a mansab in return for which they were expected to perform military duty, whether they were a poet, a painter, a physician, or a philosopher, in addition to carrying out any task the Padshah demanded of them. In the beginning, all mansabs were given to individual men only after a personal interview with Akbar and the mir bakshi, chief of military personnel, who reported directly to the Padshah. In rare instances, officers would be paid a direct salary, or inam, but in most cases they were assigned the land revenue of an area. Upon the death of a mansabdar, his property would return to the khalisa, though some concessions would be made to the heirs. Thus the cumbersome process of land administration and revenue collection, from what would become an immense empire over the next decade, was shifted onto the mansabdars. The system of promotions of the mansabdars was somewhat arbitrary, and could be in recognition for a particularly valorous piece of action in battle, or for a well-executed work of calligraphy.

No longer would mansabdars make a living from bounty captured during war, but were paid a fixed salary through their jagir appointments. These yearly salaries were extremely generous, 'much higher than those paid to officers of comparable rank in the armies of contemporary powers like the Safavid or Ottoman Empires'.

Apart from the other duties assigned to them, the mansabdars and their men and horses provided the bulk of the Mughal army. There were also ahadis, single men with no military troops, but who nonetheless demonstrated skill and talent. Akbar kept them nearby, as a body of personal servants, and they too had to maintain a certain number of horses. In addition to these cavalrymen were the foot soldiers. They included porters, runners, guards, gladiators, wrestlers, slaves, bearers, labourers, and matchlock bearers.

Ever since the sultans of Delhi had brought Islamic law to northern

Hindustan, the monarch was bound to rule as the guardian of Islamic revelation and the sharia, which was based on Koranic injunctions, and the hadiths, or traditions, of the Prophet Muhammad. If any new interpretations of the sharia were required with changing times, these could be addressed by jurists (mujtahids). This was, in theory at least, applicable to criminal law for Muslims and Hindus and to civil law for Muslims. Akbar, as khalifa of the age, was the ultimate authority in the administration of justice, especially in criminal cases. At court, and as he travelled across the country, people would approach him for redress, and Akbar took his duties very seriously, asking to be reminded three times before he would finally confirm capital punishment. But as access to the Padshah was essentially limited, qazis, or judges, were appointed to try both civil and criminal cases throughout the empire.

Sharia made an unequivocal distinction between the Muslim and non-Muslim peoples of the country. All non-Muslims were tolerated as dhimmis, or 'the protected people', who were subject to the discriminatory jiziya tax. Two hundred and fifty years before Akbar, Alauddin Khalji had created the office of the sadr us-sudur, in whom rested the highest authority in disputes regarding religious laws. A hundred years before that, Iltutmish had established the office of the shaikh al-Islam to deal with religious issues, administration, and the delegation of the religious duties of the rulers. Akbar appointed Shaikh Abd un-Nabi to the important post of sadr while Shaikh Abdullah Sultanpuri, who had been appointed as the makhdum ul-mulk and shaikh al-Islam under Humayun, also remained in office under Akbar. These two men, who enjoyed at this stage an untouchable prestige as the leaders of the ulema, would be the ones whose fall would be most spectacular, once Akbar took stock of the reality of Hindustan and the many faiths and beliefs that surrounded him. In an earlier age his grandfather Babur had also mused about the people he found in Hindustan:

> Most of the inhabitants of Hindustan are pagans; they call a pagan a Hindu. Most Hindus believe in the transmigration of souls. All artisans, wage-earners, and officials are Hindus. In our countries, dwellers in the wilds (ie, nomads) get tribal names;

here the settled people of the cultivated lands villages get tribal (caste) names. Again every artisan there follows the trade that has come down to him from forefather to forefather.

The most populous people, as noted by Babur and then by Akbar, were the Hindus, among whom a strict caste system existed. For them, justice at the local level, in the form of councils and panchayats, continued untouched. Hindu and other non-Muslim communities also offered legal advisers when one of their community was involved in a case. But there were also Armenians, Portuguese, Ethiopians, Jews, Christians, Parsees, Sikhs, Buddhists, and more. Even among the Muslims there were people of many ethnicities and origins. There were Arabs and Persians settled in the coastal areas, there were traders in every seaport and there were also the Turks, Uzbeks, Afghans, and Indian shaikhzadas. Other differences existed between the Shias of the Deccan and the Sunnis of the North, and then again there was a great movement of each into the other's area. In due course, the Padshah would find novel ways, and use unique symbols and formulations, to weld all these diverse people and religions into a single empire.

Shamsuddin Ataka Khan at this point held the highest posts—wakil and diwan (finance minister). But, ultimately, according to the Timurid model of sovereignty, all power resided in the emperor himself. All important assignments remained the prerogative of the emperor and Akbar would spend a great deal of time and energy learning to judge the true nature and potential of his men. He would be unswayed by glorious pedigrees and unmoved by lowly origins. His great skill, honed over years of careful observation of those around him, would be to spot the unique talent of each man he encountered and enable the greatest expression of that talent. For that he would go far beyond the narrow limitations of sharia law and the charmed circle of Turani noblemen. And fate, too, would play her capricious part.

A SUFI SHRINE, A RAJPUT PRINCESS, AND A NOTORIOUS MURDER

On a cold January night in 1562, Akbar and a small group of courtiers were out hunting in the lands around Agra which bristled with deer, birds, cheetahs, tigers, and leopards. Near Mandhakur, a village halfway between Ajmer and Sikri, they came upon a group of singers, probably qawwals, singing the praises of the Sufi saint Khwaja Muinuddin Chishti,* whose dargah was in neighbouring Ajmer. The dargah of the thirteenth-century Sunni mystic was an important pilgrimage site in the sixteenth century, attracting both commoners and kings. Muhammad bin Tughlaq had paid his respects here and because the only Brahma temple was in nearby Pushkar, Muinuddin Chishti's dargah 'became a place where Hindus placed their head and sent nazr every year', according to Shaikh Jamali Kamboh. So Akbar would have heard of the miraculous power of the Ajmer shrine and he decided that he would go there that very night. His courtiers tried to dissuade him as it was a long and dangerous journey but Akbar refused to listen. He sent word that Maham Anaga was to bring the harem via Mewat to join him at Ajmer and the small party left immediately. At the village of Kilaoli, Akbar was informed that a certain Raja Bharmal, the very same raja who had stood steadfastly in front of Akbar's rampaging elephant, now wished to greet him. 'The Raja stands out for his great intellect and courage,' Akbar was told, 'and he had constantly striven in allegiance to this exalted dynasty...' Raja Bharmal and all the important members of his clan were presented to Akbar at the town of Sanganer.

In the sixteenth century, the Rajput kingdoms in western India remained fairly isolated since the defeat of Prithviraj Chauhan by Muhammad Ghori in 1192. Indeed the entire region, a collection of small, intermittently warring principalities, was relatively culturally homogeneous with neighbouring Sind and Gujarat. Oral tradition tells us that major Rajput clans like the Kachhwahas, Rathores, and

---

*Founder of the Chishti Sufi order of India.

Sisodiyas originally came from outside Rajasthan and took over lands held by ruling tribes like the Bhils and the Meenas. The need for expansion and consolidation kept the clans constantly battling each other, and so to provide a cohesive military structure a system based on kinship (bhai-beta) and clan (gotra) was developed. Because these repeated, ferocious battles to the death could sometimes mean the end of several generations of clansmen, polygamous marriages were introduced to supply a sufficient quantity of men. The Rajputs unabashedly compared themselves with the native plant richke (lucerne), a fodder plant for horses, which grows more vigorously the more it is grazed. Dying extravagantly in battle became something of a Rajput specialty, extolled by bards and encouraged by wives and mothers. So resolute was the bravery of these Rajput warriors that neither had the Delhi Sultanate, nor any of the other rulers of north India, the Khaljis, the Lodis, or the Surs, been able to subdue these Rajasthani tribes or incorporate their lands into their empires.

The Kachhwahas of Amer were a small, resolutely insignificant family plagued by the pedestrian Rajput problem of polygamous households leading to succession disputes. They were also vulnerable to repeated acts of territorial expansion by their more powerful Rathore neighbours. Raja Bharmal was contesting the seat of Amer with Puran Mal, one of his many brothers, who had usurped the support of the Mughal governor, Mirza Sharafuddin Hussain. Bharmal, at over fifty years of age, was a patient strategist and a careful judge of men. He now sought Akbar's help in dislodging Puran Mal and in exchange offered him a daughter in marriage, thereby altering the fate of the province of Amer forever.

The Rajput clans had used marriages as signs of submission to victorious chiefs for a long time. Apart from Hindu and Rajput rulers, defeated chieftains had already married daughters to Muslim rulers such as the Ghoris and the Tughlaqs of Delhi. In more recent times, Rao Maldeo of Marwar had married a daughter to Sultan Mahmud of Gujarat and another daughter to Islam Shah Sur. But the Mughal–Rajput alliance that would arise out of this first, unassuming relationship between Akbar and the Kachhwahas, making the Rajputs stakeholders in the fortunes of the Mughal Empire, would lead to conquests and glory that neither side could have anticipated at the time. Akbar agreed to Raja Bharmal's proposal and in return induced Mirza Sharafuddin Hussain to hand over the raja's relatives he had kept hostage. Akbar then carried on to Ajmer while the raja went to Sambhar to arrange for his daughter's wedding, complete with all the elaborate Hindu rites. In Ajmer, Akbar met up with the ladies of the harem, who had been brought there by Maham Anaga, and the Mughal party arrived for the first time at this ancient site of pilgrimage with its camphor lamps, murmuring voices, and the staccato claps of qawwali singers. Akbar then travelled to Sambhar where he stopped for a day and acquired not just a bride, but the unswerving loyalty of her entire clan.

The bride who left her natal Rajput clan in Amer to enter the unknown world of the Mughal harem was Harkha Bai.[*] But the young woman did not enter unaccompanied into her new world, for she had a veritable cuirass of brothers and nephews to walk beside her. At Ranthambore, as the Mughal party proceeded towards Agra, they were greeted once again by Raja Bharmal and his sons and brothers. There was also present a young boy, twelve-year-old Man Singh, now released from the isolation that had been suggested by an astrologer.[†] Popular legend has it that when Man Singh greeted Akbar for the first time, the Padshah looked affectionately at the sprightly but dark-complexioned young boy and jovially said to him, 'Well, Man Singh, where were you when God was distributing beauty in heaven?' To which, it is believed, Man Singh replied with verve and panache, 'Shahenshah! I was in my prayer room at that time but I was present to receive valour and manliness when the almighty in her mercy was distributing the same.' Apocryphal or not, the story illustrates the legend of Akbar and Man Singh's great bond of loyalty and love which would make the Rajput one of the greatest noblemen of the Padshah. Man Singh would travel far from his natal clan into the furthest corners of the Mughal Empire, the Padshah's most trusted liegeman.

The large retinue that accompanied Harkha Bai and the Mughal

---

[*] Also known in some sources as Maanmati and Shahi Bai. Her mother was Bharmal's Solanki wife, Rani Chandravati.
[†] At Man Singh's birth, an astrologer had predicted a troubled start for the child. So he was sent away 40 miles south of Amer, to a palace built specially for him at Muazzamabad, along with his mother and a hundred boys for company.

party included the bride's brother, Bhagwant Das, her nephew, Man Singh, as well as a large number of female attendants to perform the various tasks that Harkha Bai would require: dhai maas (wet nurses), dholans (female drummers), purohits (priests), nayans (barbers), darjans (tailors), varies (cooks), and davis (maids), collectively called the zenana amla, accompanied their princess to her new marital home. For the Rajputs kept their women in seclusion in a space called the zenana deorhi in which female staff provided all the services required. As Harkha Bai was carried along in her sequined palanquin and her brothers and relatives accompanied her on horseback, this entire microcosm of Rajasthani culture also headed to Agra, bringing with them their songs, their dances, their food, their customs, and their tenacious dreams.

◆

After Akbar's return to Agra in 1562, he set about rapidly consolidating the empire. From the time of the conquest of Malwa, and for the following decade, Akbar expanded the size of his dominions at a blistering pace, driven by a fierce will and a conviction that if he did not subdue his neighbours, they would rise up against him. Akbar sent Mirza Sharafuddin Hussain to subdue the province of Merta and Abdullah Khan Uzbek was appointed to bring the province of Malwa under control where Baz Bahadur was once again stirring up trouble. Baz Bahadur was expelled once again and he remained in exile at the courts of various princes till he eventually submitted eight years later and was given an honourable mansab of 1,000.

Meanwhile, at Agra, the Mughal court was effervescent with the excitement of hosting a highly eminent guest. Sayyid Beg, the ambassador of Shah Tahmasp of Persia himself, had arrived to meet with the young Mughal Padshah and elaborate arrangements were made for him. A large royal tent was set up in the Padshah's garden and the noblemen had also added their own tents, all suitably decorated. The townsfolk would go every day to the fort to amuse themselves by gawking at the visitors and admiring the decorations. Rafiuddin Shirazi, the Persian merchant, too decided to try and see the Padshah and he was standing in a tent with a crowd of spectators when all of a sudden loud shouts of 'Badshah Salaamat!' rang out. The Padshah had arrived, clearly, 'but however much left and right I looked, I did not see anyone who by appearance gave any signs or marks of royalty' wrote the puzzled Shirazi. 'When I looked behind,' he added, 'I saw that a youth of twenty years was leaning on a favourite, with his hand resting on the other's shoulder.' This nonchalant youth, Shirazi realized, was the emperor of Hindustan but he was astonished to see that no one prostrated themselves or gave the Padshah any special treatment whatsoever. Shirazi, taken aback, asked the crowds whether this casualness was normal in Hindustani courts to which he was told, 'the etiquette for courtiers and salutations at this Court is much more elaborate than those of other rulers: but the King himself is more informal. Often he comes out in ordinary dress and mixes with his confidants and makes no distinction between companions and strangers.' Shirazi ruminated over this strange explanation but agreed that he had himself seen Akbar flying a kite on the roof of his palace at Agra. On that occasion, he noted that 'his head was bare and he was wearing a lungi. From this I was convinced that His Majesty was of an open bent of mind and extremely informal.' A later Jesuit visitor to Akbar's court, too, would be astounded by the Padshah's accessibility, even after the rules of etiquette had coalesced into something much more rigid. 'It is hard to exaggerate how accessible he makes himself to all who wish audience of him,' wrote Father Monserrate, the Jesuit, 'for he creates an opportunity almost every day for any of the common people or of the nobles to see him and converse with him; and he endeavours to show himself pleasant-spoken and affable, rather than severe, toward all who come to speak with him.' Jesuit reports from this period give us an excellent description of the young Padshah. According to them, he was 'a fine-looking, broad-shouldered man, but bow-legged, and of a swarthy complexion. His eyes are large but with narrow openings, like those of a Tartar or Chinaman. He has a broad, open forehead; and his nose, except for a slight lump in the centre, is straight. The nostrils are large, and on the left one there is a small wart. He is in the habit of carrying his head slightly inclined to the right side. Like the Turks, he shaves his beard; but he wears a small neatly trimmed moustache.'

These traits that Akbar displayed as a young emperor—his intense curiosity, his ferocious courage, and his warm approachability with both commoners and noblemen alike, would run like a thread throughout his long reign, allowing him to make bonds of friendship with the most unlikely of allies. But there were shows of unexpected anger, rare but explosive; one such episode erupted in a particularly spectacular manner, scorching the very heart of Akbar's ancient bonds of love—his foster family.

Ever since Adham Khan had been recalled from Malwa and Ataka Khan named wakil, violence had simmered under the surface of courtly life at Agra. Adham Khan, most tempestuous of Akbar's kokas, considered himself beyond chastisement because of the young Padshah's unfailing courtesy towards members of his foster family. But a reckoning was about to come for Adham Khan on a blazing day in May.

When Ataka Khan was made wakil he, along with the eunuch Itimad Khan, set about improving the state's revenues by increasing the state's share in jagirs which had long been in default. Plans were put in place to improve revenue administration and 'the royal revenues, which were in the hands of embezzlers' were handed over to Itimad Khan. The influence of Maham Anaga, Munim Khan, and Adham Khan was curtailed and reduced and this was a new reality that Adham Khan could not tolerate. In the middle of May 1563, Adham Khan strode into the council hall of the Agra Fort where the nobility were occupied with state affairs. The men stood up to greet Akbar's powerful koka but Adham Khan gestured to his liegeman, who stabbed Shamsuddin Ataka Khan. As the old man stumbled into the sun-bleached courtyard, Adham Khan's men set upon him and murdered him, while Adham Khan climbed up the stairs towards the inner apartments. Hearing the shouts and the commotion, Akbar came out from the harem, tying a lungi around his waist and seizing a sword. When he realized whose bloodied body was lying in the courtyard below, he was filled with rage: 'Son of a bitch!' he cursed Adham Khan. 'Why have you killed our Ataka?' Seizing Adham Khan by the hair, Akbar struck him on the face and then ordered him to be thrown from the top of the stairs. When the first fall left Adham Khan mangled but still alive, Akbar ordered him brought up and thrown down again, head first. Akbar then went to Maham Anaga's quarters to inform her himself of the fate of her beloved but turbulent son. 'Adham killed our Ataka,' he told Maham Anaga, 'we have taken revenge on him.' Controlling her devastation with exceptional courage, Maham was able to whisper, 'You did well'. But Akbar did not allow her to visit her son's broken and ruined body, perhaps not wishing his old milk mother to know the terrible violence of Adham Khan's end. But this woman, who had lived through all the uncertain dangers of the early days of the Mughal Empire, was unable to bear the death of her son. Forty days after Adham Khan's death, Maham Anaga died, too, in grief and despair. Akbar mourned her deeply and publicly, accompanying her bier out of Agra and weeping next to her body, and commissioned a noble tomb for mother and son. The dome of the tomb is unusually vast and a light breeze blows gently through the tomb because of an intricate system of ventilation. It lies neglected in the Mehrauli area of Delhi today, having been repurposed several times by new conquerors in the following centuries. In a sort of dubious poetic justice for the ruffianly Adham Khan, though not, it must be said, for his highly accomplished mother, it has been reclaimed today as the rather louche haunt of delinquents. Maham Anaga's exceptional destiny is more clearly seen in the few miniatures in which she would later be depicted, always close to Akbar, in her distinctive yellow robes. In time, all the important Mughal noble families would jostle to be buried near the exalted dargah of Nizamuddin Auliya, within a short distance of Humayun's tomb. By burying Adham Khan near Qutbuddin Bakhtiyar Kaki's dargah, at the opposite end of Delhi from Nizamuddin's dargah, Akbar seemed to send a silent rebuke to his foster brother for his terrible crime.

Meanwhile, the other great foster family, the family of the murdered Ataka Khan, had gathered together in a fury, demanding vengeance. The Ataka Khail had to be shown Adham Khan's broken body before they could be dissuaded from taking immediate and bloody retribution. They were still potentially dangerous at court, however, and to neutralize them temporarily Akbar sent them away on campaign against the rebellious Sultan Adam Gakkhar in the Salt Range. Then they returned to their jagirs in the Punjab, watched carefully by Akbar until such time as he was able to conclusively decimate their dangerous power.

MY SOUL WAS SEIZED WITH EXCEEDING SORROW

When Badauni would later write his covert, critical, and despairing biography of Akbar, the *Muntakhabh al-Tawarikh*, he would place considerable blame for Akbar's un-Islamic practices on Hindus, whom Badauni roundly and unapologetically detested, including Akbar's Hindu wives. '[Akbar] had introduced a whole host of the daughters of the eminent Hindu rajas into his haram,' he noted darkly, 'and they had influenced his mind against the eating of beef and garlic and onions, and association with people who wore beards—and such things he then avoided and still does avoid.' However, as a very young man, Akbar was considered a rather orthodox Islamic Padshah, performing namaaz five times a day, and he believed his Hindu subjects to be sadly deluded. Referring to that period in his life, Akbar would later write regretfully: 'Formerly I persecuted men into conformity with my faith and deemed it Islam' (he was referring here to a few incidents of forced conversion). 'As I grew in knowledge, I was overwhelmed with shame.' That one of the sources of knowledge that Akbar referred to were his Hindu wives is clear from the subtle shift in policies implemented around the time he first married Hindu women.

One of the first such measures, attributed by Shirazi to one of Akbar's Hindu wives, was the prohibiting of enslavement of prisoners of war, and indeed an order to end the slave trade altogether. Abu'l Fazl was honest when he wrote about imperial soldiers 'making captive the women, children and kinsmen of the opposing soldier and selling them, or keeping them as slaves'. According to Shirazi, some two lakh persons were captured every year in the Mughal Empire and exported as slaves. Now, though Akbar still believed that 'killing, imprisoning and whipping' rebellious persons was necessary, any attempt to torture their innocent women and children was deemed abhorrent. 'If husbands take to wretchedness, what fault is it of their wives?' Akbar is noted as having said, 'if fathers tread the path of rebellion, what sin is it of their children?'

On one occasion, Akbar had gone hunting in the vicinity of Mathura with a small group of his closest companions, including Mirza Aziz Koka. The men enjoyed a vigorous day of hunting, killing five lions in a single day and capturing two alive. Akbar then found out about the pilgrimage tax imposed upon Hindus visiting the temples, a tax which brought in millions of rupees to the royal exchequer every year. Akbar abolished this tax throughout the empire saying 'however obvious the error of some people is', referring to Hindu beliefs, 'since the error of their ways is not obvious to them, to demand anything from them and to place a stumbling block in their path to whatever leads them to the threshold of divine unity and the worship of God are less than praiseworthy to the wise, since it will necessarily lead to divine disfavour'. Farmans were issued forbidding the practice and each time a new region was integrated into the Mughal Empire, the farman would be reissued.

It is not surprising that Akbar, visiting Mathura, would have been struck by the devotion of the visiting pilgrims. Mathura attracted swarming numbers of pilgrims to its temples on the banks of the Yamuna, where more than 300 barbers stood in waist-deep water on the steps leading into the river. There they would swiftly shave the hair off the bowed heads of pilgrims, both men and women, who would then sink into the warm water of the river before emerging, cleansed and bald, to present themselves for blessings at the temple.

And, indeed, the temples of Mathura would become an important focus of imperial attention. In a few years, Akbar would issue a farman granting 200 bighas of land as a revenue-free gift to the Govind Dev temple. Many more such gifts would follow, including from his Hindu courtiers and from his mother, Hamida Banu. It is quite likely that a new sensitivity was also stoked by Akbar's Rajput bride, Harkha Bai. The Kachhwahas were Vaishnavas from the time of Prithviraj Kachhwaha and their particular deities were Shri Sitaramji and Govind Devji. Bhagwant Das and later Man Singh would lavishly patronize temples at Mathura which was, along with Brindavan at that time, the vortex of the high-voltage passion of the Bhakti movement.

Akbar, on this occasion after the lion hunt, decided to walk back from Mathura to Agra in one day, a distance of some 60 kilometres.

His enthusiastic companions all set off with their Padshah but only three, it was said, kept up with his blistering speed and were able to reach Agra the same day. Were these repeated tests of strength and endurance just youthful exuberance, or was there a deeper disquiet, an intolerable questioning of purpose and meaning? 'On the completion of my twentieth year,' Akbar said of this time, 'I experienced an internal bitterness, and from the lack of spiritual provision for my last journey, my soul was seized with exceeding sorrow.' This had been a tumultuous time for Akbar for he had lost three members of his foster family in a particularly violent way. The old order had scattered, their familiar love now gone. For Akbar it would now be a time of new alliances and unexpected friendships.

These years were also a time of gradual but momentous changes in the very fabric of the Mughal court. Possibly as early as 1556, an erudite Brahmin named Mahesh Das from a village near Kalpi was introduced to Akbar's court. Badauni, who was often tormented about what he felt was the erosion of Islamic beliefs from Akbar's heart, tried to understand the genesis of this failing. 'The emperor from his youth up had shown a special predilection and inclination for the society of religious sects such as brahmans and musicians and other kinds of Hindus,' he wrote, before going on to focus his wrath on one particular Brahmin. 'Accordingly at the beginning of his reign a certain brahman musician, Gadain Brhmaindas by name, whose whole business was perpetually to praise the Hindus and who [was] possessed of a considerable amount of capacity and genius, came to court. By means of conversing with the emperor and taking advantage of the idiosyncrasies of his disposition, he crept day by day more into favour until he attained to high rank, and was honoured with the distinction of becoming the emperor's confidant.' This man, acknowledged even by the critical Badauni as having innate genius, would later gain fame at Akbar's court under the name Bir-Bar (renowned warrior) or Birbal.

Of the much reviled musicians that Badauni regretted came to the court there was one, in particular, whose name and immortal, yearning music would come to be associated forever with Akbar. In 1562, Akbar heard of the talent of one Tansen Kalavant Gwaliyari, singer at the court of Raja Ramachandra of Baghela. This raja was exceedingly fond of his musician, to whom it was said he once gave one crore gold pieces after a particularly mesmerizing raag. Tansen, too, Badauni noted, did not want to leave the court of Ramachandra but the young Padshah was no longer a man whose summons could be ignored. There is the possibility that this tussle over Tansen may not have been entirely due to musical yearning. As Akbar began to expand his influence deeper into the hinterland, claiming for himself the greatest gem of the Baghela court was also an exercise in power. The symbols of legitimacy, for the young Mughal Empire, came in various hues and colours.

Oral tradition has it that unable to stop the departure of his beloved musician, Raja Ramachandra carried his palanquin on his shoulders himself, incognito, one last act of devotion. Tansen, who would later have a remarkably lifelike portrait made of himself at the imperial court, was a tall, angular man with a dark complexion, a hook nose, and melancholic eyes. With Tansen there would come to the Mughal court the ancient, haunting raags of Dhrupad. Far from his Baghela patron, the musician now sang for the young Akbar in a new Hindustan, in the warm and perfumed evenings of Agra.

In early 1564, Akbar attempted a further expansion of his power base that could have ended rather more calamitously for him. Wanting to marry into the shaikhzada families, the old Indian Muslim nobility of Delhi and Agra, Akbar travelled to Delhi without the harem and sent eunuchs and intermediaries to these families to find out about their marriageable daughters. According to Badauni, it was at this time that Akbar chanced to see a beautiful married woman from one of these established families. The husband, bowing to the inevitable, divorced his wife and went away to Mecca and the woman was integrated into Akbar's harem. This sudden and muscular attempt to impose Chingizid yassa law understandably alienated the Delhi Muslim nobility and 'a great terror fell upon the city', according to Badauni. Following this somewhat misguided attempt to bring the shaikhzadas into the empire's fold, Akbar was passing in front of the Khair-ul-Manazil mosque after having visited Nizamuddin Auliya's dargah when an arrow whispered through the air and struck Akbar on the shoulder. The would-be assassin was a young man named Falud, a freed slave of the disaffected Ajmer governor, Mirza Sharafuddin

Hussain. Though his noblemen wanted the young Falud arrested and questioned, Akbar ordered him executed immediately. The timing of the assassination attempt, and Akbar's refusal to hear Falud's accusations, hint at the possibility that the attempt was linked to Akbar's indiscretions with the women of Delhi's Muslim nobility. All further attempts to secure alliances in this manner were stopped and, unable to ride his horse due to his injury, Akbar travelled back to Agra by litter. 'Alas that in the first flush of youth our inestimable lives are unworthily spent,' Akbar said ruefully, much later. 'Let us hope that in future they may virtuously terminate.'

Almost immediately upon his return to Agra, Akbar abolished the jiziya tax. The jiziya had been an overt symbol of inferiority for the Hindus, establishing through law that the Muslims were the favoured ruling class and the Hindus the dhimmis, tolerated and protected by the Muslim rulers. While previous Muslim rulers had used a great deal of discretion when adhering to the sharia, the jiziya had remained. The jiziya, according to historian John F. Richards, also 'placed a real burden on the poorest taxpayers who paid an annual sum equivalent to a month's wages for an unskilled urban laborer'. Akbar had to face the vehement opposition of the ulema, 'the disapproval of statesmen' and 'much chatter on the part of the ignorant'. The abolition of the jiziya was done when Akbar was only twenty-one years old, ten years before he ever met Abu'l Fazl, who is sometimes credited with complete influence over Akbar in his humanitarian transformation. At this point in time, in fact, Akbar may have been seeing these discriminatory practices through the eyes of his young Rajput bride and his Kachhwaha noblemen.

The darbar that Akbar held at this time, between his war camps and Agra, was informal and filled with bonhomie, as the young Padshah met with his trusted men and discussed the state of affairs with his wakil and diwan and dispensed justice, directed departments of state and inspected the army. The Padshah's entrance into the darbar was announced by the beating of a drum, and all the noblemen assembled performed the kornish, raising the palm of the right hand to the forehead, and bending the head. This early court was vastly different from the hushed darbars of some of Akbar's heirs, in which the muted rustle of a courtier's garment was loud as a gunshot.

All the mansabdars and amirs were expected to attend on the Padshah regularly, and failure to do so was considered a very grave dereliction of duty. All officers served at the court for a month, mounting guard duty once a week. At the darbar, the men professed their undying loyalty to Akbar in a complicated ritual of symbolism and the Padshah was able to look at his amirs closely and judge the truth that lay in their hearts. Despite his warm approachability and genially relaxed manner, Akbar was strict with those who presumed on his youth and inexperience, his flaring nostrils and flashing eyes sure signs of his sudden, explosive temper, which his courtiers quickly learned to read. Failure to maintain decorum in court could lead to harsh punishments. Shah Abu'l Maa'li, a personal friend of Humayun's, was imprisoned for the temerity of not dismounting when greeting the young Akbar a few years earlier, in 1560, and performing the kornish while seated on his horse. The punishment was even more humiliating for one Lashkar Khan who appeared in court visibly drunk in the daytime. Akbar had him tied to a horse's tail and paraded through the town, and then sent to prison, to serve as a lesson to 'himself and to others'.

Even when the amirs were away from court, Akbar kept a very close watch on his men. They were only ever allowed to be in their jagirs, or in the areas they were administering, and contact was maintained at all times, through farmans, messengers, and other orders and appointments. If Akbar wanted to particularly distinguish one of his men, he might send a khillat, a sumptuous robe of honour. In its most extravagant form, a khillat could include a long coat, a gown, turban, jacket, shawl, patka, payjama, qaba, and scarf. When receiving such a mark of favour, the chosen amir, wherever he was in the empire, had to prostrate himself in submission before the khillat, as if in the presence of the emperor himself.

Every subah within the Mughal territory also had a miniature replica of the imperial government, with a governor, diwan, bakshi, sadr etc., who had duties similar to their imperial counterparts at the centre. The governor reported directly to the emperor while the provincial diwans communicated through the imperial diwan.

The far corners of the empire were also linked by a network of intelligence, through 'experienced spies and traders' who were dispatched to blend in with the local population and collect information. Spies were likewise sent abroad, in anticipation of military excursions, to map roads and terrains. When the army was on the move, spies were sent to infiltrate the enemy troops, posing as soldiers. Itinerant merchants and holy men were also deployed, as they could travel widely while not raising any suspicion. All this information was then written up by waqia nevis, or news writers, assigned around the country and dispatched to the court.

Messages between the court and the provinces were relayed extremely rapidly, either by carrier pigeons or by fleet-footed runners, spurred on by opium and bhang. These runners would train with lead weights on their feet to make them swifter. Since the runners needed to use the roads even by night, 'at every 500 paces small pieces of stones are fixed, which the inhabitants of the nearest villages are bound to whiten from time to time so that the letter carriers can distinguish the road on dark and rainy nights'.

A particularly useful officer at the provincial level was the kotwal, appointed to the provincial capitals and large cities. Fulfilling the functions of a police chief, accompanied by 200–300 policemen, the kotwal was meant to keep the peace by carrying out a bewildering number of tasks, as listed by Badauni:

> That he would keep a close watch on every one who came in or went out, of whatever degree he might be, whether merchant, soldier or otherwise; that he would not allow troublesome and disorderly fellows or thieves to take up their abode in the city; that if he saw any one whose expenditure was greater than his receipts, he would follow the matter up, and represent to the Emperor, through the chief police officer that this extravagance of his was probably paid for with money irregularly acquired...

Entirely unsurprisingly, the kotwal was 'the most dreaded government official during the Mughal period, whose very appearance in a public place at the head of a dozen horsemen or foot-soldiers was enough to make the people tremble with fear'.

The Padshah remained the ultimate bestower of justice, however, and for this it was crucial that he remain on the move, accessible at all times. Even in his war camp, he met every day with supplicants and one day in 1564, when he was encamped near Malwa, he was approached by a woman whose daughter had been raped by Abdullah Khan Uzbek's arms bearer. Akbar promised the woman justice and when the man was subsequently captured, during a confrontation with Abdullah Khan, he was executed.

In many ways Akbar was still at this time a rather orthodox Muslim, even as he was beginning to understand the complexities of the land. When the first embassy from Shah Tahmasp of Persia arrived bringing Persian and Anatolian horses, precious textiles, and rare objects, the shah also included a letter in which Akbar was cordially described as the 'unsurpassed adherent of God's word and extirpator of polytheists'.

It is clear from these many episodes that the Mughal Empire was not a preordained entity, emerging flawless from the inspired Padshah's thoughts, as Abu'l Fazl would rather posterity imagined, but a progressive creation, evolving through discordant mistakes and brave, unforeseen changes. And even the 'polytheists' that the Shah of Persia fondly hoped would be extirpated by Akbar, would instead find a place of dignity and honour in the Mughal Empire.

BOOKS FOR A PADSHAH

If Akbar was effectively illiterate it did not mean that he was cut off from the seductive world of ideas and stories. Every evening, at the court in Agra, books would be read out to him, books of Islamic, Persian, or Indian origin and, as he grew older, the manuscripts he would listen to would become more eclectic and philosophical, a veritable compendium of the sixteenth-century learned man's library. But as a young man Akbar loved to listen to stories which reflected his own extraordinary destiny—tales filled with valour, excitement, intrigue, and physical prowess. His very favourite story in his teenage years was the somewhat obscure *Hamzanama*, a ninth-century Persian epic which used the character of the hero Amir Hamza, uncle of the Prophet, to spin a rollicking fable that mixed folk tales, religious meanderings, and familiar legends. These stories were narrated by a professional qissa-khwan (storyteller), who not only memorized, recited, and improvised these texts but performed them, using a judicious mix of gestures, expressions, and oral modulation which kept alive the exquisite suspense of the story. The stories were performed at the court but a qissa-khwan also accompanied the royal retinue on its travels and on its hunts. It is easy to imagine all the noblemen gathered around the fireside, exhausted after a day's hunt. They may even have been eating kebabs roasted on skewers over the fire, a remnant from Babur's days wandering in the company of nomadic Central Asian horsemen. Under the vaulted sky, the listeners would be entranced as the story unfolded, the shadows shifting across the storyteller's face, his eyes glittering as his hands and words created worlds far beyond the limits of the fireside shadows.

Akbar's favourite qissa-khwan was Darbar Khan whose father, Takaltu Khan, was himself a storyteller in the service of Shah Tahmasp. As a native speaker of Persian, Darbar Khan's facility with the language would have been essential to his popularity because Persian was already greatly prized as the courtly language par excellence. Darbar Khan was given a mansab of 700 and when he died, an eighteenth-century biography noted, he had asked to be buried near the tomb of Akbar's faithful dog, showing a degree of cherished intimacy not many other noblemen could have claimed. Akbar was so fond of the story of Hamza that he had memorized large sections of it, and as he walked through the corridors of his palace, he recited reams of it, 'in the style of the storytellers', with voice modulations and gestures. Sometime in 1562, Akbar decided that these storytelling sessions would be even more enjoyable with images to depict the events that were being described and gave the order for the largest single commission in Mughal history, changing the course of Mughal painting forever.

The taswir khana that Akbar had inherited from Humayun included a few Persian master artists such as Abd al-Samad and Mir Sayyid Ali; Dust Muhammad had died, possibly on the journey back to Hindustan. These artists had created only a handful of paintings since coming to Hindustan, but one of those paintings was a quite extraordinary image entitled 'Mughals Visit an Encampment of Sadhus'. In this painting, Mir Sayyid Ali, a troubled, complicated artist, who, it was whispered, did not entirely have the Padshah's favour, created a fantastical scene where elegant yogis were surrounded by a bustling horde—'stately plump elephants; camels; flunkeys milking goats; cooks making bread and preparing meals; and musicians trumpeting fanfares to the family of Mughal visitors'. The great Persian emigré artist was clearly responding to this mesmerizing scene with foreign eyes and the art historian Stuart Cary Welch writes that '[Akbar] responded badly to Iranian graces; and he would not have been pleased to see Indian holy men transmuted into foppish courtiers, not even when they were Mughal ones'. But even if the Padshah was dissatisfied, the painting glows with the quintessential Persian fine attention to detail, exquisite ornamentation, and superb control that Mir Sayyid Ali and Abd al-Samad would transmit to their Hindustani students.

Now with the commissioning of the *Hamzanama*, a project that would take fifteen years, and would result in 1,400 paintings, the Mughal taswir khana was about to be reformed in the brazier of Akbar's colossal ambitions. More than a hundred Hindustani artists, mostly Hindus from Gujarat, were trained in the miniature style in a surge of creativity and effort. An army of poets, gilders, bookbinders, and calligraphers were also hired and trained. By the mid-1560s, four volumes of images were completed and Mir Sayyid Ali, perhaps unsurprisingly, bowed out of the project and proceeded to Mecca. Abd al-Samad now took over and, by about 1577, all twelve volumes were completed. Each volume took about a year to complete and two lakh copper tankas were spent on each. The project was so large and courtiers were so enthralled by the images that court chroniclers meticulously recorded the progress of the work. 'Verily it is a book the like of which no connoisseur has seen since the azure sheets of the heavens were decorated with brilliant stars...' wrote a courtier, quite overcome.

The paintings were extraordinary for their large scale, over a metre tall, and for the use of a cloth rather than paper ground. They were to be used as props during the recitations of the qissa-khwans, held up in front of the storyteller as the corresponding sections were narrated. Akbar was personally involved in the themes of the images and the minutiae of the painting process. He chose the scenes to be painted himself and enquired about the quality of the raw materials used, insisting on the very best. The outlines were painted by either one of the Persian masters, or another leading master, following which a junior artist coloured in the images. Every week the images were presented before Akbar and the Padshah gave out rewards and increased allowances according to the brilliance of the work. 'As a result,' wrote Abu'l Fazl, 'colouring has gained a new beauty and finish a new clarity...delicacy of work, clarity of line and boldness of execution...have reached perfection, and inanimate objects appear to come alive.'

According to art historian John Guy, though the *Hamzanama* contains glimpses of various north Indian and Deccani styles, understandable because of the varied backgrounds of the artists employed, there is nonetheless a unifying theme of energy, vitality, and action, no doubt because of the overall creative vision of a single master artist. Here, for the first time, we see the two worlds of the Mughals, the Persianate–Timurid world and the Hindustani one, fused to form a unique, new creation. Persian delicacy and flat linear forms jostle with Hindustani vigour and exuberant colour. Angular, precise shapes are intruded upon unexpectedly by typically Hindustani animals, birds, and flowers. One of the Hindustani artists discovered during this period was young Daswant, son of a palki-bearer.* 'Urged by natural desire,' wrote Abu'l Fazl, 'he used to draw images and designs on the walls.' Akbar chanced upon this graffiti one day and was impressed with the young scribbler, who was commended to the master artist of the taswir khana. 'In just a short time,' added Abu'l Fazl, 'he became matchless in his skills', pointing both to Daswant's genius and the outstanding social mobility possible at Akbar's court. Once the *Hamzanama* was completed, Akbar released a number of the painters who had been trained and used for this manuscript. This would lead to the first wave of dissemination of the emerging imperial style to new patrons, courts, and connoisseurs, both Hindu and Muslim, across the country. Thus the three painters of the Chunar *Ragamala* were said to have trained under the master Abd al-Samad himself, before leaving for the court of the Rajput prince in Chunar, where they then followed the prince to Rajasthan and served as catalyst for the spread of the Mughal style to Bundi and then Kota.

If the *Hamzanama* with its stories of exciting travels and grandiose battles resonated with Akbar because of his own experiences, there was another manuscript which was also revealing in its implicit message. Early on in his reign Akbar had another story illustrated, the *Tutinama*. This was a fourteenth-century Persian tale within a tale in which a parrot tells a woman whose husband is away a different story each night to prevent the woman from meeting her lover. This work was possibly meant for Akbar's harem which, in addition to the senior Timurid women, now included the Padshah's wives and their many attendants. In this ever-expanding, boisterous company of women, Akbar might have felt the need for some subtle messages on chastity and order.

This early Mughal court of Akbar's had already changed a great deal since the days of Babur and Humayun. There now was a polyphony of voices where earlier Turki had been the beloved mother tongue. The Timurid women, especially Gulbadan, Bega Begum, and Salima Sultan Begum would still be conversant in Turki but now there was a growing influx of Persian-speaking noblemen and scholars and

---

*A palanquin-bearer, traditionally considered lower caste.

craftsmen, enticed to the court by Akbar to serve as a bulwark against the old, irreducible Turki nobility. There was Brajbhasha, spoken not only by Akbar's Hindu courtiers such as Birbal and Bhagwant Das, but also by his Rajput wives. It was hardly surprising that the young Abdur Rahim, Bairam Khan's son, who grew up in this audacious atmosphere of experimentation and vibrant creativity would go on to become one of the greatest patrons of Persian poetry at the court and would enjoy stories in Turki, Persian, and Hindi while also writing excellent poems in all three languages.

But even as this cauldron of creativity gave rise weekly to masterpieces at court, far away on the southern border of Akbar's empire was a rani who dreamed of lions.

DURGAVATI, RANI OF THE GONDS

The land of Gondwana in central India was inhabited in the sixteenth century by Dravidian-speaking tribes who, according to Abu'l Fazl, 'live in the countryside, where they occupy themselves with eating, drinking and copulating'. He further points out that 'they are a base tribe and the people of India despise them...' The truth, however, was more complicated, for Gondwana was ruled by Rani Durgavati, who even Abu'l Fazl had to admit was an exemplary leader. 'In courage, tactics and generosity she had attained a high level and through these good qualities she had unified the whole country.' She led her troops into battle herself, 20,000 expert cavalrymen and 1,000 fierce elephants. She was a good shot with the bow and arrow as well as the musket and it was her habit, whenever she heard that a lion had appeared in her kingdom, to drink no water until she had shot it.

Rani Durgavati was born into the prestigious but impoverished dynasty of the Chandels, and her father was compelled to marry her to Dalpat Shah, of the less illustrious but considerably wealthier Gond dynasty of Garha Katanga, which at that time included some Rajput and Gond principalities. When Dalpat Shah died in 1548, Rani Durgavati's son, Vir Narayan, was only five years old but the rani took over as regent of the kingdom with aplomb and ruled her kingdom wisely and well for sixteen years, amassing riches and treasures. She defended her kingdom with admirable courage, repulsing the attacks of Baz Bahadaur and some ambitious Timurid mirzas. She also had, according to Nizamuddin Ahmad, 'a complete share of beauty and grace'. Her only fault, sighed Abu'l Fazl, was that 'she was overly proud of her success and was not obedient to the imperial threshold'.

When Akbar decided to bring these prosperous and fertile kingdoms, rich in forests and in war elephants, into the Mughal Empire, he sent Asaf Khan, a Persian courtier, to subdue the region after initial negotiations had failed. Asaf Khan first conquered Panna and then turned towards Gondwana. Rani Durgavati strapped on her armour and, using her knowledge of her country, the steep ravines, the thundering Narbada, the unknowable forests, lured the Mughal forces into a trap and inflicted a resounding defeat on them. She wanted to conclusively decimate the Mughals through a surprise night attack but her councillors, fatally, refused. Inevitably, as anticipated by the rani, they were then outnumbered by the cresting Mughal forces as many of her subordinate rajas defected to the enemy. In the end, when the troops were fighting hand to hand, with the rani's men dying in gallant numbers beside her, and as the arrows began to thud into the rani herself as she directed operations from her war elephant, she decided that to flee this scene of defeat would be a dishonour she could not live with. Rani Durgavati gauged the span and heft of her glory and all that she stood to lose, and killed herself with her dagger and her vast lands and enormous treasure fell to the Mughal Empire.

When Asaf Khan then took the neighbouring Chauragarh fortress, defended to the death by the rani's son, as gallant as his mother, there were further, more aberrant deaths. 'There is a custom among the Rajputs of Hindustan,' wrote Abu'l Fazl, 'called jauhar: in such situations wood, cotton, chips, oil and the like are piled together, and the women, willingly or unwillingly, are burned.' In Chauragarh fortress, the fire blazed for four days and any woman who shirked from the flames was beheaded by two attendants assigned to this task. At the end of four days, when 'the harvest of roses had turned to ashes', two women, miraculously, were found alive, shielded by a large piece of timber. They were Rani Durgavati's sister, Kamlavati, and a princess of Puragadh. Both the women were taken to the Mughal court.

The treasure that Asaf Khan discovered at Chauragarh was staggering. It included paintings, statues inlaid with jewels, gold idols, a hundred pots of gold coins, and 1,000 elephants. So beguiling was this wealth that Asaf Khan 'sifted the dust of misfortune' over his head and sent a paltry 200 elephants to Akbar, burying the rest of the treasure for himself. When Akbar learnt of this dishonesty, Abu'l Fazl tells us that he 'disregarded the objects and overlooked his treachery'. However, it is more likely that at only twenty-two years of age, Akbar did not think he was strong enough to censure all who defied him, and preferred to allow Asaf Khan to believe he still enjoyed the Padshah's confidence. 'He never gave anybody the chance to understand rightly his inmost sentiments,' Daniello Bartoli, a Jesuit writer, would write later about Akbar, '...a man apparently free from mystery or guile, as honest and candid as could be imagined: but in reality, so close and self-contained, with twists of words and deeds so divergent one from the other, and most times so contradictory, that even by much seeking one could not find the clue to his thoughts.' The Jesuits would have reason to lament their failure to understand the Padshah's innermost thoughts, even unto his deathbed. But even at a much earlier stage, Akbar was an enigma, and those who grew complacent in their certainty, like Adham Khan, found themselves taken unawares by his unpredictable outrage. And while Akbar chose to ignore Asaf Khan's treachery, in due time, it was not only his foster family but even his own family members who would be called upon to explain their every dubious action.

Khwaja Muazzam, brother of Hamida Banu, had always been an unstable character, gloating in his infallible closeness to the imperial family and showing, in shocking acts of violence, a simmering insanity. He had murdered servants of the family and had been banished to Mecca. Now he had returned and lived outside Agra 'in utter immoderation', married to the daughter of Bibi Fatima, the superintendent of the royal harem. Bibi Fatima came to plead with Akbar one day, saying that Muazzam was threatening to go to his fief and drag his wife with him where, she was certain, he would harm her. 'He is so mean and suspicious,' wept Bibi Fatima, 'that he will kill the poor innocent.' Akbar consoled the woman and said he would forbid Muazzam from taking his wife away and sailed down the Yamuna with a group of courtiers to confront his uncle. Two men were sent ahead to warn Muazzam of Akbar's arrival but this infuriated Muazzam who screamed at them: 'I will not go before the Emperor!' He then strode into his wife's quarters and stabbed her to death. Throwing the dagger out of the window he shouted out to the men below saying 'I have shed her blood. Go tell him that.' When Akbar was shown the bloody dagger he was enraged and stormed into Muazzam's inner quarters. 'What manner is this?' shouted the Padshah. 'You have a hand on the hilt of your sword. If you move it, know that I will give you such a blow that your head will go flying,' threatened Akbar and, noticing that one of Muazzam's men looked menacing, shouted out an order to his courtier who swung his sword and cut off the man's head.

Muazzam was then bound and taken down to the river, screaming incoherently. The courtiers tried to drown Muazzam, 'with whom they had shared cups in drunkenness', but the man was resilient. Every time he came up for air, 'knowing that to curse the great men of religion shocks Akbar, he keeps up a stream of curses'. Here again, even if obliquely via Muazzam's curses, is proof of the fact that Akbar was at this young age, a fairly God-fearing and orthodox man. Muazzam was finally imprisoned in the fort of Gwalior where 'melancholia overwhelmed him and he departed the world unsound of mind'.

But these family vicissitudes in Agra were almost pedestrian compared to the maelstrom gathering in the east. For far away in the border regions of the Mughal Empire, an entire clan was gathering in rebellion.

UZBEK CLANSMEN AND A KING IN THE NORTH

When Humayun rode back to Kabul from Persia in 1545, there were six Uzbek noblemen with him including the two brothers Ali Quli Khan and Bahadur Khan. They remained loyal during Humayun's many battles with his brothers and fought with distinction in the battles for Hindustan. By the time Akbar became Padshah in 1556, they were second only to the Timurid mirzas in hierarchy and their tight-knit family group gave them a unity of purpose rare in this shifting, mercurial early empire. The Uzbeks were given charge of the eastern region as well as the Punjab and Multan, giving them more land than any other clan in the Mughal Empire. When the Afghans of the east attempted rebellion under the banner of Sher Shah Sur, the Uzbeks defeated them at Jaunpur but then maintained worryingly friendly relations with them. The Afghans, with their own pretensions to empire since the Sur dynasty, could never be incorporated into the Timurid-led Mughal Empire and so this rapprochement between the Uzbeks and the Afghan rulers of Rohtas, Bihar, and Bengal not only made them a formidable group but one that made the Persians and the Turanis profoundly uncomfortable.

Akbar had realized early in his reign that the concentration of jagirs held by clans in one particular region was dangerous. It made the nobility territorial, recalcitrant, and made it harder to control revenue transfer to the crown. Akbar started taking measures relatively early to fragment the jagirs of the nobility and to ensure frequent transfers of these powerful men. He brought in administrative reforms, requiring the nobility to submit accounts of revenues—especially galling to the clans controlling outlying provinces, who had enjoyed a considerable absence of oversight. Akbar also now separated the department of finance (diwani) from the jurisdiction of the wakil, Munim Khan, and instead placed it under a separate official directly responsible to the Padshah. This new post, the wazirat-i-diwan-i-kul, was an important departure from Humayun's reign and brought financial and administrative control to the centre. He also brought in the office of the mir bakshi, to oversee the army, the khan-i-saman, in charge of the royal household, and the sadr with powers over the judiciary. All these changes would have been entirely unwelcome to the Uzbeks as the most powerful clan with the largest assigned lands and would have been a sign, for them, of a new dawn.

In 1564, in the middle of the monsoon season, Akbar set off for an elephant hunt in the Narwar forests of Malwa. With lightning flashing across the lowering skies, the Mughal train made its way across the slippery mud, through sheets of rain, crossing the foaming Chambal River till it reached Gwalior. In the forests around Gwalior, 'in which human had never set foot' carpenters built wood scaffolding over which tents were stretched and carpets were laid out on the floor for the emperor. These tracts of largely uninhabited forests were notoriously lawless, as noted by the Jesuit Monserrate, who wrote that their 'savage inhabitants, knowing that they can commit robberies with impunity, are wont to attack travellers from ambush and to carry off their goods as plunder'.

Around the imperial tent, the Padshah's closest companions and kokas pitched their own tents and, in the watery dawn, Akbar listened to Darbar Khan narrate a rousing episode from the *Hamzanama*. The men then set off on foot in every direction to capture wild elephants. When wild elephants were spotted, they were chased on tame elephants, all day, till the exhausted beasts were lassoed and captured. This was an early example of the use of so-called 'Judas' beasts, tame animals that were used to lure and capture their wild counterparts and Akbar would use them in innovative ways. Gentleness was then essential, wrote Abu'l Fazl, so that 'by giving it straw, grain and water appropriate to its nature', the captured animal could be calmed. One day, as the hunters made their way through forest so thick that light barely filtered through the canopy, a herd of seventy wild elephants was spotted, to Akbar's delight; the animals were captured and each was tied to a different tree. Finally, since Akbar 'desired to hunt some more wild beasts', as Abu'l Fazl meaningfully wrote, the emperor exposed the true reason behind this expedition and rode off towards Mandu to confront one of the Uzbek chieftains, Abdullah Khan Uzbek, Governor of Malwa. In the scouring rain the horses 'swam like sea horses and the camels crossed the floods like ocean-going ships'. By the time they neared Mandu, only Munim Khan, Aziz Khan Koka and a few other amirs' tents had arrived, the imperial retinue having got hopelessly bogged down in the shifting mud. Finally, when a small retinue of men, including the qissa-khwan, Darbar Khan, and the eunuch, Itimad Khan, were sent to Abdullah Khan Uzbek asking him to submit to Akbar and demonstrate his loyalty, the Uzbek chieftain decided to flee to Gujarat instead, seeking the protection of that powerful sultanate, marking the beginning of open hostilities between Akbar and the Uzbek clan.

When Abdullah Khan had initially tried to prevaricate, before his flight to Gujarat, there were skirmishes and battles and Akbar himself led the imperial troops in a charge. When a foolhardy amir suggested that Akbar not endanger himself, Akbar was so enraged that he turned his horse around to face the man, his hand immediately on his sword. The man, one Khaksar Sultan, understanding his folly at once, jumped nimbly off his own horse and ran away through the stampeding horses of the other soldiers. But Akbar's vast anger would not be contained and he charged after the man. Akbar struck Khaksar Sultan with his sword but 'since the blade was an Indian Khanda',* Abu'l Fazl pointed out, 'it did not kill him' and the man lived to regret the impertinence of trying to question the young Padshah.

The Mughal troops harassed and chased Abdullah Khan till one day, with the ancient golden ruins of Champaner in the distance, they hurtled down a hillside, banners fluttering with the Timurid symbols of the lion and the sun, scimitars gleaming, screaming out their battle cry, 'Allahu Akbar!' and the Uzbek chief fled, abandoning his valuables, his goods, his horses, his elephants, and all his womenfolk, and Malwa was conclusively annexed to the Mughal Empire. After this decisive victory, Akbar gave high promotions to those who had distinguished themselves, for the first time since 1560, strengthening a core of noblemen whose loyalty to the Padshah was now proven. Some of the men recorded as having taken part in these battles included two kokas, Aziz Khan and Saif Khan, in addition to Munim Khan, the eunuch Itimad Khan, Asaf Khan and, for the first time, a certain Raja Todar Mal.† Qara Bahadur Khan

---

*Indigenous double-edged straight sword.
†Akbar's finance minister, who first served under Sher Shah Sur, then joined Akbar's court

was appointed to the governorship of Mandu and, in the middle of pouring rain, with the drummers leading the procession, the imperial retinue headed back to Agra. One particularly fascinating manuscript is believed to have entered the Mughal imperial library at this time along with other treasures from Mandu. This was the *Nimat-khana* (Book of Pleasures), an illustrated collection of recipes, aphrodisiacs and perfumes, commissioned by the aesthete and gourmet ruler of Mandu, Sultan Ghiyath Shah, earlier in the sixteenth century. Akbar rode mast elephants most of the way back, including one particularly ferocious animal named Khandi Rai. En route the king of Khandesh, Miran Mubarak Shah, offered a daughter to Akbar as a sign of allegiance. Finally, in October, followed by hundreds of captured elephants, a new bride, and a bolstered sense of confidence and purpose, the Mughal train reached Agra.

Late in 1564, twins were born to Akbar, Hussain and Hasan, but the boys died within a month of their birth. Almost immediately, Akbar began work on the first of his construction projects. First a hunting lodge was built outside Agra called Nagarchain (City of Rest), then orders were given to build a new stone fort at Agra, to replace the now decrepit brickwork of the earlier Badalgarh Fort*. According to art historian Jeremiah Losty, this early Akbari architectural style was 'a synthesis formed from the Indo-Islamic regional styles of Gujarat and Bengal, combined with earlier Hindu ideas on architectural symbolism...' Akbar was willing to borrow and innovate to develop an aesthetic which would be a true reflection of his rule. Under the supervision of Qasim Khan, Mir-Barr-u-Bahr (Lord of the Land and Sea), 1,000 cartloads of red sandstone were brought daily from Sikri Ridge to Agra. According to Shirazi, some 3,000 qalandars and other mendicants were rounded up and used as labour at Agra Fort under the supervision of 300 expert craftsmen at a daily wage of one Akbari tanka. These ex-mendicants could now afford simple meals of khichdi, with pickle, and possibly even ghee, as the cost of goat meat, ghee, and milk was relatively low in the sixteenth century. Slavery had already been abolished by Akbar a

---

sometime in the early 1560s.
*Beginning with Sikandar Lodi, a number of the Lodi Sultans held the fort and added to its structures.

few years previously and Shirazi, travelling through Agra, now had the opportunity to see how the measure was being implemented.

> During those days I set out from Agra for Gujarat. I had a companion. He sold a slave (at Agra). On coming to know about this (transaction) the Kotwal of the city arrested the (original) owner of the slave and carried him to the gate of the fort where his ears were pierced with a pin so that it should serve as a warning to other men.

In Agra, hewn stones of a fiery red colour were used to raise colossal walls and imposing gates. The palace complex, according to historian Michael Fisher, was built using Akbar's early architectural aesthetic—uniform red sandstone surfaces highlighted with white marble. Apart from the palace itself, Monserrate wrote of the 'mansions of his nobles, the magazines, the treasury, the arsenal, the stables of the cavalry, the shops and huts of drug-sellers, barbers, and all manner of common workmen'. According to Abu'l Fazl, some 500 buildings were added 'in the fine styles of Bengal and Gujarat'. Apart from supervising these construction works, Akbar continued to hunt and, now, to play polo. He had devised a way to play the game even after nightfall, by using a ball made of the dhak or palas tree, which smouldered once it was lit, allowing for a glimmering, smoky light between the thundering hooves. Courtiers were all required to play the game and when one nobleman demurred, reluctant to join in this admittedly dangerous pastime, he was roundly censured. For polo playing, like many other aspects of Mughal social life, was a visible reminder of a cherished and heroic past, the Central Asian inheritance that Akbar was a proud claimant of, the same heroism that was narrated repeatedly in the *Hamzanama*.

Agra was now a city that was about to enter its full resplendence. Already in the time of Babur, orders had been given to his noblemen to build riverfront garden residences in the Persian style so beloved of Babur. The heart of Agra lay in these gardens lining the banks of the Yamuna on either side, the pavilions of the Mughal family, and the great noblemen of the empire. The houses of the rich, wrote Monserrate, had 'ornamental gardens in their courtyards and tanks and fishponds which are lined with tiles of various colours'. Their roofs and ceilings were decorated with carvings and paintings but there were no windows looking out 'on account of the filth of the streets'. The true beauty of these river-front gardens was to be admired from the gently flowing river, from where one could admire the fruit trees and the flowers, the dense green trees, and the fluttering brocade tents. The homes of the simpler folk, merchants and the like, were made of brick or stone, or mud covered with a brilliant white plaster, much admired by foreign travellers. Writing in this very year, the chronicler Muhammad Arif wrote of a cosmopolitan city, its riches attracting people from around the world. 'The multitude of foreigners from all sorts of nations, from the corners of the four sides of the world,' he wrote, 'have gathered for trade and fulfillment of necessities, in such a country that the capital city of Agra has become all of India.'

◆

Far away in the kingdom of Naples, meanwhile, a young nobleman, Rudolf Acquaviva, was dreaming of angels and Hindustan. Born into the famously saintly family of Atri, young Rudolf spent his childhood praying on the damp and cold stone floors of his castle's chapel till ulcers formed on his knees. He fasted every Saturday, even as a teenager, and his avoidance of all sinful thoughts and activity 'and his dislike of fine clothes won him from his brothers the nickname of the Stoic'. By the time he was sixteen, he scourged himself every day, wore a hair shirt against his skin to torment the flesh and was fasting almost continually. He told his servants that he dreamed of going to a faraway place like Hindustan and dying for Christ. The choice of Hindustan was not an altogether whimsical one for the young Acquaviva, for that country was the very raison-d'etre for the Order of Jesuits, which he dreamed of joining. The founder of the order, Ignatius of Loyola, had sent Francis Xavier in 1542 to Goa where he took over the running of the College of St Paul by the teal Mandovi River. When Francis Xavier died ten years later in 1552, there were sixty-four Jesuits working in Hindustan and the object of all Acquaviva's lonely scourgings was to join their number.

It was at this time, late in the winter of 1564, that Bega Begum left to perform the hajj. Akbar was reluctant to see his stepmother go so this was clearly a religious obligation Bega Begum was keen to perform for herself. Having started the building works at Humayun's tomb by this time, Bega Begum sailed away to Mecca and disappeared from Mughal records for the next three years. Akbar also turned his attention to the temples of Mathura once again. On a report submitted by Raja Bharmal in 1565, Akbar gave 200 bighas of land in inam (revenue-free gift) to Gopaldas, priest at the Govind Dev and Madan Mohan temples, both of the Chaitanya sects.

In the spring of 1565, Akbar set off once again for Narwar, purportedly to hunt elephants but also to finally requisition the treasure from Gondwana that Asaf Khan had misappropriated and to check on the loyalty of this famously flighty officer. It was around this time that, without much fanfare, Akbar ordered the execution of Kamran's son, his cousin Abu'l Qasim Khan, a prisoner in Gwalior these many years. According to the contemporary writer Muhammad Arif Qandahari, the man appointed to carry out this execution was the son of Raja Bharmal, showing the extraordinarily high confidence Akbar now had in his Kachhwaha relatives. With his empire simmering with rebellion, a hostile prince of royal blood would have been considered potentially too dangerous, and could no longer be allowed to languish at Gwalior. The cause of Akbar's many alliances and actions at this time was mainly to neutralize the danger posed by the old Timurid system of co-sovereignty in which all princes had an equal right to rule. Akbar seemed to fear no enemy as much as he dreaded a challenge from a prince of the royal blood. After all, Humayun's many humiliations were almost entirely due to challenges from his own brothers, especially Kamran, which Akbar would have known about. Now those challenges appeared before Akbar, too, in the shape of Kamran's sons, and Akbar's half-brother, Mirza Hakim. It did not matter that the princes themselves were inconsequential, or that Mirza Hakim was only twelve years old at the time. What mattered was the legitimacy they could claim in the name of Timur and Babur, and the dangerous factions they could gather around themselves from among those dissatisfied by Akbar's measures to bring his nobility under control. In time, as we will see, Akbar would disband the Timurid co-sovereign system altogether but at the moment, it was the Uzbeks, proud, independent, and fierce, who were rebelling in the name of Mirza Hakim.

The Uzbek clansmen, who had understood the shape of the Padshah's ambition after his action against Abdullah Khan, now decided to summon all their liegemen and supporters against what they believed was an attack against the very fabric of their clan. Ali Quli Khan began gathering an army of mercenaries that included Uzbeks, Turkmen, Afghans, and Hindustanis, an explosive assembly of some 30,000 veteran horsemen. Akbar now moved to try to isolate the Uzbeks from some of their other clansmen. He sent an emissary to Fath Khan Uzbek at Rohtas, who promised to help Akbar if he came to Jaunpur. Another emissary, to Sikandar Khan Uzbek, jagirdar of Awadh, was less successful—Sikandar defected to Ali Quli Khan. With the Uzbeks now in open revolt, Akbar led his troops from Narwar towards Jaunpur, marching at night to avoid the catastrophic heat of June, and chased the rebels into the territory of the Afghans in Bihar.

With the Uzbeks successfully out of Akbar's territory, a force was required to guard the ferry across the Ganga so that the rebels could not cross back into Mughal lands. Munim Khan, more sympathetic to the Uzbeks because of their old kinship from the time of Humayun, wanted control over the ferry. Asaf Khan, Persian immigrant and much less indulgent of the Uzbeks, was another contender to guard the crossing but the eternally vacillating Asaf Khan chose this moment to finally desert. The conversation between Munim Khan and Akbar that followed this desertion, reported by Bayazid Beg, is telling in its recording of old racial tensions and ambiguities, especially the resentment between the old Chaghatai Turkmen and the newer Persian clans.

Akbar summoned Munim Khan and asked him apropos the deserting Asaf Khan, 'Khan Baba, do you know what that Tajik* dwarf has done?'

To which Munim Khan railed, 'How could a clerk dare do such a thing? It was you who gave him so many promotions.'

Akbar reasoned with Munim Khan saying, 'Khan Baba, he was trained by Khwaja Jahan (a Persian). What knowledge could we have about his character?'

'At the time he (Asaf Khan) was appointed,' continued Munim Khan bitterly, 'Khwaja Jahan had remarked "even a single hair of Asaf

---

*A derogative term for a Persian, considered a scribe.

Khan is better than the whole of the Chaghatai clan". But now the Khwaja would not tell which of the hairs of Asaf Khan is better than the Chaghatai clan.' Saying this, Munim Khan started weeping and Akbar comforted him and said it 'was nonsensical and mischievous' of Khwaja Jahan to have spoken thus.

Munim Khan now tried for many months to broker peace with the rebellious Uzbeks, a peace which Todar Mal stoutly opposed, preferring confrontation, while Akbar negotiated with various parties to put pressure on Sulaiman Karrani, the Afghan, to withdraw his support of the Uzbeks. Finally, it was when the independent Raja of Orissa* ominously promised to 'do such things to Sulaiman that he would be a warning to all strife-mongers' that the Uzbeks were sobered somewhat in their ambitions and agreed to a meeting with Munim Khan. Ali Quli Khan and Munim Khan agreed to meet in neutral territory, in the middle of the Ganga. Near Baksar, Munim Khan embarked on a boat from one side of the river while Ali Quli got into another boat from the other side. Troops were lined up on both banks, looking at the unusual scene playing out in front of them. 'As the two boats approached each other in the middle of the Ganga,' remembered Bayazid, who was present at the time, 'Ali Quli Khan rose to his feet in the boat saying, "peace be on you kaifiyat lagh". Then he jumped into Munim Khan's boat. 'They embraced each other and wept bitterly to mourn...(Humayun's) death as they had not met since then.' A great deal had changed since these two old liegemen of Humayun's had come to Hindustan with the previous Padshah, and the Uzbeks railed against the new order which demanded a reconfigured allegiance they deplored.

Ali Quli refused to go to court personally but he sent his mother along with Ibrahim Khan, most senior Uzbek, to meet with Akbar. An uneasy peace was accepted by all and Ali Quli was warned not to cross the Ganga as long as imperial forces remained in the east. Almost as soon as Akbar left for Benares, however, Ali Quli defied the Padshah and crossed the Ganga. Akbar was furious and turned his army around and headed back for Jaunpur, calling peremptorily for all his noblemen to leave their jagirs and join him there. Munim Khan negotiated a peace once again but it was clear to all that a

---

*Raja Mukunda Deva.

reckoning would come for the Uzbeks, for Akbar would now never allow them to hold vast areas of lands in jagir as they had done in the past.

At the end of 1566, with Akbar concentrating his forces on the Uzbeks in the east, an unexpected challenge appeared in the north, with the contender being someone who shared the Padshah's blood. Mirza Hakim, youngest son of Humayun, and now thirteen years old, left Kabul and attempted to occupy Lahore. As a Timurid prince Mirza Hakim was no fugitive pretender but a legitimate source of power, able to rally disaffected noblemen to his cause. Indeed, Ali Quli Khan added further heft to the challenge by having the khutba read out in Mirza Hakim's name, thereby proclaiming him a sovereign. Akbar placed Munim Khan in charge of Agra and set off for the north in November 1566. By the time he reached Lahore in February 1567, Mirza Hakim had wisely reconsidered his challenge and retired across the Indus. Akbar now proceeded to demonstrate his power and his might to all those who had claims to rule in Hindustan by organizing a hunt, the enormous, dangerous, and bloody qumargha.

A vast plain outside Lahore was chosen and several thousand foot soldiers, 50,000 according to a history of the time, were assigned to drive birds and beasts from the outlying regions into the centre of the plain, several kilometres in circumference. All the great amirs and courtiers were posted at the outer edges of the field, in their tented encampments, while for a month, deer, cheetahs, hares, leopards, and birds were driven relentlessly into the circle. Every day, and through the cold, watchful nights, entertainments were held at the amirs' tents. Finally, at the end of the month, Akbar mounted his horse and entered the hunting ground. For five days, accompanied only by Aziz Koka, Akbar galloped through the field using the arrow, the spear, the sword, and the musket. The smaller animals he snatched by hand while thundering past on his horse while others he snared by lasso or shot with his lethal arrows. Every day soldiers at the edge of the circle moved in, holding lengths of bamboo fences, and the field became smaller, the area dense with blood, and fear, and the warm bodies of the frightened beasts. After five days, the great amirs and special courtiers were allowed to hunt and next came the attendants until, on the last day, ordinary foot soldiers and cavalrymen charged into the tight circle in a final, screaming orgy of bloodlust. At the end of the qumargha, the air rang with the silence of the dead animals, the earth was scorched and bloody, and there could have been no more effective demonstration of Akbar's might, the skill and fury of his warriors, and the wealth of Hindustan's great amirs.

The qumargha was not only extremely effective at demonstrating imperial power, it served as a training ground for the cavalry and infantrymen. There were few spaces more dangerous at the time than the dense, heaving circle of a qumargha, where swords flashed and arrows from the deadly accurate composite bows thudded into moving targets. It was a drill exercise in near battle conditions, and tested the soldiers' expertise as much as their bloodlust. Indeed, scores were sometimes settled in this incendiary field, an enemy quietly killed off amid the carnage.

Returning to Lahore after the qumargha, the Mughal troops arrived at the river Ravi, wide and unsoundable after the spring snow melt. Akbar plunged his horse into the river, obliging his retinue to do the same. As the horses swam against the current and the treacherous eddies, two men drowned. At each stage Akbar appeared to test not just himself but also his men, their loyalty to their emperor, and their courage which, when the Padshah was Akbar, was the very same thing.

At some point during his stay in the Lahore region, Akbar paid a visit to a venerable old man, the third Guru of a young religion which had gained followers with great speed. This was Guru Amar Das, ninety years old at the time, living at Goindwal on the banks of the river Beas. There are no records in the Persian biographies of the time regarding this meeting, but it is entirely plausible that Akbar would have wanted to visit this elderly man whose reputation for saintliness and social service was well established. It is Sikh tradition, rather, that lovingly recorded the meeting of the young Padshah and the old Guru. Guru Amar Das invited the Padshah to share in the communal kitchen, the langar, which was one of the three sanctioned activities of the faith, in addition to a place for worship (dharamsala) and congregational worship (sangat). The Guru's langar was especially famous for its use of fine flour and ghee, in addition to serving a sweet dish of rice boiled in milk. Akbar was impressed with the food, and the number of people fed at the langar, for the followers of the Guru had increased rapidly, attracting men and women of all classes and backgrounds because of his egalitarian message of brotherhood, love, humility, and a God above all earthly distinctions. Akbar too was impressed with the order and wanted to make an offering to the Guru, who refused the offer.

After finally settling affairs at Lahore, Akbar and the Mughal camp headed back to Agra. North of Delhi, near Kurukshetra, the Mughal party camped outside a town called Thaneshwar. There was a large tank with a pavilion in the middle and hundreds of yogis and ascetics of different sects had gathered for a pilgrimage. The ascetics were a fearsome collection of men, bare-chested, with large, lopsided topknots, faces cloudy with ashes, and carrying swords, bows and arrows, and sticks. A large number of pilgrims had arrived too. A dispute arose between two sects, the ascetic Sannyasis and the tantric Naths, described by Abu'l Fazl as the Puris and the Kaurs. As the bemused Mughal party watched, the sadhus began to argue over the best spot from which to collect alms from the pilgrims. Akbar tried to reason with the men but it was like 'casting pearls into the dust'. The men grew angrier and demanded to be allowed to fight each other which Akbar eventually agreed to. Both groups lined up to face each other and one man from each sect swaggered up, sword drawn, to fight the other. In an instant, all the yogis had rushed at each other in a terrible melee of flailing limbs and smashing stones and swishing swords. Akbar watched the proceedings with keen interest and when he saw that one side, the Puris, were outnumbered, he sent some of his own followers to join in and balance out the fight. The Kaurs were then roundly defeated with their chief, one Anand Kaur, 'ground into the dust'. The Padshah, we are told, 'thoroughly enjoyed the spectacle'. That Akbar was fascinated by this encounter with the yogis, as he would be later in life, too, is borne out by paintings made of the episode in at least four separate biographies of the time.

Once the imperial train had reached Agra, Akbar was confronted with a delicate problem. One of his officers, Jalal Khan Qurchi, was seized with passion for a 'beautiful youth and was immoderate with regard to him'. Very annoyed, Akbar attempted to separate the two men but then Jalal Khan Qurchi ran away with the youth. Akbar had them caught and brought back to court and Jalal Khan was 'confined under the public staircase so that he could be trodden on by the feet of everyone entering it' until such time as the emperor remembered his old affection for the man and released him. The following year it was another officer, Muzaffar Khan, who developed an attachment for a smooth-faced youth and Akbar had the boy removed from court. Scholar Rosalind O'Hanlon has shown that there was a certain racial stereotyping of Uzbeks by the Mughals with both Abu'l Fazl and Badauni talking of 'the filthy manners of Transoxiana', while referring to homosexual attachments deemed 'neither burning nor melting, neither love nor friendship'. A certain homoerotic sensitivity was admitted by the Mughals, but of a rarefied and exalted sort, preferably leading to the writing of charming couplets. It was not considered within everyone's power to control it and keep it within acceptable boundaries as Jalal Khan had demonstrated.

Much more worryingly for Akbar, however, was news of the Uzbeks' renewed efforts to foment rebellion in the eastern regions. Ali Quli Khan had not only had the khutba read out in Mirza Hakim's name, he had also had coins minted, all irrefutable signs of a treacherous realignment. Efforts at peace and compromise had clearly failed and Akbar spent a month gathering his forces before leaving, at the beginning of summer in May 1567, at the head of an army of 2,000 war elephants. At Rae Bareli, Akbar decided to take the shortest route, through forested scrubland, and arid, benighted tracks, so that by the time he reached Manikpur, there were only eleven courtiers left with him. When they reached the Ganga, it was rumbling and frothing with rain water as the monsoon had begun but Akbar plunged into the river on his elephant, forcing his courtiers to do the same. Behind them, three elephants in their train, Khuda-Baksh, Bal-Sundar, and Toofan-Masti, bellowed and trumpeted in agitation and the men rejoiced, seeing in this a sign of imminent victory. After his forces had caught up, Akbar attacked. In the final confrontation with the Uzbek clan, there were 500 Mughal soldiers and 500 war elephants and the Uzbeks were finally decisively routed. Ali Quli Khan was thrown off his horse and crushed by an elephant which 'ground his bones to powder and made his body like a bagful of chess-pieces'. Bahadur Khan Uzbek was captured and decapitated and the heads of the two Uzbek brothers were sent to Agra. The soldiery would be forgiven, treated simply as brave and valuable warriors who were not responsible for their generals' choices, but there would be no clemency this time for the officers and Akbar reserved the strongest punishments for all the rebels who had defected from the Mughals to the Uzbeks. Mirza Mirak Mashhadi, who had defected from the imperial camp, was tortured for five days by an elephant, who 'twisted him in its trunk, stepped on him...and shook him from side to side', until he was finally pardoned, possibly more dead than alive.

After the Uzbek rebellions were conclusively crushed, there would be a reappraisal of ancient ties and old ways of shaping the Mughal nobility. Earlier in the decade, Akbar had begun recruiting other Indian Muslims, the Sayyids of Baraha, migrants and brave warriors from Persia who had settled in Sirhind since the thirteenth century. Now Munim Khan himself would be transferred to the provincial capital of Jaunpur, effectively ending his career as a powerful wakil at the centre. A Chaghatai nobleman of the old guard, he had proved himself too intractable in his ways and too forgiving of disaffection when it originated from men from the old order. In the first twenty years of Akbar's reign, the number of Persian noblemen of high rank would reflect this change of guard, and would swell to 38 per cent, almost at a par now with the Turanis at 39 per cent.

There was another family deemed too powerful at this time to remain in their concentrated jagirs in the Punjab—the Ataka Khail. Soon after the Uzbek rebellion, the members of the Ataka Khail were summoned to court and reassigned jagirs so that they were dispersed throughout the empire 'like the constellation of the Bear in the sky', as Akbar himself proudly claimed. Only Aziz Koka, Akbar's beloved old playmate from his Kabul days, was allowed to retain his jagir. As for the Uzbek nobility, the clan was scattered and fragmented and would never again challenge Akbar's supremacy. Akbar now also pragmatically restored Gondwana to its earlier ruling family, represented by a brother of Durgavati's deceased husband, keeping only ten forts from Gondwana and making them a part of the subah of Malwa.

In the course of this year Akbar was petitioned by the ulema, the body of Islamic scholars appointed to the court, regarding the burial site of one Mir Murtaza Sharif Shirazi. The two main members of the ulema, Shaikh Abd un-Nabi and Abdullah Sultanpuri, were narrow-minded men and scholars whose religious learning was shallow and suspect but at the beginning of Akbar's reign, their power was incontrovertible. Abd un-Nabi had been given wide-ranging powers and a great deal of resources to use at his discretion for 'deserving people' while Abdullah Sultanpuri's fatwa (religious decree) was considered law. Now these men brought forward the case of Shirazi, a Persian Shia, who had died the previous year and was buried in the neighbourhood of the famous Delhi poet, Amir Khusro. The ulema maintained that being a Hindustani Sunni, Khusro would 'be very much annoyed' by the posthumous company of Shirazi, 'a native of Iraq and a heretic'. Akbar agreed to these demands and had Shirazi dug up and buried elsewhere, an act which Badauni himself, usually orthodox in matters of religion, found 'was a great act of injustice to both of them'. During this decade, it is clear that Akbar acquiesced to a repressive attitude towards all Muslim sects which were condemned by the orthodox Muslims as heretical. Badauni meanwhile had spent most of the decade in the employ of Shaikh Hussain Khan, once Governor of Lahore. Hussain Khan had one day stood up to greet a visitor, not realizing that he was a Hindu, not a Muslim. Enraged at having shown an 'infidel' this passing courtesy, Hussain Khan ordered that Hindus stitch a patch of cloth, or tukra, of a different colour near the bottom of the sleeve so that they could be distinguished easily from Muslims and he would not inadvertently honour a Hindu. Having thus earned the sobriquet 'Tukriya', when Hussain Khan was transferred to Rohilkhand, a demotion, he retaliated by raiding Hindu temples and appropriating their hidden treasures to make up for his diminution of pay. This spirit of casual intolerance and bigotry was by no means uncommon at the time and Akbar, as he gauged his many challenges and especially the dangerous one from Mirza Hakim, preferred to keep the ulema pacified for the time being. When Akbar would finally confront the ulema, the fall of these men would be spectacular, the theologians completely unaware for many years of the true nature of the Padshah's spiritual quest.

After the Uzbeks had been crushed in the east, many of the disgruntled survivors simply relocated to the prosperous sultanate of Gujarat, counting on its ruler for support and patronage. Akbar realized that the time would come when he would have to confront this powerful province, too, but between the Padshah's territory and Gujarat lay an arid country filled with indomitable warriors, Rajasthan. Akbar, therefore, immediately after subduing the Uzbeks decided to attack a legendary fort that had never been taken. Its legacy was intertwined with his own Mughal ancestry but it was famously associated with one of the greatest warriors of the era, long dead but still revered—Rana Sangha. 'One eye was lost in a broil with his brother,' wrote the nineteenth-century historian James Tod approvingly, 'an arm in an action with the Lodi king of Delhi, while he was a cripple owing to a limb having been broken by a cannon ball. From the sword or lance, he counted eighty wounds on various parts of his body.' And the fortress that this exemplary warrior had once defended in an earlier age was Chittor.

LEGENDS OF RAJASTHAN

In October 1567 a large Mughal force arrived in Mewar during a thunderstorm so furious that, as the imperial tents were pitched, the rain scuffed the countryside around them into watery shadows. The next morning, however, the clouds dispersed and rising from the rainswept plains the troops saw a fortress made by giants, nearly 5 kilometres long and rising from a hill, a ship of stone in an endless sea. This was Chittor, capital of Mewar, and scene of extravagant acts of gallantry in past centuries by both men and women. It was also, more prosaically, on the trade route from Delhi to Gwalior, and a worthy adversary for Akbar in the battle for Rajasthan. All the palaces, havelis and bazaars of Chittor were within its fortifications and high on the hill were two great towers, the Jai Kirti Stambh (Pillar of Fame) and the Jai Stambh (Pillar of Victory), eloquent symbols of a past glory. Enormous stone reservoirs were filled with rainwater and Udai Singh, Rana of Chittor, 'knew his own strength and felt at ease about Chittor because the Emperor's force had but little siege apparatus and it did not seem likely that he would attempt to reduce the place'. So sanguine did Udai Singh feel about the safety of Chittor that he left it in the care of the Rathore chief Jaimal 'Mertia' of Badnor while he and his entire court removed themselves to their other capital at Udaipur.

Though historian James Tod, a great proponent of the history of Rajasthan, would bitterly criticize Udai Singh for his failure to exhibit the exemplary Rajput bravery expected of him when he wrote scathingly that 'the absence of the kingly virtues in the sovereign of Mewar filled to the brim the bitter cup of her destiny', the rana was not altogether deluded in placing his faith in Chittor's natural defences. The fortresses of Hindustan were formidable structures, constructed with great quantities of stone and rising to imposing heights. Built on a substantial hill, Chittor was the largest fort at the time, its stone walls bristling with watch towers and iron-spiked doors. The fortress was well stocked with supplies, ammunition, water, and a garrison of 8,000 warriors. The garrison, it is said, 'uttered cries of derision', when they saw the paltry force that had had the audacity to besiege their mighty fortress. The Rajputs hunkered down to watch what they believed would be another derisory attempt against their fortress of legend but Akbar was not just another attacker and his dreams were far greater than just the subjugation of a spiky neighbour.

Once the Mughal camp had been pitched, Akbar got onto his horse and rode around the entire circumference of the fortress, accompanied by the surveyors who always travelled with the army. He had the distances carefully assessed and then ordered battle stations assigned and entrenchments dug. According to historian de la Garza, as a weapon, 'the shovel was nearly as important as the musket'. The soldiers now dug slit trenches and constructed sandbag barricades, and individual fighting holes which were soon manned by reinforcements that arrived every day. Within a month, the entire fortress was ringed by the besiegers, while three main batteries were stationed around it. The Mughal troops had built a circumvallation, a line of fortifications around the fortress including not only 'zigzag trenches and sunken gun emplacements but also sirkob, or siege towers'. All the while, individual amirs in shows of braggadocio, charged at the fortress, shooting their muskets from their galloping horses at the defending soldiers. But the besieged soldiers within the fort were far from defenceless. From behind the safety of Chittor's stone walls, snipers hit the Mughal forces with deadly accuracy. The Rajput soldiers used the crossbow, which was not as advanced as the Mughal composite bow but was easy to use and especially effective when used from a prone position. They also had muskets, which a group of crack shots, led by their chief musketeer, Ismail, used from within Chittor's walls to great effect. Meanwhile, Akbar was unable to deploy his most deadly weapon, the mounted archers. As proud descendants of Central Asian Timurid warlords, the most skilled and versatile element of the Mughal army, the one favoured by the elite, was the horse archer, who combined deadly accuracy with the composite bow with speed of movement. But in the siege conditions of Chittor, Mughal artillery and arrows sailed harmlessly over the fort walls so Akbar decided to engineer sabats, covered trenches, to bring his fierce firepower closer to the walls of the fort.

Raja Todar Mal and Qasim Khan supervised the construction of the sabats and 5,000 carpenters, stonecutters, blacksmiths, excavators, earthworkers, and shovelmen set to work digging trenches with walls and roofs of wood, canvas, and leather so that sappers and elephants could approach the walls of the fort to place their heavy guns. In the pouring rain, and under the constant fire of the Rajput soldiers, deep trenches were dug with mud walls to shelter the workers. Even so, casualties on the Mughal side were bruising, and 100–200 labourers a day were killed by snipers. Akbar rewarded the survivors so handsomely that people exclaimed that the worth of silver and gold had reduced to dust. Thousands of men and animals were employed in these tasks, with many tons of ration and fodder required. Mughal access to the heartland and resources meant that as Rajput rations dwindled over the winter months inside the fortress, Mughal supplies and men kept arriving.

For the soldiers within the fortress, the earlier mood of confidence and elation would have progressively slid into bemusement, and then a sort of horror, as they saw the very landscape outside Chittor moulting and morphing into something monstrous: in every direction were the tunnels and mounds of earth leading inexorably towards the fort, like a disarticulated beast, unstoppable even after they had pounded them with cannons and fired all their musket rounds; there would have been elephants trumpeting impatiently in the distance, hauling cannon, daggers strapped to their tusks; dust rising from the artillery shots; men, armies of them, inexhaustible, straining at ropes and scaffolding as they built siege towers and sabats; and high towers studding the siege perimeters, from which officers surveyed the work; archers in full armour, wheeling on their pure-blood horses, were shooting arrows in every direction. The horses themselves looked like beasts from a nightmare, entirely covered in plates of armour, even their heads, their braided manes pulled through openings in their neck armour. Rumbling through the air would have been the ominous, syncopated rhythm of many drummers, each signalling the presence of a high-ranking Mughal officer. Most shocking of all were the siege guns, monsters which could fire projectiles weighing more than a ton. But there were also smaller, more manoeuvrable ones, including cannons large enough for half-maund balls which Akbar had cast on the battlefield itself, in his presence, to avoid having to drag the larger ones forward. And the noise would have been incessant, a weapon in itself, the relentless whine and thud of cannon shots and muskets, and the whistling of arrows.

On 17 December, two mines were laid against the walls of Chittor and set off, but they misfired and, in a deafening explosion of stone and dust and blood, the storming party itself was blown up, some 200 men, while 40 Rajputs were killed. Akbar constantly patrolled his frontline, as cannon balls fell scattershot all around him, in a hail of dust and screams and blood. He took aim at the besieged soldiers using a musket, much improved since the crude brass contraptions used by Babur's men. Akbar's muskets were sophisticated weapons made of iron or steel, designed for accuracy, and he tested every musket in his arsenal himself. He kept 101 muskets within the harem and, in times of peace, he tested each one, in rotation. Mughal matchlocks were able to pack more gunpowder than their European counterparts and were considerably deadlier. Now Akbar gave orders for work on the sabats to continue, and by end February 1568, four bruising months after the siege began, in a final superhuman effort by the Mughal soldiers, the sabats were completed. The Mughal army now attacked the pounded walls of Chittor and Akbar got out his favourite musket, Sangram, and shot at a Rajput officer 'with a spiked breastplate who looked like a commander'. Jaimal, it was later learnt, had been killed and now, desolation in their heart, no more Rajput soldiers advanced to shore up the breaches in the fort walls. As the Mughal officers looked on at the suddenly quiet walls of the fortress, they saw three ominous plumes of smoke drifting up into the cold January evening. 'This is the fire of jauhar,' explained Raja Bhagwant Das to Akbar, telling him of the custom that the Rajputs had of having their women immolate themselves when they faced certain defeat. Three hundred women died in three separate pyres that night—one for the Sisodiya clan, one for the Rathores, and one for the Chauhans.

At first light, the following day, the Mughal troops, some 5,000 men, stormed the breach, followed by their war elephants in full armour, swords strapped to trunks and tusks. The elephants also had steel plates on their brows, to use as battering rams. Some had yak tails and animal pelts attached to them making them appear even more terrifying. Akbar, sitting on the largest elephant of all, joined the attack shouting his new war cry 'Ya Muin!'* The elephants raged and trumpeted and threw enemy soldiers into the air with their trunks and slashed at them in a fury. The 8,000 Rajputs fell to a man, either in the narrow winding lanes of Chittor, crushed by the elephants, or in combat with the Mughal troops, at the rana's haveli or in front of the Mahadeva temple. In addition, some 30,000 civilians who had 'fought fiercely' to defend their fortress were also put to the sword while more were taken captive. The expert snipers, some 1,000 marksmen, who had caused havoc and ruin in the Mughal troops, managed a most daring escape, though Akbar sought them out particularly. Tying up their women and children like captives, and driving them out noisily in front of them, they made their escape among the Mughal foot soldiers who were also leading out prisoners.

The massacre of the civilian population of Chittor would be the only instance in which Akbar would indulge in this aberrant scorched earth policy in what would be a long and eventful reign. It remains a profoundly disquieting episode for modern readers but the Mughal Empire was still being formed, in the furnace of battles, mystic episodes, and past legacies. In February 1568, Akbar had fought personally for four long months, increasingly incensed by what he saw as the obduracy of the besieged forces and the great loss of lives the Mughal troops suffered. De la Garza points out that 'it was expected that a besieged enemy would surrender soon after a practicable breach was made in their defences. If the assailants were forced to take their objective by storm, the consequences for the defenders were usually dire.' There was also an elemental misalignment between the two sides in the understanding of bravery and battle tactics. For the Central Asian warriors, tactical defensive strategies and withdrawal in case of overwhelming odds were essential battle skills. They were contemptuous of what they saw as heedless aggression as exemplified by notions of European chivalry and Rajput valour. As a later Padshah, Aurangzeb, would explain:

---

*In deference to his new allegiance to the Sufi Muinuddin Chishti, Akbar changed his war cry at this time to Ya Muin, a shortened form of Muinuddin.

The Turani people have ever been soldiers. They feel no suspicion, despair or shame when commanded to make a retreat in the very midst of a fight, which means, in other words, 'drawing the arrow back,' and they are a hundred stages remote from the crass stupidity of the Hindustanis, who would part with their heads but not leave their positions.

For the Rajputs, meanwhile, the battle was a divine furnace, a conduit to an immortal life which was the destiny of those who died on the battlefield. For Akbar, the defeat of Chittor and the massacre of all those who resisted, coming after three years of persistent Uzbek and mirza rebellions, was intended to be seen as a fiery and clear message to all those who stood against him.

Akbar stayed for three days in Chittor, declaring it a sarkar of the Mughal Empire, and placing it in the charge of Asaf Khan. It is said he removed the symbols of its sovereignty, its great wooden doorways, and the great naqqaras, or kettledrums, whose doleful bass reverberations proclaimed the comings and goings of the rana. The royal library of Chittor was destroyed, too, its manuscripts reduced to ashes.

During his three days in Chittor, Akbar rewarded the bravest fighters. One of the men thus singled out for his exemplary service was a khatri, one Rai Rayan, who had begun his carrier as an accountant in the elephant stables.* Akbar then set off on foot in the rising heat of March to offer thanks for his great victory at the dargah at Ajmer, accompanied by some of the harem women and his closest courtiers, also on foot. At Ajmer, Akbar issued a Fathnama-i Chittor, a letter of victory, to be sent to the officers in the Punjab. In language full of bombast, the defeat of Chittor was stridently proclaimed to be the victory of Islam over infidels. In his fathnama, Akbar declared:

> We, as far as it is within our power, remain busy in jihad... we have succeeded in occupying a number of forts and towns belonging to the infidels and have established Islam there. With the help of our bloodthirsty sword we have erased the signs of infidelity from their minds and have destroyed temples in those places and also all over Hindustan.

---

*Rai Rayan would have a very distinguished career, and was made Diwan of Bihar, and then of Kabul, earning the title Raja Bikramjit and a mansab of 5,000.

Babur, after his famous victory over Rana Sangha at Khanua, similarly evoked the image of the Ghazi conqueror and, like Akbar, would quietly put it aside with equal nonchalance once it had served its purpose. Moreover, Iqtidar Alam Khan has argued that a lot of this overtly orthodox posturing, like the fathnama and the visible deference to the sadr, Shaikh Abd un-Nabi, were in fact a calculated move by Akbar to appeal to the Indian shaikhzadas. In any event, as we will see later, this was a path that was soon forsaken, quietly assigned to past mistakes and experiments. Akbar would understand the need for a much more robust and inclusive idea of empire, one that would truly reflect and incorporate the multiple identities of Hindustan.

After the defeat of Chittor, Akbar remained in Ajmer for ten days before returning to Agra. After the capitulation of what was considered one of the mightiest fortresses of Hindustan, Akbar was now ready to attack Ranthambore. To be able to subdue the entire province of Rajasthan it would be crucial to take its great fortresses, eloquent symbols of its invincibility.

By the end of 1568, Akbar had gathered an army together to march on Ranthambore, which was held by Surjan, the chieftain of the Hada clan. Travelling via Delhi to visit Nizamuddin Auliya's dargah, and Humayun's tomb, Akbar organized a qumargha near Palam, outside Delhi. Hunting was a supremely effective way of moving large numbers of soldiers and weapons without warning, to be able to quell resistance when required. Quite often no actual confrontation was ever required, potential troublemakers growing more circumspect in the face of these great hunting parties and their casual display of power.

Akbar arrived at Ranthambore in December 1568 and encircled and besieged the fort with ominous precision. A siege tower was constructed under Raja Todar Mal's supervision and huge mortars were dragged up the hill by 200 pairs of oxen. One particularly fearsome cannon required 1,000 oxen and several elephants to drag it uphill, and was 'reported to launch a payload of over 3000 pounds'. The Mughal guns started pounding the walls of Ranthambore but resistance, this time, was much less determined. Intimidation was clearly as effective as actual warfare and the absolute terror created by the sight of these monstrous cannons was dramatic. In less than two months, Surjan Hada sent his sons, Bhoj and Doda, to serve at Akbar's court and handed over the silver and gold keys to the fortress. In addition to the sobering effect of the calamitous fate of Chittor, Surjan Hada would have been reassured by the presence, in the Mughal army, of two Kachhwaha neighbours, Raja Bhagwant Das and Kuar Man Singh, both now respected Mughal officers. The relatively easy capture of Ranthambore after the violence of Chittor was recognized later by the Mughals as a moment of reckoning. There would be a very fine miniature painted of the submission of Surjan Hada in the *Akbarnama*. The painting is full of compassion for the chieftain, who bows before the young Padshah while Akbar gently puts his hand on his vanquished foe. A contemporary Sanskrit text, the *Surjancarita*, presents an alternate reality. According to this text Akbar was so impressed by Surjan's courage that he gifted him three territories in lieu of Ranthambore—nimbly converting defeat into victory.

The capture of the great fortresses of Chittor and Ranthambore would fundamentally alter the shape of the Mughal Empire. Until these two strongholds fell, only the relatively minor Kachhwahas and the Rathores of Merta, a junior branch of the Rathores of Jodhpur, had aligned themselves with the Mughals. But now for Akbar there would be a novel means of Rajput conquest, the offering of honourable and profitable inclusion into the empire. Raja Ramchand, the Baghela Rajput from Bundelkhand, decided that discretion was the better part of valour after hearing of the capitulation of Chittor and Ranthambore and handed over the fortress of Kalanjar, gaining a jagir near Allahabad in lieu. The Rathores of Bikaner and the Bhatis of Jaisalmer also submitted to Akbar in the slipstream of the two great Mughal victories. And so, all the great fortresses in the north-west submitted to Akbar and became part of the Mughal Empire. This area became incorporated into the subah of Ajmer, which included seven sarkars: Ajmer, Jodhpur, Chittor, Ranthambore, Nagaur, Sirohi, and Bikaner and included within it the territories of Mewar, Marwar, and Hadauti.* The area was bound by Agra to the east, Delhi to the north, Gujarat in the south-west, while to the west lay Multan. To

---

*A tract formed of the territory of Kota and Bundi.

the south lay the Aravalli hills, a natural barrier.

Before returning to Agra, Akbar went to Ajmer to pray and offer alms at Muinuddin Chishti's tomb. He then travelled via Amer where, for the first time, a Hindu chieftain, his brother-in-law, Raja Bhagwant Das, hosted the Padshah of Hindustan. A mosque was built especially for the Friday prayers of the Padshah and his noblemen, the Akbari Mosque, which stands to this day in Amer. By 1569, however, Akbar was praying for something that no amount of bravery could guarantee him—a living heir. All his sons had died as infants and the children recently born to him were daughters. So now, with an empire to bequeath and limned dreams, he looked for assistance to a man living on a hill, a man of god and a soothsayer, Salim Chishti.

PART 3

THE WORLD IS A BRIDGE
{1569–1578}

~

THE MAKING OF A COMPLICATED HAREM

When the city of Agra had been rebuilt by Akbar, and he went to live there, Monserrate wrote that 'he found the place overrun with ghosts, which rushed to and fro, tore everything to pieces, terrified the women and children, threw stones, and finally began to hurt everyone there'. The ghouls may have been tolerated, we are told, if the matter had stopped there. 'But the cruel spite of the Evil One began to wreak itself on the children of the King who were slain a day or two after birth.' Akbar was twenty-seven years old now and found to his dismay that his children kept dying. The people of Agra had begun muttering darkly about malevolent spirits and evil forces, so when Harkha Bai became pregnant in 1569, Akbar decided to beg for divine intervention. Not far from Agra, on an isolated hillside, in a small town called Sikri, with wheeling kites and soft-stepping leopards for company, lived a Sufi pir, Salimuddin Chishti. Shaikh Salim lived a life as frugal as his surroundings, wearing a single layer of thin cotton clothes even in winter and keeping fasts during which he would eat only half a watermelon. Shaikh Salim promised the Padshah a son and Akbar immediately had Harkha Bai shifted to Sikri and built a palace for her near the khanqah of the shaikh. On 31 August 1569, a son was born to Harkha Bai. Dressed in a flowing black jama, Shaikh Ibrahim, Salim Chishti's son-in-law, conveyed the news to the Padshah in Agra. Akbar named the child Salim, in honour of the shaikh. To further declare his allegiance to the Hindustani order of Sufis, the Chishtis, Akbar appointed a number of women from Shaikh Salim's family to the prestigious post of milk mother to the infant.

When Salim was born, Akbar did not immediately visit the child, in deference to local customs. As recorded by Abu'l Fazl, 'as the common people of this country have an old custom according to which whenever God, after long expectation, has bestowed an auspicious child, he be not produced before the honoured father till after a long delay'. The celebrations to mark this longed-for birth, however, were unprecedented both around the mother in Sikri and at the court in Agra. The entire darbar was caught up in a frenzy of excitement. Both Greek and Hindu horoscopes were cast, poems and odes composed, prisoners released, and alms distributed. The drummers began a clangorous music as dancers swayed and twirled in front of the Padshah. Scented water was poured on the heads of courtiers as blessing and royal banquets were arranged for seven days of celebrations. At Sikri, meanwhile, the baby Salim was much admired by adoring ladies. The birth chamber was a place of subdued joy, as the new mother was gently tended to by an older woman in Timurid dress. The women surrounding the mother and infant would have heard music spilling out from the courtyard, where drummers played large naqqara drums, while behind them men blew into trumpets, and enthusiastically smashed cymbals together.

In January 1570, Akbar set off on foot from Agra to fulfil a vow he had made to walk to the Ajmer shrine if ever he were granted a son. Members of his harem, including Harkha Bai, and the infant Salim also travelled to Ajmer. When Akbar arrived at Ajmer, he gave such a huge donation in gold and money to the shrine that it resulted in charges of misappropriation and embezzlement and a general outcry among the attendants of the dargah. A dispute arose over the question of who among the shrine's several attendants was most deserving of the huge donation. Hearing of this unseemly behaviour, Akbar dismissed all the attendants and appointed his own officer, Shaikh Muhammad Bukhari, 'a wise and respectable saint', and a nobleman of the court, as keeper of the dargah. Mosques and a khanqah were built at the dargah and, in the course of the year, Akbar would begin work on a fortress and palace at Ajmer. He would also gift kettledrums to the dargah and would initiate customs at the shrine that mimicked those of the Mughal court. In these many ways Akbar cleaved to his own persona, and bequeathed to his son the lustrous legacy of the Sufi saints. What was remarkable was that Akbar had emphatically turned away from the Naqshbandi Sufis, traditional partners of Central Asian rulers, and had chosen the Chishtiya Sufis of Hindustan.

Beginning in the Mawarannahr* region that the Timurids came from, the Naqshbandi khwajas believed they had a clear duty to

---

*Central Asian region comprising modern-day Uzbekistan, Tajikistan, and parts of Kazakhstan.

protect all Muslim subjects from oppression even if that meant 'trafficking with Kings and conquering their souls'. Babur himself wrote of dreams in which he saw the powerful Naqshbandi Sufi Khwaja Ahrar in dreams. But by the time Akbar was strengthening his empire in the 1570s, the milieu had become decidedly uncongenial for the Naqshbandis, who not only advocated the protection of Muslims but encouraged a robust condemnation of non-Muslim social practices. Akbar, meanwhile, was encouraging the entry of Persian Shia and Hindu Rajput noblemen into the Mughal aristocracy as part of his long-term plan to reduce the worrying influence of the large and fractious Turani clan, and was also marrying Hindu women. In this climate of social churn, the Chishtis of Hindustan were found to be a great deal more accommodating. They maintained a greater ascetic distance from kingship and flirted more openly with the idea of a religious cauldron, an amalgamation of various ideals and, in its more extreme variant, maintained that the world was a manifestation of ishq, love, above and beyond any religious limitations. 'There is no precedence of one religion over the other', they wrote, 'after you experience the limitlessness of unbounded Beauty you can see His Grace present both in a kafir and a Muslim.'

In the harem at Agra, meanwhile, there was a flurry of further additions. A daughter, Khanum Sultan, was born to Akbar and then in 1570, a second prince, Murad. In November 1570, Rao Kalyanmal of Bikaner and his heir, Kuar Rai Singh, accepted Mughal overlordship and were brought into the Mughal fold. Rao Kalyanmal then offered a daughter and two nieces, Raj Kanwar and Bhanumati, in marriage to Akbar. At the same time Har Raj of Jaisalmer also submitted to Akbar and offered a daughter, Rajkumari Nathi Bai, as a wife for the Padshah while his son, Kuar Sultan Singh, was accepted as a nobleman at the Mughal court.

When the Rajput brides entered the Mughal harem they brought with them their holy fires and their sparkling language, their busy gods, and their swaying clothes. For Akbar did not require these women to convert to Islam and they were allowed to fully participate in their Hindu rituals as they had in their own homes. And yet, in an astounding sleight of hand, these women would disappear completely from the Mughal records, smoothed into impossible standards of purity and chastity, all individuality removed. So very rigorous would this vigilance be that there is only one record that clearly states that the mother of the much longed-for Mughal heir, Salim, was indeed Harkha Bai Kachhwaha. For these women, there would be no intimate accounts of labours arrested by plain-faced midwives or compassionate recordings of a young girl's mixed feelings towards her determined groom. The name of Prince Murad's mother was not noted and the celebrations following births were negligently narrated, formal and bloodless. The purdah, which had been cursory in the case of the Timurid women, who rode on horseback, participated in mixed gatherings at banquets and feasts, and travelled with their husbands and sons, had now suddenly become opaque. This was noted in a history of the reign of Akbar's grandson, Shah Jahan, when it was written that 'ever since the reign of Akbar, it had been ordained that the names of the inmates of the seraglio should not be mentioned in public, but that they should be designated by some epithet derived either from the place of their birth or the city in which they might have first been regarded by the monarch with the eye of affection'. That there was a growing Mughal desire to circumscribe the harem within an ordered space as a reflection of the exalted charisma of the Padshah, which now removed the harem from the sight of ordinary people, is clear from Abu'l Fazl's writings. But there may also have been something the Rajput brides brought with them, along with their gods, dancing girls, and feasts, that made this process inevitable.

In the turbulent, fractious environment of Rajasthan, the clan structure of ruling families was the scaffolding upon which layers of loyalty were constructed. On the one hand there were the rulers, linked to their thikanedars and small jagirdars in an intricate web of blood and obligation called bhai-beta, or clan. A further unit of relationship and strength increasingly became the saga, the in-law family, who were also expected to provide warriors and fealty in times of strife. Marriages between two weaker clans could provide ballast against more formidable neighbours while clans could try to appease encroaching pretenders by offering daughters in marriage, thus securing bonds and alliances. As a result, polygamy became rampant in the ruling houses of Rajasthan, the women often inconsequential beyond their ability to produce brave sons to fight and die magnificently in their endless battles. In an extreme example, Rawat Durga Das of Deogarh married strong horse-riding women and then kept them in seclusion to breed sons who would, it was hoped, be as fearless as their mothers had once dreamed of being. In genealogies and chronicles, the Rajput women lost their names, their individuality now smooth as river stones, hidden behind the name of their fathers' clans. As Rajput kinship networks evolved through the centuries, regulating the place of these elite Rajput women and their chastity became deeply embedded in the honour of the clan; this also became an increasingly confounding problem for these polygamous households. Widow remarriage, also known as nata marriages, which did occur in earlier, more forgiving times, were now deemed impossible for elite women who had to be irreproachable in their purity. And so to further ensure that all these many women with their female attendants were kept beyond the temptation of any sexual lapse, a physical space was devised, the zenana deorhi or rawala, which was the equivalent of the Rajput purdah.

The zenana in a Rajput household did not open directly into the main entrance of the home. Instead, a wall known as a pardi hid the main entrance to the women's apartments. Not even a glimpse of these women could now be seen by anyone outside of the zenana. As the rules of the feudal structure became stricter, the purdah of elite women became a symbol of a ruler's prestige and power. The more exalted the ruler, the higher were the zenana walls and the smaller the windows, the women obliterated behind the stone walls. The entrance to the zenana was guarded by deorhidars and eunuchs. The only males who were allowed entrance, apart from the ruler and the immediate family of the women, were priests, and the sons of davris, the hereditary female slaves who were part of the women's dowries. Curtains would be held up at the entrance to the zenana if state matters needed to be discussed. Purdah was also used to enforce rules of hierarchy within the bustling zenana and so the wives of a ruler were made to use the ghoonghat, a cover for the head, in front of their mothers-in-law and senior women of the zenana, whom they were not allowed to speak to directly for years after their marriage. In this the Rajput women differed from the Mughals, who were never expected to hide themselves from other women. So forbidding did the idea of purdah become that even in Rajput art, while hundreds of portraits of men would be produced in the following decades, almost no paintings of actual women were ever produced, this invisibility itself, as described by historian Molly Aitken, 'a form of purdah that served to promote elite men's and elite women's different accesses to public visibility'.

In the colliding worlds of the Rajput and the Mughal, it is difficult to be sure exactly who learnt from whom, as they now increasingly had intertwined cultures and destinies. Did the Mughals adopt the Rajput notion of seclusion or did the Rajputs bolster their women with additional layers of coverings when they encountered the Mughals? Was this a defensive measure or an imitation as elite behaviour in a feudal society began to mirror the other? What is clear is that in the alchemy of this meeting, the idea of honour became inextricable from a woman's chastity, both Mughal and Rajput. When Abu'l Fazl would begin work on the *Ain-i Akbari*, he would, for the first time in the history of the Mughal Empire, declare that the Mughal women were pardeh-giyan, the veiled ones. The women would be further hidden behind grandiose titles which made them indistinguishable, Hindu, Persian or Turk. Hamida Banu would be transformed into Maryam Makani* and Harkha Bai into Maryam uz Zamani† and when they were mentioned at all in the records, they were now always resolutely 'chaste'.

There were other ways in which the Rajput women brought their culture into the Mughal world. As their life in seclusion was physically constrained, Rajput women often turned to religion both as emotional sustenance and as a source of entertainment. There were almost daily functions, distracting with their rituals and their effervescent colour. There was Basant Panchami, Holi, Rakhi, Dussehra, Diwali, Teej, and Janmashtami, breaking the monotony of their years and colouring the background of their lives. They had access to the royal priests as well as female Brahmins so they could conduct these rituals with panache and fervour. 'From early youth, in compliment to his wives, the daughters of the Rajahs of Hind,' railed Badauni bitterly, 'he had within the female apartments continued

---

*Of the household of Mary.
†Mary of the World.

to offer the hom, which is a ceremony derived from sun-worship.' To Badauni it was clear that this nefarious influence on Akbar was at least partly due to these Rajput women. He grumbled gloomily about the 'jewelled strings tied on his wrists, by Brahmans, by way of a blessing' and the abhorrent 'current custom also to wear the rakhi on the wrist, which means an amulet formed out of twisted linen rags'. Still later Badauni would note that even Akbar's sartorial choices were influenced by Hindus. 'Certain pandering pimps,' he clarified, 'brought forward proofs in favour of shaving the beard.' The Rajput wives 'had influenced his mind against...association with people who wore beards. And in order to gain their love and goodwill, and that of their castes, he abstained entirely from anything which was a natural abhorrence to these people, and looked on it as a mark of special devotion to himself if men shaved off their beards—so that this became a common practice.' And indeed Akbar never did keep a beard, only a small moustache, and he grew his hair long out of deference to the habits of his Hindu subjects.

If religious festivals were an important part of the lives of Akbar's Rajput wives, then so were fasts, which were essential to elite Rajput women. The entire zenana deorhi would be routinely involved in the rituals of 'vrats', fasts, which punctuated the seasons. Akbar, too, started keeping fasts regularly and the number of days of fasting increased steadily throughout his reign, though he never imposed it on his subjects. 'Of the austerities practised by my revered father,' wrote Jahangir in his memoir, 'one was not eating the flesh of animals. During three months of the year he ate meat, and for the remaining nine contented himself with Sufi food...' Some of the specifically vegetarian dishes made for Akbar, as noted by Abu'l Fazl, included khushka, plain boiled rice; pahit, lentils cooked with ghee, ginger, cumin seeds, and asafoetida; khichdi, made of equal parts rice, mung dal, and ghee; and thuli, sweet, spicy cracked-wheat porridge.

Vegetarianism was a common trait amongst Rajput noblewomen, even when the men ate meat. For the men, especially the Rajput aristocracy, game was a highly appreciated food and there were numerous recipes for cooking shikar, 'such as boar cooked with onions, coriander, cumin, garlic and ginger over an open fire'. Among the vegetarian dishes, a favourite was the dal batti churma, which consisted of a dal made from five kinds of lentils cooked in ghee, battis which were wheat-flour balls roasted in coals until hard, then cracked open and eaten with ghee, and churma which was ground wheat crushed and cooked with ghee and sugar. Besides his Hindu wives, there were others who introduced Akbar to greater austerity in his eating habits—the Hindus at his court, notably Birbal and Todar Mal, and the religious groups such as the Jains and the Jogis. But one of the very first times that Akbar would come into contact with fasts and the careful control over food in religious practice would be in the intimacy of the zenana, with his Rajput wives. Indeed, one of the first instances of Akbar taking a vow of austerity was when Harkha Bai was expecting Salim and failed to notice a quickening in her womb on a Friday. The anxious Padshah immediately declared that he would never hunt again on a Friday, to ensure the good health of his much longed-for child.

In the early years, when Akbar visited Sikri, he stayed, according to Abu'l Fazl, 'in the lodgings of Shaikh Salim'. Badauni adds that '[Shaikh Salim] allowed the Emperor to have the entrée of all his most private apartments' and that this led to some dismay among his sons and nephews who complained that 'our wives are becoming estranged from us'. Badauni's bracing conclusion from this was that you 'either make no friendship with an elephant driver, or make a house fit for an elephant'.

By the end of 1571, Akbar had decided to move permanently to Sikri, 'to silence the babble of the common throng' regarding the maleficent ghouls haunting Agra Fort. 'The Emperor built a lofty palace on the top of the hill of Sikri,' wrote Badauni, and 'a high and spacious mosque of stone so large that you would say it was a part of a mountain...in the space of about five years the building was finished and he called the place Fathpur and he built a bazaar and baths and a gate.' In addition to the palaces and gardens and bazaars, Sikri would solve the 'vexatious question' that Akbar's growing harem posed. A separate, sequestered space was built especially for the women, 'a large enclosure with fine buildings inside where he reposes', wrote Abu'l Fazl, and which now would be carefully guarded. From the clearly bombastic claims of 5,000 women that Abu'l Fazl speaks of to the more modest number of 300 that Monserrate puts forward, it is difficult to assess exactly how many women there really were. Abu'l Fazl was undoubtedly exaggerating so as to highlight the Padshah's power and benevolence in gathering all these women, symbolically representing the different peoples of Hindustan. As for Monserrate, he would never have had access to the women's quarters himself. Nonetheless, there were clearly dozens of wives and concubines, with their attendant large retinues, as well as all the other women—the foster mothers, the aunts, the sisters, the visitors, the dispossessed relatives and so on.

There were other eclectic visitors to court at this time and one of the first Jain visitors Padmasundara wrote 'one of the first Sanskrit works ever to be commissioned by the Mughals'. This was a work called the *Akbarasahis Garadarpa* (Mirror of Erotic Passion for Shah Akbar) and, according to historian Audrey Truschke, the Jain was one of the first authors to openly reflect a cross-cultural milieu. In his introduction, Padmasundara created one of the first Sanskrit texts to use a Koranic name for God, Rahman, to describe Akbar...

> The entire world shines with his splendor such that
> it blinds the eyes.
> Our welfare rests in him like a genuine jewel, always
> and forever.
> He stands beyond the darkness and is called Rahman,
> the highest point.
> O Akbar, crown jewel of Shahs! May that light
> always protect you.

Most of the noblemen at court at this time were caught up in the frenzy of chaupar, a dice game that had become an obsession. There were often 200 players at a time playing the game at court and we are told that no one was allowed to go home till he had completed sixteen games, which could last up to three months. If anyone lost their patience, they were to drink a cup of wine, presumably to calm them down. One nobleman lost so much money on bets during a game, and became so angry and vociferous that he greatly annoyed Akbar, so much so that he was told to remove himself to Mecca.*

Serious work continued nonetheless for the Padshah as he

---
*Muzaffar Khan Turbati. Akbar later revoked the order.

continued efforts to overhaul the land revenue system. He appointed Raja Todar Mal to assist the diwan, Muzaffar Khan. Todar Mal suggested a dramatic departure from the earlier method of using a rough estimate of the produce and instead called for actual measurements of all cultivable land by the qanungos.* Tax would be calculated on the basis of the estimated average yield per unit of land, taking into account local variations in productivity in different parganas. The emperor himself was to determine prices of assessed crops separately and the revenue settlement was made directly with the ryot† and so came to be called the ryotwari system.

While Raja Todar Mal would travel the length and breadth of the empire measuring the cultivable lands, over the next ten years, Sikri would become an extraordinary place—a hotbed of ideas and experimentation and creativity possibly unmatched in the world at the time. But at the same time, the Mughal Empire would face many challengers, both in the west and in the east.

The rich province of Gujarat had profited enormously in the fifteenth century from the stable rule of erstwhile advisers to the Delhi Sultanate. As the sultanate itself disintegrated following Timur's invasion, just one such governor, Zafar Khan, restyling himself Muzaffar Shah, set about bringing prosperity to the region. His descendants made Ahmedabad their capital and developed trade and export thanks to their access to the sea and the large seaports of Cambay and Surat. After Akbar had crushed the power of the mirzas in Jaunpur, the survivors, both Timurid and Afghan, fled to Gujarat seeking the patronage of Muzaffar II, the Sultan of Gujarat, and began defying Mughal authority.

Almost simultaneously with unrest in Gujarat, at the other end of the country, Bengal would flare up too. Ever since the Afghan Lodi dynasty had been crushed by Babur, many Afghan horsemen had galloped east, to the territories held by the Bengal sultan Nair al-din Nusrat Shah. Nusrat Shah welcomed all these Afghan warriors, happy for them to set up a buffer zone in Bihar between the alarmingly expansionist Mughals and Bengal. One Taj Khan Karrani had set up a dynasty in that buffer zone, all the while keeping a keen lookout

---

*The hereditary registrar of landed property in a subdivision of a district.
†A cultivator.

on events unfolding in Delhi. A descendant of Taj Khan, Daud Khan Afghan, would no longer be so cowed by Mughal power and would rise to challenge Akbar.

For the next few years Akbar would confront all these enemies in battle, for to fail to do so would be to fail his destiny and his Timurid legacy. At the same time, Akbar would carefully forge a composite identity for Mughal noblemen so that their dangerous clan allegiances would be diffused. But first, with Rajasthan now secure within the Mughal Empire, and the way thus cleared all the way to the Arabian Sea, Akbar set off to conquer Gujarat.

THE FIRANGIS AND THE SALT SEA

If elephants had been one of the major attractions of Malwa and Gondwana for the Mughals, then in Gujarat it was something much smaller and a great deal more intangible—indigo dye. This precious and valuable product was exported in its raw form, and was also used to colour locally produced textiles—velvet, brocades, and cotton— with the extremely sought after and distinctive deep blue colour.

It was not only indigo and textiles, which brought wealth to the province, it was also locally produced high quality weapons (swords, daggers, bows, and arrows), perfumes, mother of pearl articles, and boats, which were constructed in Sarkhej, near Ahmedabad. Merchandise was loaded onto small vessels in the port of Ghogha and sailed down the Gulf of Khambhat* where it was transferred to large ships off the town of Cambay, bound for Turkey and Iraq; Gujarati block-printed textiles were exported to Egypt. With exports bringing in revenue, the sultans were able to import silver and war horses. All this had been accomplished through the rule of the sultans of Gujarat, who had secured land routes from the coast to the rich agricultural hinterlands.

In July 1572, Akbar set off for Gujarat himself, accompanied by some of the women of the harem and select noblemen. Raja Birbal and a few other officers were sent to the Punjab to bolster the forces of Husain Quli Khan, a kinsman of Bairam Khan, while the imperial party proceeded, via Sanganer, to hunt cheetahs. 'He was quite taken with cheetah hunting,' admitted Abu'l Fazl but this lukewarm assessment does not capture the intense love that the Padshah had for this solitary, elusive animal. He would eventually have a thousand cheetahs in the imperial stables of which fifty 'khasa' (special) ones were kept at the court itself. His very favourite cheetah, Samand Malik, was carried in a litter, wore a jewelled collar and was accompanied by its own servants in full livery running alongside the litter while another servant walked in front, beating a large drum.

---

*Also known as the Gulf of Cambay.

In Sanganer, Akbar was so delighted when an imperial cheetah named Chitranjan leaped across a wide ravine while chasing a deer that it was immediately promoted to head cheetah, with a drummer marching ahead of it.

The imperial train then headed for Ajmer, to seek the blessings of the saint for the Gujarat campaign. One of Akbar's concubines, who was heavily pregnant, was left in Ajmer where she soon gave birth to a boy, Daniyal, named after the shaikh in whose house he was born. When the child was one month old, Akbar had him sent to Amer, to be looked after by Raja Bharmal's wife. Shielded now with the blessings of Khwaja Sahib and a lustrous son, Akbar sent an advance guard of 10,000 horsemen ahead of the army and began marching towards Patan. This was the first time that Akbar had visited the town since the murder of his old ataliq, Bairam Khan. Even more poignant was the fact that he was accompanied by Bairam Khan's son, Abdur Rahim, now sixteen years old. Abdur Rahim was a precociously intelligent, sensitive, and alert young man who would no doubt have remembered the terrible day when his father had been murdered before his very eyes. The Padshah questioned the young man gently about the terrible tragedy he had witnessed, and perhaps Abdur Rahim remembered enough to tell the Padshah of the horror of witnessing the Afghan youth stabbing his father with such fury that the dagger had gone through him and come out of his back. Akbar promised the young man the fief of Patan once he came of age and then rode towards Ahmedabad to relieve Itimad Khan Gujarati, who had been besieged by mutinous Mughal nobles. But news of the approaching imperial army was enough to chasten the rebels, who quietly left the city and Ahmedabad was taken without a fight. The great noblemen of Gujarat, Ikhtiyar ul-Mulk, Itimad Khan Gujarati, and Shah Turab Abu, among others, now submitted to Akbar. Also present were some Ethiopians such as Ulugh Khan Habshi,* and Jajar Khan Habshi, some of whom would become great amirs at Akbar's court while others were entrusted with the guarding of the imperial harem. Having settled the affairs of Ahmedabad and handed over its governorship to Mirza Aziz Koka,† Akbar marched to the port of Cambay, to see the ocean.

---

*The Arabic word Habashi, for Abyssinia, the old name for Ethiopia.
†Now titled khan azam.

When Akbar turned towards the ocean in Gujarat, it would also have been to survey the ambitions of the firangis, the Portuguese, who had long posed a violent threat as they tried to establish a foothold in the area. From the time in 1502 when Vasco da Gama 'set alight, and watched burn, a crowded pilgrim ship', the Portuguese were rapacious in their interactions with Muslim traders. A rich and highly developed region, Gujarat and its coast and traders had been kept safe from the firangis as long as Malik Ayaz, a Christian from Russia, kept careful vigil over its pewter seas. From the island of Diu he had built a chain-link barrier across the shallow waters to prevent access to firangi ships and it was said that 'during the government of the Malik, the Firangi was unable to enter the Gujarat ports'. But Malik Ayaz had died and the Portuguese appetite for the pepper which had made the fortunes of the Portuguese king, would no longer be denied. They seized Diu in 1535 and imposed the cartaz, which was a pass issued by the Portuguese against which they promised protection for Indian trade ships from plunder at the hands of other Portuguese pirates. This was a move stoutly resisted by all the traders in the Indian Ocean, as it was considered humiliating and implied the payment of debilitating taxes, but the Portuguese were unstoppable. At the time of Akbar's first encounters with the Portuguese, they had already established a lucrative trade in African slaves. Between 1575 and 1595, tens of thousands of Africans were sent from West Africa to Brazil, to lead lives of abomination and degradation.

In faraway Naples a different kind of firangi, Rudolf Acquaviva, was continuing on his exalted and stricken path which was to lead him, however improbably, to the opulent Mughal court. He had been admitted to the Jesuit novitiate in Rome where he loved to work in the kitchens and in the infirmary. While he practised austerities in his bleak cell, he offered his sacrifices in the hope that he would be sent on a mission to Hindustan where lost souls were crying out for salvation.

As soon as Akbar arrived in Cambay 'the merchants of Rum, Syria, Persia and Turan' came to pay their respects to the Padshah. Akbar may have sampled some of the Gujarati food which was peculiar to the region. Historian Aparna Kapadia has studied the list of foods mentioned in a fifteenth-century text of the region called the

Varnak Samucay. She writes of a truly bewildering number of courses presented during a meal which was usually served on a large platter reminiscent of the present-day thali. The text suggested starting a meal with fresh fruits, dry fruits, and nuts, followed by a variety of laddus, jalebis, and fried snacks such as dahi vada. This would be followed by laapsi, a liquid dessert made from wheat, almost in the way of cleansing the palate, before an avalanche of main courses—rice dishes, dals, ghees, vegetables, more fried snacks, and breads. Finally, it was suggested that the sated and presumably incapacitated diner be served fragrant waters, and betel leaves filled with betelnut, saffron, and spices.

If there were many merchants from various countries in Cambay then there were also 'baniyas'* from Cambay in foreign ports, conducting business. The Italian traveller Pietro Della Valle wrote about meeting such merchants in Isfahan, where they regaled him with stories of their home town, and their religion. They told him about the most observant among the Indians, who would 'neither eat nor kill any living thing'. That they 'esteem it a good and holy deed to save the life of animals and set them free and very often they buy at high prices birds that other people are keeping in cages...so as to save them from death and set them free...' They told the Italian about charitable hospitals in Cambay to treat animals and birds, and of the many cows, 'very beautiful with their horns decorated with gold and jewels...' So evocatively did they speak about their land that Della Valle finally visited Surat, in 1623, and wrote long letters describing the country.

At Cambay, Akbar was not only able to view the sea but was also able to assess the port and the trade that took place by sea. The annexation of Gujarat was to give to the landlocked Mughal Empire its first access to the sea. There were some fifty or sixty private Portuguese traders as well in Cambay, engaged in buying Gujarati goods to send to Goa, the rest having fled upon hearing of the impending arrival of the Mughal army. Cambay was a prosperous town with fine streets and buildings, and beautiful structures, whose streets were closed off at night with gates. The town had large storage tanks for water and a public hospital to take care of sick and crippled

---

*Hindus of the merchant class.

birds of all kinds. Interestingly, a traveller to the region wrote that the Gujaratis of the area were more concerned with ritual purification and pollution through eating than locals in other regions of Hindustan. They dressed in long, thin white gowns and wore red leather shoes, turned up at the ends. Before leaving Cambay, Akbar would cut taxes on the export and import of goods passing through the port, and would allow artisans to settle on the outskirts of the city, measures which would further boost the economy of Cambay, making it the most important Mughal port in Gujarat.

Akbar then 'boarded a fast-moving boat and ordered that an assembly of pleasure and enjoyment be arranged' and, according to Qandahari, enjoyed a round of drinks in the briny sea breeze. But, before long, rebellion was brewing again among the Gujarati noblemen whom Abu'l Fazl condemned, describing them as 'evil-conditioned men' in whom 'timidity, deceit, and falsehood have been mixed up with a little honesty, simplicity and humility and made into a paste to which the name of Gujarati has been given'. This time it was Ibrahim Sultan, a Timurid mirza and descendant of Timur, who was railing against the control of the Padshah at Sarnal. Akbar left his two young sons and harem in Cambay and galloped in the night against the insurgents with a small force of only 200 men that included his Kachhwaha noblemen.

When they arrived at the Mahi, Akbar and his men plunged into the river and scrambled up the steep banks on the other side and were told that Ibrahim Sultan Mirza had run away from Sarnal. His men had remained to fight, however, and now Akbar's small band of warriors found their horses stumbling on the broken ground bristling with thorny bushes and trees. Seeing his men falter, Akbar spun his horse around to face them and 'roared loudly like a lion and called his men...and their courage returned'. For Akbar there could be no countenancing of defeat or fear and he found in his Rajput officers an equal and clear gallantry. Man Singh, now twenty-two years old, begged to be allowed ahead in the coveted vanguard while Bhagwant Das rode bridle to bridle with the Padshah as they charged and sliced at the enemy in the narrow ravines and passes. The two men fought with lance and scimitar as time seemed to stand still amid the panting horses and the slashing blades and the curving of the sun through the sky, but finally the enemy was defeated on 23 December 1572. Bhagwant Das was awarded a banner and kettledrums, the first Hindu officer to obtain these significant honours. There was a sad loss for the Kachhwahas, however, in the death of Bhupat, one of Raja Bharmal's sons, who was killed in the fierce fighting. Bhupat's sister, Harkha Bai, waiting with the harem in Cambay would have been devastated. When the imperial retinue returned to Agra after the Gujarat campaigns, Akbar would send Harkha Bai to her natal home in Amer, a consolation for her bereaved parents.

While Akbar was occupied in Gujarat, he was also closely involved in supervising operations in the eastern reaches of his kingdom. A letter to Munim Khan written at this time shows the Padshah's meticulous attention to detail. In the letter Akbar lists to Munim Khan the artillery and munitions he is having sent to him from the capital. 'We have ordered that Rumi Khan should make ready 500 pieces of Daudi cannons and fifty pieces of Islam Shahi cannons, with fuses and carriages and send them...' wrote Akbar. '5000 chandra bans and kahak-bans Mazamdarani (a type of rocket made of an iron tube and bamboo rod, packed with combustible material which was lit and then directed by hand and launched primarily at horses and elephants) and 12,000 boats were available at Agra in full preparedness.' Akbar also urged Munim Khan to be extremely vigilant and to prevent dereliction of duty amongst the soldiers. Munim Khan himself was instructed to pay special attention to the royal elephants, and to supervise their diets personally. The Padshah even listed the names of the elephants being sent to Munim Khan—these included Dodi, also known as Mal Jamal Bahadur Shahi, who was the Padshah's personal elephant.

Akbar's ability to react instantly to events happening in the different corners of the empire even as he remained constantly on the move, depended, as we have seen, on an extensive system of couriers and informants who relayed information to the Padshah. Qandahari has described this extremely efficient system:

> He [Akbar] is such an expert in espionage that he keeps four thousand* foot-runners, who in Hindi are called Meurah. They

---

*Abu'l Fazl, more reliable, puts this number at 1,000 at this stage. It would reach 4,000 at the time of Akbar's death.

are on His Majesty's service day and night so that news and reports reach regularly everyday from all sides of the world. This class of men run as fast as lions, so that within ten days news comes from Bengal, which is at a distance of seven hundred karohs (kos) from Agra. His Majesty gets all information of good or bad and profit or loss.

Akbar then turned his attention to the town of Surat where, it was learnt, the inconstant Ibrahim Sultan Mirza was strengthening the defences of the city. Akbar besieged Surat in January 1573 and it was here, during the siege, that he met the Portuguese for the first time. The meeting with the Portuguese envoy, Antonio de Cabral, was conducted with great bonhomie and Akbar questioned the Portuguese closely 'about the wonders of Portugal and the manners and customs of Europe'. The Padshah was already watching the distant horizons beyond the heaving ocean to learn what the wide world had to offer. Akbar was delighted with gifts of Portuguese cloaks and hats and, according to Qandahari, there were also cartloads of Portuguese wine, whose 'scent turned the lions of skies dead-drunk'. But an important concession was made by the Portuguese when they issued passes to members of Akbar's family to go on pilgrimage to Mecca. For it was not only trade that Surat was vital for, it was also the 'Gateway to Mecca', so called because of the pilgrim ships that set off for the hajj from this port. The Portuguese authorities were known to harass the hajj ships and Akbar now needed to ensure that pilgrims would be safe. Extraordinary attention, it was clarified, had to be paid to the vessel which would be carrying the imperial family to Mecca. It is very possible that the persons being singled out in this way were Gulbadan and her party of Mughal women, who would leave for the hajj in 1575. In return, Akbar gave the Portuguese important tax concessions and instructed Mughal officials in the area not to harass the Portuguese merchants.

As the siege of Surat continued, Akbar met with another interesting local personality, the Parsee priest Dastur Meherji Rana. Akbar questioned the priest about his religion and traditions and the man, stately in his spotless white robes and long white beard, made a favourable impression on the Padshah.

Surat was captured and occupied easily and the imperial train settled into the city to administer its affairs. One evening when Akbar was enjoying a round of drinks with a select group of noblemen, some of the Rajput warriors began regaling the audience with tales of exemplary Rajput heroism. To settle issues of rivalry, they claimed, a rather unusual method was followed: someone would be deputed to hold a double-headed spear steady, and then the two contending Rajput men would charge at the weapon from either end 'so that the latter would transfix them and come out at their backs'. Piqued by talk of this admittedly insane act of physical prowess, Akbar immediately fixed his own sword in a wall and 'declared that if Rajputs were wont to sell their valour in their way, he too could rush against this sword'. Immediately sobered, the assembly watched in horrified silence until Man Singh rushed at the sword and flung it away, injuring Akbar's hand. The enraged Padshah threw Man Singh upon the ground and began beating him roundly until one of the courtiers pulled him off. Akbar's wound healed, we are told, and he would reserve further feats of bravery for the battlefield.

Surat, on the banks of the river Tapti, was already a large and prosperous town. Manuel Godinho, a later traveller and writer, remarked about the houses of the Muslim noblemen that 'the best of these houses from the roadside look like hell but once you enter them, they seem like paradise, because they are laced all over with gold, with magnificent paintings on their ceilings...' The Hindu 'baniyas', on the other hand, 'build their houses more for the benefit of the onlookers from outside rather than the advantage of those living inside.' But for all the fine mansions, the crowded bazaars and the ships lurching on the ocean, Surat, and Gujarat itself, possessed a mysterious and enigmatic side that would even impact the court of the Padshah.

The sixteenth century was a time of fizzing fervour in the Islamic world. A belief began to gain currency that the Prophet would return once the old millennium was past, as the Mahdi.* The origins of Mahdavi belief could be traced to Sayyid Muhammad Jaunpuri, a charismatic Chishti Sufi of extreme piety who came to Ahmedabad

---

*In popular Muslim belief, a spiritual and temporal leader who would restore religion before the end of the world.

in 1497 to preach the heretical and incandescent message that he was the Mahdi. 'Proclaim the manifestation of your Mahdiship,' he claimed to have heard, 'and do not fear the people'. Shaikh Jaunpuri died in 1505 but his followers gathered in Gujarat and preached the rejection of formalism in Islam and instead founded communes called dairahs where they spread a message of devotion, renunciation, and meditation to achieve a perfect and direct vision of God. Implicit in the Mahdavi message, however, was a much more dangerous idea. Charged with a fin-de-siecle malaise and an intimation of a forsaken world, the Mahdavis were driven by a divine mission to proselytize, to take up jihad, if necessary, and to give a clear direction to the religious and political elite at a time of impending chaos. This inevitably brought them into confrontation with the orthodox ulema but in Gujarat they were remarkably successful, for a time, in converting the Afghan clans.

The Mahdavi who was to have the most direct impact upon the Padshah, first through Aziz Koka's court at Ahmedabad, then in Sikri, was Shaikh Mustafa Gujarati. Shaikh Mustafa was born in 1525 and gained notoriety from a young age. Combining the usual Mahdavi charisma with a formidable intellect, he founded his own dairah near Patan and married into the family of an important Afghan jagirdar. One of the persons who carried on a correspondence with Shaikh Mustafa on matters of religion was Shaikh Mubarak, Abu'l Fazl's father. But Shaikh Mustafa's radiating popularity, combined with his influential Afghan in-laws, made him dangerous to the Mughals. During Akbar's conquest of Gujarat, encouraged by the sadr, Abd un-Nabi, Mustafa's dairah was plundered and eight members of his family were executed and his women and children imprisoned. Mustafa was captured and brought in chains to the court of Mirza Aziz Koka at Ahmedabad where he was tortured and questioned.

Meanwhile, having settled the affairs of Surat, Akbar set off towards Agra in April 1573, stopping en route at Ajmer. Harkha Bai was sent to Amer to be present at the mourning ceremony for her brother Bhupat and the child Daniyal was brought back into the royal retinue. Now, as the victorious troops headed towards Sikri, the royal astrologer advised them to wait three days for the auspicious moment to enter the city. The Hindu astrologer who bore the title

Jyotik Rai was possibly the priest Nilakantha, a protégé of Raja Todar Mal. Akbar used both Muslim and Hindu astrologers and Nilakantha was a learned scholar who would write a commentary on Islamic astrology called the *Tajikanilakanthi*. While Akbar waited for the planets to align themselves, Shaikh Salim Chishti and all the great noblemen of the court came to congratulate him. Shaikh Mubarak, recently arrived at court, greeted him by saying that Akbar had been accorded glorious victories so that he may become peshwa of the spiritual world, words which resonated deeply with Akbar. Finally, on 3 June 1573, a year after he had left the city, Akbar returned home in triumph.

No sooner had he returned, however, than news reached Akbar that the uneasy truce in Gujarat had collapsed and that the same rebels had mutinied again upon his departure. As before, they were led by Ikhtiyar ul-Mulk who was joined this time by Muhammad Husain Mirza.* The rebels had taken Broach, Cambay, and Surat and had besieged Mirza Aziz Koka himself in Ahmedabad. Akbar was furious at this cavalier and incessant questioning of his authority but there was a further depth to the emotion that would drive what was to become the most blistering campaign of Akbar's long life. This time it was Aziz Koka, childhood companion of his Kabul years, whose life was in danger. Aziz Koka, who was the only nobleman ever allowed to share the takht on the imperial elephant, and who galloped alongside the Padshah inside the raging qumargha circle. And at the harem in Sikri there was Aziz Koka's mother, Jiji Anaga, who would have come to Akbar to lay before him her great grief and her worry. 'His Majesty,' wrote Jahangir, 'in consequence of the distracted state of Jiji Anaga, the mother of [Aziz Koka], started for Gujarat with a body of royal troops without delay from the capital of Fathpur.' Jahangir, who had witnessed these events as the four-year-old Salim, realized that it was clearly the faultless love that Akbar had for his milk mother that now made him act as he did. Indeed, according to Jahangir, who admittedly had a more circumspect view of Aziz given his role in the tussle for succession, Mirza Aziz Koka's meteoric rise at court was only due to Akbar's great affection for his mother. Akbar, he wrote in his memoir, 'had favoured him from his

---

*A Timurid nobleman.

very infancy because of the service his mother had rendered...' Jiji Anaga who was so beloved of Akbar as a child that the other milk mothers, jealous, accused her of using witchcraft to lure the infant.

Since the previous expedition to Gujarat had lasted a year, the courtiers had run out of resources and money. Akbar now disbursed money to everyone from the royal coffers, for salaries and rewards, and also planned the operation with the meticulous personal attention which was to become a decisive factor in all his military campaigns. The Padshah appeared to be everywhere at once, his loud voice booming through the halls and courtyards as he hustled his men and shouted out orders to his servants. Sun-darkened from years of campaigns, Akbar was shadowed with worry for Aziz and he rapidly sent imperial tents and horses in advance, and ordered his officers in charge of the diwani to make every effort to react with promptitude to all demands. Noblemen were chosen for the mission and escorted to the advance camps the very same day, as was the harem, accompanied by trusted men such as Raja Bhagwant Das, Kuar Rai Singh of Bikaner, and Shujat Khan. Akbar was heard assuring everyone that though they might be leaving ahead of him, he had a premonition that he would reach Ahmedabad before anyone else.

On 23 August, barely a month after his return to Sikri, Akbar headed out towards Gujarat again, this time leaving his young sons in the charge of Raja Bharmal and Raja Todar Mal, amongst others. Accompanied by 3,000 men, all on dromedaries, Akbar mounted a camel called Jummuza and the men rode out at dusk as the heat rose from the baking earth. The great north Indian summer heat was a force that had struck terror into the hearts of the most hardened warriors. The dust storms that accompanied the ferocious heat had been described by Babur, in an earlier age. 'It gets up in great strength every year in the heat...when the rains are near...so strong and carrying so much dust and earth that you cannot see one another. People call this wind andhi, the darkener of the sky.' But for his grandson, Akbar, the elements themselves would be swept aside.

Akbar first stopped at Ajmer, to pray at Khwaja Sahib's dargah, focusing his thoughts and his will on victory. The men rode all night through the suffocating Rajasthan desert, where the heat was like a furnace even under the vaulting night skies. On the way they saw a blackbuck and Akbar declared that if their cheetahs caught the antelope, it meant that victory was theirs. A cheetah was released and the antelope was caught, confirming not only Akbar's unshakeable belief in his own destiny, but his men's implacable faith in their Padshah's quasi-divine powers. The men covered a staggering 50 miles per night; there were twenty-seven chosen noblemen with Akbar, amongst them the most trusted and true men of his empire including Abdur Rahim, Bairam Khan's son, and Akbar's kokas, Saif Khan Koka and Zain Khan Koka. After a few days, Akbar switched to a horse and 'like the full moon, traversed an immense distance in the night'. In nine days, Akbar and his men reached the outskirts of Ahmedabad, having covered a distance of 800 kilometres on camels and horses with intimidating speed.

Akbar mounted a favourite white horse, Noor Baize, strapped on his moulded armour made of Damascus steel, and kept 100 men under his own command. Fifteen were Hindus and included Raja Birbal, Man Singh Darbari, Raja Bhagwant Das, Ram Das Kachhwaha, the musician Lal Kalawant, and four painters, Sanwal Das, Jagannath, Har Das, and Tara Chand. He then inspected all his noblemen and soldiers, his great amirs resplendent and fearsome in their armour. Each of the noblemen wore a cuirass of finely-tempered steel, 'including a breastplate, backplate, and two smaller pieces for the sides—all carved and engraved, decorated with tassels, and held together by leather straps. Underneath was a coat of mail with mail sleeves. Helmets were carved with visors and nose-guards and a network of mail which protected the neck.' Akbar's helmet was decorated with delicate gold damascene and had a spike at the top.* The horses too were similarly armoured 'front, back, head, and neck with crafted steel pieces'. At the front of the army was a man holding the imperial alam,† a lion and a sun against a moss green background. Then with the roll of the drummers leading the way and the trumpeters sounding their chilling wail, the Mughal army

---

*Akbar's armour can be viewed at the Chhatrapati Shivaji Maharaj Vastu Sangrahalaya. The reader will allow me a little liberty of a few years, as this particular armour is dated 1581.
†The imperial standard, used since the time of Timur.

headed for the Sabarmati River.

On the opposite bank of the river, Muhammad Husain Mirza had come to enquire about the army that was heading his way.

'This is the army of the Emperor, which has come from Fatehpur to exterminate those who have been faithless to their salt,' responded Subhan Quli, a Mughal soldier.

'My spies only fourteen days ago left the Emperor at Fatehpur,' shouted back Muhammad Husain Mirza, clearly discomfited. 'And if it is the imperial army, where are the imperial elephants?'

'How could elephants with mountain-like bulk traverse four hundred karohs with the army in the space of nine days?' shouted back a scoffing Subhan Quli.

Muhammad Husain Mirza returned to his camp and readied himself for battle, doubtless with a premonition of disaster in his heart. The mirzas were defeated roundly with the Mughal army killing 2,000 of the 20,000-strong rebel army. Very few Mughal soldiers were killed but one of the few who died, Saif Khan Kokaltash, had shared an unexpected and tender destiny with Akbar. When the Padshah was a young boy, he encountered one of his milk mothers, flustered, coming back from meeting Hamida Banu Begum. On being questioned, she admitted to Akbar that having given birth to many daughters, her husband was unhappy and had warned her, 'if this time too a daughter comes I shall never cohabit with you again.' Distressed, the woman had just obtained permission from Hamida Banu to abort the child she was carrying. 'If you wish to retain our affection,' the young Akbar now told her, 'you will not touch this matter. God will bestow upon you a son of a happy star.' The woman acquiesced and the child she gave birth to was Saif Khan Kokaltash. Now Saif Khan Kokaltash had died heroically in a battle that had ended in victory for his Padshah and the legend of Akbar grew.* He literally appeared to control the destinies of his men in the palm of his hand—their divine births and their perfect deaths. His campaigns themselves were touched by an effulgence that appeared beyond the reach of ordinary mortals. Muhammad Hussain Mirza was doomed even before the battle started, when he realized that Akbar had

---

*On learning that the dead man was heavily indebted, Akbar paid all Saif Khan's dues on his return to Agra.

accomplished something that had never been done before, that he had bent time and space to his will and it was partly this psychological advantage that had won Akbar the victory before the battle had even been joined. In Hindustan, kings were wont to wait for the end of the monsoon, for the cool, short winter, to declare hostilities, in pre-ordained formations. But now the rules had scattered like dust before the monsoon storms. Now armies could cross deserts in the middle of the night and abandon war elephants if they no longer suited their purpose. Now raging rivers and unbreachable walls were there only to be conquered. As for the Padshah, he was an implacable, irresistible force who seemed to commune with the spirits and the fates. 'This Prince,' wrote Monserrate, 'is of a stature and of a type of countenance well-fitted to his royal dignity, so that one could easily recognise, even at the first glance, that he is the King.... His eyes so bright and flashing that they seem like a sea shimmering in the sunlight.' And Akbar would demand of his men a similar, unconditional courage, even the poets, the musicians, the historians, and the philosophers.

After the battle was won at Ahmedabad, Muhammad Hussain Mirza was captured and brought before Akbar where Raja Birbal asked him, 'Which of these men captured you?' The question was asked because a number of soldiers were crowding around the prisoner, claiming to be the champion of the moment. Muhammad Hussain Mirza, however, replied with simple fatalism that 'the salt of His Majesty has captured me'. Akbar spoke kindly to his defeated foe and then handed him into the custody of Rai Singh. There was no such equanimity a moment later, however, when Akbar saw another group of prisoners. Included in this bedraggled group of men was the koka of Ibrahim Hussain, one Mard Azmai Shah. This was the man who had killed Bhupat, Raja Bhagwant Das' brother, and Akbar's flaring rage demanded immediate retribution. He spun around, grabbed a spear, and flung it at the man, who was immediately set upon by the crowd of jeering soldiers who slashed him to death.

As he grew older, Akbar would become aware of the need to control his sudden, unpredictable rages and he would write long letters to his own sons, advising temperance and patience. But in Gujarat, faced with the man who had killed one of his closest courtiers, his own brother-in-law, Akbar's wrath was beyond reason.

A tower of heads was constructed with some 1,000 heads of the fallen enemy, as a warning to all rebels. The heads of Muhammad Hussain Mirza and Ikhtiyar ul-Mulk* were sent to Agra. Masaud Husain Mirza, captured alive, would later be brought before Akbar along with 300 of his followers. They were dragged into court, to the horror, bemusement, and chilled amusement of the courtiers, bound in chains with collars around their necks, covered in filth and flies, and wearing the skins of animals over their bodies and heads—'the skins of asses, hogs and dogs', specified Badauni. Some of them were put to death and the rest were freed.

The years of warfare required to bring about the decimation of the empire's enemies had an effect on the province of Gujarat as well. Ravaged by years of war, as the huge imperial army swept through the country repeatedly, the province suffered a catastrophic famine in 1574 of which contemporary writer Qandahari leaves us a moving account.

> During the same year plague and famine visited Gujarat. The rulers considered these the spoils of battle, caused by filth and rotten stench. The pestilence continued for five or six months. People had not witnessed such awful disaster for a long time, they felt utterly helpless and dreadful. Many people left the province and became exiles. The intensity of pestilence was such that every day a hundred cart-loads of dead bodies were taken out of Ahmadabad, which were thrown into ponds and covered with mud. Those were in addition to the dead who were carried on biers and bedsteads and were properly buried. Commodities became so dear that men had to be content with a single loaf of bread per day... Graves could not be dug for burials... Ultimately the deadly pestilence spread over the districts of Pattan, Baroach, Baroda and indeed engulfed the whole of Gujarat... Provision for horses and camels was nowhere to be had. So they scraped the bark of trees, crushed it and made it soft by soaking it in water and fed their cattle on it. Its after effects were numerous.

Gujarat became a subah of the Mughal Empire and the chief zamindar

---

*They were put to death by order of Rai Singh.

was a Brahmin, one Narain Das who, according to Abu'l Fazl, was 'of such austere life that he first feeds his cattle with corn and then picks up the grains from their dung and makes this his food, a sustenance held in much esteem by the Brahmans. He is regarded as the head of the Rathore tribe and has a following of 500 horse and 10,000 foot [soldiers].'

The indefatigable Raja Todar Mal was appointed Diwan of Gujarat, to rejuvenate its shattered economy and finances. Todar Mal ordered a complete survey of the cultivable land of Gujarat using a uniform method.* Land was now measured using lengths of bamboo instead of the old method of using rope. He also perfected the system of classification of lands on the basis of their actual productive quality and this would result in detailed survey reports which would form the basis for all future tax calculations.† From now on this zabt revenue system, based on regular collection of data on cultivated area, crop prices etc., would be implemented throughout the empire.

In 1573, after being reunited with Mirza Aziz Koka, Akbar returned to Sikri in just three weeks, triumphant. In honour of his tremendous Gujarat victory, the city would be renamed Fathpur Sikri or Fatehpur Sikri (City of Victory). As the victorious Padshah approached the city, the joy of the people spilled over like a pomegranate cracked open. The musicians of the naqqar khana, above the entrance to the city, prepared their drums, cymbals, and curved and long trumpets. Akbar waited for all his warriors outside the capital; on 5 October, the Padshah mounted a grey horse and, with a spear in his hand, directed all his liegemen to ride behind him holding spears or lances. In the saturated dusk, the victorious Mughal warriors rode into Fatehpur Sikri where Hamida Banu Begum, the other begums, the three princes, and all the impatient amirs and soldiery broke into cheers and cacophonous music and exuberant joy.

---

*The gaz or yard, which was 4 digits or 33 inches in length, was adopted as a national measure.
†All land would be classified into four categories on the basis of the continuity of its cultivation.

THE GILDED PRINCES

On a perfect day in November 1573, as winter conjured up a high blue sky, the four-year-old prince Salim sat cross-legged in front of a distinguished audience in his father's court. A Koran was placed on the prince's lap, and his newly appointed tutor, Maulana Mir Kalan, led the Bismillah prayer, 'In the name of the gracious, merciful God. The Merciful One taught the Koran.' Immediately the waiting nobles broke into raucous cheers and the 'assembly erupted in such a roar of congratulations that the foundation of the assembly hall shook'. Mir Kalan then lifted the young prince onto his shoulders as the gathered noblemen threw coins into the air and roared out their approval. This short ceremony marked the beginning of Salim's formal education and Akbar had ordered that all the noblemen be present at this momentous occasion.

This resplendent gathering in Fatehpur Sikri was, in its essence, vastly different from similar occasions in Akbar's childhood. The nobility now present included not only Chaghatai and Uzbek Turanis but increasingly Persians, Indian shaikhzadas, Rajput Hindus, Indian Muslim clerics, Chishti descendants, Barahas, and Hindu Kayasthas. Reflecting this new melange of men and styles, the courtiers were dressed in costumes that derived from the accommodating genius of Akbar, who had designed a court dress that both unified and distinguished the men. Under earlier Muslim dynasties, Hindu men of rank at court were obliged to wear the costumes of Muslim noblemen, often leading to resentment. Akbar, on the other hand, designed the jama, probably using an earlier indigenous style called the takauchiya, 'a coat without lining of the Indian form'. These garments were tightly fitted up to the waist and then flowed out in a full skirt with tight sleeves, paired with churidars or payjamas. The Hindus and the Muslims wore jamas which subtly yet easily told them apart—the Muslims wearing the jama with fastenings under the right armpit and Hindus with fastenings under the left armpit. In this way any inadvertent faux pas of etiquette or courtesy was averted while maintaining outward uniformity.

Akbar also proposed a style of jama which, instead of having a straight hem at the bottom, had four pointed ends which could be tucked into the belt of the wearer, allowing greater freedom of movement. This 'absurd style' according to Badauni, did not find favour for very long but the jama itself slowly infiltrated the courts, the towns, and the villages in the furthest reaches of the empire. Over the jama the courtiers wore the choga, a loose wool or silk overcoat. Akbar was especially fond of shawls from Kashmir and had begun the fashion of wearing them thrown over the shoulder, loose or folded. They were made from shahtoos, the soft wool from the underbellies of mountain goats collected from bunches of thorns the animals had run over. To further make these clothes familiar and acceptable to all his subjects, Akbar developed new Hindavi terms for these items of clothing, and introduced the word sarbgati (covering the whole body) for jama, sis-shobah for cap, parmnaram, for shawl, and, for the burqa, the decidedly whimsically named chitra-gupita. Rajput courtiers in an earlier time used to wear only crisp white dhotis, elaborately pleated; their torsos bare, with a cloth sometimes thrown around the shoulders. Under the influence of the Mughal court, Rajput clothes became more elaborate and included a long coat, in the style of the Mughal jama, with a lining in the winter. The clerics meanwhile wore traditional long costumes and members of the Sufi order wore distinguishing ochre yellow and cinnamon robes. The courtiers all wore the small, compact, 'atpati' turbans, preferred by Akbar, decorated with ornaments, with clerics and scholars favouring voluminous, large headdresses. Courtly etiquette dictated that courtiers emulate the Padshah so styles would quickly adapt themselves to Akbar's tastes, all the noblemen wearing the styles and jewels preferred by the Padshah.

On this auspicious occasion Akbar may have worn in his turban a special ruby presented to him by Hamida Banu on the birth of Salim, and which he took to wearing as a sarpech (turban ornament). For all the distracting ceremonial around the beginning of schooling, the education of the royal princes, as indeed of all the mirzas and the children of the noblemen, was an extremely vital element of courtly culture. 'In society,' warned the eighteenth-century Mirza Namah to a nobleman, 'he should try to guard against the shame of committing any mistake in conversation, for such incorrectness in speech is considered a great fault in a Mirza.' A faultless knowledge of the great texts of the time, in Persian and Arabic, and even Hindustani, was considered de rigueur to be able to carry out scintillating and erudite conversations, introducing apt quotes from the texts at relevant moments. The young mirzas began by memorizing some verses of the Koran, and then were taught grammar, Islamic law, logic, mathematics, and some elements of medicine. At the same time, calligraphic skills were developed, as an elegant hand was considered an essential skill. Akbar's thoughts on education were quite clearly elucidated by Abu'l Fazl:

> A great portion of the life of the students is wasted by making them read many books. His majesty orders that every schoolboy should first learn to write the letters of the alphabet, and also learn to trace their several forms. He ought to learn the shape and the name of each letter, which may be done in two days, when the boy should proceed to write the joined letters.

After learning writing skills the emphasis was on comprehension of the material, with the teacher only there to direct the pupil. The princes were encouraged to read books that dealt with morals, arithmetic, accountancy, agriculture, mensuration, geometry, astronomy, physiognomy, household matters, rules of government, medicine, logic, physical sciences, sciences, spiritual sciences, and history.

At the same time, young mirzas and amirs began their training in the martial skills at the age of nine. They would acquire skills in archery, horsemanship, and wrestling. Progressively harder training increased endurance and instilled competitiveness. Wrestling was a very developed art, with masters teaching their charges special tricks 'to overcome deficiencies in weight or height'. Training in hand-to-hand combat taught the young men how to defend against dagger attacks; they were even shown how to disarm an opponent with a handkerchief.

The careful and unremitting attention paid to the education of princes and children of nobility, was by no means usual in other parts of the world at this time. A full century later, when Peter the Great began his education in Russia in 1675 at the age of three, he was simply handed a primer to learn the alphabet. 'At that time in Muscovy,' writes the biographer Robert K. Massie, 'most people, even among the gentry and the clergy, were illiterate. In the nobility, education rarely consisted of more than reading, writing and a smattering of history, and geography.' The Mughals' reverence for education and learning was part of their Timurid ancestry, which valued a cultured and aesthetic sensibility as highly as military accomplishments. As we know, Salim's great-grandfather Babur wrote a memoir of great sensitivity and wit, demonstrating a curious mind and a fascination with the natural world.

A few months before the formal start of their education, the circumcision ceremony of the young princes had been carried out in equally grandiose style. As Akbar built his new capital at Fatehpur, he was careful to place his sons in the midst of the imperial image-building, thereby binding the allegiance of the noblemen to his heirs. However, as scholar Munis Faruqui has shown, the dangerous old Timurid system of appanages for princes was quietly abandoned. Now contenders for the throne could only arise from among the Padshah's own sons. Moreover, the new system was designed in such a way that princes were expected to work tirelessly at cultivating their networks of influential noblemen so that when the time came for them to stake their claim to rule, they would be ready. As we shall see later in the book, this system was not without its disadvantages and imperfections but it would safeguard the empire against fragmentation upon the death of a Padshah.

'The wise sovereign,' noted Abu'l Fazl approvingly, 'kept his children under his own care and did not appoint any guardian to them, and was continually educating them in the most excellent manner of which there are few instances in ancient times. Their holy minds have been enlightened daily by the sciences.' Akbar did appoint ataliqs to the princes but these men were inextricably bound to the Padshah through ancient ties of loyalty. In 1577, Akbar appointed Shaikh Ahmad, one of Shaikh Salim Chishti's sons, to be tutor to Prince Salim and many of the Shaikh's family members now lived in the prince's household, as milk mothers, kokas, tutors, and imperial officers. The daughter of Shaikh Salim Chishti was a beloved milk mother and, when he became emperor, Jahangir would write about this woman that 'I have not so much affection for my own mother as for her. She is to me my gracious mother.' Akbar would also take Salim, from the time he was a baby, to be presented at the dargah of Khwaja Muinuddin Chishti, thus aligning the prince's fate with that of this Hindustani order of saints. It would have been a silently eloquent symbol for Salim, a Mughal prince born to a Rajput mother, to be seen in the strategically important site of Ajmer in Rajasthan.

In 1579, when Salim was ten, Akbar appointed a member of his own Ataka clan, Qutbuddin Khan, brother of Shamsuddin Ataka Khan, as ataliq to the prince. Another Ataka clan member, Sharif Khan, was appointed tutor to Murad in 1580. It was a complicated calculation to appoint powerful courtiers who nonetheless would never challenge Akbar's own position during his lifetime. And though they were powerful, the Ataka clan's loyalty to Akbar had never been questioned. The princes would remain at court under the vigilant eye of their father and were not sent out as governors to develop dangerous and powerful alliances. When Salim was thirteen, Abdur Rahim was appointed as his ataliq and this young man, fostered and saved by Akbar after the terrible murder of his own father, would always show an unshakeable allegiance to the Padshah who had given him the title 'farzand', or 'son'. He was, nonetheless, an accomplished courtier and an excellent choice to teach the young prince the workings of the empire. He was fluent in Arabic, Persian, Turki, and Hindi and was 'famed as a consummate gatherer of rumour, gossip, news and intelligence'. A few years previously, at the age of fourteen, Abdur Rahim had composed a work of astrology called the *Kheta Koutukam*, in a mix of Persian and Sanskrit, confidently stating that 'many of my predecessors composed works in a mixed language—Sanskrit and Persian'. One of these literary predecessors would have been Amir Khusro, whose illustrated work, *Duval Rani va Khizr Khan*, was in the collection of his stepmother, Salima Sultan Begum.

While his children were still very young, Akbar, besides keeping a close watch on their upbringing and education, was a loving and doting father. Jahangir would write that 'after my birth they gave me the name of Sultan Salim but I never heard my father, either drunk or sober, call me Muhammad Salim or Sultan Salim. He always called me Shaikhu Baba', in a tender reminder of the shaikh after whom he was named. Murad was similarly always called Pahari, because he was born on the hilly heights of Fatehpur Sikri. From their pedestrian childhood ailments, like the coughs he treated with alcohol mixed in a little rose water, to guarding them against future rebellions by appointing men who would be 'protectors for his children from the malice of his life-long enemies', Akbar's vigilance was constant. Salim was also sent to the madrasa of the sadr, Shaikh Abd un-Nabi, where he learnt the teachings of the Persian Sufi mystic, Maulana Jami. About the princesses Monserrate added that '[Akbar] gives very great care and attention to the education of the princesses, who are kept rigorously secluded from the sight of men. They are taught to read and write, and are trained in other ways, by matrons.'

The children grew up in a court composed of an eclectic mix of people—their older, adoring Timurid matriarchs, Rajput mothers and attendants, Shaikh Salim's relatives, Persian noblemen, and Hindu courtiers, musicians, and artisans. They would be raised amidst a polyphony of languages and customs and Shaikhu Baba would grow up to become an elegant writer of Persian who also composed Hindi verses. As Emperor Jahangir he would develop an appreciation for Hindi verses. He was once so moved by a poet who wrote verses praising him, calling him the son of the Sun, that he gave him an elephant in reward. Jahangir would later even offer grudging admiration of Daniyal, who 'was fond of Hindi songs and would occasionally compose verses with correct idiom in the language of the people of India, which were not bad'.

Akbar's care did not stop with just his sons and daughters. '[Akbar] maintains, and gives a liberal education to many noble boys and youths who have lost their fathers'. Whenever Akbar spied a glimmer of talent or goodness in any deserving waif, like Daswant the artist, he would take them in and put personal effort into forming them. Jahangir would later write of one 'Lal Kalawant, who from his childhood had grown up in my father's service, who had taught him every breathing and sound that appertains to the Hindi language'. There was also Manohar, of the clan of the Shekhawat Kachhwahas, on whom, 'in his young days my father had bestowed many favours. He had learned the Persian language and, although from him up to Adam the power of understanding cannot be attributed to any one of his tribe', was Jahangir's brisk assessment, 'he is not without intelligence'. However, of all the princes and youth at Fatehpur it was Shaikhu Baba who would be, for a while at least, the adored and chosen heir. His would be the grandest celebrations and the greatest honours, and he would be repeatedly sent to greet or accompany journeying royal women. And the harem, in turn, would always be united in their efforts to bolster the sometimes faltering trajectory of this complicated prince. For the candescent gaze of Padshah Akbar was not always easy to bear, especially as the princes grew older. 'He used to give them orders rather roughly whenever he wanted anything done,' wrote the Jesuit priests about Akbar and his sons, 'and he sometimes punished them with blows as well as with harsh words.' This made Murad 'so submissive that he sometimes did not even dare to raise his eyes to his teacher's face when he was reproving him'. It may not be altogether surprising that Jahangir noted that his father's 'august voice was very resonant'. For both Murad and Daniyal this fatal mix of their father's own soaring achievements, his impossible expectations of them, combined with a beguiling and increasingly luxurious courtly life, would result in their undoing and both would succumb to alcoholism early in life.

But these early years for the princes were undoubtedly a time of indulgence and joy. Almost every day there were new celebrations and innovations as the masons and craftsmen constructed a vision in red sandstone all around them. In 1573, following Akbar's great victories in Gujarat, Haji Begum came to court from Delhi to congratulate her stepson and there was a grand banquet. These great celebrations would become increasingly elaborate as the years went by while the etiquette surrounding the Padshah's every meal also gained in spectacle and was meticulously described a few years later by Monserrate:

> His table is very sumptuous, generally consisting of more than forty courses served in great dishes. These are brought into the

royal dining hall covered and wrapped in linen cloths, which are tied up and sealed by the cook for fear of poison. They are carried by youths to the door of the dining hall, other servants walking ahead and the master of the household following. Here they are taken over by eunuchs, who hand them to the serving girls who wait on the royal table.

Supplying these gargantuan meals was the imperial kitchen, a department consisting of a head cook, a treasurer, a storekeeper, clerks, tasters, and more than 400 cooks from all over India and Persia. According to food historian Salma Husain, the hakim (royal physician) planned each menu to include medicinally beneficial ingredients. Each grain of rice for the biryani was coated with silver oil, which aided digestion and acted as an aphrodisiac. According to historian Lizzie Collingham, biryani itself was a fragrant and fortuitous Mughal mix of delicately flavoured Persian pilau and the pungent and spicy rice dishes of Hindustan. Ice, for the cooling of drinks and making frozen desserts, was brought daily from the Himalayas by an elaborate system of couriers.

Some of the food served at banquets, in dishes of gold, silver, stone, and earthenware, would have included yakhni, a meat stock; musamman, stuffed roast chicken; dopiaza, meat prepared with large quantities of onions; dampukht, meat cooked slowly with aromatic spices in a pot with a sealed lid, all served with naan-like large breads, yoghurt, lime, and up to thirty kinds of pickles, which could include pickled quinces, bamboo, ginger, brinjal, sour lime, and mustard. There may have been dishes like murg zamindoz, popular at this time, which showed the fusing of Mughal and Rajput cooking traditions. The chicken, a quintessential Mughal ingredient, was well spiced and wrapped in dough, and then cooked under the earth using charcoal, a traditional Rajasthani technique for cooking vegetables. The food was flavoured with spices such as ginger, cinnamon, black pepper, cumin, cardamom, cloves, saffron, and coriander but would not have contained red chillies, potatoes, or tomatoes, which had not yet reached north India from the New World. Nor did the food contain kalonji, mustard seeds, sesame seeds or curry leaves, found in local market places but not incorporated into the Mughal kitchens, these indigenous spices probably still foreign to Central Asian and Persian palates.

There were fruits, however, for as Abu'l Fazl noted the Padshah 'looks upon fruits as one of the greatest gifts of the Creator, and pays much attention to them'. He brought the best horticulturists from Central Asia and Iran to supervise his orchards, which were watered with rose water to improve the flavour of the produce. To enhance the taste of the much-appreciated mangoes, milk and treacle were poured around the base of the trees. Akbar encouraged the cultivation of melons, peaches, apricots, walnuts, apples, pears, cherries, and pineapples, which were especially expensive, and sold in Delhi's market for the price of ten mangoes. With the passing decades, Akbar became more frugal in his eating habits restricting himself to just one meal a day, at no fixed time. This was not the case with the women in the harem and their complicated fasts, their many visitors, their varied cuisines. 'The food allowed to the women of the seraglio,' clarified Abu'l Fazl, 'commences to be taken from the kitchen in the morning and goes on till night.'

If the Padshah became more austere in his eating habits over the years, then the care and attention that went into the royal cuisine became ever more rigorous, as the fear of poison settled like a noxious stain in the fabric of Mughal life. Ever since the mother of the slain Ibrahim Lodi had tried to poison Babur after the Battle of Panipat, the fear of death by poisoning became an obsession that required constant vigilance. After the meals were prepared in the kitchens at Fatehpur Sikri, the cooks covered their mouths and noses with their hands as the food was taken out. The food was then tasted by the cooks as well as the mir bakawal (master of the kitchen) after which the dishes were wrapped in cloth, sealed, and tagged with the name of the contents; then an inventory of all the dishes was drawn up. Once all the dishes were sealed, mace bearers led a procession of male servants bearing the food, keeping all onlookers away. The dishes were then transferred to eunuchs, who carried the food part of the way before handing it over to young girls who brought the dishes into the presence of the Padshah. In the dining area, tentatively identified by historian Rezavi as the building erroneously called 'Maryam's house' over the ages, a crisp white cloth was laid on the ground and the dishes were unsealed and tasted a second time. The mir bakawal and the table servants remained in attendance on the emperor as he ate his meal which, in addition to the many dishes cooked, was accompanied by breads including hot chapattis, fresh ginger, limes, various greens, and fresh yoghurt. At the end of the meal, Akbar prostrated himself for a prayer of thanks.

And everywhere in Fatehpur Sikri, in ever greater numbers, were the animals. The elephants, horses, and camels in their stables but also the pigeons in their dovecotes, the companionable dogs, the noiseless cheetahs roaming free through the courtyards at dusk, and the silent, ferocious hawks.

For all these various activities, for the women in their seclusion, the children at their studies, the kitchen, stables, armoury, and soon, religious discussions, Akbar built in the arid landscape a glowing city of dreams.

CITY OF DREAMS

Of all the characteristics that Akbar shared with his semi-nomadic Timurid ancestors, perhaps the most enduring one would be his habit to gather up his men, his harem, his soldiery, and his animals, and move. For Timur, as indeed for Babur, a tent in a fragrant garden next to a flowing stream was home. For the Mughals of Hindustan, this tenacious need to be on the move would continue, even as their tented encampments grew ever more elaborate and stately. They would travel to hunt, on battles, on pilgrimages, on adventure, and sometimes just on a whim. The tent in a garden setting was therefore a profoundly evocative image for the Mughals and in Akbar's first great monumental project, after the re-building of Agra, it is not surprising that the layout of Fatehpur Sikri resembles, in its vast, open spaces and centrally located, vertical masses of flat-topped buildings, that same image translated into sandstone.

There is much that remains a mystery about Fatehpur Sikri—the order in which the buildings were constructed, the layout and planning, the purpose of some of the buildings, today often misleadingly named. Many of the original buildings, made of rubble bonded with lime, and gypsum mortar, have crumbled. These include the nobles' houses, the offices of the bureaucrats, the stables, the shops and the bazaars. But from what remains it is easy to gauge the wealth of the empire and the creative vision and energy of the man who willed the city into being when spirits and ghouls were threatening the peace of his house.

The ecstatic impression of visiting travellers gives us some sense of the wonder that this city was in its time. 'Agra and Fatepore,' wrote Ralph Fitch, English traveller to Hindustan in the sixteenth century, 'are two very great cities, either of them much greater than London and very populous... The King hath in Agra and Fatepore as they do credibly report, 1000 elephants, 30,000 horses, 1400 tame deer, 800 concubines: such store of ounces, tigers, buffalo, cocks and hawks that is very strange to see.' And Monserrate thought that 'the splendour of [Akbar's] palaces approaches closely to that of the royal dwellings of Europe. They are magnificently built, from foundation to cornice, of hewn stone, and are decorated both with painting and carving.' About the building of Fatehpur Sikri, Jahangir would write that 'in the course of fourteen or fifteen years that hill, full of wild beasts, became a city containing all kinds of gardens and buildings and lofty, elegant edifices and pleasant places, attractive to the heart'. One of the first buildings to have been completed was the Jami mosque, which incorporated features from Hindu temples, making it unique in the Islamic world. Like the triplication of the domes of a Hindu temple, the Jami mosque has a triad of domes and is located on a high platform, with a lofty and wide view of the city below. When Shaikh Salim Chishti died, in 1571, his dargah was built in the courtyard of the Jami mosque, adding another layer of mystical sacrality to the space. An enormous Buland Darwaza, a victory gateway built to commemorate the Gujarat victories, has a surprising inscription in Naskh calligraphy that purports to quote Jesus: 'The World is a Bridge, pass over it, but build no houses upon it. He who hopes for a day, may hope for eternity; but the World endures but an hour. Spend it in prayer, for the rest is unseen.' Though not part of any canonical Christian text, this quote is from a body of Jesus's sayings from Islamic lore, possibly from early oral Christian traditions. It is a silent and enigmatic witness to some of the most audacious experiments in cultural and philosophical syncretism that were to ever take place in India.

As the various buildings of Fatehpur Sikri came up, they reflected a joyous mix of Timurid, Rajasthani, and Gujarati sultanate architecture. The haramsara, or ladies' quarters, the so-called Birbal's palace, the so-called Jodh Bai's palace, and then later the diwan-e-aam and innumerable more buildings combined the arch and dome of Islamicate architecture with delicate lattice-work jaalis and chattris (umbrellas) as well as Gujarati trabeation—beams. Akbar himself took a keen interest in the works, with Monserrate noting that '[Akbar] is so devoted to building that he sometimes quarries stone himself, along with the other workmen.' The fearsome flirted with the decorative as when one of the great gates of the city was festooned with 'chains, manacles, handcuffs and other irons' to deter all possible crooks and brigands. The Jesuits agreed that this was to 'inspire terror than for actual use' because the chief executioner too was wont to present himself at court positively brimming with 'leather thongs, whips, bow-strings fitted with sharp spikes of copper, a smooth block of wood used for pounding the criminals' sides or crushing to pieces his skull and scourges in which are tied a number of small balls studded with sharp bronze nails', accoutrements which were, however, never actually used.

Technological innovations developed alongside the ornamentation and a water tank, the Hauz-i Shirin, was built on a sharp slope and supported on inverted arches to hold the enormous weight of the stored water. Sweet water was required for human consumption and for cooking, to which Gangajal was added because Akbar strongly believed in the beneficial qualities of water from the Ganga. Wherever he happened to be in the empire, Gangajal was brought to Akbar in sealed jars, transported sometimes over long distances, because that was the only water he would drink. Akbar would have heard of the qualities of Gangajal, long revered in the country, through his Hindu wives and his Rajput noblemen. To Akbar, who would be haunted by the noxious spectre of poison, this would be one more measure, a divine one, to protect himself from harm.

An enormous workforce of labourers, stonemasons, stonecutters, stonecarvers, carpenters, diggers, wickerworkers, glassmakers, bricklayers, and various other craftsmen was mobilized as the city took shape at a rapid pace. To reduce the amount of noise created near the living quarters, Akbar ordered 'everything cleverly fashioned elsewhere, in accordance with the exact plan of the building, and then brought to the spot, and there fitted and fastened together'. As each building was completed, it was furnished too, with rich carpets on the floors and draperies on the walls and silk bolsters and cushions.

The unadorned red surfaces that bake in the summer sun today at Fatehpur Sikri give an inaccurate idea of what the palaces and buildings would have looked like. Instead of the unremitting expanse of red, there would instead have been colours and textures and textiles in glorious profusion as every surface and space was covered in paintings or wall hangings, carpets and tent awnings. There were frescoes and decorations on every surface, today sadly almost all degraded. Syed Ali Nadeem Rezavi has shown that the artists of Fatehpur Sikri used wall paintings extensively to cover almost every surface of the buildings with vibrant images. Wall paintings had been used since the time of Babur but it was under Akbar that these paintings were considered an essential part of architecture itself and encouraged accordingly. Artists used red ochre or black carbon to outline the paintings, filling in colours using minerals like lapis lazuli, sulphides of mercury, lead, and other arsenic and copper ores as well as plant extract dyes like indigo, lac, and dhak. The artists used mainly the tempera method of applying paint to dried plaster. The murals in the Khwabgah, the Khizana-i *Anuptalao* and the Sonahra Makan (Maryam's House) glowed with narrative paintings including figures, angels, landscapes, elephants, cheetahs, and horses. While the figurative paintings were reserved for the more private spaces, the public spaces were decorated with flowers and trees including jasmine, marigold, champa, poppy, rose, and tulip. There would also have been masses of fragrant flowers in vases: chameli in the monsoon, mogra in the summer, nargis in the spring, and champa all year round. The court was kept scented with incense too, ambergris and aloe wood, using ancient recipes or new inventions. In the background, as the water channels were built, and the fountains installed, water quietly flowed, a consoling music as the heat soared.

During this maelstrom of activity in 1574, an elderly man was brought in chains from Ahmedabad to Fatehpur Sikri, to be interrogated by the Padshah and his ulema. This was the famous Mahdavi Shaikh Mustafa Gujarati whose family and dairah had been decimated, and who had already spent some months at Aziz Koka's court, being brutally questioned. Now Akbar, his noblemen, and the ulema sat in a circle and placed the shaikh in the centre. One of the Gujarati noblemen disdainfully commented on the unkempt aspect of the old man. 'Shame on you,' was Akbar's sharp rebuke, 'he is an elderly person and one should talk to him respectfully.' Akbar then asked the shaikh to clarify his stand on Mahdavism, explaining that 'the ulema and (religious guides) are very hostile to you.... It is because of the efforts of the ulema that you have fallen into this predicament. How far is your heart afflicted by this?' The shaikh explained his philosophy emphasizing the Sufi, mystical aspect of Mahdavism, veering away from a political role. In a long discussion lasting many days, Akbar seemed to be using the shaikh to subtly question and undermine the ulema themselves. 'We are fifty or sixty people here trying to corner the Shaikh by our questions,' the Padshah said. 'The Shaikh, despite his poverty, shackles, being away from his father or brother and relatives and friends, sits in our court as if he is our master. He is answering each and every one of our questions with dignity, aplomb and steadfastness.' During another session, while trying to explain his allegiance to the Mahdi, the shaikh asked Akbar who his spiritual guide was. Bowing his head in veneration and touching his ear lobes the Padshah said, 'I am the disciple of Hazrat Khwaja Moinuddin Chishti.' The shaikh then asked him what he would do if someone challenged the legacy of Hazrat Muinuddin. 'I would call such a person a kafir,' maintained Akbar stoutly, 'and kill him with my own hands.' Similarly, argued the shaikh, the Mahdi was his spiritual guide, equally mystical and equally benign. At some point in the discussions, which the shaikh would later transcribe himself in his cell, the ulema reacted to the shaikh's persuasive and charged message by saying, 'If we, the learned people in the Emperor's assembly, hear even a little of his words, we might imagine that he is right, for his words made an impression on our heart. For this reason, one must not permit fitnah [actions threatening the stability and power of a Muslim state]'. The ulema were unwavering in their condemnation of the shaikh who, in turn, refused one day to follow the sadr, Abd un-Nabi, in the midday prayer, accusing the ulema of being 'false men' who 'appear before the king, flatter him and his nobles, and accept his largesse'. These false men, he thundered, would never see God.

Shaikh Mustafa would remain more than a year at Akbar's court, infuriating the ulema and being carefully questioned by the Padshah. These discussions were only the beginning of an extraordinary series of religious and philosophical explorations by Akbar, a deeply personal search by the Padshah for a truth that reflected his growing maturity. Shaikh Mustafa's health, meanwhile, deteriorated rapidly and when Badauni went to visit him where he was staying at Abd al-Samad's house, the charismatic and dynamic preacher had become a frail and feeble man, suddenly old, and vomiting blood. Akbar eventually released him, allowing him to return to Gujarat but the shaikh never did reach Gujarat, dying en route, at Bayana in 1576.

In the midst of this curdle and churn, two men arrived at Akbar's court, childhood friends who were reunited at Fatehpur Sikri but whose trajectory at the Mughal court would torque in vastly different directions. Both men were troubled, searching for answers in Akbar's glittering new court into which men of worth and talent were being voraciously assimilated each day. The first to arrive, in 1574, was Badauni, now thirty-four years old, and scoured and bruised by personal tragedies. He had recently witnessed a terrible fire at Badaun, where 'many Hindus and Musulmans perished in the flames... carts filled with the charred remains were driven down to the river and none could tell who was a Moslem and who an infidel'.

At Fatehpur Sikri, Badauni was presented to Akbar by one Jalal Khan Qurchi, 'a master of mirth and wit, and a confidential and personal friend of the Emperor'. Jalal Khan introduced the serious young scholar to the Padshah saying, 'I have discovered an imam for your majesty, whom you will be pleased with.' This was a crucial interview for Badauni as all appointments to imperial service were made by the Padshah personally, and the rank and salary were determined case by case, depending on circumstances, and a great deal rested on Akbar's discernment:

> In ordinary cases...a candidate had to find a patron who would introduce him to the Emperor and if he won favour, his appointment followed after a somewhat lengthy series of formalities. There appears to have been no recognized test of fitness... Akbar had great faith in his own powers of discerning character, and he appears to have acted uniformly on his own judgment. In the same way there were no rules regarding promotion; an officer might be advanced or degraded, or dismissed at the Emperor's pleasure.

Badauni himself admitted that 'as learning was a merchandise much in demand, I had the privilege of being addressed [by His Majesty] as soon as I reached (his presence). I was included among the members of the assembly and was thrown into the discussion with the ulema...

By the grace of God, the power of my mind, the sensitiveness of my intelligence and that boldness which is a natural quality of youth, I often proved myself the superior.' Badauni, not in the least bashful, also noted that 'the Emperor, on account of the beauty of my voice, which was comparable with the sweet voice, and ravishing tones of a parrot, made me the Reader of the Prayer on Wednesday evenings, and entered me among the seven Imams.' Badauni was poised at this time to become a valued member of Akbar's court. He was undoubtedly knowledgeable in orthodox Islamic literature but he had many other accomplishments which would have been greatly cherished at the Mughal court. 'Mullah Abdul Qadir,' wrote Faizi, 'in addition to his accomplishment in learning, has an inclination towards poetry and taste in prose composition both Arabic and Persian. He is also acquainted with Indian astrology and mathematics. He has knowledge of Indian and Persian music and is not ignorant of chess, both two-handed and four-handed. He has also made commendable practice on the bin (flute)'.

The other addition to the court was twenty-four-year-old Abu'l Fazl, whose father, and elder brother, Faizi, had already been received by Akbar. The precocious young intellectual was initially very loath to join the imperial court, abhorring what he saw as the venality of courtly life and a renouncing of higher intellectual and spiritual pursuits. But Faizi, who had already gained a reputation as a talented poet, as well as Shaikh Mubarak, worked hard to persuade the doubting young man. 'From [Akbar] comes the solution of spiritual and temporal matters,' explained Shaikh Mubarak and indeed under the magnetic influence of Akbar, 'I experienced a bit of relief from that stubborn illness', Abu'l Fazl later wrote, 'which my father, despite his great ability, had been unable to cure.'

As Shaikh Mustafa Gujarati argued with eloquence and fervour for a return to a more perfect idea of Islam before the corruption of the ulema and the beguiling allure of kings, Akbar was creating a new department at Fatehpur Sikri to translate into Persian a whole range of unorthodox texts in Sanskrit, Arabic, and Turki, which would have certainly seemed of highly dubious origin to the beleaguered shaikh.

DUHU DEEN KO SAHIB

While the labourers strained and the cattle heaved to put together the chiselled sandstone buildings at Fatehpur, each new quarter was immediately filled with incessant activity and noise. As we have noted, in 1574 Akbar established a translation bureau (maktab khana) in which he gathered together scribes, clerks, translators, theologians, and pundits. A large number of texts, both well known and obscure, were chosen for translation into Persian. These included a number of Sanskrit texts such as the *Rajatarangini* (History of the Kings of Kashmir), and the *Panchatantra*, known in its translation as the *Anwar-i Suhayli*. Arabic encyclopaedias were also translated into Persian as was the *Baburnama*, Babur's memoirs, which he had written in Chaghatai Turki. This was the beginning of Akbar's long-term plan to make Persian the official language of the Mughal Empire and the language which would bind together not only the disparate nobility at court but would also infiltrate into the lower levels of the bureaucracy.

Persian had already arrived in Hindustan with the Ghaznavids, the Ghurids, and then through an influx of writers, poets, and thinkers fleeing Chenghiz Khan's conquest of the Perso–Islamic world. That it was already the language of the Hindustani elite can be gauged from the line of Hafiz of Shiraz when he claimed that 'all the Indian parrots will turn to crunching sugar with this Persian candy which goes to Bengal'. But Persian patronage stagnated for a while in the fifteenth century and the Afghans in the sixteenth century were uninterested in the language too. It was with Humayun that a slow influx of Iranian refugees began which was then greatly encouraged by Akbar. The enormous impetus that Akbar would give to Persian would make it the language of literate Hindustanis from the Indus to the Bay of Bengal, and would bring into the fold of the Mughal Empire people from varied religious and social groups. Extraordinary social mobility was possible for those fluent in Persian as in the case of the qissa-khwan Mir Muhammad Hashim. Hashim began his career as part of the retinue of 'slaves and servants' of Abdur Rahim, and then became a 'panegyrist, storyteller, master of the stables and jagirdar'. It would make Akbar, in the words of the Sanskrit poet and scholar Keshavdas, 'duhu deen ko sahib' (master of both religions).

While Akbar most enjoyed literary soirées during which books of Hindavi, Persian, Greek, Kashmiri, and Arabic were read out to him, in the towns of the empire it was the ghazal that was rapidly gaining popularity as the medium of choice for amateur poets. They would recite these at gatherings of aficionados which now included 'sufis, women and general townspeople' and brought together people from very different backgrounds. Badauni wrote that the poet Qasim Ali 'Ghubari' was 'very handsome and used to sing at social gatherings and had pretentions to be a Quraishi', but was 'embarrassed that his father was a grocer', showing that social mobility and the importance of lineage were both aspects of Mughal society at the time. Of the poet Qasim Kahi he was more scathing still, disapproving of his association with dervishes, courtesans and, intriguingly, dogs, though he admitted that he sang in a reasonably good voice and that some lines of his ghazals had become all the rage. These musical assemblies, or mushairas were 'not only complex competitive arenas and technical workshops but hothouses of gossip and general social rivalry as well', where charges of plagiarism were bitterly contested and a single excellent line of poetry would be carefully noted down by attendees and then shared widely.

Jostling alongside the translators at Fatehpur Sikri were also hundreds of artists for each document translated was to be elaborately illustrated. Akbar's argument for his love of painting human forms, usually deemed un-Islamic, was evocatively noted by Abu'l Fazl:

> I cannot tolerate those who make the slightest criticism of this art. It seems to me that a painter is better than most in gaining a knowledge of God. Each time he draws a living being he must draw each and every limb of it, but seeing that *he* cannot bring it to life must perforce give thought to the miracle wrought by the Creator and thus obtain a knowledge of Him.

Akbar had studios built for his painters and with his usual enthusiasm and curiosity, would watch the artists at work. 'He has built a workshop near the palace where there are studios and work rooms for the fine and more reputable arts such as painting, goldsmith work, tapestry making, carpet making and the manufacturing of arms', wrote Monserrate. 'Hither he frequently comes and relaxes his mind with watching at their work those who practice these arts.' The painters in their small cells would have sat on the floor, their drawing boards resting on their raised thighs, or placed slanting against the ground. Set around the artists would be just a few objects, of the very highest quality: twenty mussel or clam shells containing pigments, brushes made of kitten or squirrel hairs, a pot of water, and a pot of glue. The pigments were made of pounded gold or silver. Crushed minerals such as lapis lazuli mined in Afghanistan produced a vivid blue, cinnabar and copper salts a bright crimson, saffron from the crocuses in Kashmir, ground-up shells a chalky white, soot a deep black, and the urine of cows fed on mangoes a bright, arresting yellow.

Miniature painting was a long and laborious process, a moderately elaborate painting sometimes taking up to a month to finish. The paper would be first brushed with a light priming coat of white pigment then turned over and burnished to provide a smooth ground. The paintings were often a collaborative effort, in which one artist would draw the sketches and another would colour in the painting with a third artist reserved for painting faces. Mughal artists sometimes painted from life but usually worked from earlier sketches, with an emphasis on opulence of colour and fineness of details. Depth of colour was achieved by applying repeated layers of paint. 'Sometimes actual jewels—rubies, emeralds, diamonds—or jewel-like beetle-wing-cases were attached to miniatures for special opulence.' Hunched over their canvases, using a magnifying lens for fine detailing, the men would grow old, and would lose their eyesight, from the precision of the tiny works of art they created, worlds within worlds of fluttering movement, emotion, and splendour. Other artists would pay an even higher price for their years of precise and sustained effort. Daswant, untrained genius, and fragile of mind, would eventually commit suicide, perhaps overcome at the end by these dreams of spinning gold.

Alongside the painters were the calligraphers and scribes, who were especially revered not only for their artistic skill, but because they copied the sacred Koran and of whom it was said that 'whoever writes "in the name of God the Merciful and Compassionate" in fine lettering will enter paradise'. The calligraphers worked with reed pens and their own special inks. Ambar Qalam (sweet pen) used a jealously guarded formulation which gave him a lustrous brownish-black ink, easily identifiable. And alongside the artists and illustrators were ateliers for jewellery, for textiles, for the ironsmiths and welders who wrought armour and arms, and for lapidary workers who were 'kept busy creating not only delights for the emperor but also gifts for family members, favoured courtiers and rival rulers'.

At their peak, Akbar's taswir khanas would have 145 Hindu painters and 115 Muslim painters, far more than the next great collector of artists, Jahangir, who would only have 43 and 41 respectively. With his usual unbridled enthusiasm Akbar would indiscriminately promote a large variety of artists as opposed to the smaller number of 'master artists' preferred by his heirs. The wages of artists were comparable to that of soldiers, and they could be rewarded extravagantly for outstanding work, such as with grants of villages or even elephants. Artists did not remain in the studios but accompanied Akbar wherever he went, to battlefields, pilgrimages, on hunts, and extended campaigns. The art being produced at Akbar's ateliers now was different from the earlier large-scale projects—the *Hamzanama*, for example. Now the works of art were usually only a few inches across, meant to be held in the hand, and scrutinized closely in their fine details, and were exceptional 'masterpieces', the work of a single master artist rather than a collaborative effort between several painters.

The *Anwar-i Suhayli*, painted at this time, was one of the first examples of this style in which overall directions were given by the Safavid artist Abd al-Samad but then individual artists, usually local in origin, such as Basawan and Miskin, carried out the actual work. These Hindustani artists brought an exuberance to their brushwork and a soaring imagination, especially in their paintings of animals, that seemed to visibly struggle to stay within the elegant framework of the Persian masters. Though Akbar admired his Safavid masters, he was particularly moved by the work of his Hindu painters, some of whom had come to court as spoils of war, as in the case of the booty from the campaign against Rani Durgavati. Lacking a formal education himself, he would have thrilled to see the raw, untethered talent of these artists, some from very humble backgrounds—palki-bearers, stonecutters, water carriers. 'Judge the nobility of any one's being and great lineage,' wrote Akbar to his son Daniyal many years later, 'from the essence of his merit, and not from the pedigree of his ancestors or greatness of the seed.' Most tellingly, the names of these artists were written in red ink near the lower margin of the painting, silent testimony of the high regard Akbar had for his painters, remarkable and rare for his time. Even more intriguingly, three of the names are those of women—Nadira Banu, Sahifa Banu, and Ruqiya Banu. The presence of these female artists allows one to ponder the access they may have had to the imperial harem and whether they were able to paint some of the royal women from life. That the royal women were collectors and patrons of manuscripts is well known. Salima Sultan Begum had in her personal collection a copy of Amir Khusro's *Duval Rani va Khizr Khan*, illustrated during the early reign of Akbar, perhaps even under her direct guidance. Hamida Banu Begum was another voracious collector of books and manuscripts and as for Gulbadan, she would write a book herself. The *Anwar-i Suhayli*, with its animal fables and moral messages from the *Panchatantra*, was deemed to be highly suitable to teach Salim and his siblings the nuances of human nature and Akbar commissioned a simpler version of the same stories called the *Iyar-e Danesh* (Pearls of Wisdom) for the education of the princes.

At the same time, as this effervescent activity had begun to flourish in Fatehpur, Akbar saw an opportunity to finally rout the troublesome Afghan menace. Afghans had been settling in Bengal for a while, as we saw, keeping away from imperial authority in the north-west. They had been encouraged to migrate by the Bengal sultan Nusrat Shah who used them to create a useful buffer zone between himself and the Mughals. In 1564, Taj Khan Karrani had founded an Indo-Afghan dynasty in this region where he cautiously maintained a submissive attitude towards the increasingly powerful Mughals. But when Sulaiman Karrani Afghan had died in 1572, creating a power vacuum in Bengal and Bihar, his son Daud, as the new Sultan of Bengal, no longer even pretended to wear the 'outer garment of submission' to Akbar and had struck coins and had the khutba read in his own name. This was insolence that could not be tolerated and Akbar went first to Ajmer to seek the blessings of the saint for the war he was proposing to wage. At this time he organized the building of kos minars (milestones) and the sinking of wells at regular intervals along the Agra-Ajmer road. At Ajmer, Akbar appointed Rai Ram Das to the diwani of Ajmer sarkar and then returned to Fatehpur to prepare for battle.

Chenghiz (Genghis) Khan, founder of the Mongol Empire which became the largest contiguous empire in the world.

Timur feasts in the gardens of Samarkand. The Mughals revered their ancestor Timur and emulated many of his habits such as this tented banquet in a garden setting.

Padshah Babur. After he was exiled from his homeland of Ferghana, Babur founded the Mughal Empire in Hindustan in 1526.

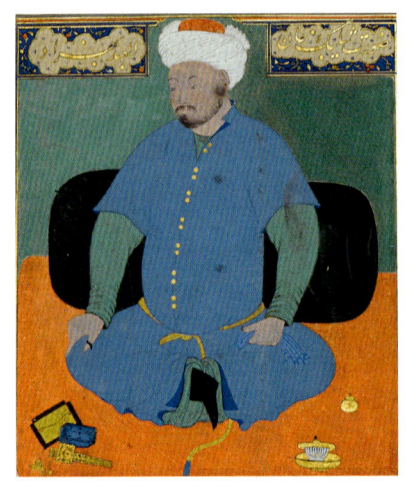

Shaibani Khan Uzbek, detested foe of Mirza Babur, who chased him out of his homeland of Ferghana and then Samarkand.

Allegory of celebrations around Akbar's circumcision ceremony, 1546.

Young Prince Akbar and noblemen hawking—by Abd al-Samad. A rare early work from Humayun's atelier, 1555.

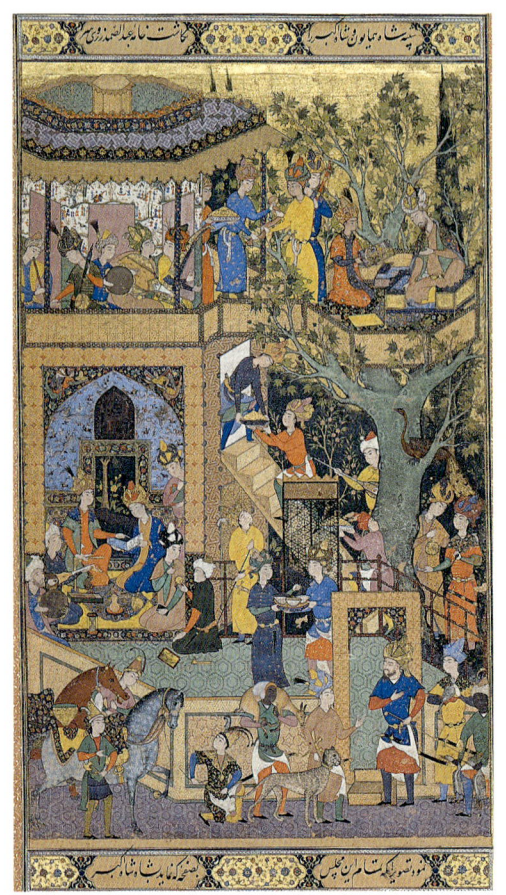

Prince Akbar presenting a painting to his father, Humayun—by Abd al-Samad, 1550–1556, from the Gulshan Album. Painted in a Persianate style, Akbar may have contributed to the painting as a student of the Persian master painter.

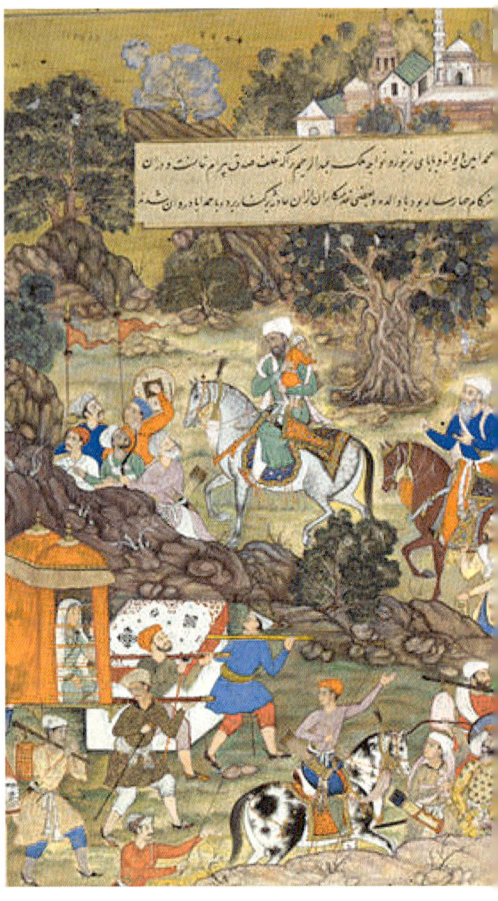

Following the murder of Bairam Khan, his widow, Salima Sultan Begum, and his son, Abdur Rahim, were brought to the Mughal court. Akbar then married Salima Sultan Begum, a Timurid princess.

Tansen Gwaliyari joined Akbar's court in 1562 and his Dhrupad raags would enchant the court for decades.

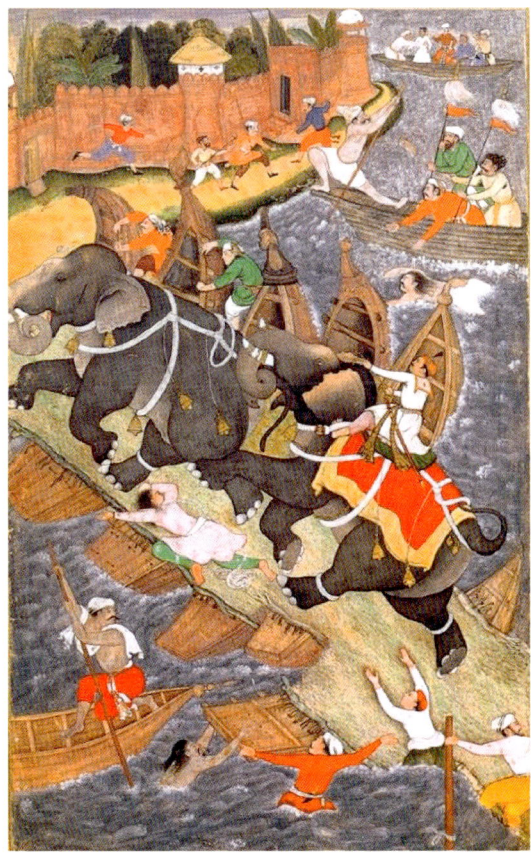

Akbar leads an attack mounted on the elephant Hawai. Folio from the Akbarnama.

Akbar hunts in the neighbourhood of Agra using tame cheetahs—by Basawan.

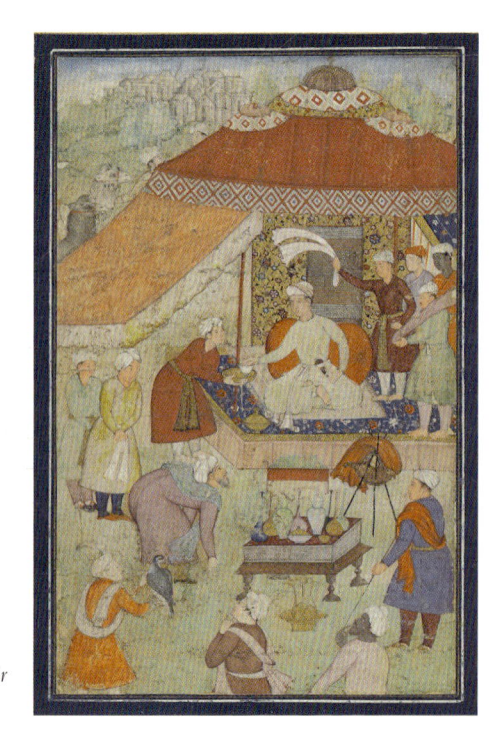

Like their Timurid forebears, the Mughal Padshahs spent a considerable part of their life on the move, in tented encampments.

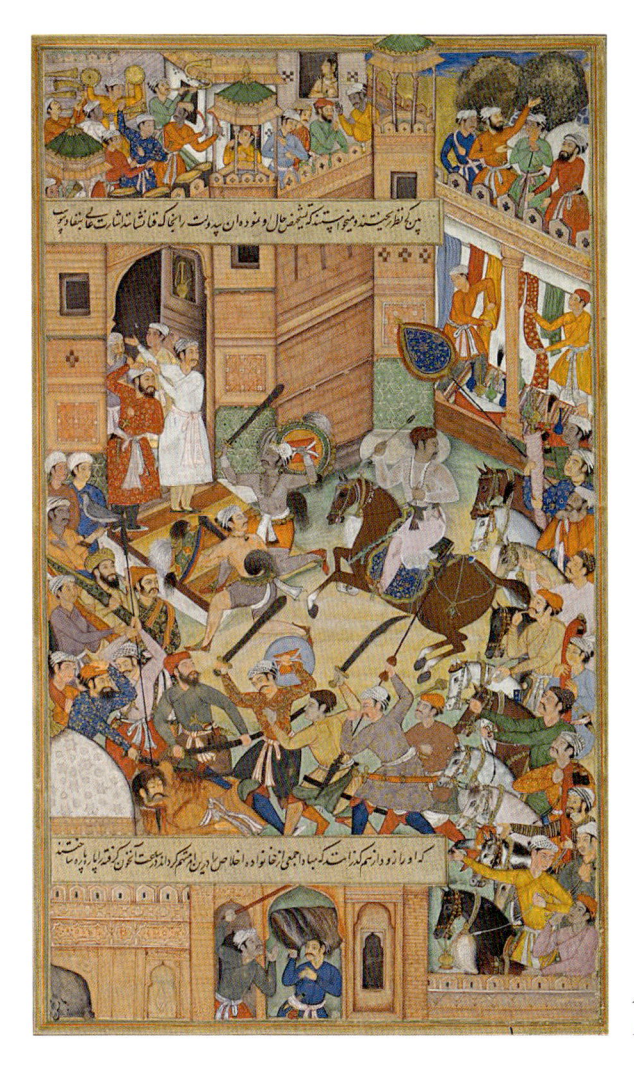

An attempt on Akbar's life at the Khair-un-Manazil, Delhi, in 1564.

Ataka Khan's mausoleum in Delhi contains the tombs of Akbar's milk mother, Jiji Anaga, and her husband, Shamsuddin Ataka Khan.

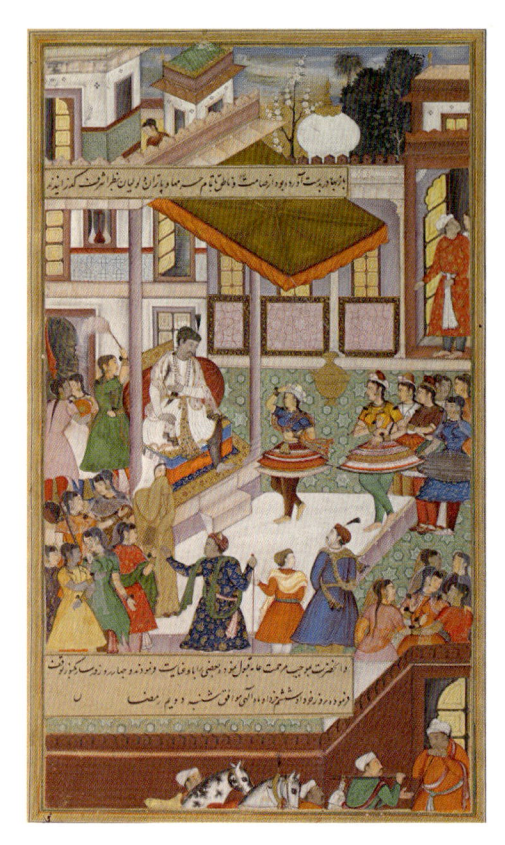

(Left): *The dancers from Mandu presented to Akbar after the defeat of Baz Bahadur, while a worried Maham Anaga hides her face behind her yellow sleeve.*

(Left, below): *The Tutinama, commissioned early in Akbar's reign, was a tale within a tale told by a parrot.*

(Right, below): *Umayya frees Umar, who has been imprisoned by Iraj—folio from the Hamzanama (The Adventures of Amir Hamza), the first large work commissioned by Akbar.*

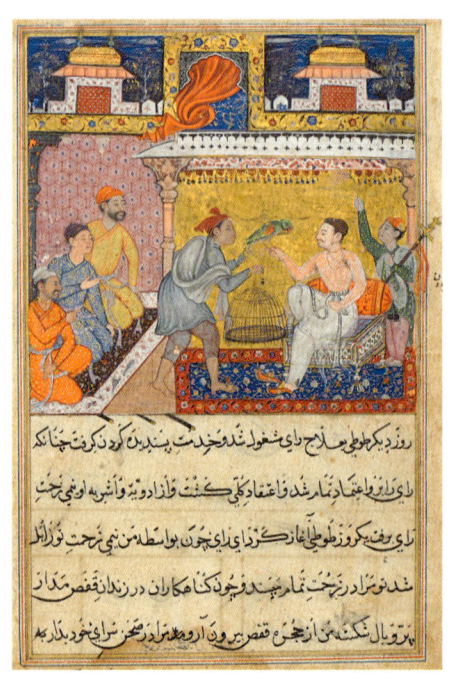

The siege of Chittor. Some 300 women are believed to have committed jauhar after the defeat of Chittor.

The qumargha or ring hunt. Qumargha hunts involved thousands of soldiers, and lasted many days, and were a powerful demonstration of Akbar's wealth and his soldiers' might.

Akbar's sword.

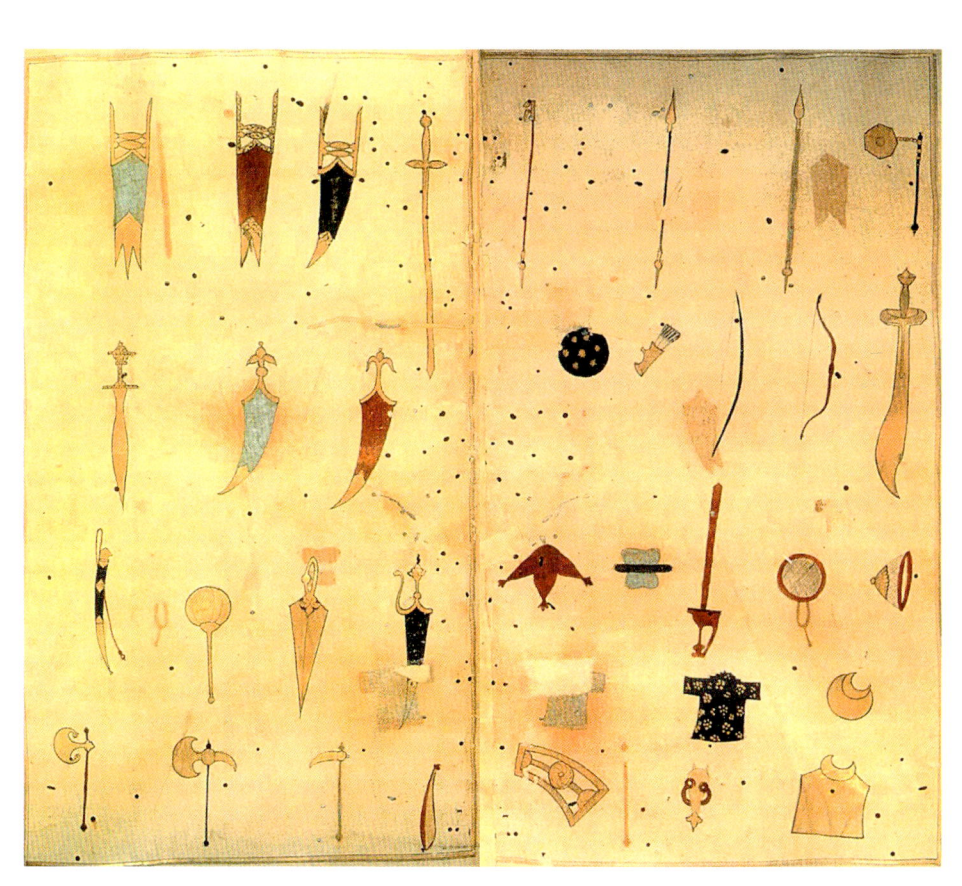

Weaponry from the Ain-i Akbari.

Akbar's personal moulded armour made of Damascus steel. Akbar's helmet was decorated with delicate gold damascene and had a spike at the top.

Considered the battle tank of its day, the elephant was an important part of Indian armies, even under Akbar. This armour is the most complete set to be found in the world today.

Detail from the Battle of Sarnal showing heavily armoured horses and generals using the lance and sword.

The diwan-e-khas building at Fatehpur Sikri. With its flat-top, the diwan-e-khas brings to mind the travelling tent of the Timurids.

Akbar visits Muinuddin Chishti's dargah in Ajmer—by Basawan. Akbar became a devotee of Muinuddin Chishti and changed his war cry to Ya Muin!

Birth of Akbar's first son, Salim.

Akbar receiving his sons at Fatehpur Sikri after the Gujarat campaign—Akbarnama, 1573.

Detail from the battle scene with boats on the Ganga, 1565. Akbar expanded his navy, and ships were armed with forward firing guns and swivel guns.

LORD OF THE STORM

In Fatehpur Sikri it was the beginning of the monsoon season when an urgent summons arrived from Munim Khan in Bihar, requesting assistance in quelling the rising ambition of Daud Khan Afghan. Akbar decided that together with 'the princes and a few of the ladies and the cream of the courtiers', a river expedition down the Yamuna for the royal retinue would be organized while the army marched alongside on land. By 15 June 1574, a large fleet of boats was readied for the royal party. The two largest boats had enormous carved prows, one in the shape of a lion, and one in the shape of a crocodile. Even 'gardens, such as clever craftsmen could not make on land' were constructed on some of the boats for the pleasure of the harem while the 'bows of every one of those water-houses were made in the shape of animals so as to astonish spectators'. Two bull elephants, Bal Sundar and Saman, were also to be a part of the river fleet, each in his own boat along with two female elephants. Bal Sundar was a particularly beloved imperial elephant, for he had 'the strength to pull down mountains and break the ranks of armies, but always retained perfect control of himself and obedience to his driver, never losing his judgment even in the height of mast'. These were supremely valued qualities, ones believed to be embodied in Akbar himself.

Akbar had given a huge boost to his navy's operations which in earlier times had consisted of a motley assembly of hastily requisitioned crafts, discarded after every season. Now the navy had been rationalized and expanded, and accepted any 'experienced seamen acquainted with the tides, the depths of the ocean, the time when the several winds blow' and the imperial sailor was urged to be 'hale and strong, a good swimmer, kind hearted, hard-working, capable of bearing fatigue and patient'. The ports of Gujarat and, soon, Bengal, would give the Mughals access to centres of ship-building with their proximity to forests rich in teak and sundari, native woods which would prove much more durable than European oak and pine. Most Mughal warships, because they were primarily used in river and coastal operations, were smaller and not as heavily armed as the European ships. They usually carried four to eight forward-firing guns and a number of smaller swivel guns in addition to oversized muskets and rockets.

In 1574, Akbar was accompanied on the river by a small party of his best officers, both Hindu and Muslim, including Raja Bhagwant Das, Man Singh, Birbal, Shahbaz Khan, and Qasim Khan, the mir bahr (admiral). When the party was finally ready to sail, the very face of the river was hidden by the huge number of boats. Banners were hoisted up the creaking masts as the clouds skidded across the sky and the monsoon winds began to gust. As the boats set sail, the watching fishermen let out such loud shouts and ululations that 'the birds of the air and the fish of the water were well-nigh made to dance'.

The boats headed down the Yamuna towards Prayag and every day Akbar would call a halt for hunting and in the evening they would cast anchor and the party would be entertained by poetry recitations, singers, and other entertainments. Heroic deeds were recalled, musicians sang and banquets may have included Akbar's favourite fruits—melons, grapes, and pomegranates which he enjoyed eating along with opium and wine. The mangoes cultivated in Hindustan were always the soft pulp variety, which would be squeezed in the hand and the pulp sucked out. (The Portuguese, needing firmer mangoes that could be cut for the table for consumption in Europe, had begun experimenting with grafts in Goa and had developed a new, fragrant, and firm variety which they named the Alphonso, in honour of Alfonso de Albuquerque, the man who had conquered Goa in 1510.) In the enchantment of these wind-swept evenings, Akbar was sometimes moved to tears by the touching pathos of the stories recited by the qissa-khwans.

Every day the storms grew fiercer and the boats struggled in the strong rain and the sudden wind. Many boats sank near Etawah and eleven more were lost at Ilahabas near Prayag, and the naqqar khana (orchestra) was damaged and nearly lost. Badauni noted about Prayag that this was where 'the waters of the Ganga and Jumna unite. The infidels consider this a holy place and, with a desire to obtain the rewards which are promised in their creed...they submit themselves to all kinds of tortures'. Ralph Fitch, the English traveller, was equally bewildered and only marginally more sympathetic when he wrote that there were 'many beggars in these countries which go naked, and the people make great account of them'. He wrote of naked sadhus with long beards, matted hair, and monstrous nails. 'There are many tigers,' he also noted, 'and many partridges and turtle doves and much other fowl.' For Akbar, this ancient site of pilgrimage and devotion was deeply moving, and he began the construction of a great fort here. 'For a long time, His Majesty's desire was to found a great city in the town of Piyag,' agreed Abu'l Fazl, 'where the rivers Ganges and Jamna join, which is regarded by the people of India with great reverence and which is a place of pilgrimage for the ascetics of the country and to build a choice fort there.'

From Prayag the fleet sailed down the Ganga, broad as an ocean. 'Here is [a] great store of fish of sundry sorts,' wrote Ralph Fitch, making the very same journey a few years later, 'and of wild fowl, as of swans, geese, cranes and many other things. The country is very fruitful and populous.' But by the time the Mughal fleet arrived at Benares, after sailing for twenty-six days, the waves were crashing against the boats as the coir ropes groaned against the wind. Many chose to disembark at this point, undone by the violence of the storms. After staying three days in Benares, the Mughal fleet sailed on and anchored near Sayyidpur, where the land army joined them. The harem and the princes were dispatched to Jaunpur and now as the fleet sailed down the Ganga towards Patna, the army kept pace on land and in the evening camped opposite the anchorage of the royal boats.

Akbar disembarked one day to ride one of his royal elephants, Mubarak Qadam, and through sheets of rain he plunged the elephant into the foaming water of the Ganga, now miles wide because of the torrential rain, followed by 500 elephants and their riders. All the camp followers were astounded at this powerful demonstration of the Padshah's authority over the elements themselves. The message sent out to those who would dream of rebellion was equally clear. Every evening Akbar stopped to hunt with his cheetahs, keeping the machinery of war and empire running efficiently and smoothly at the same time. At Hajipur, the Mughal troops were joined by

Munim Khan and it was decided to first capture this town because it supplied Patna and the rebellious Afghans. Akbar dispatched 'into the midst of the raging stream 3000 fully equipped horsemen in boats with such ornamentation and display, that at the sight of it the eye was rejoiced...[and the boats were] filled with all store and munitions necessary for taking the fortress of Hajipur'. The fort was taken despite strong resistance and the heads of the Afghan leaders killed in the battle were brought by boat to Akbar who forwarded them to Daud Khan, a wordless intimation of the fate that awaited him, if he persisted in his resistance.

Munim Khan invited the Padshah to come to Patna and organized a noisome reception, designed to intimidate the enemy. Akbar sent a fleet of boats bearing cannons and gunners and 'the noise, the smoke and the concussion shook the earth and the neighbourhood... became dark... The horrific noise wound its way into the brains of the darkened foe and their gall-bladders became water.' Daud Khan almost immediately sued for peace but this was an option that Akbar was well placed to refuse. He offered, instead, to fight Daud Khan in single combat, with arms of his choice. He also offered to send a strong warrior against a chosen man of Daud Khan's and, as a last resort, suggested that they could send an elephant from each side to fight the other. But perhaps sensing that he was in the presence of an unstoppable force of nature, Daud Khan demurred and chose to flee.

Once again, Akbar had performed the unthinkable. He had brought an enormous army, with elephants and horsemen and cannons and gunpowder, by river through the worst of the monsoon storms right across the empire. He had planned his march with meticulous precision, controlling the movements and the lives of thousands of men and animals, on land and on the water, in the scouring rain, with seamless power. Patna was taken without a fight and enormous treasure fell to the Mughal army. 'Though he had 20,000 horsemen and fierce war elephants without number,' wrote a sneering Badauni, present among the troops on land, '[Daud] fled shaking with terror.' Indeed, Daud Khan was believed to have possessed an enormous army of 40,000 cavalry, an infantry of 1,50,000, thousands of elephants and guns, in addition to a respectable number of war boats.

Bihar was described admiringly by Abu'l Fazl as a province in which 'agriculture flourishes in a high degree.' Rice, especially, was of the highest quality and quantity, while there was also sugarcane, an important cash crop. Paper was produced, precious stones from foreign shores were traded, gilded glass was manufactured and there were also some more whimsical specialities—parrots were in abundance as well as Barbary goats, who were fattened to such an extent that they had to be carried around on litters.

Akbar now assembled a large army at Patna and entrusted its command to Munim Khan who was appointed Governor, while Raja Todar Mal and Ram Das Kachhwaha were appointed diwan and naib diwan, with instructions to pursue Daud Khan and subjugate Bengal. On the road back to Jaunpur, Akbar was very annoyed when a precious elephant drowned at Chausa and severely punished the officer in charge, Sadiq Khan. Sadiq Khan's jagir was confiscated, he was excluded from attendance at court, and was told to find another good elephant to replace the lost one. Sadiq Khan responded with panache to the order, returning in two years' time with 100 elephants and was immediately restored to favour.*

Akbar then returned to Jaunpur where he met with the harem and his sons and spent a pleasant month of ease and rest. Akbar, like all the Mughal emperors before and after him, took his harem with him everywhere he went, on military campaigns, and on hunts and other excursions. The presence of these women was often crucial in maintaining his political networks through the information they collected from their politically powerful relatives and agents. The harem was also a place of refuge and safety for the Padshah. When he was ill, or wounded, it was the women who tended to him, their lives intricately tied up in his safety and well-being. In the month that they spent in Jaunpur, there would have been a great deal for them to see and do, for Jaunpur was a thriving city and though no longer a capital city of the sultanate, a local trader listed it as having fifty-two bazaars, fifty-two wholesale markets, and fifty-two caravanserais as testimony to its vibrancy and size.

As the Padshah and his retinue were making their leisurely way back to the capital, Akbar called for Badauni at Kannauj and gave

---

*Considered one of Akbar's best officers, Sadiq Khan was made a high mansab of 5,000 and appointed Governor of Shahpur.

him a book called the *Singhasan Battisi* (32 Tales of the Throne) a collection of moral tales about the legendary Vikramaditya, King of Malwa. 'I received his Majesty's instructions,' wrote Badauni, 'to make a translation of it in prose and verse. I was to begin the work at once, and present a leaf of my work on that very day.' Akbar appointed a Brahmin to translate and interpret the Sanskrit verses for Badauni, who set to work immediately and read out the first section in Persian that very evening. The completed book was called *Namah-i Khirad-Afza* and it became part of the imperial library. Akbar had gauged in Badauni the talent to be an excellent translator, a much more talented scholar than he ever was a warrior.

Akbar went on to Delhi, to offer thanks at the Sufi shrines there. He now received the glorious news of Munim Khan having chased Daud Khan all the way to the Afghan capital of Tanda, which was relinquished without a struggle, and Bengal was won. The Mughal party then headed towards Ajmer where, some 20 kilometres outside the city, Akbar dismounted and walked on foot to Hazrat Khwaja's dargah. He presented Daud Khan's kettledrums, which became part of the dargah's naqqara khana, and every day while the Padshah remained, 'seances for dancing and sufism took place'. In the cool winter evenings, the qawwals sang their songs of ecstatic love, accompanied by the syncopated claps of the accompanists, and gold coins glittering with starlight as they were flung over the singers. Finally, in January 1575, after an absence of seven months, during which he had 'done the work of many years in conquering new countries, administering the old', according to an admiring Abu'l Fazl, Akbar returned to Fatehpur Sikri.

THE MAN WHO SET THE WORLD ON FIRE

As the Mughal Empire grew dramatically during this period through Akbar's extensive military campaigns, the Padshah instituted precise administrative measures to bring these territories into the Mughal fold. Hindustan had long been an agricultural economy and, through the centuries, appropriation of agricultural surplus was the primary means of revenue generation for the rulers. Under the Tughlaqs, and then under the Afghan Lodis especially, control over revenues of territory increasingly became hereditary, leading to a dangerous leavening of power bases, as had happened with Sulaiman Karrani Afghan and then his son, Daud Khan. After his return from the Bihar campaign, Akbar brought in a number of changes in the administration, some of which he had been working on previously, to centralize power and control the influence of his ever-widening nobility. It was at this stage that Akbar systematized the administration of the mansab, or number-rank, for every imperial officer, or 'man of the sword'. Instead of being given a salary with its attendant obligations in an arbitrary manner, officers now had a very specific place in a hierarchy of numerical ranks which determined the salary of the official and the number of horses that he was expected to maintain in case military duties arose. Thus, a mansabdar of 500 rank, for example, would have to maintain a force of 500 horses and he would be assigned a salary which would allow him to raise that force.* The salary could be given in cash but was usually in the form of a land revenue assignment, the jagir. The jagirs were assigned strictly for revenue collection and these were now regularly transferred. Neither the mansab rank nor the jagir land were hereditary, thereby encouraging personal loyalty to the Padshah, and not to any regional grouping or dispensation. While there were other aspects of the administration—the land-revenue system and the branding of animals—that were legacies of

---

*A mansabdar could be paid in cash, or by the assignment of a jagir, in which case he was also a jagirdar of that land. There was, therefore, a close correlation between jagirdars and mansabdars. If the mansabdar was paid in cash, then he could not also be called a jagirdar.

earlier dynasties, the mansab system was truly unique and, according to historian M. Athar Ali, 'an unrivalled device for organizing the ruling class'. 'These men were specialists,' according to historian Stephen P. Blake, 'devoting their lives to the arts of war.' The low ranking mansabdars, of 20-400, were vital to the Mughal army and filled 'minor posts in imperial, princely, or great amiri contingents'. Single cavalrymen and ahadis were the backbone of the army and received a decent salary of about 200 rupees a year. 'Theirs was an honourable profession in Mughal India,' writes Blake, 'and both ahadis and cavalrymen were respectable men in Muslim society.' The men holding ranks upto 500 were all called mansabdars while those from 500 to 2500 were called amirs and those from 2,500 and above were amir-e-azam.

Akbar had already divided his empire into subahs, sarkars, and mahals and he would now replicate exactly the entire administrative structure of one subah with another, so that they would be virtually identical from one end of the empire to the other. Because of the expense involved in maintaining the designated numbers of horses, elephants, and camels for a mansabdar, there was a temptation by officers to present animals that might not actually belong to them and receive pay for the non-existent animals. Some officers went to remarkable lengths to pass off 'borrowed' men and animals as their own, as described by Badauni:

> ...Amirs did as they pleased...[putting] most of their own servants and mounted attendants into soldiers' clothes, brought them to musters... Hence...a lot of low tradespeople, weavers and cotton-cleaners, carpenters, and green-grocers, both Hindu and Musulman...brought borrowed horses, got them branded, and were appointed to a command...and when a few days afterwards no trace was to be found of the imaginary horse and the visionary saddle, they had to perform their duties on foot.

So Akbar also introduced a system of dagh, or branding of horses, to prevent corruption in the muster of animals. All mansabdars were now required to brand their animals and present themselves to Akbar with the exact number of horses that corresponded to their numerical rank.

The mansabdari system was equally applied to Hindu chieftains, in a move that co-opted these men into the Mughal Empire and made them equally invested in its success. Under earlier sultans, Hindu chiefs were required to raise a peshkash, a payment of tribute, and to supply an army whenever required. This peshkash was usually raised by the chieftains by taxing their dependants, and could be debilitating for the peasantry. Now the chieftains were incorporated into the mansabdari system, being steadily promoted and gaining more honours as they provided loyal service to the Padshah, 'making loyalty more profitable than rebellion', according to historian Rima Hooja. The kingdoms of Rajasthan slowly became more peaceful, as Akbar condemned and discouraged the wars between states for expansionist purposes. The jagirs that the Rajput chieftains were awarded usually included the assessed revenue of their ancestral lands, the watan jagirs, while Akbar maintained the right to confirm each successive ruler in his domain. This granting of the coronation teeka by the Mughal Padshah was a powerful symbol, fracturing some of the old clan structures between the rulers and their clansmen. One of the famous instances of the Padshah confirming a besieged contender to rule was for his favourite, 'Mota Raja' Udai Singh of Marwar. Most of the time, however, Akbar rarely interfered in the Rajput succession process, the Mughal Empire profiting from the symbiotic relationship of the chieftains with their clansmen, who could raise strong armies from among their kinsmen. A great many Rajput chieftains would not only have exemplary careers, travelling the length and breadth of Hindustan, and thereby changing the very topography and culture of their home states, but would forge deep personal bonds of friendship with Akbar.

The administration of the kingdoms of Rajasthan would be profoundly influenced by their incorporation into the Mughal Empire. In Marwar, Raja Udai Singh was assisted in this task by his pradhan, or adviser, one Govind Das Bhati, 'who was fully conversant with Akbar's administrative system'. The office of diwan was instituted, and it was usually held by a member of the elite Mutsaddie group, from the Oswal Jain business community, and the diwan gradually became the most powerful officer of the state. There were also bakshis, or military commanders, kotwals, and a wakil, who was the state's representative at the Mughal court with the force of the Mughal Padshah behind him.

Another state which was transformed by its alliance with the Mughal Padshah was Bikaner. Bikaner had been peacefully incorporated into the empire, and a daughter of Raja Kalyanmal had married Akbar. Kalyanmal's son, Kuar Rai Singh, then proved his courage in battle during the Gujarat wars and when Mughal authority was resisted by Marwar's Rao Chandrasen and Mewar's Rana Pratap, Akbar assigned the administration of Jodhpur to Rai Singh. During the three years that Jodhpur remained under Rai Singh, 'various villages were endowed to Brahmans, Charans, and Bhats'. Upon the death of his father in 1574, Rai Singh was the first ruler of Bikaner to be given the title Maharaja. So widely and relentlessly did this formidable warrior travel to maintain order in the empire, from his home state in the desert to the high plateaus of Kabul and the forests of the Deccan, that it was said of him that 'his saddle is his throne'. Another favourite of Akbar's was Rai Singh's brother, Kuar Prithviraj, popularly called Peethal, who was not only an exceptional warrior, but also a flamboyant poet and scholar, and would become a beloved and much appreciated member of the Mughal court. Peethal and the Padshah also became brothers-in-law when two daughters of the Raja of Jaisalmer, Champa Dey and Nathi Bai, married Peethal and Akbar respectively.

The incorporation of Bikaner and other Rajasthani regions brought rich trade routes and market centres into the Mughal Empire. A dizzying variety of goods were traded through caravans including 'ivory, copper, dates, gum-arabic, borax, coconuts, silk, chintzes, muslin, shawls, sandalwood, camphor, dyes, drugs, spices, dried fruits, cumin seeds, dyed blankets, potash and salt'. Various transit taxes brought further riches into the empire's coffers. In western Rajasthan, merchandise was placed under the protection of Charan bards who, in courageous imitation of the Rajputs whose bravery they extolled, were willing to defend these goods to the death in an act of suicide known as performing chandi. Indeed, the killing of a Charan who was protecting a caravan was considered as heinous as killing a Brahmin, 'with all its post-life connotations of hell-fire and damnation'.

All these many changes that Akbar was bringing about were all meticulously recorded, the Padshah's every pronouncement noted down. For this, Akbar would have a group of scribes, fourteen in total, who were in attendance upon the Padshah, two at a time. The scribes had a kalam-daan (pen box), containing reed pens, an inkwell, sand, etc. At court, they sat cross-legged on the ground close to the Padshah with their reed pens at the ready, to note down his every order.

> All applications and documents presented to the court, and all orders and enquiries from the ruler, were written down by the particular scribe responsible, to be read out in court the following day. No imperial order could be executed without confirmation from the scribe that the case had been presented to the ruler as recorded. This confirmation then had to be recorded in the farman...the correct transcription of the farmans on the appropriate paper and with the designated seal could take days, even months.

This elaborate system made impetuous decisions much more difficult to make, and the scribes, for their part, took care not to accidentally step on the Padshah's shadow, a most boorish act.

The writing, sending, and receiving of these royal messages were elaborate tasks themselves, since it was the sacrosanct word of the Padshah or his family that was being conveyed. A command from the emperor himself was called a hukm*, while commands issued by the other members of the royal family were called nishans. The elaborate ways in which farmans were folded, the seals, the paper, were all part of the ritual of authority, meant to convey the imperial presence in absentia.

> The farman is folded so that both corners touch, then a paper knot is tied and then sealed in so that the contents are not visible. The sealing gum is made from the sap of kunar, bar, pipal and other trees which, like wax, becomes soft when warmed, but hardens when cold. After the farman has been sealed, it is placed in a golden envelope, for His Majesty regards the use of such external signs of greatness as a service to God.

---

*The word hukm is still used today in some states when addressing an erstwhile maharaja.

Nor could the recipient of such an exalted farman irreverently rip it open. He would have to halt before the messenger at a certain distance, in a suitably submissive manner, place the document upon his head, prostrate himself, and then give the messenger an apt reward for his service. A particular honour was when the Padshah might affix his fingerprint upon the document, as when he pardoned a Rajput chieftain for some misbehaviour.

While Akbar was bringing in these profound and long-lasting changes in Mughal administration, as we have seen, the Mughal forces under Munim Khan and Todar Mal in Bihar and Bengal had achieved stunning successes against the Afghan forces of Daud Khan. 'A tremendous battle took place,' wrote Badauni, 'when the elephants of Daud (all of which were fed on good grass and were madder than can be imagined) were put into motion.' In the Battle of Tukaroi, in southern Midnapur district, the eighty-year-old Chaghatai warlord, Munim Khan, fought with furious bravery, lashing out at Gujar Khan Afghan with a whip when he found his sword-bearer missing, and had to be carried out unconscious from the battlefield due to his many wounds. Fighting not only the enemy but also the unfamiliar, swampy terrain, and the faltering resolve of the Mughal troops, Munim Khan nonetheless rallied his forces and achieved a decisive victory. Daud Khan submitted, and in a specially constructed ceremonial tent, formally surrendered to Munim Khan. In an elaborately orchestrated ceremony Daud Khan, once Sultan of Bengal, untied his sword and set it aside while Munim Khan presented the Afghan with a Mughal sword, an embroidered belt, and a cloak purportedly worn by Akbar, thus 'incorporating' Daud Khan into the body of the emperor. Wearing the cloak and the sword, Daud Khan then turned his face to the faraway Mughal capital at Fatehpur Sikri and prostrated himself.

Despite the freighted symbology of Daud Khan's surrender, conditions on the ground in Bengal would remain explosive for decades:

> ...seizing the capital and possessing the land were two different matters. While Mun'im Khan and Raja Todar Mal...were in Tanda reorganizing the revenue administration of the newly conquered

province, thousands of Afghans melted into the forested Bengali hinterland, where for the next forty years they continued to hold out against the new regime. There they attracted a host of dissidents, including Muslim and Hindu zamindars, Portuguese renegades, and tribal chieftains, all of whom perceived the Chaghatai Turks from Upper India as foreigners and usurpers.

On a more prosaic note, to achieve victory, bribery had also been resorted to, bringing many of the Bengal noblemen over to the Mughal cause and diluting the power of the Bengal army. Raja Todar Mal had advocated the use of bribes, writing that 'the method to restrain the faction was to send money by one who was loyal and smooth-tongued'. Abu'l Fazl noted with satisfaction that this had 'quieted the slaves to gold'.

In Fatehpur Sikri his many victories and successes, dreams made reality, seemed to weigh on Akbar. So much had been obtained, seemingly effortlessly, in the past few years. Akbar had subdued Rajasthan, Gujarat, Bihar, and Bengal. He had scattered the Uzbeks, the mirzas, and the Afghans. He had wrought a huge empire into a cohesive unit. He had three golden sons, a glittering new capital, and he was only thirty-three years old. Always supremely confident of his purpose on earth, Akbar now wanted further confirmation of his divine mission. 'His Majesty spent whole nights in praising God,' wrote Badauni. 'He continually occupied himself in pronouncing Ya huwa (O God), and Ya hadi (O Guide) in which he was well versed.' Akbar isolated himself from the swirl and skitter of his court and would spend nights sitting on a stone slab in a quiet cell, gratitude filling his heart 'with his head bent over his chest, gathering the bliss of the early hours of dawn'. According to Badauni, Akbar had learnt that Sultan Sulaiman Karrani had been in the habit of praying every night in the company of religious men, and discussing matters of spirituality and philosophy with them, and so decided to build a separate hall in which to discuss the many questions that weighed on his soul and troubled his heart. 'Discourses on philosophy have such a charm for me that they distract me from all else,' he was to say later, 'and I forcibly restrain myself from listening to them, lest the necessary duties of the hour be neglected.' Akbar now ordered the building of an ibadat khana* at the site of the Mahdavi Abdullah Niyazi Sirhindi's old quarters 'consisting of four porticoes with separate seating arrangements for the nobles, sayyids, theologians (ulema) and the mystics'. Here Akbar began to hold weekly discussions on Thursday evenings when incense perfumed the air while the Padshah waited impatiently to offer gold coins to those who would dazzle with their arguments and articulate speech.

Also present at the meetings was Abu'l Fazl, now calling himself 'allami'. 'He is the man,' wrote Badauni bitterly, 'that set the world in flames.' But that was much later, after Badauni had been humiliated and repudiated by Akbar and cast out from the warm glow of the Padshah's attention. Of the two young men, it was initially Badauni who was the more intemperate and argumentative. When the two scholars happened to meet the orthodox jurist Abdullah Sultanpuri in 1572, it was Badauni who argued provocatively with him about the supposed heretical nature of a text, while Abu'l Fazl attempted discreetly to silence him. 'You have passed through a great danger,' Abu'l Fazl chided Badauni after the meeting, 'but (fortunately) he did not set himself to persecute you. Had he done so, who could have saved you?'

For now, however, both men, untethered and wandering, were looking to be saved from their many demons by this Padshah who promised new horizons and brighter futures. They were both given a mansab of 20 to begin with and thus these two old schoolmates were 'both baked in one kiln'. Abu'l Fazl, by Badauni's own admission, 'worked so strenuously at the dagh-u-mhali (branding) business that he managed by his intelligence and time-serving qualities to raise himself to a mansab of 2,000 and the dignity of a Wazir'. As for Badauni, he would be shackled by something much more intangible—his own obduracy and a certain fatal stubbornness. But in 1575, both the men were eager, interested participants in the discussions at the ibadat khana, proud of their massive erudition and keen to display their wit and sharply incisive thinking.

The most important members of the ulema at this time were Shaikh Abd un-Nabi, and Abdullah Sultanpuri. For a long while,

---

*The ibadat khana has been located by Syed Ali Nadeem Rezavi as the structure erroneously known as the Daftarkhana.

the young Padshah had been especially solicitous and respectful of the older theologian, Abd un-Nabi. Akbar would visit the sadr, and stand barefoot before him to listen to his lectures on the traditions of the Prophet. He would bring the sadr his shoes as an act of devotion and place them before the shaikh's feet. But most of these theologians, as pointed out by historian John F. Richards, 'were neither speculative intellectuals nor serious religious thinkers'. Abd un-Nabi, in particular, was abrasive and rude. On one occasion, when the Padshah presented himself on a Friday to listen to the sadr's lectures, Abd un-Nabi grew infuriated because Akbar was wearing yellow, considered to be against the sharia. The sadr furiously rebuked the Padshah and even threw his staff at him, offending him deeply. The distressed young Padshah did not react but later went to complain to his mother, Hamida Banu, about the appalling behaviour of the sadr. Abd un-Nabi also took satisfaction in humiliating the great amirs of the court. He would sit down after midday prayers, wash his hands and feet and, while carrying out his ablutions, spit on the faces and clothes of assembled courtiers, feigning inadvertence. Moreover, though the office of the sadr was that of the highest religious dignitary in the land, it was attached to other duties, such as the distribution of royal charities, making the position open to corruption. Even Badauni admitted that the shaikh had become insufferably arrogant in his habits, dealing with people in an 'infamous manner', because of the power he commanded as sadr towards those who came asking for patronage. As for Abdullah Sultanpuri, it was discovered that he too was corrupt and avoided paying the obligatory charitable tax on property by transferring his assets to his wife's name every year when the time for tax inspection came around. Moreover, these two men were 'at loggerheads with each other, and had been responsible for the fall of people's faith in the scholars, past and present, amounting to a disinclination towards the Religion itself'.

It was not surprising, therefore, that Akbar found the tenor of the discussions in the ibadat khana initially very disappointing. 'A horrid noise and confusion ensued,' admitted Badauni, as the ulema started arguing with one another. Akbar angrily told Badauni to inform him of any ulema 'who talks nonsense and cannot behave themselves, and I shall make him leave the hall'. Badauni whispered to Asaf Khan, sitting next to him, that if he were to obey the Padshah, most of the ulema would have to leave. Akbar, who insisted on hearing what Badauni had said, was much amused by this remark and merrily repeated it to those around him. But the crass aggression and vicious, low manner of the ulema continued to disappoint Akbar. On one occasion, Haji Ibrahim of Sirhind declared that the wearing of red and yellow clothes, usually reserved for women, should be allowed for everyone, upon which Sayyid Muhammad, the chief qazi (judge), grew incensed with rage, abused Haji Ibrahim in Akbar's presence, and 'called him an accursed wretch, abused him, and lifted up his stick to strike him'.

One of the very first issues discussed in the ibadat khana was the number of freeborn women a man was allowed to marry by way of nikah. When Akbar was told that the Prophet had limited such marriages to four, he is said to have remarked that 'in our youth we had not felt bound by this rule, and whatever number of freeborn women and concubines we wanted we have collected. What should be done now?' Furthermore, 'in justice to his wives... he wanted to know what remedy the law provided for his case', because he had not kept to the legal number permitted. That this was a matter that troubled Akbar is not surprising. In the convulsion of empire formation, Akbar had married a large number of women: Timurid princess, Rajput rajkumaris, Afghan noblewomen and more. From Monserrate's estimate of 300 women to Abu'l Fazl's fulsome description of 5,000 women in the harem, these large numbers were meant to reflect Akbar's munificence and splendour. Even a cursory examination of the quarters at Fatehpur Sikri make these excessive numbers entirely unrealistic and, moreover, of all the women in the harem, most were not sexually available to the Padshah. They included his aunts, his stepmothers, his Timurid relatives, and the retinues that accompanied the wives—their entourage of childhood friends, singers, cooks, masseuses, tailors etc. Even so, Akbar had far exceeded the stipulated number of wives permitted by the sharia when he was using marital connections to stabilize his empire and now sought to remedy the situation. After much discussion, it was agreed that, according to the Shia custom of mut'ah* marriage, a man

---

*A temporary marriage that unites a man and woman as husband and wife for a limited time.

may marry any number of wives. Shaikh Abd un-Nabi, who seemed to prevaricate upon this matter, earned Akbar's sharp displeasure and finally the Padshah appointed a new qazi, the Shia Qazi Maliki, more amenable to his particular matrimonial problems, who decreed that Akbar's mut'ah marriages were legal.

From these discussions at the ibadat khana it was clear that Akbar was concerned with the legality of the status of his wives and his own standing in the eyes of God and in society. There is a sense of Akbar struggling to right the wrongs committed during the vagaries of his youth and of accepting his own fallibility. This was quite in contrast to the views of an orthodox man like Shaikh Ahmad Sirhindi,* for example, who believed that Islamic laws regarding marriage and concubinage were there expressly to protect men's enjoyment of women. The four wives, the instrument of divorce, the provision for nikah marriage, were primarily to allow men as many sexual liberties as possible. For Shaikh Sirhindi, women's views were quite inconsequential for they were naqis ul-aql, without intellect.

Another theologian whose fall was imminent was Abdullah Sultanpuri, the makhdum ul-Mulk. When the discussions had started at the ibadat khana, Akbar had summoned him 'in order to annoy him' and pitted him against the precocious Abu'l Fazl. Sensing the winds of change, and following the lead of Akbar, who would keep interrupting Abdullah Sultanpuri, the other courtiers also interjected to ridicule the theologian so that he soon became, according to Badauni, a living example of the Koranic warning—'and some of you shall have life prolonged to a miserable age'. Badauni also believed that 'from this day forward the road to opposition and differences in opinion lay open, and remained so, till Akbar was appointed Mujtahid of the Empire'. This mood of sharp-edged bonhomie seems to have extended to the court, too, for Badauni narrates an incident in which Deb Chand Rajah Manjholah caused great amusement among the courtiers by jokingly suggesting that Allah had a great respect for cows since that animal is mentioned in the first chapter of the Koran.†

There were other signs of a change in the texture of the court at

---

*An Indian Sunni theologian of the Naqshbandi order. He would later join Akbar's court as a junior member, and would become a vocal critic of Akbar's 'heretical' practices.
†The Sura of the Heifer.

Fatehpur Sikri. Attracted by Akbar's new capital, its dazzling wealth, and the climate of religious and cultural experimentation, learned and talented men from less accommodating regimes in the Muslim world began drifting to Fatehpur Sikri. Hakim Abul Fath, Hakim Humam, and Hakim Nuruddin were three brothers who had had to flee the increasingly intolerant rule of Shah Tahmasp. The shah had seized Gilan and tortured and murdered their father, who had served as sadr of Gilan. These brothers had acquired training in medicine from Persia which was, at the time, famous for its tutor-based model of medical education. The brothers now came to Fatehpur Sikri where Abu'l Fazl remarked of Hakim Abul Fath that he was 'specially remarkable for his tact, his knowledge of the world and for his power to read the lines of forehead'. Even Badauni admitted that his manners 'were exceedingly winning' and that he became an intimate friend of the Padshah, though he grumbled that this was because 'he flattered him openly, adapted himself to every change in the religious ideas of His Majesty, or even went in advance of them'.

As the philosophical debates continued in the ibadat khana, the men alternatively exalted and furious, in the haramsara a discussion of a different sort had been occupying the women for many months, and would result in a journey that would take a large number of the women very far from the safe confines of their sandstone city and away from the 'proper order' that Abu'l Fazl yearned for the women of the harem.

THE HARAMSARA AND THE HAJJ

When Abu'l Fazl would write his magisterial biography of Akbar a few years later, he would strive very hard to justify all the earlier foibles of Akbar—his transgressions, his vulnerabilities, and his inconsistencies explained away by an enduring 'veil' behind which he hid his true, divinely inspired nature, to be revealed only after he had thus tested those around him. And if the Padshah, the army, and the empire had to be ordered and tabulated, then so did the much more capricious institution of the harem. In earlier, more capacious, times, the harem was not so separated from the men, and in Kabul, as testified by Gulbadan, 'the women were not veiled, they rode, went on picnics, followed shikar, practiced archery'. It was from the time that Fatehpur Sikri was built, and Abu'l Fazl conjured up a perfect, secluded space, that the women of the Mughal Empire became much more invisible, assigned for the first time to quarters separate and apart. When they were written about at all, as we have seen, which was only very rarely, they were now all 'pillars of chastity' and 'cupolas of chastity'. And, yet, despite the very considerable effort expended by Abu'l Fazl, there were times when that veil was rent aside, when the shadowy, insubstantial presence of the Mughal women grew dense and full of purpose. One of the most extraordinary instances of the women of the Mughal harem stepping far beyond their designated cloistered space was the royal women's hajj of 1575.

Royal women had gone on the hajj before, and we have noted Bega Begum's journey in the previous decade, but the royal hajj of 1575 differed in the scale of the enterprise, the number of women involved, and the elaborate arrangements made for them. According to Abu'l Fazl, Gulbadan had 'long ago made a vow to visit the holy places' and now that the Portuguese 'had become submissive and obedient', performing the hajj pilgrimage had become a reality. Apart from Gulbadan, the large party included two daughters of Kamran, Sultanam Begum, the wife of Askari who had looked after the child Akbar when he had been held hostage by his uncles, a granddaughter and a stepdaughter of Gulbadan, a widow of Babur, three dependents of Humayun (about one of whom we know the charming detail that she 'sang in the moonlight on the road to Lagham in 1549') and Salima Sultan Begum, widow of Bairam Khan and wife of Akbar.

Apart from Salima Sultan Begum, who was the only wife of the Padshah to be included, these were all senior Mughal women, enormously respected by Akbar. They carried with them the Timurid legacy of journeying from the time of Babur and Humayun. It is a testimony to the respect and influence these women commanded that Akbar allowed them to make the pilgrimage, for the hajj was a dangerous and unpredictable journey. There was the risk of piracy, of shipwreck, of abduction, of drowning, as well as the many dangers of travelling in the Holy Lands themselves. In fact, this party of women would be delayed for a year at Surat while the Portuguese prevaricated with the cartaz, they would flounder off the coast of Aden on the way back, and be marooned for a year while they waited for a ship to rescue them. They would bring back from the Holy Lands tales of many exciting adventures, the satisfaction of bestowing largesse on the devout that was so ostentatious that they were chastised by the Ottoman authorities themselves, and also the confidence of pious Muslim women who had completed the hajj. When they returned to Fatehpur Sikri, they would make the stay of the Jesuit priests untenable.

It is generally believed that the women's hajj was organized and headed by Gulbadan, the irrepressible and beloved aunt of Akbar's who had endured so many reversals as she followed in the wake of her father and brother, Padshahs of Hindustan. Akbar, too, was no doubt eager to sponsor the hajj, a visible and opulent symbol for a Muslim ruler to display. Akbar 'sent with her [Gulbadan] a large amount of money and goods' and indeed he 'poured into the lap of each the money that they wanted and so made the burden of their desires light'. He enlarged the pious trust (waqf), which had been set up by the last Sultan of Gujarat to send the revenues of a number of coastal villages as donations to the Holy Lands. Several thousand robes of honour and enormous sums of money for charity were also sent by Akbar with the party. Akbar sponsored the building of a hospice in Mecca and from 1575 onwards would send a hajj caravan under a special Mughal officer known as the mir hajj every year from Hindustan, rivalling the great hajj caravans of Egypt and Syria and threatening the very power of the Ottoman Sultan, whose sole prerogative it was to arrange for these caravans. 'A general permission was given to the people' agreed Badauni, 'so that at great public expense, with gold and goods and rich presents, the Emperor sent them on a pilgrimage to Makkah.' It is possible that as incendiary talks began in the intimacy of the ibadat khana, Akbar also wished to reassure his more orthodox populace of his being a true Muslim monarch. At the same time, Akbar was sending an emissary to Goa armed with money and gifts, always keen to learn about 'the curiosities and rarities' of different places, with instructions to bring back 'the wonderful productions' that the Portuguese may have brought with them to Goa.

The women, meanwhile, were sent off in a magnificent cavalcade and orders were sent to 'the great Amirs, the officers of every territory, the guardians of the passes, the watchmen of the borders, the river-police, and the harbour-masters' to make the journey of this chosen party as smooth as possible. The only senior Timurid woman not to be included in this party was Hamida Banu Begum, who remained at Fatehpur Sikri to keep vigil over her son, the Padshah.

That there was still considerable apprehension about the trouble the Portuguese might cause for the ladies at Surat can be inferred from the fact that Qulich Khan, the Governor of Surat, was deputed to attend to them there. Qulich Khan was familiar with Portuguese dealings and was not reassured when he reached the port city. Moosvi has examined a farman which showed that following Qulich Khan's appraisal, Akbar was 'unnerved, and wrote to his "Esteemed Mother"...to consider her journey to Surat as equivalent to hajj and defer the voyage at least for a year. He openly expressed his fear for a blow to the honour of the Imperial Family, and his own great pain, if something happened to the party at the hands of the Portuguese.' But Gulbadan and the ladies had not come so far on the journey of their lives to be put off by fear of the loathed 'firangis' and a cartaz was finally obtained.

While the hajj party was at Surat, they would have received sad news of the death of an old ally of the harem from the days of the early forays into Hindustan. One of their number, Bibi Saruqad, was now widowed, for Munim Khan khankhanan had just died, far from his home and his family, in Bengal. 'He rendered his account to the guardian of Paradise,' was Badauni's truculent assessment, 'or to the guardian of Hell (God knows!)'. After the surrender of Daud Khan, Munim Khan had made the disastrous decision to shift the seat of the government from Tanda to the ancient city of Gaur. But the river Ganga had changed her course and now the rushing river had become a stagnant, maleficent backwater which bred diseases, like nightmares. 'The thought of death took hold of everyone,' wrote Abu'l Fazl as thousands of Mughal troops and villagers died of disease. 'Things came to such a pass that the living were unable to bury the dead,' agreed Badauni, 'and threw them head foremost into the river.' The elderly warlord Munim Khan died, too, undone, in the end, not by any flashing sword or betraying clansman but by the plague, noxious and invisible. According to historian Eaton, this catastrophic plague occurring right at the beginning of Mughal inroads into Bengal, 'contributed to the stereotype, soon accepted throughout the imperial service, that Bengal was a hostile and foreign land'.

As the Mughal women prepared to board the great hajj ships, the *Salimi* and the *Ilahi*, either built or bought by Akbar in the three years since Gujarat was taken, Akbar sent Khan Jahan and Raja Todar Mal to Bengal, to deal with Daud Khan who, with Munim Khan now dead, was once again flirting with the idea of rebellion. In the lavish rain of the monsoon of 1576, Daud Khan Afghan was finally defeated. His horse got trapped in the sliding mud and he was captured. Apparently, Khan Jahan hesitated to behead him as per imperial orders 'for he was a very handsome man'. The deed was done, however, and his head, stuffed and perfumed, was sent to the emperor while his trunk was gibbeted at Tanda.

Once in the Holy Lands, the Mughal ladies, having travelled far away from the gaunt topography of their lives at Fatehpur Sikri, were determined to participate fully in all that this great occasion had to offer. These widows and daughters of Babur could reclaim those earlier, less constrained, times when they had wandered in the wake of their peripatetic husbands and brothers across the country. In the next few years, the women would participate in the communal aspect of the hajj and would distribute the extravagant wealth that Akbar had provided for the occasion—six lakh rupees and many robes of honour as gifts. This wealth was so ostentatious that it would cause a sharp reaction from the Ottoman authorities. Between 1578 and 1580 five documents were sent from Sultan Murad III, the Ottoman sultan, to the authorities at Mecca, complaining about the extended stay of the Mughal ladies and the 'anti-Sharia' activities indulged in by them. They railed against the overcrowding of the Holy Cities due to the enormous retinues of the ladies and the large number of pilgrims attracted by their largesse. The sultan further gave instructions to the Sharif of Mecca to encourage them to leave the Holy Lands as soon as they had completed the pilgrimages and even prohibited the distribution of the alms sent by Akbar in the Haram Sharif. It would appear that Gulbadan and her Mughal party's largesse, which challenged the Ottoman authorities' prestige, in addition to the hustling crowds attracted by them, made Sultan Murad III keen to be rid of the Hindustani pilgrims. The royal ladies would finally depart from Mecca in 1580, much against their wishes, and return to Hindustan, bringing back mementos and curiosities, Arab servants, and a lifetime of memories of ecstatic passions and cacophonous celebrations.

At Fatehpur Sikri, meanwhile, the women of the harem continued their involvement with more domestic duties in increasingly guarded spaces. 'Several chaste women have been appointed as darogahs and superintendents over each section,' noted Abu'l Fazl primly, about the women in the harem, who were moreover guarded by 'sober and active women, the most trustworthy of them placed about the apartments of his Majesty'. While the inside of the palaces were guarded by strong women called the urdubegis,* the outside was guarded by eunuchs; the next outer perimeter was guarded by Rajputs, and then there were the porters at the gates and, on all four sides, squads of Ahadis. The women were assigned salaries, 'sufficiently liberal, not counting the presents, which his Majesty

---

*The urdubegis were a class of women, often Turki or Abyssinian, robust and trained in the use of bows and arrows and daggers, to protect the women within the harem and when they travelled outside the harem.

most generously bestows'. The salaries ranged from Rs 1,610 per month to the most senior women to Rs 20 to the servants.

The Rajput women, too, when they married and left their homes, were given jagirs called hath kharach jagir (personal expenses land) which they administered directly through their own officers, thus maintaining some financial independence, vital in a polygamous society. An important wedding organized at this time was the marriage of Abdur Rahim, eighteen years old now, to a daughter of Jiji Anaga, Mah Banu Begum. This was an important alliance for the young nobleman, and it brought him the considerable influence of the Ataka Khail, and also made him the brother-in-law of the temperamental but talented and powerful Mirza Aziz Koka. Akbar now gave Abdur Rahim the title 'khan', usually only reserved for princes of the blood, and henceforth always addressed him as 'Mirza Khan'.

It was at this time that Aziz Koka, in his long and tumultuous career, temporarily fell from favour. Akbar's orders regarding the branding of animals was resented by the old Central Asian nobility, who saw in this system of inspection a further curbing of their power. Aziz, it was felt, had grumbled rather too openly at the branding order. 'Everything that he knew about these things,' wrote Badauni about Aziz's criticism of branding, 'he mentioned with unqualified disapprobation.' Akbar 'could not endure this unpleasant plain-speaking' and Aziz was removed from his post as Governor of Gujarat and temporarily confined to his garden quarters in Agra.

With Aziz Koka and his intemperate criticisms dealt with, Akbar and the entire city of Fatehpur Sikri got ready to receive a visitor who brought with him all the nostalgia of the Timurid homeland—Mirza Sulaiman of Badakhshan*. After a long career spent skirmishing at the edge of the Hindustani empire in Badakhshan and Kabul, this old warlord from the time of Babur himself had been brought low by his own grandson who, in fine Timurid tradition, was planning to assassinate him. Keen to demonstrate Mughal resplendence to this scion of the Timurids, Akbar organized a magnificent display of Hindustani splendour. Five hundred elephants were lined up for 10

---

*It will be recalled that this Timurid cousin had been given the fief of Badakhshan upon the death of Babur.

miles from the great gates of Fatehpur Sikri, 'adorned with European velvet and embroidered fabric from Constantinople' and 'with chains of gold and of silver'. There were also fine, shimmying Arabian and Persian horses wearing golden saddles and, between every pair of elephants, there was a cart containing a velvet-eyed cheetah wearing a collar of gold and sitting on a carpet of embroidered gold. Raja Bhagwant Das, Governor of Lahore, accompanied the visitor to court and Akbar himself rode out several miles to greet the mirza. When they came face to face, Akbar dismounted and walked up to the mirza to embrace him and to prevent the old man from prostrating himself.

The palaces at Fatehpur Sikri were decorated with rich carpets, golden vessels, and tents of gold cloth, and when the young princes were presented to the elderly exiled ruler, Mirza Sulaiman was delighted and took them into his lap and kissed their cheeks. Old Chaghatai customs were hurriedly revived to impress the mirza. 'They spread royal tables in the audience-hall,' wrote Badauni, 'and the officers of high grade gathered the soldiers together, and took to themselves the trouble of arranging the customary food.' Qandahari noted that 'bejewelled and golden plates, big bowls, made of Chinaware, sugar pots and countless other delicious dishes were served'. 'But when the Mirza departed,' Badauni sniffed contemptuously, 'all these [revived customs] departed too.' Clearly these old Turki–Chaghatai customs and foods were now present only as a memory, used as potent symbols when required, and then pragmatically set aside. Akbar's changing nobility no longer justified the perfect remembrance of Chaghatai customs. This was especially so because in 1576 it was not the old Timurid mirzas who were posing a threat to Akbar but a lone Rajput chieftain who was preparing to battle the Padshah of Hindustan on a field of gold, and carve for himself a place in the long and glittering scrolls of Rajput braves.

THE SAFFRON FIELDS

On a warm spring day in 1576, Akbar brought Kuar Man Singh to Khwaja Muinuddin Chishti's tomb at Ajmer and, in the sanctified precinct of the saint's grave, surrounded by the murmuring of the praying pilgrims, wisps of incense, and the charged atmosphere of more than three centuries of benedictions, presented the young Rajput prince with a robe of honour and sent him to war. For what was to become one of the most contested battles between the Mughal Empire and a Rajput king, one whose legacy would reverberate into the twenty-first century, was in fact fought between two Rajput leaders and it would be most extravagantly glorified by a British chronicler and an agent of the British Empire, Colonel James Tod.

By 1576, large swathes of Rajasthan including Amer, Bikaner, Jaisalmer, and Sirohi, had become part of the Mughal Empire through a mix of military force and marriage alliances. But Mewar was a land with a particularly blood-drenched past in which the fires of jauhar had smouldered on three separate occasions. This was a land of uncompromising valour in which the honour of the Sisodiya clan was deeply, violently invested in the chastity of its women. When Rana Pratap ascended the gaddi of Mewar in 1572 upon the death of his father, Udai Singh, substantial parts of Mewar, including Chittor and Mandalgarh, were already part of the Mughal Empire. In fact, Rana Pratap's half-brother Jagmal, favourite of their father, Udai Singh, was an honoured jagirdar in Akbar's empire. Akbar had also tried on at least three separate occasions to persuade Rana Pratap to integrate into the empire with honour, sending Kuar Man Singh, Raja Bhagwant Das, and Raja Todar Mal to parley with him. According to historian Rima Hooja, during one of these attempts, Rana Pratap had contemplated compromise. He put on the imperial robe forwarded to him by Akbar and sent his eldest son Amar along with Bhagwant Das to wait upon the Padshah. He baulked, however, at the idea of going in person to the Mughal court and negotiations broke down. For Rana Pratap there would now be a complete rejection not only of the Mughal Empire but also of those Rajputs who had 'polluted' their pure blood by marrying daughters to the Mughals. There were also signs that the rana never did seriously entertain the idea of submission to the Mughals, for he had done much to strengthen defences in the territories he controlled. He guarded his southern border rigorously, improved fortifications in the Aravalli ranges, and ensured amicable relations with the local Bhil tribes. He also induced the farmers of the fertile plains around Chittor and Mandalgarh to relocate, leaving the plains barren and desolate: the farmers were told to settle in inaccessible hilly areas. He ensured his orders were carried out with 'unrelenting severity', according to James Tod. It was said that when a poor goatherd dared to bring his animals to pasture in the plains, he was killed, and his body hung up to serve as a warning to others. According to folklore, Rana Pratap took vows of austerity, to use no gold and silver dishes, nor sleep in soft beds, until Chittor was won.

In 1576, having subdued some especially resistant opponents like the mirzas and the Afghans, Akbar finally decided to send an army against the rana in his stronghold at Gogunda. Appointing the young Man Singh to head the Mughal army against Rana Pratap was a perfectly poised balancing act. Akbar not only demonstrated his complete confidence in his Kachhwaha relatives but gambled wisely that his Rajput troops, who may have fought with less than total ardour against a greatly respected Rajput foe, would now be galvanized by a Kachhwaha chieftain. Akbar was also rewarding Man Singh's personal qualities of courage, able generalship, and resourcefulness. Along with Man Singh, Akbar also appointed some reputed Mughal generals, such as Asaf Khan, the mir bakshi, Ghazi Khan Badakshi, and Shah Ghazi Khan, to lead the army. That not all the Mughal courtiers shared Akbar's foresight and meritocratic pragmatism can be seen in the reaction of one Naqib Khan, when Badauni begged him to have him enrolled in the army. 'If a Hindu had not been the leader of the army,' Naqib Khan assured Badauni, trying to dissuade him, 'I should myself have been the first to have asked permission to join it.' The presence of the cerebral Badauni among the Mughal troops was itself surprising. Badauni had not exactly covered himself with glory up to this point and may have been trying to redeem himself as he was still in 1576 eager to rise in the Padshah's court. He had been sullen about his mansab of 20, had been unable to carry out his branding duties, and had requested a jagir of land in lieu of a military rank. Akbar at this stage of his rule, was quite rigid about mansabdars maintaining the actual number of cavalrymen assigned to them according to their rank. Badauni would have been obliged to produce the 20 cavalrymen expected of him as a mansabdar of 20. In time, as men were found unable, or unwilling, to supply the actual number of horses and men, Akbar would institute the double rank system (sawar and zat). But for Badauni, at this time, asking for a fixed salary was a mistake as promotions were much more certain for talented men by rising through the military ranks, protected from the interference of the clergy. Badauni was scrambling now to remedy his earlier foolish miscalculations. 'Why, he has just been appointed one of the court imams,' grumbled Akbar when presented with Badauni's request, 'how can he go?' Finally, Badauni persuaded Akbar that he wanted to 'dye his beard in blood' for the sake of the Padshah, apparently immune to the irony of fighting jihad under a Hindu general. On 3 April 1576, the Mughal army of 5,000 chosen men marched out from Ajmer to Gogunda.

While the Mughal army camped at Mandalgarh for two months, gathering their forces, Rana Pratap was at Gogunda calculating the Mughal strength and rallying his men. It is estimated that he had '3000 horsemen, 2000 infantry, 100 elephants and 100 miscellaneous men who served as drummers, trumpeters and pick-men'. The rana's warriors included Bhil tribesmen, forest dwellers who grew up stalking prey on silent footsteps and learning the spiky topography of the Mewar landscape while hunting deer, wild boars, hyenas, jackals, hares, and bears with their bows and arrows. The rana moved the bulk of his men to the village of Khamnor, at the entrance of a narrow, ravine-like pass called Haldighati with shifting sands the colour of turmeric gold. According to James Tod, 'above and below, the Rajputs were posted, and on the cliffs and pinnacles overlooking the field of battle the faithful aborigines, the Bhils with their natural weapon, the bow and arrow, and huge stones ready to roll upon the combatant enemy'.

On a blazing day in June, Rana Pratap decided to launch an attack when he saw the Mughal forces dragging their great artillery guns across the river Banas, depleted after the relentless summer. In retaliation, Man Singh sent an advance guard of 900 skirmishers under Syed Hashim Baraha who, it was said, fought with determined gallantry. The Sayyids of Baraha were a group that had been traditionally considered somewhat rustic and boorish but who were courted and greatly valued by Akbar, who gave them the coveted and honoured position in the Mughal vanguard. Jahangir would describe them later as 'the bravest men of their time'. Skirmishers or shamsherbaz (gladiators), were specialized troops in the Mughal army, elite infantry companies who fought with 'a variety of exotic weapons like two-handed swords, halberds, and massive war clubs'. These men also carried shields, sometimes so large that they covered the body entirely. The vanguard of the rana, led by Hakim Sur Pathan, then attacked the Mughal cavalry led by Raja Jagannath and Asaf Khan. The Mughal horses struggled on the sharp, broken ground as the armies clashed. Just as Raja Jagannath was in danger of being killed, the Mughal vanguard arrived, led by Man Singh on a war elephant. Ever more warriors streamed out of the ravines and the gullies, with slashing blades and screaming fire.

Rana Pratap's left wing was led with great courage by Raja Ram Shah of Gwalior who died that day on the blood-soaked battlefield, flanked by his three sons, all of whom laid down their lives for the rana. The opposing right wing of the Mughals was led by Ghazi Khan Badakshi and Rai Loonkarn along with a number of shaikhzadas from Sikri. As the sun rose inexorably higher on this churning ochre battlefield, Mughal scimitars and Persian shamshirs clashed with straight Rajput talwars and broadswords. The horses whirled and whinnied in their armour, sweat darkening their heated bodies. The foot soldiers swung their maces and battleaxes and thrust their katars at each other. Most dangerous of all were the mounted archers of the Mughals, who were deadly in close combat. They could fire the composite bow at full gallop or swing a sword or throw a lance and were 'arguably the most formidable individual warrior on any battlefield', according to Andrew de la Garza. At one point, the Rajputs on the Mughal side got so hopelessly entangled with the

Mewar warriors that Badauni shouted out to Asaf Khan under the molten sun: 'How are we in these circumstances to distinguish between friendly and hostile Rajputs?' To which Asaf Khan joyfully yelled back, '[T]hey will experience the whiz of the arrows, be what may. On whichever side they may be killed it will be a gain to Islam.'

Elephants on both sides also joined the battle, trumpeting loudly and swinging their sharpened tusks. But there was an even deadlier aspect to the war elephants of the Mughals. Akbar had understood the need for smaller, easily portable guns and the most ingenious artillery developed was the chaturnal, or so-called 'camel gun'. This was a swivel gun attached by a harness to the side of a camel or elephant, where it could be operated by a gunner and fired in any direction. The larger of these weapons could fire 'lead shots the size of baseballs' and a contingent of camel gunners, unique to the Indian battlefield, could create deadly chaos by moving with great speed to any point on the battlefield. Both sides were pushed beyond endurance in the merciless summer sun because of which 'the very brain boiled in the cranium'. Disarray and confusion began overtaking the Mughal side. That was when Mihtar Khan, commanding the rear, beat his war drums and shouted out to the Mughal soldiers that the Padshah himself was coming so that 'this shout of his was to a great extent the cause of the fugitives taking heart again and making a stand'. So galvanizing was the thought of the Padshah that Man Singh's Rajput bodyguard rallied once more around their young leader and Badauni wonderingly noted that 'a Hindu wields the sword of Islam'. Exhausted by the relentless sun, and suddenly demoralized, the rana's men lost heart and the battle was won for the Mughals while Rana Pratap, 'despite fighting very bravely and getting many wounds', was persuaded by his men to leave the battlefield. 'The Rana turned and fled,' wrote Badauni rather more curtly, and 'betook himself to the high mountains...and there sought to shut himself up as in a fortress.'

In the blinding sun the Mughals counted their dead, some 120 men, while another 300 were wounded. Of the Rana's men, 380 lay dead on the 'Field of Blood', the Rati-Talai. The Mughal army encamped at Gogunda, having first barricaded the streets and dug a protective trench. No effort was made to pursue or capture the rana, and though the Mughal army was exhausted, it is generally believed that Man Singh was not keen to further humiliate or disgrace the rana. He even forbade the ravaging and looting of the rana's territory, which would have been standard practice at the time. The Mughal army lacked for food and grain and was reduced to eating 'the flesh of animals and the mango-fruit', which soon made them ill. Badauni was sent back to Fatehpur Sikri with the rana's special elephant, Ram Prasad, to give an account of the battle to Akbar. When Badauni told the Padshah the name of the elephant, Akbar announced that, 'since all this [success] has been brought about through the Pir, its name henceforth shall be Pir Prasad'. Akbar was considerably less pleased with Man Singh's clear reluctance to capture or kill the rana. While the other great generals like Ghazi Khan Badakshi, Mihtar Khan, Ali Murad Uzbek, and a few others, were all summoned to court and honoured, Man Singh and Asaf Khan were not. Akbar's irritation was fleeting, however, and Man Singh was received at court in late September 1576. However, the following year, when Shahbaz Khan Kamboh was appointed commander of the Mewar expedition to capture Rana Pratap, 'he sent back both Bhagwant Das and Man Singh on the ground that as "they were zamindars there might be delay in inflicting retribution on that vain disturber [Pratap]"'. Though Man Singh would go on to have a long and glorious career as a Mughal commander, he would never be sent to campaign in Rajasthan again.

Rana Pratap would go on to evade successive Mughal efforts to capture him for more than twenty years. He would lose all his great strongholds over the next few years and would be reduced to living in the Aravalli hills, in the village of Chavand, sheltered by the Bhil tribesmen. By maintaining a ceaseless campaign of guerrilla warfare and ravaging Mughal territories, Rana Pratap managed to recover some of his Mewar lands though the fabled fort of Chittor was forever forfeit. The rana's absolute refusal to come to terms with Akbar and envision peace with honour can appear baffling. After all, the rana would not have been interfered with in any way that would have affected his religion and honour for, as noted by historian A. L. Srivastava and quoted by Rima Hooja, 'there was no danger to Hinduism or the Hindu way of life from Akbar, who respected religious beliefs and susceptibilities of all classes of people and more specifically those of his Rajput allies and vassals'. Nor would the rana's land and people have suffered. On the contrary, while other Rajput kingdoms like Amer, Bikaner, and Jaisalmer had prospered through Mughal contact, evolving art and architecture in new and vibrant ways, Mewar stagnated, its fields ravaged and despoiled through decades of neglect following the rana's scorched earth policy. Perhaps the rana's actions were determined in his boyhood itself when, in the gloaming of a Rajasthani evening, as the lamps were lit and jackals howled in the distance, the Rajput families were told stories of their ancestors by the Charans—stories of impossible bravery and incandescent destinies, of purity of blood, and resistance at all costs. When those ancestors included the indomitable Rana Sangha and Lord Ram himself, as the Rajput genealogies were reconfigured to include mythical heroes, then the destinies of the boys were likely preordained. In the end, perhaps, it was about the very definition of the word honour—who wielded it and who claimed it.

In an epic poem, written by the Charan poet Durasa Adha called the *Gita Ranaji Pratapasimhaji Ro*, the poet praises the rana 'for preserving the dharma of the earth and the dharma of ksatriyas... other rulers bowed their head at the Emperor Akbar's court; the Rana however refused to hear the sounds of the kalamam (kalima), he only heard the sounds of the veda-purana. The heroic warrior refused to worship at a mosque, he only worshipped at a temple.' These lines demonstrate the poet's robust knowledge of the way in which Mewar patrons viewed themselves. However, he also wrote poems in praise of Man Singh, and of Akbar himself.

After Rana Pratap died in 1597 his son, Amar Singh, would survive as a guerrilla chieftain in the hills before finally surrendering to Khurram, Jahangir's son, in 1615. He would be treated with great courtesy by Jahangir and never made to attend the Mughal court or offer a daughter in marriage. Both his son, Karan Singh, and grandson, Jagat Singh, would attend the Mughal court and would consequently lose precedence amongst the ranas of Mewar for doing so.

As the decades and the centuries passed, this one battle, this lone Rajput, came to symbolize a great deal of collective nostalgia and yearning, reflecting a shifting attitude to Mughal rule. In an early chronicle, Amrit Rai's *Mancarit*, written to eulogize Man Singh's great achievement, the poet writes that 'the Rana was defeated in battle, having put his foot on the shoulder of death'. He celebrates Man Singh's exemplary military service, when he took up the paan offered by Akbar, thereby stepping up to the challenge of fighting for the Padshah.

> All became the dependents of our master emperor Akbar
> Those who did not touch his feet passed their days in fear.

Amrit Rai does not mention the inconvenient matter of the rana not being captured by Man Singh, nor the fact that the Kachhwaha chieftain did not allow the plundering of the rana's lands, these subtleties of conflicting loyalties and pragmatic solutions escaping the poet's recording. But later narratives were not so understanding of Mughal–Rajput alliances. More than 200 years later, at the dawn of a new century, and in the service of a new empire, a young Scotsman and soldier in the East India Company (EIC) grew enamoured with the stories of Rajput martial valour. Bringing with him his own notions of European chivalry and feudalism, of knights fighting the Ottoman Turks, James Tod constructed a history that focused largely on Mewar, and only on the Rajputs, to the exclusion of all other Rajasthani peoples. In highly charged language he spoke of Mewar's resistance to Mughal power, its 'settled repugnance...to sully the purity of its blood', and castigating all the other clans who had 'degraded' themselves. Forgotten was the fact that Rajput clans had long fought each other, and that women had committed sati and jauhar in the face of opposing Rajputs, as had happened when the Bhati Rajputs had committed saka and jauhar when attacked by the Panwar Rajputs. Obliterated was the memory of the Rajput clans offering daughters to Akbar as a show of fealty, of the Mughal Padshah taking part in Hindu rituals involved in the marriages. Now these were recast as brutal acts of coercion, of an emperor ruthlessly carrying out his desires, subjugating the Rajput peoples to his violent will.

Meanwhile, in 1576, as Rana Pratap parsed his lonely but immortal destiny as a Rajput hero, Akbar was seeding the night with light in Fatehpur Sikri and arming his empire with grace.

A LIGHT DIVINE

When the Great Comet of 1577 shimmered in the night sky over Hindustan in November of that year, it caused much consternation. Grain would be expensive, astrologers warned, but far worse was feared, and when news arrived of the death of Shah Tahmasp of Persia, and the murder of his son and heir, Ismail, at the hands of his own sister, Pari Khanim, then the extent of the maleficent influence of the celestial visitor was well understood. There were those at court who took a more flippant view of the comet and when a courtier, the Wazir Shah Mansur, 'took to wearing a long tail to the back of his turban, they dubbed him "The Star with a Tail".'

There were a great many unusual arrivals at court in this cosmically charged year, from strange and exotic places. Badauni described the arrival of the distinguished Persian Nuqtavi thinker, the Sharif of Amul, a man he uncharitably claimed had 'betrayed the filthiness of his disposition' and had therefore been dispatched from the Deccan, where he had been 'set on a donkey and shown about the city in disgrace'. The Nuqtavis were a millennial creed who based their knowledge on astrological theories and the science of alphabetical letters. Blaming the distressingly tolerant nature of Akbar's court, which welcomed such heretical thinkers, Badauni noted bitterly that 'since Hindustan is a wide place, where there is an open field for all licentiousness, and no one interferes with another's business, so that every one can do just as he please', the sharif had been able to make his way to the Mughal court. The sharif was 'ridiculous in his exterior, ugly in shape, with his neck stooping forward', and his deceitful blue eyes betrayed the falsehood and hypocrisy of his nature, according to Badauni. Jahangir, too, who wrote about him in his memoir was circumspect about the scholar. 'During my exalted father's time,' wrote Jahangir musingly, 'he left his dervish garb of poverty and attained the rank of Amir and commander.'

Akbar, however, enjoyed many animated personal interviews with the visitor, who explained to the Mughal Padshah the tenets of the Nuqtavis, even as Akbar continued to offer namaaz five times a day. Hakim Ain ul-Mulk Shirazi, who had led the delegation to the Deccan, returned with elephants, other presents, and perhaps some startling news about the Shah of Bijapur. Ali Adil Shah II had recently brought back Shiism to his state, turning away from what had become an intolerant Sunni Islamic rule* and now promoted a simpler, more mystical kingship. He 'dressed plainly...forbade the slaughter of animals at his court...held religious discussions with Hindus, and Muslims as well as Jesuits'.

Refugees from the increasingly repressive regime in Persia also began arriving at the Mughal court. One family in particular arrived in 1578 with not a great deal besides their personal talent and ambition. Ghiyas Beg was, at the time, just another nobleman fallen on hard times but he brought with him his daughter, the baby Mehr un-Nisa, who would have a remarkable destiny. She would become the most famous woman of the Mughal Empire—Noor Jahan. Another party that returned in the course of the year was an embassy that had been sent to Goa with strict instructions to bring back any European curiosities and crafts that might be of interest to Akbar. This resulted in a cacophonous procession returning to Fatehpur Sikri because the objects deemed curious included some European individuals, some Indians dressed in European clothes and playing the drums and the clarion, a man carrying an organ 'like a great box the size of a man, played by a European sitting inside', and other assorted items of interest.

Another most unorthodox event occurred when Akbar, while hunting in the vicinity of Palam outside Delhi, decided to spend the night in the house of the headman of the village, one Bhura. Bartoli, the Italian writer and historiographer, had noted that Akbar was 'great with the great: lowly with the lowly'. With his boundless curiosity about human nature, Akbar would maintain till the end of his life a charismatic ability to communicate with all kinds of people, and he would take every opportunity to live alongside them,

---

*Ali Adil Shah's predecessor, Ibrahim Adil Shah I, a Sunni, became infamous for his particularly intolerant and cruel rule. He dismissed all his Shia aristocrats and, according to Manu Pillai (see *Rebel Sultans*), indulged in a two-month reign of terror, assassinating Hindus and Muslim officials of rank.

for a fleeting instance, or for a lifetime, as when he quarried stone, painted pictures, graded his matchlocks, slept in huts, and talked to his animal-keepers.

Akbar and the court too were in a state of flux as the Padshah had just moved the imperial camp to the Punjab. Here, in special consultation with Raja Todar Mal and Khwaja Shah Mansur, Akbar made a number of important decisions, one of which concerned the royal mint. Until then, the various mints had been in the charge of minor officials called chaudhuris. Now overall control would be delegated to a responsible 'Master of the Mint' and Akbar chose Abd al-Samad, the painter from Shiraz who had given him his childhood lessons in painting, as the first official to hold this title. The very same day Akbar gave the order for the striking of square rupees. The purity of the metal used, the fullness of the weight of the coins, and the artistic execution of Akbar's varied coinage was exceptional and unmatched in the world, far superior to what was being manufactured under Queen Elizabeth I in England, for example. A great deal of the silver used in these coins came from the mines of Mexico, plundered by Spain and taken back to Europe, where merchants in England and the Netherlands would use it to buy commodities in Hindustan. Between 1586 and 1605, a staggering 185 metric tons of silver a year from overseas would pour into the Mughal heartland to become silver rupees. The influx of this silver, which made it possible to mint the coins, meant that this standard coinage would soon replace the copper-and-gold billon* and cowrie shells that were being used as currency in various parts of the country.

On the personal front, Akbar had some minor emotional issues to deal with because of his great Kayasth minister, Todar Mal. A diligent, sombre, and brilliant man, Todar Mal was one of the most accomplished examples of Akbar's 'men of the sword and men of the pen' system, a man who shone both as a warrior and an administrator. Though 'unique of the age for practical wisdom and trustworthiness', admitted Abu'l Fazl, the raja was 'at the head of mortals for superstition and bigotry'. Abu'l Fazl's disdain is clear when he notes that the raja would not begin his day before worshipping his little idols 'after a thousand fashions'. Now in the turmoil of

---

*An alloy of a precious metal with a majority base metal content.

moving, those precious idols were lost and the raja was heartbroken, neither sleeping nor eating in his grief. Whereas Abu'l Fazl was uncomprehending, speaking of his 'heartfelt folly', and calling him a 'simpleton', Akbar was a great deal more compassionate, tending to his friend and hard-working minister and consoling him for his loss till the raja recovered.

The year had been momentous for Badauni too. At the age of nearly forty, he had received the thrilling news that he had had a son, 'a happiness which I had been long anxiously expecting'. Badauni immediately went to the emperor and asked him to name the child, which he did, naming him Abdul Hadi, 'Hadi being a name which at that time was day and night upon his lips'. Hadi was, indeed, a common Sufi word and a Shiite term for God while Badauni was a declared Sunni. One of the imams of the court in fact urged Badauni not to use the name and 'commit this folly', but Badauni did not follow the advice, showing him to be, at this stage at least, not such a recalcitrant, orthodox Sunni as it was later believed. Then Badauni asked for five months leave, 'on account of certain important affairs, or rather follies', and during that time, tragically, Badauni's son died. Badauni would hold the emperor responsible for this dreadful calamity and would not return to court for a whole year. For Akbar, this was an unpardonable lapse in duty in a courtier and Badauni acknowledged this saying the Padshah 'took no further notice of me'. From here on, despair in his heart, Badauni could only watch as his old schoolmate, Abu'l Fazl, climbed inexorably through the ranks at court while he languished, ignored and ridiculed.

After their sojourn in the Punjab, Akbar and the court returned to Fatehpur Sikri where Faizi, who had by now been honoured with the title 'King of Poets', greeted the Padshah with a charming couplet:

> The breeze that cheers the heart comes from Fathpur
> For my King returns from a distant journey

In Fatehpur Sikri the ulema seemed not to have anticipated the undercurrents rippling below the smooth sandstone pathways of the palaces and courtyards. They had perhaps not understood that for the Timurids, the Islamic sharia was never as binding a force as it was in other Islamic kingdoms and that there remained the companionable presence of Chenghiz Khan's yassa laws, and their pre-Islamic guiding spirits. The yassa advised the ruler 'to consider all sects as one and not to distinguish one from another'. Shaikh Ahmad Sirhindi raged that 'every evil that appeared in those days...was due to the wickedness of these evil ulema who have been a menace to mankind and to the word of God'. Abd un-Nabi especially, because of Akbar's earlier devotion and his own obdurate arrogance, was about to make a grave error of judgement.

The qazi of Mathura came to the sadr with a complaint one day because some materials that he had gathered in Mathura for the construction of a mosque had been forcibly requisitioned by a Brahmin and used to build a temple. When the qazi had protested, the Brahmin had used offensive language against Prophet Muhammad. Akbar sent Abu'l Fazl and Birbal to investigate the matter and they found that the blasphemy had, indeed, been uttered. With the Brahmin taken into custody, the matter of the punishment to be given to the offender was debated. 'The ladies of the imperial harem busied themselves in interceding for his release,' we are told, and we can well imagine Harkha Bai of Kachhwaha, with her clan connection to the temples of Mathura, using her influence to free the Brahmin. Akbar, however, would not yet commit to directly opposing Abd un-Nabi, who wanted to execute the Brahmin, and so the Padshah said 'punishments for offences against the holy law are in the hands of you, the ulema: what do you require of me?' The sadr then peremptorily ordered the execution of the priest. Thereupon, pandemonium, we are told by Badauni, ensued both inside the harem, because of the ladies, and outside the harem, because of the Hindu courtiers.

So furious and baffled was Akbar by the decision of Abd un-Nabi that he called for a discussion that very night around the Anuptalao water tank at Fatehpur Sikri. All the jurists agreed that the Brahmin's transgression had not called for such an extreme punishment and that there was an 'obligation to safeguard infidel subjects' by Muslim rulers. Badauni, too, agreed that, in case of doubt, clemency was to be preferred but then, inexplicably, began to argue that the sadr, being a very learned man, must have had his reasons to act as he did. He argued so long that 'the Emperor's moustache now bristled like the whiskers of a tiger', and all the courtiers present hissed at him to stop.

In the flickering light of the candles, the Padshah's eyes blazed and he clenched his fists as his increasingly rare temper suddenly erupted. 'What you say is nonsense,' thundered Akbar at last and Badauni had no further option but to bow out of the assembly. Badauni, it seems, was hopelessly shackled by his need to display his erudition and contradict the apparently acquiescent jurists. 'From this time onwards,' wrote Badauni, 'the fortunes of Shaikh Abd un-Nabi began to decline', as, indeed, did those of Badauni himself.

In the year 1578, Akbar continued to tour the empire and to organize hunts wherever he went. These hunts, wrote Qandahari, 'not only created hysteria in the hearts and minds of his companions, but unleashed a wave of terror among all beasts and birds of that region'. As we have noted, the hunts were a supremely effective display of Akbar's power and were an opportunity for the Padshah to assess the loyalty of the various chieftains of the empire. In the summer of 1578 Akbar ordered a qumargha to be organized in the vicinity of Bhera, in the Punjab. Over a span of ten days the great nobles of the empire were stationed around the qumargha ring while the beaters drove in animals and birds from miles around. But just as all the arrangements were completed, the birds and animals huddled in the centre, and as Akbar prepared to gallop into the circle of fire, his gleaming sword thirsty for blood, something completely inexplicable happened. 'A divine flash of light was received by His Majesty' wrote Abu'l Fazl. 'The Divine Call had descended on the Emperor which tranced him completely', agreed Qandahari. 'A strange state and strong frenzy came upon the Emperor,' added Badauni 'and an extraordinary change was manifested in his manner…' Akbar put down his sword and ordered that not a single finch be harmed and thousands of animals were released from the qumargha. From these accounts it would seem that Akbar was overcome by a state of grace, and for a while was even tempted to abandon the affairs of the world. Badauni wrote the following couplet to describe this baffling episode:

> Take care! For the grace of God comes suddenly,
> It comes suddenly, it comes to the minds of the wise

Akbar then sat 'at the foot of a tree that was then in fruit, he distributed much gold to the faqirs and poor, and laid the foundation of a lofty building, and an extensive garden at that place'. He cut off his hair, 'which was long and beautiful and entrancing' and which he had started early in his reign to wear long because of 'an inclination towards the sincerely loyal Indians'. Some of the courtiers present immediately cut off their long hair too. That there was disquiet and bafflement around this ecstatic episode is clear from the fact that, soon after, Hamida Banu Begum arrived at the imperial camp from Fatehpur Sikri. Akbar was delighted and sent Salim and the nobles in advance to greet her and then he rode out himself and 'made the reverence to his visible God (his mother), an act of worship of the true Creator'. The ceaseless vigilance of the harem and of Hamida Banu over the Padshah was made clear by this visit which was unusual enough to be noted by both Abu'l Fazl and Badauni. That Hamida Banu would have been troubled by news of Akbar laying down his arms, and even his authority, was understandable. She knew of her son's steely ambition as well as his restless spirituality. She would have remembered earlier moments of unease, beginning at the age of fifteen. She would have come, perhaps, to remind him of his duty to his people and to his ancestors, and that renunciation was impossible for a Padshah of Hindustan.

In any case, Akbar returned very soon to the task of ruling his empire, enquiring into the land grants made to holy men, and dealing with the various demands on his time. He met with the leading Portuguese merchant from Bengal, one Pietro Tavers, renamed Partab Tar Feringi by Abu'l Fazl, and his wife Leorna who were, we are assured, 'amazed at the laudable qualities of the sovereign'; because of their 'good sense and propriety of conduct' Akbar, too, was pleased with them. But while affairs of state continued, Akbar also sent a message to Fatehpur Sikri to fill the Anuptalao tank to the brim with silver and bronze coins to be distributed to the deserving and the wise. It would take a full three years to empty the tank of its coins and, in that time, the tenor of the wise men and the merit of the deserving would have changed the fabric of Mughal thought forever.

◆

In 1578, a fleet of three vessels set sail from Lisbon, carrying a blessed and exalted cargo. Travelling in the uneasy company of Christian relics, including the bones of one Saint Boniface, was a group of missionaries. Of the fourteen missionaries on the ships one would die of poison at the hands of the 'pagan Japanese', one was decapitated by 'the natives' of the island of Java, and a third man, twenty-eight-year-old Rudolf Acquaviva, landed in Goa on 13 September, after years of austerity and grief and penance, and knelt to kiss the Indian soil in joy and gratitude. A year later, a great deal of commotion was created by the arrival in Goa of an ambassador from a most unexpected source—the Mughal court. The envoy, Abdullah, carried a letter from Akbar which read: 'To the chief Padre, in the name of the Lord. I am sending Abdullah...with the request that you will send me two learned Fathers, and the books of the Law, especially the Gospel, that I may know the Law and its excellence. For I desire to know it.... And the Fathers may be sure that I shall receive them most courteously, and entertain them most handsomely. When I have learnt the Law sufficiently to appreciate its excellence, then may they depart at their pleasure, with an escort and honoured with abundant rewards.' These words filled the Jesuits with almost uncontrollable joy and as for Acquaviva in particular, 'I should like to describe the pleasure, nay the inordinate delight', wrote the Jesuit Monserrate, 'with which Rudolf received this commission...as though it were a direct divine command'. This summons brought within reach a most precious object—the soul of the Mughal Padshah. The emperor, it was believed, was 'weary of the contradictions and absurdity of the Mullahs, the "Scribes" of Moslem law' and informed about the Christian faith by Pietro Tavers, the Portuguese officer now in his employ in Bengal, was eager to learn more about their religion.

The Jesuits were arriving in Hindustan in the sixteenth century as the Portuguese crown sought to strengthen their presence in foreign lands. Papal bulls published by the Catholic Church between 1452 and 1606 'permitted the King of Portugal the sole right to sail the sea, to conquer the new lands and extend his dominion at the expense of the Moors and other pagans'. The King of Portugal thus had monopoly over commerce in these regions over other European nations with the threat of excommunication against those who disobeyed. In return, the Portuguese state would construct churches and supply them with priests and protection and thus the Portuguese state and the Catholic

Church were bound in an uneasy alliance which had brought the Society of Jesus to the city of Goa.

When Akbar had returned to Fatehpur Sikri after his ecstatic vision of 1578, he had entered into the debates of the ibadat khana with renewed enthusiasm and energy. But to his desolation and bemusement the debates between the mullahs and theologians again descended into vile abuse. 'The antagonism of the sects reached such a pitch,' revealed a disappointed Badauni, 'that they would call one another fools and heretics.' The attacks became personal with Abdullah Sultanpuri accusing Abd un-Nabi of being undutiful towards his father, as well as afflicted with hemorrhoids, while Abd un-Nabi's response was to call him a fool. Severely disappointed with the arrogance of the theologians, men he had once been in thrall to, Akbar now put forward before them an articulate, erudite, and driven young man, who would have burned with the sharp memory of his father's humiliation and debasement at the hands of these very men. 'The Emperor,' agreed Badauni, 'expected to find in Abu'l Fazl a man capable of teaching the Mullahs a lesson.' These men had hounded Shaikh Mubarak mercilessly for twenty years and had even tried to have him executed. In an earlier time they had succeeded in having Shaikh Alai, a friend of Shaikh Mubarak, flogged and tortured to death under Islam Shah Sur on charges of being a Mahdavi. Now Abu'l Fazl, using his wit and his wide erudition, could expose the ulema for the opinionated, opportunistic, and corrupt men that they were. However, when he did as expected, Badauni lamented that Abu'l Fazl indeed 'took every opportunity of reviling in the most shameful way' the sadr and the makhdum ul-mulk, Abdullah Sultanpuri, because of which 'miseries and misfortunes broke in upon the ulema'. When these men were brought low, Abu'l Fazl was wont to quote the following quatrain, which he claimed applied to them perfectly:

> I have set fire to my barn with my own hands,
> As I am the incendiary, how can I complain of my enemy!
> No one is my enemy but myself
> Woe is me! I have torn my garment with my own hands.

Badauni further mentioned an occasion in which, troubled, he asked Abu'l Fazl, about his need to argue about the various tenets of Islam:

'For which of these notorious heresies have you yourself the greatest inclination?' To which Abu'l Fazl smiled and replied nonchalantly, 'I wish to wander for a few days in the vale of infidelity for sport.' Abu'l Fazl then 'fell boldly into disputation in religious matters with such imbecile old men as the Sadr, the Qazi, the Hakim-ul Mulk and Makhdum-ul Mulk, and had not the slightest hesitation in putting them to shame, at which the Emperor was pleased'. So roundly humiliated were the theologians that they wrote to Abu'l Fazl privately, in bafflement: 'Why are you always falling foul of us?' Abu'l Fazl answered flippantly, implying that he was just sensing the winds of change and following them. And so the theologians, supposedly the highest upholders of Islamic law, were shown to be mediocre philosophers and base men. 'His Majesty was genuinely seeking after the Truth,' admitted Badauni but because of these discussions 'doubts had been planted in his mind so that within five or six years Islam had all but disappeared.'

Disappointed by the sheer number of contradictory traditions and decrees held as infallible by the different orthodox Sunni theologians, Akbar invited proponents of the other sects of Islam, such as the Shias and the Mahdavis* to the ibadat khana. But here again the men became irrevocably entrenched in their various beliefs, to the extent of abusing the others' cherished holy figures and heroes. Even the Prophet and his companions were not spared and the discussions once again descended into recriminations and accusations. In October 1578 Akbar finally decided to invite scholars and thinkers from outside the Islamic fold to join in the discussions. 'Sufi, philosopher, orator, jurist, Sunni, Shia, Brahman, Jati, Sevra (Jain monks), Charbak, Nazarene, Jew, Savi, Zoroastrian and others enjoyed exquisite pleasure,' wrote Abu'l Fazl, 'by beholding the calmness of the assembly... The treasures of secrets were opened out without fear of hostile seekers after battle.'

An early Christian visitor to the Mughal court was Father Julian Pereira, who arrived in March 1578 at Akbar's invitation. Described as 'a man of more virtue than learning' he exposed the errors of Islam during discussions with the ulema, causing the agitated Akbar to jump up during the talks with loud shouts of, 'May God help me!

---

*A millennial sect.

May God help me!', so annoyed and upset was the Padshah at the mullahs' poor defence of Islam. Father Pereira taught Akbar a few words of Portuguese, one of which was the name of Jesus, which Akbar then took great pleasure in repeating aloud to himself in his palace.

It was in this spirit that Akbar's ambassador, Abdullah, was sent to the Jesuits in Goa where he was received by a number of Portuguese noblemen. Dressed in their finest robes and accompanied by a cavalcade of swishing horses, Abdullah was taken to the tomb of St Francis Xavier, a Catholic missionary and co-founder of the Society of Jesus, where the Mughal party removed their shoes respectfully and paid homage. A group of three Jesuits—Rudolf Acquaviva, the Spaniard Anthony Monserrate, and Henriques, a Muslim convert 'of great piety but of very slight learning', but fluent in Persian—was appointed to travel to the court of the 'Great Mogul'. 'I am writing to ask your prayers,' wrote Acquaviva earnestly to his uncle Father Claude Acquaviva, also a Jesuit. 'For we need greatly God's help, as we are being sent "like men appointed to death," into the midst of Muhammadans, whose word is always to be distrusted.' Nonetheless, Acquaviva reassured his uncle, 'we go...filled with a joy such as I have never felt before, because there is a chance of suffering something for Christ our Lord... And if we are to shed our blood for love of Him, a thing very possible in such an expedition, then shall we be truly blessed.' So with exaltation in their hearts and a Persian grammar book in their hands, the three Jesuits travelled to Fatehpur Sikri accompanied by an escort of twelve Mughal horsemen. They crossed plains 'covered with cactus, with palms, and banyan trees'. They travelled past mango trees in blossom, and fields of poppy, and flax, and noticed the frequent wells and stone tables built for the ease of pilgrims by Hindu citizens.

Travel, for the Hindu population, was an essential part of life. Pilgrimages were as much part of the texture of their lives as fasts, vows, and religious ceremonies. Very often, wealthy men from cities would send out invitations to their friends to join them on particularly redoubtable pilgrimages. The highways, though much more secure than earlier, could still be highly dangerous. Banarsi Das, a trader from Agra, once saved himself through his quick wit, pretending to be a Brahmin and reciting Sanskrit slokas and blessing the robbers so that they were either too ashamed or too fearful to rob the 'high caste' traveller. Akbar had begun making improvements to some of the major roads and highways and one in particular, the Agra-Ajmer road, was described by Badauni:

> A lofty college and high and spacious palaces were built on the road to Ajmer.... ...he ordered a palace to be built at every stage...and a pillar to be erected and a well sunk at every kos. Ever so many hundreds of thousands of stags' horns, which the Emperor had killed during the course of his life, were placed on these pillars as a memorial to the world.

While the Jesuits were making their weary journey from Goa, sixty-seven Jain monks from Gujarat, silent and barefoot, were preparing to leave for the Mughal court too. Elsewhere, Brahmins were gathering their few possessions as were Sufi monks, and aberrant, long-haired yogis, all preparing to head to Fatehpur Sikri because Akbar wanted to meet with the seekers of the sublime, the speakers of seductive truths. 'For a long time, it was the custom that the dull and superficial regarded the heartfelt words of holy souls as foolishness,' agreed Abu'l Fazl. 'They recognized wisdom nowhere but in the schools and did not know that acquired knowledge is for the most part stained with doubts and suspicions. Insight is that which without schooling illuminates the pure temple of the heart.'

This spirit of joyous enquiry was rare for the times. In England, a small nation of some four million people, Queen Elizabeth I had recently been excommunicated by the Pope after she had wrested the throne from her sister, Mary Tudor, who had been wont to burn 'heretics' at the stake, and came to be known as Bloody Mary. Under Elizabeth I, Catholics and Jesuits were those who were persecuted and Muslims, if they were acknowledged at all, were always 'Saracens', the crusading Arabs. In France, the Protestant Huguenots were waging war on the Catholics and had desecrated statues in the Gothic cathedral of Notre Dame in Paris. This was also Spain's century of conquest. In vast tracts of the Caribbean and South America they introduced a plundering mix of religion, disease, rapacity, and destruction. Meanwhile the three great empires that covered the

Dar al-Islam—the Ottomans, the Safavids and the Mughals—were crucibles of cultural creativity and cosmopolitan movement. Scholar Jerry Brotton, writing of an English soldier's first visit to Morocco at this time observed that coming from 'the monoglot world of England and Ireland and its stark religious divisions between Protestant and Catholic, the multi-confessional and polyglot world of Marrakesh... with its Berbers, Arabs, Sephardic Jews, Africans, Moriscos and Christians' would have come as a great shock.

In the sixteenth century in Fatehpur Sikri, there was a similar shearing of ideas and languages and influences between men and women from all over the Mughal Empire, 100-million strong at its peak,* and boasting thirty languages and seven religions, and from further still, from the Deccan, Persia, and from the shores of Christendom. In an equally cosmopolitan court, a new culture would be wrought which would travel, through its great courtiers, in syncopated rhythms, vernacular cadences, and jewel-bright colours, to all corners of the empire.

---

*W. H. Moreland's estimate; Shireen Moosvi's estimate is 130-140 million. Historians such as Sanjay Subrahmanyam and Ashok V. Desai consider this inflated.

PART 4

THE YEAR OF THE LION
{1579–1585}

~

PADSHAH-I ISLAM

The kites wheeling into the twisting thermals over Fatehpur Sikri in 1579 would have witnessed a highly unusual sight. Over the smooth red walls of the palace a charpoy was being slowly hoisted up, carrying a Brahmin, one Debi, a theologian and a scholar. The charpoy reached a balcony perched high on the fortress where the Padshah of Hindustan was sitting on a takht, leaning out to listen to the priest. A discussion was had, in which the Brahmin 'instructed [Akbar] in the secrets and legends of Hinduism, in the manner of worshipping idols, the fire, the sun and stars and of revering the chief gods of these unbelievers, such as Brahma, Mahadev, Bishn, Kishn, Ram and Mahama... His Majesty, on hearing further how much the people of the country prized their institutions, began to look upon them with affection.' The writer of these astounding words was Badauni, appalled witness to Akbar's increasing interest in different religions and alternative truths. Badauni also wrote that a Brahmin named Purushottam, a scholar and a translator, had been asked by Akbar to invent Sanskrit names for all things in existence. Abu'l Fazl, reflected more compassionately on Akbar's affection for his Hindu subjects when he wrote about the people of Hindustan in lyrical terms: 'Shall I describe the constancy of its inhabitants or record their benevolence of mind? Shall I portray the beauty that charms the heart or sing of purity unstained? The inhabitants of this land are religious, affectionate, hospitable, genial and frank. They are fond of scientific pursuits, inclined to austerity of life, seekers after justice, contented, industrious, capable in affairs, loyal, truthful and constant.'

Akbar had demonstrated for a long while his affinity and fondness for the people of Hindustan: his long hair, his careful etiquette, his love of Indian tales like the *Panchatantra* and *Singhasan Battisi*, his nurturing of Rajput and other Hindu noblemen, his elimination of discriminatory laws and practices were all manifestations of this fondness. Now, in October 1578, Akbar spoke openly in court of his great love for the people of 'Hind' and 'praised the truth-based nature of the people of India'.

If the manner of Akbar's enquiring into the tenets of Hinduism by suspending a Brahmin on a charpoy was altogether piquant and unusual, then there were a great many such scenes playing themselves out in Fatehpur Sikri at this time as Akbar's plastic, inquiring mind analysed everything of interest around him. When Hakim Ali Geelani, a Unani* physician of renown, arrived at the Mughal court from Persia, Akbar ordered several bottles containing the urine of healthy and sick people as well as that of cattle and asses to be presented to the hakim for the detection of disease. Fortunately for the physician, he was said to have diagnosed each one correctly and thereby became a valued and favourite courtier of Akbar. Badauni was somewhat less enthralled with the young Shia physician and he wrote that 'his excellence in acquired knowledge and especially the science of medicine is extreme...but he is a youth, self-opinionated and of limited experience.... It sometimes happens,' added Badauni with caustic wit, 'that a patient after taking one of his draughts speedily has a taste of the draught of extinction.'

Another experiment conducted around this time was prompted by the arrival at court of a man with no ears, just a flap of skin where the ears would have been. But even without ears, the man could hear everything around him provoking considerable amazement. Akbar wanted to understand if there might be a 'natural language', a zuban-i-qudrut, which would be spoken even if it wasn't heard and learnt through childhood. He then ordered that twenty infants be placed in a specially constructed sarai and attended to by wet nurses and attendants who were told strictly never to talk to their charges. As Fatehpur Sikri resonated with the many languages of the numerous itinerant visitors, in 'Gung Mahal',† as it was popularly known, the infants grew up in hushed and disconcerting silence. A few years later Akbar rode past the Gung Mahal again, and stopped by to visit the children. They communicated only in grunts and gestures and no

---

*Traditional Islamic medicine developed and refined after studying the systems of the ancient Greek physicians. Largely spread through the efforts of the tenth-century Muslim physician and scholar, Ibn Sina, more popularly known as Avicenna.
†House of the Deaf.

natural language, concluded the Padshah, had spontaneously evolved in the silence that surrounded them.

In the ibadat khana, Akbar continued to search out truths in their many beguiling forms. These philosophical discussions, initiated by Shaikh Mubarak and his sons, greatly enchanted Akbar, as we have seen, who had not had a formal introduction to these ideas in his boyhood. Now, Akbar admitted, these high voltage exchanges between articulate and learned men enthralled him. 'I have organized this majlis for the purpose only that the facts of every religion, whether Hindu or Muslim, be brought out in the open,' said Akbar, according to an early recension of the *Akbarnama*. 'The closed hearts of our (religious) leaders and scholars [have to] be opened so that the Musulmans should come to know who they are!... They only think of Muslims (i.e. themselves) as those who recite kalima, consume meat and perform sijda on the earth. (They should know) Muslims are those who wage war on their "self" and control their desires and temper; and surrender (themselves) to the rule of law.'

In September 1579, in the midst of these discussions, an extraordinary document was drafted by Shaikh Mubarak and signed by an additional six of the leading ulema of the court including Abd un-Nabi, the hakim ul-mulk, and Abdullah Sultanpuri.* This decree, or mazhar, proclaimed Akbar to be the Padshah-i Islam and the Mujtahid of the Age. Through this declaration Akbar proclaimed for himself the role of interpreter of the law, thus freeing himself from the narrow confines of the sharia as practised by the ulema, and their distressingly limited understanding. Now, when disputes arose over religious points of law, it would be Akbar who would decide the issue and have the final say. However, it is clear that in the mazhar the emperor's title as Padshah-i Islam, head of the orthodox Muslims, was sanctioned by the ulema, and not by divine providence, and Akbar only had the power to interpret Muslim law, not to create it. Moreover, every opinion Akbar proposed had to be in accordance with the Koran. He did not invent a new office for himself and in effect took over the functions and powers earlier vested in the sadr. The relatively pedestrian ambition of the mazhar can be gauged by Abu'l Fazl's silence over it. Though it was drafted by his own father, Abu'l

---

*The other three were Ghazi Khan, Qazi Jaladuddin Multani, and Sadri Jahan Mufti.

Fazl gives it a cursory recording because, for him, Akbar would go on to reveal much grander claims as his luminous destiny 'unveiled' itself. The term 'mujtahid' that Akbar adopted was, however, particularly provocative. It was a term used for a scholar of Islamic law who used judgement, or ijtihad, to resolve finely balanced points of law that had no legal precedent. Yet Akbar, as he had openly declared, was illiterate. So Akbar's impeccable knowledge, despite his illiteracy, was explained by Abu'l Fazl as being supreme and intuitive knowledge as opposed to the learning of 'paper-worshipping scholiasts'.

In addition to the mazhar, Akbar also in this year decided to recite the khutba, the Friday prayers which usually included wishes for the reigning sovereign, himself. Faizi composed some verses for Akbar to recite from the pulpit:

> In the name of Him who gave us sovereignty,
> Who gave us a wise heart and a strong arm
> Who guided us in equity and justice
> Who put away from our heart aught but equity:
> His praise is beyond the range of our thoughts
> Exalted be his Majesty—Allahu Akbar!

The Mazhar of 1579 caused considerable disquiet, both in its own time and in the many interpretations attributed to it over the centuries. Apart from Shaikh Mubarak, it is likely that most of the other ulema signed the document under duress, submitting to pressure from the court. When the ulema of Delhi, the next most important city after the capital, were asked to sign the mazhar, Shaikh Jamaluddin refused, saying 'why should we faqirs and people living in seclusion be troubled?' referring to the greater austerity of the Delhi shaikhs and their careful distance from the glamour and lure of the court. Rumours began to spread that the imperial qazis had been forced, against their better judgement, to sign the document. The reading of the khutba was viewed with even more unease. The phrase 'Allahu Akbar'* was deliberately ambiguous yet almost insouciantly provocative. Even Babur and Humayun had had the traditional khutba recited, nominally giving reverence to the Ottoman Sultan. Akbar now deliberately distanced himself from acknowledging the Ottoman

---

*Which could be understood either as 'God is Great' or 'Akbar is God!'

Sultan as overlord of all Islamic kingdoms and instead claimed for himself the role of king of the orthodox Muslims of Hindustan and for the Mughal Empire an equally righteous claim to rule in the land.

In response to these upheavals, there was a fusillade of caustic and sharp one-liners from critical courtiers and observers. Mullah Sheri, a courtier 'renowned for his devastating one-liners as much as for his Islamic orthodoxy,' according to historian Harbans Mukhia, said 'this year His Majesty has laid claim to being the Prophet, next year, if God wills, he will become God himself'. Other courtiers, loath to attack the Padshah, laid the blame on Shaikh Mubarak's sons, Abu'l Fazl and Faizi. The poet Urfi of Shiraz made an allusion to this scandalous influence when he wrote, 'O Prophet, protect the Joseph of my soul (i.e. my soul) from the harm of the brothers; for they are ungenerous and envious, and deceive me like evil spirits and lead me wolf-like to the well (of unbelief)'. Akbar was particularly piqued when any reference was made to the disapproval of Ottoman sensibilities. When Qutbuddin Khan and Shahbaz Khan objected to the mazhar saying 'what would the King of the West, as the Sultan of Rum, say if he heard all this?' Akbar reacted sharply, accusing the men of secretly being spies from Constantinople, and sarcastically suggesting they go back to that country. The debate took a rather heated turn when Birbal joined in and Shahbaz Khan rounded on him, calling him a 'cursed infidel' and threatened him—Akbar could no longer contain himself and shouted to the dissenters in surprisingly robust language saying 'would that they would beat your mouths with a slipper full of filth!'

Sensing these undercurrents of hostility and bitterness, Akbar decided to make a pilgrimage to Ajmer, as he had done so many times in the past decade in gratitude, hope, and prayer, but this time 'as a means of calming the public and enhancing the submission of the recalcitrant', according to Abu'l Fazl. Akbar dismounted several miles from the sacred spot to continue the journey on foot but 'sensible people smiled', wrote Badauni, and said 'it was strange that His Majesty should have such a faith in the Khwaja of Ajmer, while he rejected the foundation of everything our Prophet, from whose "skirt" hundreds of thousands of saints of the highest degree like the Khwajah had sprung'. Perhaps Akbar might have sensed in the elements themselves a warning. On his way back from Ajmer, torrential rains lasting for three days caused a sudden, catastrophic flood which 'washed out a large number of men, cattle and goods'.

This was to be Akbar's last visit to Ajmer, this mystical spot where he had brought the turbulence of his thoughts so many times over the past ten years. These many repeated visits to the dargah, especially in the past decade, had been crucial in guiding his trajectory, as Akbar began to look for alternatives to orthodox Islam. Akbar would have been exposed to pantheistic Sufi doctrines, including fana, or extinction of the ego or the self, where the need to overcome one's own bodily desires transcended other religious considerations. The Sufis had pragmatically accommodated themselves to the presence of other beliefs and often incorporated aspects of Hindu and Buddhist practices. 'They shunned ritual and ceremony,' according to historian Muzaffar Alam, 'and spoke the language of the common people.' Akbar had also carefully cultivated the symbology of the Ajmer dargah, along with Shaikh Salim's living blessings, and effortlessly made it a part of the legacy of the Mughals of Hindustan. Now, finally, Akbar may have felt he had outgrown the need for this constant, visible reverence, having seen other, blazing horizons and guessed at many seductive truths.

After the Mazhar of 1579, once Akbar began to free himself from the need to be defined by a narrow Islamic identity, he began the complex and complicated process of creating a new identity for himself that reflected the diverse people and faiths of the court and the country. Among the nobility alone, for example, 17 per cent were Irani and another 15 per cent were Hindu. But before he could do that he had one last great challenge to face from someone who represented the old values and purely Timurid charisma—Mirza Hakim. In the next few years, having responded to the gauntlet laid down by that brother, Akbar would invite thinkers and scholars from across the empire and beyond the seas to Fatehpur Sikri and would assess the truth of their various beliefs.

As he evolved, another previously sacrosanct authority Akbar had finally outgrown were the duo of Abd un-Nabi and Abdullah Sultanpuri. 'When two people clash together,' was Badauni's bitter assessment, referring to their constant bickering, 'they fall together.'

Despite their great reluctance and shrill protests, Akbar sent them away to Mecca, with orders never to return to Hindustan. While the two mullahs were perforce being coaxed to depart to Surat and onward to the Holy Lands, three theologians of a different faith were heading in the opposite direction, from Goa to Fatehpur Sikri, carrying the relics of long-dead saints and dreams of martyrdom in their hearts.

THE TRUTH IS AN INHABITANT OF EVERY PLACE

On an ordinary day in February 1580 the inhabitants of Fatehpur Sikri were startled by a remarkable sight. Accompanied by a Mughal cavalcade, as well as some Armenian and European traders, were some bizarre-looking travellers. Crowds lined the streets and gawked openly at these men. 'Everyone stopped and stared in great surprise and perplexity,' admitted Monserrate, 'wondering who these strange-looking, unarmed men might be, with their long robes, their curious caps, their shaven faces, and their tonsured heads.' Their smooth, pale faces glowed blotchily with sweat in the warm day and almost more striking was that none of them bore any weapons. In the Mughal court, every man had a katar (Rajasthani-style dagger) tucked into his patka, or cummerbund, and a smoothly curved scimitar hanging at the waist and perhaps a jewelled dagger for good measure. Even the gentle, otherworldly musician Tansen had a jewelled sword, and the theologians all had long staffs and rods. These foreign men, however, were unarmed and unadorned, bearing only their faith, and a burning desire to proselytize.

The Jesuit priests were hustled away from the boisterous throng and brought before Akbar, who had been eagerly awaiting their arrival. 'The Fathers found the great conqueror,' we are told by Monserrate, 'seated cross-legged on a throne covered with a velvet cushion fringed with gold, upon a raised platform.' All around him were his great amirs, splendidly dressed in silk jamas and crisp turbans studded with glittering jewels. When they looked up at the Padshah, the Jesuits found that Akbar 'was almost as fair as southern Europeans, and...upon his head he wore a turban of Hindu form, adorned with a fortune of rare gems. His dress consisted of a robe of cloth of gold, embroidered with leaves and flowers, a great brooch was on his breast. Instead of Moslem trousers, he wore the Hindu dhoti of the finest and most delicate silk, falling to his heels, and there gathered in by bangles covered with pearls.... At his side was a scimitar.' Around the Padshah were attendants bearing bows and quivers of arrows, daggers, scimitars, and muskets, were he to require them, while writers waited quietly, ready to note down anything of importance. Akbar greeted his visitors with great warmth, and conversed with them at length, before sending them to their quarters under the charge of Abu'l Fazl and Hakim Ali Geelani.

The following day the priests presented to Akbar in the diwan-e-khas the *Royal Polyglot Bible*, beautifully bound in seven volumes and containing illustrations engraved by Flemish artists and recently printed in Antwerp. Each volume had a phantasmagorical painting in an anatomically accurate and naturalistic style that would profoundly influence the future course of Mughal art. Akbar respectfully took off his turban and placed each volume on his head before kissing it. He then had the books sent to his private room and, leading Acquaviva by the hand, took the Jesuit to show him the casket he had had made specially for the holy books.

One can well imagine the great turmoil in Acquaviva's heart during these meetings—the culmination of a lifetime of ardent prayers and hopes. This was a man, twenty-nine years old now, who had spent his life in a self-imposed 'rule of silence and solitude, only coming out of his cell for purposes of religion'. He preferred to wear worn-out garments and shoes and when going about his work 'used to take pleasure in singing softly to (the Virgin Mary's) honour little extempore songs which he improvised'. He was also deeply virginal, in effect and in manner, 'devoted to perpetual chastity and invoked the aid of the Virgin Mother of God to enable him to keep this resolution'. This man, trailing faintly around him the musky, ecclesiastical odour of daily scourgings, of dried blood, of abstinence and denial, now came into the presence of Akbar, thirty-eight years old, and in the full splendour of his life and personality. A man 'sturdy, hearty and robust...exceedingly well-built and...neither too thin nor too stout' with eyes 'so bright and flashing that they seem like a sea shimmering in the sunlight'; a man who tamed cheetahs for pleasure and who invoked the love of God by facing down tigers and riding wild elephants; a monarch who unselfconsciously led his visitor by the hand in his eagerness, radiating human warmth, and hospitality while for Acquaviva all physicality was a reminder of the loathsome weakness of the flesh, to be overcome by pain and repentance and constant deprivation.

In Akbar's quarters the air would have been perfumed by the scent of his favourite ambergris, perhaps, incense burning in gold censers, and masses of fresh-cut fragrant nargis and champa. There would have been soft carpets underfoot and beautiful vases and images in every niche in the walls. About Acquaviva, Monserrate noted that 'he was of virgin modesty. For whenever he spoke to the king, he blushed deeply'. No doubt Acquaviva would have blushed that first evening, too, in the company of the 'Great Mogul', and in the expectation of all that he wished so ardently to accomplish.

Akbar invited the Jesuits to join in the discussions at the ibadat khana in the cool evenings, where the different religious groups were placed separately around the hall and Akbar walked eagerly from one group to the next, asking questions. One of the first questions discussed was the relative merits of the Bible versus the Koran. With their ecstatic mission to convert the Mughal Padshah burning in their hearts, the Jesuits unapologetically attacked the Koran, 'stuffed with countless fables full of futility and extreme frivolity' while upholding the 'accuracy and authority of the Holy Scriptures'. So impassioned and virulent was Acquaviva's attack that, after a while, the Muslim theologians fell into a complete, and ominous, silence. At the end of the evening Akbar called aside Monserrate and Henriques and, upset at the intemperance of the younger theologian's attack, asked the two Jesuits to control the tenor of their colleague's rhetoric.

The discussions continued for several weeks and while Akbar enjoyed many of the teachings of the Bible, he was most discomfited by the ideas, well known to Muslims, of the Holy Trinity, the Virgin birth, and the fact that Jesus had allowed himself the indignity of death on the cross. Akbar was extremely disappointed by his own Muslim theologians because they did not counter the Jesuits with unified arguments, and themselves offered varied and contradictory positions. At one point, seemingly tired and disheartened by these recriminatory discussions, Akbar suggested that one theologian from each party undergo a trial by fire, protected by the righteousness of their holy book, to test which scripture contained the Supreme Truth. Unsurprisingly, no one rushed to accept this proposal and the night ended with loud, conciliatory shouts of 'Peace be to the King!'

Akbar continued to be unfailingly gracious and kind to his Jesuit guests. He told them that 'it was his desire that Christians should live freely in his empire, and build their churches, as he had heard was the case in Turkey.... He made this declaration with plain signs of great love and kindliness.' To the great astonishment of the Jesuits, Akbar once put on Portuguese costume, a scarlet cloak with gold fastenings, and a Portuguese hat. He made the three young princes wear similar clothes and spent an evening listening to madrigals with them. He had the Jesuits shifted from their noisy quarters in the city to within the palace grounds, sent them food from his own table, and went to visit their chapel, at Easter, once they had settled in. When Akbar saw the images of Jesus and Mary, 'he first, in Muhammadan fashion, made a profound reverence before it'. Akbar then took off his turban and shook out his long hair, grown back after the mystic episode of 1577, and, to the delight of the Jesuits, 'like a Christian... with clasped hands, bent his knee'. Lastly, he prostrated himself in the manner of Hindus saying that 'God deserved the homage of all peoples'. A few days later Akbar arrived with his three sons and some of his noblemen and they all respectfully bowed down before the Christian images. Akbar accepted 'with the greatest delight' a painting of the Virgin, brought from Rome. This was possibly a copy of the Byzantine Virgin, a miraculous painting deemed to have been painted by St Luke himself, which can be seen today in the Borghese Chapel in Rome. Akbar appointed Abu'l Fazl, who the Jesuits decreed was a 'young man of a keen and capable mind', to help the priests learn Persian and he taught Acquaviva the Persian language within three months. Acquaviva began translating the gospel into Persian and the first reader of these translated texts was Abu'l Fazl himself, who was delighted with them. These two men, Acquaviva and Abu'l Fazl, could not have been more different—one ravaged and skeletal in his austere, bleak robes the other already plump in the gold-limned, perfumed qaba of an exquisitely dressed Mughal courtier. One with his single, tenacious, and driven spirituality and the other with his capacious, adaptable, and inclusive mind.

Akbar seemed to have been most impressed with the priests' vows of poverty and chastity, for they refused all the presents and money he tried to give them. 'He could well understand,' said Monserrate, 'that a man was especially dear to God who abjured the pleasures of the world, wife, children and possessions.' Indeed the question of his many wives appeared to be a sensitive topic for Akbar, for when Acquaviva, with considerable lack of tact, informed Akbar that apart from the first wife, 'the rest are all courtesans and adulteresses, whom the commandment of God and Christ it is wickedness to retain', Akbar replied with uncharacteristic sharpness that 'these things are in the hand of God, who grants to those who ask plain paths from which they cannot stray. I myself have no desires', he continued evasively and clearly disingenuously, 'I reckon wives, children, empires, as of no account'.

Akbar was able to bring up the question of wives with the Jesuits in another context, when discussing the practice of sati among Hindu women, when he said:

> Since you reckon the reverencing of women as part of your religion, and allow not more than one wife to a man, it would not be wonderful if such fidelity and life-sacrifice were found among your women. The extraordinary thing is that it occurs among those of the Brahman (Hindu) religion. There are numerous concubines, and many of them are neglected and unappreciated and spend their days unfructuously in the privy chamber of chastity, yet in spite of such bitterness of life they are flaming torches of love and fellowship.

Akbar had, of course, witnessed jauhar himself at Chittor when 300 women had turned to ashes and he would no doubt have heard more about sati from the Rajput women in his harem. If his Rajput noblemen were sharing with him their stories of bravery in battle then Akbar's Rajput wives would have had their own tales of exemplary behaviour to amaze him with. For the Charans did not confine their epic stories only to men. They also had to instruct Rajput women in their kulreet, the cultural norms which evolved over centuries to prop up the Rajput system. The implicit support of women was essential in ensuring that brave sons were raised to become equally brave husbands whose only destiny was often to embrace death. 'Oh friend! By taking a royal umbrella and chavar (ceremonial whisk) one cannot be called a Rajput nor by inheriting the title of Rajput', was one popular Charan refrain. 'It is only one who sacrifices himself for the benefit of the country who is a true Rajput'. In this way, the notion of sacrifice above all else, above personal happiness certainly, was subtly but inexorably passed on to women from a very young age. During the discussion with the Jesuits, Akbar was clearly admiring of the love the Hindu women seemed to demonstrate by performing sati, but Akbar's ideas on sati were to change drastically, as he became ever more compassionate and aware of the impossible and conflicting demands made on the women in this system. The visiting Jesuit priests the following year were to describe the abomination of the practice when they witnessed it, to which Akbar responded that such fortitude could only come from God:

> The wretched women are rendered quite insensible by means of certain drugs, in order that they may feel no pain. For this purpose opium is used, or a soporific herb named bang....
> ...sometimes they are half-drugged: and before they lose their resolution, are hurried to the pyre with warnings, prayers and promises of eternal fame. On arriving there they cast themselves into the flames. If they hesitate, the wretched creatures are driven on to the pyre; and if they try to leap off again, are held down with poles and hooks.

Akbar was always very sensitive to the predicament of the women around him, and regularly brought up issues concerning the happiness and safety of the women in his empire. Having discussed the number of wives permitted by Islam, Akbar now raised the issue of monogamy in the ibadat khana. 'Under the principle of attachment to one another, which is the foundation of the arrangement of the universe,' he said, 'it would be eminently preferable that one should not marry more than one wife in a lifetime.' In these discussions Akbar was beginning to demonstrate an awareness, rare for the times, of the vulnerability of women and the need to protect them in a society which inevitably favoured men.

The Jesuits were also startled to discover that one of Akbar's closest confidantes, Shaikh Mubarak, 'an exceedingly pious old man who was devoted to the study of religious commentaries and books of religious medication', had but little faith in orthodox Islam. They found that the shaikh and his two sons 'openly declared that the Koran contained many impious, wicked and highly inconsistent passages, and hence they were convinced that it had not been sent by God'. The priests, added Monserrate, 'were astonished at this old man's wisdom, authority and friendliness to Christianity'. They found others to be just as friendly. Abu'l Fazl even agreed to help out the Jesuits during the ibadat khana discussions by listening to their arguments beforehand so that he could then defend their position before the Muslim theologians more 'fully and elaborately' than they could. Indeed, Monserrate noted that Abu'l Fazl 'seemed to be inspired by a divine earnestness, so clearly did he demonstrate how we believe that God has a Son' and that the Jesuits themselves were astonished at his eloquence. One may easily surmise that Abu'l Fazl's great efforts on behalf of the Jesuits were primarily to embarrass and humiliate the ulema, due to his ancient enmity, rather than because of any cherished spiritual beliefs about Christianity.

As a great sign of Akbar's trust, young Prince Murad and a few other boys from the nobility were entrusted to the Jesuits for an education. Murad was taught to make the sign of the cross and to call upon the name of Jesus and Mary at the beginning of lessons. The young boy, ten years old at the time, 'was an ideal pupil as regards natural ability, good conduct and intellectual capacity. In all these respects,' added Monserrate, 'it would have been hard to find any Christian youth, let alone a prince, surpassing him.' The Jesuits were also delighted by what appeared to be sincere reverence from both the Hindus and the Muslims in Fatehpur Sikri towards their religious icons. They owned a statue of the Virgin Mary whose fame quickly spread through the town and throngs of Muslims and Hindus 'lifted their hands to heaven and did reverence before it'. The Jesuits were moved to note that at least in the field of idol worship, the Muslims and Hindus were superior to the Protestants of Europe.

The Jesuits at the Mughal court were deadly serious about the mission they were on. They were in Hindustan for the sole purpose of converting 'heathens' and 'moors'. The early Jesuits were limited by their ignorance of Hindu and Muslim beliefs, preventing them from going beyond what they believed was vile superstition. They repeatedly used horrified terms for the Hindus, referring to their 'false gods', their 'sect of perdition' and accused the Prophet Muhammad of the most debased behaviour. From as early as 1550 a great temple in Cochin had been destroyed by the Christians and in Divar, north of Goa, where many pilgrims came to bathe in a holy river, the place was desecrated at least once by the Portuguese in 1557 by cutting up a cow and throwing the pieces into the river. In 1567, Antony de Noronha, the Viceroy of Goa, ordered the destruction of all temples and idols in Salsette and one Father Lewis Goes went to tear down a Hindu statue of 'Manmay', the Salsette Venus, 'the centre of a voluptuous and degrading worship', with his own hands. Jesuit priests and their converts had ruthlessly destroyed temples, even while admitting they were 'highly honoured by the Hindus who treated them as living beings'. Monserrate would also be appreciative of the efforts of the Muslims to rid the Hindu population of idolatry. On their way to Fatehpur Sikri, Monserrate had written with satisfaction of the numerous destroyed 'idol temples' which littered the countryside. Many of these temples had been destroyed by earlier Muslim rulers, however, and Monserrate added with dismay that because of 'the carelessness of these same Musulmans' sacrifices have been allowed 'to be publicly performed, incense to be offered, oil and perfumes to be poured out, the ground to be sprinkled with flowers, and wreaths to be hung up, wherever—either amongst the ruins of these old temples or elsewhere—any fragment of an idol is to be found'.

In 1580, in Fatehpur Sikri, Acquaviva was both tormented and seduced by the possibility of converting the great Mughal Padshah. Mistaking Akbar's gracious interest and genuine curiosity for a desire to convert to Christianity, he became increasingly convinced that this was the divine purpose of his life. He was also deeply frustrated that this mesmerizing prize always seemed to be beyond his reach. He wrote to Father Claud about his experience at the court and noted with desolate abhorrence that the Muslim courtiers constantly glorified the name of Muhammad and 'bend the knee, prostrate, lift up their hands, give alms, and do all they do' in the name of the Prophet. And, despite Acquaviva's very best attempts to vilify the Prophet Muhammad and denigrate Islam, his fervent desire for martyrdom remained elusive and he bitterly complained: 'Will these Musalmans never martyr us?' to which the other priests used to reply, 'the King is too fond of us; no one dare touch us'.

While the Jesuits' unrelenting effort would come to naught as far as the soul of the Padshah was concerned, the greatest influence they were to have on Akbar and on the Mughal Empire was in the field of art. Akbar was genuinely delighted with the paintings they gifted him and the images in the illustrated Bibles. He already owned a few Christian images before the arrival of the Jesuit mission, which he had proudly pointed out to the priests. In his dining room were images of Christ, Mary, Moses, and Prophet Muhammad, and the priests noticed that he showed the image of the Prophet less reverence than he did to the others. This, though, may have been wishful thinking as Syed Ali Nadeem Rezavi has described these paintings to be of Timurid origin. After the Jesuit missions, however, European art would have a dramatic influence on Mughal paintings. Because most of the ships leaving Europe set off from Antwerp (which was a major centre of printing at the time) woodcuts and engravings of the Albrecht Durer tradition arrived at Fatehpur Sikri, and would heavily influence the Mughal school. There would be frescoes painted of Christ, Mary, and the Christian saints in the private chambers of Fatehpur Sikri and, indeed, in Mughal buildings across the empire. '(The Emperor) has painted images of Christ our Lord and our Lady in various places in the palace' wrote a surprised Jesuit, 'and there are so many saints that...you would say it was more like the palace of a Christian King than a Moorish one'. Akbar would show the engravings and European paintings to his favourite Hindu painters and they would learn European concepts of volume, perspective, and space in addition to the painting of angels, and of the holy figures, and use them in ingenious ways. It was probably just as well that the Jesuit priests did not live to see the use that Akbar made of their beloved sacred images as, according to Kavita Singh, 'Mughal imperial painting would eventually appropriate the tropes of Catholic devotional art to aggrandize the image of Mughal Emperors'. The lustrous halos, the taut-skinned cherubs, and the allegorical imagery would be incorporated into Mughal miniatures, using all available symbology to glorify the Padshahs of Hindustan.

Paradoxically Badauni, the acerbic critic, was the one who would most lucidly analyse Akbar's theological and philosophical bent.

'From childhood to manhood and from manhood to his declining years the Emperor had combined in himself various phases from various religions and opposite sectarian beliefs and by a peculiar acquisitiveness and a talent for selection by no means common, had made his own all that can be seen and read in books.' As a result, continued Badauni, Akbar believed that 'there are wise men to be found and ready at hand in all religions, and men of asceticism and recipients of revelation and workers of miracles among all nations and that the Truth is an inhabitant of everyplace'.

While Akbar was discussing the finer points of Christian theology with the Jesuits in the ibadat khana, he was also busy subduing what had become one of the most serious challenges to his rule. After the audacious mazhar and the reading of the khutba, there was a gathering momentum of those who believed that Islam itself was under threat because of Akbar. Far away in Bengal a disaffected mullah, Qazi Muhammad Yazdi, had denounced Akbar as an infidel and had issued a fatwa of kufr (disbelief), calling on all righteous Muslims to take up arms and to revolt against the Padshah. The contender for the throne, under whose name they would unite was that long-forgotten brother, relegated and confined these many years to Babur's old capital at Kabul, Mirza Hakim.

ALLAHU AKBAR

While the Jesuit priests were constructing their chapel and translating the gospel into Persian, another unusual text was being composed at Fatehpur Sikri. An anonymous Brahmin, at Akbar's request, had written a Sanskrit text called the *Allopanisad* (Allah's Upanishad). Riffing with unselfconscious candour on the meaning of the words 'Akbar' and 'Allahu Akbar', the text provocatively offered ambiguous interpretations of the phrases that included the Mughal Padshah's name. At the same time, mutinies broke out in Bengal and Bihar, ostensibly as a righteous movement against the rumours of un-Islamic practices being carried out by the Padshah at Fatehpur Sikri. But the cause of Islam was just a convenient rallying point for disgruntled officers, mostly Central Asian Turani noblemen and some Persians, who were deeply resentful of the measures taken by Akbar to reduce the rampant corruption and nepotism in his administration, and to centralize the fiscal system. These measures were loathed by some noblemen who, in earlier times, had been the favoured elite backbone of Mughal nobility.

As we have seen, Akbar was constantly trying to tighten the empire's revenue and administrative system. Dissatisfied with the way in which land revenue was being assessed, Akbar had ordered all lands in the central Indo-Gangetic provinces to revert to the khalisa, the crown lands, in 1575. For five years, mansabdars were paid in cash from the imperial treasury while the lands in the newly acquired territories were carefully measured following Raja Todar Mal's system, crop yields were noted down, and tax rates accurately determined. These new figures were added to older measurements and a new assessment generated. On the basis of the average prices of crops in the previous ten years, the tax claim was now fixed for each crop in each region. No longer would tax be calculated on the basis of seasonal prices and a direct communication between the government and the ryots had been established. Akbar then reassigned a large amount of the lands back to mansabdars but retained lands yielding about 25 per cent of the overall yield for the needs of his own household. Khalisa land was retained in the most productive areas, providing the emperor with some fiscal security. In gratitude for his outstanding work of the past ten years, Raja Todar Mal was made the imperial diwan in 1582.

Now a discontented group of noblemen revolted at attempts to curtail their power and the dilution of their coterie by the gradual introduction of Indian Muslims and Rajput noblemen into the mansabdari system. The Jesuits noted the pragmatic meritocracy of the Mughal court when they said that 'men of low birth, upstarts, and (as the Mongols say) "men who have risen", together with those of alien birth, are given posts in the royal household if the King finds them capable and efficient, and are gradually promoted'. But were these men ever to disappoint the Padshah they were made to 'always carry about with them the tools of their original handicraft, lest in their vulgarity and insolence they ever forget the low station from which they have sprung'. It was clear, therefore, that while it was the Padshah's prerogative to raise men when he discerned talent, it was not generally tolerated that people try and change their station of their own accord. 'Whenever a domestic servant turns to ilm (scholarly business),' Akbar said, 'much business would remain unattended'. Superintendents were therefore warned to be vigilant so that no one wantonly abandoned their profession.

There was now an equal percentage of Rajput, Indian Muslim, and Persian noblemen, and just a fraction more Turani noblemen in the Mughal Empire. By 1580, the total number of Rajput mansabdars numbered 43, out of 272, while Persians accounted for 47 noblemen, Indian Muslims 44, with Turani noblemen having the highest number at 67. In addition to feeling that their clout was waning, the disgruntled noblemen had other reasons to be discontented. The recent innovation of the dagh, or branding, of horses that mansabdars were paid to maintain was particularly disliked. The outrage of the nobility was further stoked by the sadrs, who had been so unceremoniously ousted from their previously unassailable positions by the mazhar. Now all the disaffected noblemen of the east responded with violent enthusiasm to the fatwa issued by Mullah Yazdi. The ever-fractious Afghans of Bengal joined the

Central Asian Qaqshals and the Bihar rebels. The Mughal Governor of Bengal was killed and Mirza Muhammad Hakim was recognized as the legitimate ruler of Hindustan. 'They were not troubled by the thought,' railed the historian Vincent Smith, 'that the man whom they desired to substitute for their gifted monarch was a drunken sot, cowardly and irresolute, incapable of governing the empire. It sufficed for them to know that Muhammad Hakim was reputed to be sound in doctrine.'

Not all Mirza Hakim's officers were loyal to his cause, however, and one Mir Abu'l Qasim left Kabul to join Akbar's service. Since his lands lay within the Salt Range, he presented the Padshah with a plate and cup made of salt, to demonstrate his good intentions (namak-halali). He thus earned not only the Padshah's favour but also the sobriquet Namkin, or Salty.

Akbar responded to the challenge of the Afghans by sending Raja Todar Mal to the east but as the rebellion gathered momentum, through April 1580, Akbar finally recalled his long-neglected and rambunctious foster brother Mirza Aziz Koka. Ever since his truculence over the branding of horses, Aziz Koka, now titled khan azam and a mansabdar of 5,000, had been kept far away from the court. A witty, erudite, and orthodox man, Aziz Koka could never resist the temptation to contradict the Padshah and make plain his disapproval of all Akbar's religious innovations. Brought up in the camaraderie of their youth spent wrestling and camel-racing in Kabul, Aziz was entirely at ease with Akbar, one of the few amirs to truly ever be so. With his refined intelligence, and cool elegance, Aziz offered a study in contrast with Akbar, who was stocky and powerful, and possessed of a more intuitive understanding and magnetic warmth. 'Aziz was', according to Abu'l Fazl, 'remarkable for ease of address, intelligence, and his knowledge of history'. He wrote poetry and was credited with an aphorism of dubious merit that 'a man should marry four wives—a Persian woman to have somebody to talk to; a Khurasani woman for his housework; a Hindu woman for nursing his children; and a woman from Mawarannahr, to have someone to whip as a warning for the other three.' It was through the determined intercession of the harem (where Jiji Anaga must have made her feelings clear too) that Akbar heard that Aziz Koka was 'ashamed and repentant' and finally reinstated him.

Mirza Aziz Koka was now sent off to Bengal at the head of a large army and carrying 'those black standards, the sign of war to the death, which Timur the Lame...had been wont to employ in his wars' as a fluttering warning to the rebellious forces. But even with the enormous power of the Mughal force behind him it would be a few years before Bengal and Bihar were subdued. In 1580, Bihar was finally organized as a separate subah with 7 sarkars and 199 parganas 'yielding a revenue of about 22 crore dams or Rs. 5,547,985' and Mirza Aziz Koka became the first Subedar of Bihar.

Bengal, however, was another matter. Ever since Munim Khan's disastrous attempt to relocate the capital and the ensuing plague and devastation, Bengal, isolated from the rest of India for centuries, was viewed with suspicion and fear, a place for renegades, a punishment posting, leading Abu'l Fazl to dolefully record:

> The country of Bengal is a land where owing to the climate's favouring the base, the dust of dissension is always rising, from the wickedness of men families have decayed, and dominions (have been) ruined. Hence in old writings, it was called Bulghakkhana (house of turbulence).

Everything in Bengal appeared foreign and provocative to the Mughals stationed there, from the diet of rice and fish to those used to wheat and meat, to the deluge and foetid heat of the tropical thunderstorms, to the main occupation of the locals, fishing, deemed unworthy by the warrior mansabdars. Something of even Abu'l Fazl's puzzlement can be understood through his bizarre description of the region when he writes that the 'inhabitants are as a race good-looking and addicted to the practice of magic. Strange stories are told regarding them. It is said that they build houses, of which the pillars, walls and roofs are made of men.... There grows a wonderful tree whose branches when cut, exude a sweet liquid which quenches the drought of those athirst.' A land of sorcery and danger, then, but extraordinarily fecund, for Abu'l Fazl also wrote that 'harvests are always abundant, measurement is not insisted upon, and revenue demands are determined by establishment of the crop. His Majesty,' continues Abu'l Fazl, 'in his goodness has confirmed this custom,' reflecting the ground reality wherein Mughal occupation at this time remained nominal.

While almost all the zamindars in Bengal were Kayasthas, as the province increasingly integrated into the Mughal Empire, the Mughal governors would bring in a host of immigrants from other parts of the country to help them settle the land:

> soldiers recruited from the north, Marwari merchants who accompanied and helped finance their Mughal patrons, swarms of petty clerks attached to Mughal officers, and the many artisans who supplied and equipped the Mughal military establishment.

But most of these changes would finally take shape under a different governor, Raja Man Singh, at the beginning of the next century. For now, Abd un-Nabi and Abdullah Sultanpuri, hearing of the khutba in Mirza Hakim's name, returned to Hindustan from Mecca despite Akbar's express order to the contrary. But the time for indulgence had passed and Akbar had some of the troublesome mullahs quietly killed—Mullah Muhammad Yazdi was drowned in a river, as was Qazi Yaqub from Bengal. The hakim ul-mulk, one of the signatories of the mazhar and a learned and trusted man, but one who was opposed to Abu'l Fazl and who had named him, admittedly in a puerile pun, Abu'l Fuzlah (excrement), was sent to Mecca. Abdullah Sultanpuri died in Gujarat and Qazi Ali was sent to confiscate his property. 'Several boxes full of ingots of gold,' wrote Badauni about the corrupt theologian, 'were discovered in his sepulchre where he had caused them to be buried as corpses.' All these ingots of gold and Abdullah Sultanpuri's precious library were reclaimed by the imperial treasury. Abd un-Nabi returned to Fatehpur Sikri, though the atmosphere at court was hostile towards him. He was rude to the Padshah one day and 'unable to restrain his passion', Akbar struck the mullah in the face. 'Why don't you strike with a knife?' raged the furious mullah in the court where he had once spat on the amirs in his arrogance and pride. Now there was to be no quiet submission by the Padshah and Abd un-Nabi was handed over to Raja Todar Mal and Abu'l Fazl over charges of embezzlement due to a missing amount of 70,000 rupees that Akbar had given the mullahs for distribution in charity at Mecca. A short while later the mullah was strangled in his bed, probably on the order of Abu'l Fazl, who would thereby also have put to rest the demons of his father's ancient humiliations at the hands of these very men, once all-powerful.

Akbar, however, had given clear instructions that all these actions against the ulema had to be carried out 'in such a manner that the ladies should not know of it'. The ulema had the favour of the senior ladies of the harem and Akbar would not have risked their displeasure, for the harem was a formidable force when they acted in concert. There is no doubt that the emperor would have been challenged about decisions and actions which the women considered questionable. Indeed, Abu'l Fazl admitted that Akbar had to be very careful of maintaining all the protocol due to the women of the harem and that he spent three hours in the apartments of the women every afternoon, tending to their various petitions equitably. These petitions would often involve the submission of grants for pious women fallen on hard times, the handing out of presents, promotions for men who had distinguished themselves with service and 'possibly listening to political or military intelligence gathered through networks linked to his harem'.

The year 1580 also saw the arrival of the beleaguered Kashmir sultan, Yusuf Shah Chak, at the Mughal court. Akbar had already sent ambassadors to Kashmir, in 1570 and 1578, to gather information on the state of affairs in that kingdom and to also, not inconsequently, inform the nobility and residents of the glory and wealth of the Mughal Empire. The lesson had not been lost on Yusuf Shah Chak, long used to pragmatically accepting the symbolic sovereignty of powerful neighbours. He had shown allegiance by sending princesses as brides for Salim, by reciting the khutba, and striking coins in the name of the Mughal Padshah. Over time, these placatory gestures eroded the charisma of the sultan in his own country, encouraging dissidents and now, in desperation, he had come to the Mughal court for help. Akbar greeted him warmly, courteously offering him two mistresses, and Yusuf Shah Chak stayed at the court for almost a year. Eventually, Yusuf Shah Chak was dissuaded by his noblemen from accepting Mughal military help and he escaped back to Kashmir. The damage was done, however, for once Akbar had given refuge to embattled rulers, he would only ever treat them as vassals. He began to address the sultan as Yusuf Khan, and not by his title, and the balance of power was forever altered. After regaining power, Yusuf Shah further alienated the Kashmiri people by exacting violent revenge upon his opponents, including gouging out their eyes, and exasperated his own supporters by 'excessive indulgence in merry making and gross neglect of state affairs'. Internal dissensions, volatility and rivalries, long a trait of rulers in this region, now became widespread. Haidar Chak, a rival warlord, rode over to Lahore and joined the imperial service under Governor Man Singh. From now on, defectors and soldiers would supply the Mughals with local intelligence as well as invaluable local guides and fighters.

If the year 1580 saw Akbar concerned with the furthest eastern frontiers of his kingdom, then he was simultaneously occupied with his western frontier and the teal-green seas off Surat and further away still with the firangi menace that was Portugal. Early in the year, Akbar sent a party with an uncle of Mirza Aziz Koka 'to capture the European ports' with orders 'to remove the firangis who were a stumbling block in the way of the pilgrims to the hijaz'. We have seen how the Portuguese were opposed to both trade and the hajj in the Indian Ocean, which they further discouraged by the imposition of the onerous system of cartazes, the plundering of pilgrim ships, and the harassing of Muslim traders. A statement made during the 1567 Provincial Council under the archbishop of Goa, Gaspar de Leão Pereira, made these prejudices clear:

> Many Muslims and other infidels come to our ports with books of their sects and their false relics that they bring from the House of Mecca and other places they hold to be holy, and they pass through our territories with these things to their own areas. The officials of the customs houses are ordered that when these books and relics are seen, they should not be cleared but rather examine them and if they find them to be such, should burn them.

The Mughals did not operate in isolation in Hindustan, but kept themselves well informed about happenings in the rest of the world.

Akbar was particularly interested in all major military battles and conquests beyond the frontiers of his kingdom and a European at court once overheard Akbar and his men analysing the Battle of the Three Kings, or the Battle of Alcazar al Kabir, in which the invading Portuguese forces of King Sebastian were defeated by the Moroccan Sultan of Morocco, Abd al-Malik. This was not an exercise in simple curiosity, but a way to keep informed about military technology and tactics, which the Mughals were supremely effective at adopting and adapting.

The arrival of gunpowder technology had profoundly altered Mughal battle tactics. The earlier Central Asian battle array, or yasal, was based on a centre and rear, which served as shock troops that drew in the enemy troops, accompanied by right and left flanks of mounted warriors who then encircled the enemy, galloping at high speeds, all the while firing at the trapped soldiers. Babur had already adopted the 'camp battle' technique of the Ottomans which involved the use of trenches and mobile wagon forts lashed together to protect the centre. Babur was able to combine two apparently contradictory elements—a highly mobile Central Asian cavalry with a more static entrenchment and artillery element and this 'mobile fortress combined with a swarm of swift and dangerous horsemen presented a unique problem for the defending force'.

This combination of gunpowder technology with field fortifications made Mughal tactics truly devastating. Moreover, gunpowder technology was not adopted blindly or haphazardly. The Mughals, led by Akbar himself, were obsessed with guns and their uses and tinkered endlessly with them. Akbar devised new ways to use this musket and cannon technology in response to the demands of the empire and the challenges he faced. So, for example, Akbar devised rockets,* light and easy to transport. Rockets were found to be particularly effective against enemy animals—horses and elephants, for their whistling shriek caused pandemonium among them. The Mughals then devised a special rocket with an in-built whistle to make better use of this effect and, as pointed out by Andrew de la Garza, 'rocketry is one instance where the West adopted Indian military

---

*Present in India since possibly the fourteenth century, the war rocket was now made of metal instead of wood or paper, allowing for a larger payload.

technology'. The Mughals adapted swivel camel guns and elephant guns, high-performing muskets, lethal field artillery of different sizes all in addition to the famed horse archer. 'The resulting method of warfare would appear alien to Western observers', used to linear formations and close order drill:

> ...but it was in reality a logical response to an extremely hazardous battlefield environment dominated by fire. It actually demanded a higher degree of discipline and initiative from the individual soldier and small unit commander and in many ways anticipated much later developments in Europe after the introduction of rifle muskets, breechloaders and even more lethal field artillery.

Meanwhile Akbar's sudden show of aggression in Surat in 1580 seems to have been at least partly due to more personal calculations. Though the Portuguese had indeed proved to be a constant menace, it was the coastal trading kingdoms of the south who had been most affected. The Mughals, with their focus directed towards the huge agricultural heartland, were only minimally inconvenienced. But from the time that Gulbadan and her party of Mughal women had planned to travel to Mecca, Akbar had been supremely solicitous of their safety. As we have seen, he had ensured friendly relations with the Portuguese at Surat in 1573 so that a cartaz was readily obtained. Despite this, Gulbadan and her party had been delayed for a year in Surat while the authorities prevaricated and Gulbadan had offered the Portuguese the town of Baksar to expedite matters. Then in 1577 there were reports of the Portuguese capturing Gujarati ships returning from Mecca, at a time when the Mughal women's party would have been directly concerned. The royal ladies finally reached Mecca in time to participate in the pilgrimage of 1577 following which they performed the hajj three more times. According to Badauni they also undertook many lesser pilgrimages and visited the important Shia shrines of Karbala, Qum, and Mashhad in addition to Mecca.

In 1581, once the Mughal ladies were safely back on Hindustani soil, Akbar inexplicably stopped sending the hajj caravans and the annual alms to Mecca. For six years Akbar had patronized the sending of a mir hajj, and hajj ships, and had subsidized all pilgrims at great expense, and now he forbade pilgrims from going to Mecca altogether. It has been argued that this was in line with his veering away from orthodox Islamic practices and while it is true that other practices, such as the Ajmer pilgrimage, were also discontinued, Akbar was a pragmatic man. If he did not participate in the Ajmer pilgrimage himself he sent the royal princes in lieu, to keep orthodox sentiments appeased. The withdrawal of ships and money to Mecca appear to have been motivated by a personal and sharp sliver of anger at the high-handedness of the Ottoman authorities and what would have been perceived as disrespect towards Akbar's beloved family members. There was certainly a moment of imperial frisson between the descendant of Suleiman the Magnificent, and Akbar the Great. So violent now would be Akbar's reaction at any perceived slight from the Ottomans that in 1582 he would put the Ottoman ambassador in chains and send him 'for a long period to Lahore' while the embassy itself 'vanished in a cloud of smoke' for a supposed excess of arrogance.

Gulbadan brought back with her an iron detestation of the Portuguese, whom she complained about bitterly, and she even tried to encourage the locals to take back the town of Baksar once she had returned to Surat. This hatred of the rapacious Portuguese was widespread and 'the mere name of Christian or Frank', noted Monserrate sadly, when returning to Goa in 1582, 'is horrible and hateful'. There would be no more hajj ships sent by Akbar, though Jahangir would reinstate this custom and the next ships to be sent on hajj would be under the patronage of his mother, the Rajput princess, Harkha Bai, after she had become the queen mother. Reborn as Maryam uz Zamani she would send 1,700 pilgrims on hajj in 1619. But for Akbar, Padshah of Hindustan, ruling over an empire with a population five times that of the Ottoman Empire, there was no longer any need for Ottoman recognition, for the Mughal name was lustrous enough.*

---

*As has been noted earlier, Eaton quotes an observer who, in 1615, estimated the Mughals' annual revenue at 120 million silver coins compared to forty-five million for the Ottoman Empire. (See *India in the Persianate Age*, p. 371.)

THE SLOW MARCH TO KABUL

In 1581 two brothers, kings both, faced each other across the icy Jhelum over the fate of Kabul, ancient capital of Babur. Outside the city was Akbar, thirty-nine years old, leading an imperial army of 50,000 cavalry, 500 elephants, camel corps, and infantry. Facing him was Mirza Hakim, twenty-eight years old, and self-proclaimed guardian of the luminous Chaghatai–Timurid legacy of Babur. Mirza Hakim had spent decades cultivating that legacy, upholding the Turco–Mongol code, and paying ostentatious reverence to Babur's tomb in Kabul. According to Munis Faruqui he 'portrayed himself as a Ghazi with a rough and ready Turkish steppe identity, staunch Sunni and a bold risk taker like Babur'. Now he made an audacious appeal to the Central Asian noblemen within the Padshah's besieging army at Kabul, urging them to turn on their fellow soldiers, the 'natives of Hindustan' (Hindi nazhadan), and to join him instead, the true heir of Babur. But Akbar's troops, including 'Mongols, some Persians, some Turkmen, Chagatai, Uzbegs, Kandaharis, Baluchis, Pathans, Indians and Gujaratis, Musulmans and also Hindus' were unimpressed. Akbar, too, had spent decades preparing for just such a challenge and had wrought an empire from a careful balancing act between the various clans in it. Aziz Koka, having long outlived his milk brother, would tell Jahangir about his father's strategy: 'His Majesty Akbar during the fifty years of his reign increased the number of Chaghatais and Rajputs among nobles for these people are not seditious. They know nothing but loyalty.'

Mirza Hakim had finally laid bare his ambitions to challenge his half-brother the Padshah the previous year in December 1580 when he had marched into Hindustan and invaded the Punjab, encouraged by the mutinies in Bengal and Bihar and the rallying of orthodox Islamic elements to his banner. Akbar had then decided to finally confront his brother's claims, born of their shared legacy as Timurid mirzas, and their unshakeable belief in their right to rule. In February 1581, almost a year before the brothers would eventually face each other across the Jhelum, Akbar decided to march to Kabul. But this would not be an intemperate and blistering campaign. This would be a spectacle on the move, a glorious cavalcade limned in gold, an unfurling of imperial power across the span of Hindustan from Akbar's blended capital at Fatehpur Sikri to the ancient Timurid stronghold at Kabul.

Before leaving his capital, Akbar made careful and meticulous arrangements for the administration of the empire, as he expected to be gone for a long time. Akbar had initially planned to leave Salim, twelve years old, in Fatehpur Sikri in his stead but 'the prince begged through [Hamida Banu] that he might accompany His Majesty'. The young Salim was at this stage a golden-skinned, delicate-featured boy whose face was dominated by a strong nose, which it would eventually grow into. Aziz Koka was placed in charge of Bengal and Qutbuddin Khan was in charge of Gujarat with a garrison of 10,000. Hamida Banu herself was 'to be superior to both of these' and was in charge of Delhi with a garrison of 12,000 cavalry. Despite Abu'l Fazl's considerable efforts at rendering the women 'orderly' and contained within the walls of the harem, Mughal women continued to be unexpectedly 'visible'. As for Akbar's wives, the senior Rajput queens, including Harkha Bai, were getting ready to accompany him on his campaign across the country, along with his two eldest sons, a few of his older daughters, and the Jesuit Monserrate.

Before leaving the capital, Akbar spent two days outside Fatehpur Sikri in his 'immense white pavilion' with his mother and the Jesuit priests, organizing the enormous resources and men required for the campaign. When Akbar finally set off on 8 February 1581, it was not so much an army on the move as a visible reminder of the wonder that was the wealthiest empire on earth. Akbar rode in front, followed by his elite fighting corps, the cavalry, which would swell to 50,000 after a few days march, resplendent in their armour and their wicked curving swords and bows. Behind the cavalry followed the 500 royal elephants, also wearing armour and gold and silver trappings. The royal women followed on female elephants, in colourful, swaying howdahs, surrounded by 500 white-haired senior noblemen who drove away any stragglers who should come in the way of the queens. The elephants were followed by the retinue of the queens, all on slow-stepping, lurching camels and protected by white umbrellas. The infantry and camp followers were estimated at four times the size of the cavalry and other mounted units, bringing the total size of the Mughal army and retinue to 2.5 lakh people. There was also the great tribe of animals in attendance—a hundred blindfolded cheetahs on horse-drawn carts, ears twitching and tails switching, and hawks, their ferocity contained in their claws clenched around the armguards of their keepers. Bringing up the rear was the treasury, carried on elephants and camels, and the king's furniture, all transported by mules, and twenty-eight field guns. This immense procession, soon so large that it 'seemed to hide the earth', and extending over a breadth of 3 kilometres and 'filling the woods with a crowding multitude', was led, in the front, by a single drummer who laid down the marching beat. In addition to the staccato of the horses' hooves, the occasional fluttering wing, the feral, dense bodies of the moving elephants, and the subdued shouts of the soldiery, there was always the sound of the drum beat, far away in front of the emperor, sounding out a slow, regular rhythm, a long-drawn breath.

By the time the Padshah reached the first halt, the enormous Mughal tented encampment was already set up. As he dismounted and rushed towards his imperial tent, powerful shoulders rolling beneath the fine cotton of his qaba, Akbar was greeted by two long rows of elephants and cavalry, all the noblemen saluting him as he walked by. The layout of this enormous mobile city followed an exact pattern, so that within a few days, anyone walking through would 'know his way about the bazaars as well as he does about the streets of his own city'. The crimson imperial tent was laid out on flat ground, within a large open space, which was covered by carpets; next to it were the audience hall and the naqqara, covering 1,500 metres in length. The open space was accessible only to guards, who patrolled it continuously to ensure the privacy of the women. To the right were the quarters of Salim and his attendants and to the left, those of Murad. Behind these tents were the offices and the workshops and, further still, a separate bazaar set up for the Padshah, the princes, and the elite noblemen with not just grains, maize, pulses, and provisions but all kinds of merchandise so that 'these bazaars seem to belong to some wealthy city instead of to a camp'. The merchandise was available at cheap rates as Akbar sent runners ahead to inform merchants of his impending arrival and exempt them from all taxes and promise them generous rewards on his return from the campaign. These incentives and promises were crucial, for as historian Abraham Eraly has pointed out:

> The very movement of an army through the land caused damage to property and unsettled life, so people invariably fled from the army's path, like gazelles at the scent of the tiger.... the advance of a vast horde...was like a locust invasion: they simply ate up everything on their path or trampled down stranding crops. The greatest damage was done by camp followers, the rabble that constituted the bulk of the Mughal host, who stripped whatever they found on the way.

There were also additional tented structures, some eighteen described by Qandahari, 'which have been made of boards of wood, each including an upper chamber and balcony...that are set up in a suitable and attractive place. The boards are joined up together by iron rings'. These prefabricated and movable structures were an innovation of Akbar's and used an ingenious system of posts and beams which could be used to instantly fashion wooden housing. European brocade and velvet furnished the insides of the tents and on the floors, up to a thousand carpets made it look like 'a garden had bloomed'. In the centre of the encampment was a high pole with an immense lamp known as the akash diyah, used by the camp dwellers to orient themselves, and was 'the heart and head of the whole camp'. The farrash khana, or department of tents, carpets, and materials, contained two identical sets of equipment so that while the Padshah remained in one location, a second camp was being prepared in advance at the next stop.

Four days after leaving Fatehpur Sikri the Mughal camp arrived at Mathura, where Monserrate noted that 'temples dedicated to Vishnu are to be found in many places'. These shrines were patronized by many members of the Mughal elite, and on the report of Raja Birbal, a grant of 100 bighas had been made to temples in the city. By the time the imperial army was passing through in 1581, seven temples of Mathura had been granted tax-free lands. In the course of the year,

Hamida Banu was to issue a farman from Fatehpur Sikri permitting free grazing by the cows and oxen of one Vithalrai of Govardhan. Outside Mathura was a Hanuman temple with 300 trained monkeys who fought like gladiators with miniature weapons upon the ringing of a bell, which Monserrate derided as being a venal attempt by Brahmins to fleece poor and easily beguiled pilgrims.

Each time Akbar departed from the camping ground for another day's journey, he was closely followed by officers carrying a ten-foot rod*—these officials meticulously measured the distance covered. 'These measurements,' wrote Monserrate, 'are afterwards found very useful in computing the area of provinces and the distances of places apart, for purposes of sending envoys and royal edicts, and in emergencies.' And indeed one of Akbar's great achievements was the standardization of measurement of area. For measuring distances, the kos was used.†

Six days later, the camp reached Delhi, described by Monserrate as studded with 'lofty and handsomely decorated residences' and broad and imposing streets 'planted down the middle with beautiful green trees which cast a grateful shade'. On either side of the fickle Yamuna, which would one day abandon these glorious buildings, were stately mansions and parks dense with fruits and flowers. Akbar went to visit Humayun's tomb and met his beloved stepmother, Bega Begum, who lived in the Arab Sarai quarters. When he visited his father's tomb, Akbar would have had an aching and visceral reminder of Humayun's physical presence. The tomb at that time would have been richly decorated with carpets and tapestries while an awning would have covered the central shrine itself. Within the chamber of the tomb would have been Humayun's Koran, dagger, sword, turban, and shoes, as if the Padshah had only just left the room. All these priceless mementos would quietly disappear after the British took back Delhi following the chaos of the 1857 Uprising.

In Delhi Akbar was shown incriminating letters that proved his powerful finance minister, Shah Mansur, was colluding with Mirza Hakim. Shah Mansur had begun his career as an accountant in the Perfume Department and, as so often happened in Akbar's

---

*Two hundred lengths of the ten-foot rod made up a kos.
†Hobson-Jobson's *Glossary* lists the Akbari kos as measuring 2m. 4 f. 183 1/3 yards.

meritocratic system, worked his way up through talent and ambition to become wazir. Though the veracity of these letters was later doubted, Shah Mansur was a deeply unpopular man for the brusque, tactless, and over-zealous way in which he carried out his affairs. Even Todar Mal, Akbar's exemplary officer, complained of his high-handedness, talking of his 'sharp letters...claiming a good deal of money'. Akbar was therefore constrained to publicly execute Shah Mansur, though 'the King's mournful countenance plainly showed how much pained he had been by the wretched man's fate' and the loss of a supremely efficient officer.

The execution of Shah Mansur, so troubling to Akbar, was part of the vital dispensation of justice which was carried out even while the court was on the move. The Jesuits had noted Akbar's great concern with the proper rule of law and wrote that 'the King has the most precise regard for right and justice in the affairs of government'. Cases were usually brought forward before two judges but 'by the King's direction all capital cases, and all really important civil cases also, are conducted before himself. He is easily excited to anger, but soon cools down again. By nature moreover he is kindly and benevolent and is sincerely anxious that guilt should be punished, without malice indeed, but at the same time without undue leniency. Hence in cases in which he himself acts as judge the guilty are, by his own directions, not punished until he has given orders for the third time that this shall be done.'

From Delhi, the camp set out in a northerly direction, towards the low mountains and the foothills, so as to always be close to a water source for the needs of the gigantic army. Sappers were sent ahead to level the roads over 'rocks and crags and deep torrent-beds' under the charge of Akbar's best military engineer, Muhammad Qasim Mir Barr.

Two days after leaving Delhi, the caravan reached Sonepat, more 'famous than many a city on account of the swords, scimitars, daggers, poniards, and steel points for spears, pikes and javelins, which are skilfully manufactured here and exported to all parts of the empire'. Iron and steel were mined from the lower reaches of the Himalayas and brought to the town, which was populated by many weapons manufacturers for this very reason.

In Panipat, 'the inhabitants, especially the women, filled the balconies and the roofs in their eagerness to see the King', who must have cut a very dashing figure on his fine horse, surrounded by all his noblemen. But the king was not his usual affable self during the early part of this journey. Seemingly oppressed by Mirza Hakim's challenge, he was seen frowning, and anxious, caught up in an internal turmoil that no one could distract him from.

Monserrate has left a somewhat damning description of Hindustani towns which, he wrote, were striking from afar but when inspected closely it was found that 'the narrowness, aimless crookedness, and ill-planning of the streets deprive these cities of all beauty'. However the wealthy inhabitants, he conceded, 'adorn the roofs and arched ceilings of their houses with carvings and paintings; plant ornamental gardens in their courtyards; make tanks and fish-ponds, which are lined with tiles of various colours; construct artificial springs and fountains, which fling showers of water far into the air; and lay down promenades paved with brickwork or marble'. At every halt multitudes gathered to meet the Padshah. They brought him gifts for vows fulfilled, asked him for spiritual advice, and brought cups of water. Sick children were produced before the Padshah so that Akbar could breathe on them and infuse them with his miraculous healing powers. Abu'l Fazl writes that whenever Akbar set off outside the capital, he was always petitioned by crowds who 'ask for lasting bliss, for an upright heart, for advice how best to act, for strength of the body, for enlightenment, for the birth of a son, the reunion of friends, a long life, increase of wealth, elevation in rank, and many other things'.

In the towns and villages along the way, Holi was celebrated with an ecstatic fervour that the somewhat aghast Monserrate wrote about. 'During a space of fifteen days,' wrote the Jesuit, 'they are at liberty freely to cast dust upon themselves and upon whoever passes by. They plaster with mud their own bodies and those of any persons they may meet. They also squirt a red dye out of hollow reeds.'

When they reached Thanesar, Akbar along with Abu'l Fazl and Faizi visited the khanqah of an old and respected Chishti Sufi, Shaikh Jalal al-din. The elderly shaikh, who used to remain lying down and was only semi-conscious because of his great age, asked to be lifted upright to honour the visit of the Padshah, the 'Caliph of the age'. The three men had a long conversation on 'the secrets of Divine Realities and mystical sensibilities' and then, prompted by Akbar, Abu'l Fazl asked the shaikh a question: 'You have spent a long life, and have enjoyed the society of the good. Can you tell of a cure for melancholy?' The melancholy that Abu'l Fazl enquired about may have been that of Akbar himself. The Jesuit priests had also commented on the Padshah's tendency to introspection, saying that 'Akbar was by temperament melancholy', attributing it to the 'falling sickness', or epilepsy, and argued that this was the reason Akbar kept himself constantly busy, occupied, and focused. Akbar, too, once said that 'when his understanding is still undeveloped, man is in constant change of mood: at one time taking joy in festivities, at another sitting disconsolate in the house of mourning. When his vision is raised to higher things, sorrow and joy withdraw.' This tendency to occasional melancholia, and a lingering malaise, may have contributed to what would become a constant quest for revelations and spiritual solace. In Thanesar, Akbar had an emotional discussion with the Sufi shaikh and in the recorded memory of later Chishti tazkiras,* Akbar was said to have been so impressed with the shaikh that he even wanted to give up his kingship. The shaikh, however, would have dissuaded him saying:

> First you find a person who can match you and sit (on the throne) in your place, and then come for this work...remember God. Kingship does not prevent you from remembering Him.

The Mughal camp continued towards Kumaon, and could now see 'the snow-covered Himalaya mountains...gleaming white', while a cold wind blew over the fluttering standards of the army. 'The Hindus who inhabited Kumaon,' wrote Monserrate, 'do not own allegiance to [Akbar] and are protected by exceedingly thick forests.' At Kalanaur, where he had been proclaimed Padshah twenty-five years previously, Akbar stayed in the gardens which he had had planted all those decades ago. The Mughal camp slowly passed through plains and glens, fragrant in the cool air, and crossed rushing streams filled with the flickering movement of fish and lethal crocodiles. Rivers were

---

*A biographical memoir.

crossed either by constructing wooden bridges, or by lashing boats together with grass ropes and laying branches on them to make a temporary, bobbing construction. Akbar was insistent about the army crossing carefully in single file so that no confusion was caused with 'the cavalry, the infantry, the camels, the baggage-animals, the flocks and the herds' crossing together. Monserrate was impressed with Akbar's meticulous attention to detail and concern for the soldiery, writing that 'praise should be given to [Akbar]'s carefulness and foresight in giving such earnest attention to the safety of his army that he consulted its interests not only in the matter of water supply and of cheap corn, but also in the passage of rivers'.

In the evenings, stories were told or religion discussed with the Jesuits and Brahmin priests. Conspicuous by his absence on this carefully planned journey was Badauni. Caught up, by his own admission, in a 'bond of friendship' for a youth called 'Mazhar' which so distracted him, he was absent from court for an unforgivable period of a year. Badauni, even seventeen years after the event, did not regret the illicit passion which caused him such dereliction of duty. 'The delight of that taste,' he bravely proclaimed, 'has never left my heart.' Akbar was considerably less impressed with his unpredictable scholar. 'How was he left behind on this journey?' the Padshah enquired of Abu'l Fazl angrily, and excuses of ill-health had to be quickly invented to save Badauni from being struck off permanently from the royal rolls. Badauni's dereliction of duty by not attending to the Padshah was a much more serious crime than it may appear to be. Personal attendance by courtiers, when Akbar commanded it, was imperative. Monserrate had described it as a means by which the Padshah controlled his nobility, who needed to constantly be reminded of their place in the imperial hierarchy. 'In order to prevent the great nobles becoming insolent through the unchallenged enjoyment of power', wrote Monserrate, 'the king summons [them] to court...and gives them many imperious commands, as though they were his slaves—commands, moreover, obedience to which ill suits their exalted rank and dignity'.

Having crossed Ambala, the army reached Sirhind, a large city built on a broad plain 'beautified by many groves of trees and pleasant gardens'. This was a thriving city where 'bows, quivers, shoes, greaves and sandals', were made and exported to all the cities of the empire. There was a famous school of medicine in Sirhind, which exported doctors to other parts of the country. While camped at Sirhind, Akbar received the encouraging news that Mirza Hakim had fled Hindustan, and was heading away from Lahore, back towards Kabul. Intensely relieved by Mirza Hakim's decision, Akbar went on outings around the city on his favourite two-horse chariot on which, admitted the Jesuits, he looked very imposing. Mirza Hakim would be pursued, Akbar decided, and made to fight or to submit, once and for all.

On their long march across the country, the ordinary soldiers and low-ranking mansabdars kept themselves toned and fit by organizing drills and games. Since amirs did not routinely conduct training manoeuvres, the men exercised on their own to stay in fighting shape, with 'dumb-bells, heavy sticks of wood, clubs, and chainbows. Daily rehearsal of a coordinated sequence of movements called kasarat developed agility and quickness. The men wrestled and engaged in mock fights with heavy sticks and shields, they jousted at tent-pegs with lances, shot arrows at small targets while at a full gallop, and trained their horses to stand on their hind legs and jump forward in a manoeuver designed to attack elephants.' In their spare time the soldiers would have played chess, one of the most common pastimes then.

Near the banks of the Jhelum, Akbar was taken to the top of a steep and craggy hill, the Balnath Thilla, to visit an ancient hermit, the Balnath. From the top of the Thilla the snow-capped Himalayas were clearly visible and far below, at the foot of the hill, the Jhelum sparkled. This extremely venerable religious site, predating by millennia the coming of Guru Gorakhnath, was now the most well-known base of the Kanphata yogis of the country. They derived their name from their custom of splitting the cartilage of the ear to put huge, distinctive earrings through them. Many naked ascetics, disciples of the Balnath, came out of their caves to receive the respectful salutations of the camp followers. They were a sect of sun-worshippers, according to Monserrate, and saluted the rising sun with 'the concerted sound of flutes and conches'. They lived a frugal life, eating 'only cooked lentils and ghi'. They had a reputation for communicating with the spirit world and practising magic, exorcism, witchcraft, and some primitive medicine. The Gorakhnath sect had rejected traditional religious practices and, like the Bhakts of Kabir, sought an identity that could 'somehow be both Hindu and Muslim and neither, all at the same time'. One of their sayings was 'the Hindu calls on Ram, the Muslim on Khuda, the yogi calls on the invisible one, in whom there is neither Ram nor Khuda'. Akbar walked up to the top of the hill and 'did reverence to the place and to the prophet with bare feet and loosened hair'.

It was when the Mughal camp finally reached the river Indus, known locally as the Blue Water, that the army faltered for the first time. 'Some were influenced by ignorance,' grumbled Abu'l Fazl, 'some by smallness of intellect, some by dread of a cold country...and a love for India.' The world had changed since the time Babur had to plead with his Chaghatai clansmen to remain in hot and inhospitable Hindustan while they yearned for the bracing cold of Kabul and its sweet, consoling melons. While the camp remained by the river for fifty days, Akbar went with Abu'l Fazl to visit the shrine of the Gorkhatris, near Peshawar, in a cave so deep that 'there are nowhere else in the whole world such narrow and dark hermits' cells as at this place'. The men had to crawl in darkness through a tortuous cave system to reach the sacred prayer spot; it was such a daunting and depressing task that most of the men lost heart and turned back.

When the great army finally reached the outskirts of Kabul, the Padshah took the fight to his half-brother. An advance guard under young prince Murad, only eleven years old, led the attack as astrologers had decreed that his was the brightest star at the time. Akbar followed with a small contingent while the bulk of the army was left behind with Salim, to advance slowly.

The attacking force included some of the famous imperial elephants, Gaj Mangal, Mukut, and Lakshmi Sundar. Each animal carried on its back four small wooden turrets from which soldiers fired muskets or shot their arrows simultaneously, a moving menace of fearsome firepower. About the cavalry, Monserrate noted that 'the Mongols, Persians, Parthians, Turks, Sogdians, Bachtrae and Scythians all use the same fighting tactics'. They were 'most dangerous when they seem to be flying in headlong riot for, turning round on their horses, although they are going at full gallop, they fling their javelins with such deadly aim that they can transfix the eye of an enemy'. These elite horsemen fought as light cavalry, galloping while standing almost upright in their stirrups. The Rajputs meanwhile were employed as heavy cavalry, fighting hand to hand with lance and swords while firmly seated in the saddle, legs fully extended.

While the mansabdars were sheathed in gleaming armour, the regular cavalrymen had to content themselves with long quilted coats to absorb the impact of swords and arrows. On the lower body, they wore cotton trousers tied with a shawl and folds of quilted cloth to protect their heads in lieu of helmets. Raja Man Singh, Madhu Singh, Surat Singh, and other elite noblemen threw themselves into the attack and this was when Mirza Hakim sent the offer to Akbar's soldiers, claiming that 'the Turanis and Persians...will join us without fighting and the brave Rajputs and gallant Afghans will end their days...' Abu'l Fazl was greatly scornful of this tactic, saying that 'the great deeds of the Rajputs and the Shaikh-zadas of India [were] unknown to [Mirza Hakim]'. The men disdained Mirza Hakim's call and his army was soon routed and Mirza Hakim fled the scene of battle.

After first sending heralds to announce to the 'merchants, workmen, and common people' that they need not fear any reprisals, Akbar marched into Kabul where he had spent his boyhood in the shade of the chinar trees and the riotous company of his milk brothers.

While in Kabul, Akbar attended to two particularly galling derelictions of duty in his officers. The paymaster, who had been sent ahead of Akbar's party with 15,000 pieces of gold coins to pay Mirza Murad's troops' salaries, had been ambushed and captured by Mirza Hakim's men. Despite having enough men to put up a determined resistance, he had allowed himself to be shamefully captured without inflicting or receiving a single cut or wound. For this the Padshah 'upbraided him soundly for his carelessness and cowardice'. Even more embarrassing was the routing of Shaikh Jamal Bakhtiyar, a brother-in-law of the Padshah's, who had also been ambushed and put to flight. So terrified was the man at the reaction of the Padshah that he 'adopted the scanty clothing, bare head and unshod feet of a dervish', preferring a life of banishment to the utter humiliation of Akbar's fury, for he knew that Akbar was 'severe [on] breaches of military discipline'. Both men were, however, eventually forgiven.

After a short stay in Kabul, during which Akbar visited the quiet resting place of his grandfather at the Bagh-e-Babur, and having easily made his point, he pragmatically handed over the rule of the city to the mirza's sister, Bakht un-Nisa Begum, and returned to Fatehpur Sikri. Monserrate noted that while on the long journey to Kabul Akbar had had a white tent set up in the royal enclosure within which he had performed his prayers, on the way back 'he pretended not to notice that it was no longer erected'. With Mirza Hakim, the Timurid prince, neutralized, Akbar could now define a new identity for the Padshah of Hindustan. No longer would he feel the need to ostentatiously show himself to be a pious and orthodox Muslim monarch.

Indeed, Akbar seemed released of a burden that had cast a shadow over the past year of his life and he recovered his earlier lightness of spirit. When twelve deserters were captured and brought into custody, one of the men who had been assigned capital punishment begged for a chance to approach the Padshah. 'O King,' he pleaded, 'order me not to the gibbet, for nature has bestowed upon me marvellous powers in a certain direction.' Akbar's interest was piqued. '[I]n what direction do you thus excel, O miserable wretch?' the Padshah asked the harried prisoner. The man claimed he could sing wonderfully and when asked to demonstrate his skill, proceeded to croak in a 'discordant and harsh' manner so that everyone started murmuring and laughing. 'Pardon me this poor performance,' shouted out the prisoner, sensing that the Padshah was amused, 'for these guards of yours dragged me along so roughly and cruelly, on a hot and dusty road, and pummelled me so brutally with their fists, that my throat is full of dust, and my voice so husky that I cannot do myself justice in singing.' Akbar was so entertained by the man's ready wit that he pardoned not just him but also his fellow traitors.

There was less clemency for villages in the plains across the Khyber Pass, loyalists of Mirza Hakim who had refused to sell grain and supplies to the army despite being offered large sums of money. The villagers had fled their homes as soon as they heard that the great caravan was on its way back, and watched helplessly from across the river while their villages were put to the torch.

There were some among Akbar's party who demanded that Mirza Hakim be hunted down and executed. Akbar refused to do so, saying, 'Mirza Hakim is a memorial of the Emperor Humayun though he has acted ungratefully, I can be no other than forbearing'. Mirza Hakim's revolt was to be the last great challenge to Akbar's right to rule. From here on, the glory sought would be divine.

THE LION OF GOD

The scale of the Nauroz celebrations that took place in Fatehpur Sikri over eighteen days in March 1582 was unprecedented. More than a decade after construction had begun, Fatehpur Sikri was ablaze in its final resplendence. In the golden spring light of March, all the buildings of the palace city glowed—the red sandstone of Sikri, also the royal crimson colour of Kshatriyas—the colour of kings. Within an encircling wall more than 11 kilometres in length, a series of interlocking palaces and courtyards lay along the ridge overlooking the city—a harmonious ensemble of monumental spaces and small, intimate ones. Some of the largest buildings included the main assembly hall, the diwan-e-aam, a large, majestic courtyard with 114 cloistered bays and a raised central pavilion. At the other end of the ridge was the largest gateway ever built in the country at the time, the Buland Darwaza, over 130 feet high, and vaulting even higher due to an additional flight of 123 steps leading from the street below. This majestic gateway led to an immense Jami Masjid, the first of the congregational mosques of the Mughals, built to accommodate 10,000 worshippers. In the middle of the immense courtyard of the mosque was the jewel-like tomb of Salim Chishti, plastered white. Between these two structures were connecting buildings in unusual styles, including the five-floored Panch Mahal topped with a domed chattri, the Anuptalao with its rectangular pond, and the diwan-e-khas, with its utterly mesmerizing massive sculpted column, supporting a stone throne platform.

The diwan-e-aam and the diwan-e-khas were decorated with wall hangings of gold and silk, European curtains, paintings, and high tents. The bazaars of Fatehpur Sikri and Agra were similarly ablaze with bunting and cloth and 'the Emperor sent for all sorts of troops of singers and musicians, both Hindu and Persian, and dancers, both men and women, by thousands of thousands'. Akbar sat on a golden throne, wearing a crown, and called on all the people to celebrate, to 'show their joy either by leaping, singing or dancing'.

Hindustan was a land of clamorous and varied celebrations and there were 'actors, dancers, singers, players of instruments, mime artistes, rope dancers, jugglers, tap dancers, troubadours and ganikas'. A particularly appreciated entertainment was afforded by the Bahurupi, whose performance included startlingly accurate mimicry of people and animals. 'Youths disguised themselves as old men so successfully,' marvelled Abu'l Fazl, 'that they impose upon the most acute observers.' All those who presented themselves were given gifts, wine, and a banquet of food and, not surprisingly, throngs of people jostled to view the extravagant affair and 'whole communities of jogis arrived, with their chiefs'. Monserrate was astonished to note that these jogis 'profanely and frivolously laid aside all pretense of piety, danced impudently and shamelessly, and fulsomely flattered the King in the songs they sang'. Women were allowed into the palaces and were taken to see the beautiful decorations inside and they may even have witnessed the dance performances of the celebrated Kanchani. These were dancers of the Kanjari caste to whom Akbar had given the title Kanchani, or gilded, and who performed for the ladies of the harem. According to the later French traveller Bernier, 'most of these kenchens are handsome and well dressed, and sing to perfection; and their limbs being extremely supple, they dance with wonderful agility, and are always correct in regard to time'.

Another ceremony that may have originated from Persian precedents of Nauroz in the reign of Shah Ismail took place at this time. This ceremony involved weighing the emperor at the beginning of the solar year. Other scholars see in this tuladan a revival of old Hindu customs. This ceremony, begun in the time of Humayun but gaining in importance only under Akbar, became very elaborate during the reigns of future Padshahs. On both his lunar and solar birthdays, Akbar was weighed against twelve articles such as gold, quicksilver, silk, perfumes, copper, ruh-i-tutiya*, drugs,† ghee, iron, rice-milk, and seven types of grains and salt. Once he had been weighed, the articles were distributed among the needy, both Hindus and Muslims.

On each day of the Nauroz, Akbar went to the tent of a select

---

*Zinc.
†Medicines, which were expensive and rare.

nobleman and was entertained lavishly by him. These privileged amirs would have demanded the very best banquets for the Padshah from their cooks and there would have been kebabs, marinated meats of all kinds, and elaborately spiced vegetables. Perhaps some of the Rajput noblemen would have been aware of the *Ksemakutuhalam* (Diet and Well-Being), written for a Rajput ruler in 1550, which listed a veritably overwhelming selection of meats that could be cooked for a king including boar, lamb, goat, venison, rabbit, lizard, pig, peacock, tortoise, and a variety of game birds. In addition, it was recommended that rice, dal, ghee, papads, and vegetables be served along with the meats and as for the vegetables, the author Ksemasarma seems to have brazenly favoured aubergines over all others and to have been very particular in their preparation, for he says: 'Fie on the meal that has no aubergine. Fie on the aubergine that has no stalk. Fie on the aubergine that has a stalk but is not cooked in oil and fie upon the aubergine that is cooked in oil without using asafoetida!' For eighteen days the music, the women's laughter, the swirling skirts of the dancers, the hoarse singing of the yogis, tumbled out from the courtyards of Fatehpur Sikri into the bazaars below and such celebrations, it was whispered, had not been seen in thirty years.

For Akbar, at the dawn of his fortieth birthday, this was a glittering moment. He had won a great victory, not only against Mirza Hakim but against all those who had used the mirza as ballast for their claims of heresy against the Padshah. After three years of intense turbulence, both within the ibadat khana and on the battlefields, Akbar had forced a reckoning. Opposition to his supremacy had been categorically quelled, both in the borderlands of his kingdom and in the order of theologians who had challenged him. The Jesuit priests themselves marvelled that there had been no one since Timur who had won so many battles and conquered so great an area. Starting with his subduing of Bairam Khan and the control of Delhi twenty-five years previously, Akbar had gone on to conquer Malwa, Gondwana, Rajasthan, Gujarat, Bihar, Bengal, Kabul, and would soon annex Kashmir and the Sind. All that would remain, they surmised, was the Deccan.

Now Akbar was free to formulate a more capacious world view, one which would reflect with greater accuracy the teeming clans of noblemen who made up the Mughal court, each with their own truths and divinities. For the astrologers who kept a close watch on the stars, this was a moment charged with significance because the two superior planets, Saturn and Jupiter, were in conjunction, which was as rare as it was powerful. It had occurred at the birth of Timur, and at the birth of the Prophet Muhammad. Now after a thousand years had passed, the planets were aligning themselves again, to announce the coming of the second Islamic millennium with all its possibility of renewal and rebirth.

If the celebrations of the new year were resplendent, there was also a parallel enthusiasm for change and new beginnings. One of the first decisions that Akbar took in this year was the liberating of his own slaves. 'We have freed all the imperial slaves who exceed hundreds and thousands', said Akbar. 'To count as my slaves those whom I have captured by force means stepping outside the realm of justice and discernment.' 'From that day on,' added Abu'l Fazl, 'his majesty, nurtured by divine knowledge, styled his slaves chelas.' Those former slaves who wished to leave were allowed to do so and those that remained would be given wages and duties to perform according to their capabilities. No mention, however, was made of the female slaves who, it might be assumed, remained sequestered. Akbar then asked his closest courtiers to also think on the matter and to suggest one meaningful measure that would be beneficial for the empire and its people. Prince Salim, thirteen years old now, and perhaps most aware of his father's own feelings, suggested that children younger than twelve not be allowed to marry. Akbar was pleased with this suggestion and issued orders for its implementation. Raja Todar Mal, Raja Birbal, Faizi, Abdur Rahim, the physician Hakim Abul Fath, and Aziz Koka were some of the noblemen included in the deliberations and they all suggested various measures designed to improve the well-being of the most deserving and vulnerable.

In the course of this year there would be provocative experiments and changes at Fatehpur Sikri that would be talked about and recorded by the visitors at court. It was noted by all that Akbar now began his day in a most unusual manner. At the highest point of the roof of the palace, Akbar had had a wooden building 'of ingenious workmanship' constructed and from this building, in the cool and watchful dawn, Akbar worshipped the rising sun. For Badauni, it was clear that it was 'the accursed Birbal' who had convinced the Padshah:

> ...that since the sun gives light to all, and ripens all grain, fruits and products of the earth, and supports the life of mankind, therefore that luminary should be the object of worship and veneration; that the face should be turned towards the rising and not towards the setting (towards Mecca) sun...that man should venerate fire, water, stones and trees, and all natural objects, even down to cows and their dung.

In the evenings, when all the lamps and the candles were lit, the whole court 'had to rise up respectfully'. This Badauni attributed to an equally nefarious influence—Akbar's Rajput wives. 'From early youth, in compliment to his wives, the daughters of the Rajahs of Hind,' noted Badauni, 'he had within the female apartments continued to offer the hom, which is a ceremony derived from sun-worship.' Now, continued Badauni, Akbar went one step further and prostrated himself in public before the fire as well as the sun. Akbar also began appearing in the diwan-e-aam with a tilak on the forehead and a rakhi on the wrist, tied by a Brahmin, as a blessing. Immediately all the elegant noblemen adopted the custom and it became de rigueur to wear a rakhi to court. Jahangir remembered this custom and wrote that 'the Hindu Amirs and others in imitation of them performed the ceremony of rakhi in adorning [Akbar], making strings of rubies and royal pearls and flowers jewelled with gems of great value and binding them on his auspicious arms'.

He 'prohibited the slaughter of cows and the eating of their flesh', bemoaned Badauni, 'because the Hindus devoutly worship them and esteem their dung as pure'. This restriction on eating beef was seen as a particular injunction against all Muslims and it was Badauni, once again, who also noted that since 'he had introduced a whole host of the daughters of eminent Hindu Rajahs into his haram, and they had influenced his mind against the eating of beef and garlic and onions, and association with people who wore beards—and such things he then avoided and still does avoid'. The Jesuits were clearly discomfited by all these new changes, for Acquaviva wrote a letter to the Provincial of Goa, confessing that 'the King keeps this Court in a great state of embarrassment with the novelties he introduces every day in it. For among other things,' he went on to write, 'he seems to pay much reverence to God's creatures such as the sun and the moon. And from Saturday evening to the end of Sunday he does not eat flesh-meat, and I am credibly informed that many heathens [Hindus] here do this.' A well-known quote of Akbar's also points to his gradual distaste for the eating of meat:

> It is not right that a man should make his stomach the grave of animals... Were it not for the thought of the difficulty of sustenance I would prohibit men from eating animals. The reason why I do not altogether abandon it myself is that many others might willingly forego it likewise, and be thus cast into despondency.

It was not only the Hindus who were encouraged in their rituals and practices, for the Parsees 'proclaimed the religion of Zardusht as the true one and declared reverence to fire to be superior to every other kind of worship'. They taught the Padshah the rituals of their religion and Akbar decreed that the sacred fire be maintained at Fatehpur Sikri, under the charge of Abu'l Fazl, and kept eternally burning. For 'though illiterate', agreed the Jesuits, '[Akbar] loved to hear discussions on points of theology and philosophy and with an open mind, listened to any man learned in the law, whether he was Parsee or Hindu or Christian'. Akbar had heard of the renown of the Jain priest, Hiravijaya Suri. According to Jain folklore, Akbar happened to witness a religious procession celebrating six months of fasting by a Jain monk Champa and was intrigued. The Padshah immediately sent two prominent Jain citizens of Agra, Bhanu Kalyan and Singh Ramji, to summon Hiravijaya to the Mughal court. He also issued farmans to the Governor of Gujarat to make all the necessary arrangements for a comfortable journey for the Jain monk.

As for the Christians, Akbar 'always seemed not only to favour them, but to heap honours upon them in his desire to show his affection towards them. For when 'they saluted him, which they did with uncovered heads, he answered with a nod and a bright smile... When a council was being held...he used to make them sit beside him. He shook hands with them cordially and familiarly.... Several times he paced up and down with his arm round Rudolf's shoulders.... He wished the priests to be sharers of his inmost thoughts, both in good and ill fortune—no common mark of love and kindness'. The same casualness and ease of manner that Rafiuddin Shirazi had been amazed by all those years before, when he had struggled to recognize the Padshah of Hindustan as the youth leaning against a friend, Akbar now demonstrated with the Jesuits. Grasping them affectionately by the arm, he would listen to their disquisitions, head slightly tilted as was his wont. The charm of his personality made them believe that, in that instant, Akbar's attention was entirely theirs. Acquaviva's ardent desire to convert this extraordinary Muslim king and save his soul never abated. 'It was remarkable,' admitted Monserrate, 'with what zeal he longed that [Akbar] should be converted from a wicked life to the worship of God.' And when Akbar understood Acquaviva's motivation, continued Monserrate, 'he began to love Rudolf warmly, not because he had any idea of becoming a Christian, or had much of an opinion of our religion but because (as he used to say himself), knowing that Rudolf regarded Christianity as the best of all religions, he perceived his love for himself (the King) in the fact that he tried so earnestly to induce him to accept this best of all paths to salvation'.

Quite apart from the many religious sects there were also, at Fatehpur Sikri, those who made up the many strands of Hindustani life in their teeming, provocative multitudes. There were, wrote the aghast Monserrate, 'worthless profligates, some of those who dress and adorn themselves like women' but when the Jesuits tried to convince Akbar to have them thrown out, he just laughed genially and walked away, limping slightly in his left leg, as was his habit, promising to think about what they had said. Monserrate admitted that Akbar was 'especially remarkable for his love of keeping great crowds of people around him and in his sight; and thus it comes about that his court is always thronged with multitudes of men of every type, though especially with the nobles, whom he commands to come from their province(s) and reside at court of a certain period each year. When he goes outside the palace, he is surrounded and followed by these nobles.' And it was not just the Christians that Akbar made himself available to—Monserrate also wrote about all those who prayed to meet him, both great and small, and that 'it is hard to exaggerate how accessible he makes himself to all who wish audience of him. For he creates an opportunity almost every day for any of the common people or of the nobles to see him and converse with him; and he endeavours to show himself pleasant-spoken and affable, rather than severe, towards all who come to speak with him. It is very remarkable how great an effect this courtesy and affability has in attaching to him the minds of his subjects.' Jahangir would also attest to this trait in his father, when he wrote his memoir many years later: 'He associated with the good of every race and creed and persuasion, and was gracious to all in accordance with their condition and understanding.'

If the Jesuits, the yogis, the Jains and the Parsees at Fatehpur Sikri had their more sedate garments, the nobility were all resplendent in their courtly clothes, for though the orthodox Muslim was constrained to wear clothes of 'wool, linen or cotton; and must be white', according to Monserrate, nonetheless '[Akbar] is so contemptuous of the instructions given by the false law-giver, that he wears garments of silk, beautifully embroidered in gold. His military cloak comes down only as far as the knee, according to the Christian fashion; and his boots cover his ankles completely.' 'The wearing of gold and silk dresses [at prayer-time]' agreed Badauni, 'was made obligatory.'

The kar khanas of the empire were kept busy all year round supplying robes and dresses for the Mughal court. Every year, a thousand complete suits (sar-o-pa, head to toe) were made for the imperial wardrobe, some for the Padshah and some to be given as gifts to noblemen. At any given time, 120 new robes were kept in readiness. The materials used for these qabas, payjamas, turbans, and overcoats included silk, zarbaft (cloth woven using golden thread), kamkhwab (cloth made of gold), tiladoz, mukkeshkar, and muslin from Malwa. Deccani muslins were reputed to be so fine that they were invisible when floated on water. An item of clothing which became popular at this time was the patka, which Akbar named the katzeb, or waistband. It was a simple, narrow band of cloth wound around the waist with the two ends hanging in front. With Akbar's successors, this patka would become very elaborate, detailed, and intricately embroidered. Akbar himself remained fairly austere in the way he dressed, often wearing fine white muslin shot through with gold thread. The gorgeous robes he wore on the occasion of his birthday, however, took the tailors a whole year to complete.

In September 1582, Acquaviva wrote about a new festival called Merjan (Persian Equinox) that was celebrated at Fatehpur Sikri. When Acquaviva questioned the court astrologers about it, he was told that 'it was a feast which the ancient Kings of Persia, who worshipped fire, used to celebrate'. Akbar ordered that 'all the captains (noblemen), should dress in festal attire, and there was native music and dancing'. Akbar had new coins stamped with 'Era of the Thousand' written on them and had a new history commissioned, the *Tarikh-i Alfi*, beginning with the death of the Prophet. These unusual celebrations and changes introduced to the court were noted with some bemusement by the Jesuits but it was Badauni who kept the most scandalized record of them.

He wrote his clandestine biography of Akbar long after his career at court had floundered hopelessly. It was brought out after he died in 1614 and was banned by Jahangir for being too shocking; Jahangir also had Badauni's sons arrested for good measure. For Badauni, these 'millennial celebrations' were the result of Akbar believing he could now openly criticize orthodox Islam and propose new, heretical alternatives as 1,000 years had elapsed since Prophet Muhammad's birth, and a new millennium beckoned. He quoted the following verses by a tenth-century Ismaili writer that some Shias at court were using in praise of Akbar, to illustrate his point.

> In 989 according to the decree of fate,
> The stars from all sides shall meet together.
> In the year of Leo the month of Leo, the day of Leo
> The Lion of God will stand forth from behind the veil.

In the same month, a great feast was held by Abdur Rahim to celebrate his new position as ataliq of Salim. Abdur Rahim invited the emperor to be present at the banquet and the young nobleman outdid himself in the gorgeous arrangements he organized. The path from the fort of the walled city to Abdur Rahim's haveli was strewn with flowers made of gold and silver. Outside the haveli itself, rubies were scattered along the lane. The entrance to his residence was lined with cloths of satin and velvet while, inside the grounds, Abdur Rahim had a dais made at the cost of 1,25,000 rupees. Once the Padshah was seated, Abdur Rahim offered him jewels, exquisite garments, and refined and advanced weapons of war. The feast prepared would have had the favoured combinations of meat and dried fruit, as well as large quantities of saffron and asafoetida (hing), which were all Persian staples. Asafoetida brought in by the Mughals became very popular with the vegetarian population of Hindustan because, when cooked in oil, it took on a garlicky flavour that made it a good substitute for onions and garlic. It was also a good digestive, useful in combination with indigestible pulses and beans, and quickly became an indispensable part of local cuisine. So pleased was Akbar with this celebration that he offered Abdur Rahim all the insignia of royalty normally reserved for princes of the blood. Mirza Khan was now a nobleman to be reckoned with.

That the exuberance and fevered anticipation around the coming of the new Islamic millennium led to a great deal of mystical experimentation in the sixteenth century is well known. The belief that this was when a mujaddid, or renewer, would appear to cleanse Islam of corruption, and renew its essence had been building in successive waves of fervour and fury as different sects were convinced that they were the ones to offer the final truth. For Akbar, this appeared to be a cosmically perfect time in which to finally perfect and declare the many ideas he had been experimenting with. From the time Akbar had witnessed the fallibility of the orthodox ulema in the ibadat khana, it was as though he had been freed from an earlier adherence to orthodoxy. Badauni had written that since the ulema constantly contradicted each other, and would use fallacious arguments to first support, and then disprove the very same beliefs, Akbar's faith was shaken. And just as he had once believed with devotion everything they said, now that that faith had cracked 'he inferred the known from the known and rejected also their predecessors'. Where orthodox Islam was found wanting, Akbar turned for answers to more mystical alternatives within Islam and then to the different religions in his wide kingdom. Badauni had noted with sadness that 'everything that pleased him, he picked and chose from, anyone except a Moslem, and anything that was against his disposition and ran counter to his wishes, he thought fit to reject and cast aside'.

There were a number of subterranean streams of thinking in the sixteenth century that contributed to Akbar's religious experimentation and much scholarly work has been done on the subject. There was the Sufi belief in 'Unity in Multiplicity' known as Wahdat-al-Wujud, which Akbar had long known through the Chishti Sufis and which allowed for a great deal of flexibility and cultural pluralism. There was the doctrine of the 'Unity of Existence' present in medieval Islam through the work of Ibn Arabi and the theory of 'Divine Light' of Shihab al-Din Suhrawardi Maqtul, all of which Akbar would have heard about through Shaikh Mubarak and Abu'l Fazl. There was also the Nirguna Bhakti of the Bhakti saints such as Kabir, who saw no difference between Hindus and Muslims, and whose incandescent teachings raged through the Braj heartland.

In all that he heard and saw around him, Akbar seemed to adopt only that which he could physically and viscerally experience and shape. This was entirely in character and he behaved just as he did in all other facets of his life, when he was seen making ribbons like a lace-maker, and filing, sawing, hewing, polishing and quarrying, always needing to experience the world directly.

In his quest for spiritual truths he prostrated himself in front of many gods—he prayed to the sun, he whispered mantras, he worshipped fire, he kept fasts, and he examined his conscience. And in his own manner, every assertion he came across Akbar would now submit to the test of reason or, as Abu'l Fazl put it, 'intellect (khirad)' would be elevated to a 'high pedestal (buland paigi)'. Now aql (reason) would be praised above mere taqid (imitation). There had been indications much earlier in Akbar's reign that showed the Padshah questioning long-accepted suppositions. Whether it was testing the theory of a 'natural language' through the isolation of infants or questioning the need for circumcision—'it is a remarkable thing that men should insist on the ceremony of circumcision for children' said Akbar, 'who are otherwise excused from the burden of all religious obligations'—the Padshah would now put to the test and interrogate all claims that appeared dubious.

As he reconciled these many troubling ideas into a structure with which to rule a diverse country, justly and well, Akbar took the ideas of Ibn Arabi to draw a conclusion that was abhorrent to the orthodox, whether Muslims, like Badauni, or Christians, like the Jesuits. Akbar proposed that 'all religions are either equally true or equally illusory'. In addition to his personal search for a greater truth, Akbar wanted to develop and implement, as pointed out by Irfan Habib, 'an accepted code of ethical and legal behaviour', that not only made him a better person but also a greater king to all the subjects in his land. This would make the Hindustan of the late sixteenth century a place unique in the Muslim world and, indeed, in the world at large.

UNIVERSAL CIVILITY

It had been seven years since the royal ladies' hajj party had been gone from Fatehpur Sikri so when they returned to the capital in April 1582, they were greeted with exuberant and resplendent joy. Gulbadan and her party had decided to stop en route at Muinuddin Chishti's dargah for a final thanksgiving and Salim, favourite of the harem, was sent to Ajmer to formally welcome the ladies back to Hindustan. Every day after that a different nobleman of rank was sent to salute the women as they made their way back to Fatehpur Sikri and when they reached Bharatpur, Akbar himself rode out to meet his aunt. The Padshah had had the pavements in Fatehpur Sikri covered with silken shawls and he 'conducted her himself to her palace in a gorgeous litter, scattering largesse meanwhile to the crowds'. As Gulbadan, Salima Sultan, and the other women settled back into the harem, after their many years away, they would hear from Hamida Banu and the other ladies of some truly intriguing changes at court. Perhaps the most provocative of the new visitors they were told about were the Jesuits, for from this time on, after the return of Gulbadan, the priests began to feel decidedly unwelcome at the Mughal court.

The Mughal harem had always shown a great solidarity in the causes they supported from the time of Babur, whether it was protecting the interests of a favoured prince or undermining the power of a disruptive regent or arranging marriages. In their distaste for the Jesuits and the Portuguese, the harem appeared to have been united once again and it was evident enough to have been recorded by a foreign traveller, Thomas Coryat, an Englishman at the court of Jahangir. '[Akbar] never denied [his mother] anything but this,' said Thomas Coryat, 'that shee demanded of him that our Bible might be hanged about an asses necke and beaten about the towne of Agra, for that the Portugals...tied (the Quran) about the necke of a dogge and beat the same dog about the towne of Ormuz.' Hamida Banu's fury at the Portuguese's disrespect of the Koran was understandable but this once, Akbar refused to do as she suggested for 'the contempt of any religion was the contempt of God'.

If the Timurid ladies were horrified at the blasphemous disrespect shown to the Prophet and Islam, then the Rajput wives would have found equally intolerable the repeated suggestion by the Jesuits that Akbar distance himself from all but one wife. '[H]is mother, his aunt, and many of the great lords of the Kingdom who attended him,' wrote a biographer of the Jesuits, 'left no stone unturned to discredit the Fathers and their teaching.' It was further noted that 'his bevy of wives followed their example; for they realised that all of them, save one only, would be abandoned if the King became a Christian'. The ladies, who were all dearly devoted to Salim, perhaps also feared and resented the growing influence the Jesuits appeared to have on the young prince. Many decades later Jahangir would recount an incident from this time concerning Acquaviva, 'whose intimate friend he had been'. He described how he came upon the priest when he was scourging himself, for Salim had been sleeping close enough to the Jesuit's quarters to have been disturbed by the sound of the thudding whip. When Salim entered Acquaviva's room, he found a whip 'so covered with blood that drops were falling on the floor' and when questioned, Acquaviva 'tried to cover with a laugh what the flush on his face and the modesty of his eyes plainly betrayed'. Salim was astounded both by the self-denial and flagellation as well as the modesty of the Jesuit who tried to hide the bloodied whip but the ladies, it may be supposed, would have been more leery about this threatening friendship.

In the end the Jesuits were finally undone by Akbar himself who, they admitted, 'was always pondering in his mind which nation has retained the true religion of God; and to this question he constantly gave the most earnest thought'. At the end of one of their last discussions in the ibadat khana Akbar told the assembled scholars and courtiers:

> I perceive that there are varying customs and beliefs of varying religious paths. For the teachings of the Hindus, the Musalmans, the Jazdini, the Jews and the Christians are all different. But the followers of each religion regard the institutions of their

own religion as better that those of any other. Not only so, but they strive to convert the rest to their own way of belief. If these refuse to be converted, they not only despise them but also regard them for this very reason as their enemies. And this causes me to feel many serious doubts and scruples.

The point about the conversions may have stung the Jesuits and they 'began to suspect that he was intending to found a new religion with matter taken from all the existing systems'. Jahangir also talked about this aspect of his father in his memoir when he wrote: '[T]he professors of various faiths had room in the broad expanse of his incomparable sway. This was different from the practice in other realms for in Persia there is room for Shias only and in Turkey, India (non-Mughal) and Turan there is room for Sunnis only.'

Dismayed and defeated, the Jesuits decided to leave the Mughal court, not wishing to give Akbar 'the pearls of the Gospel to tread and crush under his feet'. They asked Abu'l Fazl with some mystification why Akbar desired their presence at the court so passionately when it was clear now he had no intention of becoming a Christian. 'The King, having a desire for all kinds of knowledge, and liking to show his greatness,' replied Abu'l Fazl succinctly, '[is] delighted to have at his court people of all nations.' 'My father always associated with the learned of every creed and religion', agreed Jahangir, 'especially with Pandits and the learned of India'. As for Akbar himself, when Acquaviva told him he was planning to leave, he replied with simple sincerity: 'I love you, Father, and rejoice to have you near me; for you have taught me many things which have pleased me more than all I have learnt from others.' In a letter to the Jesuit mission in Goa, Akbar admitted that, 'the Almighty, through his eternal favours and perpetual grace, had turned (his) heart in such a way as continuously to create a craving for God' while Jahangir wrote about Akbar that he 'never for one moment forgot God'.

The pearls that Akbar did collect, despite the Jesuits' misgivings, contained multitudes. They could not be constrained within the rigorous limits of the Jesuit doctrine, for Akbar's kingdom contained almost limitless ways of worshipping the divine. It was probably just as well that the Jesuits had left by the time Akbar was taking part in the ceremonies that Badauni wrote about with despair. There were masses of people, wrote Badauni, who 'stood every morning opposite to the window, near which His Majesty used to pray to the sun, and declared that they had made vows not to rinse their mouth, nor to eat and drink, before they had seen the blessed countenance of the Emperor. And every evening there was a regular Court assembly of needy Hindus and Musalmans, all sorts of people, men and women, healthy and sick, a queer gathering and a most terrible crowd. No sooner had His Majesty finished saying the thousand and one names of the "Greater Luminary", and stepped out into the balcony, than the whole crowd prostrated themselves.'

From these many experiences of God there arose in Akbar a desire for harmony, as opposed to the conflict and the disharmony of the earlier ibadat khana discussions. Abu'l Fazl would make it his life's work to articulate and expand upon this notion in his biography of Akbar, which he would begin to write in a few years. 'As the world's Lord exercises sway over it on the principle of sulh kul, universal civility,' wrote Abu'l Fazl, 'every group of people can live in accordance with its own doctrine without apprehension, and everyone can worship God after his own fashion.' This spirit of harmony, present also in the Bhakti and Sufi movements, as well as the pantheistic philosophy of Ibn Arabi, did not, as historian Harbans Mukhia has shown, just prescribe a passive 'tolerance' of all religions but was an active ideological state. In his work Abu'l Fazl blames the 'blowing of the chill blast of inflexible custom and the low...lamp of wisdom' for being the cause of disharmony whereas 'if the doctrine of an enemy be in itself good, why should hands be stained in the blood of its professors? And even were it otherwise, the sufferer from the malady of folly deserves commiseration, not hostility and the shedding of his blood.' For Akbar, it would appear that after all his experiments and his ecstatic visions, he was beginning to relate to a concept of divinity as described in the teachings of the Nirguna Bhakti. In a letter to Murad, written in 1591, Akbar told his son:

> Devotion to the Matchless one is beyond the limits of the spoken word whether in respect of form, material attributes, letter or sound. Devotion to the Matchless one is also matchless.

The influence of these thoughts in governance, especially through the works of Tusi and Rumi, which were among Akbar's favourite texts, has also been pointed out by scholars. Akbar was particularly fond of Rumi's *Masnavi*, reciting them from memory. One such masnavi, which seemed to reflect Akbar's deepest convictions, was:

> Thou has come to unite
> Not to separate
> For the people of Hind, the idiom of Hindi is praiseworthy
> For the people of Sind, their own is to be praised.

In a proclamation of the royal code of conduct issued by Akbar to all officials, there are thoughts which echoed the same sentiments of active tolerance and compassion:

> The best prayer is service to humanity. They should welcome all with generosity, whether friends, foes, relatives or strangers. In particular they should be kind to the recluse and seek the company and advice of the pious.
>
> They should be ever watchful of the conditions of people, the big and the small (for) chief-ship or ruler-ship means to guard and protect... And they should not interfere in any person's religion. For, wise people in this worldly matter, which is transient—do not prefer that which harms. How can they then choose the dis-advantageous way in matters of faith—which pertains to the world of eternity? If he (the subject) is right, they (state officials) would oppose the truth (if they interfere); and if they have the truth with them and he is unwittingly on the wrong side, he is a victim of ignorance and deserves compassion and help, not interference and resistance.

The guiding principles reflected in sulh kul were essential for a just ruler of a plural kingdom. As Iqtidar Alam Khan describes it 'within this framework there was no scope for the operation of those provisions of the Sharia which imposed certain disabilities on the zimmis'. 'As in the wide expanse of the Divine compassion there is room for all classes and followers of all creeds,' wrote Jahangir, 'so...in his (Akbar's) dominions...there was room for the professors of opposite religions, and for beliefs good and bad, and the road to altercation was closed. Sunnis and Shias met in one mosque and Franks and Jews in one church, and observed their own forms of worship.'

In practical terms, the spirit of 'universal civility' or 'absolute peace' was reflected in the very concrete reality that all the ruling clans in Akbar's empire were now almost evenly balanced. No single group was in a dominant position to impose its will on another and even the Turanis, the largest group, now comprised just 24 per cent of the nobility. Moreover, some of the Turani and Irani mansabdars commanded units composed mostly of Rajputs and 'by the end of Akbar's reign, Kachhwaha mansabdars alone commanded more than 26,000 ordinary cavalrymen in Mughal service'. This diversity and balance within the nobility would remain the keystone of Mughal politics into the reigns of future emperors. It would result in the presence of courtiers who were very different from one another, men like Raja Todar Mal, Husain Khan 'Tukriya', Mirza Aziz Koka, Raja Bhagwant Das, Qulij Khan, and Faizi, with all their idiosyncrasies and clashing values who were nonetheless respected, loyal, and cherished members of the Mughal court.

This very personal moral code of conduct born of Akbar's understanding of the many faiths and practices which he encountered, led to a loose collection of guidelines for those who might be keen to follow them, guidelines based on reason and rationality, and encouraging temperance and moderation in everyday life. 'If people really wished it,' Akbar offered, 'they might adopt this faith, and his Majesty declared that this religion ought to be established by choice, and not by violence.' Scholars M. Athar Ali and M. Akhtar Ali have shown that by using the terms of the Sufis, referring to his disciples as murids,* Akbar was aspiring to a position similar to that of a spiritual guide, but only for a very select band of men. 'Whoever desires to be enrolled as a disciple,' specified Abu'l Fazl, 'finds great difficulty in his plea being accepted.' Indeed, this was to be a close circle of aristocratic men willing to share the Padshah's spiritual leadership, and in no way a popular mass movement. When German scholar Heinrich Blochmann was translating Abu'l Fazl's works, he mistranslated the phrase Ain-i Iradat Gazinan (literally—regulations

---

*Sufi term for follower.

for those privileged to be His Majesty's disciples) as 'Ordinances of the Divine Faith' and the idea of Din-i Ilahi and a new religion wrongly captured the popular imagination.

In reality, what took place in Akbar's time was that a ceremony was organized in which the 'disciple', or murid, took an oath and was given a special seal that had the phrase 'Allahu Akbar' written on it. They were also given a small image of the Padshah, which they often wore pinned to their turban. Disciples were encouraged to greet each other with the phrase 'Allahu Akbar' to which the other would respond 'Jalla Jallaluhu'. While these Arabic salutations were seemingly inoffensive, they also contained the emperor's name within them (Jalal-ud-din Akbar). This audacious and even irreverent play on words would lead to considerable uneasiness and angst in those who accused Akbar of conflating his definition of kingship with that of divinity since the apparent meaning of the phrases 'God is Great/May his Glory be ever Glorious' could also be interpreted as 'Akbar is God/May his Glory be ever Glorious'. This idea would be reinforced in Abu'l Fazl's *Akbarnama*, in which he would project Akbar as the Insaan-e Adil (Perfect Man) and kingship itself as emanating from a Farr-i Izadi (Divine Light). But for Akbar the essence of sulh kul was an eclectic collection of rather non-heretical thoughts. Ten virtues were encouraged (liberality, forbearance from bad actions and controlling of anger with gentleness, abstinence, freedom from excessive materialism, piety, devotion, prudence, kindness, attachment to God) of which nine were taken directly from the Koran. The recommendations for disciples were more in the manner of moral guidelines and bodily practices, such as giving up meat on certain days. As for the disciples, only eighteen were ever accounted for, making this more a collection of like-minded courtiers who were willing to go along with the Padshah on his religious quest rather than a new religion for everyone as has been suggested. They included Shaikh Mubarak and his sons, Abd al-Samad the painter and his son, Muhammad Sharif, and Raja Birbal.* These members owed a four-fold allegiance to Akbar, the Ikhlas-i-Chahargana, which

---

*The others were Asaf Khan, Qasim-i Kahi, Mullah Shah Muhammad, Sufi Ahmed, Mirza Aziz Koka (who joined later in 1594), Sadar-i Jahan and his two sons, Mir Sharif, Sultan Khwaja, Mirza Jani Beg, Taqi, and Shaikh Zada Gosala.

was defined by a willingness to sacrifice lives, property, honour, and religion. Of the eighteen disciples only one, Raja Birbal, was a Hindu.

The very small number of murids who actually followed this formulation of the Padshah demonstrates the resistance to these eclectic ideas even among the great amirs of the court. Shahbaz Khan Kamboh was an orthodox, devout Sunni, a prickly man, and a competent officer. At Fatehpur Sikri, he refused to shave his beard as was the custom among Akbar's courtiers, nor did he agree to become a disciple of Akbar. On one occasion, the Padshah was conversing with him one-on-one at the time of the midday namaaz. Hakim Abu'l Fath, watching from a distance, nudged Hakim Ali, and wondered aloud if Shahbaz Khan would be able to perform the namaaz, which was discouraged by Akbar. But while the Padshah tried to remonstrate with his courtier, Shahbaz Khan hastily laid down his dupatta and knelt to perform his prayers, while Akbar smacked him on the head the whole time, asking him to stand up.

When a few years later in 1587 Akbar brought up the subject of discipleship with another favourite courtier, Kuar Man Singh, the Kuar was unequivocal and replied with candour: 'If discipleship means willingness to sacrifice one's life, I have already carried my life in my hand, what need is there of further proof? If, however, the term has another meaning and refers to faith, I certainly am a Hindu. If you order me to do so, I will become a Mussalman, but I know not the existence of any other religion than these two.' For Kuar Man Singh, if both Hinduism and Islam were recognizable and acceptable options, the Padshah's proposed system of allegiance to what appeared to be a new religious cult was suspect, and Akbar did not push the matter further.

Another special courtier, Mirza Aziz Koka, was more scathing of Akbar's religious innovations. In a letter to the Padshah when he was en route to Mecca, Aziz Koka wrote about the extraordinary claims his old childhood companion appeared to be making: 'There have been rulers who commanded great power and authority but it never occurred to anyone of them to advance a claim for Prophet-hood and strive to abrogate the religion of Muhammad,' admonished Aziz Koka. As for those who had chosen to become Akbar's disciples, he was even more scornful. 'O my God, who are the people who claim to become the four friends,' railed Aziz Koka. 'By God and by the dust of the Emperor's feet, there is none except Aziz Koka who wants a good name, all others depend on flattery and passing out time.' Accusing all the disciples of being vain sycophants, Aziz Koka added that they 'have preferred infidels over Muslims and this will remain imprinted on the pages of the days and nights'. So disgusted was Aziz Koka at the destabilizing changes at court that he stormed away in a great sulk, claiming he needed to grow out his beard. He did not return even after Akbar grew exasperated and chided him saying, 'You are making all these delays in coming; evidently the wool of your beard weighs heavily on you.'

Despite the high bombast of Mirza Aziz Koka's letter, he would come to regret these bruising sentiments after his sojourn in Mecca. But that would be later, and for now, having lit up the night of Fatehpur Sikri with embers too hot to behold, Akbar set off for a hunt in the Faizabad region. On the way the Mughal retinue passed the 'Gung Mahal', and Akbar decided to visit it, to see how the children were faring in their hushed silence. As we have seen earlier, Akbar found that 'not a sound was emitted from the silent house nor any speech came out of that place of residence. They displayed nothing beyond the usual gestures of the dumb. Whatever his majesty had, in his wisdom, realised some years earlier', said Badauni, 'now became clear to the superficial worldly ones, and it became a source of enlightenment to a large number of people.' There was no universal language, Akbar realized, having put the idea to the test.

THE BOOK OF WAR

Every day at dawn, an hour before sunrise, the musicians of the naqqar khana would begin to play a few tentative melodies to wake up the residents of Fatehpur Sikri. An hour later, just after sunrise, the music began in earnest and an hour-long medley of tunes and refrains were played, which included the lusty use of cymbals and the deep bass of the large naqqara drums. Following the musical performance there was a reading of poems and 'beautiful sentences', again lasting an hour, and finally the residents of the city and palace were ready to face a new day. The Jesuit priests who were present at this time left a less than glowing record of these musical mornings. 'At fixed hours, namely before dawn when the cocks begin to crow...a barbaric din is kept up for the space of a full hour by means of trumpets, bugles, drums, rattles, bells and the like'. The Jesuits would have had ample opportunity to moan about the quality of the naqqara music, for the band now played according to the Hindustani system of dividing the day into eight watches, or 'ghari'. Their assessment was all the more galling as many of the tunes performed by the naqqar khana had been composed by Akbar himself, more than 200 in the style of old Khwarizmian songs. In fact, it may have even been the Padshah himself playing as Abu'l Fazl tells us that he was 'likewise an excellent hand in performing, especially on the naqqara'.

After spending some time in personal prayers, Akbar would then appear at a balcony, where an assembled crowd below the window was waiting to catch a glimpse, or darshan, of the emperor before beginning their day. The jharoka darshan would become one of the enduring symbols of Mughal authority and Abu'l Fazl described how the Padshah 'is visible from outside the awning to people of all ranks, whether they be given to worldly pursuits, or to a life of solitary contemplation, without any molestation from the mace-bearers. This mode of showing himself is called, in the language of the country, darshan, and it frequently happens that business is transacted at this time.' The power of this symbol, transcending all religion, may be seen in the fact that centuries later in 1911, the king and queen of a new empire also chose to show themselves at the jharoka of the Qila-e-Mualla (Red Fort) in Delhi, built by the grandson of Akbar.

At some point in his busy morning Akbar would have found time to visit his beloved pigeon cotes. Mullazada Mulla Asamudin Ibrahim would have found some consolation for his abrupt termination as first tutor to Akbar had he seen the lifelong obsession that Akbar had for pigeon flying, which he called ishq-baazi. There were 20,000 pigeons in the imperial household, of which 500 were khasa, or special. The most valued pigeon in this fluttering ensemble was called Mohan, and belonged to Aziz Koka. They were kept in pigeon cotes made of blue and white bricks and were cared for by eunuchs and maidservants. Some of the pigeons were used to deliver messages while others were kept for the beauty and magnificence of their iridescent plumage. A few extra-special ones were trained to perform intricate manoeuvres and acrobatics while flying, which astounded the visitors to court. 'It will seem little short of miraculous,' wrote Monserrate, overcome, 'when I affirm that when sent out, they dance, turn somersaults all together in the air, fly in orderly rhythm and return to their starting point, all at the sound of a whistle.' One hundred and one pigeons were let out at a time to perform these various skills, a blur of pearl-grey synchronicity.

At some point in his day Akbar would make time to inspect his special animals. 'He knew the names of all his elephants, though he had many thousands of them', wrote du Jarric, 'of his pigeons, his deer, and the other wild animals which he kept in his parks, and of all his horses to which names had been given. Each day, a certain number of these animals were brought before him for his inspection. He watched these from his window; and as each animal passed him, its name and that of the person responsible for feeding it was read out to him.' The attendants were rewarded if the animals were thriving, if they were not their salary was docked.

Both Agra and Fatehpur Sikri were now populous and thriving cities. The road between the two cities was made up of a market so full of produce and people that it looked like one continuous town. Fine bullock-carts, carved and gilded with gold and covered with silks and fine cloths, trundled on the road ferrying people and goods between the cities. There were merchants from Persia and Hindustan, trading in silks and precious stones like rubies, diamonds, and pearls. Many of these merchants and traders would have been serving the important courtiers of the city.

The ferocious energy that Akbar displayed during his battles and campaigns, in peacetime was channelled into the meticulous and careful attention he gave to all that was happening around him. 'He is much loved as well as feared by his people,' wrote Henriques, the Jesuit, 'and is very hardworking; to the end he is never idle, he knows a little of all trades and sometimes loves to practise them before his people either as a carpenter or as a blacksmith or as an armourer, filing and even quite often bleeding some of his captains in public as he once expertly bled a captain, who needed it, before us and his people.' Endearingly, Akbar could sometimes be distracted and enthralled by the most insubstantial things, causing Abu'l Fazl much torment as he imagined a grander purpose for everything Akbar was involved in. 'His majesty from curiosity likes to see spider fights,' admitted Abu'l Fazl, this time quite undone by the Padshah, 'and amuses himself in watching the attempts of the flies to escape, their jumps, and combats with their foe'. The Jesuits, too, described a Padshah who was distracted from time to time.

> At one time he would be deeply immersed in state affairs or giving audiences to his subjects, and the next moment he would be seen shearing camels, hewing stones, cutting wood, or hammering iron, and doing all with as much diligence as though engaged in his own particular vocation.

However, in 1582, there was a project which was entirely worthy of Abu'l Fazl's most extravagant praise, for in the maktab khana of Fatehpur Sikri, a collection of writers and theologians were starting on one of the most audacious projects of Akbar's reign—the translation of the Mahabharat from Sanskrit to Persian. Writing about this project, Faizi said:

> With a hundred charms I am bringing an
> Ancient book
> From Hindi into Persian, the language of the court

I stroll to see with friends
The idol temple of Hindustan

His brother, Abu'l Fazl, was less whimsical in his assessment. He said that Akbar 'decided to explore the reason for the hostility that divided the Muslims, Jews and Hindus and in doing so realized that their denial of one another was all too obvious'. Once Akbar had understood this problem, 'he decided to translate the authentic books of the different groups into another language, so that both groups could have the pleasure of benefitting from the perfect knowledge; thus forgetting their enmity and hostility and seeking the divine truth... Therefore,' continued Abu'l Fazl, 'it is an important task to translate the Mahabharata, which is about the many skills of kings and covers many principles, including the smaller issues and beliefs of India.' In this way, argued Abu'l Fazl in his preface, sulh kul would be encouraged because Muslims would become familiar with an ancient system of thought and Hindus would have to confront certain inconsistencies in the text so that, in an ideal world, one of 'complete civility', everyone might be brought to reflect individually on the nature of truth.

There were other Sanskrit texts which were translated over the next few years including the Ramayan, the *Rajatarangini*, and the story of Nala and Damayanti but the Mahabharat would remain the most popular, the most extensively studied and the most re-copied over the following decades. The royal family and the Mughal elite were the main audience as well as the patrons of these works. Hamida Banu, a renowned patron, also owned a priceless copy of the Persian Ramayan. Some of the Hindus at court, especially the Rajputs, became patrons as they had had to learn Persian to occupy administrative positions. This would lead to a unique strand of Indo-Persian literature coming into existence which was all the more remarkable for it was the Brajbhasha texts that were at that time blazing through central and north India, dispersed through the mysticism of the Bhakti saints.

The Mahabharat was considered by the Mughals, as indeed by earlier rulers, as 'the most authoritative, important, and comprehensive book (among the Brahmans of India)'. Badauni mentioned an additional reason for Akbar wishing to translate the Mahabharat, one that most Hindus would be familiar with, that 'the Hindu unbelievers consider it a great religious merit to read and to copy it. And they keep it hid from Musalmans.' Therefore, Badauni argued, to accrue religious merit and glory in the world, Akbar decided to have the texts translated in his name.

Because there were no scholars who were fluent in both Sanskrit and Persian, the Mughal Mahabharat was a collaborative effort between a number of Persian and Sanskrit intellectuals. The Persian translation group included the court historian Naqib Khan, the poet Mullah Shari, a fiscal administrator Sultan Thanesari, and Badauni. The Sanskrit scholars were Brahmins, who explained the meaning of the texts orally to the Persian scholars in Hindi. 'Several learned Brahmans—such as Deva Misra, Satabadhana, Madhusudan Misra, Chaturbhuja and Shaikh Bhavan, who embraced Islam because of the attention of his blessed Majesty,' wrote Naqib Khan in his colophon to the translation, 'read this book and explained it in Hindi to me, a poor wretched man, who wrote it in Persian.' Badauni also claimed that Akbar spent several nights with the translators, explaining the meaning of the epic to the Persian scholars. Abu'l Fazl would later contribute a preface to the book and Faizi would rework two books from the epic into verse. The *Razmnama*, or Book of War, would be gorgeously illustrated and the imperial master copy 'numbers among the finest, most highly valued specimens of Mughal art that survive today' according to Truschke. The paintings were altogether different from the earlier styles of the Timurid, Safavid, or Sultanate traditions that the artists came from as the work itself was that disconcerting entity—a singularity that had never been imagined before. Once it was completed, 'the Amirs had orders to take copies of it, with the blessing and favour of God', implying that Akbar wished for the Persian translation of the Mahabharat to be circulated widely.

The translation of the *Razmnama* was begun in 1582 and took about eighteen months to complete. After that began the process of copying the text in beautiful calligraphy, and of illustrating the manuscript. The final manuscript, divided into four large volumes, and containing 168 illustrations, was completed around 1586–87. The illustrations were necessarily collaborative efforts, given the large number of paintings and the detailed nature of the illustrations, and the main artists were Basawan, Lal, and Daswant. These three artists between them designed and outlined most of the illustrations, while artists like Muhammad Sharif and Farrukh Beg contributed to some of the paintings. Interestingly, thirteen of the paintings are horizontal compositions, unique among Mughal manuscripts but current in traditional Hindu religious texts. Unfortunately, the paintings of the imperial *Razmnama*, and the manuscript itself, have been off-limits to scholars and enthusiasts alike as they have remained sealed in the City Palace Museum in Jaipur by court order for more than half a century.*

Not everyone was equally enamoured of these intellectual exercises. Mullah Shari and Haji Thanesari loathed having to work on the translations, considering it an attempt to denigrate Islam. As for Badauni, writing about the two sections that he translated, he miserably said they were full of 'the puerile absurdities of which the eighteen thousand creations may well be amazed.... Such discussion as one never heard! As, Shall I eat forbidden things? Shall I eat turnips? But such is my fate, to be employed on such works.' There were further humiliations in store for Badauni because Akbar took a very keen interest in the translated pages, and one day summoned Badauni, furious over a line he had just come across in the *Razmnama*: 'Every action has its reward and every deed its recompense.'

Turning to Abu'l Fazl the Padshah damningly said, 'We imagined that this person [Badauni], was a young, unworldly adherent of Sufism, but he has turned out to be such a bigoted follower of Islamic law that no sword can slice the jugular vein of his bigotry.' It took a lot of explanation from Badauni to convince the Padshah that this was, in fact, part of the original text which taught the concepts of rewards and punishments. Akbar, it seemed, was particularly wary of any allusion to the Islamic notion of a Day of Judgement, which was how he had interpreted Badauni's line. Akbar remained deeply invested and implicated in the translation of the work, judging each line of the translated text and keeping a vigilant watch over any attempt to manipulate the message of the text.

---

*The *Razmnama*, along with other priceless documents, have been sealed by court order and it is unknown what condition they are now in.

While the scholars and the translators wrestled over the nuances of the Mahabharat in the maktab khana, Akbar conducted a second darbar after the morning's jharoka darshan. The court had not yet ossified into the rigid and minutely-detailed protocol of the later Mughals, so this second darbar was sometimes held in the morning, or in the evening, or even at night. A large drum would announce the arrival of the Padshah at the hall, while his sons and courtiers would hurry to take their places. Broad-shouldered, powerfully built, and slightly bandy-legged, limping almost imperceptibly in the left leg, Akbar would stride into the darbar. He would be armed, as were all the men. Monserrate wrote that he was especially fond of carrying a European sword and a dagger. He would be surrounded by a bodyguard of twenty men, all armed too. Akbar would sometimes use an octagonal low throne, made of pure white ivory inlaid with gold.

Standing behind him would be young servant boys holding the standard, or alam, wrapped up in an embroidered crimson cloth, to be unfurled in times of war or during parades. Salim was always meant to be placed slightly nearer his father than Murad or Daniyal but Akbar would often pull his younger sons or, later, his grandsons, affectionately closer to him. Everyone would then perform the kornish, bowing low, with the right hand placed on the head, and then settle down on to the rich, vibrant carpets that covered the floors. Jugs of drinks and other delicacies would be arranged on trays and platters and placed in front of the men and incense would burn in fragrant, wispy plumes. A favourite cheetah, jewelled collar gleaming in the flames of the candles, would watch the proceedings with an unblinking gaze while dogs would roam the courtyards. 'His Majesty likes this animal very much for his excellent qualities and imports dogs from all countries,' wrote Abu'l Fazl, adding that the best dogs were to be obtained from Kabul. Men with hawks on their arms would stand by and if the meetings were taking place at night, the water in the Anuptalao would reflect the perfect fractal geometry of the moonlight.

Akbar had also recently revived the ancient custom of sajda, or full body prostration, in court. He had renamed it zaminbos, kissing the ground, but even rebaptized, it caused revulsion amongst the orthodox theologians who had already had to tolerate a great deal of erosion in their power. Abu'l Fazl fumed that they were 'ignorant ones' who did not realize that this was a source of blessing and not, as they railed, worship before God. But Akbar quickly conceded the point and allowed zaminbos only to his closest disciples, in private.

In the darbar, meanwhile, Akbar attended to matters that were brought before him. In the diwan-e-khas, surrounded by his favourite noblemen and greatest courtiers, Akbar was relaxed and indulgent. He sat cross-legged, often wearing a dhoti of fine silk rather than the usual payjamas. The courtiers sat on their heels, hands placed decorously on their knees but the atmosphere was often easy-going and engaged. There would be Birbal, a paan tucked into his cheek, eyes sparkling and ready with a spirited remark. Aziz, deep-set eyes critical below his arched eyebrows, but affectionate and sincere. Todar Mal, sober and erudite, Man Singh, sun-scorched from his numerous campaigns, and always Abu'l Fazl, with his immense learning and keen intellect, constantly watching the Padshah, assessing, analysing, and translating everything that he saw around him. Rather discordant in this gathering of smooth courtiers was the Sayyid Mahmud of Baraha, considered 'a man of rustic habits, and great personal generosity'. While the other courtiers sometimes sniggered at his lack of social graces and plain-speaking, Akbar recognized the great courage and loyalty of the man and rewarded him accordingly.

The Jesuits noted the keen and incisive manner with which Akbar was able to deal with a variety of subjects. 'He can give his opinion on any question so shrewdly and keenly,' wrote Monserrate, 'that no one who did not know that he is illiterate would suppose him to be anything but very learned and erudite. And so indeed he is, for in addition to his keen intellect, of which I have already spoken, he excels many of his most learned subjects in eloquence, as well as in that authority and dignity which befits a King.' Akbar's clerks carefully noted down everything he said and all the while, 'skillful gladiators and wrestlers from all countries hold themselves in readiness, and singers, male and female, are in waiting. Clever jugglers and funny tumblers also are anxious to exhibit their dexterity and agility.'

If the entertainment was to be music, then there was a great deal of choice for there were a variety of artists, 'Hindus, Iranis, Turanis,

Kashmiris, both men and women', organized in a rotating system for each day of the week. By studying the miniatures painted at this time, scholars have concluded that of the musical instruments, one of the most popular was the Hindustani veena. There was also a Persian flute called the na'i, the Hindustani flute, several types of lutes, a harp, as well as percussion instruments. Of all the musicians, the most revered of them all was Tansen, still at court and still singing his haunting Dhrupad compositions. 'A singer like him,' wrote Abu'l Fazl confidently, 'has not been seen in India for the last thousand years.' Tansen was not just a singer, but also a poet-composer, and wrote his lyrics in Brajbhasha. 'The fact that Akbar patronized him and others like him,' writes music historian Françoise Delvoye, 'suggests that the Emperor was familiar with the vernacular languages in which the song-texts were composed and could appreciate [their] imagery and aesthetic values, which were quite different from those of Persian poetry.' And there is, in fact, a rich oral tradition of Akbar being enthralled by Tansen's singing a song that he thought the maestro had composed, only to discover that the Brajbhasha song he was singing was composed by a Bhakti poet. A popular incident involved the poetess Pravin Ray, a courtesan of great beauty at the court of Raja Indrajit of Orchha, and a student of the poet Keshavdas*. Hearing of her beauty and talent, Akbar summoned her to court upon which she sent him a proud retort:

> Pay heed, wise emperor, to what Pravin Ray has to say.
> Only low-caste people, cows and dogs eat off plates used by others.

While these stories may be apocryphal, the sheer volume of these popular tales demonstrates both the Padshah's appreciation for, and knowledge of, the Braj language and the Bhakti poets' resistance to appropriation by the rulers. The Brajbhasha sources also describe a more brittle reality that doesn't involve the sparkling magnificence of the court where Akbar was the faultless presence described by Abu'l Fazl. Dadu Dayal, for example, was a Bhakti poet of the sant

---

*Keshavdas Misra of Orchha was a pre-eminent Brajbhasha poet. An heir to the Sanskrit tradition, he is credited by scholars with influencing Braj poetry with classical inflection and is also celebrated as being a major influence in the efflorescence of poetry in the language.

tradition from Gujarat, who was an exact contemporary of Akbar. Dadu travelled to the Amer region of Rajasthan where Raja Bhagwant Das became a follower of the poet's message of inclusive love for all:

> He ignored all Muslim customs
> And abandoned Hindu practices
> He did not mix with other ascetics
> But stayed immersed in Ram day and night.

According to the Dadu's Hindi biography, Akbar was keen to meet with the saint and sent Abu'l Fazl and Raja Bhagwant Das to meet him first. When Abu'l Fazl questioned him on the nature of God and the worship due to him, the poet replied:

> Because He cannot be grasped, we call Him Allah,
> Because He cannot be described, we call Him Alakh.
> Because He created every thing, we call Him Sirjanhar,
> Because He is without end, we call Him Apar

When Dadu resisted going to meet the emperor on being summoned, Birbal tried to remonstrate with him:

> The king [Birbal] pointed out that the emperor is god incarnate (avatar)
> And that even Dadu should give him respect;
> 'he is looked at with great respect and worshipped
> as a god by both Hindus and Muslims'.

> Svamiji replied; 'I worship only One
> And do not bow to any other.
> All created beings are in the power of death,
> Only Brahma does not come or go.'

Finally the two met and had a long conversation about spirituality, presumably in Braj. For it was from the time of Akbar that Braj became the naturalized idiom of the Mughals. Akbar was completely conversant with spoken Hindi, in addition to Persian and Turki, as well as having a working knowledge of Arabic, and as for Salim, Braj was his mother tongue, and he would become a fine poet in the language. Even if Persian remained the official public language, in the intimacy of the harem and in their private lives, the Padshahs also spoke Braj with their Rajput wives and their Hindu courtiers.

As for Tansen, he continued to mesmerize the court for a quarter of a century, and the only courtier immune to the charm of his singing appears to have been Shaikh Mubarak. 'He compared his singing to the noise of beasts,' gloated Badauni, 'and allowed it no superiority over it,' an assessment which may have been influenced by the fact that Tansen by then was a very old man, his finest singing days long past.

Every evening before the entertainment began, there was the ceremonial lighting of lamps and candles at the end of the day, which was a sacred task. On the day when the sun entered the nineteenth degree of Aries, a lustrous white stone called the Surajkrant was held up to it, with a piece of cotton next to it. The reflected heat of the stone soon lit up the cotton, and this fire was kept burning for a year in a vessel called the Agnigir—all the candles, torches, and lamps of the palace were lit from this source. In the evening, which fell suddenly like a malediction, twelve white candles on gold and silver candlesticks would be brought to Akbar, and a 'singer of sweet melodies, with a candle in his hand' would sing a number of songs praising God while the Padshah stood in concentrated silence. Once all the lamps and candles were lit, the palaces and courtyards of Fatehpur Sikri would be ablaze with flickering light; some of the candlesticks and wax candles were so tall that a ladder was needed to snuff them out.

Every evening Akbar would also inspect the palace guards, who were comprised of an unusual tribe of men called the Chandals, described by Abu'l Fazl as 'unequalled in India for wickedness'. Considered outcastes and highway robbers, Akbar had wanted to encourage them to change their ways and he gave them the title 'Rai' and their chief was called Khidmat Rai. Akbar 'guided him towards honesty' and following the Padshah's example, all the noblemen had taken to employing these 'Khidmatiya' as guards. The mounting of the guards was an important duty and Akbar inspected these men himself. Every evening, as the Qur* was taken in to the diwan-e-khas, the golden lion on the pennant glowing in the fast-falling dusk, Akbar

---

*A collection of flags and royal insignia.

would inspect the two rows of guards standing on either side of the hall. On the right were the guards who had done guard duty all day and on the left were guards who would relieve them, ready for night duty. Both ranks of men would salute smartly as the Padshah appeared, and Akbar would stop to inspect each man, his sharp eyes noting any uniform that was awry or any guard who was missing. Absentees, unless excused with a valid reason, were fined a week's pay.

The evening then ended sometimes with horse polo using, as we have seen earlier, wooden balls that were set alight to smoulder in the dark. The ends of the chaugan or polo sticks were made of gold and silver and if they broke during a game, the players were allowed to keep them. There were other diversions and entertainments at hand including 'elephant-fighting, buffalo-fighting, stag-fighting, and cock-fighting, boxing contests, battles of gladiators, and the flying of tumbler-pigeons'. Late at night Akbar would finally retire, for a few short hours of sleep. In the very early dawn, as the last stars were fading from the night sky, soldiers, merchants, peasants and townsfolk would begin to shuffle up to and gather below the jharoka window, preparing to bow before the glorious presence of the Padshah, immutable and consoling, ready to begin a new day.

A SHIRAZI VISITOR FROM THE DECCAN

When the ruler of the Bijapur Sultanate in the Deccan, Ali Adil Shah I, was murdered in 1580 by 'two handsome eunuchs who had for a long time excited his perverse attention', this not only brought to power an extraordinary woman as regent, Chand Bibi, but also provided the necessary impetus for a famous Shirazi intellectual to leave the suddenly uncongenial court of Bijapur for the much more attractive one at Fatehpur Sikri. An enormous sum had been spent by Ali Adil Shah I to lure the scholar Fath Allah Shirazi from Persia to Bijapur where he had rapidly gained a considerable reputation. 'All the great Muslim scholars, as well as Hindu sages,' writes historian Ali Anooshahr, 'would attend scholarly discussions held at his house.' Now with the death of the Adil Shah, Akbar sent Abdur Rahim and Abu'l Fath Gilani to receive Fath Allah Shirazi and he was made joint wazir of the Mughal Empire along with Raja Todar Mal. The two men together brought about enormous changes in the organization of the revenue and other administrative departments as they brought in Persian as the language of administration at all levels, thus making of Akbar the first Indo-Islamic Padshah of north India to declare Persian as the official language of administration. An eighteenth-century historian recorded this measure in the following way:

> Earlier in India the government accounts were written in Hindi according to the Hindu rule. Raja Todar Mal acquired new regulations from the scribes of Iran and the government offices then were reorganized as they were there in wilayat (Iran).

Now Persian became the language of government at all levels, and was no longer simply an elite courtly language. Since a great deal of the administration was carried out by Hindu communities, these groups learnt Persian and worked alongside the 'wilayatis' as clerks, scribes, and secretaries. This was only possible because of the upheavals in the madrasa education system that Akbar had brought about in parallel. This reform was planned and executed by Fath Allah Shirazi and brought about an overhauling of madrasa education at all levels, transforming it from just religious instruction into a more formal and expanded course of education. At the primary level, students were taught reading, writing, medicine, history, and accountancy. Children were not required to spend too much time practising the alphabet but instead began to learn Persian couplets and moral phrases so that they instinctively learnt the texture and nuance of the language. At the middle level, 'secular' themes like logic, arithmetic, astronomy, accountancy, and agriculture were introduced which encouraged a large number of Hindus, Kayasthas, and Khichri especially, to join madrasas in large numbers, beginning with the village schools, or maktabs, so as to have a coveted career in the imperial Mughal service. In maktabs, which children joined at the age of four, Kayastha children were taught accounting skills and would grow up to serve as land registrars and village accountants while the more accomplished ones became news writers, revenue reporters, petition writers, and court readers. The maktab curriculum included classics from Persian literature such as Sa'di's *Gulistan* and Firdausi's *Shahnama* and the Kayastha clans became increasingly 'Persianized', even acquiring Persian pen names.

By the middle of the seventeenth century, the departments of accountancy, draftsmanship, and the office of the revenue minister were mostly filled by Hindu munshis, and Chandra Bhan 'Brahman' would be rated second only to Abu'l Fazl in his prose and poetry. 'A man who knows how to write good prose as well as accountancy is a bright light even among lights,' wrote Chandra Bhan in a letter, giving refreshingly timeless advice to his son about being a Mughal munshi. 'Besides, a munshi should be discreet and virtuous.' Through Persian, Akbar sought to unite the far-flung inhabitants of his empire, polyphonic and multi-faith, beyond the divisive binary of religion. This meant that a certain intangible Mughal essence, the tehzeeb, a refinement of language, manners and morals, spread outwards from Fatehpur Sikri like a flood tide to the distant corners of the empire.

Persian intellectuals, thinkers, and poets were drawn to Akbar's inclusive court in a steady stream during the 1580s. By the late sixteenth and early seventeenth century, this would become a deluge. Historian Sunil Sharma uses the example of a French traveller, Jean

Chardin, who described this situation with sweeping generalizations in 1666, to illustrate an exodus of talented Persian families from the Iranian plateau towards Hindustan:

> ...within this last century, a great many Persians, and even entire Families, have gone and settl'd in the Indies. As they are a handsomer, wiser and more polite People, beyond all comparison, than the Mahometan Indians, who are descended from the Tartars, in the Country of Tamerlane...[they] go willingly where Fortune invites them, especially into a Country, which is one of the most plentiful of the World.

A poem written as a caustic challenge to Shah Abbas of Persia demonstrated the great lure of Hindustan, which was now being called the Dar al-Aman, the abode of peace:

> That in Persia no one comes within sight,
> Who is a customer of the commodity of meaning;
> In Persia the palate of my soul has become bitter,
> Go I ought towards Hindustan;
> Like a drop towards the ocean,
> I may send my commodity to India.

The visitors to the court may have appreciated playing cards, a game popular throughout the Mughal Empire, and with Akbar and his men, for the Padshah had made suitable alterations to the suit of cards to satisfactorily reflect this new reality of Hindustan. Now each of the twelve kings was distinct and represented a particular strength or region. So Akbar played with the suit representing the King of Delhi, shown with the insignia of royalty such as the umbrella, standard etc. Then there was the King of Elephants, representing the ruler of Orissa. There was the King of Infantry, with a nod to the rulers of Bijapur, a King of Forts, Dhanpati, the King of Wealth, a King of the Fleet, and even a suit called Tipati, in which the ruler was a Queen. The most lowly was the Padshah-e-Ghulam, whose suit consisted of servants 'some of whom sit, some lie on the ground in worship, some are drunk, others sober etc.'

Besides playing cards, another form of entertainment that grew in popularity was the habit of reading. In Fatehpur Sikri, booksellers hunkered down by the roadside, beside piles of diwans of Persian immigrant poets. The most popular of these poets was Urfi Shirazi, a young poet with a sharply acerbic wit. Shirazi and the poet laureate of Akbar's court, Faizi, had a brittle disregard for each other, testing each other on the jagged edge of their poetry. Faizi had once taken on the orthographically challenging task of writing a 'dot-less' commentary on the Koran, using only those Arabic alphabets which did not contain a dot. When Abu'l Fazl told Urfi that he was writing a preface for the piece, and struggling with the name of his father, Mubarak, which contained a letter with a dot, Urfi facetiously suggested the similar word Mumarak, which did not contain a dot but did, insultingly, mean 'the indecent one'. Badauni was less appreciative of Urfi, saying of him that, despite his talents he was 'also very haughty and pompous, which caused him to lose favour with people'. He uncharitably added that 'he was said to be ugly to boot because of a pockmarked face'. Badauni also mentions the only Hindu poet of Persian to make it to his list of accomplished poets, Manohar 'Tausani', son of Raja Loonkaran of Sambhar, and a single female poet, one Nihani of Agra.

Peace reigned through most of this period but one shocking act of violence deserves mention for it led to a major reform instituted by the Padshah. It took place in the very heart of the empire—the women's harem. In the early dawn of a spring day in 1583 there was a sudden, calamitous disturbance in the harem quarters of Fatehpur Sikri. Women were wailing while others tried to comfort them, and at the entrance to the palace, the Padshah's bodyguards were in terrible disarray, hastily buckling on armour, grabbing weapons, and angrily shouting at each other. The Padshah, it appeared, had jumped onto his horse and had galloped away into the rising dawn in such catastrophic haste that the ever vigilant eunuchs and guards had not even had time to react. For terrible news had arrived late at night that one of his officers, Jaimal, had died en route to Bengal and his wife, the daughter of Raja Udai Singh of Marwar, affectionately called Mota Raja, was being forced to commit sati. Her own son and some 'bold and foolish persons' were trying to forcibly drag her onto the flames. Not wishing to waste a single minute, Akbar had ridden his horse straight to Raja Udai Singh, rescued the young widow, and imprisoned 'the misguided ones' till they thought better of their actions. This personal encounter with the horrors of sati radically altered Akbar's attitude towards the practice. Up until this time, he had admired the great fortitude of women who committed sati, accepting it as a sign of their devotion to their husbands, but had not tried to interfere with the practice as it was staunchly defended by many Hindus and Rajputs at court, including Raja Bhagwant Das, his brother-in law. But now Akbar brought in measures which reflected his new recognition of the injustice it meted out to the women. 'It is a strange commentary on the magnanimity of men,' Akbar said, now scornful of the men, 'that they should seek their deliverance through the self sacrifice of their wives.'

To ensure that women were not forced to commit sati against their will Akbar appointed officials in every town so that only 'those who of their own impulse wished to commit sati might be allowed to do so'. Akbar had already decreed that 'Hindu child-widows who had not enjoyed conjugal relations should not be burnt; but if the Hindus should find this difficult, they were not to be interfered with.' It was a fine balance that Akbar tried to maintain, between his own growing empathy for the plight of the women, and his awareness of the prickly honour of his Hindu subjects, some of whom were deeply attached to the practice of sati.

Akbar's sensitivity to the distressing vulnerability of women resulted in a number of orders and measures being passed during these years to try and protect them. He had always abhorred the marriage of children and said about it that 'it is particularly distressing under a law where a woman (being so much younger than her husband) cannot marry again'. Child marriages were rampant at this time, having been noticed by Ralph Fitch who said that 'we found marriages great store, both in towns and villages in many places where we passed, of boys of eight or ten years and girls of five or six years old.... They do not lie together until they be ten years old.' Akbar raised the minimum age for marriage to sixteen years for boys and fourteen for girls, and instructed the kotwals to establish the ages of the bride and groom before allowing weddings to take place. Unfortunately, writes Badauni, 'this greatly filled the pockets of officials such as Kotwal's men', as people began bribing the officials to allow the practice to continue.

Akbar also brought in an order in 1587 permitting widows to remarry, 'in the manner that the people of India do not prohibit'. He was greatly saddened by the notion that 'here in India among the modest, a woman once married cannot go [again] to anyone else'. That Akbar would find the idea of widows not being allowed to re-marry puzzling and distressing is understandable given the Timurids' pragmatic approach to women's chastity. Women who 'fell' to enemies in times of war were never blamed for their predicament, and were taken back with honour by their families when they were returned. In Akbar's own family there would have been the glowing example of Khanzada Begum, twice forcibly married to Uzbek men who were sworn enemies of Babur, and then received with gratitude and love at the court of Babur, who gave her the highest title of honour of the harem, Padshah Begum, in recognition of her sacrifice for her family. There were many widows, divorced women, and homeless Timurid women who were all part of the Mughal harem. Babur had sent to all these women a letter which was both invitation and imploration, offering them a place of safety in Hindustan after the destruction of the Timurid homeland by the Uzbeks, but also asking for their help in maintaining the precious Timurid legacy in this new country. The matriarchs of the Mughal Empire, mothers, widows, and grandaunts, would continue to be revered figures of authority and love through the many turbulent generations. This was why, despite the determined effort to keep the royal women nameless and faceless, Gulbadan and her sisters in the harem escaped the cloister of Fatehpur Sikri and the pardeh-giyan were never truly invisible.

Other noteworthy incidents in this period involved two of Akbar's favourite people. In faraway Naples, in the summer of 1583, the Duke of Atri was in a joyous mood. 'He ordered his household to dress in their holiday suits of white, and welcomed the news with illuminations, fire-works, and all the state which he could display.' The news that he was celebrating was the long-awaited martyrdom of his fifth son, Rudolf Acquaviva, at the age of thirty-three. After surviving the Mughal court, despite his public and profane desecration of the Prophet, Acquaviva found martyrdom when he was least expecting it, among the 'heathens'. The Jesuit, along with four companions, was hacked to death by a mob of Hindus whom they had been trying to convert, in Salcette, south of Goa. 'He gladly stretched out his neck,' averred Monserrate, 'and offered his throat to the savages who slew him'. Akbar greeted the news of the death of his young friend with vivid sorrow: 'Alas, Father! Did I not tell you not to go away? But you would not listen to me.'

The artist Daswant, too, would die in 1583, stabbed by his own hand, overcome by melancholy. But others would take his place, and Akbar's taswir khana would create works of beauty whose legacy would long outlive the mortal painters, many of whom would remain anonymous and largely forgotten.

OTHER WORSHIPPERS OF GOD

The residents of Fatehpur Sikri had become used to the presence of unusual visitors at their court but the arrival of sixty-seven Jain monks in a whispering procession, heralded by drummers and singers in 1583, must have nonetheless caused a considerable stir. '[Jains monks] wear nothing on the head and pluck out the hairs of chins and heads, leaving only a tuft,' wrote a bemused European traveller to Hindustan about the Jains. They were 'more European than Indian in colour', noted the traveller, and tied a cloth over their mouths. They carried brooms, and swept the ground clean of ants and other tiny insects as they walked. This silent procession of austere men included Hiravijaya Suri an orphan and a monk since the age of thirteen, whom, as we have seen, Akbar had invited to his court. The distinguished monk brought with him followers from the relatively minor Tapa Gaccha sect. In the poem *Jagadgurukavya*, the earliest Sanskrit text describing the Jain experience at Akbar's court, Hiravijaya is described as 'foremost among the dispassionate, best of ascetics, who had the form of glorious khuda', which was, as Truschke describes it, a flagrant adoption of Islamic hierarchy when invoking the Persian name of God (khuda) for Hiravijaya.

A Jain text, the *Hirasaubhagya*, written in the early seventeenth century, described the supposed meeting between the two scholars, Abu'l Fazl and Hiravijaya. According to Truschke, this text contains a rare, unabashed description of Islamic beliefs in Sanskrit, which had always tended to scuff out the presence of Islam in religious discourse. The conversation between the two men is transcribed in Sanskrit and Abu'l Fazl begins by describing the tenets of Islam, and asks about the validity of a creator God, a Heaven and Hell, and resurrection at the end of the world:

> O Suri, this was laid out by the ancient prophets in our scriptures—all Muslims who are deposited on earth as guests of the god of death will rise at the end of the earth and come before the court of the Supreme Lord called khuda, just as they

come to the court of an earthly king... O Suri, what is the validity of the Quranic speech: is it true, like the speech of great-souled people, or is it false like a flower in the sky?

Hiravijaya refutes this argument with panache, according to this Jain source, and firmly puts Abu'l Fazl in his place:

He who is free of dirt like a shell, devoid of defects like the sun, made of flames like fire, and without a body like the god of love is the Supreme Lord. In what form does he attend court like a living being that adopts many appearances in his wanderings through existence? There he sets a person on the path to heaven or hell for what reason?... let action (karma) alone be recognized as the creator of the world since otherwise (God) has no purpose.

While the exact tenor of the conversations may be in doubt, the *Hirasaubhagya* is a fascinating text for it describes the way in which a small religious community was able to formulate its relationship with the ruling Muslim elite, and the many vibrant routes of communication open to them. Hiravijaya remained in Fatehpur Sikri for three years, holding philosophical debates and favourably impressing Akbar. After his first meeting with the monks, which was held in the gardens of Ram Das Kachhwaha, the Jain texts go on to say that Akbar respectfully bowed down before Hiravijaya Suri and sent his chariots, horses, and imperial elephants to accompany the monks to their quarters.

The Brahmins at court eventually became jealous of Hiravijaya's influence, grumbled the Jain texts, and sent Raja Ram Das Kachhwaha to point out to Akbar that the Jains were atheists. 'Those idiot Jains,' began the accusation by an anonymous Brahmin, 'do not believe that there is a pure one, without a physical form, changeless, sinless, emancipated from rebirth, free of emotional agitations, passionless, independent, the slayer of all sins and the maker of all happiness, namely Paramesvara.' The charge was a serious one, for atheism was altogether unacceptable for a Mughal Padshah. Vijayasena, another Jain monk, responded to the challenge:

The Shaivas worship him as 'Shiva' and the Vedantins as 'Brahma'. The Buddhists, who are sharp in logic, worship him as 'Buddha' and the Mimamsakas as 'Karma'. Those who ascribe to the Jain scriptures worship him as 'Arhat' and the Naiyayikas as 'Creator'. May that Hari, the Lord of the Three Worlds, give you whatever you desire.

Vijayasena used Jain scriptures to expose the venality of the Brahmins' accusations and proved to Akbar and his courtiers the similarity of Jain thought to the Samkhya philosophy of the Brahmins. Through some sharp verbal calisthenics, the Jains equated the concept of karma to theism and thereby put the argument to rest. Pleased, Akbar gave Vijayasena the title Savai Hiravijaya Suri, i.e. a quarter greater than his master Hiravijaya. 'When the Brahmans were defeated by the Suri,' gloated the Jains, 'they became so emasculated it is amazing the townspeople did not lust after them as if they were women.'

Jain monks remained at the Mughal court continuously till 1605, altering forever the significance of this otherwise insubstantial sect. Siddhichandra's biography of his master Hiravijaya described the virtues of Akbar, in which the Mughal Padshah was firmly welcomed into the Jain worldview:

> There is not a single art, not a single branch of knowledge, not a single act of boldness and strength which was not attempted by young Akbar...thieves and robbers were conspicuous by their absence in his empire...

He further compared him to the son of Kaushaliya (i.e. Ram) and wrote that 'his religious fervour never made him intolerant as is shown by his degree of regard for all the six systems of philosophy. He took interest in all the arts and all branches of learning.'

Akbar remained fascinated by the Jain monks till the end of his reign. The Jain concepts of compassion to all living things would have resonated deeply with Akbar, especially from this time on, as his attention radiated outwards to the dispossessed and the uncounted. He extended his powerful support to this small sect, keeping them safe from attack from other religious groups that were jealous of their meteoric rise. Following requests from the Jain monks Akbar issued farmans prohibiting animal slaughter for twelve days every year, allowed tax exemptions for Jain pilgrims, protected Jain temples in Gujarat besides awarding further donations and gifts.

Abu'l Fazl, when listing the great seers of Hindustan, allowed that the Jains 'perceive the mysteries of the external and internal and in their understanding and the breadth of their views, fully comprehended both realms of thought'. Akbar also asked Bhanuchandra Suri to teach him the Suryasahasranama, or the 1,000 names to worship the sun god. In Bhanuchandra's commentary, Akbar approached the monk and asked him: 'Tell me who among good people can teach me this?' The Jains replied, 'only one who has subdued all the senses, sleeps on the ground, and possesses sacred knowledge is qualified in this manner. When he heard this, the Shah (Akbar) said, "Only you (Bhanuchandra) possess such qualities here. You alone, venerable one, will teach me this every morning."' Akbar learnt the 1,000 names, we are told, and would stand facing the east, with folded hands pressed to his forehead, and concentrate his mind on the effulgence of the rising sun.

Sun worship was a potent symbol for Akbar, as it was venerated by many people at court and across the country. Hindus worshipped the sun while reciting the Gayatri Mantra and Raja Birbal himself was a believer in sun worship. The Parsees, some of the Sufis, the Rajputs at court, Akbar's Rajput wives, and the Timurids, would all recognize the power and visible symbolism of the Padshah venerating the sun.

While Akbar worshipped the sublime light of dawn, along with the cerebral, philosophical, and austere Jain monks, he also acquainted himself with more tenebrous ascetics, adept at the mysteries of the night. 'His Majesty also called some of the Jogis,' wrote Badauni, 'and gave them at night...interviews.' Akbar would question the jogis about their methods of meditation, spiritual practices, postures, alchemical preparations, and practice of magical powers. On Shivratri, Akbar joined this ferocious, unfettered group of men in the opaque night and ate and drank with them. The worship of Bhairava, the most terrible aspect of Shiva, was said to be 'both intemperate and licentious'. On this bleak and black night, the Shivlinga was worshipped every third hour with offerings of flowers, dhatura, ketaki, and bel leaves and it was bathed, in succession, with milk, curd, ghee and honey, and Gangajal. The jogis predicted the Padshah would live three or four times as long as ordinary men. 'Fawning court doctors,' sneered Badauni, 'wisely enough, found proofs for the longevity of the Emperor'. On being told that there were hermits and recluses living in Tibet and Mongolia, who could live for more than 200 years, Akbar began practising increasing austerity in his life and habits. He 'limited the time he spent in the harem', wrote Badauni, and 'curtailed his food and drink, but especially abstained from meat'. Badauni also wrote that Akbar shaved the crown of his head, the tenth opening of the body, and let the hairs grow at the sides to allow his soul to escape freely out of the body at the moment of death.

Akbar's interactions with the jogis were scandalous, according to Badauni, but also path-breaking and resulted in Hindu ascetic practices having a pronounced and lasting impact on Indo-Islamic culture. Akbar would have the *Yog Vashisht*, the dialogue between Rama and the Sadhu Vashishta, translated into Persian and would commission miniatures of the jogis of Gorkhatri for the *Baburnama*. Babur himself had barely mentioned his visit to the Gorkhatri but his grandson would have the jogis painted with great realism, showing their distinctive physical features and their particular dress and habits because of his own first-hand observation of them. The singanad janeu, the fillets, and the necklace of coloured cloth of the Nath jogis were all meticulously painted.

In the same spirit of compassion and empathy, Akbar had two caravanserais built outside the city for the housing and feeding of the poor, one for Hindus and one for Muslims, called Dharampurah and Khairpurah respectively. Sarais were built, wrote Abu'l Fazl, 'so that the poor and needy of the world might have a home without having to look for it'. Abu'l Fazl was put in charge of these inns and so many jogis flocked to them that a third place was built, called Jogipurah. Akbar seemed to have been genuinely keen to alleviate poverty and suffering, viewing it as the duty of a king and a virtuous man. 'It was my object that mendicancy should disappear from my dominions,' Akbar claimed. 'Many persons were plentifully supplied with means, but through the malady of avarice,' he continued sadly, 'it proved to no avail.' The rampant 'malady of avarice' or corruption was one that Akbar fought long and hard against. Many of his measures, such as the branding of horses, were brought in to try and curb this deeply entrenched habit. Proof of corruption in trusted men could make him violently angry, as when he discovered that alms sent for distribution to the Haram Sharif in Mecca were unaccounted for and Shaikh Abdullah Sultanpuri's egregious venality had made him hoard gold bars in his house. This was perhaps why Akbar was so very impressed by the vows of poverty undertaken by both the Jesuits and the Jains. They never did accept the truly magnificent gifts and largesse he kept trying to give them and, in the end, this earned them Akbar's abiding respect.

Of Akbar's empathy and care for his poorer subjects the Jesuits have left a moving account:

> Amongst his great nobles he was so predominant that none dared lift his head too high; but with the humbler classes he was benevolent and debonair, willingly giving them audience and hearing their petitions. He was pleased to accept their presents, taking them into his hands and holding them to his breast (which he never does with the rich gifts brought to him by his nobles), though often with prudent dissimulation he pretended not to see them.

Many of the rulings from this period of Akbar's reign reflect this deep empathy, along with a spirit of rationality, questioning all the old traditions and rituals. There was a determined effort, too, to exercise a pragmatic tolerance for practices that would have earlier been condemned by the Padshah. Akbar had been notoriously intransigent, for example, about sexual crimes. 'The King has such a hatred of debauchery and adultery,' wrote Monserrate, 'that neither influence nor entreaties nor the great ransom which was offered would induce him to pardon his chief trade commissioner, who, although he was married, had violently debauched a well-born Brahman girl. The wretch was by the king's order remorselessly strangled.' Now, however, Akbar tried to regulate prostitution and set up quarters outside the city, called Shaitanpurah, so that the prostitutes 'who had gathered together in the Capital in such swarms as to defy counting or numbering' could be regulated. Nonetheless, the limits of the Padshah's tolerance may be seen in the order that 'if a young woman were found running about the lanes and bazars of the town, and while so doing either did not veil herself, or allowed herself to become unveiled, or if a woman was worthless and deceitful and quarrelled with her husband, she was to go to the quarter of the prostitute and take up the profession'.

The selling of alcohol was also now permitted through the opening of a wine shop though it was clarified that the wine was for medicinal purposes. Interestingly, to control boisterous behaviour at the site of the wine shop, a woman, a porter's wife, was placed there to supervise wine sales, clearly in the belief that men would control their behaviour in the presence of a woman.

Wine had always been drunk, even among the elite. The nobles had their own suchi khanas, or provisioning establishment, which no doubt Akbar would have had, too, though Abu'l Fazl was discreetly silent about this. While Akbar disapproved of his courtiers appearing visibly drunk or even smelling of alcohol in his darbar, he was much more indulgent outside the court. When one Shaikh Abdur Rahim, friend of another notorious drunkard*, from whom 'he had learned wine-drinking', and who 'drank so hard that he got frequently insane', accidentally hurt himself during just such a drunken fit, Akbar himself tended to the wounded man. On another occasion, it was no less than the sadr, Abd ul-Hai, and the chief qazi, who took part in a drinking competition during a feast, and Akbar was so delighted at thus seeing the highest religious and judicial authorities in their cups that he was moved to quote a line of poetry by Hafiz.

Badauni tells us about specific bans brought in to protect the beliefs of the Hindus at this time: 'He prohibited the slaughter of cows, and the eating of their flesh, because the Hindus devoutly worship them.' Anyone accused of cow slaughter or of having killed a peacock was punished by state authorities, long beards were frowned upon, dogs were allowed into the harem, and the hajj pilgrimage and five-times-namaaz were deemed unnecessary. Though an increasing austerity diffused into the Padshah's habits he still, nonetheless, appreciated good food. Hakim Humam in addition to being a doctor, was a calligrapher, scientist, connoisseur of poetry, and also mir bakawal, master of the kitchen. When he had to absent himself on missions, Akbar would complain that 'since Hakim Humam has gone my food has not the same taste'.

For Badauni, who was now only employed for translations and

---

*Jamal Bakhtyar, who appeared in court drunk and was sent home.

completely excluded from the high-voltage discussions with the Jains, Brahmins and Sufis, it appeared that Akbar only wanted to placate the Hindus. 'He acted very differently in the case of Hindus, of whom he could not get enough,' wrote Badauni bitterly, 'for the Hindus, of course, are indispensable; to them belongs half the army and half the land. Neither the Hindustanis nor the Moghuls can point to such great lords as the Hindus have among themselves. But if other than Hindus came and wished to become disciples at any sacrifice, his Majesty reproved or punished them. For their honour and zeal he did not care, nor did he notice whether they fell in with his views or not.' For Pinheiro, a later Jesuit to Akbar's court, the verdict was even more succinct: 'He adores God, and the Sun, and is a Hindu, he follows the sect of the Jains.' As for the Hindus and Brahmins at court, Akbar fit easily within their capacious pantheon. 'Cheating, thieving Brahmans,' moaned Badauni, 'collected another set of 1001 names of "his Majesty the Sun" and told the Emperor that he was an incarnation, like Ram, Krishna and other infidel kings; and though lord of the world, he had assumed his shape, in order to play with the people of our planet.'

For the orthodox at court these extraordinary changes would appear to be provocatively anti-Islam. The orthodox Sunni Shaikh Ahmad Sirhindi, who was most fond of repeating Prophet Muhammad's maxim that 'anything new which is introduced in my religion is condemnable', would have found the atmosphere distinctly unpalatable. Rafiuddin Shirazi, the Iranian visitor, claimed that '(Akbar) nursed a grievance against the Holy Prophet on account of his being the last of the prophets. Otherwise he could have claimed the position of a prophet for himself without facing opposition.' For Badauni, consigned to translating 'unimaginable nonsense', and unable to tolerate the tenor of the discussions at this plural, questioning court, there was no option but to retire even further from the warm glow of the Padshah's presence. On darbar days, he performed the kornish from a distance and took his place at the door, 'where the shoes are left', mourning for an uncomplicated dawn where the preferred and cherished children of God were good Muslims. For Abu'l Fazl, meanwhile, the non-Muslim peoples were simply 'other worshippers of God'.

AKBAR AND BIRBAL

In the next few years, between 1583 and 1586, the trajectory of Akbar's life would unexpectedly swerve away from what had been the glowing heart of his empire for so many years—Fatehpur Sikri and the ibadat khana. There has been a lot of conjecture about the reason why Akbar left Fatehpur Sikri at this point. There was the death of Mirza Hakim, for one, which immediately caused turmoil in the north-west frontier. But there was also the death of a courtier and a friend who had held a unique place in the Padshah's affections—Birbal.

Birbal was one of the first officers to join Akbar's court, possibly as early as 1556, when he was twenty-eight years old. A pleasant-faced man, with a glossy moustache just like the Padshah's, Birbal's increasingly privileged place at court would be reflected by his spreading girth, resulting in his qaba settling in comfortable, voluminous folds around his form. He was honoured with the title Raja and a high rank of 2,000 soon after he joined imperial service. In Birbal the Padshah found a quick and adaptable mind, a lively intelligence, and an engaging wit and, above all, a complete and sincere devotion to Akbar himself. Another title that Birbal earned early on in his career, which gives some indication of the talents he possessed, that would have attracted the attention of the Padshah, was that of Kavi Rai, King of Poets. He was a fine poet of Braj, and his poems were much appreciated at court. He also had a naturally generous nature and all these traits combined—elegant repartee, largesse, and poetical talent—made Birbal the ideal Mughal courtier.

In the eleventh century text written in Persia, the *Mirror for Princes*, the author gives precise advice for those wishing to sparkle at a Persianate court. For the close companion, the author clarifies, '(y)ou should be a raconteur, retaining in your memory a large number of anecdotes, jests and clever witticisms; a boon companion without stories and quips is imperfectly equipped'.

When Akbar was building his new city at Fatehpur Sikri, he had ordered 'the erection of a stone palace for [Birbal]'. So celebrated was the friendship between the two men that long after the Mughal Empire was history, a veritable tsunami of anecdotes of the so-called Akbar–Birbal variety lived on, lampooning the Padshah as a somewhat dim-witted though well intentioned character, regularly put in his place by Birbal. The scholar C. M. Naim has shown that while often subversive, these stories also tend to try and 'humanize' Akbar and to transform him into someone who was accessible and approachable. While there is very little evidence that any of these anecdotes were based on actual events, there is no doubt that Akbar enjoyed witty and sharp observations. When the poet Faizi happened to boast in Akbar's presence that no one surpassed him in the three Cs—Chess, Combat, and Composition—the emperor retorted that he had forgotten a fourth, Conceit. On another occasion, when Shaikh Mubarak had berated the emperor for being too extravagant, Faizi had tried to make excuses for his father saying 'our Shaikh is not much of a courtier', whereupon Akbar had teased him saying 'no, he has left all those fopperies to you'. That the qualities appreciated by Akbar included a lively intellect and pleasant, charming manners are evident, yet he also demanded complete devotion and loyalty. It is inconceivable, therefore, that any courtier would have been allowed the liberties depicted in the Akbar–Birbal stories, certainly not from one who had such a long and special career at court. For though Akbar surrounded himself with movement and clamour and discussions, he was 'full also of dignity and when he is angry, of awful majesty', according to Monserrate, with an anger that most courtiers would have been loath to provoke.

A sign of the unique bond that Akbar shared with Birbal was that the raja was never censured in the thirty years he served at court as a close confidant of the Padshah. Even his closest courtiers were rebuked or punished when found lacking, as when Man Singh had not pursued Rana Pratap after Haldighati. 'The King's severity towards errors and misdemeanours committed by officials in the course of government business is remarkable', wrote Monserrate, 'for he is most stern with offenders against the public faith.' Only three men never incurred royal displeasure in their entire careers: the poet Faizi, the musician Tansen, and Raja Birbal. 'By means of conversing with the Emperor and taking advantage of the idiosyncrasies of his disposition,' wrote Badauni bitterly, '[Birbal] crept day by day more into favour, until he attained to high rank and was honoured with the distinction of becoming the Emperor's confidant and it became a case of thy flesh is my flesh and thy blood my blood.'

An incident in 1583 in Fatehpur Sikri was further demonstration of the close bond between Akbar and Raja Birbal. During an elephant fight organized in the grounds of Akbar's court, one of the elephants, 'unique for violence', suddenly rushed towards Birbal, and seized him with his trunk. Akbar turned his horse around and galloped towards the elephant, charging at him, while all around him his soldiers and courtiers shouted out in alarm. The elephant then turned towards Akbar but, inexplicably, faltered, and Birbal was saved.

A few months later, the courtiers of Fatehpur Sikri were caught up in a much more joyous emotion. The young prince Salim, fifteen years old, was getting ready for his marriage and the prestige of the clan of the Kachhwahas was about to be burnished to high gold. 'Since (Man Singh) was constantly in my father's house,' wrote Jahangir later in his memoir, 'I myself proposed marriage with his sister', Rajkumari Man Bai. According to Abu'l Fazl, it was the Kachhwahas who desired this union as Raja Bhagwant Das 'had a daughter whose purity adorned her high extraction and was endowed with beauty and graces', and so the Kachhwahas wished that 'she should be united to the prince'. As for Badauni, it mattered little who first proposed the idea since it was all a highly regrettable habit 'in accordance with [Akbar's] established custom' to ally himself with the Hindus and raise them up at court.

And so on a cool day in February 1584, as the sun arced through the sky, the once insignificant town of Amer was about to be lit up with a magnificence it had never before witnessed. The Padshah of Hindustan, along with the leading qazis and nobles of the court, for the first time in the history of the Mughals, brought a baraat to the bride's home in Raja Bhagwant Das's palace. 'They performed all the ceremonies which are customary among the Hindus,' wrote Badauni, 'such as lighting the fire etc. and over the litter of the Princess the Emperor ordered gold to be scattered all the way from that house to the palace.' Raja Bhagwant Das gave a splendid dowry for his daughter, who would be renamed Sultan un-Nisa Begum. He gave 'several strings of horses, and a hundred elephants, and boys and girls of Abyssinia, India and Circassia, and all sorts of golden vessels set with jewels, and jewels, and utensils of gold and silver'. Akbar himself, it was noted, carried the bridal palanquin part of the way back. Nor were the noblemen ignored, for they were all gifted 'Persian, Turkish and Arabian horses with golden saddles'. And so another Rajput princess from Amer entered the harem at Fatehpur Sikri, about whom Salim would write with great affection in his memoir. 'What shall I write of her goodness and excellence?' he wrote. 'She had a mind to perfection and she was so loyal to me that she would have sacrificed a thousand sons and brothers for one hair on my head.'

At the age of fifteen, Salim was growing into a strikingly handsome youth with a faint moustache and a firm jaw. Like his father, he would never grow a beard but he would favour a much more luxurious style in jewels and clothes than Akbar, with elaborately embroidered patkas, jewelled daggers, and a profusion of ornaments and jewellery. Soon after his wedding, Akbar granted Salim full adult status in 1585 and the young prince began assiduously building a corps of noblemen who would be loyal only to him.

The very first missive from the monarch of England, Queen Elizabeth I, arrived in Fatehpur Sikri in the course of the year, brought by a delegation of three English traders representing the 'merchants of the Levant' and headed by one John Newbery, accompanied by Ralph Fitch. Elizabeth I addressed Akbar as 'the most invincible and most mightie prince, Lord Zelabdin Echebar, King of Cambaya', a sentiment the Mughal Padshah would have appreciated though it is unlikely he ever received the letter. Akbar was at the time busy getting an expedition ready to travel to the Punjab, but he was pleased, nonetheless, to retain the services of a jeweller in the English party, William Leades, to whom he gave 'a house, and five slaves, a horse, and every day six shillings in money'. The Newbery expedition was the first of many attempts by the English to circumnavigate the Portuguese monopoly of trade in the area. While these adventurers were not able to establish any trade links at this time, they produced the first description of India by an Englishman.

Akbar left Fatehpur Sikri for the Punjab in 1585. When he left, there was no indication that he would never return, and that the great lively discussions of the ibadat khana were forever silenced.

The senior members of the harem, including Hamida Banu and Gulbadan, remained in Fatehpur Sikri during Akbar's endless absence, expecting the Padshah to return any day. Nor was there an abandonment of the city itself, as was later suggested, since many courtiers and harem members remained in the city. Rather, there was a gradual leeching away of its vitality and exuberance, as the Padshah's absence lengthened to years, and then decades. It has also been proposed that there was a sudden water shortage in the city after a dam broke but Hakim Abu'l Fath Gilani, who stayed on at Fatehpur Sikri, increasingly bemused and saddened by Akbar's absence, never mentioned any lack of water which he surely would have had that been the reason for the Padshah's absence.

Akbar had left Fatehpur Sikri to tend to his fractious border in the Punjab but on this journey he was also forced to deal with the consequences of two deaths that affected him deeply. The first was the death of his half-brother, Mirza Hakim. Late in 1585, Mirza Hakim 'after much madness...fell into pains difficult of treatment' and finally died of alcoholism. Immediately, the rebellious Kabuli noblemen showed signs of discontent, requiring Akbar's attention, for an old nightmare from the time of Babur himself had resurfaced—the Uzbeks. With Mirza Hakim, a convenient buffer, now dead, Abdullah Khan Uzbek* began to dream of empires in Afghanistan and Hindustan. But another death, in early 1586, was much more personally devastating for Akbar. Zain Khan Koka and Raja Birbal had been sent on an expedition against the troublesome Pashtun Yusufzais in the Swat and Bajaur regions but disagreement and mistrust between the two leaders led to Birbal falling into a trap that the Yusufzais laid for him in the crumbling defiles of Kabul's mountains. The Mughals suffered the worst defeat of Akbar's reign, in a massacre called the Yusufzai Disaster, in which more than 8,000 Mughal soldiers, including Birbal, were killed.

It is fitting that the sombre description of the death of this great poet-warrior of Akbar's court found a place in one of the most celebrated works of Brajbhasha of this period, Narottam's *Mancarit*, with its fluid mix of Perso-Arabic words and Persianized Braj a perfect

---

*This was the ruler of Badakhshan and Balkh, not to be confused with Abdullah Khan Uzbek, who earlier served in the Mughal army and then rebelled.

reflection of Birbal's life itself:

> The emperor was seated in the royal court,
> The earth's Mlecchas and Khans stood around him,
> as did all the Raos and Rajas.
> Just then a petition from there (the Northwest) was brought
> to his attention.
> The shah called in his attendant, and asked
> what was the matter;
> 'Who died, and who was saved? Who has been wounded?'
> He (the attendant) said these words, 'Blessed majesty,
> all the imperial forces were lost.
> I've never seen such a catastrophic manifestation of divine will.'

When this terrible news was announced to Akbar, he was inconsolable. For two days and two nights he refused any food or water, did not attend to any state matters, left the bemused ambassador of Turan unattended, and turned away in grief from the jharoka window. Akbar 'grieved him exceedingly, and his heart turned away from everything', wrote Abu'l Fazl. Hamida Banu, who had come to the Punjab to meet with her son, had to entreat with the Padshah, along with his attendants, to resume his activities. The entire court mourned Birbal and the poet Keshavdas wrote verses in Brajbhasha in memory of him.

> When Birbal passed away there was great rejoicing in
> Poverty's court.
> The pakhavaj drums of Evil began to play
> The sounds of the conch shells of Grief resounded
> The songs of Falsehood, the tambourines of Fear
> A concert of all these instruments was heard
> The house of Kaliyuga was merry with the pipes of Discord
> and the streaming banners of Disgrace.

'He never experienced such grief at the death of any Amir,' wrote Badauni, 'as he did at that of Birbal.' Akbar seemed tormented by the idea of the broken, bloody body of his old friend lying unclaimed on the cold, stony hillsides on which he had died, carrying out his duty to his Padshah unto death. 'Alas,' he said, 'that they could not bring his body out of the defile, that it might have been committed to the flames.' In his grief and his fury he even wanted to rush to Kabul himself, to find Birbal's body and to punish the other officers. He was dissuaded by his courtiers, and comforted by them with the idea that the light of the sun was enough to purify the body of his fallen friend. 'By this heart-rending mishap, the memory of the pleasures of his lofty company has become very bitter,' Akbar admitted to Abu'l Fazl, 'and this sudden calamity has greatly afflicted my heart...some obstacles have prevented me from seeing the body with my own eyes so that I might testify my love and affection for him.' Rumours circulated for the rest of the year, and even longer, that Birbal was not dead, that he had been seen, among jogis and sannyasis, or wandering in his old fief of Nagarkot. Every time such a rumour reached the court Akbar, painfully hopeful, sent men to have it investigated. 'The world is like a mirage,' Akbar wrote to Abdur Rahim sadly, 'to beguile thirsty souls... at the end of this frenzy is simply a mist—a fume.'

A Hindi couplet has been popularly attributed to Akbar, describing his state of mind:

> Deen dekhi sab din, ek na dinho dusah dukh
> So ab ham kan din, kachhahun nahin rakhio Birbal
> (He saw the poor and gave them all, but never distributed sorrows
> Now that he has given even [sorrow] to me, Birbal has kept nothing for himself)

Something had broken inside the Padshah, and he would never again contemplate returning to Fatehpur Sikri, because 'the pleasant palaces of that city did not engage his heart', wrote Abu'l Fazl. Akbar kept moving further and further north, to Kabul and then to Kashmir. Perhaps the palaces and courtyards of his erstwhile capital were too painful a reminder of a friend and courtier whose presence and companionship had made bearable the heavy melancholy that sometimes weighed on Akbar's soul. The only Hindu who was so wholly devoted to the Padshah that he staked his most precious possession on the Padshah's 'religion', his own immortal soul. So Fatehpur Sikri remained, not abandoned, but bereft. But for the next decade, as Fatehpur Sikri retracted back into itself, Akbar would discover Paradise on Earth.

PART 5

PARADISE ON EARTH
{1585–1598}

~

A RAJPUT IN THE SNOW

Mid-winter in Kashmir was the season of long nights, ice flurries, and impenetrable high passes. It was a time when men sheltered in the shadows of the great mountains and dreamt of spring. So when Akbar's army of 5,000 specially-equipped war horses commanded by Raja Bhagwant Das and Shah Quli Mehram marched from Attock along the Pakhli Route through the ravine of Baramullah in December 1585, the forces of the Sultan of Kashmir, Yusuf Shah Chak, were caught unawares. Even so, skirmishing between the two armies was vicious, made even more brutal by the slicing sleet and the lack of provisions. The Kashmir sultan began to push the Mughal army back but he didn't press home his advantage. This was because the years of diplomacy by the Mughals, in which the Kashmir sultan's supremacy had been steadily undermined and dissidents supported, meant that Yusuf Shah Chak's grip on power had been eroded and he was willing to make peace as soon as he received a letter from the Rajput general ominously warning that 'although this time the royal army was defeated, next time a force thousand times larger than this would be dispatched (against you) and it would be difficult for you to save your life. Therefore,' continued Bhagwant Das, 'I suggest to you that it is better for you to proceed with me to the presence of Emperor Akbar.' The striking of coins and the reciting of the khutba would continue in Akbar's name, agreed Yusuf Shah, and he also promised to bring his son, Yakub Shah, to Akbar. It was agreed that Yusuf Shah needed only to accompany Bhagwant Das to pay obeisance before the Mughal Padshah before returning to Kashmir.

However, when the Mughal army returned to the imperial court at Attock, Akbar was in no mood for conciliation and disapproved of the treaty which Bhagwant Das had negotiated on his own. He had Yusuf Shah arrested, discomfiting his Rajput general who had brought the Kashmir sultan into Hindustan upon his honour. Bhagwant Das was so mortified by what he perceived as a slur that when Akbar appointed him Governor to Kabul a few months later, he laid down certain conditions regarding the extent of his authority before he would agree to take up office. This, recorded Abu'l Fazl, was perceived as a sort of 'madness' by Akbar, who could not countenance any questioning of his decree. Bhagwant Das was detained, and Mirza Daniyal was appointed Governor of Kabul in his stead. Perhaps realizing that he had presumed too much upon the Padshah's indulgence, Bhagwant Das withdrew his conditions and Akbar reinstated him as governor. However, Bhagwant Das appears to have been deeply troubled by what he would have perceived as a public humiliation. On his way to Kabul, having crossed the Indus, 'his intellect grew darkened and he became very giddy' wrote Abu'l Fazl. He was brought back to the imperial camp and placed in care where, to the Padshah's astonishment and alarm, he tried to kill himself with a dagger. The Padshah sent four of the best physicians at court—Hakim Hasan, Mahadev, Khangar, and Daulat Khan—for the raja's entourage to choose from and finally it was settled that Mahadev would attend to Bhagwant Das, who slowly recovered.

A second force was sent to Kashmir in June 1586, this time under the command of Qasim Khan Mir Bahr, aided by Haidar Chak, a dissident from the Kashmiri royal family, and now a Mughal commander. The army sent to Kashmir was a massive one, numbering about 50,000 cavalry and up to 100,000 foot soldiers. Conditions on the ground had suddenly become a great deal more congenial for the Mughals, made so by the violent rule of Yakub Chak, son of Yusuf Chak, who had taken over the rule of Kashmir after his father had been arrested. Yakub Chak had aligned with the ulema and had had the popular Sunni leader, Qazi Musa, executed, causing considerable disquiet between Shias and the Sunnis. Having emptied the state coffers fighting the Mughals, Yakub Chak then took to harassing and plundering the local zamindars. He also closed down important roads, fearing Mughal incursions, with the result that people could no longer travel for trade and supplies, leading to resentment and disaffection. As a result, a large number of the disgruntled Kashmiri elite arrived at the Mughal court, asking for help, and were received with satisfaction as well as royal robes and presents by Akbar who had been waiting a long time for just such a moment. The Kashmiri leadership signed a pact which guaranteed religious freedom for Kashmiris, their protection against enslavement and oppression, and the expulsion of those Kashmiri nobles who were deemed mischievous. Consequently, the army marching to Kashmir were given the following strict instructions:

> They (Mughal forces) were given directions to show consideration and favour to all people who would come across their way so that they were not forced to abandon their homes.

Faced with defections and disunity, Yakub Chak was unable to resist the combined Mughal–Kashmir army, which marched into Srinagar on 7 October 1586.

As for Raja Bhagwant Das, he would never again be asked to campaign and, from the time of his recovery till his death in 1589, he was put in charge of the royal harem. For the pragmatic Akbar the extreme action of Bhagwant Das appeared profoundly mystifying. As the Jesuits had written of Akbar, 'He is willing to consult about his affairs, and often takes advice in private from his friends near his person, but the decision, as it ought, always rests with the king'. It was perfectly in order for Akbar to reserve the final decision on the treaty with Kashmir to himself. Moreover, as the Jesuits had noted, Akbar behaved 'so sternly towards the nobles who are under his proud sway that each one of them believes himself to be regarded not only as a contemptible creature but as the very lowest and meanest of mankind. For instance, these nobles, if they commit offences, are punished more severely and relentlessly than the rest of the people, even those of the meanest degree.' Given the fact that he censured his generals routinely, it was natural for him to be surprised by Raja Bhagwant Das's reaction. However, there had been several instances when the actions of Rajput men and women were ascribed to a sort of insanity, a familial malady, by bemused Mughal chroniclers. For the Rajputs, their word and their honour as warriors and chiefs were as unalterable as the rising of the sun. Death, as sung by the Charans, was a far easier alternative to a life without honour. The Bhagwant Das episode, then, was one where the fine balance between the Padshah being the final authority on key matters and the Rajput code of honour was disturbed. However, having exerted his authority, Akbar did everything he could to take care of his courtier.

By giving Bhagwant Das charge of the imperial household Akbar was keeping the raja close at hand, where his well-being could be monitored, while, at the same time giving him one of the highest honours of the land. Only the most trustworthy officers, who enjoyed the Padshah's complete confidence, were ever given this charge, which included control of the royal bodyguard and the supervision of all provisions and articles required for the comfort and safety of the harem women. On a more personal note, these last years at court would have been deeply satisfying ones for a man who had dedicated his life to the cause of the Mughal Empire. In April 1586, Bhagwant Das's daughter gave birth to a child, a girl who was named Shah Begum, and Akbar called for celebrations which were unprecedented. Abu'l Fazl tells us that 'contrary to the usage', Akbar gathered an assembly to give thanks for the joyful news of the birth of a daughter. A great feast was hosted by Hamida Banu, who had come to court for the occasion, and gifts and money were distributed to all.

That Akbar had specifically ordered grand celebrations for the birth of a girl child was not surprising. His own daughters were raised with a great deal of love and preference, which Salim recalled with something akin to jealousy. 'Her temperament is greatly inclined to volatility and sharpness,' wrote Salim about his youngest sister, Aram Banu Begum, born just a few years before his own daughter. 'My father loved her so much that he politely tolerated her acts of rudeness, and in his blessed sight, since he loved her so much, she did not seem so bad. He often said to me,' continued Salim, who had clearly found his sister trying, 'Baba, for my sake, after I'm gone, treat this sister of yours, who is, as the Indians say, my ladla...as I do. Tolerate her coquettishness and overlook her rudeness and impudence.' Of another of his sisters, Shakr un-Nisa Begum, born after the birth of Daniyal in 1572, Salim notes the particular care Akbar took to keep her close to himself. 'Since she was brought up in the lap of my exalted father's care, she turned out very well,' wrote Salim, 'good-natured and innately compassionate toward all people.'

As his daughters and granddaughters grew up around him Akbar became increasingly concerned about the plight of girls when they got married and left their families. Criticizing Muslim laws of inheritance which allowed for a smaller share of inheritance to a daughter, Akbar argued that this was inherently faulty, for if a daughter was deemed 'weaker', then 'the weakness of the woman calls for a larger share', to ensure her own protection. As for the law which allowed a greater share of inheritance to fall to nephews in case a deceased person only had daughters, 'how could this law be justified', exclaimed Akbar. In this clear and lucid articulation of his disapproval of Muslim laws of inheritance with regard to girls, Irfan Habib considers Akbar a pioneer and a unique example of a sixteenth-century Muslim monarch wanting to safeguard the rights of girls and women through the reform of laws.

For Bhagwant Das it would have been a moment of great pride and accomplishment to have the birth of his granddaughter celebrated with all the extravagance due a Mughal shahzaadi that she was. The following year, in August 1587, Bhagwant Das's daughter gave birth to a son whom Akbar named Sultan Khusrau. Another Rajput rajkumari entered Salim's household in June 1586, when one of Akbar's favourite courtiers, Raja Rai Singh of Bikaner, married his daughter to the prince. Akbar was very fond of the Raja of Bikaner, who was not only an indefatigable warrior but also demonstrated all the ideal traits of a great Mughal courtier. He was a generous patron to writers and poets and was himself a scholar of Sanskrit, writing the *Rai Singh Mahotsav*, on the treatment of diseases, in Sanskrit. He was a magnanimous and careful ruler, protecting not only those of his own faith but those of other faiths as well, including the Jains. Like the other influential courtiers surrounding the Padshah, the raja was a patron of architecture and built the Junagarh Fort outside Bikaner, in an indigenous style with traces of Mughal influence. When in 1592 one of Raja Rai Singh's daughters was widowed, Akbar rode to comfort the raja and his daughter, and to plead with the widow not to commit sati, for the sake of her children. For the Padshah of Hindustan to condole with a courtier in his own home was a very special honour and a testament to the great affection Akbar had for the family of Bikaner.

The Marwar Rathores sent a daughter in 1586, Rajkumari Mani Bai (also known as Jagat Gosain), the daughter of Rao Udai Singh, to be married to Prince Salim. It was noted that Akbar and the ladies of the harem went to Udai Singh's house for the celebration of the marriage. Upon her marriage to Salim, Akbar gave her the title Taj Bibi though she was popularly known as Jodh Bai, for her home state of Jodhpur. Udai Singh was given the title raja, and awarded a mansab of 1,000.

Munis Faruqui has pointed out that from this time onwards, Akbar recused* himself from further marriage alliances and instead encouraged his three sons to contract a large number of marriages between them. For royal marriages were not only a way to ensure heirs but, much more potently, as demonstrated by Ruby Lal, a way to incorporate a diverse peoples into the protective embrace of the Mughal Empire. From this time onwards no non-royal pretender to the Mughal throne would be tolerated but for Akbar's sons, gilded with wealth, courtiers and powerful in-laws, the empire was theirs to claim.

It was from this period, too, for the first time in the history of the Mughals, that the royal mirzas were kept at court well into adulthood. As we have seen, Mirza Hakim would be the last Timurid prince to control an appanage. When Akbar dismantled the appanage system, he had Mirza Hakim's young sons, Kaikobad and Afrasiyab, imprisoned in Hindustan. From now on, the only candidates eligible to aspire to the throne would be Akbar's direct descendants. The Padshah would keep his heirs close to the vortex of imperial power so that he could monitor their activities himself. Akbar had already accorded his three sons mansabs in 1577, at the ages of eight, seven, and five respectively, marking their prestige at a young age. As the three boys grew into young men there was a constant eddying of noblemen around each one, as the mirzas unfolded their ambitions according to their personality and talent.

With the powerful Kachhwahas already aligned to him through his wife, Salim pushed back against Akbar's tight control by looking further afield for supporters who would one day buttress his claims to rule. He welcomed into his household former supporters of Mirza Hakim, whom Akbar did not tolerate, men like Lala Beg Kabuli and Zamana Beg. He courted members of the recently displaced Kashmiri royal family, such as Amba Khan Kashmiri, who would prove to be valuable allies in the years to come. Salim was also beginning to watch

---

*Though there are records of a couple more marriages to daughters of minor chieftains.

the two men closest to his father, Abu'l Fazl and Faizi, with a certain degree of flinty and corrosive judgement. The poet Urfi had been blocked from gaining full-time employment at the Mughal court by Faizi, and the professional frisson between the two men soon turned into a deep loathing. In 1589, upon the death of Urfi's patron, Hakim Abu'l Fath Gilani, it was Salim who became his patron, along with Zain Khan Koka and Abdur Rahim. The three men, writes Munis Faruqui, had a 'shared dislike of the brothers Shaikh Abu'l Fazl and Faizi, whose arrogance and abrasiveness', as well as their jealously guarded proximity to the emperor 'had made them notorious and unpopular figures at the imperial court'.

Besides attempting to chart his own course, Salim also had to cope with the enormous pressure of being his father's eldest son. Akbar must have appeared superhuman to his sons and this pressure was, in all likelihood, a major contributing factor to Salim becoming addicted to wine and opium at exactly this stage. 'One day I mounted to go hunting,' wrote Salim in his extremely candid autobiography. 'Since I overdid it and got exhausted, a wonderful gunner...said to me, "If you drink a beaker of wine, it will relieve the exhaustion." Since I was young and my nature was inclined to do these things, I ordered Mahmud the water-carrier to go to Hakim Ali's house and bring some alcoholic syrup. The physician sent a phial and a half of yellow-coloured, sweet-tasting wine in a small bottle. I drank it and liked the feeling I got.' Salim would come to depend on the feeling of invincibility that alcohol and opium gave him in the face of a father who needed nothing other than his own indomitable willpower to meet the various challenges he faced.

Salim may have been the most prominent Mughal at the time to develop a dependence on alcohol but he was by no means an exception. Alcohol, primarily wine, was a part of Mughal life though the pattern of consumption had changed since Babur's time. Babur had written frankly of drinking parties with his men, evenings that began with poetry and ended in drunken mishaps. But these gatherings were occasional, punctuating a busy, nomadic lifestyle. Now, as Mughal life became more settled, alcohol became a more private pastime, often indulged to excess, known to cause decrepitude and even death. Opium consumption, on the other hand, seemed to provoke no stigma and appeared to be widely used, even outside courtly circles as the poorer folk used it to ease the drudgery of their working day. Alfonso de Albuquerque had already come across the plant in 1513 and, ever the practical merchant, wrote to the Portuguese king to urge him to cover the fields of Portugal with the plant. Indeed, poppy, indigo, and sugar were listed by Abu'l Fazl in 1590 as the three products of the highest value in the land.

Mirza Murad, meanwhile, was married to a daughter of Mirza Aziz Koka in 1587, thereby securing for himself the support of one of the most powerful men in the empire. The wedding was celebrated with éclat in the house of Hamida Banu, and one can imagine the immense satisfaction of Jiji Anaga, as her granddaughter became one of the princesses of the empire. The son of a concubine, Murad was described as a quiet and serious young scholar by the Jesuits. 'His complexion was dark,' wrote Salim later in his memoir about Murad, 'and he was tall in stature, inclining to be portly. Gravity was apparent in his manner, and bravery and manliness were evident from his conduct.' Mirza Daniyal, on the other hand, was described as 'a young man of fine stature', by Salim. 'He was very fond of elephants and horses... He was fond of Indian singing.' As each prince married the daughters of eminent men, myriad ambitions and clashing desires whirled in dense circles around the mirzas, who were like planets around the sun that was the Padshah, waiting for the inexorable dawn of the next emperor.

Akbar and his sons married women from all the important ethnic groups in Hindustan except the Afghans, with the largest groups being the Persian, Turki, and Rajput families. But where the Padshah's daughters were concerned, no Mughal princess was married to a Rajput, a non-Muslim noble, or a shaikhzada. Akbar's daughters were married to exalted Turki families or to royal princes. Hypergamy was similarly exercised among the Rajput clans, with lower status families looking to marry their daughters into higher status families.

After Akbar, no non-royal groom was ever considered worthy of marrying a Mughal princess, and as the generations evolved, and cousins and uncles were routinely killed during increasingly violent succession struggles, these princesses often remained unmarried, leading to rumours, fuelled by European accounts, that Mughal emperors preferred to keep their daughters for their own perverse pleasure. The French adventurer François Bernier, never one to refrain from the most lurid rumour-mongering, would primly claim that 'it is painful to allude to the rumour of his [Shah Jahan's] unnatural attachment, the justification of which he rested on the decisions of the mullahs. According to them, it would have been unjust to deny the king the privilege of gathering fruit from the tree he himself had planted.'

As for the Rajputs, their links with the Mughal court through marriages and service ensured a corresponding change in their clans and territories. Raja Udai Singh, following the Mughal system, introduced the payment of a peshkash, later known as the hukmnama, owed by noblemen when a jagir lapsed on the death of its jagirdar. Marwar also saw the introduction of an extensive communication network at this time, linking the region with the Mughal Empire. As in other parts of the empire, dak chowkis or post stations were set up along major roads connecting towns and cities and allowed for the very rapid transmission of news, commands, and papers. Monserrate had noted in amazement that the runners along these routes could cover the same distance as a horseman at full speed. 'They practise running in shoes made of lead,' the Jesuit wrote, 'or train themselves by repeatedly lifting their feet and moving their legs till their heels touch their buttocks. When their leaden shoes are removed, they are seen to be magnificent runners, by the help of whose swiftness the King can very rapidly and regularly obtain news or send orders on any matter touching the peace of his realm.' Along with fleet-footed runners, there were caravanserais and wells provided along these highways for the comfort of travellers.

At this time, in the clan of the Kachhwahas, with Raja Bhagwant Das at court, it was Kuar Man Singh who would now fly the white pennant of Amer on distant battlefields, including at Kabul. Having defeated the main Afghan and Pathan tribes in the area and taken Kabul, tradition has it that when Man Singh presented their multi-coloured flags to Akbar, the Padshah allowed him the use of these colours as his own, to which Man Singh added the white of Amer thus creating the Dhoondhari 'panchranga' flag.

Besides the Kashmir and Kabul victories, Akbar's armies were active on other fronts. Raja Todar Mal, along with a large army, was sent to subdue the Yusufzai and avenge the unpardonable death of Raja Birbal. This indefatigable warrior built forts along the mountain passes and directed his forces to skirmish with the Afghans continuously till they were defeated. Raja Man Singh was dispatched to deal with the notorious Raushanias, a tribe of hillmen aiming to liberate Afghanistan from the Mughals. They were branded heretics, on account of the claims to prophethood of their leader, Bayazid, and 'were enslaved and sent to the markets of Central Asia for sale'. These emphatic actions taken by Akbar along the Hindu Kush were reason enough for Abdullah Khan Uzbek to send an ambassador, Sayyid Mir Quraish, to the Mughal court along with a selection of gifts including 'chosen steeds, powerful camels and swift mules; with wild animals and choice furs'. Much more effective a present, however, was a clutch of nine special pigeons from Turan along with Habib, a kabootar-baz. While the ambassador was kept waiting for an audience for many days, Akbar sent for Habib and his winged charges, was delighted with their exploits and wrote a thrilled letter to Abdur Rahim about the joys of ishq-baazi.

Sayyid Mir Quraish was kept for many months at the Mughal court, a virtual prisoner, but one who was extravagantly feted and dined. He was detained long enough to witness the victories of Man Singh against the Yusufzai and the victories of Bhagwant Das in Kashmir. He was then taken, along with the court, to Lahore, where he learned about the annexation of Kashmir. When he was finally allowed to leave in August 1586, along with the Hindustani ambassador Hakim Humam, Sayyid Quraish carried a letter from Akbar to Abdullah Khan which must have caused much rumination and introspection on the part of the Uzbek. 'What you have written with a pen perfumed with brotherhood on the subject of our mutually exerting ourselves to strengthen the foundations of peace,' wrote the Hindustani Padshah, 'and to purify the fountains of concord, and of making this Hind Koh the boundary between us, has most fully commended itself to us.' The details of the 'exertions' that Akbar had made to strengthen his borders would have been conveyed by the Turani ambassador in worrisome detail.

Abdullah Khan Uzbek was right to be nervous about Akbar's

actions, for the Mughal Padshah had just pushed the north-west frontier of the empire from the Indus, where it earlier lay, further than it had ever been. This vast and porous frontier, from the Oxus to the Beas, had only been tenuously held by successive Indian rulers. The challenges for a secure command of the area were daunting.

> The Punjab rivers were all fordable except during the season of inundations. The Indus too was difficult to defend during the winter and early summer with its long course and broad channels in the Plains. The Salt Range is really formed of low hills that could be penetrated at any number of points. To the West of the Indus, the Sulaiman Range...is pierced by numerous passes open throughout the year, for another, it was inhabited by Afghan tribes who made regular garrisoning of all the passes by any outside army impossible. A truly 'scientific frontier' in medieval conditions could be secured only if an Indian Government held the Hindu Kush mountains.

Now, at last, Akbar had secured the Hindu Kush and though Abdullah Khan Uzbek had captured Badakhshan and Balkh, he would venture no further. Akbar also stoutly defended his credentials as an Islamic leader, assuring the Uzbek that 'places which from the time of [the] rise of the sun of Islam till the present day had not been trod by the horse-hoofs of world-conquering princes and where their swords had never flashed, have become the dwelling-places and the homes of the faithful'. Akbar realized the importance of reassuring the Uzbek leader, and not isolating himself among the celebrated Muslim empires of the world. Aware that scandalous whispers may have sliced through the Khyber Pass about the unorthodox texture of the Mughal court, Akbar claimed that 'the churches and temples of the infidels and heretics have become mosques and holy shrines for the master of orthodoxy. God be praised!' And finally, about the rumours that may have reached Turan, Akbar pointed out that 'neither God nor Prophet has escaped the slanders of men, much less I'. Abdullah Khan Uzbek died in 1598, effectively bringing to an end the Uzbek menace.

In the decade from 1587 to 1597, Akbar would move first to one end of the empire, then to the other, in both cases extending the frontiers of Mughal rule further than they had ever been before.

Kashmir, Kandahar, and the Hindu Kush, were brought firmly within his dominions. Much more resistant to the Padshah's will, however, would be his own sons, grown into men, with ambitions of their own. To keep them safe from each other, Akbar would separate his sons and his amirs by sending them away from court, into the different corners of the empire, but despite all the Padshah's efforts, most would not return alive.

THE DAR AL-SULTANAT

When Akbar set off from Attock Fort on the Indus in 1586, it was believed that he was finally returning to the capital at Fatehpur Sikri. Instead, the Mughal retinue stopped at Lahore and Akbar would remain in the city for a dozen years, anchoring it forever in the Mughal imagination and bolting it onto Hindustan's expansive scaffolding. It would remain a great Mughal city and the cultural heart of the Punjab till 1748 when it was captured by the Afghans. Salim, who was travelling to Lahore with his father, would be particularly enchanted with the city and would live there many years when he became Padshah. His wife, Noor Jahan, is believed to have said; 'We have purchased Lahore with our soul; we have given our life and bought another Paradise.' Both Salim and Noor Jahan would be buried in Lahore, and Noor Jahan's family, especially, would cleave the city to their legacy through extensive architectural commissions.

Monserrate, arriving in Lahore in 1582, wrote of a lively and thriving city, fragrant with perfumes:

> This city is second to none, either in Asia or in Europe, with regard to size, population and wealth. It is crowded with merchants, who forgather there from all over Asia. In all these respects, it excels other cities, as also in the huge quantity of every kind of merchandise which is imported. Moreover there is no art or craft useful to human life which is not practised there. The population is so large that men jostle each other in the streets. The citadel alone, which is built of brickwork laid in cement, has a circumference of nearly three miles. Within this citadel is a bazaar which is protected against the sun in summer and the rain in winter by a high-pitched wooden roof—a design whose clever execution and practical utility should call for imitation. Perfumes are sold in this bazaar and the scent in the early morning is most delicious...most of the citizens are wealthy Brahmans and Hindus of every caste, especially

Kashmiri. These Kashmiri[s] are bakers, eating-house keepers, and sellers of second-hand rubbish....

Writing magnanimously about the weather and the fruit, Abu'l Fazl mentioned that 'musk melons are to be had throughout the whole year', a detail that would have delighted Akbar's grandfather, Babur. 'When the season is over, they are imported from Kashmir and from Kabul, Badakhshan and Turkestan. Snow is brought down every year from the northern mountains.' The availability of snow and ice was one of the great luxuries of the court at Lahore. These were transported from the mountains north of Lahore, and brought to the capital every day by boats, carriages, and runners. The most profitable way was to bring down the ice by river, in boats manned by four oarsmen. When carriages were used, the journey was accomplished in fourteen stages, with horses changed at each stage. A total of 50 to 120 kilograms of ice and snow arrived every day, depending on the season. While noblemen were able to afford ice all the year round, the lower ranks only bought it in the hot summers.

As the empire had expanded dramatically in the first thirty years of Akbar's rule, bringing into the Mughal fold the rich provinces of Gujarat and Bengal, had gained it access to the sea, which helped it economically. In the kar khanas that were promoted enthusiastically, 'Akbar promoted textile manufacture for foreign markets, building roads that connected Mughal weavers' workshops to seaports and abolishing inland tolls and duties'. The goods were sent to China, Arabia, Abyssinia*, and Europe; the Europeans were able to pay for the precious silks and cottons with silver mined in South America and the cities of the empire grew prosperous.

Placed along the major route leading to Central Asia, Lahore was clearly therefore already a thrumming city by the time Akbar decided to stop here instead of moving back to Fatehpur Sikri. The Padshah rebuilt the fort of the city which became known as the Shahi Qila. It included a rampart with twelve gates, an audience hall, personal living quarters, and a zenana. It is likely that Akbar's court miniaturists and artists decorated the Padshah's quarters and the zenana. There would, however, be no inferno of building as there

---

*Ethiopia

had been in Fatehpur Sikri. No layered palaces, or inscrutable minars, or intimidating expanses of stone. Akbar's great building days were over and it would be royal family members, and the courtiers of the empire, who would take on the task of architectural patronage.

'Throughout Akbar's reign,' writes urban studies scholar William Glover, 'court nobles were encouraged to build palaces, gardens, and religious institutions in and around the city, and Lahore grew rapidly both in extent and population.' Even outside the walls of Lahore, there were vast tracts covered in 'richly designed mosques, tombs, havelis and gardens of the aristocracy', though sadly no traces of these buildings remain today. Within the city walls, bazaars were built along the main roads, highly specialized according to the commodity sold. Incense and religious books were sold near the mosques, leather workers supplying book bindings were located nearby, as also the slipper bazaar. Further away were the cloth and embroidery bazaars as well as the jewellers, while furthest away were bazaars dealing in bulk commodities too cumbersome to convey through the narrow pedestrian streets such as wholesale grain and spices, wool, pottery, fresh products etc. Future generations of Padshahs and their families would add to the landscape and by the time Akbar's grandson, Shah Jahan, came to power the mythic Shalimar Gardens would be built and Lahore would become the City of Gardens.

The walled city of Lahore was built by the river Ravi, with the Shahi Qila overlooking the vast and busy river. There was a bridge of boats constructed over the river and a steady stream of vessels sailed up and down the Ravi, 'constantly carrying an infinity of supplies'. Across from the Shahi Qila was a huge tented encampment, where merchants from different countries brought their goods to sell to the people at the court in the city. There was a small mud island in the middle of the river where, every morning at dawn, crowds thronged to make their daily darshan of Akbar following which there would be animal fights arranged on the sandy banks to amuse the crowds and the Padshah.

If in Lahore Akbar was no longer as enthusiastic a patron of architecture, his devotion to miniature paintings remained undiminished. There was a change, nonetheless, in the type of works that the taswir khanas at Lahore would produce at this time. From the earlier large works that had been created, the focus would now be on a few volumes of Persian poetry, produced to a high degree of perfection, known as de luxe manuscripts. These small but exquisitely finished works, as perfect as a single liquid note of a nightingale, were produced using the very best artists and the purest and highest quality products of the land. There were new additions to the ranks of painters, local men with names like Ibrahim Lahori, Kalu Lahori, and the talented calligrapher, Muhammad Husayn al-Kashmiri, known as Zarrin Qalam (Golden Pen). In addition to these newer artists at work in Akbar's studios there were some of the most talented painters of the time, at the peak of their artistic powers. Artists like Miskin, so compassionate in his paintings of animals that he captured not only their physical exertions and muscularity but even their inner, desperate fears. And Basawan, who perfected his art at the Mughal court over more than thirty years, using his 'psychologically acute... characterizations, painterliness, three-dimensional treatment of space, and swelling roundness of form' to create works of astounding realism and subtlety.

There would have been Manohar Das, too, Basawan's young son, around Salim's age, who would have carefully observed Akbar and all the formidable courtiers at Lahore, and who would paint tender and vulnerable images of the ageing Padshah in the following decades. Manohar grew up observing and adopting each changing nuance in the artistic tenor of the court, and while not possessing the genius of some of the greatest artists, he stands out 'as a humble, painterly artist whose arabesques and drapery cavort and ripple with released vitality and express the joy he found in his work'. The art historian John Seyller has argued that Basawan began promoting Manohar as an artist at around this time. There is a portrait of Manohar that has survived. It shows a smooth-faced, large-eyed, and slightly chubby young boy dated to this period believed to be one of only three self-portraits of sixteenth-century Mughal India. Seyller believes this was in fact a joint work between father and son, Basawan wishing to promote the talents of his son, probably not imagining that his son's fame would far outshine his at the courts of Jahangir and then Shah Jahan. And then there were outliers, like Farrukh Husain, a Persian painter at the Safavid court who left Isfahan to first work at Mirza

Hakim's court at Kabul. Considered by art historians to be one of the most underrated artists of Mughal painting, he joined the Mughal court in 1585, when he was already a mature forty-year-old artist. He was much admired and given the title Farrukh Beg. At the Mughal court, Farrukh Beg was initially paired up with the artists Dharmadas and Dhanraj, to work on the *Khamsa of Nizami*. However, after this work, it was understood that Farrukh Beg preferred to work alone and this contemplative, enigmatic, and singular artist was allowed the quite exceptional privilege from 1586–96, to work on illustrations on his own. He created works of remarkable sophistication and delicacy, with a clear penchant for lissom youths and swaying cypresses. His signature element was to add a large chinar tree somewhere within his compositions, to add drama, perspective, or symbology.

The de luxe manuscripts created in Lahore were tiny, meant to be held in the hand and admired closely. They contained only a dozen or so perfect works of art as opposed to the hundreds of paintings in earlier manuscripts. The texts were works of beloved poets such as Amir Khusro, Nizami, and Jami. Unlike the earlier exuberant and rambunctious works meant to be shared and exclaimed over, these small works were intimate, almost meditative, meant for the intense and visceral enjoyment of the patron, usually the Padshah, and his close family. One of the finest examples of de luxe manuscripts is the *Divan-e-Anvari*, a tiny work measuring only 5.5 inches by 2.8 inches, with just fifteen images. Anvari was a twelfth-century poet from Turkmenistan, who is believed to have suffered from gout, leading to understandably caustic and sharp reams such as the following qit'a*:

> I asked for wine, and you gave me stale vinegar,
> Such that, should I drink it, I should rise up at the
> Resurrection like pickled meat…

Art historian Kavita Singh points out that these de luxe manuscripts, like Anvari's *Divan*, indulged in 'conspicuous luxury' in all aspects of their making, 'from the fine, gold-flecked paper and costly pigments used for the books to the superb calligraphy by master calligraphers, and the exquisite margins, elaborate illumination, and fine bindings with which they were decorated'. Historian Annemarie Schimmel

---

*Short poems best suited for epigrams, satires, and light verse.

adds the awe-inspiring detail that each figure in the paintings was 'scarcely larger than an eyelash', yet managed to convey, possibly for the first time in Mughal art, a sense of a breathing space around the people, animals, and landscape. It is believed that a reason for the dramatic change in style from the earlier large-scale and boisterous works was the presence at court of Prince Salim, nineteen years old at the time, and as yet not estranged from his father. Salim who had begun drinking wine in increasingly immoderate quantities. Soon he was drinking twenty cups a day, lacking the iron will and self-discipline of his father. But despite his dissolute ways, Salim would go on to become a legendary patron and connoisseur of art who claimed to be able to distinguish at a single glance the distinctive brushwork of different painters. He even wrote with no false modesty whatsoever that in a work involving several painters, 'I can discover which face is the work of each of them. If any other person has put in the eye and eyebrow of a face, I can perceive whose work the original face is, and who has painted the eye and eyebrow.'

The images showcased the unfettered brilliance of artists at the peak of their powers and an empire at its most capacious in terms of wealth and ambition. The manuscripts were treasured and kept within the imperial library, to be handled with care and admired by each successive emperor.

These tiny, jewel-bright manuscripts were a new direction for the Mughal taswir khanas but the translation projects begun at Fatehpur Sikri also continued in Lahore. The first Persian translation of the other famous Hindustani epic, the Ramayan, was undertaken at this time. This was the first illustrated manuscript of the epic. Earlier Rajput versions, if they had existed, would have been destroyed in the storming of Chittor and Gwalior, the major centres of art at that time. The Mughals understood the epic to be about the trials and tribulations of an ideal Indian monarch, Ram. This had great resonance with Akbar, who rather enjoyed the frequent comparisons that Brahmins made between Vishnu and the Padshah. Badauni had long lamented that Brahmins had told Akbar 'that he had descended to earth, like Ram, Krishan, and other infidel rulers'. The particular attributes that Akbar shared with Ram were piquant. 'He would honor Brahmans,' wrote Badauni about what the Brahmins were claiming, 'protect cows, and justly rule the earth.' And, indeed, Akbar, Hamida Banu, Todar Mal, and Abdur Rahim were all issuing farmans giving land and protection to the temples, priests, and cows of Mathura at this very time. While the Persian text may have stayed true to the spirit of the original, the images that accompanied the Persian Ramayan were reminiscent of sixteenth-century Mughal India. According to Truschke, in these images, 'Rama is dressed in Mughal fashion and has Central Asian facial features, remarkably similar to portrayals of the Emperor in paintings of the *Akbarnama*.' Similarly, in his Persian-Sanskrit grammar book, the scholar Krishnadasa describes Akbar in astonishing terms, comparing him with Krishna and marvelling that he protects cows.

The translated Ramayan proved very popular in courtly circles and more than two dozen Persian versions of it were created over the next three centuries. Hamida Banu owned a copy of it, and Rajput rulers, electrified by these possibilities, responded by creating their own illustrated manuscripts of the Ramayan. Maharana Jagat Singh of Mewar, Rana Pratap's great-grandson, who would submit to Jahangir in 1615, commissioned a truly stupendous work in the 1640s comprising a staggering 400 paintings of joyous colour and abandon, many of which were painted by the leading artist of the time, Sahibuddin, a Mewari Muslim. This Mewar Ramayan is considered the finest and most complete version of this epic ever commissioned by a Hindu patron.

As for Badauni, Akbar's most prolific translator despite all his many misgivings, though he admitted that the Ramayan was marginally better than the tales of the Mahabharat, he baulked at writing a preface for it. 'I seek refuge in God from that black book,' he wrote despairingly, 'which is as rotten as the book of my life.' Badauni knew that Akbar would expect from him a work like the preface of the Mahabharat, which Abu'l Fazl had written in lyrical and expansive style, praising the knowledge contained in the Mahabharat and the cross-cultural enterprise undertaken by Akbar. Unable also to conceive a work in which he would not be allowed to include praise for the Prophet Muhammad, Badauni demurred.

But now, alongside the eclectic works of translation that were taking place in Lahore, Akbar decided that his empire was finally secure enough for him to begin the monumental texts that would anchor his legacy within the history of Hindustan, the history of Islam, the history of the Timurids, and the history of mankind itself.

THE MEMORY–KEEPERS

'Write down whatever you know of the doings of (Babur) and (Humayun)'. This ordinary phrase sounded innocuous enough and gave no indication of the seismic rumble it actually was. In 1587, having decided to commission a history of his reign, Akbar sent for his beloved aunt, Gulbadan, and asked her to contribute to this history by writing down all her memories of her father and brother. Akbar summoned other memory-keepers too, such as Humayun's water carrier, Jauhar Aftabchi, and an old soldier from Humayun's army, Bayazid Bayat, amongst others. 'His Majesty Jalal al-Din Muhammad Akbar Padshah,' wrote Bayazid, 'commanded that any servants of court who had a taste for history should write.' Akbar had decided, now that he had been Padshah for more than thirty years, it was time to create a history of his rule, his lineage, and his achievements that would reflect in all its splendour a life and destiny sparked by the divine. It was Abu'l Fazl who was entrusted with this monumental task, one which would take a decade to complete, and would involve an army of compilers and assistants across the empire. The accounts of the memory-keepers were intended as source material for Abu'l Fazl to use in his remarkable work of history and it was but a fortuitous accident that Gulbadan then produced a unique and precious work—the first and only record of life in the Mughal harem through the eyes of a Mughal woman.

Gulbadan was sixty-five years old when she began writing her memoir, and had already lived through the reigns of two previous Padshahs—Babur and Humayun. With the philosophical distancing that age and time afforded her, with her own lived experience as a cherished and beloved member of Akbar's court, and due to a complete absence of any such previous recording to model her writing on, Gulbadan wrote an account that was unlike any other work produced on the subject of Mughal history. Most accounts of kings and empires focused overwhelmingly on the personalities of the emperors and their eminent amirs, as well as the battles, conquests, and territorial expansions that visibly reflected the emperor's power. In Gulbadan's account we see these same emperors, but they are backlit by the familial and the domestic, their edges are scuffed by the elucidation of family dramas, loves, hierarchies, and power structures. And Gulbadan is the only chronicler to write candidly and unselfconsciously of the unexpected and influential roles of women. She is the only writer, for example, to record events such as Khanzada Begum's diplomatic mission to Kamran on Humayun's behalf, and the moral authority this elderly matriarch wielded in the name of Padshah Babur himself. She writes about the determined wooing of Hamida Banu by Humayun that was equally stoutly resisted by the unimpressed bride for forty days.

Many of the incidents Gulbadan wrote about she would have discussed with Hamida Banu, and she often refers to Hamida Banu's memories in her writing. So we have the shadowy recording of various women's voices in this unique document. And in complete contrast to the ossified and sequestered space that Abu'l Fazl would write about in a few years, Gulbadan writes of a harem continuously on the move, of women on horseback, of women journeying and living in tents, and sharing the struggles and the victories of their men. Her tale is replete with the accounts of births while on the move, marriages of temperamental or forthright brides, the detailing of gifts as symbols of a Padshah's love, and tender remembrance. According to Ruby Lal, through Gulbadan's writing, 'we have a lost world of the court in camp brought to life in a way that no other chronicle of the time even approaches'.

Abu'l Fazl, meanwhile, would spend the next few years questioning Akbar's old family retainers and relatives, to record their memories of Babur, Humayun and, especially, of Akbar himself. 'I spoke to old and young men of right character', asserts Abu'l Fazl firmly, after which accounts were drawn up and then read out to the Padshah every day. The Padshah listened closely to these accounts and corrected the mistakes as he saw fit. Abu'l Fazl consulted the records office, farmans issued by Akbar, petitions filed by ministers, in addition to listening to the oral records of trustworthy persons including, notably, those of his own father, and of the emperor himself. The result of this enormous labour of research and compilation would be two gargantuan works—a history of Akbar's reign and his times, called the *Akbarnama* in two volumes, and an equally voluminous gazetteer, the *Ain-i Akbari*, which was a detailed compendium of imperial regulations, as well as information on the geography, social and religious customs, and administration of the land. The *Ain-i Akbari* was a unique document for its time and would serve as a model for future generations of historians. It would also be used by the British to understand a complex and foreign land. Among its many revelations was a new awareness, as pointed out by M. Athar Ali, of the geography of Hindustan as a peninsula lapped by the sea and crowned by the Himalayas. Abu'l Fazl described the people of the land in prose refreshingly free from the religious limitations of other medieval Muslim historians. 'The people of this country,' he wrote, 'are God-seeking, generous-hearted, friendly to strangers, pleasant-faced, of broad forehead, patrons of learning, lovers of asceticism, inclined to justice, contented, hard-working and efficient, true to salt, truth-seeing and attached to loyalty.' Despite being irritated by Raja Todar Mal's idol-worship, Abu'l Fazl wrote of the use of religious figures by Hindus in the following way:

> They one and all believe in the unity of God, and as to the reverence they pay to images of stone and wood and the like which simpletons regard as idolatry, it is not so. The writer of these pages has exhaustively discussed the subject with many enlightened and upright men and it became evident that these images of some chosen souls nearest in approach to the throne of God are fashioned as aids to fix the mind and keep the thoughts from wandering, while the worship of God alone is required as indispensable.

These views, which were also stated by Akbar, were in sharp contrast to Babur's dismayed recordings of his impression of Hindustan and its people: 'There is no beauty in its people, no graceful social intercourse, no poetic talent or understanding, no etiquette, nobility or manliness. The arts and crafts have no harmony or symmetry.'

The *Ain-i Akbari* reflected a determination on the part of the Padshah to delineate every aspect of life in the empire, from the mundane to the mystical. They included regulations for the tents in the farrash khana, instruction about etiquette to be followed in court, donations, education, marriages, the oiling of camels and the branding of horses. It is in just such a chapter that Abu'l Fazl also deals with the 'vexatious question' of the many women that Akbar had married, and the consequently unwieldy harem that had to be contained and sequestered. 'Several chaste women', we are reminded, guarded over each section of the harem which was further policed by eunuchs, Ahadis, and Rajput guards. The women were decorously involved in various duties and Abu'l Fazl would be careful to never allow any woman a glimpse of individuality. They would all be given titles, their names almost completely forgotten, and would be accorded the most perfunctory of descriptions—'cupolas of chastity' and 'pillars of chastity' being preferred monikers. Akbar's wives, especially, would be subjected to a ruthless and complete censorship, reduced to barely acknowledged shadows whose only noteworthy acts were to produce 'pearls', Akbar's children, from their blessed wombs. Interestingly, Abu'l Fazl would hold his own family to this very same rigorous standard, never once referring to a wife, a sister, or a daughter in his own biography. It would fall to Gulbadan's memoir, forgotten for a long time, to eventually shine a light on the complex geometry of these women's lives.

Abu'l Fazl's *Akbarnama* overshadowed medieval history for centuries with the sobering weight of his learning and conviction to the detriment of all other histories and sources of memory. At the same time, the tone of the *Akbarnama* was derided for being sycophantic to Akbar, and the Padshah himself was belatedly scolded by Western historians for tolerating such excessive flattery. But to see the *Akbarnama* as simply an exercise in obsequiousness by an overenthusiastic courtier would be short-sighted, for what Abu'l Fazl intended was far more ambitious, even incendiary. In most histories of the time, in which the ruler was Muslim, genealogies would begin with praises of Allah, and Prophet Muhammad, and then work their way through the various caliphs and sultans, through purely Islamic lineages, to the ruler in question. Abu'l Fazl, instead, after praising Allah, begins with Adam, the original 'man', omitting the Prophet and the caliphs altogether. He traces Akbar's lineage through fifty-two generations, placing the Padshah firmly in the position of the ruler of all humanity, and not just his Muslim subjects.

In addition, as scholars such as A. Azfar Moin and Ruby Lal have shown, Abu'l Fazl used a complex set of symbols to articulate a vision of the Padshah as semi-divine, appearing as he did at the cosmically and spiritually charged advent of the new Islamic millennium to be the temporal as well as spiritual guide to all the peoples of Hindustan, not only Muslims. In his genealogy of Akbar, Abu'l Fazl did not just show Akbar descending from an illustrious line of forefathers as Babur and Humayun had sought to do but instead inversed this equation to demonstrate that it was, on the contrary, Akbar's luminous destiny that tinged his predecessors with glory. This would explain the episodes of 'divine effulgence' that occurred before Akbar's birth, whether it was Hamida Banu's mysteriously shining brows, Humayun's visions, or Jiji Anaga's lucent dreams. It was in this spirit, argues A. Azfar Moin, that Humayun's astrological preoccupations and frequent auguries were interpreted as being premonitions of impending greatness. The *Akbarnama* even has a long digression to include in Akbar's genealogy the rather obscure Alanqua, a princess of Moghulistan, who was impregnated by a divine light to give birth to three 'shining sons'. The implication was clear—Akbar was above the limitations of ordinary human forefathers with their pedestrian ambitions and expected frailties. Instead, the *Akbarnama* described the life of a monarch who demonstrated miraculous powers from infancy. A monarch who commanded rampaging elephants, succumbed to visions, articulated prophesies, and cured people using his holy breath. A monarch, moreover, who did not rule only Muslim subjects. Instead, Abu'l Fazl wrote about a king who used imagery from many faiths while crafting a faultless persona. Through fire worship, the veneration of the sun, mantras and austerities, fasts, and the translation of the sacred works of the Hindus, Akbar became the insaan-e-kamil* and peshwa of the spiritual age.

Since Abu'l Fazl needed to show that the Padshah was above all limitations of religion, events described in the *Akbarnama* were relentless about showing the Padshah in a positive light. Every occurrence was interpreted in the light of Akbar's later immaculate grandeur and all earlier foibles were explained as a need by Akbar

---

*The Perfect Man.

to 'veil' his true self and to test those around him. That Abu'l Fazl was intensely admiring of the Padshah is evident and he found in Akbar a great monarch worthy of his own boundless energies and dedication. It is nonetheless tempting to wonder whether there was not also a splinter of anger in Abu'l Fazl when he poured all his fierce energy into the *Akbarnama* into making the Padshah a Mujtahid of the Age which served to eviscerate and make redundant his sworn enemies, the ulema.

For all his passionate arguments in favour of reason, or aql, above all else and above received wisdom, an incident occurred in the 1590s that showed the truth to be rather more complicated for Abu'l Fazl. The *Maasir ul-Umara** describes an episode in which Salim went to visit Abu'l Fazl in his home and was astounded to discover forty clerks busily copying the Koran, a Muslim act of piety. Salim, who was becoming increasingly leery of Abu'l Fazl's closeness to Akbar, immediately appropriated clerks and Koran and presented them to the Padshah. According to the *Maasir ul-Umara*, Akbar was thoroughly shaken by this sign of ostentatious piety in his famously rationalist friend and said, 'He incites us to other kinds of things, and then when he goes to the privacy of his home he acts differently.' The *Iqbal Nama-i-Jahangiri*† also recorded Akbar's displeasure when Shaikh Mubarak wrote a commentary on the Koran without alluding to the Padshah himself, which Abu'l Fazl then sent to various dignitaries. From then on, noted historian Shamsauddaula Shah Nawaz, there was a slackening of the earlier bond that drew the two men together. For Shaikh Mubarak and his sons, marked forever by the ulema's long-ago persecution, the true nature of their own personal faith would always remain hidden by their pragmatic adoption and brilliant exposition of the Padshah's views.

Whatever Abu'l Fazl's motivations, he worked unceasingly on the *Akbarnama*. The Padshah listened to each page of the text as it was read out to him, using his prodigious memory to verify facts and occurrences. It was said that Abu'l Fazl wrote five drafts of the

---

*Eighteenth-century Persian biography by Shamsuddaula Shah Nawaz Khan of important Mughal notables.
†A seventeenth-century account by Mutamad Khan of the history of the Timurid dynasty until the accession of Shah Jahan.

manuscript. Besides scrutinizing the text, Akbar took an inordinate amount of interest in the illustrations that accompanied the writing. Between 1590 and 1595, concurrently with the shaping of the text, miniatures were painted of various episodes described and it is believed that Akbar was closely involved in deciding which particular moments in his life were to be painted. Indeed, in the eyes of some experts, the illustrations are thought to give us a more accurate reflection of the Padshah's own view of his life than Abu'l Fazl's text.

Forty-nine artists were listed as being part of the project and they included all the leading masters of the age. These were collaborative works involving several artists working together and effortlessly using the Persian vertical use of space, European perspective, and indigenous vibrancy and luminous colour. A large number of the painters were Hindus of the agricultural Ahir caste, men with names like Kesu, Madhu, Mukund, Nand, Narayan, Paras, Shankar, Surdas, Ramdas, and Basawan. This accounts for the effervescence and dramatic energy of the paintings, a style favoured by Akbar. The famous Muslim painters of this taswir khana included Miskin, Mansur, Qutb Chela, and the Persian Farrukh Beg. The great Persian master Abd al-Samad was not included in this project and had presumably already retired, after training his two sons, Muhammad Sharif and Bihzad. Abd al-Samad painted one last painting at this time, a work created purely from memory, of a great Persian masterpiece by the maestro Bihzad. In a touching entreaty to his son Muhammad Sharif to never forget his Persian roots, Abd al-Samad wrote: 'At the age of eighty-five, when his strength has gone, his pen has weakened and his eyesight has dimmed, he has agreed to draw from memory as a memento for this album with every detail for his wise, witty, and astute son Sharif Khan, who is happy, fortunate, prosperous and chosen by the memory of the Merciful.' This painting, called *Two Fighting Camels*, is a lovely example of the Persian school, 'where technical virtuosity was prized equally with poetic sensibility', but it was one which would have been considered passé in Mughal India.

Of the extant 116 paintings detailing the period 1560–77,* the very choice of the subject matter is instructive. Twenty-seven paintings depict specific battles, sieges, and engagements, and another

---

*The miniatures of the second volume of the *Akbarnama* are lost.

twenty-five show arrests, executions, submissions, and overtures of peace. A further twenty-two paintings depict scenes of hunting, including five vibrant double-spreads. Taken together, this group of paintings is an eloquent testimony to the articulation of power and strength in the sixteenth century: the heaving scenes of furious battles showing the enormous power of the empire tempered by the compassionate embracing of the submissive party; the importance of the qumargha as an instrument of political power; the use of animals—elephants, tigers, cheetahs—as thinly veiled metaphors for the conquest and incorporation of dangerous elements into the Mughal Empire. The elemental energy of these pages point to the incessant and ruthless game of strength and diplomacy and brinkmanship that Akbar played to bring him to the point where, in the elusive dawn of Fatehpur Sikri, he could give thanks to God for allowing him to create the enormous empire of his dreams.

The remainder of the paintings are those of court scenes, celebrations, births, and marriages, and a handful of scenes of meditative contemplation, and unexpected turmoil in Akbar's life. It is in these paintings that the artists contribute most viscerally to the document, adding details of court life that are not mentioned in Abu'l Fazl's text. Some of these artists would have had first-hand experience of the scenes described, as painters often accompanied the Padshah on his journeys. It is in these unexpected and precious details that a complex and changing court is brought to life. It is a world of colour, texture, and dynamic complexity with its exquisite details of a courtier's brocaded jama or the graceful movement of the sijda salutation. In these paintings we see women stringing up bunting made of auspicious mango leaves to celebrate the birth of a child, and the energetic beating of huge drums and the blowing of trumpets to announce the victorious arrival of the Padshah. There are also troubling details such as the degraded and piteous condition of prisoners of war wearing animal skins over their faces, which Abu'l Fazl glosses over. Startlingly timeless details are shown, too, like women labourers wearing glass-studded brocade cloth in a construction scene, just like women continue to do in India today.

The paintings show a court that was always changing, incorporating different elements from its new courtiers. So from a purely Persian aesthetic painted by Farrukh Beg in the scene showing a Mughal emissary and the rebel Bahadur Khan, the court paintings become more exuberant and dynamic and incorporate Rajput clothes, Rajput courtiers, indigenous musicians and instruments, and details of courtly life that show a much more expansive interpretation of the Mughal Empire than that shown in the accompanying text. In one such example, art historian Geeti Sen has suggested that in the painting showing the court dancers of Mandu being presented to Akbar after the defeat of Baz Bahadur, we can see a possible route for the introduction of the Kathak style of dance into the Mughal court through these famous dancers from Malwa.

And, finally, there is the alluring possibility that some of the paintings of well-known amirs and courtiers, and indeed of Akbar himself, are actual likenesses in the manner of portraits. The art of portraiture in Mughal painting has usually been attributed to Padshah Jahangir, with his fascination for psychologically acute images. But Akbar, too, was intensely and passionately interested in the deep desires that motivated people and a corresponding need, his whole life, to viscerally understand and 'read' the faces and characters of people. Abu'l Fazl wrote that Akbar had commissioned an enormous portrait album in which 'those that have passed away have received a new life, and those who are still alive have immortality promised them'. Geeti Sen has proposed that a number of the paintings of key figures from Akbar's life including Bahadur Khan, Munim Khan, Mirza Sulaiman, and Azim Khan, among others, appear to be actual likenesses. There are even a handful of enigmatic images showing moments of high emotion—blistering rage, haunting introspection or grateful celebration in Akbar's life—which seem to show finely-drawn likenesses of the Padshah himself, reflecting these different moods. These images are always the work of one of just six artists, specialists in the painting of 'chehra', or the face, and they include the artists Madhu, Kesu, Miskin, Basawan, and Nanha. These beguiling portraits of this elusive emperor still mesmerize across five centuries.

THE GARDEN OF PERPETUAL SPRING

In April 1589, the music spilled out of the city of Lahore in a continuous stream. The musicians of the naqqar khana with their giant drums, smaller tambours, cymbals and trumpets, played their instruments with a feverish energy, while dancers twirled and swayed in front of them, both men and women. Some of the women wore long Turki–Chaghatai robes while others wore tight bodices and cholis with diaphanous odhanis, and stamped their feet and threw out their arms in the sharp, staccato movements of Kathak. Attendants rushed to and fro, distributing gifts, and handing around trays of delicacies and drinks. The women in the harem smiled to themselves, for they held a clean and glimmering secret, like the first snow on red leaves: a child had been born to a wife of Prince Salim, a daughter. We do not, in fact, know the exact details of the celebrations, often omitted from the texts. But Abu'l Fazl pointed out that 'contrary to the custom of contemporaries, it was made an occasion of rejoicing'. Once again, Akbar had decreed that the birth of a girl would be celebrated with the same gratitude and joy as that of a boy, and the exquisite details of such festivities can only be guessed at through the silent pages of the miniatures in the *Akbarnama*.

Only three weeks later, the very same city was hushed and silenced, for the musician of genius Tansen had died. 'His death,' said a grieving Akbar, 'was the annihilation of melody.' For Tansen was not just a singer, but a lyrical poet whose sensitive imagery Jahangir captured in his memoirs, demonstrating not only a sensitive appreciation of imagery but also a fine knowledge of Brajbhasha:

> Because the black bee is a constant visitor to these flowers, the Hindi poets consider it to be like the nightingale in love with the rose, and they produce marvelous poetic conceits based on it. One such poet was Tansen Kalawant, who was in my father's service and without equal in his own time—or any other for that matter. In one of his songs he likened the face of a youth to the

sun and the opening of his eye to the blossoming of the lotus and the emerging of the bhaunra. In another one he likened the beloved's wink to the motion of the lotus flower when the bhaunra alights on it.

To bid a fitting farewell to Tansen, whose extraordinary music had accompanied him these many decades, Akbar ordered that his funeral procession be resplendent with the best musicians and dancers of the city, and that he be sent off joyously, in melody, like a groom to his beloved, in the manner of the Sufis. Two days later, almost as if to shake off his sadness, Akbar decided to journey to Kashmir.

After its relatively straightforward annexation from the Chak dynasty in 1586, Akbar had not yet visited Kashmir. Now, suddenly, he became impatient to leave and Abu'l Fazl agreed that 'he does not fix his heart to one place...' His courtiers were unhappy about the journey, loath to see the Padshah journey so far from the heartland of the empire but Akbar would not listen to them. '[O]ur going there is...the fulfilling of (Humayun's) dream', he said. Babur's cousin, Mirza Dughlat, had, in fact, ruled the Kashmir valley on behalf of Humayun from 1541 to 1551 so it is not impossible that Humayun would have talked to his son of a desire to journey there one day.

Akbar ordered Qasim Khan, the engineer of the Agra–Lahore road, and of Agra Fort, to make the road to Kashmir passable. Qasim Khan used 3,000 stonecutters, 2,000 diggers, mountain-miners, and 'splitters of rocks' to transform what was a pedestrian-only track into a highway which could be used by the Mughal army with its lumbering elephants, cavalry, and guns. This road had earlier been used to transport salt from the Punjab to Kashmir, and was called the Namak Road. Under the Mughals it would become the most important road connecting the landlocked valley of Kashmir to Hindustan and would come to be known as the Mughal Imperial Road.

Leaving Lahore in the care of Raja Bhagwant Das, Raja Todar Mal, and Qulij Khan, Akbar set off for Kashmir in the month of May. When he reached Bhimbhar, he suddenly decided to proceed alone with only a small retinue of courtiers including Prince Salim and Abu'l Fazl. Prince Murad was left in charge of the harem and an officer was stationed at Bhimbhar Pass to prevent any other courtiers or attendants from following the Padshah. Akbar made rapid progress on horseback till he crossed Rajauri and reached the tents of Qasim Khan who was directing the operations for the clearing of the roads. Salim was sent back to Bhimbhar with orders to bring some of the ladies of the harem while Akbar and his retinue continued through snow, rain, and hail, often obliged to dismount from their horses and cross the passes on foot. Abu'l Fazl noted the dense forests covering the mountains and bridges over sparkling streams but by the time they reached the Pir Panjal Pass, the snow had become a silent, brooding presence for the inhabitants of Hindustan who had never seen such an expanse of aching white. 'Shall I describe the severity of the cold?' mused Abu'l Fazl. 'Or shall I tell of the depth of the snow, and of the bewilderment of the natives of India? Or shall I describe the heights and hollows of this stage?' As the party walked through falling snow, their breath coming in icy exhalations, their thoughts filled with dread prompted by stories of malevolent spells and djinns whispering through the passes. The locals, they found, used snow shoes, woven out of ropes of rice-straw, to walk over the powdery snow but Akbar disapproved of these so the men carried on as best they could.

Finally, the Mughal party made their way across the mountains and once beyond Hurapur came out onto a plateau. Here there were waterfalls, flowers, crisp and fragrant air, but unexpectedly, 'a cloud settled on the face of joy (Akbar)'. Salim had arrived at Hurapur without the ladies of the harem because he had deemed the conditions too dangerous for them to travel. Akbar flew into a sudden, explosive rage. A furious Padshah forbade Salim from presenting himself and raged at Abdur Rahim, who had accompanied the prince. 'If the prince, owing to his evil propensities, behaved in this way, why did you allow him to exhibit such audacity?' To the horror and great worry of his courtiers, Akbar then mounted his horse in the pouring rain and turned around with a small escort, proposing to bring back the harem himself. A thoroughly discomfited Abu'l Fazl admitted that 'I was nearly losing my senses and the dress of society was falling from my shoulders.' Terrified for the safety of the Padshah, Abu'l Fazl struggled to understand the reason for his unexpected rage. 'The whole confusion was caused by thinking why at such a time should the Shahinshah of the Universe become so angry? And why did he take upon himself this task which could be accomplished by a minor servant?' Salim, unsurprisingly, shut himself up in his tent, utterly mortified, refusing any food and drink. Akbar was eventually persuaded to return and Abdur Rahim was sent back to tend to the harem.

Akbar's terrible anger towards Salim remains something of a mystery, one that clearly confounded someone as close to him as Abu'l Fazl. Perhaps the Padshah had already been in a volatile mood due to Tansen's death, when he had planned the journey to Kashmir so precipitously. He would have been feeling the strain of several weeks' arduous journey, too, but his anger at Salim nonetheless seems to indicate an undercurrent of strain simmering between the Padshah and his sons. Akbar's reluctance to send the princes away from the court meant that there were now three additional, constantly growing princely households in claustrophobic intimacy, exacerbating potential tensions. Just as the princes increasingly baulked at the strictures on their actions, Akbar, too, appeared unwilling to accept challenges to his authority and orders. The clash between Akbar, now approaching fifty, and the refined and elegant Salim was entirely unequal. Too young and inexperienced to be able to openly withstand the fury of his father's will at this stage, Salim would begin to develop sly ways of mounting his own challenge to his father, often through secret alliances and opportunistic friendships.

The Mughal party now continued on to Srinagar, reaching the capital of Kashmir on 5 June where crowds of people thronged the Padshah. The Mughals were delighted with the city where, Abu'l Fazl noted, the houses were made of wood, up to five storeys high, with tulips planted on the rooftops. Cattle were kept on the lower floor, the family apartments were on the second floor while the topmost floors contained the various household stores. They were enchanted, too, by the dense shade of the chinar trees, the saffron flowers, and the waterfalls. Abu'l Fazl was less enchanted with the musicians. He wrote that musicians were 'exceeding many and equally monotonous, and with each note they seem to dig their nails into your liver'. Through the reigns of Jahangir, and then his son Shah Jahan, Kashmir would become, for the Mughals, a place of pastoral delight and earthly perfection.

> The country is enchanting, and might be fittingly called a garden of perpetual spring surrounding a citadel terraced to the skies, and deservedly appropriate to be either the delight of the worldling or the abode of the dervish. Its streams are sweet to the taste, its waterfalls music to the ear, and its climate is invigorating. The enchanting flowers fill the heart with delight. Violets, the red rose and wild narcissus cover the plains. Its spring and autumn are extremely beautiful.

Historian Sunil Sharma has shown that Abu'l Fazl was also able to find a text relating to Kashmir in a more unusual source, the twelfth-century Sanskrit epic *Rajatarangini*, that had been translated to Persian at the Mughal court. In this text, Kashmir is described as the eternal sacred place of Hindus:

> In winter there are hot baths by the river, in the summer the cool river-banks; and the rivers are calm, and not infested with water animals. It is a country where the sun shines mildly being the place created by (the sage) Kashyapa as if for his glory. High school-houses, the saffron iced water, and grapes, which are rare, even in heaven are common here. Kailasa is the best place in the three worlds. Himalaya the best part of Kailasa and Kashmir the best place in the Himalayas.

The best people in Kashmir, according to Abu'l Fazl, despite their lamentable dependence on the 'bonds of tradition', were the Hindus:

> The most respectable class in this country is that of the Brahmans, who notwithstanding their need of freedom from the bonds of tradition and custom, are true worshippers of God. They do not loosen the tongues of calumny against those of their faith, nor beg nor importune. They employ themselves in planting fruit trees, and are generally a source of benefit to the people.

Meanwhile Salim, who 'was ashamed of his former mistake, and was continually showing a desire to obtain this service', was finally able to bring the ladies of the harem to the Mughal camp. Akbar was delighted to be reunited with his family and not long after, 'felt a desire for the coming of Miriam Makani (Hamida Banu)'. He sent envoys to Fatehpur Sikri to escort them to Kashmir with a verse as supplication:

> The pilgrim may go to the K'aaba to perform the haj
> O God! May the K'aaba come towards us!

After several weeks in Kashmir, Akbar reluctantly agreed to leave as the monsoon was about to break. Instead of heading back to Lahore, however, the Padshah decided to go to Kabul, to settle the area. While in Kabul, news arrived that Hamida Banu, Gulbadan, and some of the other ladies from the capital had received Akbar's summons and were on their way. Daniyal was first sent out of the city to wait on the ladies, after which Murad was sent and then, finally, Salim. Akbar then went out of the city himself to welcome the ladies and a grand feast was held in honour of their arrival. Akbar was always very solicitous of the welfare of the older ladies, and was careful about the deference owed to them. The English traveller Thomas Coryat was astounded to note that, on one occasion, when Hamida Banu was returning to Agra from Lahore, Akbar and his amirs lifted the queen mother's palanquin on to their shoulders and carried her out of the city themselves.

After several pleasant months in Kabul, and though Akbar wished again 'that the active young men should behold the spectacle of the falling of snow, and should tread the ice, and that the natives of India might enjoy this', the Padshah was finally persuaded to head home. It was while they were camped at Begram, in November 1589, that news arrived of the death of an old and loyal courtier. Sensing that the end of his life was drawing near, a sick and feeble Raja Todar Mal had asked permission to retire to Haridwar, and he was on his way to the holy city when Akbar unexpectedly changed his mind, saying that 'no worship of God was equal to taking care of the weak. It was therefore better that he should look after the affairs of the oppressed.' Just as he had given up the practice of regular namaaz and ritual worship, Akbar believed that the worship of idols was not to be placed above duty towards the weak. Raja Todar Mal turned sadly back to Lahore, and died a few months later. Abu'l

Fazl's somewhat uncharitable assessment of this grand old man, the backbone of Akbar's administrative reforms, was that 'he was unique of the Age for uprightness, straightforwardness, courage, knowledge of affairs and the administration of India. If he had not had bigotry, conventionalism, and spite, and had not stuck to his own opinions, he would have been one of the spiritually great.'

Raja Bhagwant Das went to attend to the funeral of his friend and returning to his house had a vomiting fit, and himself died five days later, in the cold Lahore winter far from his desert home. Badauni's report of the deaths of these two stalwarts of Akbar's court was positively gloating. They 'hastened to the abode of hell and torment,' was his assessment, 'and in the lowest pit became the food of serpents and scorpions, may God scorch them both!' For Badauni, all those Hindus at court who were honoured and rose to prominence while he himself languished in neglect were a far simpler target of his loathing than the Padshah himself. On these men, and on all those like them, and on Akbar's Rajput wives, Badauni squarely put the blame for Akbar's wandering away from the path of orthodox Islam.

Perhaps even more provocative for thinkers like Badauni were signs that Akbar would not now tolerate anti-Shia behaviour. The previous year Mirza Fulad, 'a hot headed young man', and a Sunni, had murdered a Shia theologian, one Ahmad Thattawi. Ahmad Thattawi had been notoriously outspoken and 'was a firm adherent of the Imami doctrines, and talked largely about them, continually brought forward discourse about Sunnis and Shias, and from a despicable spirit used immoderate language'. Nonetheless, in the spirit of sulh kul, clarified Abu'l Fazl, 'every sect can assert its doctrine without apprehension and everyone can worship God after his own fashion'. Akbar had Mirza Fulad executed, despite the opposition from high-placed noblemen and even members of the harem, sending out a clear signal that he did not approve of such conflicts. As a result 'the contest between Sunni and Shia subsided'.

The deaths of Todar Mal and Bhagwant Das were grave losses for the Padshah, however. Bhagwant Das, especially, had been a staunch and unflinching ally since Akbar had been twenty years old. The raja had always responded with exemplary chivalry to the Padshah's frequent calls to demonstrate personal courage on the battlefield and

Abu'l Fazl admitted that 'he was endowed with uprightness, weight of counsel, and courage' for which he had been rewarded by the high mansab of 5,000. Akbar had suffered a further loss on the trip to Kashmir when the intellectual and sadr, Shah Fathullah Shirazi, had died. Akbar was wont to say that the 'mir was his vakil, philosopher, physician and astronomer and that no one can understand the amount of his grief for him'. As for Raja Todar Mal, his personal seal reflected an entire cosmos of complicated loyalties, spelling out his allegiance to the two figures in his life, his God and his Emperor—Banda-i Dargha, Ram ki Panah (Servant of the Court and of God).

As the Mughal party made their slow way towards Lahore, tragedy and sorrow continued to stalk them. When hunting a hyena, Akbar was thrown from his horse and smashed his face on the rocky ground. Hakim Ali Gilani treated his wounds with a healing oil and, despite his courtiers advising against it, Akbar decided to continue the onward march in a litter. Then, in January 1590, Abu'l Fazl received the news that his mother had died in Lahore and 'became somewhat deranged and fell into great grief'. By the time they reached Rohtas in February 1590, the party was thoroughly demoralized. Moreover, as it was the rainy season, Hamida Banu suggested that they rest awhile within the fort but her son, so long used to bending even the elements to his will, refused, saying that 'honour did not allow that he should be in comfort and the world in trouble'. Nor could Akbar allow his amirs and soldiery to see any weakness in him. Instead, he organized a qumargha hunt, as he had done so many times in the past, where no fear or uncertainty would be tolerated. A few days later, after crossing the Jhelum, Akbar was thrown off an elephant while trying to subdue a mast animal and, for a while, to the terror of his amirs, remained unconscious. Indeed, Akbar's condition was so critical that there were sporadic acts of plunder in the area, as the Padshah was believed dead. When he regained consciousness, he was bled in the arm and then continued his journey by elephant litter. Finally, in March 1590, after an absence of more than ten months, Akbar rode back into Lahore.

The city that Akbar returned to would have appeared sadly altered over the year. Two of his great statesmen had died in addition to his favourite musician, and Akbar would have felt bereft. A Brajbhasha lyric is popularly attributed to Akbar in Rajasthani legend which might very well have reflected his feelings at this stage in his life:

> Peethal so majlis gayee, Tansen so raga,
> Hansibo-ramibo-bolibo, gayo Birbal saath
>
> (With the death of Peethal have gone the pleasures of the majlis, with Tansen music itself has fled
> With the passing of Birbal have gone laughter, good company and conversation.)

Hamida Banu, Gulbadan, and the other ladies in the entourage returned to Fatehpur Sikri in October of 1590, despairing of Akbar's ever coming back to the city. Abu'l Fazl admits that at this stage, Hamida Banu had thought that Akbar would return to the capital. This belies the belief that Fatehpur Sikri was ever 'abandoned' by Akbar due to some sudden, unexpected catastrophe. It was, rather, his continued stay at Lahore which was inexplicable.

Meanwhile, Kuar Man Singh, who had been serving as Subedar of Bihar since 1587, learning of the death of his father now made the journey to Amer. The residents and officials at Amer, too, would have been informed of the sad news as Amer and the Mughal court were linked by an incredibly swift and reliable system of news carriers.

Raja Bhagwant Das's body was taken to his watan jagir where his last rites were conducted at Amer and his ashes interred in the royal cemetery. Akbar sent a teeka to Amer and, in a formal coronation ceremony, the kuar became Raja Man Singh with a mansab of 5,000, the highest in the land. With the blessings of the Padshah and buttressed by the wealth of the empire, Raja Man Singh would be instrumental in taking Mughal culture to the most distant outposts of the empire, in his unique position as both Mughal mansabdar and Hindu raja.

Akbar holds a religious assembly at Fatehpur Sikri; the two men dressed in black are the Jesuit missionaries Rudolf Acquaviva and Francisco Henriques— Akbarnama, *miniature painting by Nar Singh, 1605.*

Akbar standardized weights and measures, and the coins in the empire became famous for their purity and weight.

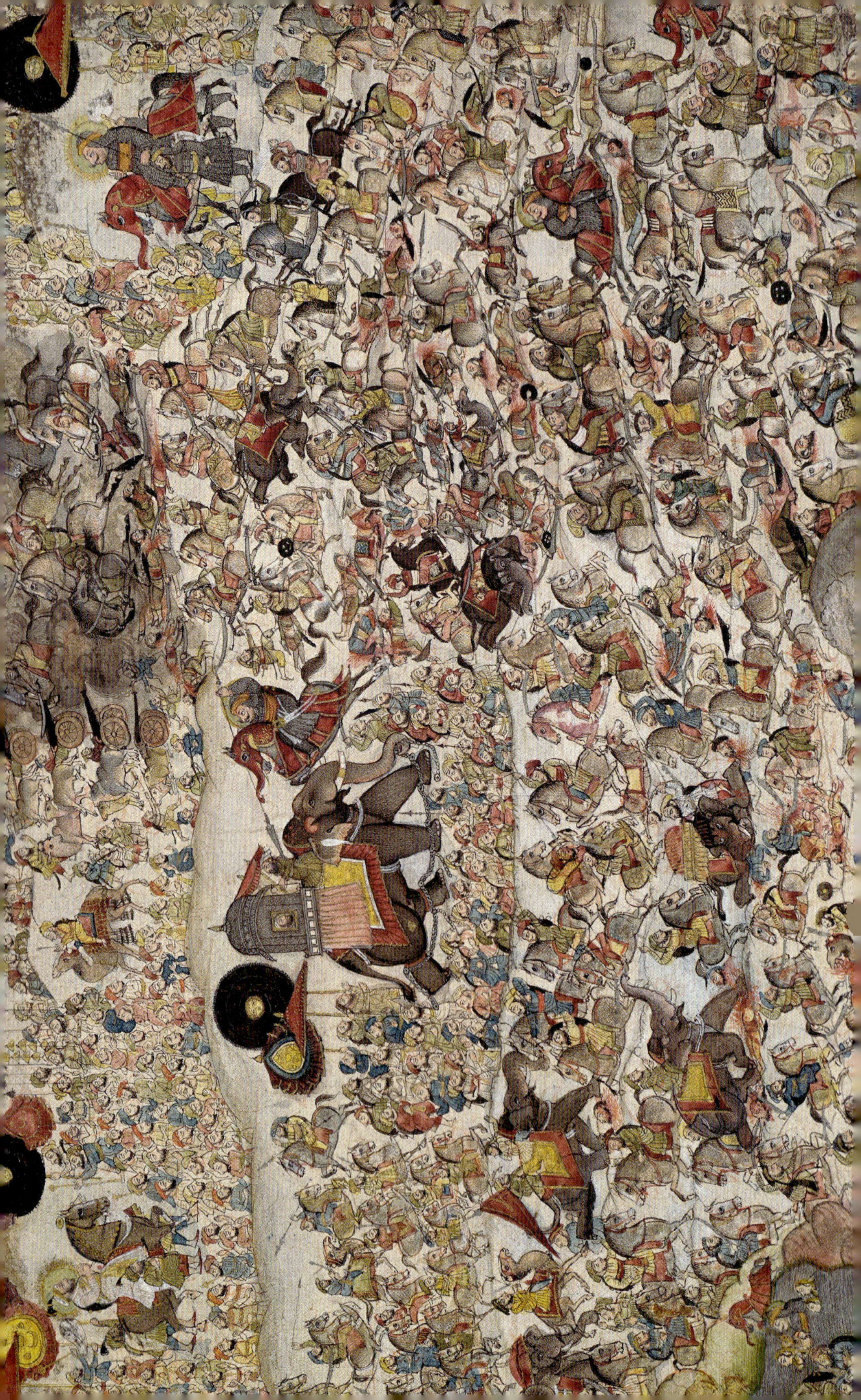

Kumbhakaran Asleep. Folio from the Jagat Singh Ramayana, also known as the Mewar Ramayan, the finest Ramayan ever commissioned by a Hindu patron. Painted in classic Rajasthani style with a bright background and vivid, flat figures, it was commissioned as the patron was inspired by the Mughal Ramayan. The manuscript is the most heavily illustrated version of the epic, originally containing as many as 450 images, painted during the period 1649–1653.

(Left): *The Battle of Haldighati. The Mughal forces, led by Kuar Man Singh, defeated Rana Pratap. The rana would continue to wage guerrilla war against the Mughals for many years.*

Akbar in disguise visits Swami Haridas with Tansen, Kishangarh, Rajasthan, 1760.

In this folio from the Persian Mahabharat, the Razmnama, there is an eclectic mix of styles as the teacher and students are painted like Mughal courtiers while the woman is painted in a purely Gujarati style.

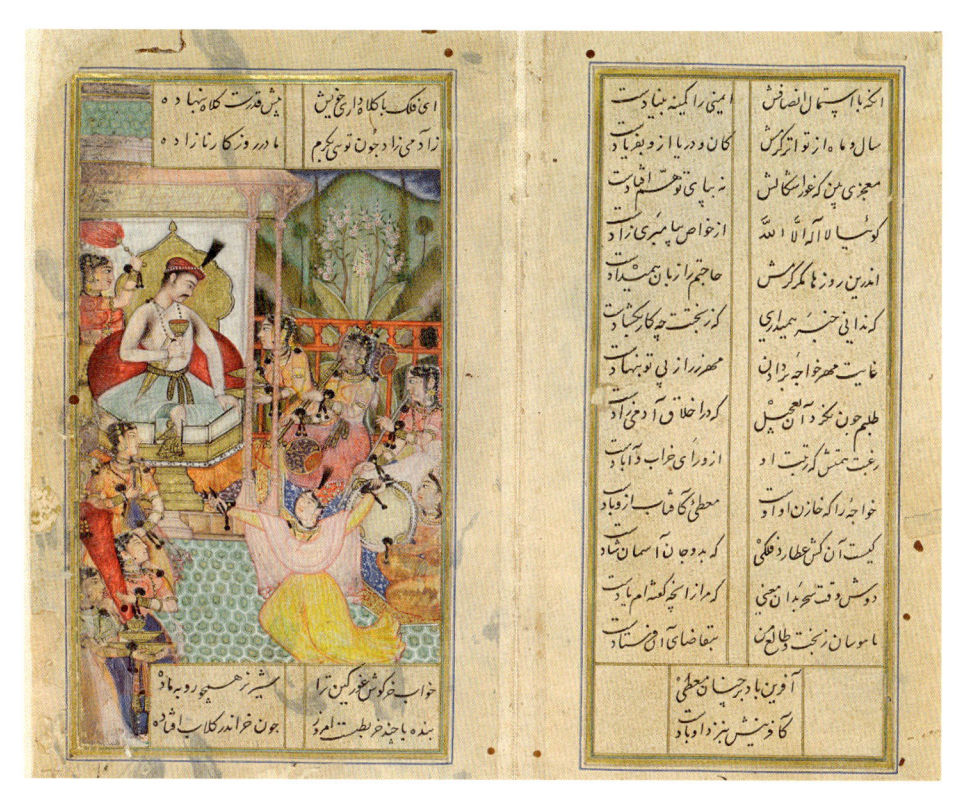

Heavenly Joys Come to Earth—attributed to Khem Karan. Folio from the jewel-like Divan-e-Anvari, *produced in 1588.*

Folio from the Persian translation of the Ramayan, *painted in Lahore in 1594. Ram and Lakshman wear ascetic robes but their moustaches betray their Mughal origins.*

(Left): *The young artist Abu'l Hasan, who began his career at Akbar's court but went on to become the favourite artist of Jahangir—by Daulat.*

(Right): *A portrait of Manohar—by Daulat. Son of the master painter Basawan, Manohar later joined Jahangir's atelier.*

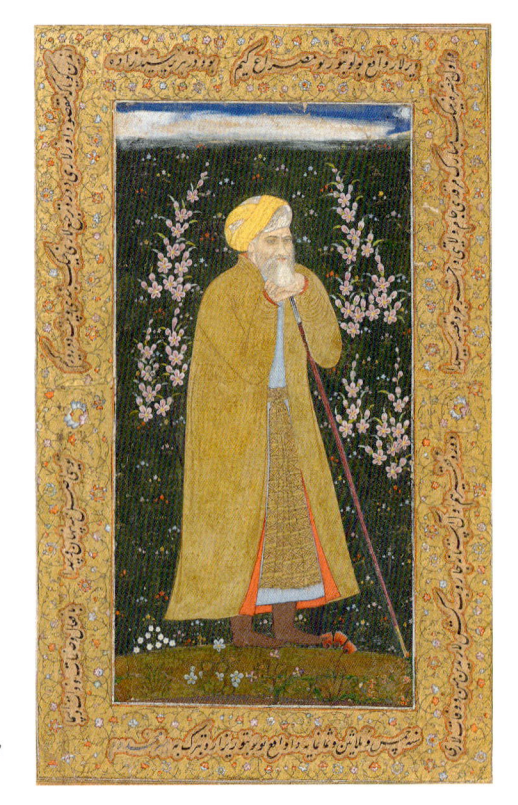

Farrukh Beg, self-portrait. He was a Persian miniaturist who worked first at the court of Mirza Hakim, then at Akbar's court before leaving for the Deccan. He returned north only after Jahangir became emperor.

Folio from the Baburnama, *painted in 1598 at Lahore, when Akbar commissioned a translation into Persian of Babur's autobiography, written in Turki.*

Abu'l Fazl presents Akbar with the second volume of the emperor's biography, the Akbarnama.

Babur crossing the River Son. Folio from the Baburnama, *1598.*

Chand Sultan playing polo with her attendants, unveiled.

Bir Singh Deo of Orchha, painted here in a transparent white jama, sided with Prince Salim in the war of succession against Akbar.

Prince with a hawk. Though only 6 inches by 3 inches, this exquisite painting (1600–1605) shows extraordinary, precise details like the animals on the prince's qaba.

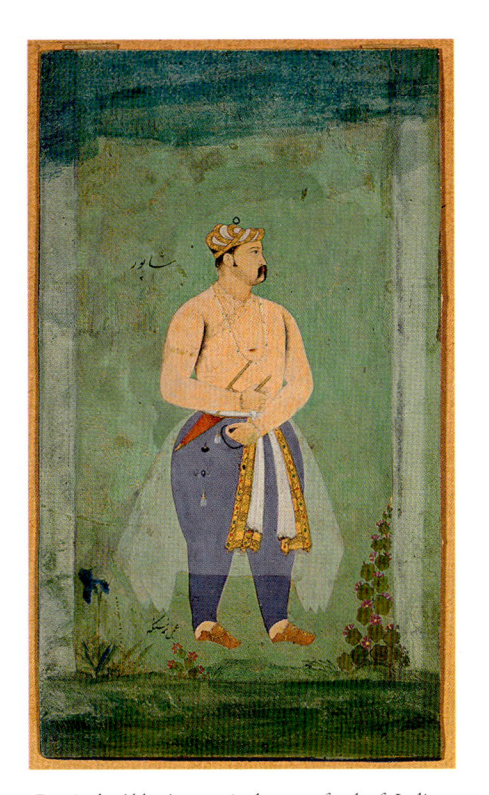

Daniyal, Akbar's son. '...he was fond of Indian singing': Jahangirnama

Murad, Akbar's son. '...gravity was apparent in his manner, and bravery and manliness were evident from his conduct': Jahangirnama

Folio from the Gulshan Album. Considered one of the world's greatest books, it was assembled for Salim when he was still at his father's court. He added to it at Allahabad and after he had become Emperor Jahangir.

Nath Yogis, painted at Salim's rebellious court at Allahabad in 1600.

Art at Salim's rebel court showing European influence.

The western gateway to Akbar's tomb at Sikandra.

Akbar with lion and calf—by Bichitr. Folio from the Shah Jahan album, 1630. Posthumous portrait of an elderly Akbar with the European motifs of lion, calf, and cherubs.

Prince Salim, the future Jahangir, enthroned.

Akbar and Jahangir.

SHRI MAHARAJADHIRAJA MAHARAJA OF THE MUGHAL EMPIRE

Brindavan had long been a holy site of pilgrimage associated with the pastoral childhood of Krishna, but it had gained prominence in the sixteenth century when the Chaitanya sect began preaching its message of complete and ecstatic devotion to Krishna. The explosive rise of the Bhakti movement in the region and its proximity to Agra and Fatehpur Sikri meant that the Mughal court was familiar with the sacrality of the place. Akbar, Hamida Banu, Raja Todar Mal, and Raja Birbal had all extended their patronage to temples and priests in Mathura and Brindavan. In a series of farmans issued in the 1590s, Akbar specifically ordered that the Brahmin Vithal Rai, priest of the temple of Govardhan Nath, not be harassed about questions of faith and be allowed to pray for the welfare of the empire as he had always done. Officers were to desist from demanding any form of tax from Vithal Rai and not harm him in any way. Vithal Rai was no ordinary priest: he had a long and illustrious list of disciples including Harkha Bai, Todar Mal, Birbal, Baz Bahadur, Tansen, Man Singh, and, in an earlier time, Rani Durgavati of Gondwana. Despite the emperor's farman, Hamida Banu had to issue further farmans confirming the demands of the emperor since some Mughal officers had ignored the earlier decrees. Hamida Banu's farman was detailed and explicit:

> May it be known that according to the farman of the exalted and the just Emperor, the cows belonging to the indisputable prayer offerer (well wisher) Vithalesharai Brahmin, may graze wherever they are and not a single individual out of the khalis or jagir should molest them or prevent them from grazing. They must permit his cows to graze (wherever they are). The above mentioned (Vithalrai) should therefore remain easy at heart. It is incumbent that they must act according to the order and carry it out.

It would appear that when officials created trouble for the people, they then appealed to royal Mughal women to ensure that the Padshah's farmans were obeyed.

There exist farmans that demonstrate Akbar's interest in the site considered the yogapitha or centre of Brindavan, at which Raja Man Singh began building works for a large new temple at Brindavan in 1590. This temple, like others in the area, became replicas in miniature of the Mughal court. The naubat* performed here as it did at the royal palace and indeed as it did at the Ajmer dargah. Statues of the deities Krishna, Balram, and Radha were presented to devotees at set times, like a royal darshan. In building the Govind Deva temple, which then adopted these 'imperial' practices, the raja was not only proclaiming his own stature as a Hindu Kachhwaha raja whose watan jagir was at nearby Amer, but was also visibly celebrating Mughal imperial grandeur in a way that had the Padshah's blessing.

Historian Catherine Asher has shown that there were many unique features in the Govind Deva temple that Raja Man Singh built at Brindavan, reflecting the eddying and swirling currents that increasingly bound together Rajput and Mughal aesthetic values. The temple was never completed, according to the *Jahangirnama*, so lacks a superstructure, though later accounts erroneously claim it was desecrated by Aurangzeb.† At nearly 80 metres in length, the temple is by far the largest constructed in north India after the thirteenth century, and the dressed red sandstone used in the temple is typical of Muslim-sponsored architecture. While the temple's exterior is largely aniconic (without idols), the interior has figures associated with Krishna lore—gopis, Radha, cows, etc. Asher further points out that while Raja Man Singh used classically Mughal arcuated, domed, and vaulted interior corridors flanked by bracketed pillars, the manner in which the temple used long barrel vaults, domes, and intersecting vaults to create a sense of arcing space and expansive grandeur actually anticipated trends in Mughal architecture, making Raja Man Singh something of a visionary and trendsetter. So admired was this temple that Abdu'l Latif, visiting in the seventeenth century, wished that it were a mosque and not a temple.

---

*Orchestra.

†Tour guides and local priests today still claim the temple's superstructure was deliberately destroyed.

The inscriptions on the temple are eloquent in demonstrating the rising status of the Kachhwaha clan within the Mughal Empire. This is the earliest inscription from Man Singh's reign and claims for him a title greater than that used for his father and grandfather. Historian Ramya Sreenivasan has shown that the Brajbhasha inscription accords Man Singh the title Maharajadhiraja whereas his father had only been accorded the status of Maharaja. Moreover, in a feat of useful amnesia in tracing the lineage of the clan, the Kachhwahas are shown as descending directly from Prithviraj Kachhwaha to Bharmal Kachhwaha, effacing all the troublesome contending factions and cousins in between.

Raja Man Singh did not restrict his patronage of architecture to his watan jagir. He built temples on a far larger scale, covering a much wider geographical range than any other pre-modern patron in India, and this was a testament not only to the wealth he commanded as a Mughal mansabdar but also to the ambition he rightly claimed as a highly successful commander and as the Padshah's cherished farzand. Raja Man Singh was governor of Bihar from 1587 to 1594 during which time he established Mughal power firmly in the region. Most of his temples were built in Bihar—in Rohtas, Patna, Baikatpur, and Manpur, on the outskirts of Bodh Gaya. For Raja Man Singh the celebration of his status as a Hindu raja did not clash in any way with his identity as Mughal mansabdar. Indeed, the two seemed to overlap and intertwine in such a way that imperial visibility was increased even as the raja used Hindu symbolism. Raja Man Singh performed an elaborate and ostentatious shraddha at Gaya for forty-five days following his father's death, much longer than the stipulated period of sixteen days. He then built a town, now largely destroyed, on the opposite bank of the river from Gaya called Manpur and began work on the Govind Deva temple. In addition to Hindu temples, the raja built mosques in Lahore and at Rajmahal, and maintained the shrine of a Sufi saint in Hajipura.

Raja Man Singh also built structures commemorating important victories in his capacity as Mughal subedar, the most significant of which were his buildings at Rohtas Fort in Bihar. This fort, well-situated and strategically important, was considered essential in controlling Bihar, Bengal, and Orissa. On the highest spot of the hill was a temple dedicated to the area's legendary patron, Rohitsava. Raja Man Singh had a smaller structure built at the foot of the Rohitsava temple that looks remarkably like the tomb of Salim Chishti at Fatehpur Sikri. This temple resembling the tomb of a Sufi saint in the distant east, is a fascinating co-opting of a local deity using multiple and complex symbols.

In the fort itself, Raja Man Singh built an enormous palace complex, based loosely on the plan of Fatehpur Sikri, which was the largest non-imperial palace built in the entire Mughal Empire. This was clearly not meant as a private residence alone as it had administrative sections, such as a viewing balcony for public audiences, private and public audience halls and elaborate office buildings. In this way, Mughal court ritual could be seamlessly enacted even far away from its capital at Lahore. Catherine Asher calls it 'the first structure to introduce the courtly Mughal style of architecture to eastern India'. At the time, local zamindars only had crudely constructed rudimentary forts to show so the visual reminder of the might and wealth of the Mughal Empire was silently but eloquently expressed. A large stone slab at the entrance of the palace gates bears two inscriptions that show that the raja was quite aware of his dual role. One inscription, in Persian, is addressed to the emperor, Sultan Jalal-ud-din Muhammad Akbar Badshah Ghazi, and mentions the raja only very briefly, stating rather blandly that he 'has built a strong building'. The longer Sanskrit inscription on the same slab does not mention Akbar at all and instead celebrates the raja as head of the Kachhwaha Rajputs and refers to him, with fulsome celebration, as Sri Maharajadhiraja Maharaja (king of kings). Today, sadly, the Rohtas Fort and all Raja Man Singh's ambitious buildings lie in a state of ruined neglect.

As has been noted, after the magnificent creative explosion of Fatehpur Sikri, Akbar would never again commission buildings on the same scale. From now on, it would be his amirs and mansabdars who would take on the job of translating Mughal splendour into stone in the distant hinterlands of the empire. It was these favoured courtiers who carried imperial aesthetics and culture into dusty desert towns and swampy outposts, negotiating local traditions both Hindu and Muslim. And it would be Raja Man Singh, brought up at the Mughal court since he was twelve years old, who would carry out this work with the most panache and audacity.

While Man Singh's career would outstrip the others, there were many other Rajput rajas and chieftains who would now travel throughout the empire as Mughal mansabdars and remain for months and even years away from their home towns. Sometimes the rajas appointed Jains or Brahmins to administer to their states in their absence, since 'Rajput rulers realised the pitfalls of leaving the governance of their kingdoms in the hands of close male relatives during their own absence'. But often, as noted by historians Rima Hooja and Varsha Joshi, it was the most senior rani who carried out the work of governing the kingdom in the absence of her husband. In the case of Raja Man Singh, it was his chief Bhattiyani rani, Kanakwati, who ruled his thikana and controlled the state's finances. In Bikaner, Rani Ganga Bai was the most powerful of Maharaja Rai Singh's wives and used her influence to secure the throne for her son. The ranis had their own set of staff, loyal to them, known collectively by the name of the rani, such as Bhattiyaniji ki sarkar, who carried out the work under her supervision. Like the Mughals, the rajmata was often the most powerful woman of the zenana, acquiring more influence as a queen mother than she ever did as a wife. These women often owned land in their own names, the haath-kharach jagir, which they controlled through administrators. Agents kept these ranis informed about conditions in their jagirs, 'the state of agriculture, famine, law and order, or social problems'—such as those related to the peasantry and so on. In a few years' time, Harkha Bai would be similarly kept informed about the state of indigo cultivation in her own jagir, and she would send agents to buy the precious harvests, at one stage getting into a confrontation with Portuguese buyers, which would have rather dire consequences for the Portuguese.

Articulating the fine-grained imagery of these complicated personas was the *Mancarit*, a biography of Raja Man Singh written in a mixture of Brajbhasha and Rajasthani by Amrit Rai. In one part of the *Mancarit*, Amrit Rai deals with the genealogy of the Mughal Padshah using unassailable Hindu imagery:

Born in the lineage of Timur, the son of Humayun
Is revered in the three worlds by heroic men
He is a portion of the supreme being (avatara) descended to earth

To destroy the suffering of others
He is the rightful universal emperor of the Chaghatay clan
A protector of the entire earth
Long live Shah Jahal al din the world conqueror
The Jewel of the World.

The *Mancarit* was just one of a profusion of writings in Rajasthani and Brajbhasha dialects that were produced at the regional courts in the late sixteenth century. Indeed the Kachhwaha court at Amer has been deemed crucial by scholars in the genesis of Riti literature.* The Kachhwahas did not usually patronize Persian literature but instead supported Rajasthani and Riti styles of writing, sometimes in addition to Sanskrit. Mostly ignored by Abu'l Fazl and the Mughal records because of the preference given to Persian texts, these manuscripts offer fascinating insights into the ways in which sub-imperial courts imagined their place in this new world order. In these accounts, we can see how the writers used their skill and imagination to describe their heroic patrons who had been fully absorbed into the Mughal Empire. On the one hand, they had to make sure that a suitable deference was observed where the Mughal Padshah was concerned. On the other, the writers had to present their Rajput patron as a heroic and virile figure for two other groups of intended listeners—other elite Rajput clans and the patron's dependants. Therefore these texts were rarely 'histories' in the conventional sense, or in the sense that the Mughal court was producing them, but they are nonetheless a glimpse into the ways in which the regional courts and rulers built a new scaffolding for their unfolding ambitions.

Sreenivasan has shown that the *Mancarit* is also possibly the earliest account of an exalted Kachhwaha genealogy. Using Puranic symbols, the Kachhwahas are described as descending from Brahma himself, via Raghu. Puranic genealogies had been produced for Rajasthani chiefs from the late fifteenth century onwards, naming the patrons as descended either from the sun or the moon. In the sixteenth century, the audience for these genealogies now included the Mughal emperors, who were also interested in the notions of ancestry—as a result, the construction of Puranic genealogies became

---

*A tradition of early Hindi literature, associated with the late medieval court.

further validated. Indeed, since the Mughal Padshahs were now confirming the succession of Rajput rulers, as Eaton has pointed out, these detailed genealogies supported by Charans and poems 'had the effect not only of sharpening the boundaries between Rajput clans, but also—because there were fierce struggles with other peoples in the region—of shaping the identity of Rajputs as against non-Rajputs'.

Written in 1585, at a time when Akbar's rise was inexorable, the *Mancarit* for all its staunch praise of the equation between its Rajput patron and the Mughal emperor nonetheless, almost inadvertently, hints at a sense of disquiet and even foreboding at the immense changes that had taken place in the Hindustani landscape, and speaks of the age as Kaliyug.

Just as he would carefully weigh the messages in Persian and Sanskrit outside his palace walls at Rohtas for a wider Hindustani audience, in the *Mancarit*, Raja Man Singh would also patronize a Brajbhasha text that would celebrate the splendour of a Rajput raja while parsing the truth wherever it proved altogether unacceptable.

Braj poets in the regional courts began to experiment with the vernacular in innovative ways in the late sixteenth century using Persian imagery and Sanskrit classicism—these poetic forms would become immensely popular and widespread by the early seventeenth century. One of the reasons for the efflorescence of this vernacular poetry was the enthusiastic patronage by the Mughals. This patronage has been almost completely overlooked because Mughal chroniclers themselves took note of Persian writings over all other languages and so the presumption that Hindi writing was predominantly Hindu became largely accepted. But Alison Busch describes this Mughal patronage as 'early, copious and critical to the consolidation of Hindi's courtly style'. The Braj dialect of Brindavan and Mathura, driven by the Vaishnava Bhakti movements of the late sixteenth century, would have been familiar to the Mughal court due to the physical proximity of Fatehpur Sikri and the extensive patronage of these towns not only by the emperor but by his family and courtiers as well. These enormously popular poems in Braj would have certainly not been unknown to Akbar, who was not only familiar with Braj, but according to Abu'l Fazl even composed the occasional verse in the language. Harkha Bai herself had a profound interest in the region as did her entire family and, as for Salim, Braj was his mother tongue. We hear of courtiers composing in Braj, or Hindi, too—Birbal, Todar Mal, Faizi, and, most famously, Abdur Rahim.

Of the Braj poets known to be associated with the Mughal court the most well-known was Gang. Later equated alongside Tulsidas as one of two sardars among Braj poets, Gang wrote poetry for Mughal patrons including Akbar, Abdur Rahim and his sons, Prince Daniyal, Raja Man Singh, and Birbal.

Other significant works of Hindi kavya to be produced at a mansabdar's court were by the poet Keshavdas Misra in Orchha. Orchha had become subsumed into the Mughal Empire in the 1570s when Raja Madhukar Shah was defeated relatively easily and his sons, including one Ratnasena, were sent to serve at the Mughal court. These incontrovertible facts were, however, quite summarily dismissed and using virtuoso technical skill and verbal calisthenics in Brajbhasha the poet Keshavdas Misra created for his patrons a much more pleasing world in terms of martial values demonstrated. In the *Ratnabhavani*, written soon after Orchha's capitulation in the 1570s, the Mughals are roundly censored and abused as being 'Mlecchas', 'Turks' and 'Pathans' whereas Prince Ratnasena is compared to Ram, Angad, and Hanuman. Ratnasena, in true heroic Kshatriya style, dies magnificently on the battlefield, trying to defend his father's kingdom. Ratnasena, in fact, did not die fighting the Mughals in this battle but died some years later, fighting *for* the Mughals. The *Ratnabhavani* shows us how, as the world began to reconfigure itself in the 1570s, a proud Bundela clan tried to reconcile itself to a new order. In the words of Busch, the text demonstrated 'the fervent wish that the Mughals could be resisted in the face of a new historical reality where resistance is no longer possible'.

By the time Keshavdas wrote his second historical poem, the *Virsimhdevcarit*, twenty-five years later, the political landscape had altered considerably. The pejorative term 'mleccha' was no longer acceptable and the words Pathan and Turk no longer evoked the alienating 'otherness' they had in the *Ratnabhavani*. Raja Madhukar Shah had died in 1592 and Akbar had recognized the right to his position of his eldest son, Ram Shah. However, the raja's youngest son, Bir Singh Deo, contested this claim and spent a decade skirmishing with his brother and with the Mughal forces. It is Bir Singh Deo's rise to power that the *Virsimhdevcarit* celebrates but the events it would gloss over were scandalous and would involve the murder of one of Akbar's beloved friends and would implicate Prince Salim.

POISON IN PARADISE

Bhaktamara!

With this sombre Sanskrit word began the recitation of the Bhaktamara-stotra, a sacred hymn in honour of Adinath Jain, which the scholar and Jain priest Bhanu Chandra recited, the lilting cadences rippling through the magnificent Jain temple inside Lahore Fort. In front of Bhanu Chandra stood Akbar and Salim, head bowed, as they allowed these ancient verses to calm them, for a cold fear had settled in their hearts. Salim had just had a baby girl and the astrologers had quite disastrously decided that the constellation she was born under was harmful for Akbar. 'Perform whatever is the purifying rite in the Jain philosophy!' Akbar had ordered and Bhanu Chandra had suggested that they perform the Ashtottara-Sata-Snatra, a ceremony involving 108 baths to be given to the idol of Jina in the temple. After the completion of the hymn, the monk took some of the holy water from a gold pot and applied it to the Padshah's eyes while his harem, Harkha Bai and his other Hindu wives, bowed before the pot and prayed for his health.

After his experience with Jain monks at Fatehpur Sikri, Akbar would continue to nurture the relationship between these priests and the Mughal court. Bhanu Chandra would stay at court well into the reign of Jahangir, and many other Jain scholars would continue to sporadically visit the Mughal court. These encounters, not mentioned in the Persianate texts, were meticulously recorded in Jain biographies.

While this incident shows the Padshah and his eldest son united in a common cause, both equally comfortable in seeking benediction from an unusual place, there is nonetheless a sense of a slow curdling of old, familiar affection. That danger to the Padshah's life had been calculated as coming, even indirectly, from Salim's family was unfortunate. It would have increased the prince's sense of vulnerability and perhaps stoked Akbar's paranoia.

Sometime in the year 1590, Akbar fell ill with a stomach upset and colic, which no remedy seemed able to alleviate. Badauni writes about this episode, during which 'in this unconscious state (Akbar) uttered some words which arose from suspicions of his eldest son, and accused him of giving him poison'. According to Badauni Akbar then said to Salim:

> Shaikhu Baba, since all this Sultanate will devolve on you,
> why have you made this attack on me...
> To take away my life there was no need of injustice
> I would have given it to thee if thou hadst asked me

Akbar even began to suspect the physician Hakim Humam, previously above suspicion, of having poisoned him. Death by poisoning was an old fear, one that the Mughal Padshahs would try to guard against with increasingly elaborate rituals. With Akbar seemingly close to death Salim, according to Badauni, then appointed some of his close allies to spy on his brother Murad. When Akbar recovered, the women of the harem and Murad himself complained to the Padshah about Salim's offensive behaviour, and Akbar realized that he could no longer keep his three sons under his claustrophobic care.

The three princes were young men now, with families of their own, and powerful connections through marriage. Murad, especially, married to the daughter of Mirza Aziz Koka, would have been considered a potentially dangerous threat to Salim. Akbar decided that it was finally time to separate his sons to try and diffuse the increasing tension of their close proximity. Murad was appointed Governor of Malwa and given 'pennant, kettle drum, martial music, and a royal standard and all the paraphernalia of royalty'. He was also given 'a royal sleeveless dress of honour, which is an honour conferred only on princes', specified Badauni. Akbar gave him detailed instructions on how to conduct himself during this first major trial of his life. He was to be moderate in his behaviour, his food and drink, his sleep, and his interactions. Leniency and clemency were advised: 'A frown will effect with many what in other men requires a sword and dagger' and 'if apologies are made, accept them'. Murad was encouraged to surround himself with good people, and to listen to their advice. He was to 'secure the affection of contented hermits and of the matted-haired and barefooted' and 'not lose sight of an old servant'. Murad thus went off in resplendent state, attended by noblemen and the advice of his father, first to Malwa, then to Gujarat, and finally to the Deccan. Many ambitious members of the ruling clans and soldiers joined him, believing him 'superior to the other princes in majesty and pomp'.

But twenty years in the presence of the charisma, power, and talent of his father had not been conducive to fostering humility and wisdom in Murad, and little by little his supporters grew disenchanted by 'his bad conduct in all relations of life, and court and ceremonial, and in his over-weening pride and arrogance, in which he imitated his illustrious Father, and which he carried beyond all conception, boasting of being a ripe grape when he was not yet even an unripe grape...and it became known that all that transient pomp and circumstance was caused by his ignorance rather than his knowledge'.

As for Salim, remaining at court in Lahore, Munis Faruqui has shown that he spent this decade slowly cultivating the friendships that his father could not tolerate. In addition to Mirza Hakim's supporters, whom he had already befriended, he would continue to cultivate men from clans considered quite unacceptable by Akbar—Afghan men like Shaikh Rukn ud-din Rohilla and Pir Khan, of the Lodi dynasty; also men from the Naqshbandi order of Sufis, whom Akbar had marginalized in favour of the Chishtis. In this manner, Salim not only gradually gathered around him influential men who owed their allegiance only to the prince but in doing so undermined his father's authority.

In other ways, however, Akbar and Salim seemed to share some common enthusiasms, notably in fostering unconventional religious practices. In 1590, learning that the Christians were celebrating the Feast of the Assumption of the Virgin Mary, Akbar decided to hold a similar celebration in Lahore. He had an elaborate throne made on which he placed the picture of the Virgin Mary gifted to him by Acquaviva. He then asked all his courtiers to show their respect to the image and kiss it but the courtiers, no doubt used to the eccentricities of the court, first demanded that Salim lead the way. This Salim did 'at once and very willingly', followed by all the courtiers.

The following year, Lahore saw the arrival of the second Jesuit mission at the Mughal court, Akbar having sent an invitation to the viceroy at Goa. In his letter to the viceroy Akbar wrote that he wished 'that they may dispute with my doctors, and that I by comparing the knowledge and other qualities displayed on either side, may be able to see the superiority of the Fathers over my own learned men'.

The Jesuits left a heartfelt account of the difficulties they faced in making the arduous passage from Cambay to Lahore. The journey, they wrote, lay 'mainly through deserts and dry, sandy tracts, where neither springs nor streams are to be found, but only sand everywhere, which is often lifted into the air by the wind, so that people are enveloped in it, and sometimes buried for ever'. Due to the additional dangers of highway bandits, the common folk and the poor often travelled in large caravans, which the Jesuits have described:

> ...they choose a captain to lead and command their troop, which often contains two or three thousand persons. That which the Fathers joined consisted of four hundred camels, a hundred carts, and as many horses, and there were besides many poor folk who followed the others on foot.... When travelling by night, in order that the people may not become separated from one another, the drummers lead the way, beating their drums continuously.

The caravans halted along the way wherever wells were to be found, deep wells from which water was raised through carts dragged by bullocks. And so two priests, Father Edouard Leioton and Father Christofle de Vega, arrived at the Mughal court in 1591, somewhat bedraggled, where the Padshah greeted them effusively and lodged them within the palace itself. He urged the Fathers to build a school and promised to send the sons of his courtiers as well as a son and a grandson of his own to learn Portuguese. But less exalted and, perhaps, more realistic than Father Acquaviva, these two Jesuits realized '[Akbar] had no intention of making up his mind' and returned to Goa, 'having accomplished nothing of what they had intended'.

Salim's household was growing at this stage and his young son Khusrau began his schooling at the age of four. Abu'l Fazl was appointed to 'teach him something every day' while the rest of his education was left to the charge of Abu'l Fazl's younger brother, Abu'l Khair. In January 1592, a son was born to Jagat Gosain, the daughter of Mota Raja. Akbar handed over his grandchild to the care of his first wife, Ruqaiya Begum. Ruqaiya Begum had remained childless these many decades after marrying Akbar at the age of nine following the death of her father, Hindal. In Lahore, an astrologer had predicted greatness for Jagat Gosain's as yet unborn son and Ruqaiya Begum had asked of Akbar the gift of raising a future Padshah. Mirza Khurram* as he was named, was raised in Ruqaiya Begum's care who, Salim later wrote, 'loved him a thousand times more than if he had been her own'. Salim also noted that Khurram had the exclusive attention of his grandfather, the Padshah, and 'little by little as his years progressed real potential was noticed in him. He served my exalted father more and better than any of my sons and my father was very pleased with him and his service. He always commended him to me. Many times he said "There is no comparison between him and your other sons. I consider him my true son".' Salim may have found it galling that Akbar considered Khurram his true son, given the increasing disappointment the Padshah expressed in his own sons.

Khurram would remain in Ruqaiya Begum's care until Akbar died and Salim became Padshah Jahangir, when Khurram was thirteen years old. So while Akbar may have been honouring Ruqaiya Begum by giving her what she had requested, he was also demonstrating, yet again, the faith he had in the senior Timurid matriarchs. Hamida Banu, Salima Sultan, Gulbadan, and Ruqaiya were the ones who were often trusted with the care and education of the Mughal children. And if many of them were now born of Rajput mothers, their upbringing was strictly Timurid. It was these women who surrounded them with the language, the etiquette, the food and the nuances of culture that they were the guardians of.

All the major celebrations at court, the births and the marriages, were also supervised by these senior women and it was Hamida Banu, helped by the other matriarchs, who decided on the giving of gifts, the dances, the decorations, and all the festivities as they became ever more elaborate. The women had many occasions to admire and

---

*The future Shah Jahan.

acquire new luxuries and innovations, for Akbar, intensely curious about every new development, created occasions for the women of the harem to enjoy these too:

> On the third feast-day of every month, His Majesty holds a large assembly for the purpose of inquiring into the many wonderful things found in this world. The merchants of the age are eager to attend, and lay out articles from all countries. The people of His Majesty's Harem come, and the women of other men are also invited, and buying and selling is quite general. His Majesty uses such days to select any articles which he wishes to buy or to fix the prices of things, and thus add to his knowledge. His Majesty gives to such days the name of Khushruz, or the joyful day, as they are a source of much enjoyment.

◆

The highest-ranking noblemen of the court contributed to increasing the visible glory of the court and empire. At this time, it was Akbar's foster brother, Zain Khan Koka, who begged of Akbar for a visit to his house. As we have seen, a personal visit by the Padshah was the greatest honour that a nobleman could hope for and when Akbar agreed to visit him, Zain Khan Koka arranged for celebrations that matched in extravagance and exquisite detail the magnitude of this honour. The homes of these elite noblemen were themselves lavish, with gardens and water tanks and many apartments. Often built of rubble and mud, they were covered with a white plaster that was the envy of visiting Europeans. Dutch merchant Francisco Pelsaert has described this plaster, of unslaked lime mixed with milk, gum and sugar, applied on the walls with a trowel and polished until the walls shone like mirrors. As the emperor and his retinue arrived, baskets filled with jewels were presented as peshkash, in addition to elephants. An entire terrace was covered with rare and expensive toosh shawls. Instead of water sprinklers, Zain Khan Koka had the grounds of the courtyard sprayed with a syrup of milk, sugar, and Yazd roses to settle the dust. Three tanks were dug in front of the terrace—one filled with rose water from Yazd, one with water coloured yellow with saffron, the third with argaja, a perfume. A thousand courtesans were thrown into the tanks so that their fine garments were all stained different colours.

By the end of the sixteenth century, these mansabdars of the Mughal Empire were extremely wealthy men. According to one estimate, all the officers together, some 1,671 persons, controlled 82 per cent of the net revenue resources of the empire, with the top 25 mansabdars alone accounting for 30 per cent.* As the noblemen of the Mughal court became wealthier, they spent increasingly large amounts on charities, endowments, and patronage, especially in their own parganas. Shaikh Farid Bukhari had made a list of all the Sayyids of Gujarat and gave them money, met the wedding expenses of their sons and daughters, provided subsistence to all the residents of khanqahs and darweshes,† and looked after the widows of all the men who died in his service. Mir Abul Qasim Arghun devised a rather novel method for charity in Sind. He would have entire panels of cloth hung from the branches of trees in the forest and would have herds of horses, cows, and buffaloes released into them so that poorer folk could help themselves to what they needed. Ram Das Kachhwaha donated money to communities of Charans, bards, and courtesans—they could collect from his cashier, a fixed amount annually.

Not all officers found that the life of a mansabdar suited them, however. One Husamuddin, son of Ghazi Khan Badakshi, while on campaign with Abdur Rahim and still a young man, decided that he wanted to become a fakir and devote his life to the service of Nizamuddin Auliya. Though Abdur Rahim tried to dissuade him, the young man 'smeared his body over with clay and mud and wandered about in the streets and bazaars'.‡ Akbar allowed him to resign his post and Husamuddin asked his wife, who was the sister of Abu'l Fazl, to donate all her jewellery to dervishes.

While Akbar held court in Lahore, he sent Abdur Rahim to settle a promising region that had not displayed the sort of submission that Akbar required of his territories. The region of Sind was a rich land, famous for its cotton and silk cloth, ivory work, wooden

---

*Shireen Moosvi's figures. Other scholars, notably Sanjay Subrahmanyam, David Washbrook, and Ashok V. Desai contest these figures as inflated.
†Mystics.
‡He lived for thirty years as a fakir in Delhi and became a disciple of Khwaja Baqi Billah.

furniture, leather, palanquin and chariot makers, salt-pits, and indigo. It had access to the sea, always an important consideration as the Portuguese were in possession of Goa. Sind had been controlled by relatives of the Mughals, the Tarkhans,* who had even sent a daughter, Sindhi Begum, for Akbar to marry. But the Padshah had refused the bride, as a clear indication of his disapproval at the way Sind was being governed. So, in 1590, Abdur Rahim was sent to Sind where he was able to overcome the stiff resistance of Mirza Jani Beg Tarkhan, who was then obliged to appear at court and accept his position as banda-i dargah (servant of the court). He was no longer to consider himself an independent ruler, Akbar explained to Jani Beg, but a mansabdar of 3,000 of the Mughal court, and was given the subah of Multan in lieu of Thatta. However, when reports reached Akbar that the entire Arghun clan of Jani Beg, some 1,000 men, women, and children were boarding boats and travelling in great distress to Jani Beg's new subah, the Padshah relented and reassigned Thatta to the Tarkhans. Akbar also accepted a daughter as bride for Abdur Rahim's son, Mirza Irij. Jani Beg, a talented poet who wrote verses under the pen name of 'Halimi', went on to become a favourite of Akbar's, who was impressed by 'his character, religious views, pleasing manners and practical wisdom', no doubt helped by the fact that Jani Beg became a 'murid' of Akbar's.†

But Akbar was altogether less pragmatic when it came to the happiness of his family. In 1592, when his daughter Shakr un-Nisa fell gravely ill, Akbar was unable to watch helplessly as death, his one, redoubtable foe, stalked his beloved daughter. Abu'l Fazl confessed that Akbar suddenly 'took a dislike to (Lahore)' and decided to leave for Kashmir. He left in such haste that he had crossed the river Ravi by the time news arrived that his daughter had recovered and Akbar agreed to return to Lahore. Kashmir continued to haunt him, however, and in July 1592, in 'spite of clouds of rain and the opposition of men', Akbar set off once again for the valley of Kashmir.

---

*Jani Beg Tarkhan traced his lineage to Chenghiz Khan himself.
†He managed to offend Akbar just before his death by declaring that had he commanded a fort such as Asir, he would have held it for 100 years.

MIRZA AZIZ KOKA IN MECCA

When Akbar reached Kashmir in 1592, he was once again delighted with the country. 'On my first visit, I saw the bridal chamber of spring,' he said, 'now I behold the coquetry of autumn.' The harem and the imperial camp had been left behind at Rohtas Fort because of inclement weather, in the charge of Mirza Daniyal. En route, Salim's son Khusrau was suddenly taken so ill that 'he was committed to the care of God and [Akbar] made up his mind to part from him'. Though Khusrau would soon recover, Akbar rushed away from his beloved grandson, seemingly unable to stand helplessly by while the child languished. Instead, Akbar and a small group of men, including Salim, made their way through snow, rain, and wind to reach Srinagar. There they discovered an enormous chinar tree with a hollow trunk, into which thirty-four persons were easily made to sit. 'If they had sat closer,' grumbled Abu'l Fazl, 'more might have been accommodated.'

These bucolic pastimes notwithstanding, the situation in Kashmir was uncertain. Srinagar was found to be ominously deserted and the villages similarly abandoned. Enquiries had been made after the conquest of Kashmir into the amount of revenue collected from the region, which was meant to be one-third of the produce. However, a number of irregularities had crept in with jagirdars in the past using coercive methods and appropriating a great deal more than they were entitled to. So Akbar had sent officials to assess the situation and implement the correct revenue. Yadgar, the governor's cousin, had been executed on charges of embezzlement and his head was presented to the Padshah. Expecting further troubles and punishments, the locals had all melted away into the countryside. 'Although the root of the rebellion had been dug up,' wrote Abu'l Fazl, 'yet, owing to a report that His Majesty had ordered the punishment of high and low, people had scattered, and there was no population in any of the villages.' Now efforts were made to placate the terrified population and those who had not participated in the rebellions were richly rewarded.

Akbar then went to visit the saffron fields with Salim, who would remember these visits in his father's company when writing his memoir. The endless fields were harvested and the fragrance was overpowering. Salim wrote that when he visited Kashmir again, the fragrance was so cloying that it gave him and all his close companions a headache. The locals, however, appeared immune and when questioned, 'it was obvious that it had never occurred to them in all their lives to have a headache'. It was October and Diwali was celebrated with enthusiasm. Lamps were lit along the riverbanks, on the boats, and on the roofs of the houses, and 'they presented a splendid appearance'. When in Agra and Fatehpur Sikri, Abu'l Fazl had described how on Diwali 'several cows are adorned and brought before His Majesty. People are very fond of this custom.'

Akbar wanted to remain in Kashmir through the winter but since the soldiery and 'the inhabitants of hot countries' were uncomfortable with the idea, it was decided to return to Lahore. Akbar decided to leave Kashmir in the charge of Khwaja Shamsuddin but Salim petitioned for the reappointment of the disgraced Yusuf Khan Rizvi, who had conspired with other Kashmiri noblemen to rebel against the Mughals. Akbar acquiesced, unwilling to engage in a battle of wills, and Salim thus continued to nurture men whom the Padshah disapproved of, and whom he could bind to his own cause when the need, and the time, arose.

When the Mughal party returned to Lahore, a grand celebration was organized by the ladies of the harem because Salim was to be married to a granddaughter of Mirza Kamran, Humayun's brother. Kamran's daughter, Gulrukh Begum, had asked Akbar permission in the spring of 1592 for her daughter to be married to Salim and now this marriage was celebrated in Hamida Banu's quarters. Salim had always been a favourite of the senior ladies of the harem and in the planning of the wedding there seems to have been a consensus and common purpose between them. Gulrukh Begum, granddaughter of Babur, was clearly a woman of considerable prestige. While her daughter married Salim, her son, Mirza Muzaffar Hussain, later married Akbar's eldest daughter, Khanum Sultan, providing a suitably exalted Timurid lineage for the Padshah's daughter. Mirza Muzaffar Hussain would have a charming garden tomb built for himself immediately adjacent to Humayun's mausoleum. Reclaimed from the neglect of the twentieth century, it has been restored to its serene quietude in the Sundar Nursery grounds today.

While noting this marriage, Abu'l Fazl takes care to point out that 'just as for other people more than one wife is not suitable, so for great persons more are necessary, so that their dwellings may be more splendid, and a large number of people may be supported'. For, as we have seen, Akbar had recommended in 1586 that a man should seek to have only one wife, unless his wife was barren. For kings and princes, a large number of wives and children were deemed necessary but apparently for others, marrying more than one wife 'ruins a man's health and disturbs the peace of the home'. A marriage was described as a sober and sacred union, essential for the good functioning of society:

> Every care bestowed upon this wonderful tie between men is a means of preserving the stability of the human race, and ensuring the progress of the world; it is a preventive against the outbreak of evil passions, and leads to the establishment of homes. Hence His Majesty, inasmuch as he is benign, watches over great and small, and imbues men with his notions of the spiritual union and the equality of essence which he sees in marriage.

As pointed out by scholar Rosalind O'Hanlon, through these regulations, Akbar 'aimed at promoting a particular model of ideal marriage, in which mature men could realize the ethic of imperial service, women enjoy peace and companionship, and homes fructify with children and sons to worship God'. This form of morally sanctioned marriage, bedrock to a stable society, could only promote sexual union for procreation, and there was no space for liaisons with women past menopause or pre-pubertal girls. Nor was there, indeed, license for homosexual love. Though various forms of homosexuality had been part of Hindustani and Timurid landscapes, it was now presented as a peculiarly Transoxianian malaise that sapped men's strength and undermined the proper functioning of society.

'Here in India,' continued Abu'l Fazl, 'where a man cannot see the woman to whom he is betrothed, there are peculiar obstacles; but His

Majesty maintains that the consent of the bride and bridegroom, and the permission of the parents, are absolutely necessary in marriage contracts.' Through this decree Akbar seems to have been well aware of the coercive nature of some marriages and stressed the equal importance of all the concerned parties to the arrangement. Interestingly, Akbar disapproved of older women taking younger husbands, grumbling that it went against all modesty which, while showing a rather orthodox Padshah, tells us that this was a common enough occurrence for it to have been commented upon. These incidents, in addition to Badauni's frequent, gloating commentary and indeed Badauni's own lasting infatuation with a youth, showed the limits of the Padshah's attempts to regulate and control his officers' behaviour and inculcate a reliable standard of male virtue.

Badauni's own conflicted views on women reflected a common social malaise regarding the kinds of behaviour that were acceptable in women. In his view, a 'pious and veiled woman' was always to be lauded and he proposed a punishment of eighty lashes for anyone who unjustly accused such a woman of adultery, for women, he argued, were less prone to such lust than men. Badauni's solution to protect women from the unsolicited passions of men was to ensure they were veiled, quiet, and invisible. And, he argued paradoxically, it was women who were the fatal distraction for men and they were the 'robbers whom we encounter on our road to God'. Even more violently critical of women was Shaikh Ahmad Sirhindi who said that 'their nature is so wicked that in every adultery the woman must be regarded as the main culprit, since the act would not, for example, be possible without her consent'.

In this milieu Akbar's views were decidedly more nuanced and if he sought to regulate people's sexuality within the confines of heterosexual unions, it was nonetheless with a greater degree of awareness of the pressures that vulnerable women were subjected to and a more robust acceptance of men's share of responsibility in their unions.

As he grew older, Akbar's thoughts on his own marriages underwent a great change because he now often mentioned to Abu'l Fazl that 'had I formerly possessed the knowledge which I now have, I would never have chosen a wife for myself, for upon old women

I look as mothers, on women of my age as sisters, and on girls as daughters'. As for young women, there were many instances in which he showed a protective and solicitous concern for their well-being:

> He is grave and very gentle and is always cautious with maidens and is in no way lost in lust for them. He does not pay attention only to their appearances and has in several instances also prevented lustful men from being overly desirous of them.

These were clearly the thoughts of the older Padshah, a father whose daughters were cherished above all, and who now, after a more tempestuous youth, had the sobriety and sensitivity to see in all young women his own daughters' faces.

In 1593, Akbar recalled to Lahore another old family member, one who had not been seen at court for a worrisome number of years.* Mirza Aziz Koka, capricious and outspoken on many occasions, had stormed out of the court some years previously muttering about the need to grow his beard, unhappy with the liberties Akbar was taking with Islam. Now Akbar summoned him from his subah of Gujarat but Aziz Koka, pretending to be marching against the Portuguese at Diu, prepared to board a hajj ship and make his way to Mecca.

Brought up an orthodox Muslim man, Aziz Koka had long been critical of the 'innovations' at Akbar's court, and those persons that he blamed for encouraging the Padshah in this disastrous direction. In this court Islam was not accorded preference, and the Padshah said to his mother that in the spirit of sulh kul, 'the contempt of any religion is the contempt of God'. This would have been a galling point of view for Aziz Koka, not made more palatable by Akbar's questioning of Islam being the sole repository of religious truth when he said that 'truth inhabited every religion...how was it then that one religion and one community that was relatively young—it had not been around even for a thousand years—should receive preference at the expense of others?'

Naturally this challenge was also directed at Hinduism, but it was never really perceived as such, perhaps because no Hindu sect felt the need to respond to the Padshah's enquiry. Sulh kul was primarily seen as a questioning of orthodox Islam, and the supremacy vested

---

*Different sources differ as to the exact number of years, from two to ten years.

in the ulema. Certainly, a letter that Akbar wrote to Murad at this time would give a great deal more to an orthodox Islamic man to be circumspect about:

> Devotion to the Matchless One (Bechun) is beyond the limits of the spoken word whether in respect of form (jism), material attributes (jismanaiat), letter (harf), or sound (saut). Devotion to the Matchless One is (also) matchless.

Scholars have remarked that these thoughts were rather more reminiscent of the Nirguna Bhakti saints such as Kabir and Guru Nanak than in keeping with orthodox Islam. In another letter to Murad, who asked for direction when he found a camp follower performing namaaz 'in the manner of imitating theologians', whether he was to be 'forbidden' or 'left in his way', the prince was told that such a person was not to be forced to abandon his practices, but instead deserved 'admonition' to bring him to 'the path of reason'. These instances show that the court was moving in a direction that would have been uncongenial to a man of Aziz Koka's persuasions. And yet, there is enough evidence to suppose that it was not simply the matter of religious innovations that caused Aziz Koka to take such a drastic step in 1593. After all, a man of his talent, wealth, and stature could have continued unmolested in his jagirs and Akbar would never have tried to impose any change in his beliefs. It was rather that Aziz Koka believed that there were those at court who were advancing at his expense, who were using their position to influence the Padshah against him and his family, the Ataka Khail, and these persons were, namely, Abu'l Fazl and Faizi.

From the time that the 'dagh' had been instituted, Aziz Koka had been vocal about the injustice in undermining the old nobility in favour of persons he would have judged much more suspect. In an earlier letter written to Akbar, Aziz Koka did not only criticize the Padshah's religious beliefs but he also accused Akbar of raising Abu'l Fazl and Faizi to the position of the Caliphs Usman and Ali. 'Some of the hypocrites about Court,' agreed Badauni when writing of Aziz Koka's fall, 'told tales of him and got him removed from his post.' In his letter Aziz Koka fulminated that 'his enemies had influenced the Emperor's mind against him and sought his ruin'.

'Slanders and calumnies', he stormed, had been brought to the royal ears by 'one who is the guide of the world-adorning opinion', by which Aziz Koka was clearly implicating Abu'l Fazl. If somewhat tactless and undiplomatic, Aziz Koka remained courageous in the strength of his beliefs and in his ability, almost unique at court, to speak his mind without ever parsing his words.

Aziz Koka boarded the *Ilahi*, a ship that he had had built when he was Governor of Surat, and set sail for Mecca in sufficiently grandiose style. He left with his six younger sons, six daughters, his wives, about one hundred attendants and a great deal of treasure. When Akbar heard what Aziz Koka had done, wrote Abu'l Fazl, the Padshah, though saddened, forgave him for this impertinent disobedience. 'Inasmuch as I have trod the path of peace with Jews and Christians and others, how can I rise up against my own protegé?' said Akbar. 'I so love Aziz that though he shows evil thoughts, we can think of nothing but good of him.' Akbar wrote to Aziz Koka, recalling their lifelong bond of affection, saying that the mirza was abandoning 'two Kaabas of flesh and blood; that is, his mother and Akbar, for a Kaaba of stone and mortar'. Even the Jesuits agreed that 'though often offended by his boldness, Akbar would seldom punish him. He used to say "Between me and Aziz is a river of milk which I cannot cross".'

That celebrated bond of milk and affection now appeared before Akbar in the form of Aziz Koka's long-suffering mother, Jiji Anaga. The old woman circled the Padshah's head with a cup of water and then drank the water. 'This night I had a dream that something untoward had happened to the Shahenshah,' she told the perplexed Akbar—she had taken upon herself the consequences of her errant son's actions. Akbar fretted greatly on behalf of Jiji Anaga. 'Should his mother die of grief for his absence,' he said of Aziz Koka, 'it will be hard for him to be delivered from the harshness of the world.' He wrote letters to Aziz Koka, chastising him for not seeking his mother's permission before leaving on such a perilous journey. He urged him to return immediately to console his grieving mother. On a more prosaic note, Akbar would also have been worried about the effects of the outspoken Aziz Koka's accusations against the Padshah's religious innovations on the larger Muslim world. In the end, Aziz

Koka was undone by the venal greed of the sharifs of Mecca and, disgusted by their rapacity and considerably lighter in treasure, he returned to Hindustan. When he presented himself at court and prostrated himself before the Padshah, Akbar embraced him with tears in his eyes and immediately called for Jiji Anaga to relieve her of her 'dangerous sorrow'. Akbar restored to Aziz Koka his mansab of 5,000 and the mirza became one of the Padshah's disciples, much to Badauni's disgust:

> At this time A'zam Khan returned from Makkah, where he had suffered much harm at the hands of the Sharifs, and throwing away the blessing which he had derived from the pilgrimage, joined immediately on his return the Divine Faith, performing the sijdah, and following all other rules of discipleship; he cut off his beard, and was very forward at social meetings, and in conversation. He learned the rules of the new faith from his reverence Allami...

Aziz Koka would now remain at court till 1600, one of many formidable men and women who orbited around the Padshah and his sons, in an increasingly unstable dance of alliances and fractures, betrayals and suspicions. For Akbar was merciless with his heirs, crushing their fledgling ambitions and forcing them, through his own enormous charisma and vast net of his influence, to bend to his will. This would have, in different ways, calamitous consequences for all three sons.

THE ROAD TO THE DECCAN

On a summer's day in 1594, Akbar stood by the banks of the river Ravi outside Lahore and witnessed a magnificent sight. A thousand men strained at ropes and pulleys and, finally, a huge ship, more than 90 feet long, lurched from the banks and into the river to the loud acclamation of all the onlookers. This ship, an ocean-going vessel, had taken the labour of 240 carpenters and ironsmiths, and had required almost 3,000 planks of wood—pine and sal—for its construction. After the sarkar of Thatta had become part of the empire with the annexation of Sind, Akbar decided to make use of its port, Bandar Lahiri. Since the region lacked good timber forests, the emperor had had the ingenious idea of building ships in Lahore, which was close to the Himalayan timber forests, and sailing the ships 650 miles south through the Indus river systems to Bandar Lahiri and into the ocean. On this occasion, the ship struggled in the waters of the Ravi, which were not deep enough for a seaworthy craft. So Akbar then devised the idea of an enormous barge upon which the next ship was loaded and floated down the river to the port. Once at the port, the barge was scuttled and the ship slipped easily into the sea. Through this contraption Akbar anticipated by a hundred years the 'camel' invented in the dockyards of the Netherlands in 1688, which was a submersible barge that floated ships over the shallows. This ship was to have been the first of a fleet of ocean-worthy ships—but as the Mughal court moved away from Lahore, these plans did not materialize. It is often believed that the Mughals had no interest in a navy but the large river fleet and the extraordinary experiment with this ship from Lahore show that this was not so.

Akbar's keen interest in new technology had led to a number of innovations, as we have seen, especially in gun-making, cannon, and water contraptions. This fascination was understood by all visitors, who strove to capture the Padshah's interest by presenting new, unusual things to him. When the Raja of Kumaon arrived at Lahore, much to Badauni's contempt, for 'he had never, nor his father or grandfather before him (God's curse be on them) seen an Emperor even in imagination', he brought animals from his hill country that amazed the Mughal courtiers. He brought a yak and a musk-deer and rumours flew 'that there were men in that country who had wings and feathers and could fly'. The Portuguese viceroy of Ormuz brought two ostriches, who 'treated pieces of stone as if they were fruits'.

It was at this time that Akbar created a new genealogical seal, whose popularity would spread far beyond the Mughal Empire and would later be copied in the seal of the sultans of Sumatra. This seal was, according to scholar Annabel Teh Gallop, 'a masterpiece of imperial symbolism'. A potent symbol of Mughal power and legitimacy, this 'orbital' seal had the name of the reigning emperor in the middle, surrounded by smaller circles containing the names of his ancestors up to Timur. The seal was engraved by the master engraver, Maulana Ali Ahmad 'Nishani', who was a friend of Badauni's. His engraving skills were the least of his talents, according to Badauni, who praised his learning in 'astronomy and natural history'. So saintly and exceptional was Nishani considered to be that his dies were carried as talismans by courtiers travelling abroad, to Khurasan and Transoxiana.

Even as the ostriches and yaks roamed in uneasy proximity with cheetahs and elephants, Akbar was busy arranging two weddings which were indirectly a rebuke and a punishment for Salim. Akbar and his eldest son had been involved in an unspoken imperial tussle over the allegiance of key mansabdars and allies of the court. As we have seen earlier, Salim had been actively courting the support of men considered louche and unreliable by Akbar. Angered by Salim's jostling for power by nurturing these dangerous and unworthy friendships, Akbar now retaliated by removing two significant voices of support for Salim from within the royal harem. Salim's sisters, Shakr un-Nisa Begum and Khanum Sultan Begum, were devoted to their brother and the coterie of women from within the harem thus exercised a considerable influence in favour of Salim. Now Akbar married them to Timurid cousins—men with pretensions to independent power themselves. These ambitious men would never tolerate being vassals to the prince's cause and in this way Salim lost the powerful support of his two sisters.

Akbar added another grain of worry for Salim when he openly began to favour the prince's own sons over their father. When Khusrau was seven years old, and had just begun learning 'Indian philosophy' under one Shiv Dutt Brahman, he was appointed to a rank of 5,000, equal with high-ranking amirs of the empire such as Raja Man Singh and Mirza Aziz Koka. Further, Akbar allowed Khusrau to use the financial resources of the province of Orissa, and appointed the powerful Raja Man Singh as his ataliq. Salim's younger son, Khurram, who had been brought up by Ruqaiya Begum and the Padshah, only ever referred to his father as 'Shah Bhai', or older brother, thereby introducing a worrying degree of equality in their dynamic. Another grandson, Mirza Rustam, the son of Murad, was said to listen to the council of neither father nor mother, so ruled was he by his grandfather. Indeed, the Padshah declared in open court that he 'loved grandchildren more than sons'. These developments were a direct challenge to Salim and his brothers, demonstrating to the heir apparent and to the royal mirzas that there were other potential candidates to the Mughal throne.

The 1590s had proved to be a decade of consolidation for the Mughal Empire. In his fifties, Akbar was at the peak of his powers. After a decade in Lahore, Kashmir had been incorporated into the empire and the north-west frontier had been secured through the conquest of Sind and would cause no further trouble for the rest of the Padshah's reign. Similarly, the eastern frontier had been stabilized largely through the heroic efforts of Raja Man Singh. With Bihar secured to the empire, Raja Man Singh had turned to the neighbouring state of Orissa in 1590. Orissa had been ruled by an Afghan family of the Lohani tribe but Raja Man Singh was able to force Nasir Khan Afghan into submission and 150 elephants were part of the large tribute offered by the Afghans when they accepted Mughal supremacy. They also ceded the temple of Lord Jagannath at Puri, a powerful symbol of the Orissa rulers. The Afghans would offer some further resistance but would be conclusively beaten by Raja Man Singh in 1592. The last of the rebellions in Gujarat had been crushed as well. Now with a huge contingent of 1,823 mansabdars, with the capacity to raise 141,000 cavalrymen, the Padshah looked southwards to that most alluring of places—the Deccan.

In 1527, the Bahmani sultanate had fragmented into the five Deccani sultanates of Ahmadnagar, Berar, Bijapur, Bidar, and Golconda, making the region a great deal more politically volatile, as Persian Shias jousted with Afghan Sunnis and local shaikhzadas for dominance. In addition, there was Khandesh, with its capital at Burhanpur, a prickly buffer between the northern territories and the Deccan. When succession struggles began in Ahmadnagar in 1588, a younger sibling, Burhan Shah, fled to the Mughal court for assistance. Burhan Shah successfully claimed the Ahmadnagar throne in 1591 and re-styled himself Sultan Burhan Nizam Shah II but then resisted all efforts by Mughal ambassadors, including Faizi, to submit to Akbar, allowing Abu'l Fazl the opportunity of an irritated rant against him:

> When Burhan al-Mulk prevailed over Ahmadnagar, he should have increased his devotion and gratitude, and been an example of obedience to other rulers in that quarter. The wine of success robbed him of his sense, and he forgot the varied favours he had received from the Shahinshah.

Fortuitously for the Mughals, Burhan Shah died in 1595, leading to a fractious and unstable environment, which Akbar was now ready to exploit. He directed Mirza Murad to proceed from Gujarat to Ahmadnagar. En route to Ahmadnagar Murad met some Jesuit priests at Surat, heading in the opposite direction. This was the third Jesuit mission summoned by Akbar. The mission included three hand-picked Jesuits and was headed by Father Jerome Xavier, an older man and a grandnephew of Saint Francis, a man of 'enthusiastic asceticism' who would spend twenty-three years at the Mughal court 'sometimes in favour, sometimes in prison'. There was also Father Emmanuel Pignero, and a coadjutor* called Benoist Goes who had 'lived a somewhat dissipated life' and joined the mission 'in consequence of some youthful escapade'.

Murad summoned the Jesuits to his travelling camp where he received them in impressive state in his grand war tent, reclining on a takht. All his attendants, wrote the Jesuits, 'were standing as

---

*Helper to initiated Jesuit priests.

silent as statues with their eyes fixed on him'. Murad was gracious and informal with the three men and asked them 'if there was snow or ice in Portugal, and whether bears, hares and other wild animals were to be found there, or birds of the chase, such as falcons and hawks'. Satisfied with the answers he received, the twenty-five-year-old mirza insisted the Jesuits accept some money and then mounted an elephant, from which he jumped onto a much larger one, 'which seemed like a tower'. He was accompanied by 4,000–5,000 horsemen, 400 elephants, 40 dromedaries, 4,000 bullocks and 15 large pieces of cannon. 'He went to this war,' agreed the Jesuits, 'with good courage, and with great hopes of gaining possession of the kingdom of the Deccan. But as he was as yet inexperienced, and as he allowed himself to be guided by the young, paying no attention to the counsels of his elders, his actions were not of the wisest.' They went on to write that though 'by nature mild, kind, liberal and good-tempered', his entourage of youthful retainers 'had corrupted him', and so 'his sole pleasure was in the chase, in love-making and in running hither and thither'.

At the Mughal court, meanwhile, the situation remained turbulent and precarious between the two remaining princes. It was at this time that Daniyal was caught up one night in a most mysterious ruckus. Abu'l Fazl writes about an incident in which due to 'some carelessness on the part of the sentinels', an intruder managed to infiltrate into the royal harem. Daniyal saw a 'madman', threw him to the ground and tussled with the man, creating a huge uproar which attracted all the female guards, the 'Circassians, Qalmaqs, Russians and Abyssinians'. Akbar himself rushed upon the men and 'thinking that the prince was a stranger', seized him by the hair and was about to kill him with his sword when he realized that it was his own son. The intruder was judged to be a lunatic, and allowed to leave. This incident leaves many questions unanswered, primarily because of the near impossibility of a 'lunatic' being able to stumble upon the closely guarded imperial harem. Fifty men carrying torches were assigned simply to patrol the riverbank, day and night, to ensure no intruder could scale the fort walls to enter the palace. Moreover, if Daniyal had been in the harem officially, there would have been no reason for the guards not to recognize him, and immediately assault him as a stranger, nor for his father to attack him. Almost immediately following this incident, Daniyal's marriage was arranged with the daughter of the powerful courtier, Qulij Khan, and he was then dispatched to deal with the insufficiently submissive Burhan Shah.

This incident, during which it would appear that Daniyal had slipped into the royal harem unannounced, may lie at the heart of the famous Anarkali myth. The first mention of this possibly fictitious but enormously popular Anarkali was by the English traveller, William Finch, who came to Lahore in 1608. He claimed that Anarkali was the mother of Daniyal, and that Salim had had an improper relationship with her, causing Akbar to have her walled up alive in a fit of jealousy. The heartbroken Salim, when he became Padshah Jahangir, continued the story, would then have a tomb built for Anarkali in Lahore. There were, however, no further accounts of this story either in the Persian histories, or by foreign travellers over the next 200 years, nor indeed by Jahangir himself in his remarkably frank memoir. This did not prevent the myth from taking a tenacious hold on the imagination and enduring through the centuries to the present day.*

From the few glimpses that Abu'l Fazl allows, it appears not impossible that it was Daniyal who was involved in some indiscretion in the admittedly large imperial harem, for which Akbar then tried to remove him from the court. One might even surmise that if Daniyal did, in fact, arrange for a clandestine meeting in the harem it may even possibly have been with an influential sister or matriarch to gauge the support he had in an increasingly unforgiving battle for supremacy between Salim and his siblings. By having him married to the daughter of the extremely powerful Qulij Khan, Akbar may even have been bolstering his younger son's ambitions vis-a-vis Salim. By the time William Finch arrived at Lahore, Daniyal was long dead and it was Jahangir, as Prince Salim, that the popular imagination would remember as having tussled with Padshah Akbar. And, as with all bazaar gossip and European fantasies, the tussle was presumed to have been over sexual liaisons and the story was conflated to make of Salim the hero of the Anarkali saga.

Daniyal, however, was proving very resistant to the idea of

---

*The popular Bollywood film *Mughal-e-Azam* (1960) is based on this legend.

marching to the Deccan. Along with Abdur Rahim, the khankhanan, who had been assigned to the mission, the men dithered at Sirhind, citing inclement weather conditions, till Akbar, irritated and impatient, recalled the prince to court. It was decided, moreover, that with Murad already in the region, it would perhaps prove impossible to have both the brothers leading the expedition, exacerbating rivalries.

At the court in Lahore the mood was sombre as Faizi was dying, at the age of only forty-eight. One night Akbar went to visit the poet and held the dying man's head in his lap and tried to revive him. 'O Shaikh Ji,' said Akbar, broken-hearted, 'I have brought Hakim Ali with me, why do you say nothing?' Receiving no answer, Akbar in his despair flung his turban on the ground but Faizi was beyond the help of the courtly physicians, and even the prayers of the Padshah, and passed away from complications brought on by the asthma he had suffered from throughout his life. Badauni's cantankerous assessment of his death was that 'since he had, in despite of Musalmans, associated and been mixed up with dogs day and night, they say that at the moment of death they heard him bark like a dog'. These words, noted down in Badauni's covertly written account, are all the more graceless because Faizi had been unfailingly kind to the temperamental scholar. When Badauni had fallen from Akbar's favour yet again due to a prolonged absence from court a few years previously, Faizi had written an eloquent and sympathetic appeal to the Padshah. 'He is not avaricious,' wrote Faizi about Badauni, 'has a contented mind, is not vacillating, is truthful, straightforward, respectful, unambitious, humble-spirited, meek, moderate in his requests and entirely devoid of the dissimulation so common at court, and entirely faithful and devoted to the Imperial Court.'

About his death, Badauni wrote that Faizi left behind 4,600 'valuable bound books all corrected', that became part of the Padshah's collection. Akbar had them catalogued in three sections— the first section had 'books of verse, medicine, astrology and music, the middle place to works on philosophy, religious mysticism, astronomy and geometry, and the lowest place to commentaries, the traditions, books on theology and all other subjects connected with the sacred law'.

Badauni would not long outlive Faizi. He died the following year, probably in 1596, having completed his memoir in which he wrote of all the bitterness and misery which had stalked his life, and of the Padshah of whom he had had such high hopes and who so disappointed Badauni by not being the great Islamic leader he wanted him to be.

The last year of Badauni's life would no doubt have been made even more miserable by the presence of the third Jesuit mission at Lahore. The Fathers wrote with joy about the sincere affection with which both Akbar and Salim greeted them, embracing the men when they arrived at court. Akbar gave them lodgings in a large house close to the riverbank, under the windows of the palace, and far from the noisy distractions of the town. The night after their arrival, Akbar summoned the Jesuits and showed them the various holy images of Christ and the Virgin Mary which earlier missions had given him. Akbar was holding the paintings, wrote the Jesuits, 'as reverently as though he had been a Christian'. Seeing the holy pictures the Jesuits immediately fell upon their knees following which the little grandson of the king also knelt down and clasped his hands together. This was the young Khusrau, and Akbar was greatly pleased by his behaviour and turned to Salim and said, 'Look at your son.' Salim was extremely cordial with the Jesuits, helping them locate a suitable house within the royal grounds and showing enthusiasm for their religious activities. On a particularly sweltering day in summer, he sent the Jesuits a precious box of snow, as a mark of particular favour.

Akbar lent to the Jesuits the European books that he had acquired over the years. The books included the works of Pope Sylvester, of Cardinal Cajetan, the Chronicles of Saint Francis, the History of the Popes, the Laws of Portugal, the Commentaries of Alfonso Albuquerque, the works of Saint Ignatius, and a Latin Grammar book. Fragments of European books travelled extensively through Hindustan at this time, sometimes finding themselves in unusual surroundings. The Jesuits wrote of a Hindu raja in 1648 who was a proud possessor of a brightly illumined Portuguese book, which he had fondly hoped contained the secrets of alchemy. When the Fathers explained that it was a holy book, it caused, not altogether surprisingly, 'great disappointment'.

At court, too, Akbar showed the Jesuits exceptional kindness, sometimes making them share the royal takht with him. They noticed with pleasure that Akbar sometimes wore a reliquary around his neck, suspended by a gold chain, which had on 'one side of it an Agnus Dei, and on the other an image of our Lady'. The Jesuits described a court which had altered and become more rigid since the time the bemused Persian merchant Rafiuddin had struggled to distinguish the young and debonair Padshah from his clamouring youthful companions many decades earlier. Now the courtiers and amirs maintained a respectful distance and an attentive posture before the Padshah; where they stood in court depended on their rank. All officers, unless specifically exempted, were to be present at court. The greatest punishment for an amir was to be forbidden attendance at the darbar of the Padshah. At the darbar, the more elegant among the amirs stood with the fingertips of the left hand touching their right elbow or vice versa, and they sometimes also crossed the right foot over the left, with the toes of the right foot lightly touching the ground. When Muzaffar Hussain Mirza* arrived at court to surrender Kandahar in 1595, he prostrated himself several times before the Mughal Padshah before inching his way forward on the carpet and placing his head at Akbar's feet. Many of the new measures had been devised by Akbar in order to curtail his ambitious and wealthy courtiers by ensuring suitable deference.

The treasures now being offered to Akbar were dazzling. Although Kandahar was but a small city, it was a wealthy one as it was on the main trade route between India and Persia. Its fortress would serve as an excellent frontier base, making the Mughal Empire a truly Asian one. Muzaffar Hussain Mirza also presented the Padshah a pair of swords, girdles of gold set in precious stones, a pair of golden vases, a horse with a saddle set in gold and rubies, 150 more horses, fifty camels and four carpets 'each of which was worth 2000 crowns'.

At the same time, the Subedar of Bengal sent 300 elephants. This was no ordinary courtier, but Raja Man Singh himself, who had been transferred from Bihar to Bengal in 1594. He had recently concluded a successful expedition against Kedar Rai of Jessore,

---

*Persian Governor of Kandahar, who, having been bribed, betrayed Shah Abbas the Great and handed over Kandahar to the Mughals.

whose tutelary deity he had seized. Man Singh had seen the image of Sila Mata in a dream, floating underwater. He interpreted this omen as a divine order to seize Kedar Rai's black stone idol of Sila Mata and build a temple for it. Man Singh would bring back the idol with him when he returned to Amer in 1608 where he would have it ceremoniously installed at a small, north-facing temple in Amer palace where it remains to this day, a symbol of Kachhwaha victory. Thus Man Singh expertly denied Kedar Rai not only his own natal territory but also his protective goddess. To ensure that the goddess continued to be worshipped the way she used to be, and presumably so that she would transfer her blessings to Man Singh, he brought back ten Brahmin priests from Jessore to Amer, where they served the goddess with daily blood sacrifices; descendants of these priests were recorded in Amer till the twentieth century. This episode explains the significant and rather surprising Bengali population of Jaipur.

Man Singh shifted the capital of Bengal away from Tanda, site of Munim Khan's disastrous and plague-ridden campaign. The new site Man Singh had chosen was strategically significant. It was the site, long guarded by the Gaur Sultans, considered the ancient pass to Bengal, today in a city called Rajmahal, in present day Bihar. It was also the place where Akbar's forces had defeated the last Afghan ruler of Bengal, finally anchoring this site as a Mughal stronghold. When Man Singh first proposed the name Rajnagar for the site, clearly after himself, Akbar was not convinced and ordered the city renamed Akbarnagar, showing the limits of even a powerful mansabdar's prerogative. Today, only Mughal texts contain the name Akbarnagar while the populace still refers to the site as Rajmahal, in stubborn recognition of their charismatic Rajput patron. Man Singh also built a Mughal Jami mosque in Akbarnagar. Local traditions claim Man Singh wished to build a temple, but Akbar ordered him to build a mosque which would better suit the requirements of this distant and troublesome outpost. If that was the case, then the raja, undaunted, 'accepted this order with enthusiasm' writes Catherine Asher, for it was the largest mosque ever built by a non-imperial patron.

During the Nauroz festival at the court at Lahore, meanwhile, the amirs jostled to outdo each other in the extravagance of their presents, with one courtier giving Akbar a present 'worth at least 500,000 crowns'.

It was at about this time that Akbar brought in the dual rank of zat and sawar for mansabdars. Bowing to the reality that the mansabdars never did keep the complete muster required by their mansab, Akbar allowed for both the stipulated, as well as a lesser number. The zat rank corresponded to the personal pay and status of a nobleman, and the sawar rank was the actual number of horsemen he needed to maintain. So a mansabdar of 5,000 zat and 2,500 sawar had a rank of 5,000 but was actually only required to maintain 2,500 horsemen. Only Mughal and Rajput noblemen were allowed to employ horsemen solely from their own ethnic group. All others were required to keep mixed contingents. The high-ranked noblemen were paid generously and men came from across the empire, and from overseas, to try and obtain the best posts. At the turn of the seventeenth century, according to French missionary Pierre du Jarric, there were 2,941 mansabdars holding ranks from 10 to 5,000. Of these, some 150 noblemen held ranks of 2,500 or above, and these were the men, carefully selected for their talent and skill, who held all the important military and civil posts.

It was at this time that Akbar encouraged the Jesuits to build a church, though when the Jesuits asked for a written order to the effect, the Padshah answered with sudden sharpness that he himself was a living document and so his word was sufficient. According to the astounded Fathers, Akbar had 'banished the sect of Mahomet from this country; so that in the town of Lahore there is not now a single mosque'. Every Friday, he 'has brought before him forty or fifty boars which are provoked to fight with one another; and he has their tusks mounted in gold'. Badauni had despaired that 'ceasing to consider swine and dogs as unclean, he kept them in the haram and under the fort'. Akbar had brought in these many innovations in his spirit of reasoning, attempting to demonstrate the irrationality of blind beliefs. But to orthodox Muslims, these would have been horrifying and deeply disturbing trends.

One day in March of 1596, the Jesuits looked across the Ravi from their riverside residence and were alarmed to see a dishevelled congregation of yogis on the opposite bank, huddled in groups of ten and twenty to keep warm in the cold air. They were told that these yogis gathered in this manner every year, begging for alms. Akbar, his courtiers, and the Jesuits crossed the Ravi to speak with the yogis, the noblemen in their silks, jewels, and soft woollen shawls presenting a glittering contrast to the yogis in their drab rags. After spending a few days in companionable discussions, the yogis 'scattered and left as quickly as they had come'.

The Jesuits were thoroughly confounded by what Akbar was, or considered himself to be. '[O]ne does not know for certain what law he follows. For though he is certainly not a Mahometan, as his actions show plainly enough, and though he seems to incline more to the superstitions of the Pagans, Gentiles (Hindus) being more welcome at his court than Mahometans, he cannot be called an Ethnique (Hindu), for he adores and recognises the true God, the maker of heaven and earth, and yet, at the same time, he worships the sun.' They had noticed, of course, that Akbar began his day by worshipping the sun, repeating 'as many as a thousand and fifty names' of the sun, using a japmala made of precious stones.

This very personal search of the Padshah's for a divine truth above all the sectarian differences that convulsed his empire would perplex the Jesuits, who saw in this a sign of weakness or, even more worryingly, delusion. For they noted that 'it is more or less certain that he has a strong desire to be looked upon, and esteemed as a God, or some great Prophet'. Unlike the rigid protocol at court, they said, as had others before them, that Akbar allowed throngs of lesser folk to approach him, many of whom believed that the Padshah could perform miracles, 'healing the sick with the water with which he washes his feet'. Young women 'pay vows to him to get their children cured, or that they may have children. And if these things come to pass, they bring him offerings as to a saint, which, though they may be of little worth, are willingly received and highly valued by him.' The Jesuits were possibly unaware of the ideas of sacred kingship in which the ruler was a legitimate source of divine power—in neighbouring Persia, kings had sought to add heft to their claims by taking on semi-divine and Sufi-tinged auras.

Perhaps the Jesuits would have found some explanation for Akbar's enthusiastic adoption of Christian, Jain, and Hindu practices had they read his letter of advice to Shah Abbas II of Persia the year before. 'It must be considered that the Divine mercy attaches itself to every form of creed,' wrote Akbar, 'and supreme exertions must be made to bring oneself into the ever vernal flower-garden of "peace with all". ...Hence it is fitting that kings, who are the shadow of Divinity, should not cast away this principle. For, the Creator has given this sublime order (that of kings) for the discipline and guardianship of all mankind, so that they may watch over the honour and reputation of every class.'

The Jesuits of the third mission, like those before them, would be fatally beguiled by the possibility of the Padshah's conversion and would remain at court for decades, into the reign of Jahangir. The Jesuits in the sixteenth century, like the observers in the twenty-first century, would fail to gauge the unfathomable depths of Akbar's faith.

THE PRINCE, THE PAINTER, AND THE PRIESTS

In March 1597, as the excitement of the Nauroz celebrations gripped the city of Lahore, a catastrophic blaze, possibly caused by a lightning bolt, broke out in the palace. The tents set up in the courtyard caught fire and the flames then spread to Akbar's quarters. As the servants and courtiers watched helplessly, the roaring flames burnt to ashes the pavilion of Salim, then spread from tent to tent, till the wooden structures of Akbar's palace were crackling and crashing in the cool spring air. The fire burnt uncontrolled for two days at the end of which a throne of gold had been melted down, as had 'large quantities of draperies of cloth of gold and silk'. What distressed Akbar the most, wrote the Jesuits, 'was the loss of all his treasures, both those which he had inherited from his ancestors, and those he had amassed during his own reign'. Immediately after this disaster, Akbar decided to leave Lahore for Kashmir. Even Abu'l Fazl admitted that the Padshah now had no wish to remain in the city to celebrate the Nauroz festival and that the only way that Akbar could deal with his grief was to gather his harem and his men and leave.

Before leaving for Kashmir, Akbar decided to send the twenty-five-year-old Daniyal away from the imperial court, for the first time, to Allahabad. Daniyal was made a Hafthazari*, and given many honours. Qulij Khan was appointed as ataliq. As he had done for Murad, Akbar gave Daniyal a long list of instructions and advice. The Padshah reiterated the need for temperance, moderation, measured action, and clemency. Akbar stressed repeatedly the wisdom in surrounding oneself with worthy people and underlined the need to gauge the true nature of people. 'Consider nobility of caste and high birth as an outcome of a person's character, rather than goodness inherited from grandfathers or the greatness of the family,' wrote Akbar to his son. 'You can understand this truth by knowing that although smoke comes from fire, it has no light.' These were truths that Akbar had crafted his empire upon—the ability to judge men

---

*A mansabdar of 7,000, the highest at the time.

of talent beyond their dubious births and uncertain pedigrees; the vast confidence to promote men from outside the orthodox Muslim Sunni fold, and the iron strength with which to bestow clemency and forgiveness on those deserving it. But, as we've noted, the princes, especially Murad and Daniyal, had been shackled by Akbar himself, fostered and dependent on the seductive riches of the court, and the velvet-smooth courtesies of young courtiers with ambition. He had bound them inexorably to his own will, appointed ataliqs to govern them, even when they were men in their mid-twenties, with growing families of their own. As a result of this, they would not be the men their father expected them to be.

Soon after the fire in Lahore, Akbar, Salim, and the court proceeded to Kashmir, this time accompanied by Fathers Jerome Xavier and Benoist Goes. The Jesuits were charmed by the 'groves, orchards, gardens' of Kashmir and wrote of the flocks of wild geese which had arrived in Srinagar from the mountains of Afghanistan, settling in exotic abundance on the rivers of the capital. They wrote of wheat and rice grown in the country, and vines planted at the foot of the mulberry trees, so that bunches of pale green grapes hung from the branches of the trees. The leaves of the mulberry trees were used to grow silk worms, the eggs of which were brought from Tibet and Gilgit. The wine from the grapes was deemed 'sour and inferior' by Salim, though he recognized that 'after gulping down several goblets of it [the Kashmiris] get really excited'.

Between 1597 and 1600, when Salim would openly revolt, tensions continued to simmer between Akbar and Salim, beneath the allure of the clustering flowers and the soothing streams. Abu'l Fazl cryptically mentions several incidents when Salim or his attendants indulged in 'improper' actions, for which they were reprimanded by the Padshah, who then seemed to be overtaken by remorse, and tried to make amends. In one instance, a man who had spoken rudely to Salim had the tip of his tongue cut off on Akbar's order.

The Mughal family was struck by a number of personal tragedies at this time. Daniyal's young bride, the daughter of Qulic Khan, gave birth to a baby boy who died soon after. Murad's nine-year-old son Rustam, who was being raised by his imperial grandparents, also died. Infant deaths were remarkably common during this period, occurring all around the country as the wives accompanied their restless husbands in the travelling camps. Moosvi has studied the alarming rate of infant mortality in the Mughal family, rated as 'exceptionally high' at 43.3 per cent, especially when compared to British ducal families of the same period, which had infant mortality rates of just 31.5 per cent. The Mughal infants would have received the best care available at the time, yet they died at a far higher rate than in other countries. No suitable explanation has yet been found but one factor may have been the constant journeying these young mothers were subject to, in swaying howdahs and lurching camels.

The country was at the time in the grip of a terrible famine, which lasted for more than three years. It brought epidemics, which 'depopulated whole houses and cities, to say nothing of hamlets and villages'. Grain was so scarce 'that men ate their own kind, and the streets and roads were blocked with dead bodies'. Desperate parents were allowed to sell their children, a long-standing practice in times of famine; Badauni wrote that they could buy back their children if they were able to repay their price. In Srinagar, Akbar ordered food kitchens to be set up in twelve places. He also began the building of a stone fortress at Hari Parbat, a hill overlooking Srinagar, for which a large number of labourers were employed; through their pay, it was hoped that some of the effects of the famine would be alleviated. It was around this time, as pointed out by Irfan Habib, that Akbar began to have reservations about the practice of forced labour. He abolished fifty-five 'un-praiseworthy practices' such as being forced to clean the saffron flowers during harvest season. An inscription was put up in 1598, at the wall of the fort he built, clarifying that the Padshah 'sent one crore and ten lakh from the Treasury, and 200 Indian masters as workmen. No one did work by way of be-gar (forced labour) here. All received money from his treasury.'

Akbar wanted to remain in Kashmir through the winter of 1597 but by September the cold was so intense that 'the inhabitants of hot countries became somewhat inconvenienced' and so the Mughal party set off by boat, first to survey the saffron fields being harvested. The Jesuit party had gone ahead of the Mughals, and arrived in Lahore on 13 November, where 'the people of the town exhibited towards the Father and his companion a more friendly attitude than was their wont. It had previously been their practice,' wrote the resigned Jesuits, 'to throw stones at them and offer them other insults.'

In December of this year the Jesuits celebrated Christmas in their new church at Lahore with much fanfare, to the entertainment of the locals. They presented a play around the birth of Christ liberally interspersed with 'Indian' language phrases and this 'was greatly appreciated by the people of the country'. The people of Lahore enthusiastically joined in the celebrations, praying to the baby Jesus 'as though He were actually lying in the manger'. The Hindus, noted the Jesuits, were rather more inclined than the Muslims to join in these pastoral and mystical celebrations. But there was one exalted visitor whom the Jesuits were delighted to find was very curious about these celebrations. The Prince Salim, they wrote, 'publicly expressed his devotion to our Lord and our Lady, and placed their pictures, on which he delighted to gaze, in his own chamber'. They further noted that 'whenever the Portuguese, or other Christians at the court, obtained good copies of such pictures from India or Portugal, they used to present them to the Prince, knowing that this would greatly please him'. When the Jesuit mission had arrived at Lahore in 1595, Salim had been 'very angry with those who had conducted the Fathers, because they had not brought him any picture of our Lady from Goa'. The Jesuits had, however, brought a Portuguese painter along and Salim immediately commanded him to make a copy of the painting the Jesuits owned of the Virgin Mary. When Salim then visited the Jesuits' chapel he saw an embossed image of the baby Jesus and one of a crucifix and ordered similar ones 'to be made for himself in ivory by his own craftsmen'.

Desperate to find a convert in the Mughal family, the Jesuits failed to see that it was not so much their religion that enticed Salim, but their art. It was perhaps only when surrounded by the painters in the taswir khanas and among the gilded and glowing paintings that Salim felt himself to be the equal of his illustrious father. For Salim had an impeccable eye for beauty and his own studios, when he had become Padshah Jahangir, would create intricate worlds of immaculate precision and beauty. Salim would use the influence of the very works of art he was gleaning from the Jesuits and through them, the wider European art world, to enhance the work produced in his ateliers. And yet precisely at this time, contrary to the direction his own studios would take in the following decade, Salim began to sponsor a capriciously different style of painting.

Kavita Singh has pointed out that the paintings sponsored by Salim at this time from the late 1590s until the time he became emperor in 1605, 'harked back to Safavid painting of the mid-century and were in a style that had long been out of fashion in Akbar's atelier'. Akbar's artists, as has been seen, now expertly fused Hindustani effervescence and virility with rounded European forms and Persian restraint. But Salim began patronizing a new group of artists—recent immigrants to Lahore from Persia. These men included Muhammad Riza, Mirza Ghulam, and Salim Quli but the most well known of these was Aqa Riza, whom Salim referred to in his memoir as 'Aqa Riza of Herat'. Aqa Riza had worked for a time for Akbar's half-brother Mirza Hakim at Kabul and his accomplished style 'was marked by the use of vivid, flat colours, elaborate surface patterning, crystalline forms and elegant, elongated figures typical of Safavid painting'. Mirza Hakim had, as we have seen, styled himself as the Timurid prince par excellence to counter Akbar's 'Hindustani' image. By shunning the miniature style Akbar was developing, and patronizing painters with Persian and 'Timurid' credentials, this may have been 'an Oedipal gesture of rejection' by Salim as he looked for subtle ways to challenge his father's power.

Despite these shows of rebellion, standing up to the resplendence of his father's legacy seemed to have taken its toll, as noted earlier, for, by 1596, Salim was drinking 'twenty phials of double-distilled spirits, fourteen during the day and rest at night'. Salim would write candidly, that 'during those days my only food was the equivalent of one meal with bread and radishes. In this state no one had the power to stop me. Things got so bad that in my hangovers my hands shook and trembled so badly I couldn't drink myself but had to have others help me. Finally I summoned Hakim Humam...and informed him of my condition. In perfect sincerity and compassion he said with no beating around the bush, "Highness, the way you're drinking, in another six months—God forbid—things will be so bad it will be beyond remedy."' Following this advice, Salim started taking opium to reduce his dependence on wine.

A painter Salim was especially close to was Muhammad Sharif, the son of the Persian maestro, Abd al-Samad. Like his father, Muhammad Sharif was an accomplished painter in addition to being a poet, calligrapher, and miniaturist. His great achievement was being able to draw two armed horsemen on a grain of rice but apart from these flamboyant skills, he supervised copies of the *Razmnama* and the *Khamsa of Nizami* at Akbar's court. Muhammad Sharif had grown up with Salim, and the two young men shared an exceptionally close bond, one that Akbar failed to notice, for Salim remained covert and discreet in his dealings.

Salim would also maintain a symbiotic relationship with the other two co-patrons of the poet Urfi, Abdur Rahim and Zain Khan Koka. In 1596, Salim strengthened this bond by apparently insisting on marrying the daughter of Zain Khan Koka. He 'became violently enamoured', agreed Abu'l Fazl, and went ahead with the marriage despite the fact that Akbar 'was displeased at the impropriety'. Abu'l Fazl implied that the impropriety arose from the fact that Salim was already married to the niece of Zain Khan Koka. Nonetheless, by marrying his daughter, Salim was further binding to his cause the powerful milk brother of Akbar and the three men, united by the unlikely and whimsical bond of poetry, formed an enduring partnership.

If Salim had managed to outmanoeuvre his brothers and had them sent away from court, there still remained one man whose influence on his father the prince detested and whom Salim increasingly blamed for Akbar's disappointment in him. Abu'l Fazl was by now a mansabdar of 2,000 and a man whom many were jealous of because he had won the Padshah's trust and affection. 'He kept constant company with Akbar, like the setting to a pearl,' wrote a contemporary biographer about Abu'l Fazl, 'and nothing was done without his approval.' This made Abu'l Fazl the target of sustained rancour from other powerful courtiers but also, fatally, from Salim. It was at this time that a triumphant Salim had chanced upon Abu'l Fazl surrounded by mullahs copying the Koran and Abu'l Fazl further earned Akbar's displeasure by forwarding copies of a commentary written by his father, which did not have the Padshah's approval. In his biography Abu'l Fazl admitted that he had also angered the Padshah by not being attentive in his duties to Salim. 'From not fully considering the matter he [Salim] became somewhat angry and base and envious people had their opportunity,' complained Abu'l Fazl. 'The anger of that hot-tempered one [Salim] blazed forth, and meetings were held for troubling his [Akbar's] heart'. As soon as Abu'l Fazl earned the Padshah's wrath, he was sent off in early 1599 on the first major expedition of his life, to the Deccan, to assist Murad, for the Mughal expedition to the south would become unexpectedly complicated by the uncompromising valour and foresight of a woman.

FROM BIBI TO SULTAN

In the first forty years of Akbar's reign, the Mughal Empire had grown to a size which had been inconceivable when the Padshah took over as a distracted thirteen-year-old boy in 1556. By 1596, according to Abu'l Fazl, the kingdom was divided into sixteen subahs, each subah as large as a European kingdom of the same time and generating a revenue of over nine crore rupees. Historian George Keene has summarized Abu'l Fazl's description succinctly: In the east were Bengal and Orissa, with the capital at Gaur. Equally large were the provinces of Allahabad and Awadh while the province of Agra was smaller but strategically important, with the capital city at Agra. Malwa province had its capital at Mandu and Gujarat province brought important access to the sea. Ajmer, though a large province, was poorer than the others, while Delhi and Lahore brought in an equal share of revenue.

Four additional subahs were Multan, Tattah, Kashmir, and Kabul. The fifth, Khandesh, was yet to be incorporated for a warrior queen stood in the way of Akbar's ambition.

Charged by his father to subdue the Deccan in 1595, Murad had fetched up in Ahmadnagar to remind the heirs of the ungrateful Nizam Shah of their duties of allegiance to the Padshah Akbar. There he found a woman in charge of a chaotic and violently simmering group of suspicious and jealous noblemen, soldiers, and slaves. This was Chand Bibi, who had been married to Ali Adil Shah of Bijapur in 1564, as part of a rash of alliances made to bind the five sultanates of the Deccan in common cause against the kingdom of Vijayanagar. Vijayanagar had been defeated at the Battle of Talikota in 1565 but after that the sultanates resumed bickering and quarrelling with one another. In 1580, Ali Adil Shah had been put to death and Chand Bibi returned to Ahmadnagar, the city of her birth.

Chand Bibi was the daughter of Hussain Nizam Shah of Ahmadnagar and appeared to have enjoyed much freedom in her upbringing and in her marriage to Ali Adil Shah. She has been depicted in miniature paintings playing polo, riding horses, and hawking, always unveiled. She was a consummate diplomat and strategist, ruling Bijapur as regent after the death of her husband and dealing with the clashing aims and murderous loyalties of the region's noblemen. Now, in 1595, with the fearsome dust of the Mughal army staining the horizon, the forty-five-year-old Chand Bibi worked hard to get the various factions in Ahmadnagar to unite against the might of the Mughal Padshah of Hindustan. For, as pointed out by historians Muzaffar Alam and Sanjay Subrahmanyam, the succession struggle that arose at this point was only the final act of a complex drama involving, among others, the strong Habshi (Ethiopian) element in the state, and the Mahdavi millenarial movement at the approach of the new Islamic millennium. Chand Bibi was finally allowed to assume the regency of Ahmadnagar, and an appeal for help was sent to Golconda and Bijapur.

But all was not well within the Mughal forces. Murad, as the twenty-five-year-old son of the Padshah, should have been in command of the army but Akbar, as was his habit, had appointed Abdur Rahim, the khankhanan, as joint commander. From all accounts of the time, Abdur Rahim and Murad did not enjoy a trusting relationship. It is highly likely that Abdur Rahim, ataliq to Salim, would have become implicated in the ruinous and covert battle for succession that had begun simmering at the Mughal court.* He would have been leery of wholeheartedly supporting Salim's biggest rival, his brother Murad, and thereby ensuring a spectacular victory for him in the Deccan. The Jesuits deemed Murad the most soldierly of Akbar's sons and, by all accounts, while Murad wished to act quickly and decisively, Abdur Rahim prevaricated, advising caution and patience. By the time Ahmadnagar Fort was besieged in December 1595, even the enemy had heard of rivalry in the Mughal ranks so that a spirited defence was mounted and the siege, sighed Abu'l Fazl, 'became a tedious affair'. Even more worryingly, the enemy appeared to have found a gallant champion for themselves who, 'in glittering armour, mounted on an elephant and, disregarding the barrage from the Mughal guns and archers' visibly moved among the troops, galvanizing them. Chand

---

*Matters were further complicated by the fact that Abdur Rahim was Daniyal's father-in-law—his daughter, Jahan Begum, was married to Daniyal.

Bibi, it was agreed by all, had earned the title Chand Sultan.

Finally, with the possibility of a Golconda, Bijapur, and Ahmadnagar alliance looming, the Mughal forces laid mines at the walls of the fort of Ahmadnagar. Though the defenders were able to destroy most of the mines, the walls were breached nonetheless. The Mughals now prepared to storm the fort but Chand Sultan, 'clad in armour...with a drawn sword in her hand, dashed forward to defend the breach'. She remained in the breach all day, harrying her men to repair the wall while musket shots punctured the air all around her. The Mughals were repulsed, with Abdur Rahim, once again, being blamed for less than enthusiastic support for the army. 'The end of the day,' wrote a despairing Abu'l Fazl, 'shone upon failure.' In the end, an uneasy truce was agreed. In February 1596, Berar was ceded to Murad's forces and Chand Sultan's protégé, Bahadur, was recognized as nizam ul-mulk though he had to accept Mughal suzerainty.

At Akbar's court at Lahore, the truce was deemed to be a shameful defeat. Prince Murad's mighty Mughal forces had been defeated by what would have been considered a paltry and inconsequential party. Murad certainly seemed to have viewed the failure to take Ahmadnagar as a grievous personal failure. From now on, despite insistent orders from an increasingly worried Akbar to return to court, Murad would succumb to drink and would refuse all contact with the court or its ambassadors.

While these complicated Mughal calculations were playing out in the Deccan, further north, in what had been the badlands of Hindustan, Bir Singh Deo was resisting the path that fate had ordered for him. A later portrait of Bir Singh Deo shows us a somewhat roguish man looking ill at ease in the fine diaphanous jama of a Mughal courtier. As only the sixth son of Madhukar Shah of Orchha, his was to have been an unremarkable life, but when Ram Shah, the eldest son, inherited the throne upon the death of his father in 1592, Bir Singh Deo refused to submit to his brother. Now the old ways of succession and rule had become complicated by the new Mughal reality. As Orchha was part of the Mughal Empire, the claimants to the throne had to contend with the tumultuous world of Mughal politics. Bir Singh Deo skirmished with the forces of his brother and the Mughals throughout the 1590s. But now the Mughal Padshah was no longer the only source of imperial power, there was also Salim, and the paths of these two, impatient, and tempestuous princes—Bir Singh Deo and Mirza Salim—would cross, and they would forge a pact sealed in blood.

The volatile ambitions of all these princes, his three sons in addition to Bir Singh Deo, would finally take Akbar away from his northern capital. He would leave Lahore, never to return, for a precarious game of imperial politics was about to be played out as a new century dawned on the horizon of Mughal Hindustan.

PART 6

CROUCHING LION, RISING SUN
{1598–1605}

~

THE LAST CAMPAIGN

On a cold November night in 1598, Padshah Akbar mounted an elephant and left the city of Lahore, never to return. In the icy darkness, the Padshah had much to ruminate over. All his sons were refusing to obey his orders, though always obliquely, so it was hard to gauge where suspicion ended and presumption began. In the Deccan, it was difficult to pin Murad down, or get him to return to court. Daniyal had left his post at Allahabad and Salim was staunchly resisting his mission to march to Turan and reclaim their 'ancestral'* dominions, no doubt wary of distancing himself from a court in which the situation was so volatile with the other princes. So Akbar had decided to go to the Deccan himself, unnerved by persistent rumours of dissension and disobedience within the Mughal forces led by Murad.

Akbar crossed the Sutlej by elephant before proceeding by boat to Delhi, to visit the tomb of his father, Humayun. When he finally arrived at Agra, thirteen years after he had left the region with such haste following the death of Birbal, he decided to halt in the city and consider the weight of his sons' transgressions.

Abu'l Fazl had been sent from Agra with instructions to bring Murad back to court. But Murad was mortally ill, in body and mind. His beloved son, Rustam, had died a few months previously in Lahore, while in the care of his grandparents. That the boy, nine years old at the time, was a great favourite of the royal harem, and the Padshah, can be guessed at by the enormous grief of his family, as described by Abu'l Fazl. The child, according to him, was exceptionally gentle and sensitive and 'any excess of anger made him ill'. Though Rustam was brought up in the care of Akbar and Hamida Banu, it would appear that Murad, quite understandably, was devastated by the death of his son. Salim wrote in his memoir of a garden, the Rustam Bari, that Murad named in memory of his son near Ahmadnagar. The death of

---

*The lure of the fabled cities beyond the Khyber Pass would remain an enduring Mughal obsession.

his son, in addition to his failure in successfully taking Ahmadnagar, and thereby disappointing his father, seemed to destroy Murad. This prince, of whom so much had been expected, and who seemed to possess innate talents since, according to Abu'l Fazl, 'he had an open heart, and a liberal hand, and had courage along with gravity' was brought low in the Deccan, in the shadow of Ahmadnagar. 'When his son died,' wrote Abu'l Fazl about Murad, 'the jewel of wisdom grew dim, and he set himself down to drink in company with foolish sensualists.' Abdur Rahim had already complained to the Padshah of Murad's excessive drinking but now Murad drank even more in a suicidal bid to escape his pain. 'Excessive drinking brought on epilepsy, and he did not apply his mind to getting better. He concealed his pains and did not digest his food,' wrote Abu'l Fazl about the prince who was getting progressively more debilitated. Learning that Abu'l Fazl was on his way to meet him, Murad left Shahpur 'out of shame for his drunkenness' and marched towards Ahmadnagar, in a last, desperate bid to take the city. In Jalnapur, near Daulatabad, Murad suffered from a final fit and died of delirium tremens at the age of twenty-nine.

When Abu'l Fazl arrived at Murad's war camp near Daulatabad, he found it in a near mutinous condition. 'There I saw what may no other person see!' exclaimed Abu'l Fazl, for Murad's men were deserting in droves, from confusion and lack of pay, in a country deemed utterly foreign and unfathomable. Abu'l Fazl, with considerable aplomb and skill began to try to turn the situation around. He sent Murad's body to Shahpur with trusted servants and gathered together all the money he could to pay the soldiers and stem the exodus of men. 'The management of the troops was carried on in an excellent way,' he wrote with evident satisfaction, 'and beyond the expectations of contemporaries.' Abu'l Fazl used the 3,000 horsemen under his command to restore confidence and order among the soldiers, and thus bolstered, the retinue headed towards Ahmadnagar. Abu'l Fazl even had the time to ruminate on the irony of his condition when 'the tongue of suspicion...had sent me far away from court but (God) had made this a source of high promotion and marked them with enduring shame'.

Meanwhile, the Mughal harem had finally arrived from Lahore

to the court at Agra. Akbar was delighted and called for Khurram and Hamida Banu but his mother had terrible news for the Padshah. Abu'l Fazl's report from the Deccan had not been conveyed to Akbar, and it fell to Hamida Banu to inform the Padshah of the death of his son. Akbar mourned the death of his child, who had once shown such promise, in the discreet company of the grieving women.

After the death of Murad, Akbar wanted to dispatch Salim to the Deccan but the prince, once again, dithered. In frustration, Akbar decided to send Daniyal instead. He accompanied the prince on the first leg of the journey, giving him all the advice he could. He also gave him the signal honour of being allowed a crimson tent, a prerogative of the Padshah, and then returned to Agra.

Raja Man Singh, now Subedar of Bengal, arrived at court bringing extravagant presents including fifty large diamonds. It was Man Singh who would finally be able to integrate Bengal into the Mughal Empire within a few years. In 1602, he established Dhaka as his military headquarters and soon 'rice was being exported throughout the Indian Ocean to points as far west as Goa and as far east as the Moluccas in Southeast Asia'. Fine muslin cloth from Bengal came to be called Daka in the export markets of Asia and Bengal became 'a major producer for the imperial court's voracious appetite for luxury goods' such as raw silk and cotton cloths.

Hearing of the favour being shown to Daniyal, Salim hurried to court and wanted to present himself to his father but Akbar refused to receive him because Salim, 'from drunkenness and bad companionship did not distinguish between his own good and evil'. It finally took the efforts of Hamida Banu to soothe the annoyance of the Padshah before Salim was allowed to pay obeisance at court. If Akbar was angry at the prince for not having obeyed instructions to march to the Deccan, then Salim would have been humiliated and shaken to hear of Daniyal having been granted the royal crimson tents. The symbols of imperial authority were sacrosanct and untouchable. Objects like the Padshah's throne, his umbrella, fan, flags, and standards were exclusively his to use and were an explicit visual reminder of his blessed presence. The fluttering crimson tents, immediately recognizable to all from a distance, would have been powerfully symbolic and Salim would have clearly understood the significance of this immense honour. Akbar directed Salim to proceed to Ajmer to tend to the situation with Mewar* along with Raja Man Singh which Salim did but the prince, now bristly with frustration, began brooding over a final confrontation with his father.

Since Daniyal was not proceeding towards the Deccan with the alacrity and dedication expected of him, Akbar decided to go to Malwa, where Daniyal was camped, to organize a hunt and thereby bolster the prince's faltering resolve. Akbar's foray into the Deccan would be the last significant military expedition of his reign. With his western and north-western frontier settled and Bengal temporarily quiet, the next logical direction for the Mughal Padshah was south. Indeed, it was not only Ahmadnagar that the Padshah expected allegiance from but also the sultanates of Bijapur and Golconda, while Khandesh was already practically a Mughal dominion. As Bijapur and Golconda watched the Mughal behemoth roll towards them they looked to Safavid Perisa for assistance. From the early sixteenth century, Bijapur and Golconda had intermittently recognized a form of 'ritual suzerainty' towards the Safavids, inserting the names of their rulers in the Friday prayers. The huge influx of Iranian migrants to the Deccan in the last half of the sixteenth century had further contributed to a dynamic in which the Shia Safavids were expected to counterbalance the increasingly dangerous Sunni Mughals.

Hearing reports from Abu'l Fazl of the thoroughly impoverished state of the army in the Deccan, Akbar first dispatched orders for the Subedar of Gujarat to transfer to the Deccan all the surplus monies from the Gujarat treasury and Akbar sent 300,000 rupees from Agra too. Then, accompanied by some of the women of the harem, as well as the princes Khusrau and Khurram, Akbar left Agra for Malwa at the head of a huge army of about 80,000 to 100,000 horse, and 1,000 war elephants, in September 1599. In Malwa, the Mughal camp was joined by a sad cortège. Abu'l Fazl had organized for Murad's body to be sent back along with his harem of women and children, his treasure, and his belongings. From Malwa, Murad's body was sent to Delhi, where he joined the quiet company of his forefathers in the mausoleum of Humayun's tomb.

---

*The Sisodiyas of Mewar were the last Rajputs still resisting Mughal authority.

It was then the turn of the Kachhwaha tribe to be hit by personal tragedy. Raja Man Singh's oldest and favourite son, Kuar Jagat Singh, died suddenly at the age of thirty-two while preparing to take over the governorship of his father in Bengal. The raja was 'discomposed by grief for his son', wrote Abu'l Fazl, and Akbar sent him a horse and a robe of honour. Man Singh had lost his son, Himmat Singh, in 1597 and now the loss of his heir apparent, the son of his chief wife, Rani Kanakwati, was an almost intolerable tragedy. Rani Kanakwati suggested they build a temple in memory of Jagat Singh and so the Jagat Shiromani Temple was built outside Amer, on the main road leading from the Delhi gate of the walls to the base of Amer Fort. Built high above street level, unlike other temples, this exquisite Vaishnavite temple, as pointed out by Catherine Asher, has a mandap of red sandstone, white marble and grey stone, heavily influenced by Akbari architecture. With a gorgeous flight of white marble stairs leading to a marble gateway, the temple is suffused with an ethereal light and an air of uncontained emotion. The exterior walls dance with beguiling figures, very unlike the raja's other temples, and may have been due to the influence of Rani Kanakwati, the main patron. The raja had married many other women, including the sister of Raja Lakshmi Narayan of Cooch Behar, Abla Devi. (The Kachhwahas, however, did not recognize this marriage with a Bengali princess, so her son and descendants were always called rao sahib, never raja.) Man Singh sent Jagat Singh's young son, Maha Singh, to take over as Subedar of Bengal.

While the Padshah and the huge imperial army continued on their stately march towards the Deccan, Abu'l Fazl, who had remained in the south after Murad's death, and who had organized and stiffened the resolve of the troops under his command, began marching towards Ahmadnagar. Abu'l Fazl wanted to test the will of Chand Sultan and to see whether she might be willing to parley since, he wrote, 'though the boy [Bahadur] was considered as the ruler yet secretly that chaste lady was ruler'. The city of Ahmadnagar had been described a few years earlier by Faizi, during his diplomatic mission to the court of Burhan ul-Mulk. There was a stone fort outside the city, he had said, and there were open fields around. Water was provided to all the houses in the city via a canal which linked Ahmadnagar to a lake on the outskirts. The air was pleasant, he noted, but good melons not to be found...

> ..rather they were sour, and lacking in taste. Of all the fruits, the figs were not bad; grapes were there in abundance... Pineapples were imported in quantities from nearby and they were not bereft of good taste...roses were to be found only with difficulty, and... lacked in fragrance. On the other hand, champa and other Indian flowers were found in abundance. Sandal trees were seen there, as well as an abundance of white pepper.

The region was clearly rich in economic potential for the Mughals because Faizi also praised the excellence of the goldsmiths, weavers, and the high-quality cloth made in the Deccan.

But the fort of Ahmadnagar was a maelstrom of rivalry and suspicion. The Ethiopian Ahang Khan was camped outside the town, threatening Chand Sultan while, within the fort, she commanded the loyalty of only a few of the men. Golconda and Bijapur refused to join the fray and continued to remain resolutely neutral while the horizon grew dense with the implacable force of the Mughal army. Chand Sultan understood the limits of resistance in the face of formidable odds and, pragmatic, sent letters to Abu'l Fazl, promising help if Ahang Khan were defeated. She asked for Bir to be made her fief following which she would hand over the keys to the city and 'go to court whenever it was wished, and would send Bahadur to wait upon His Majesty'. In the midst of these negotiations, an order arrived from the approaching imperial army that Abu'l Fazl was to wait for Daniyal to arrive with his forces. With the stampeding forces of the Mughal army at her door, Chand Sultan finally decided to make overtures to the Mughals. But this was just the opportunity her enemies were waiting for. Officers of rival factions ran into the streets of Ahmadnagar, screaming that the queen had betrayed them to the Mughals, and collected an armed mob. Storming Chand Sultan's private residence the mob cut her to pieces with their swords and knives.

The Mughal army led by Daniyal, and accompanied by Abu'l Fazl, attacked Ahmadnagar Fort with concentrated effort. After a siege of four months, the moat was filled up and mines detonated at the walls which caused huge cracks in the outer defences. The soldiers stormed the breaches and 1,500 of the garrison of Ahmadnagar were put to the sword. A great deal of treasure was captured, 'valuable jewels, embroidered articles, a noble library and many other things, and 25 elephants were obtained'. Young Bahadur, the Nizam Shah, was captured and sent to Akbar, and imprisoned for the rest of his life in Gwalior Fort.

After Ahmadnagar fell, resistance spread to the countryside where two men rallied the majority of the leaderless soldiers to their standard. Raju Deccani had once been in the service of a nobleman of Ahmadnagar while the other leader was Malik Ambar. While professing allegiance to the Nizam Shahis, these two men, sworn enemies, would nonetheless harbour sprawling ambitions of their own. Malik Ambar, notwithstanding his genteel title, had had an obscure birth but his career had displayed a remarkable trajectory. Born Shambu, or Chapu, in Ethiopia around 1550, he was sold into slavery by his impoverished parents. Shambu's precocious intelligence was noticed and rewarded by his Baghdadi owners. He was converted to Islam, taught Arabic, trained in administration, and given the name Ambar, meaning 'precious jewel'. Ambar travelled with his owner to the Deccan, probably on business, and was sold to a Deccani called Malik Dabir. Fortuitously for Ambar, Malik Dabir was an Ethiopian, and peshwa to Murtaza Nizam Shah I of Ahmadnagar. Malik Dabir treated the talented young boy like a son and, upon the death of his master, Ambar became a free man. He raised an army of 150 loyal Arab soldiers and became known by the title Malik. When Ahmadnagar was taken by the Mughals, Malik Ambar escaped with his forces and devised a scheme for the survival of his family and the sultanate he had served.

In the neighbouring Sultanate of Bijapur, however, the ruler Ibrahim Adil Shah II was considerably sobered by the complete destruction of Ahmadnagar's sovereignty. He composed an ode to the memory of his courageous aunt, Chand Sultan, while also tending his congratulations to Akbar with some warmth and alacrity:

Though in battle's dreadful turmoil her courage never failed,
In the softer arts of peace she was gentle and serene.

> To the feeble, tender-hearted; to the needy, ever kind,
> Was the noble Chand Sultana, Bijapur's beloved Queen.

As for Akbar, at the head of the largest army ever mustered by the empire, he was marching to war again.

FRONTIER LANDS

At the age of nearly sixty, Akbar was still a force of nature, the wounds from a lifetime of battles soldered together by his iron will and robust health. To his sons and his soldiers he appeared indestructible, for no sign of weakness was ever allowed to show. The army that Akbar rode in front of was just as formidable as the Padshah. It would have included hundreds of camel guns and many thousand rockets, in addition to conventional artillery, muskets, and archers. 'The lumbering siege trains of the stereotypical "Gunpowder Empire," tethered to a few gigantic cannon, were nowhere in evidence.' Despite the rough and unknown nature of the countryside as they marched to the Deccan, the Mughal army was able to move huge numbers of soldiers almost seamlessly across the country because of the extensive and detailed organization of its supplies and equipment. An additional tax was levied on all agricultural holdings, the proceeds of which were used to stock thanas* throughout the empire. These could be mobilized in times of famine but, more often, were used to supply rations for the travelling army. Manufactured goods required for the army, such as weapons and ammunitions, were made in kar khanas. A great deal of the provisions were carried with the army, organized by the mir bakawal. In addition, ready cash was carried to pay for all supplies that would need to be bought along the way. Armies were accompanied by merchants, who sold commodities, and bankers, like the Marwaris in Bengal, who sometimes advanced money to the governor of campaigns to be able to finance the battles. The existence of immense mobile encampments meant that the troops did not have to forage, plunder, or requisition quarters in villages along the way, the entire army being provided for and moving en bloc.

The size of the army was meant to serve as a deterrent to all those who contemplated resistance. The sharp end of the fighting was being carried out by Daniyal, and his substantial but smaller forces. Having subdued Ahmadnagar, the prince travelled first through Khandesh,

---

*Supply depots.

and arrived at the capital, Burhanpur, where there were ominous signs that the Raja of Burhanpur, Bahadur Shah, supposedly an ally of the Mughals, was not in a sufficiently conciliatory frame of mind. Bahadur Shah did not send a message of condolence to the Mughal prince on the death of his brother, as would have been expected, nor did he come down from his imposing fortress at Asirgarh to receive Daniyal. Unimpressed with this behaviour, Daniyal proposed attacking Bahadur Shah immediately but Akbar, waiting with the bulk of the imperial forces at Ujjain, forbade him from doing so and decided to march to Burhanpur himself.

The erosion of Bahadur Shah's amity towards the Mughals had occurred because of the tragic fate of his father, Raja Ali Khan of Khandesh. With his small kingdom of Khandesh surrounded by powerful neighbours such as Gujarat, Malwa, Ahmadnagar and then, the Mughals, Ali Khan had had to play a dangerous and constantly evolving game of brinkmanship between these various parties. Torn between his allegiance to the Deccani cause, and the pragmatic reality of Mughal might, the raja finally decided to help the Mughals during one of their battles against Chand Sultan and died fighting for the Mughals. Unfortunately for Khandesh, though, the Mughals were unaware of the raja's sacrifice. As his body lay unclaimed on the sodden battlefield, the Mughals decided that his sudden disappearance signalled traitorous abdication to the Deccani faction, and plundered and looted his camp and possessions. When his body was discovered among the fallen, 'the evil-thoughted and the foolish talkers were ashamed', scolded Abu'l Fazl. The Mughals restored the raja's banners and kettledrums hurriedly and buried his body with full honours in Burhanpur. But the damage had been done and the raja's son, Bahadur Shah, now seethed at the idea of submission to Akbar.

News of Bahadur Shah's defiance had been conveyed to Akbar through Abu'l Fazl, whom the Padshah had summoned to Ujjain from Ahmadnagar. Pleased to see his old friend after an unusually long absence, Akbar raised Abu'l Fazl to a mansab of 5,000 so that this loyal but often maligned and criticized courtier could write with satisfaction of his critics that 'many sate down in the blackness of envy'.

Akbar, Abu'l Fazl, and the Mughal travelling camp now left Ujjain, and made their way south, cutting a path through the hills of the Satpura range. The accompanying Jesuit priests struggled to maintain their routine of prayers in this 'confusion worse than Babylon' but thanks to a 'portable church', they reassured their readers of being able to celebrate mass satisfactorily while on the road. When they reached Burhanpur, Akbar sent a succession of emissaries to Bahadur Shah to convince him of the wisdom in submitting to the Padshah. But Bahadur Shah sent unsatisfactory gifts of 'four inferior elephants' and did not come from the Asirgarh fortress in person to pay obeisance.

Abu'l Fazl was sent out to guard the frontiers of Khandesh by setting up military posts throughout the kingdom. Soon all of Khandesh, apart from the fort of Asirgarh, was Mughal territory. Abu'l Fazl was accompanied in his campaign by his son, Abdur Rahman, and his brother, Abu'l Barkat. During his Deccan campaigns, Abu'l Fazl seemed to grow into the full extent of his expansive, generous, and surprisingly worldly nature. It had always been his habit, on the day of the Islamic new year, to make a detailed inventory of his household items and to give away all his clothes to his servants, apart from his payjamas which he had burnt in his presence. Now, in the Deccan, 'his arrangements and establishments', wrote the author of the *Maasir ul-Umara*, 'were beyond anything that could be imagined'. He had a large tent pitched in which was a divan for the shaikh, and every day 1,000 plates of food were cooked and distributed among the officers. Outside the tent was a canopy, within which khichdi was cooked all day long for any soldier or hungry person who presented themselves. Abu'l Fazl himself, we are told, 'had a wonderful appetite', with an impressive daily intake of almost 20 kilograms of food, not including water and broth. His son, Abdur Rahman, waited upon his father while he ate, while the superintendent of his kitchen stood by. Whichever dish Abu'l Fazl served himself from a second time would be cooked again the following day. If any dish was not to his liking, he wordlessly passed it along to Abdur Rahman, who would then taste it and upbraid the cook accordingly. While Abu'l Fazl's arrangements were particularly grand, they were not exceptional. All the prominent Mughal mansabdars prided themselves on their establishments when they were travelling to war. Islam Khan Chishti, a foster brother of Salim and Subedar of Bengal, kept an austere diet of millet, vegetables, spinach, and dry rice, but ordered for his soldiers the preparation of 1,000 trays of the best quality food daily. Many employed a variety of cooks—Persian, Turani, Kashmiri, and European, with Brahmins employed to cook separately for the Hindu soldiers. Foot soldiers, naturally, often made do with a drastically simpler diet, as noted by a later traveller:

> The horseman as well as the infantry soldier supports himself with a little flour kneaded with water and black sugar, of which they make small balls, and in the evening...they make khichari, which consists of rice cooked with grain...in water with a little salt.

While Akbar remained at the Mughal stronghold of Burhanpur 20 kilometres away, Abu'l Fazl prepared to besiege Bahadur Shah at Asirgarh Fort. This fort was Bahadur Shah's 'chief stronghold', wrote the Jesuits, 'which on account of its site, and as possessing every other feature that could render a fortress strong, appeared to be impregnable, being placed on a high mountain five leagues in circuit and surrounded by three concentric lines of fortifications.... Besides water from a living well, there was within the fort sufficient wood, vegetables and other provisions to support for many years the 70,000 soldiers who defended it. It was fortified with 3,000 pieces of artillery, most of which were so large that the noise of their discharge was like terrific thunder.' Safe in the embrace of this forbidding fortress, Bahadur Shah girded himself for war.

In the early stages of the siege of Asirgarh, Akbar suffered a debilitating loss, away from the battlefield. Jiji Anaga, who had travelled with the army, as had the rest of the harem, 'died after much suffering' and Akbar was inconsolable. He shaved his head and his moustache in a sign of grief, the first time in his life he was recorded as doing so. Though he expressly forbade it, all his servants followed their Padshah, united in their grief for one of the grand old ladies of the harem who had followed every step of Akbar's turbulent life with selfless love. Even 'while old', agreed Abu'l Fazl, 'she had a youthful mind. She was very well-disposed, and gracious of heart.' Akbar carried her bier on his shoulders for part of the way to her temporary grave. Jiji Anaga would later be buried next to her husband in a jewel-like tomb called Ataka Khan's tomb near Nizamuddin Auliya's dargah, as Delhi became crowded with the ghosts of the matriarchs of the Mughal Empire. Even today Delhi sparkles with the memory of the singular destiny of Jiji Anaga's family. There is her daughter Mah Banu's tomb, known today as Abdur Rahim's tomb; there is Ataka Khan and Jiji Anaga's tomb, and there is her son Mirza Aziz Koka's Chausath Khamba, all within 1 kilometre of each other with at their spinning heart the holy presence of Nizamuddin Auliya's dargah.

Mirza Aziz Koka and Shaikh Farid joined Abu'l Fazl in the attack on Asirgarh Fort. Almost immediately, a number of officials from within the fort quietly defected. In May 1600, Bahadur Shah pretended to sue for peace by sending to the Mughal camp his mother and young son, along with sixty elephants and the offer of a bride for Khusrau. But these offers were understood by Akbar for what they were—delaying tactics while the garrison wore down the Mughal forces by attrition. Instead, Akbar countered with a diplomatic move, summoning an officer from Agra who was also the grandson of Raja Ali Khan. In the presence of this member of the Khandesh royal family, a number of the Deccani officers capitulated.

The resistance of Asirgarh, however, stuttered wearily along. As the neighbouring forts fell, Ahmadnagar and Maligarh amongst others, survivors crowded into Asirgarh, until it was crammed with about 34,000 people. The overstretched resources of the fort began to crumble and eventually led to an epidemic within the fort, eroding even further the morale of the defending garrison. Asirgarh Fort was already packed with royal prisoners, for it was the custom to imprison all other pretenders to the throne apart from the reigning monarch, and seven princes of the Faruqui dynasty were imprisoned at the time. Bribery was resorted to on both sides, to undermine the strength of the resistance, and to convince vacillating parties to desert. By this stage of empire formation, diplomacy, bribery, and intimidation were commonly resorted to because the Mughal military capability was so formidable that those ranged against it often preferred to avoid war. Bahadur Shah was a notable exception.

At one point, Akbar decided to use siege guns, but very few had been brought along with the Mughal army since it had not been thought likely that Bahadur Shah would refuse to submit. The details of the final fall of Asirgarh remain obscure, as there were contradictory reports written by the Jesuits and the Muslim chroniclers. Bahadur Shah, demoralized by the conditions within the fort and uncertain of the loyalty of his officers, finally submitted to Akbar in December 1600 and agreed to appear before him, accompanied by the Ethiopian officer, Muqarrib Khan. Akbar accepted this surrender and effectively placed Bahadur Shah under arrest, and then asked him to write a letter to the garrison, which was still holding out under the leadership of Muqarrib Khan's father, Yaqut Khan. But Yaqut Khan, valorous till the end, was furious with his son for having brought such a letter to the fort. Unable to bear the humiliation of his father's disappointment, Muqarrib Khan committed suicide. The elderly Yaqut Khan then tried to hustle one of the Faruqui princes in the fort into taking up the leadership of Asirgarh but with the tents of the mighty Mughal travelling camp snapping in the wind on the scorched battlefield outside the fort, the princes demurred. Disgusted by how low nobility had fallen, Yaqut Khan decided that such a faithless world was not for him. He retired to his haveli within the fort to bathe, pray in his mosque, and prepare his shroud. Having set his worldly affairs in order, Yaqut Khan swallowed a large quantity of opium and lay down to die.

In January 1601, after a debilitating siege of ten months, the keys of the fort were finally handed over to Akbar, and Bahadur Shah was imprisoned and sent with his family to Gwalior Fort, to join the young Nizam Shah of Ahmadnagar while all the other officers and soldiers were pardoned. Daniyal was received at Ahmadnagar in April 1601 and was given the kingdom of Khandesh, which was renamed Dandesh in his honour. The Deccan plateau would become the base for the subsequent thrust of the Mughals into the south. But that would be a task for Akbar's descendants, for the Padshah himself had more pressing and personal problems to attend to. The enemy, it transpired, had been nurtured in the very heart of the empire. Away in the north, in the city of Allahabad, Shaikhu Baba had pronounced himself Shah Salim, an incendiary and most traitorous claim.

THE ART OF REBELLION

When Akbar had directed Salim to proceed to Mewar at the time of the imperial campaigns in the Deccan, his eldest son did not do as he was ordered. He remained instead at Ajmer where 'from self-indulgence, wine drinking and bad company' he prevaricated and contemplated his future course of action. The prince was now in his thirties and was beginning to slide away from his youthful good looks. As he gave in to all kinds of indulgences, in food, in wine, and in opium, his square chin would sag into jowly folds, and his gorgeously patterned silk robes would stretch alarmingly over his increasing girth. His body wasn't the only thing about him that had languished, so had his certitude of becoming Padshah. Most worrying was the fact that his growing sons were being openly favoured by Akbar. The teenaged Khusrau, now a high mansab of 10,000, was further bolstered by the support of the powerful courtiers Mirza Aziz Koka and Raja Man Singh, through ties of marriage and blood.* With Akbar showing no signs of slowing down, Salim must have despaired of ever ruling Hindustan.

Munis Faruqui has pointed out that Ajmer, right in the centre of the Mughal Empire, was an important city geographically, straddling major trade routes and commanding access to 'both seasonal military labour and the riches of a thriving pastoral economy, especially horses and camels'. However, Ajmer's significance radiated well beyond its location and economic heft. In choosing to make his stand there, Salim must have recalled the legends of the fervour and joy surrounding his own birth, mediated by Shaikh Salim himself, and celebrated with joy and gratitude by Akbar. Ajmer, which for the entire duration of Salim's boyhood, had been the sacred destination of Akbar's yearly pilgrimages.

Having decided to revolt in the middle of the year 1600, with Akbar and the army far away in the Deccan, Salim made an unconvincing attempt to march upon the treasury at Agra. When he crossed the

---

*Khusrau was their son-in-law and nephew, respectively.

Yamuna and reached the outskirts of Agra, Hamida Banu, who was in Fatehpur Sikri, heard of her beloved grandson's erratic and suspicious behaviour. Determined to confront him, and bring him to his senses, the old lady rode out of Fatehpur Sikri to meet Salim. The prince, unable to bear her questioning gaze, hurriedly sailed away on the Yamuna back to Ajmer while Hamida Banu, heartbroken, returned to the city. Akbar had also sent instructions to his officers at Agra to guard the city against the prince and its massive gates had been slammed shut, its stone walls bristling with heavily armed soldiers.

Salim now made the decision to proceed to Allahabad where 'he seized people's fiefs, took possession of the Bihar treasury...and gave himself the title of emperor'. For the next four years, from 1600–1604, Salim set himself up almost as an independent ruler in Allahabad with a parallel court, having the khutba read in his name, appointing officers, distributing titles, and giving himself the appellation 'Shah'. The city that Salim had chosen as his refuge was no ordinary one. Built at the Triveni Sangam, the holy confluence of the Ganga, Yamuna, and Saraswati, this was a most sacred place. It was the favoured destination of those who were at the opposite end of the spectrum from the jewelled and mannered officers of Salim's court—the sadhus and yogis of Hindustan.

At first, Akbar did not appear unduly perturbed by this denouement, preferring to send the officer and painter Muhammad Sharif to reason with the prince. But Muhammad Sharif, the son of the painter Abd al-Samad, had grown up with Salim in Lahore. The two young boys had haunted Akbar's ateliers, equally enchanted by the magic of the crystal colours and the exquisite and supple forms bleeding life into the folios. In Allahabad, therefore, Salim quickly convinced Muhammad Sharif to join his own fledgling court. For Salim, this would have been a further act of conscious provocation and rebellion as Muhammad Sharif was no ordinary artist and officer. He was the son of the founder of Akbar's taswir khana—one of the two men to have trained all the future artists of Hindustan. With his impeccable Persian lineage, and his father's association with Humayun, Muhammad Sharif added heft to Salim's claim to Timurid rule.

◆

A digression would be in order here to deepen our understanding of Salim, the man who would eventually succeed Akbar as the Padshah Jahangir. Overshadowed by Akbar, he has come across as a rather unprepossessing figure and the only area in which he rivalled and even outdid his father was, as we have noted briefly, in the patronizing of artists and creation of art. In his entourage Salim already had a number of artists including the Persian Aqa Riza but also some of the younger Mughal artists, the sons and nephews of some of the grandmasters of Akbar's court such as Manohar, the son of one of Akbar's favourite artists Basawan, and Govardhan, the son of Bhavani Das. There were also Mansur, Nadira Banu, Mirza Ghulam, Nanha, Bishen Das, and Quli, as also the calligrapher Mir Abdullah, and the illuminator, Lutfullah. Indeed, the most successful aspect of Salim's rebellion was possibly the wordless challenge he extended to his father through the luminous works of arts created at Allahabad.

One of the very first paintings created at Salim's court was eloquent in its symbolism. Created by Manohar and Mansur, this striking work, called 'Prince Salim Enthroned', showed no diffidence whatsoever in plainly painting the prince as a powerful monarch. It was painted in a style that self-consciously distanced itself from Akbar's court's Hindustani melange of vibrancy, dynamism, and colour. Moreover, whereas Akbar was always painted in the midst of historical moments teeming with animals and people, in this portrait Salim is conspicuously, and grandiosely, alone upon an elaborate throne. The painting itself is in a 'deliberately flat, ornamental, Persianate style' completely at odds with Akbar's Hindustani style, and art historian Milo Beach has pointed out that it also anticipates a number of spectacular portrait series painted after Salim had become Jahangir. This was an altogether different idea of kingship than that embraced by Akbar's paintings. In the *Akbarnama* paintings, the figure of Akbar is no doubt surrounded by a respectful space but the Padshah is always swept up and surrounded by other actors. Moreover, the painters of the *Akbarnama* gave as much tender attention to a dying animal's fear or a submissive courtier's contrition as to the Padshah himself. Salim, however, is remote, untouchable, and unfathomable, his majesty is distancing and awe-inspiring. Ironically, with his long, straight nose, his square jaw, and his almond-shaped eyes, it is Salim who is shown, almost inadvertently, as the unmistakable result of a Timurid–Hindustani alliance.

The apparatus of kingship in the image 'Prince Salim Enthroned' is unmistakable. About the massive and intricately carved coronation throne, Kavita Singh writes that Salim 'was likely to have been delighted by this elaborate and outsize royal seat whose gold and lapis lazuli ornamentation perhaps mimicked on paper the materials that may have adorned the rebel prince's actual bejeweled throne'. There were minute and potent symbols in the image, 'the lion victorious in hunt, the mythical simurgh, and the falcon that soars close to the sun, all indicating the greatness of the occupant'. Understatement, for Salim, was not an option. If the image was eloquent enough then the verses surrounding the painting made their intent even more undeniable:

> In the time of the lion-capturing prince... In a year when the treasure-bestowing prince rode his steed out to chastise the Rana (the artist) Manohar, who with a stroke of his princely-approved pen would cause sperm to take shape in the womb, drew a likeness of a king as glorious as Jamshid. Mansur's brush worked on it (also). Now...without error seek the year from (the words) 'likeness of the emperor'.

The chronogram* from the painting dates it to 1601, a time when this 'Emperor' was definitely de trop, for the kingdom already had a Padshah, and Salim's claim was therefore treasonous.

Salim's pointed patronage of the Persianate style at the time of his rebellion can be seen in a work of prodigious scope and imagination—the *Muraqqa-e Gulshan*, or the Gulshan Album.† Kavita Singh has described the album as 'primarily an archival project that was designed to bring together rare and precious works on paper, including calligraphy, paintings, drawings and engravings'. These works had probably been accumulated in the imperial library through generations of Timurid rulers, as individual folios and documents. Salim began collecting these documents from the time he was at Akbar's court, many of them dating from the time of

---

*An inscription or sentence in which certain letters refer to a particular date.
†A large section of the album is today in the Golestan Palace Library, Tehran.

Humayun and before, thus allowing the prince to reach back in time and claim a legacy that bypassed his father's. At the atelier in Allahabad these folios were not just randomly put together but carefully and imaginatively assembled to demonstrate historicity, story-telling, inventiveness, and craft, much in the manner of a modern-day museum curator. Since these pages of calligraphy and paintings were of different sizes, the folios in the album had to be large, and so the empty spaces in the margins around the works were filled with images drawn by the painters of Salim's nascent studio. The paintings in the margins of this album are marvellous worlds within worlds. In them, birds tumble through the sepia pages, flowers bloom, men and women toil and labour at various tasks, muscles straining, faces grimacing, giving us a unique insight into everyday life in the seventeenth century. There are noblemen and courtiers, fantastical animals and domesticated ones, jostling and heaving with vitality. And all the pages are limned with gold, giving the album its original name, the *Muraqqa-e-Zarr-Negar*, the Album of Golden Beauty.

That Salim was using Persianate aesthetics primarily to oppose Akbar's own sensibility is clear from the fact that after he became emperor, he unceremoniously put aside both the style and the painter Aqa Riza. While Aqa Riza continued to work on the Gulshan Album, it was his son, the young Abu'l Hasan, who would become one of Salim's favourites. There is a portrait of Abu'l Hasan by Daulat, which depicts him as an intense young painter, hunched inches away from his drawing board, frowning in complete absorption. The young Abu'l Hasan quickly mastered European techniques, using a style unprecedented in Mughal India, according to Milo Beach. This incorporation of European techniques into Mughal art was what would fascinate Salim once he became Padshah Jahangir. He quickly lost interest in the flat Persianate style and enthusiastically began patronizing artists such as Abu'l Hasan. About this young artist Jahangir would write in his memoirs that '[Abu'l Hasan's] work is beyond comparison in any way to his father's. They cannot even be mentioned in the same breath... He is truly a rarity of the age.'

Despite his intense and life-long interest in paintings, Salim would maintain all his life a froideur towards the great art produced at

Akbar's court, perhaps as a silent admission that art was the only field in which he considered himself equal to his illustrious father. As pointed out by historian John Seyller, when Salim inherited his father's enormous imperial library, he made numerous notes on the margins of books praising the calligraphy or the art but he never once singled out any work from Akbar's ateliers, despite the presence of hundreds of such paintings.*

In understanding the way in which Salim manipulated artistic techniques to suit his political purposes, it becomes clear that the evolution of Mughal art did not follow a simple, linear pattern from Persian stylization to European naturalism. Scholars had earlier viewed this as a criticism of Mughal art, and cavilled about its inability to truly 'master' European techniques and remaining somewhat naïve in its use. Instead, art historians like Kavita Singh have shown that Mughal artists and patrons had a much more nuanced and flexible relationship to art styles and techniques, using different forms with virtuosity and creativity as it suited them, unhindered by a European notion of a unified style over time. 'Stylistic hybridity,' writes Singh, 'was a pervasive device in Indian painting and was the result of a conscious, willful, and self-reflexive choice.' Indeed, painters could, and did, use a variety of styles even within a single painting.

The scale and nascent ambition of the works undertaken by Salim's taswir khana at Allahabad are an indication of the changes that occurred in this city during the five years of the prince's rebellion. He introduced courtly culture into the region, and extended the influence of the Mughal Empire by bringing the area between Patna in the east and Kannauj in the west firmly within his power. Salim's court became a haven for officers who were disaffected with service within either Akbar's court, or Daniyal's, and talented men such as Abu'l Hasan Mashhadi and Khan Jahan Lodi joined the prince's entourage. As Munis Faruqui has explained it, princely rebellion and competition brought about after ending the appanage system thus actually helped in consolidating Mughal influence. It made the princes work harder at forming lasting alliances and helped spread Mughal culture into sub-imperial regions. The impact may have created minor tremors from time to time but made the Mughal Empire stronger and more

---

*I am grateful to Professor Kavita Singh for bringing this to my attention.

dynamic, for in the end, whether it was Salim or Akbar who emerged victorious, it was always going to be Mughal power that benefitted.

As news of Salim's rebellion grew more insistent Akbar decided, somewhat reluctantly, to return to his capital. The Mughal army left the Deccan in April 1601 but, outside Ujjain, Akbar made a detour to visit a hermit who had begun to gather a potent reputation for asceticism and wisdom. This was the hermit referred to by Jahangir in his memoirs as Jadrup, identified by Moosvi as one Chitrarupa, a Nagar Brahmin from Gujarat. According to the detailed description left by Jahangir, Chitrarupa lived in a tiny pit dug out of a hill, where he lived in complete darkness and solitude. 'He spends his time alone in that dark narrow hole,' wrote Jahangir admiringly. 'In winter and cold weather, although he is absolutely naked and has no clothing except a piece of rag with which he covers himself in front and behind, he never lights a fire.' Chitrarupa only left his cave to bathe in a river and to go once a day to a chosen Brahmin's house in Ujjain where he contented himself with eating five morsels of food, which he swallowed hurriedly so as to derive no enjoyment from it. Of his philosophy, Jahangir wrote that he 'had excellently mastered the science of (Vedanta), which is the science of tasawwuf', through which statement Jahangir shows that he regarded Muslim mysticism as a pantheistic doctrine similar to Vedanta. About Akbar's visit in 1601, Jahangir wrote that 'he often mentioned it with fondness'. Akbar finally reached Fatehpur Sikri in August 1601 where he spent eleven days in the company of his mother and Salima Sultan Begum before moving to Agra.

Akbar was accompanied back to Agra by the two Jesuit priests, Xavier and Pignero, who began immediately and persistently petitioning the Padshah for a written farman stating that he allowed his subjects the freedom to convert to Christianity. When the Jesuits presented themselves to Akbar in the palace at Agra, they found the Padshah surrounded by some 150 dishes full of gold pieces, which he had had made. Having examined the coins, he had them tied up in bags and deposited in the treasury. Agra Fort and all its elites were now sparkling with the lustre of what would become a Mughal obsession—precious stones. The royal kar khanas now included a bustling jewellery department, and unusual and beautiful stones from all corners of the empire were sent to Agra where they would be cut, polished, and mounted and sent to court where they were used for adornment. The Padshah and his courtiers wore them as turban decorations, necklaces, earrings, armbands, bracelets, rings and to decorate the hilt of swords and patkas. Akbar gave them as gifts to favoured courtiers, and to his wives, and distributed them to the poor on the occasion of his tuladan or that of his sons'. The stones were found everywhere...

> on royal thrones encrusted with rubies, emeralds, and diamonds;
> on the walls and ceilings of the imperial buildings, which gleam with inlaid jade, amethyst, turquoise and mother of pearl.

The Jesuits brought with them presents which were quite as valuable in Akbar's eyes: two paintings, one a portrait of Albuquerque, and the other of the Portuguese Viceroy, Ayres de Saldagna, which the Padshah was very pleased with. Akbar listened to the Jesuits' request and granted their wish for a written farman and 'for some days little else was talked of at the court' wrote the Jesuits, 'for never before had such a dispensation been granted in a (Muslim) country'. The most vociferous voice of opposition was that of Mirza Aziz Koka and uneasy rumours slipped along the corridors of the palace to the effect that Akbar was no longer a practising Muslim.

The Padshah asked the priests to translate into Persian the story of the life of Christ, which Pignero was able to do. Called the *Mirat al-Quds* (The Mirror of Purity), the book was full of the miracles and teachings of Christ, which Akbar enjoyed listening to. It was Mirza Aziz Koka who was usually asked to read the book aloud to the Padshah, and the mirza, despite his opposition to the farman, was so pleased with the book that he asked the priests for a copy for himself. Some of the other Muslim courtiers were more cynical, and scoffed that Christ's miracles were due to his excellent skills as a physician, rather than his miraculous powers. But what caused the greatest interest at court, and in the city, was a painting, a copy of the 'miraculous' Virgin of Santa Maria del Popolo, said to have been painted by the evangelist St Luke.

The Jesuits had obtained this image two years previously but had dared not exhibit it earlier because they were altogether too aware of the Padshah's voracious appetite for European paintings, and feared he would requisition it. Now, in January 1601, they exhibited their precious painting, more than 5 feet tall, in their makeshift chapel and the effect it had on the city was electrifying. People left their shops and their work to rush to the chapel and by the evening there was a jostling throng of more than 2,000 in the streets outside the chapel. With a fine flair for the dramatic, the Jesuits placed the image on the altar between two tall lighted candles and covered it with two veils. When the people saw the painting of a pale, moon-faced, melancholic Virgin pointing towards the child Jesus, who stared directly out of it, they were affected, said the Jesuits, 'in a manner that was wholly miraculous'. By the third day, the mullahs and the noblemen were rushing to see the image as well. This set off a deluge of people clamouring to view the image, 'people of every sort and quality', and those who would have 'deemed it discreditable to enter a Christian church' so that soon daily attendance had exceeded 10,000. It was not long, naturally, before Akbar heard about the image and asked for it to be brought to the palace. This the Jesuits did in the middle of the night, so as not to cause any commotion. They carried the image, draped and veiled as before, and presented it to the Padshah in his private quarters. Akbar came down from his throne and bowed low to the image, calling forward all his noblemen to approach the painting too. The Padshah told the Jesuits pointedly that his father, Humayun, would have greatly appreciated such an image if it had been presented to him but the Jesuits feigned sudden deafness and turned the conversation to other matters. Nonetheless, the Jesuits agreed to leave the painting in the palace overnight so that Akbar might show it to his wives and daughters, while telling them about the story of the Virgin Mary. All the ladies, Hindu and Muslim, came to see the image in the morning and were similarly pleased with it. On another occasion, Akbar asked for the image because the elderly Hamida Banu had asked to see it too. Akbar carried it in his arms into her quarters himself, and called for his wives and children to see it again.

Finally, having understood perhaps that the Jesuits would not relinquish the image to him, Akbar asked to borrow the painting so his artists could study it. He called for all the best artists in the city, placed the image in a well-lit position, and commanded his painters to make copies of it. As many Hindu and Muslim courtiers were in attendance, the Jesuits seized the opportunity to talk to them all day about the mysteries of their faith. Though the courtiers usually regarded 'with great contempt' all that related to Christianity, this time, wrote the Jesuits, the Muslims were 'willing listeners... and seemed to be pleased at what they heard'. Perhaps what the Muslim noblemen were best pleased at was that the Jesuits could now speak perfectly in Persian. Having struggled for many years with the language barrier, Father Xavier was now fluent in Persian, having spent years learning the language. Akbar had urged one of the Jesuits years ago to learn Persian, and advised them that a mastery of the language would 'loose a great knot that now held him bound'. By 1601 Xavier was fluent enough 'that the Persians themselves take pleasure in hearing him talk and all but admire the propriety of his vocabulary and the choiceness of his diction'. They were also much pleased with the particular accent he imparted to Persian words.

After the Padshah had kept the painting a few days, the Jesuits were obliged to part with their beloved painting twice more, to men of the highest standing in the land, one of whom was Mirza Aziz Koka. Aziz petitioned the Jesuits for the image so that his wives and daughters and daughters-in-law would have a chance to see the blessed Virgin and so these women, who had journeyed all the way to Mecca, were now able to gaze upon a holy Christian icon. This supremely urbane and cultured courtier then returned the painting, and sent his highest officer to the thoroughly unsettled Jesuits 'to assure them that his services were at all times at their disposal'. He offered to pay the Jesuits whatever sum they asked for to buy the painting, even going so far as to express an interest in 'the mystery of this Lady'. Aziz's acute interest in European books and paintings despite his scathing religious indictment of their faith should have given the Jesuits a premonition about the ultimately doomed nature of their evangelical quest. In the multi-cultural Mughal court art, no matter the imagery, reigned supreme.

As for the image itself, it was yet again in the field of art that it would have the most palpable and long-lasting effect. The naturalism and sense of perspective that Mughal artists studied through European paintings in Akbar's, and then later in Jahangir's court, would be adapted by them in innovative and creative ways. The 'harvest of heathens' that the Jesuits had fondly dreamed of in Hindustan would remain, at least in the Mughal courts, only a mirage. 'In the conversion of souls,' admitted the Jesuits ruefully, 'there was not so much progress in this land of the (Muslims) who are hard as diamonds to work upon, as in other lands where this sect has not taken root.' It might have helped if the Jesuits, with their obdurate and almost fanatical hatred of other religions, had been able to look within themselves for reasons for their failure. When the diplomatic son of Muzaffar Hussain Mirza of Badakhshan conversationally asked them what they thought of Prophet Muhammad, 'the Father told him that we regard him as one of the greatest imposters that ever entered the world'.

Over the next few months, missives fizzed between Agra and Allahabad, as Akbar tried to reason with his son and understand the cause of his dissatisfaction. In March 1602, Salim intimated that he wanted to visit his father but Akbar decided that his petition 'did not possess the glory of sincerity' and refused his son's request. Ominously, news reached the capital that Salim was headed towards Agra at the head of 30,000 horses, 1,000 elephants, and 2,000 boats. This was no longer an entourage, but an army. By the time Salim had reached Etawah, 100 kilometres from Agra, Akbar sent him an ice-cold message. The prince was either to present himself unattended to his father, else 'his peace and prosperity lay in returning to Allahabad'. Unable to countenance disobeying a direct order from the Padshah, Salim turned around.

One who was assiduously written out of the records was Harkha Bai. It is impossible to know what this Rajput queen felt about this relentless battle between her husband, the Padshah, and her son, Salim, since both Persian and Rajput records are silent on this matter. And the records would remain silent until the time her son became emperor. Up until 1605 she remains elusive, like a half-forgotten dream. But the story of a Mughal Padshah and a Rajput rani proved irresistible to the twentieth century, however, and it was mythologized in the famous Jodha–Akbar movie of 2008, the legend proving a great deal more enduring than gritty reality.

From Allahabad Salim then continued his attempts to reconcile with his father, exploring the idea of presenting himself at court. But Akbar remained unconvinced of the sincerity of the prince and decided to send for someone whose counsel and loyalty was beyond reproach. Abu'l Fazl was given orders to proceed to the court at Agra immediately, leaving his soldiers with his son in the Deccan. Responding to the Padshah's summons, Abu'l Fazl began to make his journey north with a small retinue but his path, from the Deccan to Agra, was to lead him through Bundelkhand, the territory of a certain 'highway robber' who had been waiting for ten years to challenge the cards that fate had dealt him.

AN ASSASSINATION

Abu'l Fazl marched through the hilly and broken countryside of central Hindustan with a small detachment of soldiers. After a lifetime spent at court in the intense pursuit of intellectual glory, he had now, at the age of fifty-two, proved himself almost inadvertently a most capable and courageous military commander. He had brought low one of the sultans of the Deccan; on that occasion he had shown himself able to inspire loyalty and a new sense of purpose in a force of dispirited soldiers. Now that Akbar himself had summoned Abu'l Fazl to court, there would be no dereliction in his duty to his friend and Padshah. His critics would be forever silenced, all those who had doubted his sincerity and his commitment. So when news reached him outside Ujjain that there were men waiting to ambush him en route to Agra, Abu'l Fazl was dismissive. 'I cannot flee from this unwashed thief,' scoffed the shaikh, when his long-time servant Gadai Khan Afghan suggested that Abu'l Fazl seek the help of Rai Rayan and Raja Suraj Singh and their 3,000 horses in nearby Antri. 'My gracious sovereign has raised me from the rank of a student to the lofty position of an amir, a wazir, and a general,' he is said to have added. 'On this day if I act contrary to His Majesty's opinion of me, by what name shall I be called among men…?'

Undaunted by news of what might lie in store for him, Abu'l Fazl continued on his path. Some distance outside Narwar, he was ambushed by Bir Singh Deo and a party 'of bestial, savage Bundelas', 500 horsemen in armour. Abu'l Fazl had pitched his tents and was in the white garments and gold-embroidered robes of Friday when his camp was attacked. Abu'l Fazl fought bravely, we are told. Most of his small band of companions fell trying to protect their master. Abu'l Fazl was speared in the chest as he urged his horse forward and was thrown off his mount. The Ethiopian Jabbar Khassa-khail dragged the wounded shaikh to safety. Abu'l Fazl was still alive when Bir Singh Deo rode up. The Orchha prince dismounted and, taking Abu'l Fazl's head onto his lap, told him gently that 'Jahangir' had sent for him. The mortally wounded shaikh still had enough spirit in him to abuse the 'unwashed thief' while Jabbar Khassa-khail, enraged, attacked the Rajput soldiers. But the Ethiopian was soon overwhelmed, and Abu'l Fazl too was killed in this bleak and desolate setting in August 1602. Bir Singh had Abu'l Fazl's head cut off and sent it to Salim who, it was said, was delighted and had it 'thrown into an unworthy place'.

Bir Singh Deo of Orchha was one of the many rajas and noblemen who had clustered to Salim's rebellious court at Allahabad. In Salim, Bir Singh found a sympathetic repository for his stories of unfulfilled ambitions, and the prince had promised to help Bir Singh once he had become Padshah. But the price he demanded was blood. Salim understood that if Abu'l Fazl were to reach Agra, then any chance of reconciliation with his formidable father would evaporate. In his memoirs, Salim would write candidly about this less than illustrious episode of his life. 'Shaykh Abu'l Fazl...who was outstanding in his learning and wisdom,' he wrote, 'was suspicious of me (and) was always making snide remarks. At that time, because of the corruption of mischief-makers, my exalted father's mind was quite turned against me, and it was certain that if (Abu'l Fazl) succeeded in reaching him he would create more discord...' It was necessary, therefore, that Abu'l Fazl be prevented from meeting Akbar and so, wrote Salim, 'I sent (Bir Singh) a message that he should waylay the miscreant and dispatch him to non-existence, in return for which he could expect great rewards from me.'

Salim's forthright style notwithstanding, Bir Singh's murder of Abu'l Fazl seems to have caused some dismay and disquiet amongst the Bundelkhandis themselves, for Keshavdas, Bir Singh Deo's court poet, struggled to justify this action in his *Virsimhdevcarit* in praise of his patron. Indeed, when he came to write about this fateful and bloody pact, Keshavdas proposed that Bir Singh tried to dissuade Salim from his dreadful decision:

Considering political expediency
Overcoming fear, and maintaining clarity of thought
Bir Singh folded his hands and entreated,
'You are the master and he (Abu'l Fazl) the slave, Excellency.

Is it therefore fitting to display such wrath?
A lord shows leniency towards his servants.
It is a mark of lordship to protect.
Please don't harbour a grudge against him.
Give up your anger, and make peace.

Scholar Allison Busch has demonstrated that in this Brajbhasha epic, when the prosaic and sordid truth failed to match up to exalted literary ideals of what a hero should look like, Keshavdas allowed the readers to see alternative truths that arose, inevitably, from the seam of discord in the poet's mind. In the new reality where Mughal might now controlled the destiny of Orchha and Bundelkhand, Keshavdas not only wrote of Bir Singh's unwillingness to carry out the murder, but also portrayed Abu'l Fazl in glowing terms, and described with empathy and tenderness the Padshah's deep sorrow upon learning of the death of his old friend:

Spoke Khan Azam consoling words
Which the emperor could not discern
Azam exhausted himself consoling the emperor
Who understood not a word
Who understood not a word
His eyes streamed like clouds releasing rain
Says Keshav, the cloud burst forth with maddening grief
How could the flooding ocean of the emperor's grief be contained?
Whoever tried to console the emperor over and over,
Exhausted himself with the words he spoke.

The account of the inconsolable grief of Akbar at the death of Abu'l Fazl is borne out by Persian sources. The author of the *Maasir ul-Umara* states that reports of the deaths of royal princes were never announced aloud but were wordlessly signalled through the wearing of a blue armband. So, too, for Abu'l Fazl, since no courtier dared to announce the devastating news to the Padshah directly. Shaikh Farid Bakshi Beg wore a blue armband and bowed before Akbar who was watching his beloved pigeons tumble through the sky. The Padshah took one look at the dreaded armband, uttered a loud cry, and fell to the ground unconscious. For several days Akbar was utterly grief-stricken, weeping and piteously telling Asad Beg* 'if Salim wished to be Emperor he might have killed me and spared Abu'l Fazl'. He was extremely grieved, disconsolate, distressed, and full of lamentation' wrote a shaken Asad Beg who was present at court. 'That day and night he neither shaved, as usual, nor took opium, but spent his time in weeping and lamenting.' Akbar wept for many days and 'severely censured the prince for what he had done, and often blamed him'. According to Inayatullah, who completed the *Akbarnama* after the death of Abu'l Fazl, Akbar never in his heart forgave Salim for this crime. Salim had, on the other hand, pragmatically if somewhat cynically believed that 'although this caused distress to (Akbar), in the end it resulted in my being able to proceed to kiss the threshold of my exalted father's court without fear, and little by little the bad blood between us subsided'.

These were sorely disappointing times for Akbar, for now news reached the court that Daniyal, who on his father's insistence 'had for a time given up wine-drinking, and had broken his wine-vessels, and had taken an oath against drinking wine', had once again descended into abject alcoholism in the Deccan. He sent recommendations and strong instructions to the prince through Abdur Rahim, that he should desist from alcohol, and urged him to remember the tragic fate of his brother Murad. But Daniyal seemed to find it easier to be seduced by the temptations that his companions were only too willing to offer to him, now that they were far from the stern gaze of his father, the Padshah. Instead, in an example of princely equivocation, Daniyal sent his father as peshkash a 15-carat diamond and a 120-carat ruby.

The members of the harem were devastated by news of the assassination of Abu'l Fazl and terribly anxious over the fate of their favourite prince, Salim. They realized that a sacred line had been breached and that the Padshah had been deeply wounded by this cowardly blow. Hamida Banu and Gulbadan now appeared before Akbar to plead for forgiveness on behalf of the prince. Akbar finally relented, never able to refuse these two ladies. He ordered that Salima Sultan Begum be sent to Allahabad to convince the prince of his father's forgiveness and to bring him to court. Taking one of Akbar's

---

*Abu'l Fazl's officer and friend.

elephants, Fath Lashkar, a special horse, and a robe of honour, Salima Sultan set off to bring back the prodigal son.

As for Gulbadan, at the age of eighty-two, she had carried out her very last duty to the Timurid line with grace and dignity, as she had done her whole life. Gulbadan had led a turbulent, exciting and unfettered life. She had lived a life surprisingly without constraints, true to her family, and her God. As she lay in her room, her old companion-in-arms, Hamida Banu, stood over her, trying to revive her friend, repeatedly calling out to her in terms of endearment, 'Begum Jio!' Gulbadan opened her eyes one last time to say to the weeping Hamida Banu, 'I am dying, may you live long', before dying on 7 February 1603.

After reaching Salim's court, Salima Sultan sent happy tidings of her mission. She assured Akbar that she had 'cleansed the stain of savagery and suspicion from his heart' and that she was bringing his son back to Agra. As the penitent convoy reached the capital, Salim sent a message begging that his grandmother Hamida Banu be sent out to accompany him into his father's presence. No doubt Salim believed that in view of the abhorrent assassination of Abu'l Fazl, he would require the sacred protection of the Padshah's mother herself. With Hamida Banu guiding him by the hand, Salim came into his father's presence and threw himself at the Padshah's feet. Akbar hugged his son and placed his own turban upon the prince's head but things had changed irrevocably between them and it appeared that Akbar found it hard to truly forgive his son for his latest unforgivable crime. Salim offered his father a peshkash of 12,000 mohurs and 977 elephants, of which Akbar accepted only 350, a subtle sign of his icy displeasure. When Abu'l Fazl's brother and son appeared at court soon after, to lay their grief and their tears at the Padshah's feet, in addition to a peshkash of three elephants, four swords, seven strings of pearls and decorated vessels, the atmosphere must have turned distinctly uncomfortable for the prince. Not long after, Salim left Agra, ostensibly to pursue the Rana of Udaipur, but instead went to Fatehpur Sikri, and asked his father's permission to return to Allahabad. This Akbar was constrained to do and Salim proceeded to Allahabad, 'joyfully, drinking wine, and pleasuring himself'.

Despite his fervent commitment to enjoying himself with wine and song, grief entered Salim's house. Khusrau's mother, the Rajput princess Shah Begum, daughter of Bhagwant Das, grew weary of the atmosphere of suspicion and hostility between her son and her husband. Khusrau, bolstered by the support of the powerful Kachhwahas including Shah Begum's brother, Man Singh, had become a tangible alternative to those looking for a Padshah to succeed Akbar, and Shah Begum was undone. 'She constantly wrote to Khusrau,' said Jahangir in his memoirs, 'and urged him to be sincere and affectionate to me. When she saw that it was of no use and that it was unknown how far he would be led away, she from the indignation and high spirit which are inherent in the Rajput character determined upon death.' Unable to live the life of unstained honour she had promised herself, Shah Begum took opium and embraced the immortality that the Rajput code demanded of her. 'Several times she went berserk,' agreed Salim, 'it must have been a hereditary trait since her father (Raja Bhagwant Das) and brothers (Man Singh, Madho Singh) all used suddenly to appear quite mad, but after a while they would calm down.' Salim found himself laid low by the death of his first bride, who 'would have sacrificed a thousand sons and brothers for one hair of mine'. He was unable to eat or drink for days, and the pleasure leached out of his life. Akbar, who had been very fond of Shah Begum, heard of his son's distress and sent him a kind letter of condolence accompanied by a robe of honour and his own turban. The turban would have been a comforting sign to Salim of the Padshah reconfirming Salim's position as his heir apparent.

While Salim mourned his Rajput bride, the artists in his taswir khana began works in a style shaped by the holy city the images were born in. After all, just below the great fort of Allahabad were the banks of the holy rivers which were haunted by the sacrifices, penances, practices, and truths of the yogis and mystics. The Sufi mystic Shaikh Muhammad Ghaus of Gwalior had compiled a Persian translation of an Arabic text called the 'Pool of Life', rendered as the *Bahar al-Hayat* (Ocean of Life) describing twenty-one yoga asanas. Salim had this text copied and illustrated in his ateliers and his artists drew the different asanas of yoga, showing the fascination that Salim had for the unusual contortions that he must have observed for himself from the fort of Allahabad. Akbar, too, had had paintings of yogis made but in Salim's case, the artists would have had regular access to practising yogis on the banks of the river and the images in the *Bahar al-Hayat* are careful and sensitive portrayals of the yogis in different asanas, surrounded by their meagre possessions. The paintings are simply drawn, with a light wash through which the underlying paper can be seen. They are the works of young artists, still immature, and are the grist around which the pearls of Jahangir's mature taswir khana would be created.

While Salim was consoling himself with drink, opium, and art in Allahabad, unsatisfactory reports continued to arrive in Agra from the Deccan, not only of Daniyal's intemperate drinking but also of his inability to rapidly secure a bride, as promised, from Ibrahim Adil Shah II of Bijapur. A Mughal officer, a Persian scholar called Mir Jamal-ud Din Husain Inju Shirazi, had been sent some years previously to Bijapur as an envoy to arrange for the marriage between Daniyal and Ibrahim Adil Shah II's daughter. But Ibrahim Adil Shah II had decided, in the face of overwhelmingly superior Mughal forces, in addition to gritty resistance from splinter Ahmadnagar groups led by generals of genius such as Malik Ambar, that 'passive resistance through diplomacy' was the most prudent path for him. There were those, such as the Flemish jeweller Jacques de Coutre, who found himself at the Bijapur court at this time, who were scathing about Ibrahim's strategy. Coutre referred to him as 'a coward, tyrant, arbitrary, and obsessed with his harem of over 900 concubines "who served him carnally when he wished"'. When Akbar finally grew frustrated at Mir Jamal-ud Din's inability to resolve the matter, he sent Abu'l Fazl's officer and friend, Asad Beg, to get to the truth of the matter. The truth, it turned out, was money, for Asad Beg found out that Mir Jamal ud-Din was making some '300,000 or 400,000 huns' of money which corresponded to a jagir of 5,000, and that even Akbar's trusted courtier Abdur Rahim was receiving sums of money to delay matters. Akbar had instructed Asad Beg to bring back the mir without even 'giving him a chance to take a sip of water'.

Before Asad Beg arrived in Bijapur, however, he met with a personage who was recognized as someone whose support should be cultivated—Malik Ambar. The Mughals gifted an elephant and a fine horse to the Ethiopian general as well as a farman from Akbar.

Malik Ambar, it was said, was looking for patronage and was eager to serve the Mughal emperor. In fact, wrote Asad Beg approvingly, 'Ambar was the paragon of all good qualities, a wonderful host, and a devout Muslim. Indeed, were he to recount the qualities of this bravest of the men of the time, a chapter—nay, a book—would be needed.' Relations, at this time at least, were entirely cordial between Malik Ambar and the Mughals.* After feting the Mughal envoy with suitably grand festivities, Malik Ambar sent his young nephew to accompany Asad Beg as he headed south towards Bijapur.

When Asad Beg arrived in Bijapur, he discovered a prosperous, thriving city. The bazaars impressed the Mughal envoy with their variety of exquisite goods. He wrote of jeweller's shops with daggers, knives, mirrors, and necklaces all in the shapes of birds studded with jewels. There were liquor shops filled with crystal bottles and china vessels. There were fruit shops groaning with 'fruits and sweetmeats, relishes, sugar-candy and almonds'. The bazaar was spotlessly clean, a long boulevard lined with green trees. He described even more enchanting enticements next to the bazaar:

> On another side may be a wine-merchant's shop, and an establishment of singers and dancers, beautiful women adorned with various kinds of jewels, and fair-faced choristers, all ready to perform whatever may be desired of them. In short, the whole bazar was filled with wine and beauty, dancers, perfumes, jewels of all sorts, palaces and viands. In one street were a thousand bands of people drinking, and dancers, lovers and pleasure-seekers assembled; none quarreled or disputed with another, and this state of things was perpetual. Perhaps no place in the wide world could present a more wonderful spectacle to the eye of the traveller.

Throughout his stay, Asad Beg was deluged with gifts, ceremonies, and hospitality, in an attempt to delay his meeting with the Adil Shah. He was given 200,000 huns, which he refused. He was feted with

---

*Malik Ambar went on to become a very prickly thorn in Jahangir's side. He founded the city of Khadki as a base to mount resistance to the Mughals under Jahangir, and would use guerrilla warfare very effectively to continually harass the Mughal troops. Khadki would be renamed Aurangabad by Aurangzeb after the death of Malik Ambar in 1626.

'food, drinks, and fresh fruits, and good fodder for the animals' and two noblemen were sent daily to 'converse' with Asad Beg and keep him entertained. Finally, there was an extravaganza of entertainment in which two firework castles were set alight, and 'it was as if they were firing arms and cannon at each other, with an effect that was so frightening that the horses, camels, and elephants in Asad Beg's camp entered into a panic'. But Asad Beg was made of sterner stuff than the mir and, unflustered, he insisted on a meeting with Ibrahim and the providing of a bride for Daniyal. After a great deal more resistance, the Bijapuri bride was obtained and she was married to Daniyal in the Sona Mahal of Ahmadnagar Fort. Asad Beg took back to the Mughal court a royal female elephant called Chanchal, who had been the mate of the sultan's favourite elephant, Atash Khan. Chanchal, in true royal style, required two Akbari maun of wine a day, preferably Portuguese. Asad Beg also returned with a valuable Arab horse called Chini, in addition to a fortune in jewels and precious objects.

At Bijapur, Asad Beg may have been surprised to discover the presence of Farrukh Beg, erstwhile painter at the Mughal court. Around the year 1597, Farrukh Beg, for some unexplained reason, left the Mughal court for the Deccan where he joined the service of Ibrahim Adil Shah II. Mughal sources, not overly anxious to elaborate on this absence, never mention the departure of Farrukh Beg from the court. Perhaps he, too, was offered gifts he found himself unable to refuse in Bijapur or perhaps the painter found the atmosphere of hostility between the Padshah and Salim uncongenial but, whatever the motivation, Farrukh Beg's sojourn in the Deccan left a permanent imprint on Deccani art. Art historians have marvelled at 'his transformation from a competent but conventional painter into a master of great imagination and unique style during his Bijapur years', a transformation all the more remarkable as the painter was now over fifty years of age. Farrukh Beg would only return to the Mughal court in 1609, bringing with him a denser colour palette and a certain fascination for outsized tropical flowers.

Also of consequence to the Mughal court was the introduction of tobacco by Asad Beg who had discovered it in the Deccan. He brought back with him a handsome pipe whose stem was studded with jewels and enamel at both ends. The mouthpiece was made of crimson carnelian and the burner was made of gold. Asad Beg also had a fine betel bag which Ibrahim Adil Shah II had given him and this he filled with tobacco and arranged everything pleasingly on a silver tray to present to the emperor. Akbar's curiosity was piqued, and he asked to try some. When he had begun smoking the tobacco his physician rushed to his side and, taking the pipe away from him, asked Mirza Aziz Koka to try it first. 'This is an untried medicine,' grumbled the physician, 'about which the doctors have written nothing. How can we describe to Your Majesty the qualities of such unknown things?' But Asad Beg chided the physician saying, not unreasonably, that 'every custom in the world has been new at one time or another'. Akbar was pleased with his reasoning and told Aziz Koka, 'Truly, we must not reject a thing that has been adopted by the wise men of other nations merely because we cannot find it in our books, or how shall we progress?' After trying tobacco once, however, Akbar did not adopt the practice, though all the noblemen of the court were soon smoking it appreciatively.

At his rebel court at Allahabad, Salim continued to torment the Jesuits at Akbar's court with signs of great favour. He had spoken in private with the priests earlier, in such intimate terms as to 'justify the hope that God would one day work in him a great miracle'. He sent a servant from Allahabad carrying carpets and other gifts for the priests and requested them to leave his father's court for his own. He wrote letters to them in his own hand, signed with a cross, and told an Italian visitor to his court that 'I have a very great affection for the Lord Jesus'; saying these words, Salim showed the Italian a cross of gold suspended from his neck. He sent the priests further gifts—an image of Jesus in silver and a reliquary attached to a golden chain with an image of Jesus in enamel, which he had worn himself. Through all these signs Salim excited in the Jesuits the hope that he might convert to Christianity. However, Salim's real reasons for his interest in Christianity were the twin possibilities of obtaining great European art and undermining his father.

Under the glittering veneer of art, the potentially explosive game of succession was taking its toll on the major players. The undercurrent of jealousy, hate, and suspicion spilled over as courtiers stoked their secret hopes and certainties suddenly turned to dust.

AN ENGLISHMAN AT THE MUGHAL COURT

In the early 1600s, in Allahabad, Salim found himself surrounded once again by his easily complicit companions. Crumbling under the strain of the ongoing tussle with his father, the prince became erratic and volatile. Already addicted to wine, Salim now added opium to the mix when he found the intoxication of alcohol insufficient. Under the influence of these intoxicants Salim's behaviour, ever unpredictable, now descended into sadism. In one particularly horrific incident, a writer of Salim's developed an infatuation for one of the pages at court who, in turn, was smitten with a third servant. The three young men, hoping to find a more clement atmosphere at Daniyal's court, fled to the Deccan. When Salim heard of this, he became enraged, his anger no doubt exacerbated by mention of his brother Daniyal, who was now a hated rival for the throne. He had the men captured and brought to court where the writer was skinned alive in his presence, one servant was castrated, while the third young man was subjected to lashes.

When he heard of this grotesque incident, Akbar said, 'We have conquered a whole world by the sword, but until today we have not ordered so much as a sheep to be skinned in our presence. My son is unimaginably hard-hearted if he can have a man skinned in his presence.' But Akbar too was not altogether immune from violent anger at this time of enormous uncertainty and tension. On one occasion Akbar emerged from his chambers after evening prayer earlier than was his wont. He walked into the diwan-e-aam to find all the servants missing except for one unfortunate lamplighter who was curled up, asleep, next to the Padshah's throne. Furious at this dereliction of duty, Akbar had the lamplighter thrown from the tower of the palace where he 'was dashed into a thousand pieces'. Still fuming with anger, Akbar severely reprimanded the officer whose watch it was and the other officers on guard. Tellingly, Akbar sarcastically ordered them to join Salim's camp instead of remaining at Agra. It appeared that under the strain of this succession drama, even Akbar's iron self-control was cracking.

As for Daniyal, reports kept arriving from the Deccan confirming his increasing dependence on alcohol and deteriorating health. Akbar sent Hakim Fath Ullah, son of Hakim Abu'l Fath, to tend to the prince. He then sent him a horse named Ayas and, finally, when physicians and gifts failed to work, sent an old milk mother from his childhood to try and turn things around. An idealized miniature of Daniyal from this period shows a tall, broad-shouldered, fair-complexioned young man with features reminiscent of his father's Turkic legacy. Salim, too, would later admit that Daniyal 'was a young man of fine stature, with a pleasing build and good-looking'.

After Salim had returned to Allahabad his penitential attitude towards his father, and his seeming remorse over the murder of Abu'l Fazl seemed to have evaporated. He ignored his father's summons to return to Agra and pay obeisance to the Padshah. Instead, he continued to posture as an independent monarch. Akbar decided that the time for open confrontation with his son had finally arrived. In August 1604 he sailed down the river at the head of a fleet of boats while his imperial gold-embroidered tents were pitched near Fatehpur Sikri. However, no sooner had the boats sailed off down the river than they got bogged down in the loamy sand due to the low water levels. As Akbar disembarked and waited in the royal tents, news arrived that Hamida Banu was critically ill. Akbar thought that this was a diversionary tactic, since Hamida Banu had been very disapproving of Akbar setting off to fight the prince. He sent Khurram to assess the truth behind this illness but 'heart-striking news came... that she was seriously ill and that the physicians had given up issuing medicines'. By the time Akbar rushed back to the capital, Hamida Banu was unconscious. She had asked to see her own imperial copy of the Ramayan upon her deathbed one last time. Scholars believe she may have had a particular affinity for the trials of Sita because of her own long-ago period of exile in Rajasthan, and then Persia, when she had had to abandon her infant son. Hamida Banu died on 29 August 1604, leaving behind considerable treasure in her house.

Mughal noblewomen were becoming increasingly wealthy, as the empire itself became a colossus. Unlike most of their contemporaries in the west, as well as other Hindustani women, Mughal women owned their property and wealth outright, and could spend it according to their wishes and ambitions. They were given a monthly stipend, in addition to annual gifts upon different occasions, such as birthdays, Nauroz, military victories, and could further grow their wealth by investing in trade, or through inheritance upon the death of a wealthy relative or courtier. Hamida Banu had requested that her fortune be divided between her male descendants.

At the death of Hamida Banu, we are told in the *Akbarnama*, the harem was in complete disarray. And we may believe the truth behind this as the women grieved for this remarkable matriarch of the Timurids, the last of them. All her life she had been unconstrained by the changing norms which required women to be invisible and voiceless. From the time she had jumped onto the horse which had carried her to Persia alongside Humayun, Hamida Banu, fiercely independent, had never stopped journeying according to her whims and her spirit. She was often to be found unexpectedly setting out from a capital, accompanied by her constant companion, Gulbadan, to surprise her son on one of his campaigns or hunts. While Akbar and the court had spent long years in Lahore, Hamida Banu waited, undaunted, in Fatehpur Sikri, tending to her affairs and travelling relentlessly between the two imperial cities. On his part, Akbar had accommodated her every desire and had gloried in worshipping her publicly, like he would the Divine.

Now, for the second time in his life, Akbar shaved his hair and moustache, in the manner of the Hindus, and all his courtiers followed suit. Akbar set the bier of his mother's body upon his shoulder, and carried it out of the city whence it journeyed, for the last time, to Delhi, to be buried in the family mausoleum of Humayun's tomb. At the end of the day, Akbar came out of his chamber and stood quietly for a moment; the servants were surprised by his pensive and calm demeanour. It is impossible to know the Padshah's thoughts as he watched the storm clouds gather over Agra and contemplated the loss of another indispensable figure from his life. He had lost many of the men and women who had accompanied his turbulent journey through more than sixty years of turmoil and grace. Only Salima Sultan Begum, Ruqaiya Begum, and Aziz Koka, from the old guard, remained at court. Now there was a new generation of Mughals, especially the princes Khusrau and Khurram, who accompanied their grandfather everywhere, and witnessed his terrible, corrosive rage at the disobedience of their father.

In November 1604, Salim finally decided to present himself at court, to offer his condolences to his father and to assess the depth of the Padshah's disaffection. Salim would write in his memoirs that this was one of the decisions he was most proud of, despite determined opposition from his own courtiers. Salim brought fabulous gifts with him as peshkash, including a diamond worth a lakh of rupees, 200 elephants, and trays full of gold mohurs. All Salim's courtiers similarly presented themselves, and offered gifts. Conspicuous by his absence was Muhammad Sharif, who had been sent as ambassador by Akbar to Allahabad, but who had then betrayed the Padshah's cause. Muhammad Sharif would stay away from Agra till Salim became Padshah, unable to face Akbar's disapproval and disappointment.

Akbar hugged his son and received him with warmth in the diwan-e-aam but later appeared convulsed by distress which would not be contained. He had Salim arrested and brought to him and struck him on the face, upbraiding him for all the intolerable crimes he had committed. Salim hung his head in shame and fear, weeping. Akbar had him imprisoned for a few days in the inner apartments, and forbade the servants from bringing him any wine. All the while, Salim's sisters rushed from father to son, attempting to bring peace and, eventually, Akbar forgave Salim, brought opium to the abject prince himself, and restored his lands and command to him.

That Akbar was conflicted over the decision to forgive Salim is clear, the murder of Abu'l Fazl still an unresolved and festering wound between them. But Akbar was running out of choices for an heir to the Mughal throne, for the reports from the Deccan about Daniyal's alcoholism were increasingly dire. Akbar had appointed guardians to watch over Daniyal and keep him away from alcohol but his companions found ways to smuggle in wine nonetheless, sometimes inside gun barrels, and sometimes in the bladders of animals. When Abdur Rahim managed to enforce the ban, Daniyal began to weep, and implored his servants to 'let them bring me wine in any possible way'. He called his musketeer, Murshid Quli Khan, and gave him his favourite gun and told him to bring some wine inside it.

The musketeer did as he was bid, and 'poured double-distilled spirit into the gun, which had long been nourished on gunpowder and the scent thereof, and brought it. The rust of the iron was dissolved by the strength of the spirit and mingled with it, and the prince no sooner drank of it than he fell down.' Daniyal died of alcohol poisoning on 11 March 1605, at the age of thirty-three. It is not an impossibility, though, that Salim managed to have his brother poisoned. Daniyal's dependence on alcohol was well-known, and it would have been relatively easy for Salim, with his wide network of allies, to have poison slipped into his drink. We are told that Daniyal's widow, Jahan Begum, the daughter of Abdur Rahim, grieved him endlessly and lived each day of her long widowhood as if it were the first.

Salim stayed on at Agra, watching his father and his sons with cold calculation. In a discordant use of his energies at such a politically sensitive time, he appeared to become entirely obsessed with art, and the European paintings that were available to him. He continued to maintain warm relations with the Jesuits, 'with whom he was on very intimate terms'. They offered the prince holy images and Salim had all their images copied by skilled painters. He had the image of a crucified Christ engraved on to a large emerald, the size of a quail's egg, which he liked to wear attached to a gold chain. Xavier offered Salim a copy of the *Mirror of Purity*, which the prince read cover to cover. It was only the arrival of an Englishman, one John Mildenhall, that disrupted these harmonious exchanges.

The arrival of Europeans from now on in ever greater numbers was due to the enormous allure of the manufactured goods of Hindustan. Indeed, the entire region was one of the great centres of manufacturing, much before the coming of the Industrial Revolution in Europe. Traders and adventurers came in search of textiles and other finished goods, and visited cities that were among the wealthiest and most populous in the world, with a huge task force of skilled artisans. Indian swords and daggers were considered the best to be had anywhere and steel bows, requiring high quality metal and exceptional craftsmen, were a specialty of the country*. Travellers were also amazed at the purity of the coins manufactured.

---

*Steel bows were an Indian invention—less flexible than the composite bow, but more durable, and not prone to warping and splitting in India's hot and humid climate.

When an attempt had been made in 1599 to set up a charter for the establishment of an East India Company in London to exploit the great possibilities for trade in the East, Queen Elizabeth I had been reluctant, unwilling to risk the peace treaty with Spain which appeared imminent. But there were some who were emboldened at the thought of the riches to be made in the 'Orient', one of whom was a certain John military innovations. Mildenhall believed that if he could secure trading privileges with the East to equal those of Portugal, he would be richly rewarded for his troubles when he returned to England. With this unshakeable optimism, a letter from Queen Elizabeth I, and the fictitious title of ambassador, he set off for Hindustan.

At the Mughal court in Agra, Mildenhall was well received by Akbar, to whom he presented twenty-nine good horses as well as 'diverse jewels, rings and earrings to his great liking'. Akbar appointed a house for his use and was his usual gracious self. It may be assumed that Mildenhall was plausibly dressed as a sixteenth-century European ambassador despite being a charlatan. In the midst of one of the most cosmopolitan and opulent courts in the world, in which the men would have been wearing flowing jamas in the finest of materials, delicately embroidered and jewelled, Mildenhall would have been a study in stiffness and angles. He would have been wearing hose and breeches on his lower body to present his calves to their full advantage, male legs at the time being a particular measure of beauty. He would have been wearing a doublet, and a padded overshirt, and outsized, attached sleeves. The piece de resistance of this outfit would have been the frilled ruff around the neck that had recently become de rigueur for men and women of fashion, and perhaps even a mandilion, or cloak, draped negligently over one shoulder. Luckily for all concerned, the codpiece had recently gone out of favour.

When Mildenhall submitted his request for England to be granted the same trading privileges as Portugal, and to be allowed, in addition, to attack Portuguese ships if required, Akbar listened to the Englishman carefully and then sent for the Jesuits. After Akbar's conference with the Jesuits, 'whereas before we were friends', wrote Mildenhall about his relationship with the court, 'now we grew to be exceeding great enemies'. Not surprisingly, the Jesuits, who were always working in accord with the commercial and secular arm of the Portuguese enterprise at Goa, would have been aghast at this English Protestant interloper. When Akbar asked them about the matter, wrote Mildenhall, 'they flatly answered him that our nation were all thieves and that I was a spy, sent thither for no other purpose to have friendship with his Majesty but that afterward our men might come thither and get some of his ports, and so put His Majesty to much trouble'.

When Mildenhall grew upset at the Jesuits' intemperate language, Akbar spoke to him kindly, told him not to be sad, and sent for fine European garments for him from his own wardrobe. Mildenhall waited for months for trade concessions. All this while, he wrote, the Jesuits 'day and night sought how to work my displeasure'. According to the Englishman, the Jesuits bribed Mughal officers with large sums of money and attempted to sully his reputation and his honour with all those who were well disposed towards him. They even lured away Mildenhall's translator, an Armenian who had worked with him for four years. Pinheiro, especially, described as 'a thoroughly unscrupulous man', worked tirelessly to discredit Mildenhall.

A later European writer wrote not much more glowingly about Mildenhall:

> John Mildenhall was not an estimable character. In plain words, he was a dishonest scoundrel. He cheated, or tried to cheat, Akbar with an assumption of ambassadorial dignity; he tried to cheat the Company with concessions that, in all probability, he had never received; he ended up by cheating his own employers, the merchants in London.

Nonetheless, admitted the writer, 'he was a pioneer of Anglo-Indian enterprise, no less enterprising than his many enterprising successors'. So insignificant was Mildenhall's passage at the Mughal court that there is no record of it in the Persian chronicles. Of his 'enterprising successors', however, the impact was all too evident. Ever since King Philip II's Spanish Armada had been defeated in 1588, the domination of the Iberian powers was doomed. Now, the English and the Dutch, with their vastly superior navies, and an increasing demand from the

English middle classes for luxury goods, looked determined to step into the breach. The English were especially buoyed since the return in 1580 of Francis Drake, after having successfully circumnavigated the globe. Depending on whose account you listened to, Drake was a privateer, pioneer, slaver, or pirate. King Phillip II was especially furious at his plundering of Spanish ports in the Caribbean, but Elizabeth I knighted Drake, and England was ready to inhabit her role as the next big European colonizing power.

The road that brought these English traders and adventurers to Indian shores was a decidedly bloody one. The sixteenth century had seen England convulsed by religious wars, resulting in her being considered something of a rogue and a pariah by Catholic Europe. As a result, the excommunicated* Elizabeth I found herself looking to more exotic shores for trade and commerce. She had sent one Jenkinson, a mercer by profession, to quite a list of dignitaries with grand titles including Shah Tahmasp of Persia, Suleiman the Magnificent of the Ottoman Empire, and Ivan the Terrible of Russia, seeking trade concessions. The particular goods that England was looking for at the close of the sixteenth century were sugar, spices, silk, cotton, and potassium nitrate, for gunpowder. These were the goods, and this was the climate, then, that brought a group of merchants to the court of the 'Great Mogor'.

In 1600, Elizabeth I had granted a charter to a group of 218 men, the Governor and Company of Merchants trading to the East Indies[†], allowing them a trade monopoly with the 'East' for fifteen years, and giving them the right to wage war where necessary. Unlike their competitors, the Dutch, the Portuguese, and the French, this small group of unprepossessing merchants would prove to be spectacularly successful in extending these original powers into something so vast it would make of England, at the time a somewhat underwhelming, insignificant power, the greatest empire on earth in a couple of centuries. As historian William Dalrymple describes it:

> Over the next 200 years [the EIC] would slowly learn to operate skilfully within the Mughal system and to do so in the Mughal

---

*This also, not inconsequentially, led to England being released from Papal edicts forbidding trade with Muslim nations.
†The East India Company was founded in 1599.

idiom, with its officials learning good Persian, the correct court etiquette, the art of bribing the right officials, and, in time, outmanoeuvring all their rivals...for imperial favour.

With the crumbling of Mughal power in the eighteenth century, and after Nadir Shah's coup de grâce in 1739, it would no longer be imperial favour that the EIC would court, but imperial power.

But in 1605 the Mughal Padshah was entirely unconcerned with the doings of his inconsequential English guests. Well pleased with Asad Beg's fine selection of unusual and eclectic souvenirs from the Deccan, Akbar directed him to return to Bijapur, Golconda, Bidar, and the Carnatic with instructions to search specifically for rare elephants and jewels. 'You must not relax your efforts,' clarified the Padshah, 'as long as there is one fine elephant or rare jewel out of your grasp in the Dakhin.' Before leaving, Akbar told Asad Beg to stay on a while at the court to enjoy the fine spectacle of elephant fights he had ordered. But Asad Beg declined the invitation and left the court, a decision for which he was later very grateful, for the elephant fight would trigger violence during which subterranean channels of jealousy and hate would erupt spectacularly.

DEATH OF AN EMPEROR

In 1605, the Mughal court at Agra found itself with an excess of pretenders to one of the richest empires in history. The Mughal Empire was now greater in size than any previous Indian kingdom bar the Mauryan Empire of nearly two millennia previously, far larger than any contemporary European kingdom, and was rivalled only by China. It included much of modern-day Afghanistan, Pakistan, and Bangladesh, including the cities of Kandahar, Kabul, and Dhaka. It contained Kashmir and southern Kumaon, and stretched upto Bengal, along the line of the Himalayas. In the Deccan, Khandesh and Ahmadnagar were part of the empire and Berar was about to be incorporated too. Up to a million people lived within it. A hundred metric tons of silver flowed every year into the empire, brought in by Europeans buying manufactured goods and natural resources from Hindustan, which accounted for about a quarter of all global manufacturing. The Mughal emperor, with an annual income estimated at 100 million pounds* was by far the richest ruler in the world. An army of 300,000 men defended the empire's frontiers while an additional four million infantry could be mobilized when required. This glittering empire, moreover, had been carefully reconfigured as an indivisible entity, to be inherited by a single, chosen heir. No longer would brothers be equal co-rulers, with lands of their own. This was now an empire worth fighting and dying for.

With Daniyal dying in March 1605, Akbar had only one living son remaining but, importantly, he had two grandsons. Akbar had always favoured Salim's younger son, Khurram, finding in him an heir true to his own talents and ambition. In this the Padshah showed himself an excellent judge of character, as Khurram would go on to become Shah Jahan, most magnificent of all the Mughals of Hindustan. But in 1605, it was eighteen-year-old Khusrau who was a legitimate contender for the throne, an alternative for those who had serious doubts about the temperamental, cruel, and volatile Salim.

---

*Over 10 billion pounds today.

With his own father still living, Khusrau's pretensions to rule should never have been a possibility at all. Tall and elegant like his father, but with his Rajput mother's large eyes and pleasantly regular features, Khusrau's challenge was suddenly made alarming for Salim by the support of two powerful noblemen. Mirza Aziz Koka, Khusrau's father-in-law, was already present at court, long rehabilitated since his wanderings in Mecca. Now, in August 1605, Raja Man Singh arrived at court from his subah in Bengal and Akbar raised his mansab to 7,000, previously reserved only for princes of the royal blood. For a while, Man Singh was the highest mansabdar of the land, Hindu or Muslim. His grandson Maha Singh had also been raised to a mansab of 2,000. Man Singh was the maternal uncle of Khusrau and now the prince had the backing of the two most powerful and influential noblemen of the empire. The fifty-five-year-old Man Singh, barrel-shaped and eternal like the forbidding stone fortresses he liked to build, had earned for himself something of a fearsome reputation. All the mansabdars of the empire used amils, officers who were appointed to collect revenue on their behalf from their jagirs. Man Singh, it was said, almost never had to remove or transfer an amil but if anyone happened to complain about one of his officers, the 'poor fellow's house was given to plunder and taken over and with his neck tied he was thrown over the Rohtas Kalan fort. The transfer of the amils was the termination of their life and wealth.'

Even though the raja had spent decades away from the court, his informers would have kept him updated about the unravelling relationship between Akbar and Salim, and he would have been confident of the Padshah's support for Khusrau as his heir. The raja now tried to have Salim removed from the court by suggesting to Akbar that he be appointed to take over as Subedar of Bengal. But Salim, long accustomed to playing these deadly games at court, refused to move and leave the field open for Khusrau.

These simmering tensions were suddenly exposed in all their raw violence, aberrantly, during an elephant fight. Akbar had arranged for a fight between Chanchal, Ibrahim Adil Shah II's elephant newly arrived from the Deccan, and Giranbar, Salim's elephant. Salim and Khusrau were watching the fight seated on their horses while Akbar was looking down from the jharoka window, young Khurram seated next to him. While the two animals were crashing into each other and raising fine yellow dust, the servants of Salim and Khusrau got into a bitter fight, and 'both overstepped the bounds of courtesy'. A group of Salim's unruly servants threw stones at the imperial elephant-keepers, striking one of them on the forehead and wounding him. Akbar was furious at the behaviour of his heirs, no doubt exacerbated by the thought that they were now openly and shamelessly fighting for the throne while he himself was still very much alive. He sent Khurram down from the fort with a message for Salim: 'Shah Baba (Akbar) says this elephant bout is yours. What is the reason for violence and immoderation?' Salim pleaded ignorance in the matter and the elephants were finally cooled down by driving them into the placid waters of the Yamuna. The insolence of Salim and his servants' behaviour seemed to deeply wound the Padshah.

At the age of sixty-three, Akbar's iron will and his grasp on the affairs of state were finally slackening after almost half a century of rule, his indefatigable and elemental strength suddenly undone. Miniatures depicting him at this time show that his hair had turned white, his expression melancholic, almost resigned. In October of the year, as the summer heat finally resolved itself into a golden light, and the champa trees flowered in the gardens, Akbar fell ill with a stomach complaint. He called his physician, Hakim Ali Gilani, and the hakim, not unwisely, told the Padshah to fast for a day before trying any medicines. The next day, a simple broth without ghee was advised but Akbar felt very weak and retired to the zenana quarters. Khurram tended to his grandfather tirelessly for the entire length of his illness. For ten days no treatment was attempted as the physicians argued among themselves about the best possible remedy to administer to their exalted patient. Weak and debilitated, Akbar continued to present himself for darshan at the jharoka window, as the nobility and townsfolk struggled to think the unthinkable—that the Padshah might be coming to the end of his days. Akbar continued to issue orders by dictating hukms to his writers but, after ten days, a fever began to rage in the Padshah's weakened body. As the physicians decided on who should treat the emperor, probably terrified of doing more harm than good at this critical stage, Akbar favoured Hakim

Ali. 'We have trusted our person to Hakim Ali,' he said. 'Let him do what he thinks right.'

In the midst of this maelstrom of suspicion and distrust, the thirteen-year-old Khurram demonstrated an unshakeable resolve, remarkable in someone so young. Khurram was, at this age, a smooth-faced boy with his father's long, straight nose and the large eyes and arched eyebrows of Rajput miniatures. 'Prince Khurram stood his ground in the midst of enemies and malevolents,' wrote an admiring Salim, 'and refused to leave his grandfather. Although his mother sent numerous messages telling him that it was not prudent to remain where he was in such a time of turmoil and unrest, he remained firm and refused to leave.' It is easy to imagine Jagat Gosain's concern for the well-being of her son. She had been separated from him all his life, as he had been entrusted to Ruqaiya Begum. Now, as the possibility of reclaiming him became a reality at last, his life appeared to be in danger. Rumours of poisonings and assassinations spread among the courtiers and the townsfolk, and people began distancing themselves from the dying Padshah. Khurram was commanded to present himself before his parents, which he did, but then told them 'as long as there is a breath of life left in my grandfather, there is no possibility of my being separated from him'.

Raja Man Singh, meanwhile, continued in his efforts to eliminate Salim as a contender for the throne. He tried to have the prince arrested when Salim came by boat to Agra Fort but, alerted, Salim was able to evade his would-be captors and sailed back down the Yamuna to his haveli. The raja then gathered the powerful noblemen at court within one of the halls of the palace and made an impassioned speech asking them to support Khusrau against his violent and unpredictable father. But the other nobles demurred, led by Sayyid Khan Baraha, who had long been a supporter of Salim, and Shaikh Farid, the mir bakshi. They said, among other things, 'that to give the throne to a son during the lifetime of his father was not in keeping with tradition, particularly the canons and customs of the Chagtai clan from which the Mughal royal family was descended'.

Day by day Akbar's health continued to fail. Hakim Ali's medicines worsened his condition and the Padshah was finally unable to rise from his bed, even to attend the daily darshan. It was at this stage that the Jesuits went to see Akbar, hoping for a deathbed renunciation of all his religious wrongs and a final acceptance of Christianity. As they entered his chambers they were convinced that they would find the emperor moribund, penitent, keen to make his peace with Jesus Christ and embrace the Lord. 'But they found him,' they wrote in amazement, 'amongst his captains, and in so cheerful and merry a mood, that they deemed the time unsuitable for speaking to him of the end of his life, and decided to await another opportunity. They came away, fully persuaded that he was making good progress, and that rumour, as ordinarily happens when kings are sick, had exaggerated the seriousness of his malady.'

But the emperor *was* dying and it was only his supreme will that enabled him to engage with his men and his courtiers as he lay on his sickbed. Man Singh in desperation now attempted to seize the treasury of Agra but Ram Das Kachhwaha had posted his Rajput soldiers to defend it, and once again Man Singh was foiled. The raja accepted that he had failed in his mission to secure the throne for Khusrau and prepared his boats to sail away from Agra to Bengal the following morning, along with his nephew.

All this while, Salim had been shut up in his quarters outside the fort, paralysed by fear and uncertainty. He debated the idea of meeting his father, although he was certain that he would be accused of poisoning him. He was enraged by reports of the attempt to place Khusrau on the throne, and suspected everyone around him of treachery and malice. Finally, triumphant news arrived in Salim's quarters of the decision of the nobles. Shaikh Farid soon arrived, along with the Sayyids of Baraha, and many other courtiers to assure the prince of their support. All they asked of Salim, according to possibly suspect reports by the Jesuits, was that he be a true guardian of Islam, and that he not punish his sons or those who had supported them, and this the prince agreed to do. As news spread of this momentous decision, people streamed into Salim's house, eager to align themselves to his ascending star. A crestfallen and abashed Mirza Aziz Koka too appeared, late in the evening, greatly ashamed, but Salim was magnanimous with him now that the Mughal throne was finally within reach. Assured of the safety of his nephew, Man Singh, too, would bring Khusrau back to his father.

The next day, Salim presented himself at last to his dying father. Akbar opened his eyes and gestured for Salim to be given the imperial turban, robes, and dagger. Salim then performed the sijda, prostrating himself on the floor one last time to lay his head at his father's feet. Seeing that his father was quite beyond speech, Salim hustled his son Khurram out of Agra Fort and took him back with him to his own palace.

In the waning day of Tuesday, 26 October, with the premonition of winter in the cooling air, the world shrank around Padshah Akbar. All his great noblemen had died, or had left him, sensing the dawn of a new age. Some had quit brazenly, others had melted quietly away, all of them distancing themselves from the aura of death. It was the turn of Hakim Ali to desert, fearing the wrath of the harem and he hurried to join Shaikh Farid. Akbar's great taswir khanas were still, the artists dispersed. Some would join the next emperor but many would be dismissed, left to peddle their wares in the bazaars and markets of the kingdom. Some would join the households of the great amirs of the empire like Abdur Rahim, Aziz Koka, Bahadur Khan Uzbek, and also Raja Man Singh, Raja Bir Singh Budela, Rao Surjan Singh Hara of Bundi, Rana Amar Singh of Udaipur as well as the rulers of Jaisalmer, Jodhpur, and Bikaner. According to art historian Asok Kumar Das, 'these rulers constructed new palaces in their respective capitals, borrowing heavily from Mughal architectural features, like elaborate murals on the inner walls of chambers and halls and decorations on the dados, facades and chhajas. Traces of these are still visible in the forts and palaces of Amer, Orchha, Datia and Bundi and on the garden pavilion of Bairat and in some havelis in Rajasthan, Haryana, Punjab and Madhya Pradesh.' Akbar had dreamed of a new Hindustani identity, merging local painting idioms with a Persian one. This luminous Mughal identity would slowly sweep back into the provincial courts, brightening up local styles like a comet trail of light.

As the Padshah began to slip away, the last of the imperial workshops grew quiet, and the noise of construction ceased. Only the animals remained: the lumbering elephants, the watchful cheetahs, and the loving dogs. The harem remained, too, and a small coterie of attendants, faithful to the last. The Jesuits had again tried one last time to visit with the Padshah but had been turned away by the noblemen guarding the fort. The Jesuits maintained that the attendants were trying to remind the dying emperor of the need to utter Prophet Muhammad's name, but that he had made no sign of assent, though Akbar tried to whisper the name of God. What they may have been doing, however, was quietly muttering the kalima. 'In the end,' wrote the Jesuits, for fear of the Padshah 'neither [Muslims] nor [Hindus] nor Christians would claim him as theirs, so that he had the prayers of none.'

At the other end of the city, in Salim's palace, there was a great clamour. The raucous crowds of men were loud in their congratulations and frenzied in their attempts to carve out a place for themselves in the new order. The drummers began a deafening, frenetic beat but Salim quickly silenced them, so as not to disturb the peace of his father's last night with such obscene joy. The world knew the Padshah had died when a long, aching lamentation spilled out from the women's quarters in the middle of the watchful night. Akbar had died and there was now a new emperor, Padshah Nuruddin Muhammad Jahangir.

RISING SON

The effect of Akbar's death on the general population, after almost half a century of rule, has been movingly described by Banarsi Das, an Agra merchant who was in Jaunpur at the time of the calamity. Most of those living in the empire at the time would have had no recollection of any Padshah other than Akbar. 'The alarming news of his death spread fast and soon reached Jaunpur,' wrote the merchant. 'People felt suddenly orphaned and insecure without their sire. Terror raged everywhere, the hearts of men trembled with dire apprehension, their faces became drained of colour.' Banarsi Das was so overcome by the news that, shaking and light-headed, he fell down a flight of stairs and smashed his head on the stone floor. His parents rushed to tend to him, and he was 'quickly put to bed with my sobbing mother at my side'. In the rest of the city...

> The whole town was in a tremor. Everyone closed the doors of his house in panic; shop-keepers shut down their shops. Feverishly, the rich hid their jewels and costly attire underground, many of them quickly dumped their wealth and their ready capital on carriages and rushed to safe, secluded places. Every householder began stocking his home with weapons and arms. Rich men took to wearing thick, rough clothes such as are worn by the poor, in order to conceal their status, and walked the streets covered in harsh woollen blankets or coarse cotton wrappers. Women shunned finery, dressing in shabby, lustreless clothes. None could tell the status of a man from his dress and it became impossible to distinguish the rich from the poor. There were manifest signs of panic everywhere although there was no reason for it since there were really no thieves or robbers about.

It was feared that without the Padshah's benevolent and powerful shadow over the country, chaos would ensue. The terror and insecurity are palpable in Banarsi Das's description, no doubt aggravated by the possibility of an outright war of succession, but so too is a genuine sorrow and distress. After ten days of anarchy and fear, the city breathed a sigh of relief when a proclamation arrived informing the populace that there was now a new Padshah, Sultan Nuruddin Jahangir, whose 'power reigned supreme and unchallenged throughout the land. This news,' added Banarsi Das, 'came as a great relief and people heartily hailed the new King.'

The years of rebellion and uncertainty for Jahangir before he finally became Padshah at the age of thirty-six, after having once been the chosen prince, seemed to have taken their toll on the new emperor. Jahangir's son, Khusrau, immediately went into open rebellion; his actions were entirely predictable and yet Jahangir crumbled. 'What's to be done?' asked the Padshah piteously when he was given this news. 'Should I set out on horseback, or should I send Khurram?' After the trauma of his own battle for succession with Akbar, Jahangir could not countenance rebellion in his son. He decided to pursue his errant son himself, and in his autobiography, the Padshah would write that this was one of the greatest decisions he ever took in his life. So rapidly did he set off against Khusrau, wrote Jahangir, that he did not wait for an auspicious hour, forgot to take his daily dose of opium, and was only able to consume one spoonful of a delicious biryani he was given en route. When Jahangir eventually captured Khusrau, he was unforgiving with all those who had supported his son, indulging in extremes of cruelty. He had some of these supporters trampled by elephants, and some were suffocated to death by being sewn up inside donkeys' skins. Others were lined up by the side of the road to Lahore and impaled, while a weeping Khusrau was placed on an elephant and made to witness the suffering of his wretched followers.

And yet, despite his own long rebellion and overt rejection of Akbar's Hindustani vision, when Jahangir became Padshah he did, in fact, demonstrate that he was, in many ways, his father's son. In an ostentatious display of his regard for justice, one of his first orders was to have a golden 'chain of justice' strung from Agra Fort to the near bank of the Yamuna so anyone looking for redress could ring the bells on the chain and summon the emperor. He forgave the amirs who had acted against him, and he also persisted with Akbar's Rajput policy, finally overcoming the very last bastion of resistance to the

Mughals—the Sisodiyas of Mewar—by allowing them concessions never before granted to the Rajput clans. Jahangir exempted the Sisodiya rulers from sending daughters in marriage to the Mughals and from attending the Mughal court.*

Despite a few displays of religious bravado such as the destruction of the temple at Kangra, Jahangir continued to show a remarkable eclecticism in his religious views, which prompted Edward Terry, an Anglican at his court, to say that at the Padshah's court, 'all religions are tolerated'. He continued to patronize the family of Shaikh Salim Chishti, he was devoted to the hermit Jadrup, and he allowed three sons of Daniyal to be baptized, to the abiding delight of the Jesuits, though within four years the boys had reconverted to Islam. Many of the symbols Jahangir continued to use were derived from Akbar's notion of sacred kingship, such as the halos he was always painted with, and the Sufi pirs he assiduously courted.

Akbar's extreme experiments with the orthodox tenets of Islam were bound to provoke a backlash, and it was during Jahangir's reign that a certain disgruntled element began to coalesce. The Naqshbandi saints who had lived in Hindustan during Akbar's reign felt keenly their lack of influence and prestige with the Padshah and the nobility, especially when compared with the spectacular success of the Chishti pirs, and the past glory of the Naqshbandi lineage in Central Asia. Naqshbandi thinkers such as Khwaja Baqi-Billah and his disciple Shaikh Ahmad Sirhindi launched a determined attack on the Hindustani Chishti pirs, accusing them of distorting the message of the Prophet. According to these men, there could be no foolish attempt to abandon the sharia or to seek unity between believers and infidels. There were noblemen at court who were seduced by this message, including Mirza Aziz Koka, Shaikh Farid, Qulic Khan, and even Abdur Rahim. In a letter to Aziz Koka, Shaikh Sirhindi wrote that 'the degradation of Islam has reached a stage that infidels mock Islam and its followers, and without let or hindrance celebrate their own pagan rites in bazars, whereas Muslims are restrained from the observance of their religious law'. He was critical of many of Akbar's rules, such as the prohibition of cow slaughter, seeing in them an

---

*He balanced these favours by having life-size statues of Amar Singh and his son Karan Singh on horseback placed below the jharoka window at Agra, a sign of submission.

attack on the religious freedom of Muslims.

According to historian Irfan Habib, it was not only a desire to purify Islam but a seething malaise and resentment at the way non-Muslims were treated that drove men like Shaikh Sirhindi. Wrote the shaikh: 'The glory of Islam consists in the humiliation of infidelity and the Infidels. Anyone who held an Infidel in esteem caused humiliation to Islam. Holding in esteem does not simply mean that one pays respect to them or seats them in a higher position: giving a place to them in one's company, sitting and talking with them, all are means of showing esteem. They (the infidels) should be kept at a distance like dogs.' In fact the real purpose of the imposition of jiziya was not just to tax non-Muslims, but 'to humiliate them (the non-Muslims); and this humiliation should reach a stage where owing to the fear of the jiziya, they should not be able to wear good clothes and should never enjoy any peace of mind and be in constant dread and fear of the King's taking away of their property'. In a claustrophobic definition of acceptable orthodox behaviour he said that 'the harm of being in the company of a heretic exceeds that of being in the company of an Infidel: and the Shias are the worst of the heretics'. In a court where Hindus and Persians had held the very highest honours, and formed a substantial part of the mansabdari, Shaikh Sirhindi was denouncing the very fabric of society that Akbar had fashioned—it was the spirit of sulh kul that the shaikh was railing against.

After the death of Akbar, it has been said that Shaikh Sirhindi had a great influence on a penitent Jahangir, who recanted all the more tolerant policies of his father. This was untrue. Jahangir would have Shaikh Sirhindi imprisoned, and hand him over to the care of a Rajput officer in order that 'the confusion of his [Shaikh Sirhindi's] senses and the disorder of his brain be reduced a little'. The scaffolding of Mughal rule as laid out by Akbar would prove to be durable, used by many future Mughal rulers. To the Mughals, writes Muzaffar Alam, 'the Sharia came to be synonymous with the namus-i ilahi (divine law) the most important task of which was to ensure a balance of conflicting interests, of harmony between groups and communities, of non-interference in their personal beliefs'.

The enduring appeal of Akbari ideals can be seen in the long life many of them had. The prohibition of cow slaughter and the killing of peacocks continued to be enforced into the early years of Shah Jahan's reign. The jiziya remained continually abolished for about a hundred years following Akbar's second 1579 edict, including in the first twenty years of Aurangzeb's reign. When it was revoked, many among the Mughal elite disapproved of this, including Jahanara Begum, Shah Jahan's daughter, and it was finally abolished again in 1712.

These measures were organically linked to the great success of Akbar's policy of including non-Muslims in the ruling polity of the empire, and indeed the proportion of Rajput and other Hindus in the ruling class continued to increase steadily after Akbar. In the last twenty years of Aurangzeb's reign, the Mughal elite included 31.6 per cent Rajput and other Hindus of 500 zat and above because of the recruitment of Marathas and other Hindus from the Deccan. This diverse nobility meant that even for Aurangzeb, who would make many more overtures to the orthodox factions of Islam, the duty of a ruler, as he stated in a letter to Rana Raj Singh of Mewar in 1658, was to ensure 'that men belonging to various communities and different religions should live in the vale of peace and pass their days in prosperity and no one should interfere in the affairs of another'.

That Aurangzeb had to make this appeal to garner support reflects how deeply evocative the supra-religious theory of sovereignty was in the Mughal governing class. Opposition to the reimposition of the jiziya was based on the tenacious idea of the Mughal emperor as ruler of both Hindus and Muslims, the duhu deen ko sahib, which Akbar had so openly embodied. But if these ideals proved resilient, then the Mughal Empire itself began to crumble, in the way of all empires. After the death of the last of the Great Mughals, Aurangzeb, a number of weak rulers came to power while regional players and zamindars like the Rohilla Afghans, the Marathas, and the Nawabs of Awadh grew militarized, powerful, and loyal only to themselves.

In this chaotic and uncertain environment, with no powerful central authority, the European trading companies saw an opportunity to entrench themselves. By the early seventeenth century, the Dutch East India company (1602) joined the EIC, followed by the Danish (1616) and French (1664) overseas trading companies, initially conducting trade purely on Mughal terms. But as competition between the European companies over Indian textiles grew more fierce, they became militarized, training their own sepoy-armies which were then co-opted by regional powers in exchange for revenue-collection rights which were slowly ceded to the Europeans. The French and the English eventually got locked in skirmishes, and then deadly battles over trading rights, mirroring the Anglo–French wars that were taking place at the other end of the world. Finally, by 1757, the French had been summarily outmanoeuvred, the true rapacious ambitions of the EIC were exposed at the Battle of Plassey, and a new empire proudly unfurled its colours on the embers of the Mughal one.

◆

As we have seen in this book, Akbar was an extraordinary monarch in many ways. He was a military leader of genius, an exceptional judge of men and character, a builder of cities, a connoisseur and patron of art, an innovator, a man of reason and ideas, and much more. But perhaps the secret of his enduring appeal, that which made him 'the Great Mughal', and one of only two Indian monarchs to be considered 'Great', was his determination, in a complex and complicated land, to negotiate a place of dignity for each person and every creed through the idea of sulh kul. 'He was a prince beloved of all, firm with the great, kind to those of low estate,' wrote Monserrate, 'and just to all men, high and low, neighbour or stranger, Christian, (Muslim) or (Hindu); so that every man believed that the King was on his side.'

The only other Indian emperor to command such widespread acclaim is Ashoka, of the third-century BCE Maurya dynasty, with whom Akbar shares a number of intriguing similarities. Both men were third in the line of their dynasties, and both were remarkably successful warriors and leaders, conquering vast swathes of the subcontinent through personal bravery and able generalship. Both men had to overcome personal and political obstacles in the early years of their kingship, before they settled on ways of being and ruling that would be praised for millennia. And both men experienced an epiphany that would mark them for the rest of their lives. While any detailed comparison between these two monarchs is necessarily limited by the eighteen centuries between them, it is evident that both men strove to rule their empires justly and well during their long reigns, emphasizing the rational over blind superstition, and moved by an enormous spirit of compassion. And what has endured through the vaulting centuries is Ashoka's clearly enunciated humanity and remarkable notion of respect for all faiths and all religions, not simply as a passive act of tolerance but as a 'public culture in which every sect honours every other' by learning and respecting one another,*— traits that are mirrored almost exactly by Akbar.

The central beliefs of Ashoka and Akbar continue to be relevant today. India is a uniquely diverse and complicated country made even more tangled by a bloody and vicious post-colonial legacy. A profoundly disturbing trend today is the attempt to try and rectify perceived wrongs by 'revising' and 'reinterpreting' the past and its legacies, and to formulate an increasingly narrow definition of 'Indianness'. It is perhaps inevitable that people in each age are in search of certitudes. But the essential truths about people and societies, whether in India or elsewhere, are intricate, messy and often impenetrable. They cannot be made to conform to any particular ideological persuasion, no matter how strident the argument becomes. Our very DNA refuses to be categorized into one geographical location, or privilege one particular culture. Akbar understood this through his sulh kul, through his refusal to be claimed by one certitude and one truth. If we are to visit our rich past to understand our complicated present, then Akbar's is a life worth studying.

◆

Akbar's tomb is enigmatic, complicated, and unfinished, somewhat like the emperor's legacy itself. Originally built along the banks of the Yamuna, there is no clear consensus on when exactly the tomb was begun, or who the patron was. Scholars now agree that it may have been started by Akbar himself, towards the end of his reign, then partly broken down, redesigned, built, and left unfinished by Jahangir reflecting, also, the twisted and entwined destinies of the two men.

---

* Ashoka famously propounded his philosophy of Dhamma through a series of edicts inscribed on rock surfaces. Among other things, these edicts advocated non-violence, respect towards elders, and tolerance amongst sects.

The main gateway leading to the tomb complex is a towering structure in red sandstone entirely covered in geometrical patterns in white marble, black slate, and coloured stones. There would have been clerics housed in the rooms within the enormous gateway, quietly murmuring endless prayers for the soul of the Padshah. At the top of the gateway is a naqqar khana, where drumbeats would have marked the rising and the setting of the sun. In contemporary sources the mausoleum was called Bihistabad (Abode of Paradise) and that theme was reflected in its paradisiacal charbagh structure with four canals running beneath the mausoleum. Laura E. Parodi showed that the paradisiacal motif was reflected in the symbology of the decorations used in the structure: '...cypress and fruit trees standing for immortality and the abundance of fruit promised to the believers; bottles alluding to the purified wine drunk by paradise-dwellers; birds like the peacock (the Paradise bird par excellence) and parakeet'. Even today, after 400 years of indifferent care, the entrance vault glows with the ochres, blues and gold of the swaying leaves in the hazy afternoon sun. The last line of the verses inscribed on the gateway reads:

These are the gardens of Eden, enter them to live for ever.

In many ways, however, the numerous layers and textures of styles make the monument almost impossible to define. There is the sprawling, horizontal spread of the mausoleum, the repeating chattri elements, the jaalis, the palace-like appearance of the tomb as it rises up in a stepped pattern, the elaborate decorations, and the horizontal trabeated lines that have scholars scrambling for precedents and allusions from the Panch Mahal of Fatehpur Sikri to Muhammad Gauth's* tomb, to the tomb of Sher Shah Sur, amongst others. Perhaps the most perplexing and unusual element of the mausoleum is that there is no superstructure, no classic resplendent Timurid dome. Instead, there is a flat courtyard pavilion on the roof of the monument, fashioned entirely from a single block of white marble, inscribed with the ninety-nine names of Allah. In the centre of the courtyard lies Akbar's cenotaph, which marks the exact position of the Padshah's actual grave in a crypt far below.

---

*A sixteenth-century Sufi shaikh of the Shattari order in Gwalior.

Jahangir noted in his memoir that in the third year of his reign, he visited the construction site of the mausoleum and was displeased with what he saw. He said that he then consulted with other architects and remodelled the building and spent large sums of money on having it completed. This would explain the white marble pavilion at the top of the structure, marble being Jahangir's favourite material. Whether the structure was intended to ever have a superstructure is unknown but it is possible that it was meant to be covered with a huge tent, the contemporary traveller William Finch alluding in his writings to just such a 'rich tent'. If it was instead unfinished, then Jahangir was nonetheless proud of this building:

> I had intended it to be such that world travelers wouldn't be able to point to another such building in all the world.

A narrow, cool, and dark corridor leads deep into a crypt which contains the actual grave of the Padshah. This crypt chamber once contained the very best and most extensive of the mausoleum decorations, all of which were meant to extol the glory of the dead Padshah. The chamber would have been well-lighted by lamps which would have been kept burning constantly. The paintings included Christian imagery, such as a crucifix with the Virgin Mary and Child, and a depiction of St Ignatius, while the 'ceiling of the dome were (covered with) great angels and cherubim and many other painted figures'. If we know about some of the details of these decorations it is because a contemporary traveller, Niccolao Manucci, saw the mausoleum and described it. Today they are lost to us, for Akbar's great-grandson, Aurangzeb, had all these paintings white-washed, to efface the offending human figures.

The crypt would have been richly furnished with fine carpets, gold and silver plates, and would have displayed the books, sword, weapons, and armour of Akbar. But in 1691, while Padshah Aurangzeb was far away in the Deccan, a group of disaffected Jats looted and pillaged the tomb of Akbar, robbing the mausoleum of its precious stones, gold and silver plates, and other valuable objects, and set fire to what they could not remove.

There are far grander monuments to the great Mughal emperors and their consorts, but it is almost fitting that the greatest of them all lies today in relatively austere and reduced splendour, and that his unique capital remains in genteel neglect. For Akbar doesn't need ostentatious memorials to burnish his memory, his extraordinary life is memorial enough. His legacy remains in the supreme courage he displayed, far greater than on any battlefield, in believing that the vast multitudes of India could be brought together through active efforts of tolerance and understanding. That through reason, empathy, and good faith, misunderstandings between different religious groups and ethnicities could be resolved, and a new horizon unveiled. A horizon that could be lit up by the light from many different faiths, the best of each, to guide India's path to a more luminous and resplendent future.

ACKNOWLEDGEMENTS

Writing is a contrary thing. It is at once a deeply solitary activity but also, especially in the case of narrative history, profoundly connected to existing scholarship and the help of generous experts in the field. Giants in the field of history have written about various aspects of the Mughal Empire and this book could never have been written without relying on their work—these are all included in the bibliography for interested readers.

Many other people have helped me, in ways little and large. They have shared insights and recipes, offered solutions, encouragement, and sustenance of all sorts.

My grateful thanks to Mini Menon, Professor Mubarak Ali, Professor Giles Tillotson, Aparna Andhare, Arpana Bhargava, Professor Catherine Asher, Paul Abraham, Colleen Taylor Sen, Professor Ruby Lal, Manu S. Pillai, Zareen Bukhari, Professor Harbans Mukhia, Lavneet Gyani, Dr Karni Jasol and Dr Mahendra Singh Tanwar from the Mehrangarh Museum, Jodhpur, Karamjeet Malhotra, Rachna and David Davidar, Ayesha Mago, Caroline and Ashwin Juneja, Anjuli Bhargava, Air Marshal Brijesh Dhar Jayal and Mrs Manju Jayal, Rathin and Juhi Mathur, and Mandira Mohan.

All the recipes in this book are dedicated to Marryam Reshii, writer and food blogger, who hoped for a book that she could 'sink her teeth into'. She offered encouragement and warm support to a perfect stranger, for which I am enormously grateful.

Special thanks to Rana Safvi, writer, blogger, and all-round repository of Delhi's unique culture. She is the embodiment of the Ganga-Jamuni tehzeeb and has been a most generous friend and mentor.

To Kavita Singh, art historian and professor at JNU, heartfelt thanks. She has shown patience and generosity to a persistent and pesky stranger, above and beyond the call of duty. I am truly grateful to the insights and tips she has shared unstintingly with me.

Huge thanks to the entire team at Aleph Book Company, who

have been caught up in producing this rambling monster of a book. Thanks to Pujitha Krishnan, Simar Puneet, Isha Banerji, Aienla Ozukum, Bena Sareen, and Vasundhara Raj Baigra.

Any responsibility for errors of fact or interpretation remain mine alone.

Thanks to my daughters, Yashoda and Devaki, who make everything worthwhile.

And, to Mohit, for a lifetime of love and encouragement, thank you.

IMAGE CREDITS

Page i: Akbar hunting deer by Manohar, opaque watercolour and gold on paper, c. 1586–89. Courtesy Wikimedia Commons.

Page iii: The central pillar in diwan-e-Khas at Fatehpur Sikri. Courtesy the author.

Page vi: Akbar visits the tomb of Khwaja Muinuddin Chishti at Ajmer, c. 1562. Courtesy Wikimedia Commons.

Page xx: Akbar mounted on Hawai, pursuing Ranbagh across a bridge of boats over the Yamuna, composed by Basawan and painted by Chitra. ca. 1590–95. Courtesy Wikimedia Commons.

Page 1: The Prince and His Regents
Akbar riding his favourite elephant, detail, 1609–10, opaque watercolour and gold on paper © Staatliche Museen zu Berlin, Museum für Islamische Kunst / Christian Krug.

Page 61: The Young Padshah
Adham Khan pays homage to Akbar at Sarangpur, 1561, by Khem Karan. Courtesy Wikimedia Commons.

Page 125: The World is a Bridge
Tent Encampment, 1580–95. Opaque watercolor and gold on paper, Courtesy Brooklyn Museum, Gift of the Ernest Erickson Foundation, Inc.

Page 223: The Year of the Lion
Folio from the Persian Ramayan. From The David Collection, Copenhagen, Denmark.

Page 321: Paradise on Earth
Abu'l Fazl presenting the *Akbarnama* to Akbar. Courtesy Wikimedia Commons.

Page 411: Crouching Lion, Rising Sun
Akbar in Jahangir in Apotheosis, folio from the St Petersburg Album, about 1640, attributed to Bichitr. Opaque watercolor, ink, and gold on paper. Courtesy Wikimedia Commons.

COLOUR INSERTS

Genghis Khan by an anonymous court painter. Courtesy Wikimedia Commons.

Timur feasts in the gardens of Samarkand. Courtesy Wikimedia Commons.

Padshah Babur. Courtesy Wikimedia Commons.

Shaibani Khan Uzbek. Courtesy Metropolitan Museum of Art, New York.

Allegory of celebrations around Akbar's circumcision ceremony at the Sacred Spring of Khwaja Seh Yaran near Kabul by Dust Muhammad, c. 1546. Courtesy Wikimedia Commons.

Young Prince Akbar and noblemen hawking by Abd al-Samad. Opaque watercolour and ink on paper. Courtesy Metropolitan Museum of Art, New York.

Prince Akbar presenting a painting to his father, Humayun, by Abd al-Samad. c. 1550–56, Golestan Palace Library, Tehran. Courtesy Wikimedia Commons.

Bairam Khan's widow, Salima Sultan Begum, and his son, Abdur Rahim, being taken to the Mughal court. Courtesy Wikimedia Commons.

Tansen Gwaliyari, c. 1585–90, National Museum, New Delhi. Courtesy Wikimedia Commons.

Akbar mounted on Hawai, pursuing Ranbagh across a bridge of boats over the Yamuna River, composed by Basawan and painted by Chitra. ca. 1590–95. Courtesy Wikimedia Commons.

Akbar hunts in the neighbourhood of Agra using tame cheetahs by Basawan. Courtesy Wikimedia Commons.

Tent Encampment, 1580–95. Opaque watercolor and gold on paper, Courtesy Brooklyn Museum, Gift of the Ernest Erickson Foundation, Inc.

An attempt on Akbar's life at the Khair un-Manazil, Delhi, in 1564. Courtesy Wikimedia Commons.

Ataka Khan's mausoleum in Delhi. Courtesy the author.

The dancers from Mandu presented to Akbar after the defeat of Baz Bahadur. Courtesy Wikimedia Commons.

Folio from the *Tutinama*. Courtesy Wikimedia Commons.

Umayya frees Umar, who has been imprisoned by Iraj, c. 1557–77, from the *Hamzanama*. Courtesy Museum of Applied Arts, Vienna.

The siege of Chittor. Courtesy Wikimedia Commons.
The qumargha or ring hunt. Courtesy Wikimedia Commons.
Akbar's sword. Courtesy Xenophon/Creative Commons.
Weaponry from the Ain-i Akbari. Courtesy Wikimedia Commons.
Akbar's personal moulded armour made of Damascus steel. Courtesy the Trustees of the Chhatrapati Shivaji Maharaj Vastu Sangrahalaya, Mumbai.
Elephant armour. Courtesy Gilgamesh/Creative Commons.
Detail from the Battle of Sarnal. Courtesy Wikimedia Commons.
The diwan-e-khas building at Fatehpur Sikri. Courtesy the author.
Akbar visits the tomb of Khwaja Muinuddin Chishti at Ajmer, c. 1562. Courtesy Wikimedia Commons.
Birth of Akbar's first son, Salim. Courtesy Wikimedia Commons.
Akbar receiving his sons at Fatehpur Sikri after the Gujarat campaign. Courtesy Wikimedia Commons.
Detail from the battle scene with boats on the Ganga, 1565. Courtesy Wikimedia Commons.
Akbar holds a religious assembly at Fatehpur Sikri. Courtesy Wikimedia Commons.
Coins from Akbar's empire. Courtesy Sarmaya India.
The Battle of Haldighati. Courtesy Wikimedia Commons.
Folio from the Mewar Ramayan, c. 1650s. Courtesy Wikimedia Commons.
Akbar in disguise visits Swami Haridas with Tansen, Kishangarh, Rajasthan, 1760. Courtesy Wikimedia Commons.
Folio from the *Razmnana*, the Mahabharat in Persian. Courtesy Wikimedia Commons.
Heavenly Joys come to Earth attributed to Khem Karan. Courtesy Wikimedia Commons.
Folio from the Persian translation of the Ramayan. Courtesy Wikimedia Commons.
The young artist Abu'l Hasan. Courtesy Wikimedia Commons.
A portrait of Manohar. Courtesy Wikimedia Commons.
Farrukh Beg, self-portrait. Courtesy Wikimedia Commons.
Folio from the *Baburnama*. Courtesy Wikimedia Commons.
Abu'l Fazl presenting the *Akbarnama* to Akbar. Courtesy Wikimedia Commons.

Babur crossing the River Son. Courtesy Wikimedia Commons.
Chand Sultan playing polo. Courtesy Wikimedia Commons.
Bir Singh Deo of Orchha. Courtesy Wikimedia Commons.
Prince with a hawk. Courtesy Los Angeles Museum of Art.
Daniyal, Akbar's son. Courtesy Metropolitan Museum of Art.
Murad, Akbar's son. Courtesy Wikimedia Commons.
Folio from the Gulshan Album, Golestan Palace Library, Tehran.
Nath Yogis, painted at Salim's rebellious court at Allahabad in 1600. Courtesy Wikimedia Commons.
Art at Salim's rebel court showing European influence. Courtesy Wikimedia Commons.
The western gateway to Akbar's tomb at Sikandra. Courtesy Swapnil Saxena.
Akbar with a lion and a calf by Govardhan, c. 1630. Courtesy Metropolitan Museum of Art, New York.
Prince Salim, the future Jahangir, enthroned. Courtesy Wikimedia Commons.

NOTES

INTRODUCTION

xxv **Mirak howled in terror at the endless night:** H. Beveridge (trans.), *The Akbarnama of Abu-L-Fazl*, Vol. 1, Calcutta: Royal Asiatic Society, 1907, 2000 (repr.), p. 454.
xxv **'lights of joy,' we are assured, 'showed themselves in his cheeks':** Ibid.
xxv **beheld the 'lustrous forehead':** Ibid., p. 203.
xxvii **Akbar's illiteracy may have stemmed from dyslexia:** Ellen Smart, 'Akbar, Illiterate Genius', *Kalādarśana: American Studies in the Art of India*, edited by Joanna G. Williams, New Delhi: Oxford & IBH Publishing Co, 1981.
xxviii **'one observer estimated the Mughals' annual revenue at 120 million silver coins':** Richard M. Eaton, *India in the Persianate Age: 1000-1765*, London: Allen Lane, 2019, p. 371.

PART 1: THE PRINCE AND HIS REGENTS (1526-1561)

3 **dressed in silk robes and wore a high white hat:** Ruy González de Clavijo, *Narrative of the Embassy of Ruy González de Clavijo to the court of Timour, at Samarcand, A.D. 1403-6*, translated by Clements R. Markham, London: The Hakluyt Society, 1859, p. 132.
4 **for they do not consider:** Ibid., p. 139.
5 **Lord of Conjunction was a potent and sacred symbol of power:** For a detailed discussion on the subject of astrologically potent symbols, see A. Afzar Moin, *The Millennial Sovereign: Sacred Kingship and Sainthood in Islam*, New York: Columbia University Press, 2012, p. 26.
5 **'conjunction of the two superior planets':** Ibid, p. 29.
5 **'massacring a reported 80,000 inhabitants...':** Eaton, *India in the Persianate Age*, p. 104.
6 **'northern two-thirds of the subcontinent':** Ibid.
6 **'For nearly 140 years':** Wheeler M. Thackston (trans. and ed.), *The Baburnama: Memoirs of Babur, Prince and Emperor*, New York: The Modern Library, 1996, p. 100.
6 **'Mischief and devastation':** Harbans Mukhia, *The Mughals of India*, New Delhi: Blackwell Publishing, 2004, p. 3.
6 **'300 lightly armed men':** Eaton, *India in the Persianate Age*, p. 199.
6 **Like many Chinggisid khans or Timurid mirzas:** Jos Gommans, 'The Warband in the Making of Eurasian Empires', *Prince, Pen and Sword: Eurasian Perspectives*, edited by Maaike van Berkel and Jeroen Duindam, Leiden: Brill, 2018, p. 341.
7 **'the country which from old had depended on the Turk':** Annette S. Beveridge (trans.), *The Babur-nama in English (Memoirs of Babur): Translated from the original Turki text of Zahiru'd-din Muhammad Babur Padshah Ghazi*, Vol. 1, London: Luzac & Co, 1922, p. 385.
8 **'a new style of combat built around gunpowder':** Andrew de la Garza, *The Mughal Empire at War: Babur, Akbar and the Indian Military Revolution, 1500-1605*, Oxon: Routledge, 2016, p. 6.
8 **'more than a million soldiers under arms':** Ibid., pp. 10-11.
8 **the 145 noblemen who served under Babur:** Iqtidar Alam Khan, *India's Polity in the Age of Akbar*, New Delhi: Permanent Black, 2016, p. 9.
8 **'five-time prayers' and the Hindus their 'hours of worship':** Quoted in S. Z. H. Jafri (ed.), *Recording of the Progress of Indian History: Symposia Papers of the Indian History*

	Congress, 1922–2010, Delhi: Primus Books, 2012, p. 483.
9	**'a strip of territory stretching from eastern Afghanistan'**: Eaton, *India in the Persianate Age*, p. 204.
9	**sent 'letters in all directions'**: Gulbadan Begum, *The History of Humayun: Humāyūn-Nāmā*, translated by Annette S. Beveridge, London: Royal Asiatic Society, 1902, New Delhi: Munshiram Manoharlal Publishers, 2001 (repr.), p. 97.
10	**'heated by ague or by the heat which the titanic and glowing planet causes'**: Jonathan Gil Harris, *The First Firangis: Remarkable Stories of Heroes, Healers, Charlatans, Courtesans & Other Foreigners Who Became Indian*, New Delhi: Aleph Book Company, 2015, p. 55.
10	**it was estimated at 100 million**: W. H. Moreland, *India at the Death of Akbar: An Economic Study*, London: Macmillan & Co., 1920, pp. 9–22.
10	**130–140 million by historian Shireen Moosvi**: Shireen Moosvi, *The Economy of the Mughal Emperor, c.1595: A Statistical Study*, New Delhi: Oxford University Press, 1987, pp. 389–406.
10	**15 per cent of the population lived in cities**: Irfan Habib, 'Population', *The Cambridge Economic History of India*, Vol. 1, c.1200–c.1750, edited by Tapan Raychaudhari and Irfan Habib, Cambridge: Cambridge University Press, 1982, p. 169.
10	**'Cotton textiles (calico, dyed and printed), silk fabrics'**: Moosvi, 'The World of Labour in Mughal India (c. 1500–1750)', *International Review of Social History*, Vol. 56, No. 19, 2011, p. 245.
11	**Central Asia's semi-pastoral culture**: Eaton, *India in the Persianate Age*, p. 197.
12	**mirzas were granted lands, or appanages**: For a detailed explanation of the appanage system and princely behaviour under the Mughals, see Munis D. Faruqui, *The Princes of the Mughal Empire, 1504–1719*, Cambridge: Cambridge University Press, 2012.
12	**Babur's peremptory and irrevocable request to never spill the blood of a brother**: Gulbadan, *Humāyūn-Nāma*, p. 33.
13	**'not only immensely popular local saints'**: Moin, *The Millennial Sovereign*, p. 165.
14	**'What was the good of my courtesy'**: Lisa Balabanlilar, *Imperial Identity in the Mughal Empire: Memory and Dynastic Politics in Early Modern Central Asia*, p. 115.
14	**'At Mandu, a deserter presented himself'**: Annamarie Schimmel, *The Empire of the Great Mughals: History, Art and Culture*, London: Reaktion Books, 2004, 2010 (repr.), p. 28.
14	**'unfurled the carpet of pleasure'**: Ibid.
14	**'They were good at conversation, arranging parties and in social manners'**: van Berkel and Duindam, *Princes, Pen and Sword*, p. 228.
14–15	**'His blessed heart was cast down'**: Gulbadan Begum, *Humāyūn-Nāma*, p. 145.
15	**'he saw the moon come into his arms'**: Beveridge (trans.), *The Akbarnama of Abu-L-Fazl*, Vol. 1, p. 4.
15	**'divine light so streamed from the shining brows'**: Ibid., p. 44.
15	**'a great light approached me and entered my bosom'**: Ibid.
15	**'I and my family,' she admitted candidly**: Ibid.
16	**'resisted and discussed and disagreed'**: Gulbadan, *Humāyūn-Nāma*, p. 151.
16	**'took the astrolabe into his own blessed hand'**: Ibid.
16	**'the country through which they fled being an entire sandy desert'**: Lieutenant-Colonel James Tod, *Annals and Antiquities of Rajasthan, Or the Central and Western Rajpoot States of India*, Vol. 1, London: Smith, Elder and Co., 1829, p. 321.
16	**'so ungenerous was this man and so low'**: Ibid., p. 270.
16	**'was a rough old soldier'**: Erskine quoted in Elliot (ed.), *The History of India, as Told by Its Own Historians*, p. 216fn.
17	**most senior woman of the household at this time was Khanzada Begum**: For details of her extraordinary life, see Ira Mukhoty, *Daughters of the Sun: Empresses, Queens and Begums of the Mughal Empire*, New Delhi: Aleph Book Company, 2018, p. 20.
17	**'The moon was in Leo,' wrote Gulbadan**: Gulbadan, *Humāyūn-Nāma*, p. 158.
17	**Maulana Chand 'was perturbed'**: Beveridge (trans.), *Akbarnama*, Vol. 1, p. 19.

17	'fell a'dancing, and from excess of exultation': Moin, *The Millennium Sovereign*, p. 199.
17	'This is all the present I can afford to make you': Jauhar, *The Tazkereh Al Vakiāt, Or Private Memoirs of the Moghul Emperor Humāyūn*, Written in the Persian Language, translated by Major Charles Stewart, London: Oriental Translation Fund, 1832, p. 45.
18	ten additional women were listed as having suckled Akbar: Beveridge (trans.), *Akbarnama*, p. 131.
18	'takht revan': Edward Ives, *A Voyage from England to India*, London: Edward and Charles Dilly, 1773, p. 278.
18	'much rejoiced by the arrival of so celebrated': Jauhar, *The Tazkereh Al Vakiāt*, p. 47.
19	'The people of Hindustan': Ibid., p. 51.
19	'there was not a chink of time': Gulbadan, *Humāyūn-Nāma*, p. 165.
19	it was Humayun who found it 'requisite': Jauhar, *The Tazkereh Al Vakiāt*, p. 52.
19	'the weather was very hot, so he [Akbar] was left behind': Henry Miers Elliot, *The History of India, as Told by Its Own Historians: The Muhammadan Period, End of the Afghan Dynasty and the First Thirty-Eight Years of the Reign of Akbar*, edited by John Dowson, Vol. 5, London: Trübner and Co., 1873, p. 216.
19	'under the protection of Divine love': Beveridge (trans.), *Akbarnama*, Vol. 1, pp. 391–92.
20	'he went hunting long ago': Gulbadan, *Humāyūn-Nāma*, p. 165.
20	speak of a 'river of milk': Abraham Eraly, *Emperors of the Peacock Throne: The Saga of the Great Moghuls*, New Delhi: Penguin Books, 2000.
20	'this striking and falling, are visibly before me': Beveridge (trans.), *Akbarnama*, Vol. 1, p. 397.
21	'They are the very hands and feet of my brother': Gulbadan, *Humāyūn-Nāma*, p. 174.
21	ordered the child to be weaned immediately: Beveridge (trans.), *Akbarnama*, p. 456.
22	'merely to look at him': Gulbadan, *Humāyūn-Nāma*, p. 178.
22	painting a polo match on a grain of rice: Surya Tubach, 'The Astounding Miniature Paintings of India's Mughal Empire', *Art sy*, 30 April 2018.
22	As art historian J. M. Rogers describes it: Ibid.
22	'situated in an exceptionally elevated place': Thackston (trans.), *The Baburnama*, p. 152.
23	The circumcision ceremony was an important rite of passage: See Faruqui, *Princes of the Mughal Empire* for more details on rites of passage of Mughal princes.
23	The banquet would have included biryan: Colleen Taylor Sen, *Feasts and Fasts: A History of Food in India*, London: Reaktion Books, 2015, p. 184.
23	'A few spoonfuls of fat are melted': Arminius Vámbéry quoted in Lizzie Collingham, *Curry: A Tale of Cooks and Conquerors*, New Delhi: Oxford University Press, 2006, p. 19.
24	'fruit pilaus, turmeric and saffron ones, chicken pilaus': Ibid., p. 26.
24	'fine sherbets of lemon and rosewater': Taylor Sen, *Feasts and Fasts*, p. 182.
24	the Kabul years were essential to the development of the Mughal school: For in-depth discussion see Laura E. Parodi, 'Earliest datable Mughal painting', *Staatsbibliothek zu Berlin - Preussischer Kulturbesitz, Libr. Pict. A117, fol. 15a* [accessed: 2 January 2020].
24	which employed Khurasani trained artists: Ibid.
25	'fondness for wine, which he was unable to give up': Parodi and Wannell, 'The Earliest Datable Mughal Painting' available at <https://www.asianart.com/articles/parodi/index.html> [accessed: 2 January 2020].
25	Dust Muhammad painted a masterpiece of refinement: For more information, see Laura E. Parodis, 'Tracing the Rise of Mughal Portraiture' in *Portraiture in South Asia Since the Mughals*, edited by Crispen Branfoot, I. B. Tauris, 2018.
26	'a well educated prince combined the best qualities of a man': Faruqui, *Princes of the Mughal Empire, 1504–1719*, p. 78.
26	'acute astrologers and time-knowing astrolabe-conners': Beveridge (trans.), *Akbarnama*, p. 519.

26 'scholar of God's school': Ibid.
26 'continually giving his attention to that wondrous creature the camel': Ibid., p. 589.
27 Akbar is shown presenting a painting he has made to his father: Golestan Palace Library, Tehran.
27 being due to a dyslexic condition: Smart, 'Akbar, Illiterate Genius', p. 108.
28 'the minds of those present were set at rest': Faruqui, *Princes of the Mughal Empire*, p. 72.
28 'the kindness and affection which she showed to me': Quoted in Moosvi, *Episodes in the Life of Akbar*, p. 12.
28 'would to Heaven that merciless sword': Gulbadan, *Humāyūn-Nāma*, p. 198.
28–29 'The marriage of a young child is displeasing to the Almighty': Abu'l Fazl, 'Happy Sayings of Akbar', *Ain-i Akbari*, Part 5, Vol. 3, translated by H. S. Jarrett, Calcutta: Royal Asiatic Society, 1894.
29 Sit not idle 'tis not the time for play: Beveridge (trans.), *Akbarnama*, Vol. 1, p. 317.
29 'God be praised that things which cannot be replaced are safe': Kavita Singh, *Real Birds in Imagined Gardens: Mughal Painting between Persia and Europe*, Los Angeles: Getty Publications, 2017, p. 11.
29 'was ideally a figure of fierce authority': Faruqui, *Princes of the Mughal Empire*, p. 76.
30 'Brotherly custom has nothing to do with ruling and reigning': Gulbadan, *Humāyūn-Nāma*, p. 201.
30 'disputed among themselves who was to perform the cruel act': Jauhar, *The Tazkereh Al Vakiāt*, p. 105.
30 'seeing the prince in such pain and distress': Ibid., p. 107.
31 'pleasantly floated down the river to Pyshavir': Jauhar, *The Tazkereh Al Vakiāt*, p. 109.
31 'and was so delighted and happy': Ibid., p. 110.
31 'Alas that the Emperor Humayun died so early': *Akbarnama*; 'Happy Sayings of Akbar', *Ain-i Akbari*, Part 5, Vol. 3.
32 'Before this,' writes historian Iqtidar Alam Khan': Iqtidar Alam Khan, 'The Nobility under Akbar and the Development of His Religious Policy, 1560–80', *Journal of the Royal Asiatic Society of Great Britain and Ireland*, No. 1/2, April 1968, p. 35.
32 'My father esteemed much things like this': Sir Edward Maclagan, *The Jesuits and the Great Mogul*, London: Burns, Oats and Washbourne Ltd, 1932, p. 231.
32 'the range of colours used suggests': Singh, *Real Birds in Imagined Gardens*, p. 19.
33 'became as much a master of this art as masters of a single art and craft are': Wheeler M. Thackston (trans.), *The History of Akbar*, Vol. 2, New Delhi: Harvard University Press, 2016, p. 383.
33 'eccentric dilettante' of modern rhetoric: See Moin, *Millennial Sovereign*.
33 'These included...division of the kingdom's administration': Eaton, *India in the Persianate Age*, p. 214.
34 'was upset beyond human imagination': Thackston (trans.), *Akbarnama*, Vol. 2, p. 408.
35 'Akbar's territories were hemmed in by rivals': Annemarie Schimmel and Stuart Cary Welch, *Anvari's Divan: A Pocket Book for Akbar*, New York: Metropolitan Museum of Art, p. 19.
35 'seven or eight military zones, commanded by leading nobles': Khan, *India's Polity in the Age of Akbar*, p. 26.
35 'to placate the self-sacrificing heroes who had recently entered India': Thackston (trans.), *The History of Akbar*, Vol. 3, New Delhi: Harvard University Press, 2016, p. 55.
35 Tardi Beg immediately handed over the custody of Mirza Kamran's second son: For a detailed analysis of the nobility at Akbar's court, see Khan, *India's Polity in the Age of Akbar*.
36 'outwardly he had neither rank...nor race': Kanwal Kishore Bhardwaj, *Hemu: Napoleon of Medieval India*, New Delhi: Mittal Publications, 2000, p. 10.

36	'evil speaking, plotting and calumny': Ibid., p. 12.
36	Abu'l Fazl had to admit that 'ill-starred': Beveridge (trans.), *Akbarnama*, Vol. 2, p. 71.
37	'Men of wealth and position had to close their houses': Abd al-Qadir Badauni, *Muntakhabh al-Tawarikh*, translated and edited by George S. A. Ranking, Vol. 1, Calcutta: Asiatic Society of Bengal, 1898, first edition, Delhi: Idarah-i-Adabiyat-I, 2009 (repr.), p. 549.
37	'the seeds of the Egyptian thorn, wild dry grass and cowhides': H. C. Verma, *Harvesting Water and Rationalization of Agriculture in North Medieval India: Thirteenth-Sixteenth Centuries*, New Delhi: Anamika Publishers, 2001, p. 60.
37	'The writer of these pages': Badauni, *Muntakhabh al-Tawarikh*, Vol. 1, p. 550.
37	'two years [of] continual anarchy and terror': Ibid.
37	Hemu rode towards Delhi with his enormous army: Satish Chandra, *A History of Medieval India*, New Delhi: Orient Blackswan, 2007, p. 237.
37	'While people were crying for bread and taking each other's lives': Badauni, *Muntakhabh al-Tawarikh*, Vol. 1, p. 551.
37	removal of powerful Mughal amirs from the region by Bairam Khan: For a detailed analysis, see Khan, *India's Polity in the Age of Akbar*.
38	Of the small group...almost all were foreign-born: John F Richards, *The Mughal Empire*, Part 1, Vol. 5, Oxon: Cambridge University Press, 1995, p. 19.
38	'esteemed himself at least equal to Keikobad': Vincent A. Smith, *Akbar the Great Mogul 1545–1605*, Oxford: Clarendon Press, 1917, p. 36.
39	'When it was reported to him': Thackston (trans.), *The History of Akbar*, p. 43.
39	'uniform yellow-gray waste of sterile earth': Gulbadan, *Humāyūn-Nāma*, p. 94fn.
39	'sparse grasses and stunted thorn-bushes': Ibid.
39	'pugnacious Rajput and Afghan horsemen': Bhardwaj, *Hemu*, p. 64.
40	'their blood-dripping blades like hungry lions': Thackston (trans.), *The History of Akbar*, Vol. 3, p. 119.
40	he wishes that Akbar had 'unveiled' his true nature: Ibid., p. 127.
41	'For eighty years I have been worshipping my God': Ibid., p. 137.
42	'peasants and people of low standing': B. N. Goswami, *Indian Costumes in the Collection of the Calico Museum*, Ahmedabad: The Sarabhai Foundation, 2013, p. 14.
42	'body was viewed as an integral aspect of the person': Balkrishan Shivram, 'Court Dress and Robing Ceremony in Mughal India', *Proceedings of the Indian History Congress*, Vol. 66, 2005–06; *Court Dress and Robing Ceremony*, p. 409.
43	'neither men nor women should wear a tight robe': Ibid.
43	Bairam Khan had neutralized the Turani nobility in Hindustan: For more details explaining Bairam Khan's actions, see Iqtidar Alam Khan, *The Political Biography of Mughal Noble*, New Delhi: Munshiram Manoharlal Publishers, 1991.
43	'indulging in recreation and pleasure': Thackston (trans.), *The History of Akbar*, Vol. 3, p. 145.
44	'who had grown homesick during the long drawn-out siege': Ibid., p. 169.
44	'until Nasir ul-mulk informed him': Ibid., p. 175.
44	'of what sort of crime have trouble-makers': Ibid., p. 183.
44	'sick of the sight of shortsighted people and flown into a rage': Ibid.
45	'since from time to time I find': Ibid., p. 89.
46	'dispensing justice and indulging in revelry': Thackston (trans.), *The History of Akbar*, Vol. 3, p. 203.
47	'the river itself had been decorated for a festival': Ibid., p. 229.
47	'the water and air of which put Baghdad': Ibid.
47	'the grounds were so bad and unattractive': Beveridge (trans.), *Baburnama*, p. 278.
47	'of great eloquence, and of excellent disposition': Omar S. Pound, 'The Emperor Akbar as a Religious Man: Six Interpretations', p. 3.

47   'accused in Persia of being a Sunni': Ibid.
47   **God told the Prophet Moses that he had been sent to unite mankind:** Saiyid Nurul Hasan, *Religion State and Society in Medieval India: Collected Works of S. Nurul Hasan*, New Delhi: Oxford University Press, 2005, p. 72.
48   'a dog has assumed the status of a sweet seller': Khan, *India's Polity in the Age of Akbar*, p. 111fn.
48   'at every opportunity they said to His Majesty': B. De (trans.), *Tabaqat-i-Akbari of Nizamuddin Ahmad*, Vol. 2, p. 241.
48   'who was a marvel of sense, resource and loyalty': Thackston (trans.), *The History of Akbar*, Vol. 3, p. 131.
49   **For reassuring you, we had written that though there may arise:** Shireen Moosvi, *Episodes from the Life of Akbar Contemporary Records and Reminiscences*, New Delhi: National Book Trust, 1994, p. 19.
50   **I have taken refuge with the infidels urged by necessity:** T. C. A. Raghavan, *Attendant Lords: Bairam Khan and Abdur Rahim, Courtiers and Poets in Mughal India*, New Delhi: HarperCollins, 2017, p. 60.
50   **Akbar dismissed Bairam Khan with honour:** Only Arif Qandahari mentions this in *Tarikhi-i Akbari*, edited by Sayed Moinuddin Nadwi, Saiyeed Azhar Ali and Imtiaz Ali Arshi, Rampur: Raza Library, 1962, p. 88.
51   **grains were an important part of Turki diet:** Taylor Sen, *Feasts and Fasts*, p. 185.
51   'banner, drums and tuman tugh...a fur garment': Thackston (trans.), *The History of Akbar*, p. 371.
52   'He was of medium stature but inclining to be tall': Schimmel, *The Empire of the Great Mughals*, p. 32.
52   'both the good and the bad assemble[d]': Moosvi, *Episodes in the Life of Akbar*, p. 11.
52   'suddenly some ruffian recognised me': Enayatullah Khan, 'Akbar and his Cheetahs', *Proceedings of the Indian History Congress*, Vol. 73, 2012, p. 463.
53   'whose inhabitants were of a rebellious bent': Quoted in Ibid., p. 21.
53   'rice boiled with green ginger, a little pepper': Ibid., p. 29.
53   'gave him a few lashes and told him to get out of the place': Taylor Sen, *Feasts and Fasts*, p. 190.
54   'Uzbeks in the Jaunpur region; Qaqshals in Kara-Manikpur': Khan, *India's Polity in the Age of Akbar*, p. 34.
54   'restore the sinking faith to its pristine freshness': Pound, 'The Emperor Akbar as a Religious Man: Six Interpretations', p. 13.
54   'with his powerful knowledge': Thackston (trans.), *The History of Akbar*, Vol. 4, p. 563.
55   'In early life he observed many austerities': Abd al-Qadir Badauni, *Muntakhabh al-Tawarikh*, Vol. 3, translated and edited by Sir Wolseley Haig, Calcutta: Asiatic Society of Bengal, 1925, Delhi: Idarah-i-Adabiyat-I (repr.), 2009, p. 118.
55   'gave everyone who came to the threshold...hopes of rank and jagir': Beveridge (trans.), *Akbarnama*, Vol. 2, p. 151.
56   'for this noble work, wisdom and courage was necessary': Ibid.
56   **A time will come on men, when none will become favourites:** Badauni quoted in Afshan Majid, 'Women and a Theologian: The Ideas and Narratives of Abdul Qadir Badauni', *Proceedings of the Indian History Congress*, Vol. 71, 2010–11, p. 249.
57   **Maham Anaga claimed for herself an ancient role:** For a discussion on performance of piety by Muslim women, see Gavin Hambly, *Women in the Medieval Islamic World: Power, Patronage, and Piety*, New York: St. Martin's Press, 1998. To see the role of Shah Jahan's wives and daughters in the building of mosques in Shahjahanabad, see Mukhoty, *Daughters of the Sun*.
57   **surprising that so much of it remains shrouded in mystery:** For different interpretation by scholars, see Swapna Liddle, *Delhi: 14 Historical Walks*, New Delhi: Westland, 2011; Monica

Juneja, *Architecture in Medieval India: Forms, Contexts, Histories*, New Delhi: Permanent Black, 2001.
58 **a fiercely independent woman who did not hesitate to speak her mind**: See Gulbadan, *Humāyūn-Nāma*.
58 **'in spite of the ties of love between her and H. M. [Akbar]'**: Beveridge (trans.), *Akbarnama*, Vol. 3, p. 107.
59 **'one of his wives had loved [Humayun] so faithfully'**: J. S. Hoyland (trans.), *The Commentary of Father Monserrate, S. J. on His Journey to the Court of Akbar*, New Delhi: Asian Education Services, 2003, p. 96.

PART 2: THE YOUNG PADSHAH (1561–1569)
63 **'enter the harem and after his meal'**: Leslie M. Crump, *The Lady of the Lotus: Rup Mati, Queen of Māndu: A Strange Tale of Forgiveness*, Milford: Oxford University Press, 1926, p. 49.
63 **'advised her lover to sacrifice pleasure'**: Crump, *Lady of the Lotus*, p. 48.
63 **'too drunk to recognize day from night'**: Thackston (trans.), *The History of Akbar*, Vol. 3, p. 417.
63 **'unlawful and vicious practices'**: Satish Chandra, *Medieval India: From Sultanat to the Mughals, 1526–1748*, Part 2, New Delhi: Har-Anand Publications, 1999, 2006 (repr.), p. 103.
63 **'to spread justice and be balm for the wounds of the oppressed'**: Ibid., p. 191.
63 **'tyranny and injustice Baz Bahadur had wrought upon the people of Malwa'**: Thackston (trans.), *The History of Akbar*, Vol. 3, p. 411.
64 **'had the captives brought before them'**: Abd al-Qadir Badauni, *Muntakhabh al-Tawarikh*, translated and edited by W. H. Lowe, Calcutta: Asiatic Society of Bengal, 1884, p. 47.
64 **'put them all to death and burnt them'**: Ibid., p. 48.
64 **'in one single night all these captives have been taken'**: Ibid., p. 47.
64 **'began to indulge in pleasure'**: Thackston (trans.), *The History of Akbar*, Vol. 3, p. 423.
65 **'everything he had taken from Baz Bahadur's estate'**: Ibid., p. 437.
65 **mother's servants to bring away two 'rare beauties'**: Ibid., p. 439.
66 **'they are dirty and do not know the civilized ways'**: Ibn Battuta, *The Travels of Ibn Battuta, A.D. 1325–1354*, Vol. 3, edited by H. A. R. Gibb, Cambridge: Cambridge University Press, 1971, 2017 (repr.), p. 741.
66 **women slaves in the households of noblemen were called paristaran**: Shadab Bano, 'Women Slaves in Medieval India', *Proceedings of the Indian History Congress*, Vol. 65, 2004, pp. 314–23.
66 **the strength of 'the Lion of God'**: Stuart Cary Welch, *India Art and Culture, 1300–1900*, New York, Metropolitan Museum of Art, p. 148.
66 **'Maham Anaga's heart which was distressed by the separation'**: Beveridge (trans.), *Akbarnama*, Vol. 2, p. 235.
67 **Powerful Afghan chiefs held considerable territory**: Eaton, *India in the Persianate Age*, p. 216.
67 **A broad band of land across the sweep of the Indo-Gangetic plain**: Abraham Eraly, *The Last Spring: The Lives and Times of the Great Mughals*, Part I, New Delhi: Penguin Books, 1997, p. 139.
68 **'choler, passionateness, fierceness and wickedness'**: Schimmel and Welch, *Anvari's Divan*, p. 22.
68 **'Although I was sober and the elephant was very easy to handle'**: Wheeler M. Thackston (trans.), *The Jahangirnama: Memoirs of Emperor Jahangir*, New York: Oxford University Press, 1999, p. 219.
68 **'If you don't stop acting like that'**: Thackston (trans.), *The History of Akbar*, Vol. 3, p. 463.

68	'neither was I drunk nor was the elephant out of control': Ibid., p. 279.
68–69	'must have some sort of imbalance in his mind': Ibid., p. 219.
69	'for we cannot bear the burden of existence': Colonel H. S. Jarrett (trans.), 'Happy Sayings', *Ain-i Akbari*, Vol. 3, Calcutta: The Asiatic Society, 1891.
70	most estimates putting them at less than 10 per cent of the total earnings: Shireen Moosvi, *People, Taxation, and Trade in Mughal India*, New Delhi: Oxford University Press, 2008, p. 122.
70	handed out huge cash incentives to bind men to his cause: Michael H. Fischer, *A Short History of the Mughal Empire*, London: I. B. Tauris, 2016, p. 95.
70	The collector was directed to be the friend of the agriculturist: *Ain-i Akbari* quoted in Stephen M. Edwardes and H. L. O. Garrett, *Mughal Rule in India*, New Delhi: Atlantic Publishers, 1995, p. 205.
71	'Without the support of Hindu agrarian magnates and officials': Khan, *India in the Polity of Akbar*.
72	integrated decimal hierarchy for top officer administrators: Ibid., p. 100.
72	'much higher than those paid to officers of comparable rank': de la Garza, *The Mughal Empire at War*, p. 201.
73	'Most of the inhabitants of Hindustan are pagans; they call a pagan': Quoted in J. L. Mehta, *Advanced Study in the History of Medieval India*, Vol. 2, New Delhi: Sterling Publishers, 2017, p. 108.
75	'became a place where Hindus placed their head and sent nazr every year': Hamid bin Fazlullah Jamali quoted in Motiur Rahman Khan, 'Akbar and the Dargah of Ajmer', *Proceedings of the Indian History Congress*, 2010, p. 232.
75	'The Raja stands out for his great intellect and courage': Thackston (trans.), *The History of Akbar*, Vol. 3, p. 475.
76	took over lands held by ruling tribes like the Bhils and the Meenas: Hooja, *History of Rajasthan*, pp. 417–19.
76	Rajputs unabashedly compared themselves with the native plant richke (lucerne): Varsha Joshi, *Polygamy and Purdah: Women and Society Among Rajputs*, Jaipur: Rawat Publications, 1995, p. 41.
76	The Rajput clans had used marriages: Rima Hooja, *A History of Rajasthan*, New Delhi: Rupa Publications, 2006, p. 552.
77	'Well, Man Singh, where were you when God was distributing beauty in heaven?': Rajiva Nain Prasad, *Raja Man Singh of Amber*, Calcutta: World Press, 1966, p. 20.
78	Harkha Bai would require; dhai maas (wet nurses), dholans (female drummers): Joshi, *Polygamy and Purdah*, p. 115.
79	'but however much left and right I looked': Moosvi, *Episodes in the Life of Akbar*, p. 30.
79	'his head was bare and he was wearing a lungi': Ibid., p. 31.
79	'It is hard to exaggerate how accessible he makes himself': Monserrate, *The Commentary of Father Monserrate*, p. 197.
79	'a fine-looking broad-shouldered man': Father Pierre du Jarric, S. J., *Akbar and the Jesuits: An Account of the Jesuit Missions to the Court of Akbar*, Plymouth: W. M. Brendon and Son Ltd, 1926, Oxfordshire: Routledge UK, 2014, p. 214.
80	'the royal revenues, which were in the hands of embezzlers': Beveridge (trans.), *Akbarnama*, Vol. 2, p. 277.
80	'Son of a bitch!' he cursed Adham Khan: H. Elliot, *History of India*, p. 27.
81	'Adham killed our Ataka': Ibid., p. 110–11.
82	'[Akbar] had introduced a whole host of the daughters of the eminent Hindu rajas: Badauni, *Muntakhabh al-Tawarikh*, Vol. 2, p. 312.
82	'Formerly I persecuted men into conformity': Jarrett (trans.), 'Happy Sayings', *Ain-i Akbari*, Vol. 3, p. 181.
82	'making captive the women, children and kinsmen': Irfan Habib, 'Akbar and Social

	Inequities', *Proceedings of the IHC*, Vol. 53, 1992, p. 301.
82	**some two lakh persons were captured every year**: Khan, *India's Polity in the Age of Akbar*, p. 139.
82	**'killing, imprisoning and whipping'**: Beveridge (trans.), *Akbarnama*, Vol. 2, p. 247.
83	**'however obvious the error of some people is'**: Thackston (trans.), *The History of Akbar*, Vol. 3, p. 268.
84	**'On the completion of my twentieth year'**: Jarrett (trans.), *Ain-i Akbari*, Vol. 3, p. 386.
84	**'The emperor from his youth up had shown a special predilection'**: C. M. Naim, 'Popular Jokes and Political History: The Case of Akbar, Birbal and Mulla Do-Piyaza', *Economic and Political Weekly*, Vol. 30, No. 24, 17 June 1995, p. 1458.
85	**Tansen, who would later have a remarkably lifelike portrait made of himself**: A portrait of 'Tansen of Gwalior' (1585–90), (11.8 x 6.7cm) at the National Museum, New Delhi.
85	**'a great terror fell upon the city'**: Badauni, *Muntakhabh al-Tawarikh*, Vol. 2, p. 50.
85	**a young man named Falud, a freed slave**: Thackston (trans.), *History of Akbar*, Vol. 3, p. 623.
86	**'Alas that in the first flush of youth'**: Jarrett (trans.), 'Happy Sayings', *Ain-i Akbari*, Vol. 3.
86	**'placed a real burden on the poorest taxpayers'**: John F. Richards, *The New Cambridge History of India: The Mughal Empire*, Cambridge: Cambridge University Press, 1995, p. 39.
86	**'the disapproval of statesmen' and 'much chatter on the part of the ignorant'**: Satish Chandra, 'Jizyah and the State in India during the 17th Century', *Journal of the Economic and Social History of the Orient*, Vol. 12, No. 3, September 1969, p. 331.
87	**men professed their undying loyalty to Akbar**: Thackston (trans.), *The History of Akbar*, Vol. 3, p. 553.
87	**'himself and to others'**: Beveridge (trans.), *Akbarnama*, Vol. 2, p. 529.
87	**'experienced spies and traders'**: Ibid.
88	**'at every 500 paces small pieces of stones are fixed'**: Eraly, *The Last Spring: Life in India's Golden Age*, Part 2, New Delhi: Penguin Books, 1997, 2015 (repr.), p. 230.
88	That he would keep a close watch on every one who came in: Ibid., p. 233.
88	**'the most dreaded government official during the Mughal period'**: J. L. Mehta, *Advanced Study in the History of Medieval India: Medieval Indian Society and Culture*, New Delhi: Sterling Publishers, 2009, p. 344.
89	**'unsurpassed adherent of God's word and extirpator of polytheists'**: Beveridge (trans.), *Akbarnama*, Vol. 2, p. 264.
91	**asked to be buried near the tomb of Akbar's faithful dog**: Francesca Orsini and Katherine Butler Schofield, *Tellings and Texts: Music, Literature and Performance in North India*, London: Open Book Publishers, 2015, p. 290.
91	**'in the style of the storytellers'**: Ibid., p. 289.
91	**'stately plump elephants; camels; flunkeys milking goats; cooks making bread'**: Stuart C. Welch, *The Petersburg Muraqqa': Album of Indian and Persian from the 16th and the 18th Century and Specimens of Perisan Calligraphy by 'Imad al-Hasani*, Lugano: ARCH Foundation, 1996, p. 14.
92	**'[Akbar] responded badly to Iranian graces'**: Ibid.
92	**'Verily it is a book the like of which no connoisseur'**: B. N. Goswami, *The Spirit of Indian Painting: Close Encounters with 101 Great Works, 1100–1900*, New Delhi: Penguin Books, 2014.
92	**'As a result,' wrote Abu'l Fazl**: Asok Kumar Das, *Dawn of Mughal Painting*, New Delhi: Vakils, Feffer & Simons, 1982, p. 8.
93	**'urged by natural desire'**: John Guy, 'Mughal painting under Akbar: The Melbourne Hamza-nama and Akbar-nama paintings', *Art Journal*, 26 June 2014.
95	**'live in the countryside, where they occupy themselves'**: Thackston (trans.), *The History*

	of Akbar, Vol. 4, p. 8.
95	'they are a base tribe and the people of India despise them': Ibid.
95	'a complete share of beauty and grace': Nizamuddin Ahmad, *Tabaqat-i-Akbari*, Vol. 2, p. 280.
95	'she was overly proud of her success': Beveridge (trans.), *Akbarnama*, Vol. 4, p. 27.
96	'There is a custom among the Rajputs of Hindustan': Ibid., p. 16.
96	'sifted the dust of misfortune': Thackston (trans.), The History of Akbar, Vol. 4, p. 39
96	'disregarded the objects and overlooked his treachery': Ibid., p. 41.
97	'He never gave anybody the chance': Vincent Arthur Smith, *Akbar the Great Mogul, 1542-1605*, p. 73.
97	'He is so mean and suspicious': Thackston (trans.), *The History of Akbar*, Vol. 4, p. 20.
97	'I will not go before the Emperor': Ibid.
98	'with whom they had shared cups in drunkenness': Ibid.
99	concentration of jagirs held by clans in one particular region: See Khan, *India's Polity in the Age of Akbar* for details.
99	separated the department of finance (diwani) from the jurisdiction of the wakil: Iqtidar Alam Khan, *The Political Biography of A Mughal Noble: Munim Khan-I-Khanan 1497-1575*, New Delhi: Orient Longman, 1973, p. 71.
100	'in which human had never set foot': Thackston (trans.), *The History of Akbar*, Vol. 4, p. 61.
100	'savage inhabitants, knowing that they can commit robberies': Monserrate, *The Commentary of Father Monserrate*, p. 21.
100	'by giving it straw, grain and water appropriate to its nature': Thackston (trans.), *The History of Akbar*, Vol. 4, p. 59.
100	'desired to hunt some more wild beasts': Ibid.
100	'swam like sea horses': Ibid.
101	'since the blade was an Indian khanda': Beveridge (trans.), *Akbarnama*, Vol. 2, p. 347.
102	'a synthesis formed from the Indo-Islamic regional styles of Gujarat and Bengal': J. P. Losty, 'Indian Painting from 1500–1575', *Masters of Indian Painting: 1650–1900*, edited by M. C. Beach et al., Zurich: Artibus Asiae, 2011, pp. 67–76.
102	3,000 qalandars and other mendicants were rounded up: Khan, *India's Polity in the Age of Akbar*, p. 139.
102	These ex-mendicants could now afford simple meals of khichdi: Moosvi, 'Production, Consumption and Population in Akbar's Time', *Proceedings of the IHC*, Vol. 33, 1971, pp. 260–69.
103	During those days I set out from Agra for Gujarat: Quoted in Khan, *India's Polity in the Age of Akbar*, p. 139.
103	'mansions of his nobles, the magazines, the treasure': Monserrate, *The Commentary of Father Monserrate*, p. 34.
103	'in the fine styles of Bengal and Gujarat': R. Burns (ed.), *The Cambridge History of India: The Mughul Period*, planned by W. Haig, New Delhi: S. Chand & Co., 1957, p. 537.
103	'ornamental gardens in their courtyards': Monserrate, *The Commentary of Father Monserrate*, p. 219.
103–04	roofs and ceilings were decorated with carvings: Ibid.
104	'The multitude of foreigners from all sorts of nations': Sunil Sharma, *Mughal Arcadia: Persian Literature in an Indian Court*, Cambridge: Harvard University Press, 2017, p. 111.
104	'and his dislike of fine clothes won him from his brothers': Francis Goldie, *The First Christian Mission to the Great Mogul, Or, the Story of Blessed Rudolf Acquaviva: And of His Four Companions in Martyrdom of the Society of Jesus*, Sacramento: Creative Media Partners, 2018, p. 6.
104	told his servants that he dreamed of going to a faraway place: Ibid.
105	Akbar gave 200 bighas of land in inam (revenue-free gift) to Gopaldas: Tarapada Mukherjee and Irfan Habib, 'Akbar and the Temples of Mathura and its Environs',

	Proceedings of the Indian History Congress, Vol. 48, 1987, pp. 234–50.
106	'Khan Baba, do you know what that Tajik dwarf has done?': Khan, *The Political Biography of a Mughal Noble*, p. 81fn.
107	'do such things to Sulaiman that he would be a warning': Beveridge (trans.), *Akbarnama*, Vol. 2, p. 382.
107	'As the two boats approached each other in the middle of the Ganga': Khan, *The Political Biography of a Mughal Noble*, p. 85.
108	**left Kabul and attempted to occupy Lahore:** For a detailed analysis of Mirza Hakim, see Munis D. Faruqui, 'The Forgotten Prince: Mirza Hakim and the Formation of the Mughal Empire', *Journal of the Economic and Social History of the Orient*, Vol. 48, No. 4, 2005, pp. 487–523.
108	**A vast plain outside Lahore was chosen:** Shaha Altaf Parpia, 'Imperial Hunting Grounds: A New Reading of Mughal Cultural History', PhD submitted at the University of Adelaide 2018, p. 33.
110	**the ascetic Sannyasis and the tantric Naths:** James Mallinson, 'Yogic Identities: Tradition and Transformation' available at <https://eprints.soas.ac.uk/17966/2/yogic-identities.asp> [accessed: 1 January 2020].
110	'casting pearls into the dust': Thackston (trans.), *Akbarnama*, Vol. 4, p. 257.
110	'ground into the dust': Ibid., p. 259.
110–11	'beautiful youth and was immoderate with regard to him': Ibid., p. 404.
111	'confined under the public staircase': Rosalind O'Hanlon, 'Kingdom, Household and Body: History, Gender and Imperial Service under Akbar', *Modern Asian Services*, Vol. 41, No. 5, p. 919.
111	'the filthy manners of Transoxiana': Ibid., p. 919.
111	**by the time he reached Manikpur, there were only eleven courtiers left:** Thackston (trans.), *History of Akbar*, Vol. 4, p. 267.
112	'ground his bones to powder and made his body': Badauni, *Muntakhabh al-Tawarikh*, Vol. 2, p. 99.
112	'twisted him in its trunk, stepped on him': Beveridge (trans.), *History of Akbar*, Vol. 4, p. 147.
112	**would swell to 38 per cent, almost at a par now with the Turanis at 39 per cent:** Khan, *India's Polity in the Age of Akbar*, p. 186.
112	'like the constellation of the Bear in the sky': Afzal Husain, *The Nobility of Akbar and Jahāngīr: A Study of Family Groups*, New Delhi: Manohar, 1999, p. 53.
112	**Akbar now also pragmatically restored Gondwana:** Chandra, *Medieval India: From the Sultanat to the Mughals*, Part 2, p. 106.
113	**use at his discretion for 'deserving people':** Khan, 'The Nobility under Akbar and the Development of His Religious Policy, 1560–1580', p. 33.
113	**'be very much annoyed' by the company of Shirazi:** Badauni, *Muntakhabh al-Tawarikh*, Vol. 2, p. 34.
113	'was a great act of injustice to both of them': Ibid., p. 102.
114	'One eye was lost in a broil with his brother': James Tod, *Annals and Antiquities: Or the Central and Western Rajput State of India*, Vol. 1, p. 50.
115	'knew his own strength and felt at ease about Chittor': Eliot, *The History of India, as Told by Its Own Historians*, p. 170.
115	'the absence of the kingly virtues': Tod, *Annals and Antiquities of Rajasthan*, p. 325.
116	**garrison, it is said, 'uttered cries of derision':** Eliot, *The History of India, as Told by Its Own Historians*, p. 171.
116	'the shovel was nearly as important as the musket': de la Garza, *The Mughal Empire at War*, p. 105.
116	'zigzag trenches and sunken gun emplacements': Ibid., p. 118.
117	**the worth of silver and gold had reduced to dust:** Ibid.

117 'horses themselves looked like beasts from a nightmare': Schimmel, *The Empire of the Great Moghuls*, p. 88.
118 'with a spiked breastplate who looked like a commander': John Dowson, *History of India*, Vol. 4, p. 188.
118 'This is the fire of jauhar': Thackston (trans.), *The History of Akbar*, Vol. 4, p. 363.
119 'it was expected that a besieged enemy would surrender soon': de la Garza, *The Mughal Empire at War*, p. 173.
120 The Turani people have ever been soldiers: Ibid., p. 95.
120 We, as far as it is within our power, remain busy in jihad: Khan, *India's Polity in the Age of Akbar*, p. 124.
121 'reported to launch a payload of over 3000 pounds': de la Garza, *The Mughal Empire at War*, p. 78.

PART 3: THE WORLD IS A BRIDGE (1569–1578)
127 'he found the place overrun with ghosts': Monserrate, *The Commentary of Father Monserrate*, p. 36.
127 Shaikh Salim lived a life as frugal as his surroundings: Badauni, *Muntakhabh al-Tawarikh*, Vol. 3, p. 27.
127 'as the common people of this country have an old custom': Beveridge (trans.), *Akbarnama*, Vol. 2, p. 505.
128 Akbar set off on foot from Agra to fulfil a vow: See *Akbarnama* miniature, 'Akbar receives the news in Agra of the birth of his son Salim'.
128 the infant Salim also travelled to Ajmer: Arif Qandahari, *Tarikh-i-Akbari*, p. 163.
128 'a wise and respectable saint': Ibid., p. 162.
129 'trafficking with Kings and conquering their souls': Quoted in Muzaffar Alam, 'The Mughals, the Sufi Shaikhs and the Formation of the Akbari Dispensation', *Modern Asian Studies*, Vol. 43, No. 1, p. 144.
129 'There is no precedence of one religion over the other': Ibid., p. 162.
129 Akbar did not require these women to convert to Islam: For a full discussion, see Ruby Lal, *Domesticity and Power*, Cambridge: Cambridge University Press, 2005 and Mukhoty, *Daughters of the Sun*.
130 'ever since the reign of Akbar, it had been ordained': Mukhia, *Mughals of India*, p. 129.
131 Rawat Durga Das of Deogarh married strong horse-riding women: Joshi, *Polygamy and Purdah*, p. 40.
131 Widow remarriage, also known as nata marriages: Ramya Sreenivasan, *The Many Lives of a Rajput Queen: Heroic Pasts in India C. 1500-1900*, Washington D. C.: University of Washington Press, 2007, p. 73.
132 'a form of purdah served to promote': Molly Emma Aitken, 'Pardah and Portrayal: Rajput Women as Subjects, Patrons, and Collectors', *Artibus Asiae*, Vol. 62, No. 2, 2002, p. 247.
132 Mughal women were pardeh-giyan, the veiled ones: Lal, *Domesticity and Power*, p. 176.
132 'From early youth, in compliment to his wives': Badauni, *Muntakhabh al-Tawarikh*, Vol. 2, p. 269.
133 'jewelled strings tied on his wrists, by Brahmans, by way of a blessing': Ibid.
133 'certain pandering pimps': Ibid., p. 313.
133 Akbar, too, started keeping fasts regularly: Taylor Sen, *Feasts and Fasts*, p. 189.
133 'Of the austerities practised by my revered father': Alexander Rogers (trans.), *Tuzuk-i-Jahangiri or Memoirs of Jahangir*, 2 Vols., edited by H. Beveridge, Delhi: Low Price Publications, 1909–14, 2017 (repr.), p. 45.
133 vegetarian dishes made for Akbar as noted by Abu'l Fazl included khushka, plain boiled rice: Taylor Sen, *Feasts and Fasts*, p. 184.
133 'such as boar cooked with onions, coriander': Collingham, *Curry*, p. 21.

134	a favourite was the dal batti churma: Taylor Sen, *Feasts and Fasts*, p. 251.
134	Padshah immediately declared that he would never hunt again on a Friday: George Malleson, *Akbar and the Rise of the Mughal Empire*, 36 Vols., edited by W. W. Hunter, New Delhi: Cosmo Publications, 2001, p. 179.
134	'in the lodgings of Shaikh Salim': *The Proceedings of the Indian History Congress*, Vol. 60.
134	'[Shaikh Salim] allowed the Emperor to have the entree': Badauni, *Muntakhabh al-Tawarikh*, Vol. 2, p. 118.
134	'either make no friendship with an elephant driver': Ibid., p. 113.
134	'to silence the babble of the common throng': Thackston (trans.), *Akbarnama*, Vol. 4, p. 433.
134	'The Emperor built a lofty palace on the top of the hill of Sikri': Badauni, *Muntakhabh al-Tawarikh*, Vol. 2, p. 112.
134	'vexatious question' that Akbar's growing harem: Abu'l Fazl, *Ain-i Akbari*, Vol. 1, translated by H. Blochmann, Calcutta: Asiatic Society of Bengal, 1878, p. 44.
135	'one of the first Sanskrit works ever to be commissioned by the Mughals': Audrey Truschke, *Culture of Encounters: Sanskrit at the Mughal Court*, New Delhi: Penguin Books, 2017, p. 119.
135	The entire world shines with his splendor such that it blinds the eyes: Ibid., p. 120.
138	'He was quite taken with cheetah hunting': Thackston (trans.), *The History of Akbar*, Vol. 4, p. 511
138	Samand Malik, was carried in a litter: Enayatullah Khan, 'Akbar and His Cheetahs', *Proceedings of the Indian History Congress*, Vol. 73, 2012, p. 463.
140	'set alight, and watched burn, a crowded pilgrim ship': M. N. Pearson, *The Cambridge History of India: The Portuguese in India*, Cambridge: Cambridge University Press, 2006, p. 71.
140	'during the government of the Malik, the Firangi was unable to enter the Gujarat ports': Habib (ed.), *Akbar and His India*, p. 258.
140	'the merchants of Rum, Syria, Persia and Turan': Thackston (trans.), *The History of Akbar*, Vol. 3, p. 13.
140	fifteenth-century text of the region called the *Varnak Samucay*: Aparna Kapadia, 'Why a 15th-century manuscript of Indian recipes lists eight kinds of samosas—none with potatoes', *Scroll.in*, 9 September 2019.
141	'neither eat nor kill any living thing': Guiseppe De Lorenzo, 'India in the Letters of Pietro della Valle', *East and West*, Vol. 7, No. 3, October 1956, pp. 212–13.
141	'very beautiful with their horns decorated with gold and jewels...': Ibid., p. 212.
141	engaged in buying Gujarati goods to send to Goa: Pearson, *The Portuguese in India*, p. 83.
142	Akbar would cut taxes on the export and import of goods: *Proceedings of the Indian History Congress*, Part 1, 2007, p. 244.
142	'evil-conditioned men': Beveridge (trans.), *Akbarnama*, Vol. 3, p. 9.
142	'roared loudly like a lion and called his men': Qandahari, *Tarikh-i-Akbari*, p. 194.
143	'We have ordered that Rumi Khan should make ready 500 pieces of Daudi': Iqtidar Alam Khan, 'Fath-Nama-I Gujarat (Akbar's letter to Munim Khan)', *Proceedings of the Indian History Congress*, Vol. 29, Part 1, 1967, p. 147.
143	He [Akbar] is such an expert in espionage that he keeps four thousand: Qandahari, *Tarikh-i-Akbari*, p. 62.
144	'about the wonders of Portugal and the manners and customs of Europe': Beveridge (trans.), Akbarnama, Vol. 3, p. 27.
144	'scent turned the lions of skies dead-drunk': Ibid., p. 199.
144	issued passes to members of Akbar's family to go on pilgrimage: Habib (ed.), *Akbar and His India*, p. 260.
145	'so that the latter would transfix them and come out at their backs': Moosvi, *Episodes*

	in the Life of Akbar, p. 40.
145	'declared that if Rajputs were wont to sell their valour': Ibid., p. 41.
145	'the best of these houses from the roadside look like hell': Quoted in Shireen Moosvi, 'Urban Houses and Building: Use in Mughal India', *Proceedings of the Indian History Congress*, Vol. 72, Part 1, 2011, p. 424.
145	'build their houses more for the benefit of the onlookers': Ibid.
146	'Proclaim the manifestation of your Mahdiship': Stephen P. Blake, 'Chronology: Millenarian', *Time in Early Modern Islam: Calendar, Ceremony, and Chronology in the Safavid, Mughal and Ottoman Empires*, Cambridge: Cambridge University Press, pp. 141–73.
147	'His majesty', wrote Jahangir: Rogers (trans.), *Tuzuk-i-Jahangiri*, Vol. 2, p. 40.
147–48	'had favoured him from his very infancy': Thackston (trans.), *Jahangirnama*, p. 63.
148	'It gets up in great strength every year in the heats': Eraly, *The Last Spring*, Part 2, p. 3.
149	'like the full moon, traversed an immense distance in the night': Moosvi, *Episodes in the Life of Akbar*, p. 44.
149	Fifteen were Hindus and included Raja Birbal: Parmeshwar P. Sinha, *Raja Birbal – Life and Times*, New Delhi: Janaki Prakashan, 1980, p. 58.
149	'including a breastplate, backplate, and two smaller pieces': *Journal of Asian History*, Vols. 19–20, 1985, p. 208.
150	'This is the army of the Emperor, which has come from Fatehpur': Moosvi, *Episodes in the Life of Akbar*, p. 47.
150	'And if it is the imperial army, where are the imperial elephants?': Ibid., p. 48.
150	'if this time too a daughter comes': Beveridge (trans.), *Akbarnama*, Vol. 3, p. 83.
150	'If you wish to retain our affection': Ibid., p. 83.
151	'This Prince,' wrote Monserrate: Monserrate, *The Commentary of Father Monserrate*, p. 196.
151	'Which of these men captured you?': Ibid., p. 49.
151	grabbed a spear, and flung it at the man: Elliot, *The History of India, As Told by Its Own Historians*, Vol. 5, p. 367.
152	constructed with some 1,000 heads of the fallen enemy: Badauni, *Muntakhabh al-Tawarikh*, p. 172.
152	They were dragged into court, to the horror, bemusement, and chilled amusement of the courtiers: Nizamuddin Ahmad, *Tabakat-i Akbari of Nizam-ud-din Ahmad Bakhshi*, Lahore: Sind Sagar, 1975 (repr.), p. 26.
152	During the same year plague and famine visited Gujarat: Qandahari, *Tarikh-i Akbari*, p. 232–33.
153	'of such austere life that he first feeds his cattle with corn': Jarrett (trans.), *Ain-i Akbari*, Vols. 2 & 3, p. 31.
154	'assembly erupted in such a roar of congratulations': Faruqui, *The Princes of the Mughal Empire*, p. 146.
154	'a coat without lining of the Indian form': Blochmann (trans.), *Ain-i Akbari*, Vol. 1, p. 88.
155	'absurd style': Badauni quoted in Schimmel, *The Empire of the Great Mughals*, p. 170.
155	made from shahtoos, the soft wool from the underbellies of mountain goats: Schimmel, *The Empire of the Great Mughals*, p. 170.
155	introduced the word sarbgati (covering the whole body) for jama: Blochmann (trans.), *Ain-i Akbari*, Vol. 1, p. 90.
155	courtiers all wore small, compact, 'atpati' turbans: *The British Library Journal*, Vols. 1–3, p. 159.
155	he took to wearing as a sarpech (turban ornament): Rogers (trans.), *Tuzuk-i-Jahangiri*, p. 409.
155	'In society,' warned the eighteenth-century Mirza Namah: Stephen P. Blake,

	Shahjahanabad: The Sovereign City in Mughal India, 1639–1739, Cambridge: Cambridge University Press, 1991, p. 138.
156	**A great portion of the life of the students is wasted**: Blochmann (trans.), *Ain-i Akbari*, Vol 1, p. 278.
156	**'to overcome deficiencies in weight or height'**: Stephen P. Blake, 'Courtly Culture under Babur and the Early Mughals', *Journal of Asian History*, Vol. 20, No. 2, 1986, p. 207.
157	**'At that time in Muscovy'**: Robert K. Massie, *Peter the Great: His Life and Work*, New York: Knopf, 1981.
157	**'The wise sovereign'**: Beveridge (trans.), *Akbarnama*, Vol. 3, p. 105.
158	**'I have not so much affection for my own mother as for her'**: Rogers (trans.), *Tuzuk-i-Jahangiri*, p. 78.
158	**'famed as a consummate gatherer of rumour, gossip, news and intelligence'**: Faruqui, *The Princes of the Mughal Empire*, p. 147.
158	**'many of my predecessors composed works in a mixed language'**: Raghavan, *Attendant Lords*, p. 71.
158–59	**'after my birth they gave me the name of Sultan Salim'**: Thackston (trans.), *Jahangirnama*, p. 21.
159	**'protectors for his children from the malice of his life-long enemies'**: Ibid.
159	**'[Akbar] gives very great care and attention'**: Monserrate, *The Commentary of Father Monserrate*, p. 203.
159	**As Emperor Jahangir he would develop an appreciation**: Rogers (trans.), *Tuzuk-i-Jahangiri*, p. 141.
159	**'was fond of Hindi songs and would occasionally compose verses'**: Ibid., p. 36.
159	**'[Akbar] maintains, and gives a liberal education'**: Monserrate, *The Commentary of Father Monserrate*, p. 207.
159	**'Lal Kalawant, who from his childhood had grown up in my father's service'**: Rogers (trans.), *Tuzuk-i-Jahangiri*, p. 150.
160	**'in his young days my father'**: Ibid., p. 17.
160	**'He used to give them orders rather roughly'**: Ibid., p. 53.
160	**'august voice was very resonant'**: Moosvi, *Episodes in the Life of Akbar*, p. 124.
160	**'His table is very sumptuous, generally consisting'**: Monserrate, *The Commentary of Father Monserrate*, p. 199.
161	**the hakim (royal physician) planned each menu**: Salma Husain, *The Mughal Feast: Recipes from the Kitchen of Emperor Shah Jahan*, New Delhi: Roli Books, 2019.
161	**biryani itself was a fragrant and fortuitous Mughal mix**: Collingham, *Curry*, p. 95.
161	**included yakhni, a meat stock; musamman, stuffed roast chicken**: Taylor Sen, *Feasts and Fasts*, p. 186.
161	**Nor did the food contain kalonji, mustard seeds**: Ibid., p. 186.
162	**'looks upon fruits as one of the greatest gifts of the Creator, and pays much attention to them'**: Ibid., p. 184.
162	**'The food allowed to the women of the seraglio'**: Blochmann (trans.), *Ain-i Akbari*, Vol. 1, p. 59.
164	**much that remains a mystery about Fatehpur Sikri**: For some recent scholarship on the subject, see Syed Ali Nadeem Rezavi, *Fathpur Sikri Revisited*, New Delhi: Oxford University Press, 2013.
164	**'Agra and Fatepore', wrote Ralph Fitch**: Eraly, *The Mughal World: Life in India's Last Golden Age*, New Delhi: Penguin Books, 2007, p. 8.
165	**'splendour of [Akbar's] palaces approaches closely to that'**: Monserrate, *The Commentary of Father Monserrate*, p. 199.
165	**'in the course of fourteen or fifteen years that hill'**: Thackston (trans), *Jahangirnama*, p. 22.

165	**the Jami mosque has a triad of domes:** For a discussion on the Jami mosque, see Rezavi, *Fathpur Sikri Revisited*.
165	**'The World is a Bridge, pass over it, but build no houses upon it':** Husain Ahmad Khan, *Artisans, Sufis, Shrines: Colonial Architecture in Nineteenth-Century Punjab*, London: I. B. Tauris, 2015, p. 24.
165	**'[Akbar] is so devoted to building that he sometimes quarries':** Monserrate, *The Commentary of Father Monserrate*, p. 201.
166	**'chains, manacles, handcuffs and other irons':** Ibid., p. 211.
166	**'everything cleverly fashioned elsewhere':** Ibid.
166	**it was furnished too, with rich carpets on the floors and draperies:** Rezavi, 'Mughal Wall Paintings', pp. 375–402.
167	**'Shame on you':** Shaikkh Mustafa recorded the debates at Akbar's court, they have been preserved by the Mahdavis in the Majalis-i Khamsah. The portions quoted here are from 'Beyond Turk and Hindu: Rethinking Religious Identities in Islamicate South Asia' edited by David Gilmartin and Bruce B Lawrence.
168–69	**dynamic preacher had become a frail and feeble:** Badauni, *Muntakhabh al-Tawarikh*, Vol. 3, p. 85.
169	**'many Hindus and Musulmans perished in the flames':** Ibid.
169	**'In ordinary cases...a candidate had to find a patron':** Moreland, *India at the Death of Akbar*, p. 69.
169	**'as learning was a merchandise much in demand':** Peter Hardy, *Historians of Medieval India*, p. 107.
170	**'Mullah Abdul Qadir,' wrote Faizi:** Harbans Mukhia (ed.), *Historians And Historiography during the Reign of Akbar*, New Delhi: Vikas Publishing, 1976, p. 92.
170	**'From [Akbar] comes the solution of spiritual and temporal matters':** Ibid., p. 277.
171	**'all the Indian parrots will turn to crunching sugar':** Muzaffar Alam, *The Languages of Political Islam, c.1200–1800*, Delhi: Permanent Black, 2004, p. 123.
172	**'slaves and servants' of Abdur Rahim:** Orsini, *Telling and Texts*, p. 291.
172	**'duhu deen ko sahib':** Ibid., p. 139.
172	**'very handsome and used to sing at social gatherings':** Ibid., p. 295.
172	**disapproving of his association with dervishes, courtesans and, intriguingly, dogs:** Ibid.
172	**'not only complex competitive arenas and technical workshops':** Ibid.
172	**I cannot tolerate those who make the slightest criticism:** Valerie Gonzalez, *Aesthetic Hybridity in Mughal Painting, 1526–1658*, Farnham: Ashgate, 2015, p. 234.
173	**'He has built a workshop':** Monserrate, *The Commentary of Father Monserrate*, p. 201.
173	**'Sometimes actual jewels—rubies, emeralds, diamonds':** Welch, *India*, p. 171.
174	**'whoever writes "in the name of God the Merciful and Compassionate"':** Stuart Cary Welch, *The Emperors' Album*, p. 31.
174	**'kept busy creating not only delights for the emperor':** Ibid., p. 17.
175	**he would have thrilled to see the raw, untethered talent of these artists:** Welch, *India*, p. 154.
175	**'Judge the nobility of any one's being and great lineage':** Mukhia, *The Mughals of India*, p. 59.
175–76	**'outer garment of submission':** Beveridge (trans.), *Akbarnama*, p. 96.
177	**'the princes and a few of the ladies and the cream of the courtiers':** Beveridge (trans.), *Akbarnama*, Vol. 3, p. 83.
177	**'gardens, such as clever craftsmen could not make on land':** Smith, *Akbar the Great Mogul*, p. 126.
177	**'the strength to pull down mountains and break the ranks':** O'Hanlon, *At the Edges of Empire*, p. 903.
177	**'any 'experienced seamen acquainted with the tides':** de la Garza, *The Mughal Empire at War*, p. 113.

178	'the birds of the air and the fish of the water': Badauni, *Muntakhabh al-Tawarikh*, Vol. 2, p. 178.
178	Heroic deeds were recalled, musicians sang: Schimmel, *Anvari's Divan*, p. 24.
178	they named the Alphonso, in honour of Alfonso de Albuquerque: Nene Y.L. (2001), 'Mango through Millennia', *Asian Agri History*, Vol. 5, No. 1, pp. 39–67.
178	moved to tears by the touching pathos of the stories: Badauni, *Muntakhabh al-Tawarikh*, Vol. 3, p. 89.
178	'the waters of the Ganga and Jumna unite': Ibid.
179	'many beggars in these countries which go naked': Ralph Fitch, *The First Englishmen in India*, edited by J. Courtenay Locke, London: Routledge, 2004, p. 55.
179	'For a long time, His Majesty's desire was to found a great city': Fazl quoted in Surendranath Sinha, *Subah of Allahabad Under the Great Mughals, 1580–1707*, Allahabad: Jamia Millia Islamia, 1974, p. 85.
179	'Here is great store of fish of sundry sorts': John Pinkerton, *A General Collection of the Best and Most Interesting Voyages and Travels in Various Parts of Asia*, Vol. 3, London: Longman, Hurst, Rees, Orme, and Brown, Paternoster Row, and Cadell and Davies, 1819, p. 411.
180	'into the midst of the raging stream 3000 fully equipped horsemen': Badauni, *Muntakhabh al-Tawarikh*, Vol. 2, p. 182.
180	'the noise, the smoke and the concussion shook the earth': Beveridge (trans.), *Akbarnama*, Vol. 3, p. 135.
180	Daud Khan was believed to have possessed an enormous army of 40,000 cavalry: Chandra, *A History of Medieval India*, p. 232.
181	fifty-two bazaars, fifty-two wholesale markets and fifty-two caravanserais: Tapan Raychaudhari and Irfan Habib (eds.), *The Cambridge Economic History of India*, Vol. 1, p. 325.
182	'I received his Majesty's instructions': Badauni, *Muntakhabh al-Tawarikh*, Vol. 2, p. 186.
182	'seances for dancing and sufism took place': Ibid.
182	'done the work of many years': Beveridge (trans.), *Akbarnama*, Vol. 3, p. 157.
184	'an unrivalled device for organizing the ruling class': For detailed explanations see Khan, *India's Polity in the Age of Akbar*; M. Athar Ali, 'Towards an Interpretation of the Mughal Empire', *The State in India, 1000–1700*, edited by H. Kulke, Delhi: Oxford University Press, 1980, pp. 263–77.
184	'These men were specialists': Stephen P. Blake, 'Courtly Culture under Babur and the Early Mughals', *Journal of Asian History*, Vol. 20, No. 2, 1986, pp. 193–214.
184	men holding ranks upto 500 were all called mansabdars: Chandra, *Medieval India: Delhi Sultanat, 1206-1526*, Part 1, p. 157; *From Sultanat to the Mughals*, Part 2, p. 157.
184	Amirs did as they pleased...[putting] most of their own servants: Michael Fisher, *A Short History of the Mughal Empire*, New Delhi: Bloomsbury Publishing, 2015, p. 104.
185	'making loyalty more profitable than rebellion': Rima Hooja, *A History of Rajasthan*, p. 447.
185	'who was fully conversant with': Ibid., p. 536.
186	'various villages were endowed to Brahmans, Charans, and Bhats': Ibid., p. 544.
186	'his saddle is his throne': Ibid., p. 546.
186	'ivory, copper, dates, gum-arabic, borax, coconuts, silk, chintzes, muslin, shawls': Ibid., p. 543.
186	'with all its post-life connotations of hell-fire and damnation': Ibid., p. 543.
187	All applications and documents presented to the court: Schimmel, *The Empire of the Great Mughals*, p. 73.
187	'The farman is folded so that both corners touch, then a paper knot is tied': Ibid.
187	'A tremendous battle took place': Badauni, *Muntakhabh al-Tawarikh, Vol. 2, p. 136.*
188	lashing out at Gujar Khan Afghan with a whip: Khan, *The Political Biography of a Mughal*

	Noble, p. 143.
188	**'incorporating' Daud Khan into the body of the emperor:** Richard M. Eaton, *The Rise of Islam and the Bengal Frontier, 1204–1760*, Berkeley: University of California Press, 1993, p. 166.
188	**seizing the capital and possessing the land were two different matters:** Ibid., p. 142.
189	**'the method to restrain the faction':** Eaton, *India in the Persianate Age*, p. 230.
189	**this had 'quieted the slaves to gold':** Ibid.
189	**'His Majesty spent whole nights in praising God':** Schimmel and Welch, *Anvari's Divan*, p. 25.
189	**'with his head bent over his chest, gathering the bliss':** Ibid.
189	**'Discourses on philosophy have such a charm for me':** Jarrett (trans.), 'Happy Sayings of Akbar', *Ain-i Akbari*, Vol. 3, Part 5.
190	**'consisting of four porticoes with separate seating arrangements for the nobles':** Rezavi, *Fathpur Sikri Revisited*, p. 52.
190	**'He is the man':** Badauni, *Muntakhabh al-Tawarikh*, Vol. 3, p. 116.
190	**'You have passed through a great danger':** Ibid.
190	**'worked so strenuously at the dagh-u-mhali (branding) business':** Ibid., p. 205.
191	**Akbar would visit the sadr, and stand barefoot:** Ibid., p. 204.
191	**'were neither speculative intellectuals nor serious religious thinkers':** Richards, *The Mughal Empire*, p. 37.
191	**humiliating the great amirs of the court:** Badauni, *Muntakhabh al-Tawarikh*, Vol. 3.
191	**'at loggerheads with each other':** Mukhia, *Historians and Historiography during the Reign of Akbar*, p. 96.
192	**'called him an accursed wretch, abused him, and lifted up his stick to strike him':** Ibid., p. 211.
192	**'in our youth we had not felt bound by this rule':** Irfan Habib, 'Akbar and Social Inequities: A Study of the Evolution of His Ideas', *Proceedings of the Indian History Congress*, 1992, Vol. 53, p. 303.
192	**'in justice to his wives...he wanted to know what remedy the law':** Lal, *Domesticity and Power*, p. 172.
193	**four wives, the instrument of divorce:** Majid, 'Women and a Theologian', p. 252.
193	**'and some of you shall have life prolonged to a miserable age':** Badauni, *Muntakhabh al-Tawarikh*, Vol. 3, p. 205.
193	**'from this day forward the road to opposition and differences in opinion':** Makhanlal Roychoudhury, *The Din-I-Ilahi, Or, The Religion of Akbar*, Delhi: Munshiram Manoharlal Publishers, 1997, p. 80.
194	**'specially remarkable for his tact, his knowledge':** Beveridge (trans.), *Akbarnama*, Vol. 3, p. 144.
194	**'were exceedingly winning':** Quoted in Elliot, *The History of India, as Told by Its Own Historians*, p. 524.
195	**'the women were not veiled, they rode, went on picnics':** Shadab Bano, 'Eunuchs in Mughal Household and Court', *Proceedings of the Indian History Congress*, Vol. 69, 2008, p. 418.
195	**'pillars of chastity' and 'cupolas of chastity':** See Lal, *Domesticity and Power*, for a thorough study of the changing status of Mughal women.
195	**'long ago made a vow to visit the holy places':** Beveridge (trans.), *Akbarnama*, Vol. 3, p. 145.
196	**'sang in the moonlight on the road to Lagham in 1549':** Lal, *Domesticity and Power*, p. 209.
196	**be marooned for a year while they waited for a ship to rescue them:** For more details of the women's Hajj see *Daughters of the Sun* and *Domesticity and Power*.
196	**'sent with her [Gulbadan] a large amount of money and goods':** Beveridge (trans.),

Akbarnama, Vol. 3, p. 207.
196 **He enlarged the pious trust (waqf):** Richards, *The Mughal Empire*, Part 1, Vol. 5, p. 31.
196 **Akbar sponsored the building of a hospice in Mecca:** N. R. Farooqi, 'An Overview of Ottoman Archival Documents and Their Relevance for Medieval Indian History', *Journal*, Vol. 20, No. 1, 2017, p. 207.
197 **'A general permission was given to the people':** Badauni, *Muntakhabh al-Tawarikh*, Vol. 3, p. 213.
197 **'the curiosities and rarities':** Ibid., p. 207.
197 **'the great Amirs, the officers of every territory':** Ibid., p. 206.
198 **'He rendered his account to the guardian of Paradise':** Badauni, *Muntakhabh al-Tawarikh*, Vol. 2, p. 221.
198 **'The thought of death took hold of everyone':** Beveridge (trans.), *Akbarnama*, Vol. 3, p. 227.
198 **'Things came to such a pass that the living were unable to bury the dead':** Eaton, *The Rise of Islam and the Bengal Frontier*, p. 144.
198 **'contributed to the stereotype':** Ibid., p. 144.
198 ***Salimi*** **and the *Ilahi*, either built or bought by Akbar in the three years:** Shireen Moosvi, 'Shipping and Navigation under Akbar', *Proceedings of the Indian History Congress*, Vol. 60, 1999, p. 1.
198 **'for he was a very handsome man':** Quoted in Elliot, *The History of India, as Told by Its Own Historians*, p. 48.
199 **'Several chaste women have been appointed as darogahs and superintendents':** Blochmann (trans.), *Ain-i Akbari*, Vol. 1, p. 45.
199 **Holy Lands as soon as they had completed the pilgrimages:** N. R. Farooqi, 'Diplomacy and Diplomatic Procedure under the Mughals', *The Medieval History Journal*, Vol. 7, No. 1, p. 206.
199–200 **'sufficiently liberal, not counting the presents, which his Majesty most generously bestows':** Ibid.
200 **'Everything that he knew about these things':** Badauni, *Muntakhabh al-Tawarikh*, Vol. 2, p. 218.
201 **'adorned with European velvet':** Mukhia, *The Mughals of India*, p. 80.
201 **'They spread royal tables in the audience-hall':** Badauni, *Muntakhabh al-Tawarikh*, Vol. 2, p. 220.
201 **'bejewelled and golden plates, big bowls':** Qandahari, *Tarikh-i-Akbari*, p. 243.
201 **'But when the Mirza departed':** Badauni, *Muntakhabh al-Tawarikh*, Vol. 2, p. 220.
202 **He baulked, however, at the idea of going in person to the Mughal court:** Hooja, *A History of Rajasthan*, p. 467.
203 **ensured his orders were carried out with 'unrelenting severity':** Tod, *Annals and Antiquities of Rajasthan*, p. 334.
203 **'If a Hindu had not been the leader of the army':** Badauni quoted in Bhardwaj, *Hemu*, p. 92.
204 **'Why, he has just been appointed one of the court imams':** Badauni, *Muntakhabh al-Tawarikh*, Vol. 2, p. 233.
204 **Badauni persuaded Akbar that he wanted to 'dye his beard in blood':** Ibid., p. 234.
204 **'3000 horsemen, 2000 infantry, 100 elephants and 100 miscellaneous men':** Ibid., p. 468.
204 **learning the spiky topography of the Mewar landscape while hunting deer:** Rima Hooja, *Maharana Pratap*, New Delhi: Juggernaut Books, 2018, p. 32.
204 **'above and below, the Rajputs were posted, and on the cliffs and pinnacles':** Tod, *Annals and Antiquities of Rajasthan*, p. 285.
205 **'the bravest men of their time':** Jahangir quoted in Faruqui, *The Princes of the Mughal Empire*, p. 152.

205	'a variety of exotic weapons like two-handed swords': de la Garza, *Mughal Empire at War*, p. 70.
205	'arguably the most formidable individual warrior on any battlefield': Badauni, *Muntakhabh al-Tawarikh*, Vol. 2, p. 237–38.
206	'How are we in these circumstances': Badauni quoted in Prasad, *Raja Man Singh of Amber*, p. 46.
206	'despite fighting very bravely and getting many wounds': Ibid., p. 239.
207	'he sent back both Bhagwant Das and Man Singh': Afzal Husain, *The Nobility Under Akbar and Jahāngīr: A Study of Family Groups*, New Delhi: Manohar Publishers, 1999, p. 93.
207	'there was no danger to Hinduism or the Hindu way of life': Hooja, *A History of Rajasthan*, p. 466.
208	'for preserving the dharma of the earth': Sreenivasan, *The Many Lives of a Rajput Queen*, p. 567.
209	'The Rana was defeated in battle': Allison Busch, 'Portrait of a Raja in a Badshah's World: Amrit Rai's Biography of Man Singh (1585)', *Journal of the Economic and Social History of the Orient*, Vol. 55, 2012, pp. 287–328.
209	'settled repugnance...to sully the purity of its blood': Tod, *Annals and Antiquities of Rajasthan*, p. 283.
209	when the Bhati Rajputs had committed saka and jauhar: Ibid., p. 551.
210	'took to wearing a long tail to the back of his turban': Badauni, *Muntakhabh al-Tawarikh*, Vol. 2, p. 248.
210	'betrayed the filthiness of his disposition': Ibid., p. 253.
210	'since Hindustan is a wide place': Ibid.
210	'During my exalted father's time': Thackston (trans.), *Jahangirnama*, p. 46.
211	'dressed plainly...forbade the slaughter of animals at his court': Ali Anooshahr, 'Shirazi Scholars and the Political Culture of the Sixteenth-Century Indo-Persian World', *The Indian Economic and Social History Review*, Vol. 51, No. 3, 2014, p. 340.
211	'like a great box the size of a man': Badauni, *Muntakhabh al-Tawarikh*, Vol. 2, p. 299.
211	'great with the great: lowly with the lowly': Schimmel, *Anvari's Divan*, p. 24.
212	a staggering 185 metric tons a year of silver from overseas: Eaton, *India in the Persianate Age*, p. 371.
212	'unique of the age for practical wisdom': Beveridge (trans.), *Akbarnama*, Vol. 3, p. 862.
213	'a happiness which I had been long anxiously expecting': Badauni, *Muntakhabh al-Tawarikh*, Vol. 2, p. 259.
213	'on account of certain important affairs, or rather follies': Ibid.
213	The breeze that cheers the heart comes from Fathpur: Ibid., p. 255.
214	'to consider all sects as one and not to distinguish one from another': Mukhia, *The Mughals of India*, p. 58.
214	'every evil that appeared in those days': *Studies in Islamic Culture*, Vol. 47, p. 240.
214	'The ladies of the imperial harem busied themselves in interceding for his release': Moosvi, *Episodes in the Life of Akbar*, p. 66.
214	an 'obligation to safeguard infidel subjects': Ibid., p. 67.
215	'From this time onwards': Ibid., p. 68.
215	'not only created hysteria in the hearts and minds of his companions': Qandahari, *Tarikh-i-Akbari*, p. 270.
215	'A divine flash of light was received by His Majesty': Moosvi, *Episodes in the Life of Akbar*, p. 71.
215	'The Divine Call had descended on the Emperor which tranced him completely': Qandahari, *Tarikh-i-Akbari*, p. 272.
215	Take care! For the grace of God comes suddenly: Schimmel, *Anvari's Divan*, p. 26.
215	'at the foot of a tree that was then in fruit': Ibid.

216	'made the reverence to his visible God (his mother)': Beveridge (trans.), *Akbarnama*, Vol. 3, p. 243.
216	'amazed at the laudable qualities': Ibid., p. 349.
217	'To the chief Padre, in the name of the Lord. I am sending Abdullah': Goldie, *The First Christian Mission to the Great Mogul*, p. 54.
217	'I should like to describe the pleasure': Monserrate, *The Commentary of Father Monserrate*, p. 4.
217	'weary of the contradictions and absurdity of the Mullahs': Ibid., p. 56.
217	'permitted the King of Portugal the sole right to sail the sea': Wilfred Prakash D'Souza Prabhu, 'Padroado versus Propaganda fide: The Jurisdictional Conflict between Portugal and Rome, *Proceedings of the IHC*, Vol. 66, 2005–06, p. 975.
218	'The antagonism of the sects reached such a pitch': Badauni, *Muntakhabh al-Tawarikh*, Vol 2, p. 262.
218	'The Emperor,' agreed Badauni: Ibid., p. 199.
218	I have set fire to my barn with my own hands: Ibid., p. 200.
219	'For which of these notorious heresies have you yourself the greatest inclination?': Ibid., p. 270.
219	'His Majesty was genuinely seeking after the Truth': Mukhia, *Historians and Historiography during the Reign of Akbar*, p. 100.
219	'Sufi, philosopher, orator, jurist, Sunni, Shia, Brahman, Jati, Sevra (Jain monks)': Syed Ali Nadeem Rezavi, 'Religious Disputations and Imperial Ideology: The Purpose and Location of Akbar's *Ibadatkhana*', *Studies in History*, Vol. 24, No. 2, pp. 195–209.
219–20	'May God help me! May God help me!': Maclagan, *The Jesuits and the Great Mogul*, p. 24.
220	'I'm writing to ask your prayers': Goldie, *The First Christian Mission to the Great Mogul*, p. 58.
220	'covered with cactus, with palms, and banyan trees': Ibid., p. 59.
221	A lofty college and high and spacious palaces were built on the road: Badauni, *Muntakhabh al-Tawarikh*, Vol 2, p. 176.
221	'For a long time, it was the custom that the dull and superficial': Beveridge (trans.), *Akbarnama*, Vol. 3, p. 367.
222	'the monoglot world of England and Ireland': Jerry Brotton, *This Orient Isle: Elizabethan England and the Islamic World*, London: Allen Lane, 2016.

PART 4: THE YEAR OF THE LION (1579–1585)

225	'instructed [Akbar] in the secrets and legends of Hinduism': Badauni, *Muntakhabh al-Tawarikh*, Vol. 2, p. 258.
225	'Shall I describe the constancy of its inhabitants': Jarrett (trans.), *Ain-i Akbari*, Vols. 2 & 3, p. 8.
226	'praised the truth based nature of the people of India': M. Athar Ali, 'The Evolution of the Perception of India: Akbar and Abu'l Fazl', *Social Scientist*, Vol. 24, Nos. 1–3, 1996, p. 83.
226	'his excellence in acquired knowledge': Badauni, *Muntakhabh al-Tawarikh*, Vol. 3, p. 232.
226	'natural language', a zuban-i-qudrut: Habib (ed.), *Akbar and His India*, p. 84.
227	'I have organized this majlis for the purpose only that': Rezavi, 'Religious Disputations and Imperial Ideology', p. 197.
228	term used for a scholar of Islamic law who used judgement, or ijtihad: Moin, *The Millennial Sovereign*, p. 216.
228	'paper-worshipping scholiasts': Ibid.
228	In the name of Him who gave us sovereignty: 'Smith, *Akbar the Great Mogul*, p. 177.
228	'why should we faqirs and people living in seclusion be troubled?': Maulana Abul Kalam

Azad, *Holy Angels of High Heavens*, p. 6.
229 'renowned for his devastating one-liners': Mukhia, *Mughals of India*, p. 43.
229 'O Prophet, protect the Joseph of my soul (i.e. my soul)': *Essays on Medieval India*, p. 252.
229 'what would the King of the West, as the Sultan of Rum': Hasan and Chandra, *Religion, State, and Society in Medieval India*, p. 83.
229 'would that they would beat your mouths with a slipper full of filth!': Badauni, *Muntakhabh al-Tawarikh*, Vol. 2, translated by Ranking, p. 282.
229 'as a means of calming the public and enhancing the submission of the recalcitrant': Qandahari, *Tarikh-i-Akbari*, p. 282.
229 'sensible people smiled': Ibid., p. 281.
230 'They shunned ritual and ceremony': Alam, *Languages of Political Islam in India*, p. 82.
230 17 per cent were Irani: Khan, *India's Polity in the Age of* Akbar, p. 187.
230 'When two people clash together': Ibid., p. 275.
232 'Everyone stopped and stared in great surprise and perplexity': Michael Fisher, *Visions of Mughal India: An Anthology of European Travel Writing*, London: I. B. Tauris, 2007, p. 48.
232 'was almost as fair as southern Europeans': Goldie, *The First Christian Mission to the Great Mogul*, p. 62.
233 painting in an anatomically accurate and naturalistic style: Singh, *Real Birds in Imagined Gardens*, p. 25.
233 'rule of silence and solitude, only coming out of his cell': Monserrate, *The Commentary of Father Monserrate*, p. 193.
233 'devoted to perpetual chastity and invoked the aid of the Virgin Mother of God': Ibid., p. 192.
234 'stuffed with countless fables full of futility and extreme frivolity': Monserrate, *The Commentary of Father Monserrate*, p. 37.
234 conciliatory shouts of 'Peace be to the King!': Ibid., p. 40.
235 'it was his desire that Christians should live freely in his empire': Ibid., p. 47.
235 'he first, in Muhammadan fashion, made a profound reverence': Goldie, *The First Christian Mission to the Great Mogul*, p. 69.
235 painting deemed to have been painted by St Luke himself: Maclagan, *The Jesuits and the Great Mogul*, p. 227.
235 'young man of a keen and capable mind': Monserrate, *The Commentary of Father Monserrate*, p. 49.
236 'He could well understand': Ibid., p. 52.
236 'the rest are all courtesans and adulteresses': Ibid., p. 45.
236 Since you reckon the reverencing of women as part of your religion: Beveridge (trans.), *Akbarnama*, Vol. 3, p. 372.
237 'Oh friend! By taking a royal umbrella': Joshi, *Polygamy and Purdah*, p. 91.
237 'The wretched women are rendered quite insensible by means of certain drugs': Monserrate, *The Commentary of Father Monserrate*, p. 62
237 'Under the principle of attachment to one another': Habib, 'Akbar and Social Inequities', p. 303.
237 'an exceedingly pious old man who was devoted to the study of religious commentaries': *Indian Journal of Politics*, Vol. 36, Nos. 1–4, p. 170.
238 'seemed to be inspired by a divine earnestness': Monserrate, *The Commentary of Father Monserrate*, p. 57.
238 'was an ideal pupil as regards natural ability, good conduct': Ibid., p. 52.
238 'lifted their hands to heaven and did reverence before it': Ibid., p. 60.
239 'the centre of a voluptuous and degrading worship': Goldie, *The First Christian Mission to the Great Mogul*, p. 110.

239	'the carelessness of these same Musulmans': Monserrate, *The Commentary of Father Monserrate*, p. 27.
239–40	'bend the knee, prostrate, lift up their hands': Ibid., p. 195.
240	these paintings to be of Timurid origin: Syed Ali Nadeem Rezavi, 'Mughal Wall Paintings: A Study of Fathpur Sikri', *Proceedings of the Indian History Congress*, Vol. 64, 2003, p. 384.
240	'(The Emperor) has painted images of Christ our Lord and our Lady': William Dalrymple, 'A Christmas Meditation', Qantara.de [accessed: 10 January 2019].
240	'Mughal imperial painting would eventually appropriate the tropes': Singh, *Real Birds in Imagined Gardens*, p. 29.
241	'From childhood to manhood': Eraly, *The Last Spring*, p. 195.
242–43	retained lands yielding about 25 per cent of the overall yield: Stephen P. Blake, 'The Patrimonial-Bureaucratic Empire of the Mughals', *Journal of Asian Studies*, Vol. 39, No. 1, November 1979, p. 87.
243	'men of low birth, upstarts': Monserrate, *The Commentary of Father Monserrate*, p. 27.
243	'Whenever a domestic servant turns to ilm (scholarly business)': *Proceedings of the Indian History Congress*, Vol. 53, p. 306.
243	an equal percentage of Rajput, Indian Muslim, and Persian noblemen: Husain, *The Nobility Under Akbar and Jahāngīr*, p. 35.
243	47 noblemen, Indian Muslims 44, with Turani noblemen: Khan, *India's Polity in the Age of Akbar*, p. 131.
244	'They were not troubled by the thought': Smith, *Akbar the Great Mogul*, p. 190.
244	'Aziz was remarkable for ease of address, intelligence': du Jarric, *Akbar and the Jesuits*, p. 138.
245	Akbar heard that Aziz Koka was 'ashamed and repentant': Beveridge (trans.), *Akbarnama*, Vol. 3, p. 454.
245	'those black standards, the sign of war to the death, which Timur the Lame': Monserrate, *The Commentary of Father Monserrate*, p. 73.
245	'yielding a revenue of about 22 crore dams or Rs 5,547,985': Imtiaz Ahmad, 'Mughal Governors of Bihar under Akbar and Jahangir', *Proceedings of the Indian History Congress*, Vol. 63, 2002, p. 283.
245	The country of Bengal is a land where owing to the climate's favouring: Eaton, *The Rise of Islam and the Bengal Frontier*, p. 100.
245	'inhabitants are as a race good-looking': Jarrett (trans.), *Ain-i Akbari*, Vols. 2 and 3, p. 130.
246	'soldiers recruited from the north, Marwari merchants': Eaton, *The Rise of Islam and the Bengal Frontier*, p. 167.
246	'Several boxes full of ingots of gold': Ibid., p. 572.
246	'unable to restrain his passion': Badauni, *Muntakhab al-Tawarikh*, Vol. 2, p. 321.
246	'where he had once spat on the amirs': Mubarak Ali, *The Ulema, Sufis and Intellectuals*, New York: Fiction House, 1995, p. 60.
247	'in such a manner that the ladies should not know of it': Ibid.
247	'possibly listening to political or military intelligence gathered through networks': Faruqui, *The Princes of the Mughal Empire*, p. 124.
248	'excessive indulgence in merry making': Ashraf Wani, 'Akbar and Kashmir', *Proceedings of the Indian History Congress*, Vol. 73, 2012, p. 4.
248	'to capture the European ports': N. R. Farooqi, *Mughal-Ottoman Relations: A Study of Political & Diplomatic Relations between Mughal India and the Ottoman Empire, 1556-1748*, Delhi: Idarah-i Adabiyat-i Delli, 1989, p. 149.
248	Many Muslims and other infidels come to our ports with books of their sects: Umar Ryad (ed.), *The Hajj and Europe in the Age of Empire*, Leiden: Brill, 2017, p. 27.
249	forces of King Sebastian were defeated by the Moroccan Sultan of Morocco: de la Garza, *The Mughal Empire at War*, p. 185.

249   'mobile fortress combined with': de la Garza, *The Mughal Empire at War*, p. 103.
249–50 'rocketry is one instance where the West adopted Indian military technology': Ibid., p. 48.
250   'The resulting method of warfare': Ibid., p. 310.
250–51 he forbade pilgrims from going to Mecca altogether: Habib (ed.), *Akbar and His India*, p. 264.
251   'for a long period to Lahore': Monserrate, *The Commentary of Father Monserrate*, p. 205
251   'the mere name of Christian or Frank': Ibid., p. 186.
252   ostentatious reverence to Babur's tomb in Kabul: See Faruqui, *The Princes of the Mughal Empire*, p. 138.
252   'portrayed himself as a Ghazi': Ibid.
252   'natives of Hindustan' (Hindi nazhadan): Quoted in Ibid., p. 137.
252   'Mongols, some Persians, some Turkmen, Chagatai': Monserrate, *The Commentary of Father Monserrate*, p. 83.
252   'His Majesty Akbar during the fifty years of his reign': *The Nobility Under Akbar and Jahāngīr*, p. 220.
253   'the prince begged through [Hamida Banu]': Beveridge (trans.), *Akbarnama*, Vol. 3, p. 495.
253   'to be superior to both of these': Monserrate, *The Commentary of Father Monserrate*, p. 75.
254   'seemed to hide the earth': Ibid., p. 79.
254–55 'these bazaars seem to belong to some wealthy city instead of to a camp': Ibid., p. 76.
255   The very movement of an army through the land caused damage: Eraly, *The Last Spring*, Part 2, p. 371.
255   'which have been made of boards of wood': Irfan Habib, 'Akbar and Technology', *Social Scientist*, Vol. 20, No. 9/10, September–October 1992, pp. 3-4.
255   'the heart and head of the whole camp': Monserrate, *The Commentary of Father Monserrate*, p. 77.
255   'temples dedicated to Vishnu': Ibid., p. 90.
256   'These measurements,' wrote Monserrate: Ibid., p. 78.
256   'lofty and handsomely decorated residences': Ibid., p. 97.
256   Shah Mansur had begun his career as an accountant in the Perfume Department: Ibid., p. 65.
257   Even Todar Mal, Akbar's exemplary officer: Eraly, *Emperors of the Peacock Throne*, p. 152.
257   'the King's mournful countenance': Monserrate, *The Commentary of Father Monserrate*, p. 99.
257   'by the King's direction all capital cases': Ibid., p. 209.
257   'the inhabitants, especially the women': Ibid., p. 98.
258   'the narrowness, aimless crookedness, and ill-planning of the streets': Ibid., p. 219.
258   infuse them with his miraculous healing powers: Blochmann (trans.), *Ain-i Akbari*, Vol. 1, p. 173.
258   'ask for lasting bliss, for an upright heart, for advice how best': Ibid., p. 164.
258   'During a space of fifteen days': Monserrate, *The Commentary of Father Monserrate*, p. 20.
259   'the secrets of Divine Realities and mystical sensibilities': Muzaffar Alam, 'The Mughals, the Sufi Shaikhs, and the Formation of the Akbari Dispensation', *Modern Asian Studies*, 2009, Vol. 43, No. 1, p. 163.
259   'You have spent a long life, and have enjoyed the society': Beveridge (trans.), *Akbarnama*, Vol. 3, p. 500.
259   'Akbar was by temperament melancholy': du Jarric, *Akbar and the Jesuits*, p. 9.
259   'when his understanding is still undeveloped': Jarrett (trans.), 'Happy Sayings of Akbar',

Ain-i Akbari, Vols 2 & 3, p. 427.
259 **First you find a person who can match you and sit:** Alam, 'The Mughals, the Sufi Shaikhs', p. 162.
259 'the snow-covered Himalaya mountains...gleaming white': Monserrate, *The Commentary of Father Monserrate*, p. 100.
260 'the cavalry, the infantry, the camels': Ibid., p. 110.
260 in a 'bond of friendship': Badauni, *Muntakhabh al-Tawarikh*, Vol. 2, p. 306.
260 'How was he left behind on this journey?': Ibid., p. 305.
260 'In order to prevent the great nobles becoming insolent': Balkrishan Shivram, 'Mughal Court Rituals: The Symbolism of Imperial Authority during Akbar's Reign', *Proceedings of the Indian History Congress*, Vol. 67, 2006–07, p. 339.
260 'beautified by many groves of trees and pleasant gardens': Ibid., p. 102.
261 **'dumb-bells, heavy sticks of wood, clubs, and chainbows':** Blake, 'Courtly Culture Under Babur', p. 206.
262 'somehow be both Hindu and Muslim and neither, all at the same time': Véronique Bouiller, 'Nāth Yogīs' Encounters with Islam', 2015.
262 'the Hindu calls on Ram, the Muslim on Khuda': Ibid.
262 'did reverence to the place': Monserrate, *The Commentary of Father Monserrate*, p. 116.
262 'Some were influenced by ignorance': Beveridge (trans.), *Akbarnama*, Vol. 3, p. 522.
262 'there are nowhere else in the whole world such narrow and dark hermits': Ibid., p. 528.
262 most dangerous when they seem to be flying in headlong': Ibid., p. 85.
263 'the Turanis and Persians...will join us without fighting': Beveridge (trans.), *Akbarnama*, Vol. 3, p. 538.
263 'upbraided him soundly for his carelessness and cowardice': Monserrate, *The Commentary of Father Monserrate*, p. 152.
264 'he pretended not to notice that it was no longer erected': Ibid., p. 156.
264 'O King...order me not to the gibbet': Ibid.
265 'Mirza Hakim is a memorial of the Emperor Humayun': Jarrett (trans.), 'Happy Sayings of Akbar', *Ain-i Akbari*, Vol. 3.
266 'the Emperor sent for all sorts of troops of singers and musicians': Badauni, *Muntakhabh al-Tawarikh*, Vol. 2, p. 310.
267 'actors, dancers, singers, players of instruments, mime artistes': Madhu Trivedi, *The Emergence of the Hindustani Tradition: Music, Dance and Drama in North India, 13th to 19th Centuries*, Gurgaon: Three Essays Collective, 2012, p. 11.
267 'Youths disguised themselves as old men so successfully': Ibid., p. 33.
267 'profanely and frivolously laid aside all pretense of piety': Monserrate, *The Commentary of Father Monserrate*, p. 175.
267 'most of these kenchens are handsome and well dressed': François Bernier, *Travels in the Mogul Empire*, Vol. 1, p. 311.
267 the articles were distributed among the needy: Nirmal Kumar, 'Rituals of Power and Power of Rituals: A Study of Imperial Rituals and Invented traditions in 16th Century North India, *Proceedings of the Indian History Congress*, Vol. 58, p. 249.
268 Rajput noblemen would have been aware of the *Ksemakutuhalam*: Taylor Sen, *Feasts and Fasts*, p. 171.
268 'Fie on the meal that has no aubergine': Ibid., p. 175.
269 'We have freed all the imperial slaves who exceed hundreds and thousands': Habib, 'Akbar and Social Inequities', p. 302.
269 'his majesty, nurtured by divine knowledge, styled his slaves chelas': Ibid.
270 that since the sun gives light to all, and ripens all grain: Badauni, *Muntakhabh al-Tawarikh*, Vol. 2, p. 268.
270 'From early youth, in compliment to his wives': Ibid., p. 269.

270 'the Hindu Amirs and others in imitation of them performed the ceremony of rakhi': Rogers (trans.), *Tuzuk-i-Jahangiri*, p. 246.
270 'prohibited the slaughter of cows and the eating of their flesh': Badauni, *Muntakhabh al-Tawarikh*, Vol. 2, p. 268.
270 'he had introduced a whole host of the daughters of eminent Hindu Rajahs': Ibid., p. 312.
271 'the King keeps this Court in a great state of embarrassment with the novelties': Goldie, *The First Christian Mission to the Great Mogul*, p. 99.
271 It is not right that a man should make his stomach: Jarrett (trans.), 'Happy Sayings of Akbar', *Ain-i Akbari*, Vol. 3.
271 'proclaimed the religion of Zardusht as the true one': Elliot, *The History of India, as Told by Its Own Historians*, p. 530.
271 'Though illiterate, [Akbar] loved to hear discussions on points of theology': Goldie, *The First Christian Mission to the Great Mogul*, p. 55.
271 He also issued farmans to the Governor of Gujarat: Habib (ed.), *Akbar and His India*, p. 92.
271 'always seemed not only to favour them, but to heap honours': Monserrate, *The Commentary of Father Monserrate*, p. 64.
272 'It was remarkable': Ibid., p. 192.
272 'worthless profligates, some of those who dress': Ibid., p. 62.
272 'especially remarkable for his love of keeping great crowds of people': Rogers (trans.), *Tuzuk-i-Jahangiri*, p. 38.
273 'it is hard to exaggerate how accessible': Monserrate, *The Commentary of Father Monserrate*, p. 197.
273 'He associated with the good of every race': Rogers (trans.), *Jahangirnama*, p. 37.
273 'wool, linen or cotton': Monserrate, *The Commentary of Father Monserrate*, p. 198.
273 'The wearing of gold and silk dresses': Badauni, *Muntakhabh al-Tawarikh*, Vol. 2, p. 316.
274 of his birthday: Pooja Chaudhury, *A Study of Mughal Emperial Costumes and Designs during 16th and 17th Century*, PhD Thesis, Department of History, Aligarh Muslim University, 2015, p. 16.
274 'it was a feast which the ancient Kings of Persia, who worshipped fire, used to celebrate': Goldie, *The First Christian Mission to the Great Mogul*, p. 98.
274 a tenth-century Ismaili writer that some Shias at court: Moin, *The Millennial Sovereign*, p. 152.
274 In 989 according to the decree of fate: Badauni, *Muntakhabh al-Tawarikh*, Vol. 2, p. 295.
275 Abdur Rahim offered him jewels: Shivram, 'Mughal Court Rituals: The Symbolism of Imperial Authority during Akbar's Reign', p. 343.
275 quickly became an indispensable part of local cuisine: Collingham, *Curry*, p. 28.
275 led to a great deal of mystical experimentation in the sixteenth century: For a comprehensive account of millennial history in India and Persia, see Moin, *The Millennial Sovereign*.
275 'he inferred the known from the known and rejected also their predecessors': Badauni, *Muntakhabh al-Tawarikh*, Vol. 2, p. 267.
275 'everything that pleased him, he picked and chose from': Ibid., p. 263.
276 a number of subterranean streams of thinking in the sixteenth century: For detailed analysis, see Hasan, *Religion, State and Society in Medieval India*; Habib (ed.), *Akbar and His India*, Khan, *India's Polity in the Age of* Akbar; Mukhia, *The Mughals in India*.
276 'intellect (khirad)' would be elevated: Khan, *India's Polity in the Age of* Akbar, p. 162.
276 'it is a remarkable thing that men should insist': Stephen P. Blake, *Time in Early Modern Islam*, p. 101.
277 'all religions are either equally true or equally illusory': Khan, *India's Polity in the Age of Akbar*, p. 162.

277	'an accepted code of ethical and legal behaviour': Habib (ed.), *Akbar and His India*, p. 83.
278	'conducted her himself to her palace in a gorgeous litter': Monserrate, *The Commentary of Father Monserrate*, p. 205
278	'[Akbar] never denyed [his mother] anything but this': Thomas Coryat quoted in Mukhia, *The Mughals in India*, p. 14.
279	'[H]is mother, his aunt, and many of the great lords': du Jarric, *Akbar and the Jesuits*, p. 37.
279	'whose intimate friend he had been': Ibid., p. 226.
279	'so covered with blood that drops were falling on the floor': du Jarric, *Akbar and the Jesuits*, p. 226.
279	'was always pondering in his mind': Monserrate, *The Commentary of Father Monserrate*, p. 180.
279	I perceive that there are varying customs and beliefs: Ibid., p. 182.
280	'began to suspect that he was intending to found a new religion': Ibid., p. 184.
280	'[T]he professors of various faiths had room in the broad expanse': Rogers (trans.), *Tuzuk-i-Jahangiri*, p. 37.
280	'the pearls of the Gospel to tread and crush under his feet': Monserrate, *The Commentary of Father Monserrate*, p. 184.
280	'The King, having a desire': du Jarric, *Akbar and the Jesuits*, p. 36.
280	'My father always associated with the learned of every creed and religion': Rogers (trans.), *Tuzuk-i-Jahangiri*, p. 33.
280	'I love you, Father': du Jarric, *Akbar and the Jesuits*, p. 38.
280	that 'the Almighty, through his eternal favours and perpetual grace': Akbar's letter to the wise men of Christendom, Muktabat i allami, Dafter I, letters to the emperor.
281	'stood every morning opposite to the window': Badauni, *Muntakhabh al-Tawarikh*, Vol. 2, p. 336.
281	'As the world's Lord exercises sway over it': Mukhia, *The Mughals in India*, p. 58.
281	just prescribe a passive 'tolerance': Ibid.
281	'blowing of the chill blast': Jarrett (trans.), *Ain-i Akbari*, Vol. 3, p. 3.
281	Devotion to the Matchless one is beyond the limits of the spoken: Khan, *India's Polity in the Age of Akbar*, p. 164.
282	Tusi and Rumi, which were among Akbar's favourite texts: Alam, *The Languages of Political Islam*, p. 61.
282	Thou has come to unite: Alam, 'State building under the Mughals: Religion, Culture and Politics'; *Cahiers d'asie centrale*, Vol. 3/4, Editions de Boccard, 1997, p. 119.
282	The best prayer is service to humanity: Ibid., pp. 62–64.
282	'within this framework there was no scope for the operation': Khan, *India's Polity in the Age of Akbar*, p. 16.
282	'As in the wide expanse of the Divine compassion there is room for all classes': Rogers (trans.), *Tuzuk-i-Jahangiri*, p. 37.
283	'by the end of Akbar's reign, Kacchwaha mansabdars': Eaton, *India in the Persianate Age*, p. 230.
283	'If people really wished it': Frederic P. Miller, Agnes F. Vandome, and John McBrewster (eds.), *Dabestan-e Mazaheb*, New Delhi: VPN Publishing, 2010 (repr.).
284	as 'Ordinances of the Divine Faith' and the idea of Din-e Ilahi: M. Athar Ali and M. Akhtar Ali, 'Sulhi kul and the Religious Ideas of Akbar', *Proceedings of the Indian History Congress*, Vol. 41, 1980, p. 330.
284	they also contained the emperor's name: Moin, *The Millennial Sovereign*, p. 222.
284	'God is Great/May his Glory be ever Glorious': Ibid.
285	'If discipleship means willingness to sacrifice one's life': Badauni, *Muntakhabh al-Tawarikh*, Vol. 2, p. 375.

286	'They have been rulers who commanded great power and authority': Husain, *The Nobility Under Akbar and Jahāngīr*, p. 217.
285	'you are making all these delays in coming; evidently the wool of your beard': Shāhnavāz Khān Awrangābādī, 'Abd al-Ḥayy ibn Shāhnavāz, and Baini Prashad, *The Maāthir-ul-umarā: Being Biographies of the Muhammadan and Hindu Officers of the Timurid Sovereigns of India from 1500 to About 1780 A. D.*, Asiatic Society, 1979, p. 325.
286	'not a sound was emitted from the silent house nor any speech': Moosvi, *Episodes in the Life of Akbar*, p. 91.
287	'At fixed hours, namely before dawn': Monserrate, *The Commentary of Father Monserrate*, p. 211.
287	'likewise an excellent hand in performing': Blochmann (trans.), *Ain-i Akbari*, Vol. 1, p. 51.
287	'is visible from outside the awning': Kumar, 'Rituals of Power', *Proceedings of the IHC*, Vol. 58, 1997, p. 246.
288	'It will seem little short of miraculous': Monserrate, *The Commentary of Father Monserrate*, p. 200.
288	'He knew the names of all his elephants': du Jarric, *Akbar and the Jesuits*, p. 207.
289	'He is much loved as well as feared by his people': Henriquez quoted in Moosvi, *Episodes in the Life of Akbar*, p. 81.
289	'His majesty from curiosity likes to see spider fights': Blochmann (trans.), *Ain-i Akbari*, Vol. 1, p. 296.
289	At one time he would be deeply immersed in state affairs: Shireen Moosvi, 'The World of Labour in Mughal India', (c.1500–1750), *International Review of Social History*, Vol. 56, No. 19, p. 256.
289	With a hundred charms I am bringing: Truschke, 'Reimagining the Idol Temple of Hindustan', p. 2.
290	'decided to explore the reason for the hostility': Babagolzadeh, *Understanding the Mughal Book of War*, p. 48.
290	'the most authoritative, important': Truschke, *Cultures of Encounter*, p. 139.
291	'several learned Brahmans': Ibid., p. 172.
291	Akbar himself spent several nights with the translators: Badauni, *Muntakhabh al-Tawarikh*, Vol. 2, p. 330.
291	'numbers among the finest, most highly valued specimens of Mughal art': Ibid., p. 195.
292	thirteen of the paintings are horizontal compositions: Asok Kumar Das, *Paintings of the Razmnama: The Book of War*, New Delhi: Mapin Publishing, 2005, p. 13.
292	'the puerile absurdities of which the eighteen thousand creations': Badauni, *Muntakhabh al-Tawarikh*, Vol. 2, p. 330.
292	'Every action has its reward and every deed its recompense': Ibid., p. 414.
293	'His Majesty likes this animal very much for his excellent qualities': Blochmann (trans.), *Ain-i Akbari*, Vol. 1, p. 90.
294	'a man of rustic habits, and great personal generosity': Ibid., p. 390.
294	'He can give his opinion': Monserrate, *The Commentary of Father Monserrate*, p. 201.
294–95	'Hindus, Iranis, Turanis, Kashmiris, both men and women': J. L. Mehta, *Advanced Study in the History of Medieval India*, Vol. 2, New Delhi: Sterling Publishers, p. 323.
295	'The fact that Akbar patronized him': Habib (ed.), *Akbar and His India*, p. 200.
295	Pay heed, wise emperor, to what Pravin Ray has to say: Allison Busch, *Poetry of Kings: The Classical Hindi Literature of Mughal India*, p. 133.
296	He ignored all Muslim customs: Shiri Ram Bakshi and Sangh Mitra, *Saints of India: Saint Dadu Dayal*, New York: Criterion Publications, 2002, p. 81.
296	'Because He cannot be grasped': Winand M. Callewaert, *The Hindī Biography of Dādū Dayāl*, New Delhi: Motilal Banarsidass, 1988, p. 51.
296	The king [Birbal] pointed out that: Ibid.
297	'He compared his singing to the noise of beasts': Badauni, *Muntakhabh al-Tawarikh*,

Vol. 2, p. 273.

297   'guided him towards honesty': Moosvi, 'The World of Labour in Mughal India', p. 256; *Akbarnama*, Vol. 3, p. 604.

298   'elephant-fighting, buffalo-fighting, stag-fighting': Monserrate, *The Commentary of Father Monserrate*, p. 198.

299   'two handsome eunuchs who had for a long time excited his perverse attention': Manu S. Pillai, *Rebel Sultans: The Deccan from Khilji to Shivaji*, New Delhi: Juggernaut Books, 2018, p. 127.

299   'All the great Muslim scholars, as well as Hindu sages': Ali Anooshahr, 'Shirazi scholars and the political culture of the sixteenth-century Indo-Persian world', *Indian Economic Social History Review*, 2014, p. 342.

299   declare Persian as the official language of administration: Khan, *The Language of Political Islam*, p. 128.

299   Earlier in India the government accounts were written in Hindi: Ibid.

300   the Kayastha classes became increasingly 'Persianized': Eaton, *India in the Persianate Age*, p. 382.

300   'A man who knows how to write good prose as well as accountancy': Muzaffar Alam and Sanjay Subrahmanyam, 'The Making of a Munshi', *Comparative Studies of South Asia, Africa and the Middle East*, Vol. 24, No. 2, 2004, p. 62.

301   within this last century, a great many Persians, and even entire Families: Sharma, *Mughal Arcadia*, p. 23.

301   That in Persia no one comes within sight: Raghavan, *Attendant Lords*, p. 138.

301   'some of whom sit, some lie on the ground in worship': Blochmann (trans.), *Ain-i Akbari*, Vol. 1, p. 308.

302   Manohar 'Tausani', son of Raja Loonkaran of Sambhar: Sharma, *Mughal Arcadia*, p. 42.

303   'It is a strange commentary on the magnanimity of men': Jarrett (trans.), *Ain-i Akbari*, Vol. 3, p. 449.

303   'those who of their own impulse wished to commit sati might be allowed to do so': Habib, 'Akbar and Social Inequities', p. 305.

303   'it is particularly distressing under a law where a woman': Ibid., p. 304.

303   'we found marriages great store, both in towns and villages': J. Courtenay Locke (ed.), *The First Englishmen in India*, p. 53.

304   'in the manner that the people of India do not prohibit': Mukhia, *The Mughals of India*, p. 130.

304   'He ordered his household to dress in their holiday suits of white': Goldie, *The First Christian Mission*, p. 132.

305   'He gladly stretched out his neck': Monserrate, *The Commentary of Father Monserrate*, p. 195.

305   'Alas, Father! Did I not tell you not to go away?': Correia-Afonso, Letter, p. 123-24.

306   '[Jain monks] wear nothing on the head and pluck out the hairs of chins and heads': Donald F. Lach and Edwin J. Van Kley, *Asia in the Making of Europe: A Century of Advance*, Vol. 3, Chicago: University of Chicago Press, 1993, p. 649.

306   'foremost among the dispassionate, best of ascetics, who had the form of glorious khuda': Truschke, *Cultural Encounters*, p. 289.

307   He who is free of dirt like a shell, devoid of defects like the sun: Ibid., p. 276.

307   'do not believe that there is a pure one': Ibid., p. 279.

307   The Shaivas worship him as 'Shiva' and the Vedantins: Ibid., p. 281.

308   'When the Brahmans were defeated by the Suri': Ibid., p. 282.

308   There is not a single art, not a single branch of knowledge: Habib (ed.), *Akbar and His India*, p. 104.

309   'perceive the mysteries of the external and internal': Blochmann (trans.), *Ain-i Akbari*, Vol. 1, p. 537.

309	'Tell me who among good people can teach me this?': Ibid.
309	'His Majesty also called some of the Jogis': Badauni, *Muntakhabh al-Tawarikh*, Vol. 2, p. 334.
309	question the jogis about their methods of meditation: Khan, *The Languages of Political Islam*, p. 94.
309	'both intemperate and licentious': George W. Briggs, *Gorakhnāth and the Kānphaṭa Yogīs*, Calcutta: Motilal Banarsidass, p. 159.
309	Shivlinga was worshipped every third hour: George W. Briggs, *The Religious Life of India*, p. 143.
309–10	'wisely enough, found proofs for the longevity of the Emperor': Badauni, *Muntakhabh al-Tawarikh*, Vol. 2, p. 335.
310	and let the hairs grow at the sides to allow his soul to escape freely out of the body: John Zubrzycki, *Empire of Enchantment: The Story of Indian Magic*, New York: Oxford University Press, 2018, p. 68.
310	singanad janeu, the fillets and the necklace of coloured cloth of the Nath jogis: Rachel Parikh, 'Yoga under the Mughals: From Practice to Paintings', *South Asian Studies*, Vol. 31, No. 2, 2015, p. 215.
310	'It was my object that mendicancy should disappear': Jarrett (trans.), 'Happy Sayings of Akbar', *Ain-i Akbari*, Vol. 3, Part 5.
311	Amongst his great nobles he was so predominant: Habib, 'Akbar and Social Inequities', p. 306.
311	'The King has such a hatred of debauchery': Monserrate, *The Commentary of Father Monserrate*, p. 210.
311	'who had gathered together in the Capital in such swarms': Badauni, *Muntakhabh al-Tawarikh*, Vol. 2, p. 311.
311	'if a young woman were found running about': Ibid., p. 405.
312	Akbar was so delighted at thus seeing the highest religious: Blochmann (trans.), *Ain-i Akbari*, Vol. 1, p. 468.
312	'He prohibited the slaughter of cows, and the eating of their flesh': Badauni, *Muntakhabh al-Tawarikh*, Vol. 2, p. 268.
312	'since Hakim Humam has gone my food has not the same taste': Schimmel, *Anvari's Divan*, p. 36.
313	'He acted very differently in the case of Hindus': Blochmann (trans.), *Ain-i Akbari*, Vol. 1, p. 214.
313	'he adores God, and the Sun, and is a Hindu': Smith, *Akbar the Great Mogul*, p. 262.
313	'Cheating, thieving Brahmans': Badauni, *Muntakhabh al-Tawarikh*, Vol. 2, p. 336.
313	were simply 'other worshippers of God': Qandahari, *Tarikh-i-Akbari*, Vol. 3, p. 4.
314	'(y)ou should be a raconteur, retaining in your memory a large number of anecdotes': Orsini (ed.), *Tellings and Texts*, p. 285.
314	'the erection of a stone palace for [Birbal]': Thackston (trans.), *The History of Akbar*, Vol. 3, p. 587.
315	these stories also tend to try and 'humanize' Akbar: See C. M. Naim, 'Popular Jokes and Political History: The Case of Akbar, Birbal and Mulla Do-Piyaza', *Economic and Political Weekly*, 17 June 1995.
315	emperor retorted that he had forgotten a fourth, Conceit: Sinha, *Raja Birbal: Life and Times*, p. 46.
315	'full also of dignity': Monserrate, *The Commentary of Father Monserrate*, p. 197.
315	'The King's severity towards errors and misdemeanours': Ibid., p. 209.
315	'By means of conversing with the Emperor': Badauni, *Muntakhabh al-Tawarikh*, Vol. 2, p. 164.
316	'Since (Man Singh) was constantly in my father's house': Thackston (trans.), *Jahangirnama*, p. 29.

316	'had a daughter whose purity adorned her high extraction': Thackston (trans.), *The History of Akbar*, Vol. 3, p. 678.
316	'in accordance with [Akbar's] established custom': Badauni, *Muntakhabh al-Tawarikh*, Vol. 2, p. 352.
316	'several strings of horses, and a hundred elephants': Ibid.
317	carried the bridal palanquin part of the way back: Hooja, *A History of Rajasthan*, p. 553.
317	'What shall I write of her goodness and excellence?': Thackston (trans.), *Jahangirnama*, p. 51.
317	'the most invincible and most mightie prince': Richard Hakluyt, *The Principal Navigations Voyages Traffiques and Discoveries of the English Nation*, Vol. 5, Cambridge: Cambridge University Press, 1904 (first edition), 2014 (repr.), p. 450.
317	'a house, and five slaves, a horse, and every day six shillings in money': William Foster, *England's Quest of Eastern Trade*, p. xii.
317	While these adventurers were not able to establish any trade links: Donald F. F. Lach, *Asia in the Making of Europe: The Century of Discovery*, Vol. 1, Chicago: University of Chicago Press, 1965, p. 826.
319	The emperor was seated in the royal court: Busch, 'The Classical Past in the Mughal Present', *Modern Asian Studies*, Vol. 44, No. 2 March 2010, pp. 267–309.
319	'grieved him exceedingly': Jarrett (trans.), *Ain-i Akbari*, Vol. 3, p. 732.
319	When Birbal passed away there was great rejoicing in Poverty's court: Busch, Allison, 'Hidden in Plain View: Brajbhasha Poets at the Mughal Court', *Modern Asian Studies*, Vol. 44, No. 2, Cambridge: Cambridge University Press, 2010, p. 278.
319–20	'He never experienced such grief': Badauni, *Muntakhabh al-Tawarikh*, p. 362.
320	'By this heart-rending mishap': Sinha, *Raja Birbal, Life and Times*, p. 119.
320	'and this sudden calamity has greatly afflicted my heart': Letter to khankhanan Abdur Rahim, March–April, 1586.
320	'The world is like a mirage': Ibid., p. 119.
320	Deen dekhi sab din, ek na dinho dusah dukh: Beveridge (trans.), *Akbarnama*, Vol. 3, p. 748.

PART 5: PARADISE ON EARTH (1585–1598)

323	Yusuf Shah Chak, were caught unawares: Mehta, *Advanced Study in the History of Medieval India*, Vol. 2, p. 255.
323	'although this time the royal army was defeated': Haidar Malik Chadurah, *The History of Kashmir*, Srinagar: Bhavna Prakashan, 1991, p. 85.
324	'his intellect grew darkened': Jarrett (trans.), *Ain-i Akbari*, Vol. 3, p. 745.
325	They (Mughal forces) were given directions to show consideration: Ashraf Wani, 'Sectional President's Address: Akbar and Kashmir', *Proceedings of the Indian History Congress*, Vol. 73, 2012, p. 194.
325	'he is willing to consult about his affairs': Smith, *Akbar*, p. 63.
325	'so sternly towards the nobles who are under his proud sway': Monserrate, *The Commentary of Father Monserrate*, p. 205.
326	tells us that 'contrary to the usage': Beveridge (trans.), *Akbarnama*, Vol. 3, p. 747.
326	'Her temperament is greatly inclined': Thackston (trans.), *Jahangirnama*, p. 39.
326	'Since she was brought up in the lap of my exalted father's care': Ibid.
327	'the weakness of the woman calls for a larger share': *Proceedings of the Indian History Congress*, Vol. 53, p. 305.
327	'how could this law be justified': Ibid., p. 306.
327	wanting to safeguard the rights of girls and women: Habib, 'Akbar and Social Inequities', p. 306.
327	an indigenous style with traces of Mughal influence: Hooja, *A History of Rajasthan*, p. 545.

327	**plead with the widow not to commit sati:** Ibid., p. 545.
327–28	**Udai Singh's house for the celebration of the marriage:** Thackston (trans.), *Jahangirnama*, p. 6.
328	**contract a large number of marriages between them:** Faruqui, *The Princes of the Mughal Empire*, p. 31.
328	**Akbar did not tolerate, men like Lala Beg Kabuli and Zamana Beg:** Ibid., p. 149.
328	**Amba Khan Kashmiri, who would prove to be valuable allies in the years to come:** Ibid., p. 150.
329	**'shared dislike of the brothers Abu'l Fazl and Faizi':** Ibid., p. 158.
329	**'One day I mounted to go hunting':** Thackston (trans.), *Jahangirnama*, p. 184
330	**'His complexion was dark':** Ibid., p. 37.
330	**'a young man of fine stature':** Ibid., p. 39.
330	**no Mughal princess was married either to a Rajput:** Afzal Husain, 'Marriages among Mughal Nobles as an Index of Status and Aristocratic Integration', *Proceedings of the Indian History Congress*, Vol. 33, 1971, p. 307.
331	**'it is painful to allude to the rumour of his [Shah Jahan's]:** Francois Bernier, *Travels in the Mogul Empire*, Vol. 1, p. 11.
331	**'They practise running in shoes made of lead':** Monserrate, *The Commentary of Father Monserrate*, p. 212.
331	**thus creating the Dhoondhari 'panchranga' flag:** Hooja, *A History of Rajasthan*, p. 488.
332	**'were enslaved and sent to the markets of Central Asia for sale':** Mehta, *Advanced Study in the History of Medieval India*, p. 264.
332	**'chosen steeds, powerful camels and swift mules':** Quoted in Friedrich Christian Charles August, *The Emperor Akbar: A Contribution towards the History of India in the 16th Century*, Vol. 2, translated by Annette Beveridge, London: Trübner & Co, 1890 (first edition), Calcutta: Thacker, Spink & Company, p. 183.
332	**'What you have written with a pen perfumed':** Ibid., p. 267.
332	**details of the 'exertions':** Ibid.
333	**The Punjab rivers were all fordable except during the season:** M. Athar Ali, 'Jahangir and the Uzbeks', *Proceedings of the Indian History Congress*, Vol. 26, 1964, p. 108.
333	**'the churches and temples of the infidels and heretics':** Ibid., p. 757.
333	**'neither God nor Prophet has escaped the slanders of men, much less I':** Lach, *Asia in the Making of Europe*, p. 806.
335	**'We have purchased Lahore with our soul':** Mohammad Gharipour and Nilay Ozlu (eds.), *The City in the Muslim World: Depictions by Western Travel Writers*, New Delhi: Routledge India, p. 92.
335	**This city is second to none, either in Asia or in Europe, with regard to size:** Monserrate, *The Commentary of Father Monserrate*, p. 159–60.
336	**'musk melons are to be had throughout the whole year':** Jarrett (trans.), *Ain-i Akbari*, Vol. 2, p. 310.
336	**A total of 50 to 120 kilograms of ice and snow arrived every day:** Blochmann (trans.), *Ain-i Akbari*, Vol. 1, p. 56.
336	**'Akbar promoted textile manufacture for foreign markets, building roads':** Harris, *The First Firangis*, p. 118.
336	**It included a rampart with twelve gates, an audience hall:** Dr Mehreen Chida-Razvi, 'Perception and Reality: The Mughal City of Lahore through European Eyes', p. 2 available at <https://www.academia.edu/6086394/The_Mughal_City_of_Lahore_through_European_Eyes_Reality_and_Perception> [accessed: 10 January 2020].
337	**'Throughout Akbar's reign…court nobles were encouraged':** *Urbanism Past & Present*, No. 11–16, University of Wisconsin, Milwaukee, 1981, p. 7.
337	**crowds thronged to make their daily darshan of Akbar:** Lach, *Asia in the Making of Europe*, p. 805.

338	'psychologically acute...characterizations, painterliness': Stuart Cary Welch, *India: Art and Culture, 1300–1900*, New York: Metropolitan Museum of Art, 1986, p. 177.
338	'as a humble, painterly artist': Welch, *The Emperors' Album: Images of Mughal India*, p. 111.
339	signature element was to add a large chinar tree: J. Seyller, 'Farrukh Beg in the Deccan', *Artibus Asiae*, Vol. 55, No. 33, 1995, p. 337.
339	I asked for wine, and you gave me stale vinegar: Schimmel, *Anvari's Divan*, p. 62.
339	'from the fine, gold-flecked paper and costly pigments': Singh, *Real Birds in Imagined Gardens*, p. 32.
340	'scarcely larger than an eyelash': Schimmel, *Anvari's Divan*, p. 50.
340	'I can discover which face is the work of each of them': Ibid., p. 51.
341	'that he had descended to earth, like Ram, Kishan': Truschke, *Culture of Encounters*, p. 73.
341	'Rama is dressed in Mughal fashion and has Central Asian facial features': Adamjee and Truschke, 'Reimagining The "Idol Temple of Hindustan"', p. 157.
341	'I seek refuge in God from that': Truschke, *Cultural Encounters*, p. 327.
343	'Write down whatever you know of the doings of': Gulbadan, *Humāyūn-Nāma*, p. 83.
343	'His Majesty Jalal al-Din Muhammad Akbar': Rebecca Gould, 'How Gulbadan Remembered: The "Book of Humāyūn" as an Act of Representation', *Early Modern Women*, Vol. 6, Fall 2011, Arizona State University, p. 191.
343	Gulbadan wrote an account that was unlike any other work: For a detailed, scholarly discussion of the importance of Gulbadan's work, see Lal, *Domesticity and Power*.
344	'we have a lost world of the court in camp brought to life': Lal, *Domesticity and Power*, p. 60.
344	'I spoke to old and young men of right character': Taymiya R. Zaman, 'Instructive Memory: An Analysis of Auto/Biographical Writing in Early Mughal India', *Journal of the Economic and Social History of the Orient*, Vol. 54, 2011, p. 683.
345	'This people of this country': Habib (ed.), *Akbar and His India*, p. 220.
345	They one and all believe in the unity of God: Jarrett (trans.), *Ain-i Akbari*, Vol. 3, p. 8.
345	There is no beauty in its people, no graceful social intercourse: Thackston (trans.), *The Baburnama*, p. 352.
346–47	placing the Padshah firmly in the position of the ruler of all humanity: Mukhia, 'No Conflict between Reason and Faith: Reappraising Abu'l Fazl's Rationality', p. 9.
346	Abu'l Fazl used a complex set of symbols to articulate a vision of the Padshah: For a detailed explanation, see Moin, *Millennial Sovereign* and Ruby Lal, 'Settled, Sacred and All-Powerful: Making of New Genealogies and Traditions of Empire under Akbar', *Economic and Political Weekly*, Vol. 36, No. 11, March 17–23, 2001.
348	'He incites us to other kinds of things': Samsam ud Daula Shah Nawaz Khan, *The Maathir al-Umara: Biographies of the Muhammadan and Hindu Officers of the Timurid Sovereigns of India From 1500 to about 1780 A.D.*, translated by Beveridge, p. 119.
348	the *Iqbal Nama-i Jahangiri* also recorded Akbar's displeasure: Harbans Mukhia, *Historians and Historiography During the Reign of Akbar*, New Delhi: Vikas Publishing, 1976, p. 52.
349	famous Muslim painters of this taswir khana: Geeti Sen, *The Paintings of the Akbarnama as a Source of Historical Documentation*, Dissertation, University of Calcutta, 1979, p. 9.
349	'At the age of eighty-five, when his strength has gone': John Guy and Jorrit Britschgi, *Wonder of the Age: Master Painters of India, 1100-1900*, New York: Metropolitan Museum of Art, 2012, p. 56.
349	Twenty-seven paintings depict specific battles, sieges, and engagements: Sen, *The Paintings of the Akbarnama*, p. 87.
351	scene showing a Mughal emissary and the rebel Bahadur Khan: Painting from the *Akbarnama* of an interview between the royal Mughal emissary Mir Muizzu'l Mulk and

the rebel Bahadur Khan. Seated figures are shown in a tiled royal pavilion under a chinar tree, Victoria and Albert Museum, London.

351 introduction of the Kathak style of dance into the Mughal court: Sen, *The Paintings of the Akbarnama*, p. 199.

351 'those that have passed away have received a new life': Abu'l Fazl quoted in Welch, *India: Art and Culture*, p. 173.

351 paintings of key figures from Akbar's life: Ibid., p. 370.

352 'contrary to the custom of contemporaries, it was made an occasion of rejoicing': Eraly, *The Mughal World*, p. 149.

352 through the silent pages of the miniatures in the *Akbarnama*: See the miniature entitled 'Rejoicings at Fatehpur Sikri on the birth of Prince Murad, 1570'.

352 'His death...was the annihilation of melody': Habib (ed.), *Akbar and His India*, p. 199.

352 Because the black bee is a constant visitor to these flowers: Thackston (trans.), *Jahangirnama*, p. 239.

353 'he does not fix his heart to one place...': Beveridge (trans.), *Akbarnama*, Vol. 3, p. 817.

353 '[O]ur going there is...the fulfilling of (Humayun's) dream': Ibid., p. 817.

354 'Or shall I tell of the depth of the snow, and of the bewilderment': Ibid., p. 823.

354 'I was nearly losing my senses and the dress of society': Ibid., p. 825.

354 'The whole confusion was caused by thinking': Ibid., p. 825.

355 'exceeding many and equally monotonous, and with each note': Jarrett (trans.), *Ain-i Akbari*, Vol. 2, p. 352.

356 The country is enchanting, and might be fittingly called a garden: Ibid., p. 348.

356 In winter there are hot baths by the river, in the summer the cool: Sharma, *Mughal Arcadia*, p. 76.

356 The most respectable class in this country is that of the Brahmans: Ibid., p. 74.

356 'was ashamed of his former mistake': Beveridge (trans.), *Akbarnama*, Vol. 3, p. 829.

357 The pilgrim may go to the K'aaba to perform the haj: Ibid., p. 835.

357 'that the active young men should': Ibid., p. 867.

357 'no worship of God was equal': Samsam ud Daula Shahnawaz Khan and Abd al-Ḥayy ibn Shāhnavāz, *The Maāthir-ul-umarā: Being Biographies of the Muhammādan and Hindu Officers of the Timurid Sovereigns of India from 1500 to about 1780 A.D.*, translated by H. Beveridge and Baini Prasad, Bibliotheca Indica 202, Vol. 2, Calcutta: Royal Asiatic Society, 1941, p. 954.

358 'hastened to the abode of hell and torment': Badauni, *Muntakhabh al-Tawarikh*, Vol. 2, p. 383.

358 'was a firm adherent of the Imami doctrines': Beveridge (trans.), *Akbarnama*, Vol. 3, p. 804.

358 'the contest between Sunni and Shia subsided': Ibid., p. 803–04.

359 'he was endowed with uprightness, weight of counsel, and courage': Ibid., p. 863.

359 'mir was his vakil, philosopher, physician': Ibid., p. 848.

359 'became somewhat deranged and fell into great grief': Ibid., p. 867.

360 Peethal so majlis gayee, Tansen so raga: Hooja, *A History of Rajasthan*, p. 547.

361 'May it be known that according to the farman of the exalted': Quoted in Rekha Misra, *Women in Mughal India*, 1526–1748, New Delhi: Munshiram Manoharlal Publishers, 1967, p. 154.

362 The naubat: Khursheed Kamal Aziz, *The Meaning of Islamic Art: Explorations in Religious Symbolism and Social Relevance*, Vol. 1, New Delhi: Adam Publishers, 2004, p. 1004.

362 considered the yogapitha or centre of Brindavan: Margaret H. Case, *Govindadeva: A Dialogue in Stone*, New Delhi: Indira Gandhi National Centre for the Arts, 1996, p. 216.

362 Abdu'l Latif, visiting in the seventeenth century: For a detailed study of Man Singh's patronage, see Barbara Stoler Miller (ed.), *The Powers of Art: Patronage in Indian Culture*, Delhi: Oxford University Press, 1992 and Case, *Govindadeva*.

363	Brajbhasha inscription accords Man Singh the title Maharajadhiraja: Sreenivasan, *The Many Lives of a Rajput Queen*, p. 558.
363	maintained the shrine of a Sufi saint in Hajipura: Case, *Govindadeva*, p. 215.
364	'the first structure to introduce the courtly Mughal style': C. B. Asher, 'The Architecture of Raja Man Singh: A Study in Sub-imperial Patronage', Barbara S. Miller (ed.), *The Powers of Art*, p. 191.
365	'Rajput rulers realised the pitfalls of leaving the governance': Hooja, *A History of Rajasthan*, p. 566.
365	'the state of agriculture, famine, law and order, or social problems': Ibid.
365	related to the peasantry and so on: For more information on Rajput women, see Joshi, *Polygamy and Purdah*.
365	Born in the lineage of Timur, the son of Humayun: Allison Busch, 'Portrait of a Raja in a Badshah's Worlds: Amrit Rai's Biography of Man Singh (1585)', *Journal of the Economic and Social History of the Orient*, Vol. 55, No. 2/3, 2012, p. 294.
367	'had the effect not only of sharpening the boundaries': Eaton, *India in the Persianate Age*, p. 223.
367	'early, copious and critical to the consolidation of Hindi's courtly style': Busch, *Poetry of Kings*, p. 131.
368	'the fervent wish that the Mughals could be resisted': Allison Busch, 'Literary Responses to the Mughal Imperium: The Historical Poems of Kesavdas', *South Asia Research*, Vol. 25, No. 1, New Delhi: Sage Publications, 2005, p. 37.
370	'Perform whatever is the purifying rite in the Jain philosophy!': Truschke, *Culture of Encounters*, p. 79.
370	bowed before the pot and prayed for the health of the Padshah: Habib (ed.), *Akbar and His India*, p. 100.
371	'in this unconscious state': Badauni, *Muntakhabh al-Tawarikh*, Vol. 2, p. 390.
371	'Shaikhu Baba, since all this Sultanate will devolve on you': Ibid.
371	'pennant, kettle drum, martial music': Ibid., p. 391.
371	'secure the affection of contented hermits': Beveridge (trans.), *Akbarnama*, Vol. 3, p. 913.
372	'superior to the other princes in majesty and pomp': Ibid.
372	'his bad conduct in all relations of life, and court and ceremonial': Badauni, *Muntakhabh al-Tawarikh*, Vol. 2, p. 392.
372	spent this decade slowly cultivating the friendships: See Faruqui, *Princes of the Mughal Empire*.
372	'at once and very willingly': du Jarric, *Akbar and the Jesuits*, p. 44.
373	'that they may dispute with my doctors, and that I': Ibid., p. 49.
373	'mainly through deserts and dry, sandy tracts': Ibid., p. 58.
373	they choose a captain to lead and command their troop: Ibid.
373	'[Akbar] had no intention of making up his mind': Ibid., p. 50.
374	'loved him a thousand times more': Rogers (trans.), *Tuzuk-i-Jahangiri*, p. 48.
374	'little by little as his years progressed real potential': Thackston (trans.), *Jahangirnama*, p. 30.
375	On the third feast-day of every month: Schimmel, *Anvari's Divan*, p. 31.
376	thousand courtesans were thrown into the tanks: Shivram, 'Mughal Court Rituals, p. 344.
376	Ram Das Kachhwaha donated money to communities of Charans: Husain, 'The Establishments, Households and Private Life of Mughal Nobles', pp. 377–88.
376	'smeared his body over with clay and mud': Blochmann (trans.), *Ain-i Akbari*, Vol. 1, p. 441.
377	accepted a daughter as bride for Abdur Rahim's son: Habib (ed.), *Akbar and His India*, p. 28–29.
377	'his character, religious views, pleasing manners and practical wisdom': Blochmann

	(trans.), *Ain-i Akbari*, Vol. 1, p. 303.
377	'spite of clouds of rain and the opposition of men': Beveridge (trans.), *Akbarnama*, Vol. 3, p. 943.
378	'On my first visit, I saw the bridal chamber of spring': Ibid., p. 955.
378	'he was committed to the care of God and [Akbar] made up his mind to part from him': Ibid.
379	'Although the root of the rebellion had been dug up': Thackston (trans.), *Jahangirnama*, p. 70.
379	'they presented a splendid appearance': Beveridge (trans.), *Akbarnama*, Vol. 3, p. 958.
379	'several cows are adorned and brought before His Majesty': Blochmann (trans.), *Ain-i Akbari*, Vol. 1, p. 216.
379	'the inhabitants of hot countries': Beveridge (trans.), *Akbarnama*, Vol. 3, p. 959.
380	that 'just as for other people more than one wife': Ibid., p. 969.
380	'ruins a man's health and disturbs the peace of the home': Blochmann (trans.), *Ain-i Akbari*, Vol. 1, p. 278.
380	Every care bestowed upon this wonderful tie between men: Ibid., p. 277.
380	'aimed at promoting a particular model of ideal marriage': O'Hanlon, 'Kingdom, Household and Body History', p. 911.
380	'Here in India': Blochmann (trans.), *Ain-i Akbari*, Vol. 1, p. 277.
381	'robbers whom we encounter on our road to God': Badauni, *Muntakhabh al-Tawarikh*, Vol. 3, p. 165.
381	'their nature is so wicked that in every adultery': Majid, 'Women and a Theologian', p. 251.
381	'had I formerly possessed the knowledge': Babagolzadeh, 'Understanding the Mughal Book of War', p. 39.
382	He is grave and very gentle and is always cautious with maidens: Ibid.
382	'the contempt of any religion is the contempt of God': Coryat, *Early Travels in India*, p. 278.
382	'truth inhabited every religion...how was it then that one religion': Mukhia, 'No Conflict between Reason and Faith', p. 10.
383	Devotion to the Matchless One (Bechun) is beyond the limits: Habib (ed.), *Akbar and His India*, p. 89.
383	more reminiscent of the Nirgun Bhakti saints: See Habib (ed.), *Akbar and His India* and Mukhia, 'No Conflict between Reason and Faith'.
383	'in the manner of imitating theologians': Habib (ed.), *Akbar and His India*, p. 95.
383	Aziz Koka did not only criticize the Padshah's religious beliefs: Husain, *The Nobility Under Akbar and Jahāngīr*, p. 60.
383	'Some of the hypocrites about Court': Badauni, *Muntakhabh al-Tawarikh*, Vol. 2, p. 400.
383	'his enemies had influenced the Emperor's mind': Husain, *The Nobility Under Akbar and Jahāngīr*, p. 60.
384	'Inasmuch as I have trod the path of peace with Jews and Christians and others': Beveridge (trans.), *Akbarnama*, Vol. 3, p. 980.
384	'I so love Aziz that though he shows evil thoughts': H. Beveridge, 'Aziz Koka', *The Journal of the Royal Asiatic Society of Great Britain and Ireland*, April 1921, Cambridge: Cambridge University Press, No. 2, p. 206.
384	'though often offended by his boldness, Akbar would seldom punish': du Jarric, *Akbar and the Jesuits*, p. 272.
384	'This night I had a dream that something untoward': Beveridge (trans.), *Akbarnama*, Vol. 3, p. 981.
384	'Should his mother die of grief for his absence': Ibid.
385	'At this time A'zam Khan returned from Makkah': Raghavan, *Attendant Lords*, p. 162.
386	'camel' invented in the dockyards of the Netherlands in 1688: Habib (ed.), *Akbar and*

His India, p. 144.
387–88 'he had never, nor his father or grandfather': Beveridge (trans.), Akbarnama, Vol. 3, p. 1033.
387 'a masterpiece of imperial symbolism': Annabel Teh Gallop, 'The Genealogical Seal of the Mughal Emperors of India', *Journal of the Royal Asiatic Society*, Vol. 9, No. 1, Cambridge University Press, 2009.
388 'loved grandchildren more than sons': Beveridge (trans.), Akbarnama, Vol. 3, p. 1096.
388 1,823 mansabdars with the capacity to raise 141,000 cavalrymen: Fisher, *A Short History of the Mughal Empire*, p. 138.
389 When Burhan al-Mulk prevailed over Ahmadnagar: Muzaffar Alam and Sanjay Subrahmanyam, *Writing the Mughal World: Studies on Culture and Politics*, 2002 p. 175.
389 'sometimes in favour, sometimes in prison': du Jarric, *Akbar and the Jesuits*, p. 232.
389 'in consequence of some youthful escapade': Ibid., p. 233.
389–90 'were standing as silent as statues with their eyes fixed on him': Lach, *Asia in the Making of Europe*, p. 802.
390 'if there was snow or ice in Portugal': du Jarric, *Akbar and the Jesuit*, p. 57.
390 'He went to this war': Ibid.
390 'some carelessness on the part of the sentinels': Beveridge (trans.), Akbarnama, Vol. 3, p. 994.
392 'I have brought Hakim Ali with me, why do you say nothing?': Badauni, *Muntakhabh al-Tawarikh*, Vol. 2, p. 420.
392 'since he had, in despite of Musalmans': Ibid.
392 'He is not avaricious': Badauni, *Muntakhabh al-Tawarikh*, Vol. 3, p. 420.
392 'books of verse, medicine, astrology and music': Ibid., p. 421.
393 'as reverently as though he had been a Christian': du Jarric, *Akbar and the Jesuits*, p. 62.
393 'Look at your son': Ibid., p. 63.
393 he sent the Jesuits a precious box of snow: Lach, *Asia in the Making of Europe*, Vol. 1, p. 806
393 books included the works of Pope Sylvester: Maclagan, *The Jesuits and the Great Mogul*, p. 191.
393 it caused...'great disappointment': Ibid.
394 'one side of it an Agnus Dei, and on the other an image of our Lady': Ibid., p. 72.
394 'each of which was worth 2000 crowns': Ibid., p. 65.
395 goddess continued to be worshipped the way: Ramya Sreenivasan, 'Rethinking Kingship and Authority in South Asia: Amber (Rajasthan), ca. 1560-1615', *JESHO*, 2014, Vol. 57, No. 4, p. 555.
395 populace still refers to the site as Rajmahal: Catherine Asher and T. R. Metcalf, *The Powers of Art: Patronage in Indian Culture*, p. 192.
395 'accepted this order with enthusiasm': Ibid .
396 2,941 mansabdars holding ranks from 10 to 5,000: Chandra, *Medieval India: From Sultanat to the* Mughal, Part 2, p. 162.
396 'banished the sect of Mahomet': du Jarric, *Akbar and the Jesuits*, p. 67.
396 'ceasing to consider swine and dogs': Badauni, *Muntakhabh al-Tawarikh*, Vol. 2, p. 314.
397 'scattered and left as quickly as they had come': Lach, *Asia in the Making of Europe*, p. 807.
397 '[O]ne does not know for certain what law he follows': du Jarric, *Akbar and the Jesuits*, p. 68.
397 'he has a strong desire to be looked upon': Ibid.
397 'healing the sick with the water with which he washes his feet': Ibid.
398 'It must be considered that the Divine mercy attaches itself': Beveridge (trans.), Akbarnama, Vol. 3, p. 1012.
399 'was the loss of all his treasures': du Jarric, *Akbar and the Jesuits*, p. 75.

399	**'Consider nobility of caste and high birth'**: Faruqui, *The Princes of the Mughal Empire*, p. 261.
399	**'You can understand this truth'**: Ibid., p. 262.
400	**'groves, orchards, gardens'**: du Jarric, *Akbar and the Jesuits*, p. 38.
401	**'exceptionally high' at 43.3 per cent**: Moosvi, 'Data on Mughal-Period Vital Statistics A Preliminary Survey of Usable Information', *Proceedings of the Indian History Congress*, Vol. 58, 1997, p. 346.
401	**'depopulated whole houses and cities'**: Sir Henry M. Eliot, *Bibliographical Index to the Historians of Muhammedan India*, Vol. 1, p. 296.
401	**'that men ate their own kind'**: du Jarric, *Akbar and the Jesuits*, p. 244.
401	**'sent one crore and ten lakh from the Treasury'**: Habib, 'Akbar and Social Inequities', p. 303.
401	**'the inhabitants of hot countries'**: Beveridge (trans.), *Akbarnama*, Vol. 3, p. 1095.
401	**'the people of the town exhibited towards the Father'**: du Jarric, *Akbar and the Jesuits*, p. 79.
402	**'was greatly appreciated by the people of the country'**: Ibid., pp. 80–81.
402	**'publicly expressed his devotion to our Lord'**: Ibid.
402	**'whenever the Portuguese, or other Christians at the court'**: Ibid., p. 82.
402	**'to be made for himself in ivory by his own craftsmen'**: Ibid., p. 67.
403	**'harked back to Safavid painting of the mid-century'**: Singh, *Real Birds in Imagined Gardens*, p. 46.
403	expertly fused Hindustani effervescence: Ibid., p. 48.
403	as 'Aqa Riza of Herat': Ibid.
403	**'was marked by the use of vivid, flat colours'**: Ibid., p. 46.
403	**'an Oedipal gesture of rejection'**: Singh, *Real Birds in Imagined Gardens*, p. 48.
403	**'twenty phials of double-distilled spirits'**: Thackston (trans.), *Jahangirnama*, p. 185.
403	**'during those days my only food'**: Ibid., p. 186.
404	**'became violently enamoured'**: Beveridge (trans.), *Akbarnama*, Vol. 3, p. 1095.
404	'He kept constant company with Akbar, like the setting to a pearl': Mukhia, *Historians and Historiography*, p. 53.
405	**'From not fully considering the matter'**: Beveridge (trans.), *Akbarnama*, Vol. 3, p. 1104.
406	In the east were Bengal and Orissa: Henry G. Keene, *The Turks in India: Critical Chapters on the Administration of that Country*, London: W. H. Allen, 1879, pp. x–xiii.
406	the sultanates resumed bickering and quarrelling with one another: See Pillai, *Rebel Sultans* for a history of the Deccan sultanates.
407	struggle that arose at this point was only the final act: Subrahmanyam and Alam, 'The Deccan Frontier and Mughal Expansion, ca. 1600: Contemporary Perspectives', *Journal of the Economic and Social History of the Orient*, Vol. 47, No. 3, 2004, pp. 357–89.
407	sighed Abu'l Fazl, **'became a tedious affair'**: Raghavan, *Attendant Lords*, p. 173.
407	**'in glittering armour, mounted on an elephant'**: Fazl quoted in Radhey Shyam, *The Kingdom of Ahmadnagar*, New Delhi: Motilal Banarsidass, 1966, p. 223.
408	**'clad in armour…with a drawn sword in her hand'**: Pillai, *Rebel Sultans*, p. 143.
408	'The end of the day,' wrote a despairing Abu'l: Raghavan, *Attendant Lords*, p. 174.

PART 6: CROUCHING LION, RISING SUN (1598–1605)

413	**'any excess of anger made him ill'**: Beveridge (trans.), *Akbarnama*, Vol. 3, p. 1096.
413	**Rustam Bari, that Murad named in memory of his son**: Thackston (trans.), *Jahangirnama*, p. 245.
414	**'he had an open heart, and a liberal hand, and had courage along with gravity'**: Beveridge (trans.), *Akbarnama*, Vol. 3, p. 1125.
414	**'There I saw what may no other person see!'**: Beveridge (trans.), *Akbarnama*, Vol. 3, p. 1128.

414	'The management of the troops was carried on': Ibid., p. 1129.
414	'the tongue of suspicion...had sent me far away from court': Ibid., p. 1130.
415	'rice was being exported throughout the Indian Ocean': Eaton, *The Rise of Islam and the Bengal Frontier*, p. 201.
415	'a major producer for the imperial court's voracious appetite': Ibid., p. 201.
415	'from drunkenness and bad companionship': Ibid., p. 1140.
416	recognized a form of 'ritual suzerainty': Alam and Subrahmanyam, 'The Making of a Munshi', p. 368.
416	left Agra for Malwa at the head of a huge army of about 80,000 to 100,000 horse: du Jarric, *Akbar and the Jesuits*, p. 98.
417	'discomposed by grief for his son': Beveridge (trans.), *Akbarnama*, Vol. 3, p. 1142.
417	a mandap of red sandstone, white marble and grey stone: For details on the shiromani temple, see Margaret H Case (ed.), *Govindadeva: A Dialogue in Stone*.
417	'though the boy [Bahadur] was considered as the ruler': Beveridge (trans.), *Akbarnama*, Vol. 3, p. 1143.
418	rather they were sour, and lacking in taste: Alam and Subrahmanyam, *Writing the Mughal World*, p. 184.
418	'go to court whenever it was wished, and would send Bahadur': Beveridge (trans.), *Akbarnama*, Vol. 3, p. 1148.
419	'valuable jewels, embroidered articles, a noble library and many other things': Ibid., p. 1159.
419	Though in battle's dreadful turmoil her courage never failed: Pillai, *Rebel Sultans*, p. 146.
421	'The lumbering siege trains of the stereotypical "Gunpowder Empire,"': de la Garza, *The Mughal Empire at War*, p. 77.
422	'the evil-thoughted and the foolish talkers were ashamed': Beveridge (trans.), *Akbarnama*, Vol. 3, p. 1072.
422	'many sate down in the blackness of envy': Mukhia, *Historians and Historiography During the Reign of Akbar*, p. 55.
423	'confusion worse than Babylon': du Jarric, *Akbar and the Jesuits*, p. 48.
423	'his arrangements and establishments': Beveridge (trans.), *Ma'asir al-Umara*, p. 127.
423	Fazl himself, we are told, 'had a wonderful appetite': Ibid.
424	Many employed a variety of cooks: Husain, 'The Establishments, Households and Private Life of Mughal Nobles', p. 382.
424	The horseman as well as the infantry soldier supports himself: de la Garza, *The Mughal Empire at War*, p. 251.
424	'chief stronghold', wrote the Jesuits: du Jarric, *Akbar and the Jesuits*, p. 105.
424	'while old', agreed Abu'l Fazl, 'she had a youthful mind': Beveridge (trans.), *Akbarnama*, Vol. 3, p. 1153.
426	Yaqut Khan swallowed a large quantity of opium: Ibid., p. 258.
427	'from self-indulgence, wine drinking and bad company': Beveridge (trans.), *Akbarnama*, Vol. 3, p. 1155.
427	'both seasonal military labour and the riches of a thriving pastoral economy': Faruqui, *The Princes of the Mughal Empire*, p. 218.
428	'he seized people's fiefs, took possession of the Bihar treasury': Milo C. Beach, 'The Gulshan Album and the Workshops of Salim', *Artibus Asiae*, Vol. 73, No. 2, 2013, p. 446.
429	'deliberately flat, ornamental, Persianate style': Singh, *Real Birds in Imagined Gardens*, p. 49.
430	'was likely to have been delighted by this elaborate and outsize royal seat': Ibid.
430	'the lion victorious in hunt, the mythical simurgh': Ibid.
430	In the time of the lion-capturing prince: Beach, 'The Gulshan Album', p. 445.
430	'primarily an archival project': Singh, *Real Birds in Imagined Gardens*, p. 51.

431	giving the album its original name, the *Muraqqa-e-Zarr-Negar*: Ibid., p. 54.
431	a style unprecedented in Mughal India: Beach, 'The Gulshan Album', p. 472.
431	'[Abu'l Hasan's] work is beyond comparison in any way to his father's': Thackston (trans.), *Jahangirnama*, p. 268.
432	'Stylistic hybridity...was a pervasive device': Singh, *Real Birds in Imagined Gardens*, p. 9.
432	use a variety of styles even within a single painting: For a discussion of this hybridity, see Singh, *Real Birds in Imagined Gardens*, pp. 32–37.
432	Abu'l Hasan Mashhadi and Khan Jahan Lodi joined the prince's entourage: Faruqui, *The Princes of the Mughal Empire*, p. 159.
433	'He spends his time alone in that dark narrow hole': Thackston (trans.), *Jahangirnama*, p. 209.
433	'had excellently mastered the science of (Vedanta)': Shireen Moosvi, 'The Mughal encounter with Vedanta', *Proceedings of the Indian History Congress*, Vol. 61, Part 1, 2000–01, p. 443.
433	'he often mentioned it with fondness': Thackston (trans.), *Jahangirnama*, p. 209.
434	'on royal thrones encrusted with rubies': Harris, *The First Firangis*, p. 134.
434	'for some days little else was talked of at the court': du Jarric, *Akbar and the Jesuits*, p. 158.
434	other Muslim courtiers were more cynical: Ibid., p. 271.
435	'in a manner that was wholly miraculous': Ibid., p. 161.
436	regarded 'with great contempt' all that related to Christianity: Ibid., p. 169.
436	'that the Persians themselves take pleasure in hearing him talk': Maclagan, *The Jesuits and the Great Mogul*, p. 198.
436	'to assure them that his services were at all times at their disposal': du Jarric, *Akbar and the Jesuits*, p. 169.
437	'In the conversion of souls,' admitted the Jesuits ruefully: Ibid., p. 173.
437	'the Father told him we regard him as one of the greatest imposters': Ibid., p. 171.
437	'did not possess the glory of sincerity': Beveridge (trans.), *Akbarnama*, Vol. 3, p. 1210.
437	'his peace and prosperity lay in returning to Allahabad': Ibid.
438	'I cannot flee from this unwashed thief': Ibid., p. 1218.
439	'My gracious sovereign has raised me': Ibid.
440	had it 'thrown into an unworthy place': Eraly, *The Last Spring*, p. 224.
440	'Shaykh Abu'l Fazl...who was outstanding in his learning and wisdom': Allison Busch, 'Literary Responses to the Mughal Imperium: The Historical Poems of Keśavdās', *South Asia Research*, New Delhi: SAGE, 2005, p. 42.
440	Considering political expediency: Ibid., p. 40.
441	Spoke Khan Azam consoling words: Ibid., p. 41.
442	'if Salim wished to be Emperor he might have killed me': Eraly, *The Last Spring*, p. 225.
442	'That day and night he neither shaved': Elliot, *The History of India, as Told by Its Own Historians*, p. 156.
442	'severely censured the prince for what he had done': Beveridge (trans.), *Akbarnama*, Vol. 3, p. 1219.
442	'although this caused distress to (Akbar)': Busch, 'Literary Responses to the Mughal Imperium', p. 42.
442	'had for a time given up wine-drinking, and had broken his wine-vessels': Beveridge (trans.), *Akbarnama*, Vol. 3, p. 1221.
443	'I am dying, may you live long': Ibid., p. 1226.
443	'cleansed the stain of savagery': Ibid., p. 1227.
443	a peshkash of 12,000 mohurs and 977 elephants: Mukhia, *The Mughals in India*, p. 104.
443	'joyfully, drinking wine, and pleasuring himself': Beveridge (trans.), *Akbarnama*, Vol. 3, p. 1234.

444	'She constantly wrote to Khusrau': Rogers (trans.), *Tuzuk-i-Jahangiri*, p. 56.
444	'Several times she went berserk': Thackston (trans.), *Jahangirnama*, p. 51.
445	'a coward, tyrant, arbitrary, and obsessed with his harem of over 900 concubines': Alam, 'The Deccan Frontier and Mughal Expansion', p. 379.
445	'300,000 or 400,000 huns' of money: Ibid., p. 380.
446	'Ambar was the paragon of all good qualities': Ibid., p. 381.
446	On another side may be a wine-merchant's shop: Elliot, *The History of India, as Told by Its Own Historians*, p. 164.
447	'food, drinks, and fresh fruits, and good fodder for the animals': Alam, 'The Deccan Frontier and Mughal Expansion', p. 383.
447	'his transformation from a competent but conventional painter': Marika Sardar and Navina Najat Haidar, *Sultans of Deccan India, 1500-1700: Opulence and Fantasy*, 2015, New York: Metropolitan Museum of Art, p. 102.
448	'This is an untried medicine': Elliot, *The History of India, as Told by Its Own Historians*, p. 167.
448	'justify the hope that God would one day work in him a great miracle': du Jarric, *Akbar and the Jesuits*, p. 183.
448	'I have a very great affection for the Lord Jesus': Ibid., p. 185.
449	'We have conquered a whole world by the sword': Raghavan, *Attendant Lords*, p. 190.
450	shows a tall, broad-shouldered fair-complexioned young man: 'Portrait of Prince Danyal' by Manohar, 1600, Metropolitan Museum of Art, New York.
450	'was a young man of fine stature, with a pleasing build and good-looking': Thackston (trans.), *Jahangirnama*, p. 39.
450	'heart-striking news came...that she was seriously ill': Ibid., p. 15.
453	'let them bring me wine in any possible way': Ibid., p. 36.
453	'with whom he was on very intimate terms': Ibid., p. 190.
454	'diverse jewels, rings and earrings to his great liking': John Mildenhall, *Early Travels in India*, p. 55.
454	'whereas before we were friends': Ibid., p. 56.
455	'day and night sought how to': Ibid., p. 57.
455	'thoroughly unscrupulous man': du Jarric, *Akbar and the Jesuits*, p. 115.
455	'John Mildenhall was not an estimable character': *The Cambridge History of India*, p. 152.
455	Of his 'enterprising successors': See William Dalrymple, *The Anarchy: The East India Company, Corporate Violence, and the Pillage of an Empire*, New Delhi: Bloomsbury Publishing, 2019 for an exposé of the rise of the East India Company.
456	brought a group of merchants to court of the 'Great Mogor': du Jarric, *Akbar and the Jesuits*, p. 51.
456	Over the next 200 years [the EIC] would slowly learn to operate skillfully: Dalrymple, *The Anarchy*, p. 19.
457	'You must not relax your efforts': Elliot, *The History of India, as Told by Its Own Historians*, p. 167.
458	Mughal emperor, with an annual income estimated at 100 million pounds: Dalrymple, *The Anarchy*, p. 14.
459	'poor fellow's house was given to plunder': Husain, 'The Establishments, Households and Private Life of Mughal Nobles', p. 378.
460	'both overstepped the bounds of courtesy': Elliot, *The History of India, as Told by Its Own Historians*, p. 168.
460	'Shah Baba (Akbar) says this elephant bout is yours': Thackston (trans.), *Jahangirnama*, p. 17.
461	'We have trusted our person to Hakim Ali': Moosvi, *Episodes in the Life of Akbar*, p. 113.
461	'Prince Khurram stood his ground in the midst of enemies and malevolents': Thackston (trans.), *Jahangirnama*, p. 17.

461	'as long as there is a breath of life left in my grandfather': Ibid., p. 18.
461	'that to give the throne to a son during the lifetime of his father': Hooja, *The History of Rajasthan*, p. 493.
462	'amongst his captains, and in so cheerful': du Jarric, *Akbar and the Jesuits*, p. 97.
463	'these rulers constructed new palaces in their respective capitals': Das, *Paintings of the Razmnama*, p. 23.
464	'In the end...neither [Muslims] nor [Hindus] nor Christians would claim him: du Jarric, *Akbar and the Jesuits*, p. 208.
465	'The alarming news of his death': C. M. Naim, *Urdu Texts and Contexts: The Selected Essays of C.M. Naim*, p. 246.
465	The whole town was in a tremor: Moosvi, *Episodes in the Life of Akbar*, p. 116.
466	'power reigned supreme and unchallenged': Faruqui, *The Princes of the Mughal Empire*, p. 272.
466	'what's to be done?': Thackston (trans.), *Jahangirnama*, p. 49.
467	at the Padshah's court, 'all religions are tolerated': Edward Terry, *A Voyage to East-India: Wherein Some Things are Taken Notice Of, in Our Passage Thither; But Many more in our Abode There, Within that Rich and Most Spacious Empire of the Great Mogul*, London: J. Wilkie, 1776, p. 418.
467	'the degradation of Islam has reached a stage': Aziz Ahmad, 'Religious and Political Ideas of Shaikh Ahmad Sirhindi', *Rivista degli Studi Orientali*, Vol. 36, 1961, p. 261.
468	'The glory of Islam consists in the humiliation of infidelity': Ibid., p. 211.
468	'the confusion of his [Shaikh Sirhindi's] senses': Ahmad, 'Religious and Political Ideas of Shaikh Ahmad Sirhindi', p. 214.
468	'the Sharia came to be synonymous': Alam, *The Languages of Political Islam*, p. 78.
469	elite included 31.6 per cent Rajput and other Hindus of 500 zat: Iqtidar Alam Khan, 'State in the Mughal India: Re-Examining the Myths of a Counter-Vision', *Social Scientist*, Vol. 29, No. 1/2, 2001, pp. 16–45.
469	that men belonging to various communities and different religions: *Proceedings of the Indian History Congress*, Vol. 33, p. 179.
470	'He was a prince beloved of all, firm with the great, kind': du Jarric, *Akbar and the Jesuits*, p. 205.
471	'public culture in which every sect honours every other': Nayanjot Lahiri, *Ashoka in Ancient India*, p. 196.
472	'cypress and fruit trees standing for immortality': Laura E. Parodi, 'Solomon, the Messenger and the Throne Themes from a Mughal Tomb', *East and West*, Vol. 51, No. ½, June 2001, p. 128.
473	alluding in his writings to just such a 'rich tent': William Finch, *Early Travels in India*, p. 117.
473	'I had intended it to be such that world travelers': Thackston (trans.), *Jahangirnama*, p. 99.
473	'ceiling of the dome were (covered with) great angels and cherubim': Ibid., p. 134.

BIBLIOGRAPHY

Abbas, Fauzia Zareen, *Abdul Qadir Badauni, as a Man and Historiographer*, New Delhi: Idarah-i Adabiyat-i Delli, 1987.
Abu'l Fazl, *Ain-i-Akbari*, Vol. 1, translated by H. Blochmann, Calcutta: Royal Asiatic Society, 3rd edition, 1977 (repr.).
_____, *Ain-i-Akbari*, Vols. 2 &3, translated by H. S. Jarrett, Calcutta: Royal Asiatic Society, 1949 (repr.).
Ahmad, Aziz, *Studies in Islamic Culture in the Indian Environment*, London: Oxford University Press, 1964.
Ahmad-ul-Umri, *The Lady of the Lotus: Rup Mati, Queen of Māndu: A Strange Tale of Forgiveness*, translated by Leslie M. Crump, Milford: Oxford University Press, 1926.
Akbar's Tomb, Sikandarah, near Agra, described and illustrated by Edmund W. Smith, Allahabad: Archeological Survey of India, Vol. 35, United Provinces: Government Press.
Alam, Muzaffar, *The Languages of Political Islam in India c. 1200–1800*, New Delhi: Permanent Black, 2004.
Asher, Catherine B. and Cynthia Talbot, *India before Europe*, New Delhi: Cambridge University Press 2006.
_____, *The New Cambridge History of India: Architecture of Mughal India*, Part 1, Vol. 4, Cambridge: Cambridge University Press, 1992.
Balabanlilar, Lisa, *Imperial Identity in the Mughal Empire: Memory and Dynastic Politics in Early Modern South and Central Asia*, London: I.B Tauris and Co., 2012.
Beveridge, Annette S. (trans.), *The Babur-nama in English (Memoirs of Babur): Translated from the original Turki text of Zahiru'd-din Muhammad Babur Padshah Ghazi*, Vol. 1, London: Luzac & Co, 1922.
Beveridge, H. (trans.), *The Akbarnama of Abu-L-Fazl*, Vol. 3, Calcutta: Royal Asiatic Society, 1939, 2000 (repr.).
_____, *The Akbarnama of Abu-L-Fazl*, Vols. 1 &2, Calcutta: Royal Asiatic Society, 1907, 2000 (repr.).
Bhardwaj, Kanwal Kishore, *Hemu: Napoleon of Medieval India*, New Delhi: Mittal Publications, 2000.
Bose, Mandakranta, *Faces of the Feminine in Ancient, Medieval, and Modern India*, New York, Oxford: Oxford University Press, 2000.
Burton-Page, John, *Indian Islamic Architecture: Forms and Typologies, Sites and Monuments*, Leiden: Brill, 2008.
Busch, Allison, *Poetry of Kings: The Classical Hindi Literature of Mughal India*, New Delhi: Oxford University Press, 2011.
Callewaert, Winand M., *The Hindi Biography of Dadu Dayal*, New Delhi: Motilal Banarsidass, 1988.
Case, Margaret H., *Govindadeva: A Dialogue in Stone*, New Delhi: IGNCA, 1996.
Chandra, Satish, *Medieval India: From Sultanate to the Mughals*, Mughal Empire (1206–1526), Part 1, New Delhi: Har Anand Publications, 2004.
_____, *Medieval India: From Sultanate to the Mughals*, Mughal Empire (1526–1748), Part 2, New Delhi: Har Anand Publications, 2007.
Chida-Razvi, Dr Mehreen, *The City in the Muslim World: Depictions by Western Travel Writers*, edited by Mohammad Gharipour and Nilay Ozlu, London: Routledge, 2015.
Collingham, Lizzie, *Curry: A Tale of Cooks and Conquerors*, New Delhi: Oxford University Press,

2006.

Das, Kumudranjan, *Raja Todar Mal*, Calcutta: Saraswat Library, 1979.

Datta, Rajat (ed.), *Rethinking a Millennium: Perspectives on Indian History from the Eighth to the Eighteenth Century: Essays for Harbans Mukhia*, New Delhi: Aakar Books, 2008.

de Clavijo, Ruy Gonzalez, *Narrative of the Embassy of Ruy Gonzalez de Clavijo to the court of Timour, at Samarcand, A. D. 1403–6*, translated by Clements R. Markham, London: The Hakluyt Society, 1859.

De, B. (trans.), *Tabaqat-i-Akbari of Nizamuddin Ahmad*, Vol. 2, Calcutta: Royal Asiatic Society of Bengal, 1936.

de la Garza, Andrew, *The Mughal Empire at War: Babur, Akbar and the Indian Military Revolution, 1500-1605*, Oxon: Routledge, 2016.

Desai, Madhuri, *Banaras Reconstructed: Architecture and Sacred Space in a Hindu Holy City*, New Delhi: Orient Blackswan, 2017.

du Jarric, Father Pierre, S. J., *Akbar and the Jesuits: An Account of the Jesuit Missions to the Court of Akbar*, (The Broadway Travellers Series) Plymouth: W. M. Brendon and Son Ltd, 1926, Oxfordshire: Routledge UK, 2014.

Dughlat, Mirza Muhammad Haidar, *A History of the Moghuls of Central Asia: Being the Tarikh-I-Rashidi of Mirza Muhammad Haidar, Dughlát*, translated by Sir E. Denison Ross, edited by E. Elilias, New Delhi: A. B. I. Prints and Publications Company, 1895, 2006 (repr.).

Duindam, Jeroen (ed.), *Rulers and Elites: Comparative Studies in Governance*, Vol. 8, Leiden: Brill, 2016.

Eaton, Richard M., *India in the Persianate Age: 1000-1765*, London: Allen Lane, 2019.

_____, *The Rise of Islam and the Bengal Frontier, 1204–1760*, Berkeley and Los Angeles: University of California, 1983.

Elliot, Henry Miers (ed.), *The History of India, as Told by Its Own Historians: The Muhammadan Period, End of the Afghan Dynasty and the First Thirty-Eight Years of the Reign of Akbar*, edited by John Dowson, Vol. 5, London: Trübner and Co., 1873.

Eraly, Abraham, *The Last Spring: The Lives and Times of the Great Mughals*, Part I, New Delhi: Penguin Books, 1997.

_____, *Emperors of the Peacock Throne: The Saga of the Great Moghuls*, New Delhi: Penguin Books, 2007.

_____, *The Mughal World: Life in India's Last Golden Age*, New Delhi: Penguin Books, 2007.

Faruqui, Munis D., *The Princes of the Mughal Empire, 1504–1719*, Cambridge: Cambridge University Press, 2012.

Ferishta, Mahomed Kasim, *History of the Rise of Mohamedan Power in India, Till the Year A. D. 1612*, 4 Vols, translated by John Briggs, Cambridge: Cambridge University Press, 2014.

Fisher, Michael, *Visions of Mughal India: An Anthology of European Travel Writing*, London: I. B. Tauris, 2007.

Foltz, Richard C., *Mughal India and Central Asia*, Karachi: Oxford University Press, 1998.

Foster, Sir William, *Early Travels in India, 1583-1619*, London: H. Milford, Oxford University Press, 1921.

Frankopan, Peter, *The Silk Roads: A New History of the World*, London: Bloomsbury Publishing, 2015.

Gascoigne, Bamber, *The Great Moghuls*, New Delhi: Constable Publishing, 1998.

Gil Harris, Jonathan, *The First Firangis: Remarkable Stories of Heroes, Healers, Charlatans, Courtesans & Other Foreigners Who Became Indian*, New Delhi: Aleph Book Company, 2015.

Gilmartin, David and Bruce B. Lawrence, *Beyond Turk and Hindu: Rethinking Religious Identities in Islamicate South Asia*, Florida: University Press of Florida, 2000, New Delhi: India Research Press, 2002.

Goldie, Francis, *The First Christian Mission to the Great Mogul, Or, the Story of Blessed Rudolf Acquaviva: And of His Four Companions in Martyrdom of the Society of Jesus*, 1897, Sacramento: Creative Media Partners, 2018.

Grewal, J. S. and Irfan Habib (eds.), *Sikh History from Persian Sources: Translations of Major Texts*, New Delhi: Tulika Books, 2001.

Gulbadan Begam, *The History of Humayun: Humāyūn-Nāmā*, translated by Annette S. Beveridge, London: Royal Asiatic Society, 1902, New Delhi: Munshiram Manoharlal Publishers, 2001 (repr.).

Habib, Irfan (ed.), *Akbar and His India*, New Delhi: Oxford University Press, 1997.

Hambly, Gavin, *Women in the Medieval Islamic World: Power, Patronage, and Piety*, New York: St. Martin's Press, 1998.

Harlan, Lindsey, *Religion and Rajput Women: The Ethic of Protection in Contemporary Narratives*, New Delhi: Munshiram Manoharlal Publishers Pvt Ltd, 1994.

Hasan, Mohibbul, *Kashmir Under the Sultans*, Calcutta: Iran Society, 1959.

———, (ed.), *Historians of Medieval India*, New Delhi: Jamia Millia Islamia, 1968.

Hendley, Thomas Holbein, *Memorials of the Jeypore Exhibition*, 1883.

Hooja, Rima, *A History of Rajasthan*, New Delhi: Rupa Publications, 2006.

———, *Maharana Pratap: The Invincible Warrior*, New Delhi: Juggernaut Books, 2018.

Hoyland, J. S. (trans.), *The Commentary of Father Monserrate, S.J. on His Journey to the Court of Akbar*, London: Humphrey Milford, Oxford University Press, 1922, p. 96.

Husain, Afzal, *The Nobility of Akbar and Jahāngīr: A Study of Family Groups*, New Delhi: Manohar, 1999.

Hutchison, John and Vogel, Jean Philippe, *History of the Panjab Hill States*, 2 Vols., Vol. 1, New Delhi and Madras: Asian Educational Services, 1994.

Ives, Edward, *A Voyage from England to India*, London: Edward and Charles Dilly, 1773.

Jauhar, *The Tezkereh Al Vakiāt: Or, Private Memoirs of the Moghul Emperor Humayun: Written in the Persian Language, by Jouher, a Confidential Domestic of His Majesty*, translated by Major Charles Stewart, London: Oriental Translation Fund, 1832.

Joshi, Varsha, *Polygamy and Purdah: Women and Society Among Rajputs*, Jaipur and New Delhi: Rawat Publications, 1995.

Juneja, Monica, *Architecture in Medieval India: Forms, Contexts, Histories*, New Delhi: Permanent Black, 2001

Khan, Iqtidar Alam, *The Political Biography Of A Mughal Noble: Munim Khan-I-Khanan 1497-1575*, New Delhi: Orient Longman, 1973.

———, *India's Polity in the Age of Akbar*, New Delhi: Permanent Black with Ashoka University, 2016.

Khan, M. Ishaq, *Kashmir's Transition to Islam*, New Delhi: Manohar, 2002.

Lahiri, Nayanjot, *Ashoka in Ancient India*, New Delhi: Permanent Black, 2015.

Lal, Ruby, *Domesticity and Power in the Early Mughal World*, Cambridge: Cambridge University Press, 2005.

Leyden, John and Erskine, William, *Memoirs of Zehir-ed-din Muhammed Baber: Emperor of Hindustan*, London: Longman, Rees, Orme Brown and Green, 1826.

Losty, Jeremiah P., *A Prince's Eye: Imperial Mughal Paintings from a Princely Collection; Art from the Indian Courts*, London: Francesca Galloway, 2013.

Mathur, Dr R. S., *Relations of Hadas with Mughal Emperors*, New Delhi: Deputy Publications, 1986.

Mehta, J. L., *Advanced Study In the History of Medieval India*, Vol. 2, New Delhi: Sterling Publishers, 2017.

Miller, Barbara Stoler (ed.), *The Powers of Art: Patronage in Indian Culture*, New Delhi: Oxford University Press, 1992.

Moin, A. Afzar, *The Millennial Sovereign: Sacred Kingship and Sainthood in Islam*, New York: Columbia University Press, 2012.

Moosvi, Shireen, *The Economy of the Mughal Empire c. 1595: A Statistical Study*, New Delhi: Oxford University Press, 1987.

_____, *Episodes from the Life of Akbar: Contemporary Records and Reminiscences*, New Delhi: National Book Trust, 1994.

Moreland, W. H., *India at the Death of Akbar: An Economic Study*, London: Macmillan and Co., 1920.

Mukhia, Harbans (ed.), *Historians And Historiography during the Reign of Akbar*, New Delhi: Vikas Publishing, 1976.

_____, *The Mughals of India*, New Delhi: Blackwell Publishing, 2004.

Mukhoty, Ira, *Daughters of the Sun: Empresses, Queens and Begums of the Mughal Empire*, New Delhi: Aleph Book Company, 2018.

Murshed, Meher, *Song of the Dervish: Nizamuddin Auliya, the Saint of Hope and Tolerance*, New Delhi: Bloomsbury Publishing, 2017.

Narayan, J. Stephen, *Acquaviva and the Great Mogul*, Ranchi: Catholic Press, 1971.

Orsini, Francesca and Schofield, Katherine Butler, *Tellings and Texts: Music, Literature and Performance in North India*, London: Open Book Publishers, 2015

Pearson, M. N., *The Cambridge History of India: The Portuguese in India*, Cambridge: Cambridge University Press, 2006.

Pillai, Manu S., *Rebel Sultans: The Deccan from Khilji to Shivaji*, New Delhi: Juggernaut Books, 2018.

Prasad, Rajiva Narain, *Raja Man Singh of Amber*, Calcutta: World Press Private Ltd., 1966.

Qandahari, Muhammad Arif, *Tarikh-i-Akbari*, edited by Sayed Moinuddin Nadwi, Saiyeed Azhar Ali, and Imtiaz Ali Arshi, Rampur: Raza Library, 1962, New Delhi: Pragati Publications, 1993.

Raychaudhuri, Tapan and Habib, Irfan (eds.), *The Cambridge Economic History of India: Volume 1, c.1200-c.1750*, Cambridge: Cambridge University Press, 1982.

Reshii, Marryam H., *The Flavour of Spice*, Gurugram: Hachette, 2017.

Rezavi, Syed Ali Nadeem, *Fathpur Sikri Revisited*, New Delhi: Oxford University Press, 2013.

Richards, John F., *Kingship and Authority in South Asia*, New Delhi: Oxford University Press, 1998.

_____, *The New Cambridge History of India: The Mughal Empire*, Part 1, Vol. 5, Cambridge: Cambridge University Press, 1995.

Roychoudhury, Makhanlal, *The Din-i-Ilahi or the Religion of Akbar*, Calcutta: University of Calcutta, 1941.

Ryley, John H., *Ralph Fitch: England's Pioneer to India and Burma: His Companions and Contemporaries with his Remarkable Narrative Told in his Words*, London: T. Fisher Unwin, 1899.

Sachdev, Vibhuti and Sachdev, Giles, *Building Jaipur: The Making of an Indian City*, London: Reaktion Books, 2002.

Sarkar, Jadunath, *A History of Jaipur*, New Delhi: Orient Longman Limited, 1984.

Schimmel, Annamarie, *The Empire of the Great Mughals: History, Art and Culture*, London: Reaktion Books, 2004, 2010 (repr.).

_____, and Stuart Cary Welch, *Anvari's Divan: A Pocket Book for Akbar*, New York: Metropolitan Museum of Art, 1983.

Sharma, Dr G. N., *Rajasthan Studies*, Agra: Lakshmi Narain Agarwal, 1970.

Sharma, Parvati, *Jahangir: An Intimate Portrait of a Great Mughal*, New Delhi: Juggernaut Books, 2018.

Sharma, Shri Ram, *The Religious Policy of the Mughal Emperors*, New Delhi: Oxford University Press, 1940.

Sharma, Sunil, *Mughal Arcadia: Persian Literature in an Indian Court*, Massachusetts: Harvard University Press, 2017.

Shastri, Hirananda, *The Baghela Dynasty of Rewah*, ASI, Maharaja Sawai Singh II Museum, Jaipur, 1998.

Singh, Kesri, *The Hero of Haldighati*, Jodhpur: Books Treasure, 1996.

Singh, Khushwant, *A History of the Sikhs*, Vol. 1, 2nd edition, New Delhi: Oxford University Press, 2018.
Sinha, Parmeshwar P., *Raja Birbal – Life and Times*, New Delhi: Janaki Prakashan, 1980.
Maclagan, Sir Edward, *The Jesuits and the Great Mogul*, London: Burns, Oats and Washbourne Ltd, 1932.
Smith, Paul (Trans.), *Divan of Faizi*, Australia: New Humanity Books, 2018.
Smith, Vincent, *Akbar the Great Mogul, 1542-1606*, Oxford: Clarendon Press, 1917.
Sreenivasan, Ramya, *The Many Lives of a Rajput Queen: Heroic Pasts in India C. 1500-1900*, Washington D. C.: University of Washington Press, 2007.
Subrahmanyam, Sanjay, *Explorations in Connected History: Mughals and Franks*, New Delhi: Oxford University Press, 2005.
Raghavan, T. C. A., *Attendant Lords: Bairam Khan and Abdur Rahim, Courtiers and Poets in Mughal India*, New Delhi: HarperCollins, 2017.
Tabaqat-i-Akbari of Khwajah Nizamuddin Ahmad: (A History of India from the Early Musalman Invasions to the Thirty-Eighth Year of the Reign of Akbar), 3 Vols, Calcutta: The Asiatic Society, 1927.
Talbot, Cynthia, *The Last Hindu Emperor: Prithviraj Chauhan and the Indian Past, 1200-2000*, Cambridge: Cambridge University Press, 2016.
Taylor Sen, Colleen, *Feasts and Fasts: A History of Food in India*, London: Reaktion Books, 2015.
Thackston, Wheeler M. (trans. and ed.), *The Baburnama: Memoirs of Babur, Prince and Emperor*, New York: The Modern Library, 1996.
———, *The History of Akbar*, 4 Vols, Cambridge: Harvard University Press and Murty Classical Library, 2015.
Tirmizi, S. A. I., *Edicts from the Mughal Harem*, New Delhi: Idarah-i Adabiyat-i Delli, 1979.
———, *Mughal Documents 1526–1627*, New Delhi: Manohar Publications, 1989.
Tod's Annals of Rajasthan: The Annals of Mewar, abridged and edited by C. H. Payne, M. A. Late of the Bhopal State Service, London: Routledge & Sons, Limited, Student Facsimile Reprint, 2011.
Tod, Lieutenant-Colonel James, *Annals and Antiquities of Rajasthan, Or the Central and Western Rajpoot States of India*, Vol. 1, London: Smith, Elder and Co., 1829.
Trivedi, Madhu, *The Emergence of the Hindustani Tradition: Music, Dance and Drama in North India, 13th to 19th Centuries*, New Delhi: Three Essays Collective, 2012.
Truschke, Audrey, *Culture of Encounters: Sanskrit at the Mughal Court*, New Delhi: Penguin Books, 2017.
Tubb, Gary Alan, Yigal Bronner, and David Dean Shulman (eds.), *Innovations and Turning Points: Toward a History of Kāvya Literature*, New Delhi: Oxford University Press, 2014.
van Berkel, Maaike and Duindam, Jeroen (eds.), *Prince, Pen and Sword: Eurasian Perspectives*, Leiden: Brill, 2018
Verma, Som Prakash, *Mughal Painters and Their Work: A Biographical Survey and Comprehensive Catalogue*, New Delhi: Oxford University Press, 1994.
Welch, Stuart Carey, Schimmel, Annemarie, Swietochowski, Marie L., and Thackston, Wheeler M., *The Emperor's Album: Images of Mughal India*, New York: Metropolitan Museum of Art, 1987.
Wilson, Jon, *India Conquered: Britain's Raj and the Passions of Empire*, New Delhi: Simon & Schuster, 2016.

CATALOGUES
Losty, Jeremiah P., 'Exhibition—Indian Paintings from the Heil Collection, Catalogue', With research by Joachim K. Bautze, *Asia Week*, New York.
Mazumdar, Subhra (ed.), *Indian Horizons*, Vol. 62, No. 4, October–December, 2015.
Haidar, Navina Najat, and Sardar, Marika (eds.), *Sultans of Deccan India, 1500–1700: Opulence*

and Fantasy, New York: Metropolitan Museum of Art, 2015.

Singh, Kavita, *Real Birds in Imagined Gardens: Mughal Painting between Persia and Europe*, Los Angeles: Getty Research Institute, 2017.

Tillotson, Giles and Venkateswaran, Mrinalini (eds.), *Painting & Photography: At the Jaipur Court*, New Delhi: Niyogi Press, 2016.

PAPERS

'National Seminar on Rajasthan during the time of Akbar', Institute of Rajasthan Studies, Jaipur, 7-8 July 2006.

'Visualizing the Mir'at al-quds', Cleveland Museum of Art, Acc.no. 2005.145 available at <https://archnet.org/publications/10858> [accessed: 1 January 2020].

Adamjee, Qamar and Truschke, Audrey, 'Reimagining the "Idol Temple of Hindustan" Textual and Visual Translation of Sanskrit Texts in Mughal India', *Pearls on a String: Artists, Patrons, and Poets at the Great Islamic Courts*, edited by Amy Sue Landau, Walters Art Museum, 2015, pp. 143–65.

Ahmad, Amir, 'Murder of Abul Fazl: A Re-appraisal', *Proceedings of the Indian History Congress*, Vol. 62, 2001, pp. 207–12.

Ahmad, Aziz, 'Religious and Political Ideas of Shaikh Ahmad Sirhindi', *Rivista degli Studi Orientali*, Vol. 36, 1961, pp. 259–70.

Aitken, Molly E., 'Purdah and Portrayal: Rajput Women as Subjects, Patrons, and Collectors', *Artibus Asiaae*, Vol. 62, No. 2, 2002, pp. 247–80.

Alam, Muzaffar, 'The Mughals, the Sufi Shaikhs and the Formation of the Akbari Dispensation', *Modern Asian Studies*, Vol. 43, No. 1, 2009, pp. 135–74.

____, 'The Pursuit of Persian: Language in Mughal Politics', *Modern Asian Studies*, Vol. 32, No. 2, May 1998, pp. 317–49.

Ali, M. Athar, 'Towards an Interpretation of the Mughal Empire, *Journal of the Royal Asiatic Society of Great Britain and Ireland*, No. 1, 1978, pp. 38–49, Cambridge: Cambridge University Press.

Gallop, Annabel Teh, 'The Genealogical Seal of the Mughal Emperors of India', *Journal of the Royal Asiatic Society*, Third Series, Vol. 9, No. 1, April 1999, pp. 77–140.

Anooshahr, Ali, 'Shirazi Scholars and the Political Culture of the Sixteenth-Century Indo-Persian World', *Indian Economic and Social History Review*, University of California, 2014.

Asher, Catherine B., 'Sub-Imperial Palaces: Power and Authority in Mughal India', *Ars Orientalis*, Vol. 23, Pre-modern Islamic Palaces, 1993, pp. 281–302.

Bahadur, Bishan, 'Akbar as Depicted by Prominent Contemporary Hindi Poets', *Proceedings of the Indian History Congress*, Vol. 45, 1984, pp. 458–63.

Bahuguna, Renu, 'James Tod's Portrayal of the Life and Deeds of Rana Pratap: A Critical Examination', *Proceedings of the Indian History Congress*, Vol. 74, 2019, pp. 229–39.

Beach, Milo C., 'The Gulshan Album and the workshops of Prince Salim', *Artibus Asiae*, Vol. 73, No. 2, 2013, pp. 445–77.

Bhadani, B. L., 'The Mughal Highway and Post Stations in Marwar', *Proceedings of the Indian History Congress*, Vol. 52, 1991.

Bouillier, Véronique, 'Nāth Yogīs' encounters with Islam', *South Asia Multidisciplinary Academic Journal*, 2015, May 2015, available at <http://samaj.revues.org/3878> [accessed: 1 January 2020].

Busch, Allison, 'Hidden in Plain View: Brajbhasha Poets at the Mughal Court', *Modern Asian Studies*, Vol. 44, No. 2, Cambridge University Press, 2010, pp. 267–309.

____, 'Literary Responses to the Mughal Imperium: The Historical Poems of Kesavdas', *South Asia Research*, Vol. 25, No. 1, Sage Publications, 2005.

____, 'Portrait of a Raja in a Badshah's World: Amrit Rai's Biography of Man Singh (1585)', *Journal of the Economic and Social History of the Orient*, Vol. 55, 2012, pp. 287–328.

Chandra, Satish, 'Jizyah and the State in India during the 17th Century', *Journal of the Economic *and Social History of the Orient*, Vol. 12, No. 3, September 1969.

Chida-Razvi, Dr Mehreen, 'Perception and Reality: The Mughal City of Lahore through European Eyes', 11th International Conference on Urban History, Charles University, 30 August 2012.

de la Garza, Andrew, 'Mughals at War: Babur, Akbar and the Indian Military Revolution, 1500-1605', Dissertation, Ohio State University, 2010.

Ernst, Carl W., 'Accounts of Yogis in Arabic and Persian Historical and Travel Texts', *Jerusalem Studies in Arabic and Islam*, Institute of Asian and African Studies: Max Schloessinger Memorial Foundation, Vol. 33, 2008, pp. 409–26.

Farooqi, N. R., 'An Overview of Ottoman Archival Documents and their Relevance for Medieval Indian History', *Medieval History Journal*, Vol. 20, No. 1, 2017, pp. 192–229.

Glynn, Catherine 'A Rajasthani Princely Album: Rajput Patronage of Mughal-Style Painting', *Artibus Asiae*, Vol. 60, No. 2, 2000, pp. 222–64.

Goswamy, B. N. and Krishna, Kalyan, 'Indian Costumes in the Collection of the Calico Museum of Textiles', Vol. 5, 3rd Edition, Ahmedabad, 2010.

Guy, John, 'Mughal painting under Akbar: the Melbourne Hamza-nama and Akbar-nama Paintings', National Gallery of Victoria, Art Journal, Vol. 22, 26 June 2014.

Habib, Irfan, 'Akbar and Social Inequities', *Proceedings of the IHC*, Vol. 53, 1992, pp. 300–10.

_____, 'Shaikh Ahmad Sirhindi and Shah Waliullah', *Proceedings of the Indian History Congress*, Vol. 23, Part 1, 1960, pp. 209–23.

Inayet, S., and Zaidi, A., 'Akbar's Relations with Rajput Chiefs and Their Role in the Expansion of the Empire', *Social Scientist*, Vol. 22, No. 7/8, 1994, pp. 76–82.

Jain, Shalin, 'Interaction of the "Lords"; The Jain Community and the Mughal Royalty Under Akbar', *Social Scientist*, Vol. 40, No. 3/4, March–April 2012, pp. 33–57.

Kamdar, K. H., 'Did Hiravijaya Suri Initiate Akbar's Catholic System?', *Proceedings of the Indian History Congress*, Vol. 23, Part 1, 1960, pp. 192–95.

Khan, Enayatullah, 'Akbar and His Cheetahs', *Proceedings of the Indian History Congress*, Vol. 73, 2012.

Khan, Iqtidar Alam, 'The Nobility Under Akbar and the Development of His Religious Policy, 1560–1580', *Journal of the Royal Asiatic Society of Great Britain and Ireland*, No. 1/2, April 1968, pp. 29–36.

Khan, Motiur Rahman, 'Akbar and the Dargah of Ajmer', *Proceedings of the Indian History Congress*, Vol. 71, 2010–11, pp. 226–35.

Khan, Shahnaz, 'Recovering the Past in *Jodhaa Akbar*: Masculinities, Femininities and Cultural Politics in Bombay Cinema', *Feminist Review*, No. 99, Media Transformations, 2011, pp. 131–46.

Lal, Ruby, 'Settled, Sacred and All-Powerful; Making of New Genealogies and Traditions of Empire under Akbar', *Economic and Political Weekly*, Vol. 36, No. 11, 17–23 March 2001, pp. 941–58.

Majid, Afshan, 'Emperor Akbar's Views on Women as Recorded by Badāūnī and Abu'l Faẓl, *Proceedings of the Indian History Congress*, Vol. 75, Platinum Jubilee, 2014, pp. 289–94.

_____, 'Women and a Theologian: The Ideas and Narratives of Abdul Qadir Badauni', *Proceedings of the Indian History Congress*, Vol. 71, 2010–11, pp. 248–55.

Mehta, Dr Shirin, 'Akbar as Reflected in the Contemporary Jain Literature in Gujarat', *Social Scientist*, Vol. 20, No. 9/10, pp. 54–60.

Moosvi, Shireen, 'The World of Labour in Mughal India (c. 1500–1750)', *International Review of Social History*, Vol. 56, No. 19, 2011.

_____, 'Shipping and Navigation under Akbar', *Proceedings of the Indian History Congress*, Vol. 60, 1999, pp. 251–63.

Mukherjee, Tarapada and Habib, Irfan, 'Akbar and the Temples of Mathura and its Environs', *Proceedings of the Indian History Congress*, Vol. 48, 1987, pp. 234–50.

Mukhia, Harbans, '"No conflict between reason and faith": Reappraising Abu'l Fazl's Rationality',

Academia. edu.
Naim, C. M., 'Popular Jokes and Political History: The Case of Akbar, Birbal and Mulla Do-Piyaza', *Economic and Political Weekly*, 17 June 1995.
O'Hanlon, Rosalind, 'Kingdom, Household and Body History: Gender and Imperial Service under Akbar', *Modern Asian Studies*, Vol. 41, No. 5 September 2007, pp. 889–923.
Parikh, Rachel, 'Yoga under the Mughals: From Practice to Paintings', *South Asian Studies*, Vol. 31, No. 2, 2015, pp. 215–36.
Parodi, Laura E. and Wannell, Bruce, 'The Earliest Datable Mughal Painting: An Allegory of the Celebrations for Akbar's Circumcision at the Sacred Spring of Khwaja Seh Yaran near Kabul (1546 AD)', *Staatsbibliothek zu Berlin-Preussischer Kulturbesitz, Libr. Pict. A117*, fol 15a, 18 November 2011.
Pauwels, Heidi, 'Stealing a Willing Bride: Women's Agency in the Myth of Rukmiṇī's Elopement', *Journal of the Royal Asiatic Society*, Vol. 17, No. 4, 2007, pp. 407–41.
Rezavi, Syed Ali Nadeem, 'Mughal Wall Paintings: A Study of Fathpur Sikri', *Proceedings of the Indian History Congress*, Vol. 64, 2003, pp. 375–402.
Rice, Yael, 'A Persian Mahabharat: The 1598–1599 Razmnama', *Manoa*, Vol. 22, No. 1, Andha Yug: The Age of Darkness, Summer 2010, pp. 125–31.
_____, 'Mughal Interventions in the Rampur Jami'al-tavarikh', *Ars Orientalis*, Vol. 42, 2012, Smithsonian Institution.
_____, Rice, Yael, 'Workshop as network; a case study from Mughal South Asia', *Artl@sBulletin*, Vol. 6, No. 3, Article 4, 2017.
Sarma, Professor S. R., 'Jyotisaraja at the Mughal Court', *Studies on Indian Culture*, Science and Literature, Madras, 2000.
Saxena, Pushpa, 'The Relations between Akbar and Amber (1556-1605)', PhD thesis, Agra University, 1972.
Sengupta, Dr Chandni, 'Badauni as a Source for Interpreting the History of Akbar's Period: A Critical Review of the Muntakhab-ut-Tawarikh and Najat-ur-Rashid', Vol. 6, No. 3, *International Journal of Research in Economics and Social Sciences*.
Seyller, John, 'Farrukh Beg in the Deccan', *Artibus Asiae*, Vol. 55, No. 3/4, 1995, pp. 319–41.
Shivram, Balkrishan, 'Mughal Court Rituals: The Symbolism of Imperial Authority during Akbar's Reign', *Proceedings of the Indian History Congress*, Vol. 67, 2006-07, pp. 331–49.
Smart, Ellen, 'Akbar, Illiterate Genius', *Kalādarśana: American Studies in the Art of India*, edited by Joanna G. Williams, New Delhi: Oxford & IBH Publishing Co., 1981.
Sreenivasan, Ramya, 'Rethinking Kingship and Authority in South Asia: Amber (Rajasthan), ca. 1560–1615', *JESHO*, 2014, Vol. 57, No. 4, pp. 549–86.
Subrahmanyam, Sanjay, 'The Mughal State—Structure or Process? Reflections on Recent Western Historiography', *Indian Economic and Social History Review*, Vol. 29, No. 3, 1992, pp. 291–321.
Talbot, Cynthia, 'Becoming Turk the Rajput way; conversion and identity in an Indian Warrior Narrative', *Modern Asian Studies*, Vol. 43, No. 1, January 1999, pp. 211–43.
_____, 'Justifying Defeat: A Rajput Perspective on the Age of Akbar', *Journal of the Economic and Social History of the Orient*, Vol. 55, No. 2/3, 2012, pp. 329–68.
Tubach, Surya, 'The Astounding Miniature Paintings of India's Mughal Empire', *Artsy*, 30 April 2018.
Vanina, Eugenia, 'The "Ardhakathanaka" by Banarasi Das: A Socio-Cultural Study', *Journal of the Royal Asiatic Society*, Third Series, Vol. 5, No. 2, July 1995, pp. 211–24.
Wani, Ashraf, 'Akbar and Kashmir', *Proceedings of the Indian History Congress*, Vol. 73, 2012, pp. 184–204.
Welch, Stuart Cary, 'Early Mughal Miniature Paintings from Two Private Collections shown at the Fogg Art Museum', *Ars Orientalis*, Vol. 3, 1959, pp. 133–46.
Yedullahi, Syed Ziaullah (trans.), 'Mahdi-e-Maood', Farah Committee.

DISSERTATIONS

Anwar, Mohammad Siraj, 'Mughal relations with the state of Khandesh (AD 1526-1601)', M.Phil dissertation, Aligarh Muslim University, 1990.

Babagolzadeh, Razieh, 'Understanding the Mughal Book of War: A Translation and Analysis of Abu'l-Fazl's Preface to the Razmnama', Thesis for MA, Simon Fraser University, 2015.

Hastings, James M., 'Poets, Sants and Warriors: the Dadu Panth, Religious Change and Identity Formation in Jaipur State circa 1562-1860', Dissertation, University of Wisconsin-Madison, 2002.

Khan, Iqtidar Alam, 'Life of Munim Khan, Khan I khanan', PhD under Prof. S. Nurul Hasan, Aligarh Muslim University.

Moin, A. Afzar, 'Islam and the Millennium: Sacred Kingship and Popular Imagination in Early Modern India and Iran', PhD dissertation, University of Michigan, 2010.

Pound, Omar S., 'The Emperor Akbar as a Religious Man: Six Interpretations', Thesis for Master of Arts in Islamic Studies, McGill University, Montreal, August 1958.

Salahuddin, Syed, 'Abdul Qadir Badauni and His Contemporaries and Socio-Cultural and Intellectual Milieu as Seen by a Critic', Centre of Advanced Study, Department of History, Aligarh Muslim University, 2010.

Sen, Geeti, 'The Paintings of the Akbarnama as a Source of Historical Documentation', PhD dissertation, University of Calcutta, 1979.

FILMS AND DOCUMENTARIES

Gascoigne, Bamber (presenter), *The Great Moghuls*, Channel 4 (1990).

Hughes, Bettany, *When the Moors Ruled in Europe* (2005).

INDEX

1857 Uprising, 256

Abd al-Qadir Badauni, xiv, xxx, 55
Abd al-Samad, xvii, 22, 27, 29, 32, 91, 92, 93, 168, 174, 212, 284, 349, 404, 428
Abdul Hadi, 213
Abd ul-Hai, 312
Abdullah Khan Uzbek, xv, xxiii, 78, 89, 100, 101, 318, 332, 333
Abdullah Sultanpuri, xvi, 55, 73, 113, 190, 191, 193, 218, 227, 230, 246, 311
Abdu'l Latif, 362
Abdur Rahim, xiii, xviii, 45, 59, 94, 139, 149, 158, 172, 200, 269, 274, 275, 299, 320, 329, 332, 341, 354, 355, 368, 376, 377, 392, 404, 407, 408, 414, 425, 442, 445, 452, 453, 463, 467
Abu'l Fath Gilani, 299, 318, 329
Abu'l Fazl, xiv–vi, xxii, xxiii, xxv–ix, 17, 19, 26, 27, 28, 31, 36, 37, 38, 39, 40, 46, 47, 48, 52, 54–59, 63, 68, 70, 82, 86, 89, 92–96, 100, 101, 103, 110, 111, 127, 130, 132–35, 138, 142, 143, 146, 153, 156, 157, 162, 170, 172, 179, 180, 182, 189, 190, 192, 193, 194, 195, 198, 199, 212–16, 218, 219, 221, 225–29, 233, 235, 238, 244–63, 267, 269, 271, 276, 280–84, 287, 289, 290, 291–97, 300, 302, 306, 307, 309–12, 313, 316, 319, 320, 324, 326, 329, 330, 336, 341, 343–60, 366, 367, 373, 374, 376, 377, 378, 379, 380–84, 389, 390, 391, 399, 400, 404–08, 413, 414, 415–18, 422, 423–25, 438, 439, 440–45, 450, 452
Abu'l Hasan, xvii, 431, 432
Abu'l Qasim, 30, 35, 49, 105, 244
Acquaviva, Rudolf, xvi, 104, 140, 217, 220, 304
Adham Khan, xii, xxi, xxx, 18, 48, 63–67, 80, 81, 97
Adil Shah I, 211, 299
Adil Shah II, xvii, 419, 445, 447, 448, 459
Afghans
  Lodi dynasty, 58, 76, 183
  Rohtas, 99
  in Bengal, 12, 13, 35, 44, 46, 99, 136, 175, 182, 188, 242, 243
  under Sher Shah Sur, xxvi, xxx, 13, 16, 21, 30, 31, 33, 57, 63, 70, 99, 101, 472
Afrasiyab, 328
Agra (fort-city), xxi, xxii, xxiii, xxxv, xxxvii, 7, 9, 35–37, 46, 47, 49–54, 58, 64–68, 70, 75, 77–86, 90, 97, 98, 102, 103, 104, 108, 110, 112, 121–23, 127, 128, 129, 134, 143, 144, 146, 150, 152, 164, 176, 200, 220, 221, 266, 271, 278, 288, 302, 353, 357, 361, 379, 406, 413, 415, 416, 425, 427, 428, 433, 434, 437, 438, 439, 440, 443–58, 461, 462, 463, 465–67
Ahir caste, 349
Ahmadnagar, xiii, xvi, xxiii, 389, 406, 407, 408, 413, 414, 416–19, 421, 422, 425, 426, 445–58
Ahmad Thattawi, 358
Ain-i Akbari, xv, xxxvi, 132, 345
Aisan Daulat Begum, 6
Aitken, Molly, 132
akash diyah, 255
Akbar's atelier,
  Abd al-Samad, 22, 27, 29, 32, 91, 92, 93, 168, 174, 212, 284, 349, 404, 428
  Abu'l Hasan, 431, 432
  Aqa Riza, 403, 429, 431
  Basawan, 179, 338, 349, 351, 429
  Daswant, 93, 159, 173, 292, 305
  Dust Muhammad, 24, 25, 91
  Farrukh Beg, 292, 339, 349, 351, 447
  Govardhan, 429
  Har Das, 149
  Jagannath, 149
  Kesu, 349
  Madhu, 349
  Manohar, 159, 302, 338, 429, 430
  Mansur, 349
  Mir Saiyyid Ali, 22
  Miskin, 174, 338, 349, 351
  Mukund, 349
  Nand, 349
  Narayan, 349
  Paras, 349
  Ramdas, 349

Sanwal Das, 149
Shankar, 349
Surdas, 349
Tara Chand, 149
Akbar's elephants,
  Bal Sundar, 177
  Chanchal, 447
  Dodi (Mal Jamal Bahadur Shahi), 143
  Jhalpa, 43
  Lakhna, 46
  Mubarak Qadam, 179
  Ram Prasad (Pir Prasad), 207
  Gaj Mangal, 262
  Hawai, 39, 40, 68
  Lakshmi Sundar, 262
  Mukut, 262
  Ranbagh, 68
Akbar's horses
  Hayran, 44
  Noor Baize, 149
Akbar's innovations,
  ibadat khana, 190–94, 197, 218, 219, 227, 234, 237, 238, 241, 268, 275, 279, 281, 314, 317
  jama, 127, 154, 155, 232, 350, 408, 454
  weaponry, xxxiii, 8, 453
Akbar's travels down the Yamuna, 178
Akbar–Birbal stories, xxxvii, 315
Akbarnama, xv, xxiii, xxv, xxxvi, 17, 122, 227, 284, 341, 345, 346, 347, 348, 349, 352, 429, 442, 451
Alam, Muzaffar, 32, 44, 54, 71, 121, 230, 282, 407, 468
Alanqua, 15, 347
Aleppo, 4
Ali Adil Shah, xv, xvi, 211, 299, 406
Ali, M. Athar, 184, 283, 345
Ali Quli Khan, xv, 20, 66, 99, 106, 107, 108, 111
Allahabad, xiii, xxxvii, 70, 122, 399, 406, 413, 426, 428, 429, 431, 432, 437, 438, 440, 442, 443, 444, 445, 448, 449, 450, 452
'Allahu Akbar', viii, xxii, 101, 228, 242, 284
Allopanisad (Allah's Upanishad), 242
Amba Khan Kashmiri, 328
Ambala, 260
Ambar Qalam, 174
Amer, xiii, xxi, xxix, 76, 77, 123, 139, 143, 146, 202, 208, 296, 316, 317, 331, 360, 362, 366, 395, 417, 463
amir-e-azam, 184
Amir Khusro, 113, 158, 175, 339

Amrit Rai, 208, 209, 365
Anarkali, 391
Anuptalao, 167, 214, 216, 266, 293
Anwar-i Suhayli, 171, 174, 175
appanage system, 12, 28, 70, 157, 328, 432
  dismantling, 328
Aqa Riza, xvii, 403, 429, 431
Arab Sarai quarters, 256
Aram Banu Begum, 326
Asad Beg, 442, 445, 446, 447, 448, 457
Asaf Khan, xxi, 95, 96, 97, 101, 105, 106, 107, 120, 191, 203, 205–07, 284
Ashoka, xxvii, 470, 471
Ashtottara-Sata-Snatra, 370
Asirgarh, xv, xxiii, 422–26
Askari, xi, xx, xxvi, 11, 12, 18–21, 195
Ataka Khail, xii, xiii, xviii, 67, 81, 112, 200, 383
Aurangzeb, xxxv, 119, 362, 446, 469, 473
Azim Khan, 351

Babur, xi, xii, xx, xxvi, xxxv, xxxviii, 5, 6, 7, 8, 9, 11, 12, 14, 17–23, 28, 30, 34, 35, 36, 38, 39, 42, 46, 47, 58, 67, 70, 73, 74, 90, 93, 103, 105, 118, 121, 129, 136, 148, 157, 162, 164, 167, 171, 196, 198, 200, 228, 241, 249, 252, 262, 264, 278, 304, 310, 318, 329, 336, 343–45, 347, 353, 379
  clashes with the Uzbeks, 9
  defeats Lodis, 162
  defeats the Sisodiya rulers, 8
Baburnama, 6, 171, 310
Badakhshan, 12, 28, 36, 200, 318, 333, 336, 437
Badalgarh Fort, 102
Badauni (Abd al-Qadir Badauni), xiv, xxx, xxxviii, 37, 48, 55, 56, 64, 82, 84, 85, 88, 111, 113, 132, 133, 134, 152, 155, 168, 169, 170, 172, 178, 180–82, 184, 188–98, 200–07, 210–16, 218, 219, 221, 225–30, 240–41, 246, 250, 260, 270, 273–77, 281, 286, 290–92, 297, 302, 303, 309–13, 316, 319, 340, 341, 358, 371, 381, 383, 385, 387, 392, 393, 396, 401
  conflicted views on women, 381
  death, 392
  infatuation with a youth, 381
Badshah Salaamat, 78
Baghdad, 4, 24, 47
Bagh-e-Babur, 23, 264
Bahadur Khan, xv, 20, 39, 63, 66, 99, 101, 351, 463

Bahar al-Hayat, 444, 445
Bahurupi, 267
Baikatpur, 363
Bairam Khan (Akbar's ataliq), 40, 43, 44,
    45–50, 55, 59, 67, 70, 94, 138, 139, 149,
    196, 268
  clash with Tardi Beg, 37–38
  death, 139
  marriage to Salima Sultan Begum, 46, 59
  son, Abdur Rahim, 45, 59, 94, 139, 149,
    158, 172, 200, 269, 274, 275, 299, 312, 320,
    329, 332, 341, 354, 355, 368, 376, 377, 392,
    404, 407, 408, 414, 425, 442, 445, 452, 453,
    463, 467
Bakht un-Nisa Begum, 264
Bakshi Banu Begum, xxv, 21
Balnath Thilla, 261
Banarsi Das, 220, 465, 466
Bandar Lahiri, 386
Baramullah, xxiii, 323
Bayana, 37, 169
Bayazid Bayat, 25, 343
Bega Begum, xii, 14, 21, 24, 25, 27, 28, 42,
    45, 58, 93, 104, 105, 195, 256
Benares, 13, 107, 179
Bengal, xi, xiv, xxii, 8, 10, 12, 13, 35, 43, 44,
    46, 67, 99, 102, 103, 136, 144, 171, 175,
    177, 181, 182, 188, 189, 198, 216, 217,
    241, 242, 243–46, 252, 253, 268, 302, 336,
    363, 394, 395, 406, 415–17, 421, 424, 458,
    459, 462
Bhairava, 309
Bhakkar, 17
Bhaktamara-stotra, 370
Bhakti movement, 83, 361
Bhanuchandra Suri, 309
Bhanu Kalyan, 271
Bhanumati, 129
Bhats, 186
Bhattiyaniji ki sarkar, 365
Bhils, 76, 204
Bhimbhar Pass, 353
Bibi Fatima, 97
Bibi Saruqad, 198
Bihar, xiv, 8, 12, 13, 35, 43, 46, 67, 99, 106,
    120, 136, 175, 177, 180, 183, 188, 189, 242,
    244, 245, 252, 268, 360, 363, 388, 394,
    395, 428
Bihistabad, 472
Bijapur, xv, xvi, xvii, 211, 299, 301, 389, 406,
    407, 408, 416, 418, 419, 420, 445, 446,
    447, 457

Bijapur Sultanate, 299
Bir Singh Deo, xv, xvi, xxiii, 368, 369, 408,
    409, 439, 440
Bishen Das, 429
Blochmann, Heinrich, 283
Bodh Gaya, 363
Brahmin Vithal Rai, 361
Brotton, Jerry, 222
Buland Darwaza, 165, 266
Bundelas, 439
Burhan Shah, 389, 391
  death, 389
Burhanpur, 12, 64, 389, 422, 423, 424
Busch, Allison, 367, 368, 441
Byzantine Empire, 4

cash crops,
  cotton, 10, 96, 138, 273, 336, 376, 456
  indigo, 10, 138, 167, 330, 365, 377
  opium, 10
  sugarcane, 10, 23, 181
Chaghatai clansmen, 262
Champaner, 101
Chandals, 297
Chand Bibi (Chand Sultan), 299, 406, 407
Chandra Bhan 'Brahman', 300
Charans, 186, 208, 236, 325, 367, 376
Chardin, Jean, 301
Chaturbhuja, 291
chavar, 236
Chengiz Khan (Genghis Khan) (Mongol
    warlord), 214
Chishti tazkiras, 259
Chishtiya Sufis of Hindustan, 128
Chittor, xxi, xxxvi, 114, 115, 116, 117, 118,
    119, 120, 121, 122, 202, 203, 207, 236, 340
Collingham, Lizzie, 24, 161
Coryat, Thomas, 278, 357

Dadu Dayal, 295
dagh (system of branding horses), 184, 190,
    243
Damascus, 4, 149
Damayanti, 290
Daniyal, xiii, xviii, 139, 146, 159, 160, 175,
    293, 324, 326, 330, 357, 368, 378, 390, 391,
    399, 400, 407, 413, 415, 416, 418, 421, 422,
    426, 432, 442, 445, 447, 449, 450, 452, 453,
    458, 467
  appointed Governor of Kabul, 324
  Death due to alcoholism, 442, 452
  Hafthazari, 399

marriage, 391
Dar al-Aman, 301
Dar al-Islam, xxviii, 222
Dara Shukoh, xxxi
Darbar Khan, 90, 100, 101
Daulat Khan, 324
de Albuquerque, Alfonso, 178, 330, 393, 434
de Clavijo, Ruy González, 3, 4
Deenpanah Fort, 33, 57, 58
de la Garza, Andrew, xxxiii, 116, 119, 205, 249
Delhi, iv, xii, xvi, xxi, xxxiv, xxxv, 4, 5, 6, 7, 10, 12, 31, 32, 34–37, 41, 43, 46, 49, 57, 63, 70, 72, 76, 81, 85, 86, 110, 113, 114, 115, 121, 122, 136, 137, 160, 162, 182, 211, 228, 253, 256, 257, 268, 288, 301, 376, 406, 413, 416, 417, 425, 451, 475
Delhi Sultanate, 6, 31, 76, 136
Delvoye, Françoise, 295
de Noronha, Antony, 239
Desai, Ashok V., 10, 222, 376
Deva Misra, 291
de Vega, Father Christofle, 373
Dhanraj, 339
Dharampurah, 310
Dharmadas, 339
Dhoondhari 'panchranga' flag, 331
Dhrupad, xxxix, xxxi, 85, 295
Dildar Begum, 16
dilkusha, 3
Din-i Ilahi, 284
Divan-e-Anvari, 339
diwan-e-aam, 165, 266, 270, 449, 452
diwan-e-khas, 233, 266, 294, 297
duhu deen ko sahib, 172
du Jarric, Pierre, 288, 396
Dust Muhammad, 24, 25, 91
Duval Rani va Khizr Khan, 158, 175

East India Company (EIC), 209, 454, 456
Eaton, Richard M., xxviii, 6, 11, 33, 198, 251, 367
Eraly, Abraham, 255
Erskine, William, 16

Falud, 85, 86
farrash khana, 255, 346
Farrukh Beg, xvii, 292, 339, 349, 351, 447
Farrukh Husain, 338
Faruqui, Munis D., 26, 157, 252, 328, 329, 372, 427, 432
Fatehpur Sikri, xxii, xxiii, xxxii, xxxvi, 153, 154, 159, 162, 163, 164, 165, 166, 167, 169, 170, 172, 177, 182, 188, 189, 192, 194, 195, 196, 197, 198, 199, 200, 201, 207, 209, 211, 213, 214, 216, 218, 220, 221, 222, 225, 226, 230, 231, 232, 238, 239, 240, 242, 246, 253, 255, 256, 264, 266, 268, 269, 271, 272, 273, 274, 278, 285, 286, 287, 288, 289, 297, 299, 300, 301, 302, 304, 306, 307, 314, 316, 317, 318, 320, 335, 336, 337, 340, 350, 357, 360, 361, 364, 367, 370, 379, 428, 433, 443, 450, 451, 472
Fath Allah Shirazi, xv, xxx, 299, 300
Ferghana, 6, 9
Ferishta (medieval historian), 16, 38
Finch, William, 391, 473
Firdausi's *Shahnama*, 300
Fitch, Ralph, 164, 179, 303, 317
forts,
  Agra, 68, 80, 102, 134, 353, 433, 461, 463, 466
  Ahmadnagar, 407–08
  Asirgarh, 422–26
  Attock, 323, 335
  Chauragarh, 96
  Chittor, 115, 116, 117, 118–22, 207, 236, 340
  Gondwana, 95, 105, 112, 138, 268, 361
  Gwalior, 98, 100, 105, 115, 205, 340, 419, 426
  Kalanjar, 122
  Kandahar, 18, 394
  Qila-e-Mualla (Red Fort), 288
  Ranthambore, 121
  Rohtas, 359, 363, 364, 367, 378, 459

Gang, 368
Ganga River,
  Akbar's travels, 66, 106, 107, 111, 178, 179
Gayatri Mantra, 309
Ghazi Khan Badakshi, 203, 205, 207, 376
Ghiyas Beg, 211
Glover, William, 337
Goa, xxii, xxxii, 35, 104, 141, 178, 197, 211, 217, 218, 220, 221, 231, 239, 248, 251, 271, 280, 305, 373, 377, 402, 415, 455
Goes, Father Lewis, 239
Golconda, 389, 407, 408, 416, 418, 457
Gommans, Jos, 6
Govardhan Nath, 361
Govardhan Temple, xiv
Great Comet of 1577, 210
Gujarat, xvii, xxii, xxviii, 12, 35, 37, 55, 59,

67, 75, 76, 91, 101, 102, 103, 114, 122, 136, 137, 138, 139, 140, 141, 142, 143, 145, 146, 147, 148, 151, 152, 153, 160, 165, 169, 177, 186, 189, 196, 198, 200, 221, 246, 253, 268, 271, 296, 308, 336, 372, 376, 382, 388, 389, 406, 416, 422, 433

Gulbadan Begum, xii, xiii, xxxviii, 9, 15, 17, 19, 20, 21, 22, 24, 25, 28, 30, 42, 45, 58, 93, 144, 175, 195, 196, 197, 199, 250, 251, 278, 304, 318, 343, 344, 346, 357, 360, 374, 442, 443, 451

Gung Mahal, 226, 286

Gunpowder Empire, 421

guregen or gurkani (in-laws), 4

Guru Gorakhnath, 261

Guy, John, 92

Gwalior, xiv, 98, 100, 105, 115, 205, 340, 419, 426, 444, 472

Habshi, 139, 407

Haidar Chak, 248, 324

Haidar Sultan Shaibani, 20

hajj, xii, xxii, 58, 59, 104, 144, 195, 196, 197, 198, 199, 248, 250, 251, 278, 312, 382

Hakim Abul Fath, 194, 269

Hakim Abu'l Fath Gilani, 318, 329

Hakim Ali, 226, 233, 285, 329, 359, 392, 460, 461, 463

Hakim Hasan, 324

Hakim Humam, 194, 312, 332, 371, 403

hakim ul-mulk, 227, 246

Haldighati, battle of, xiv, xvi, xxii, 204, 315

Hamida Banu Begum or Maryam Makani, xii, xiii, xx, xxxviii, 16, 17, 18, 19, 22, 24, 25, 27, 28, 41, 42, 43, 44, 45, 49, 58, 59, 83, 97, 132, 150, 153, 155, 175, 191, 197, 216, 253, 256, 278, 290, 318, 319, 326, 330, 341, 344, 347, 357, 359, 360, 361, 374, 379, 413, 415, 428, 435, 442, 443, 450, 451

Hamzanama (*The Adventures of Amir Hamza*), xvii, xxi, xxxvi, 90, 91, 92, 93, 100, 103, 174

Haram Sharif, 199, 311

Harkha Bai or Maryam uz Zamani, xiii, xiv, xviii, xix, xxi, xxix, 77, 78, 83, 127, 128, 130, 132, 134, 143, 146, 214, 251, 253, 361, 365, 367, 370, 437

Har Raj of Jaisalmer, xxii, 129

Herat, 14, 24, 58, 403

Hindal, xi, xxvi, 11, 13, 18, 21, 28, 29, 374

Hindu Kush, 332, 333, 334

Hindus, xxx, xxxii, xxxv, 8, 37, 71, 73, 74, 75, 82, 83, 84, 86, 91, 113, 133, 134, 141, 149, 154, 169, 211, 235, 238, 239, 252, 259, 267, 270, 271, 276, 279, 281, 290, 291, 294, 296, 300, 303, 305, 309, 310, 312, 313, 316, 335, 345, 347, 349, 356, 358, 397, 402, 451, 464, 468, 469

Hindustan, xi, xii, xv, xvi, xvii, xx, xxi, xxv, xxvi, xxxi, xxxii, xxxv, xxxvi, xxxviii, 5, 7, 8, 9, 11, 12, 13, 14, 15, 19, 20, 22, 30, 31, 32, 33, 34, 35, 36, 38, 40, 41, 42, 43, 47, 52, 58, 59, 63, 66, 70, 71, 73, 79, 85, 91, 96, 99, 104, 107, 108, 109, 115, 120, 121, 123, 128, 129, 135, 140, 142, 151, 161, 164, 171, 178, 183, 185, 196, 197, 198, 199, 201, 210, 212, 216, 217, 225, 229, 230, 231, 238, 240, 244, 246, 248, 251, 252, 253, 261, 262, 264, 267, 272, 275, 277, 278, 289, 290, 301, 304, 306, 309, 316, 318, 323, 327, 328, 330, 335, 342, 345, 347, 353, 354, 385, 393, 407, 408, 409, 427, 428, 437, 439, 453, 454, 458, 467

Hirasaubhagya, 306, 307

Hiravijaya Suri, 271, 306, 307, 308

Hobson-Jobson, 256

Humayun, xxv, xxvi, xxxv, xxxvi, 7, 11, 12-38, 45, 46, 57, 58, 59, 66, 67, 73, 81, 87, 91, 93, 99, 105, 106, 107, 108, 171, 196, 228, 256, 265, 267, 343, 344, 347, 353, 365, 379, 380, 413, 416, 428, 431, 435, 451
  retaking of Hindustan, 31

Humayun's atelier,
  Abd al-Samad, 22
  Mir Saiyyid Ali, 22

Hurapur, 354

Husain Khan 'Tukriya', 283

Hussain Nizam Shah of Ahmadnagar, 406

Ibn Arabi, xiv, xv, 276, 277, 281

Ibn Battuta, 66

Ibn Sina, 226

Ibrahim Adil Shah II, xvii, 419, 445, 447, 448, 459

Ibrahim Lahori, 338

Ibrahim Lodi, xx, 7, 39, 47, 70
  death, see Panipat, battle of, 162

Ikhlas-i-Chahargana, 284

Ilhahi, 284

Indus river, 386

Iqbal Nama-i-Jahangiri, 348

iqta system, 70, 71

Isfahan, 141, 338

Islam Khan Chishti, 423

Islam Shah, 30, 76, 218
Itimad Khan Gujarati, xxii, 139
Ivan the Terrible, 456

Jabbar Khassa-khail, 439, 440
Jagadgurukavya, 306
Jagat Gosain, xiii, xviii, xix, xxiii, 327, 374, 461
jagirdar, 106, 146, 172, 183, 202, 331
jagirs (land assignment), 9, 53, 54, 80, 81, 87, 99, 107, 112, 183, 185, 200, 365, 383, 459
Jahangir (Mirza Salim), 127, 128, 130, 134, 147, 154, 155, 157, 158, 151, 175, 216, 247, 253, 262, 269, 274, 278, 279, 293, 296, 316, 317, 326, 327, 328, 329, 330, 338–40, 348, 352, 353, 354, 355, 356, 357, 364, 368, 369, 370, 371–74, 378, 379, 387, 388, 391, 393, 399, 400, 403–52, 409, 413, 415, 416, 424, 427, 428–33, 437, 438, 440, 442–53, 459–63
    birth of, 155
    rebellion, 159, 413–16
    reconciliation with the Padshah, 438, 440–442
Jahangirnama, 362
Jaimal, 115, 118, 302
Jain monks, 219, 221, 306, 308, 309, 370
Jaisalmer, xix, xxi, xxii, 16, 122, 129, 186, 202, 208, 463
Jalal Khan Qurchi, 110, 111, 169
Jamal Bakhtyar, 312
Jami Masjid, 266
Jani Beg, 284, 377
Jauhar Aftabchi, 14, 19, 30, 343
Jaunpur, 54, 99, 106, 107, 112, 136, 179, 181, 465
Jesuits
    Acquaviva, Rudolf, 104, 140, 217, 220, 233, 234, 236, 239, 270, 272, 274, 279, 280, 304, 315, 372, 373
    Francis Xavier, 104, 220
    Henriques, 220, 234
    Ignatius of Loyola, 104
    Monserrate, see Monserrate, Father Anthony
jharoka darshan, 287, 288, 293, 298, 319, 460, 467
Jhelum River, 252, 253, 261, 359
jihad, xxxiv, 120, 146, 204
Jiji Anaga, xxv, 15, 17, 18, 45, 56, 67, 147, 148, 200, 244, 330, 347, 384, 385, 424
    burial, 425

    relationship with Akbar, 148
    travel with the Mughal army, 424
jiziya, xxi, xxxiii, xxxiv, 73, 86, 468, 469
Jodh Bai, xix, xxiii, 165, 328
Jodhpur, xix, 16, 122, 186, 328, 463, 475
jogis of Gorkhatri, 310

K'aaba, 357
kabootar-bazi (ishq baazi), 26, 288, 332
Kabul, viii, xii, xvii, xx, xxi, xxv, xxvi, xxxv, 6, 7, 12, 13, 21, 22, 23, 24, 25, 27, 28, 30, 31, 33, 34, 35, 36, 38, 40, 41, 42, 43, 49, 50, 99, 108, 112, 120, 147, 186, 195, 200, 241, 244, 252, 253, 261, 262, 263, 264, 268, 293, 318, 320, 323, 324, 331, 336, 339, 357, 403, 406, 458
Kachhwahas, 76, 83, 86, 105, 122, 142, 143, 149, 159, 203, 209, 283, 307, 316, 330, 362, 363, 364, 366, 376, 417, 444, 462
    clash between Raja Bharmal and Puran Mal, 330–332
    marriage with Harkha Bai, 77, 83, 127, 128, 130, 132, 134, 143, 146
    submission to Akbar, 139, 203
Kaikobad, 328
Kalanaur, 34, 36, 259
kalima, 208, 227, 464
Kalpi, 35, 84
Kalu Lahori, 338
Kalyanmal, xxi, 129, 186
Kamran, xi, xx, xxv, xxvi, 11, 12, 13, 18, 20, 21, 25, 28, 29, 30, 35, 49, 105, 195, 344, 379
Kanauj, 18
Kanchani, 267
Kandahar, xx, xxv, 12, 18, 19, 20, 21, 22, 32, 334, 394, 458
Kanjari caste, 267
Kanphata yogis, 261
Karbala, 250
kasarat, 261
Kashyapa, 356
katar (Rajasthani-style dagger), 232
Kayastha, 300
Kazakhstan, 128
Keene, George, 406
Keshavdas Misra, 295, 368
Kesu, 349, 351
Khairpurah, 310
Khair-ul-Manazil, 57, 85
Khaksar Sultan, 101
Khalisa, 243

INDEX

Khaljis, 63, 76
Khamsa of Nizami, 339, 404
Khanda, 101
Khandesh, xv, 102, 389, 406, 416, 421, 422, 423, 425, 426, 458
Khangar, 324
Khan, Iqtidar Alam, 32, 44, 54, 71, 121, 282
khan-i-saman, 100
Khan Kamboh, 207, 285
khankhanan, xi, xii, xiii, 35, 45, 46, 48, 50, 51, 52, 198, 392, 407
khanqah, 58, 127, 128, 258
Khanua, battle of, 8, 121
Khanum Sultan Begum, 387
Khanzada Begum, xx, 17, 19, 21, 24, 304, 344
khasa, 138, 288
khichdi, 102, 133, 423
Khidmat Rai, 297
khillat, 87
Khizr Khwaja Khan, 28
Khurasan, 387
Khusrau, xiii, xiv, xviii, xix, 327, 373, 378, 388, 393, 416, 425, 427, 444, 452, 458, 459, 460, 461, 462, 466
khutba, 12, 108, 111, 176, 228, 241, 246, 247, 323, 428
Khwaja Baqi-Billah, 467
Khwaja Jalal al-din Mahmud, 29
Khwaja Muazzam, 15, 17, 19, 97
Khwaja Muinuddin Chishti, xxi, 75, 158, 202
Khwarizmian songs, 287
Khyber Pass, 5, 264, 333, 413
Koka, viii, xiii, xviii, xxii, 18, 27, 83, 101, 108, 112, 139, 146, 147, 149, 153, 167, 200, 244, 245, 248, 252, 253, 269, 283, 284, 285, 286, 288, 318, 329, 330, 371, 375, 378, 382, 383, 384, 385, 388, 404, 425, 427, 434, 436, 448, 451, 459, 462, 463, 467
Koran, 5, 20, 31, 154, 156, 174, 193, 227, 234, 238, 256, 278, 284, 302, 348, 404
kornish, 86, 87, 293
Krishnadasa, 341
Ksemakutuhalam, 268
Kuar Man Singh (Raja Man Singh later), xiv, xvi, xxii, xxiii, xxx, 77, 78, 83, 122, 202, 285, 331, 360
Kumaon, 259, 386, 458

Lahore, xxiii, xxxvi, xxxvii, 32, 35, 43, 44, 45, 70, 108, 109, 110, 113, 201, 248, 251, 261, 332, 335, 336, 337, 338, 339, 340, 341, 352, 353, 357, 358, 359, 360, 363, 364, 370, 372, 373, 374, 376, 377, 379, 382, 386, 388, 391, 392, 393, 395, 396, 399, 400, 401, 402, 403, 406, 408, 409, 413, 414, 428, 451, 466
Lala Beg Kabuli, 328
Lal, Ruby, xxxviii, 328, 344, 347, 475
Leades, William, 317
Lohani tribe, 388
Lord Jagannath at Puri, 388
Lord Zelabdin Echebar, 317
Losty, Jeremiah, 102
Lutfullah, 429

Maasir ul-Umara, 348, 423, 441
Machhiwara, battle of, 32, 50, 59
Madhu Singh, 263
Madhusudan Misra, 291
Mahabharat, xv, xxiii, xxxi, xxxvi, 289, 290, 291, 293, 341
Mahadev, 225, 324
Maham Anaga, xxv, xxxv, 18, 20, 25, 31, 34, 43, 44, 45, 46, 48, 49, 55, 56, 57, 58, 60, 65, 66, 67, 70, 75, 77, 80, 81
  role in deposing Bairam Khan, 44, 46, 49
  travel to Kabul, xxv
Maharana Jagat Singh of Mewar, 341
Mah-chuchak Begum, xii, xx, 22, 30, 42
Mahdavi, xvii, 54, 145, 146, 167, 190, 218, 407
Mahesh Das, 84
maktab khana, 171, 289, 293
Malik Ambar, 419, 445, 446
Malik Dabir, 419
Malwa, xv, xxi, xxviii, 35, 63, 64, 65, 66, 67, 70, 78, 80, 89, 100, 101, 112, 138, 182, 268, 273, 351, 371, 372, 406, 416, 422
  Akbar's forces invade, 63–67
Man Bai, xiii, xiv, xviii, xix, 316
Mancarit, 208, 318, 365, 366, 367
Mandhakur, 75
Mandu, 14, 63, 100, 101, 102, 351, 406
Manohar, xvii, 159, 302, 338, 429, 430
Manohar 'Tausani', 302
Manpur, 363
mansabdari system, xxx, 185, 243, 468
Mansur, xvii, 210, 212, 256, 257, 349, 429, 430
Manucci, Niccolao, 473
Mary Tudor, 221
Mashhad, 250
Mathura, xiv, 83, 105, 214, 255, 256, 341, 361, 367
Maulana Ali Ahmad 'Nishani', 387

Maulana Pir Muhammad Shirwani, 38, 47
Mawarannahr, 128, 244
Mazhar of 1579, xxii, 227, 228, 229, 241, 243, 246
Meenas, 76
Merjan festival (Persian Equinox), 274
Mewar, xvi, xxii, 115, 122, 186, 202, 204, 206, 207, 208, 209, 341, 416, 427, 467, 469
Mildenhall, John, 453, 454, 455
military innovations, 454
Mimamsakas, 308
Mir Abd al-Latif Qazwini, 47
Mir Abdullah, 429
Mirak Mirza Ghiyas, 58
Miran Mubarak Shah, 102
Mirat al-Quds (The Mirror of Purity), 434
mir bakawal, 162, 163, 312, 421
mir bakshi, 51, 72, 100, 203, 461
mir hajj, 197, 250
Mir Jamal-ud Din Husain Inju Shirazi, 445
mir saman, 51
Mir Sayyid Ali, xvii, 22, 29, 32, 91, 92
Mir Sharif, 284
Mirza Abdullah Moghul, 44
Mirza Abu'l Qasim, 49
Mirza Aziz Koka, viii, xiii, xxii, 18, 83, 139, 146, 147, 153, 200, 244, 245, 248, 283, 284, 285, 286, 330, 371, 378, 382, 388, 425, 427, 434, 436, 448, 459, 462, 467
Mirza Dughlat, 353
Mirza Ibrahim, 21
Mirza Muhammad Hakim or Mirza Hakim, xvi, xvii, xx, xxiii, xxxvi, 30, 34, 35, 105, 108, 111, 113, 230, 241, 244, 246, 252, 256, 258, 261, 263, 264, 265, 268, 314, 318, 328, 338, 372, 403
    death due to alcoholism, 318
    Kabul, 35
Namkin, or Salty, 244
    rebellion, 105, 108, 111, 113
Mirza Murad, 263, 330, 389
Mirza Rustam, 388, 400, 413
Mirza Sharafuddin Hussain, 76, 77, 78, 85
Mirza Sulaiman, 12, 36, 200, 201, 351
Miyan Bayazid Baz Bahadur Khan, 63
Mohammad Arif Qandahari, 105, 142, 143, 144, 152, 201, 215, 255
Mohammad Sharif, xvii
Moin, A. Afzar, 33, 347
Monserrate, Father Anthony, xvi, 59, 79, 100, 103, 127, 134, 135, 151, 159, 160, 164, 165, 173, 192, 217, 220, 232, 234, 235, 238, 239, 251, 253, 255, 256, 258, 259, 260, 261, 262, 264, 267, 272, 273, 288, 293, 294, 305, 311, 315, 331, 335, 470
Moosvi, Shireen, 10, 197, 222, 376, 401, 433
Moreland, W. H., 10, 222
Mughal–Rajput alliances, 209
Mughal weaponry, 8, 40, 116, 118, 145, 204
Mughal zenana, xxxviii, 78, 131, 133, 134, 336, 365, 460
Muhammad Bukhari, 128
Muhammad Ghori, 75
Muhammad Husain Mirza, xxii, 147, 150
Muhammad Husayn al-Kashmiri (Zarrin Qalam), 338
Muhammad Qasim Mir Barr, 257
Muhammad Sharif, 284, 292, 349, 404, 428, 452
Mukhia, Harbans, 229, 281, 475
Mukund, 349
Mullah Shah Muhammad, 284
Mullah Shari, 291, 292
Mullazada Mulla Asamudin Ibrahim, 26, 288
Munim Khan, xi, xx, xxii, 30, 31, 33, 36, 42, 43, 44, 49–51, 55–56, 65, 66, 80, 99, 101, 106–08, 112, 143, 177, 180, 181, 182, 188, 198, 245, 351, 395
Muntakhabh al-Tawarikh, 82
Muraqqa-e Gulshan, 430
Muraqqa-e-Zarr-Negar, 431
Murshid Quli Khan, 452
Musicians in Akbar's court,
    Gadain Brhmaindas, 84
    Tansen Kalavant Gwaliyari, 84, 85, 232, 295, 297, 315, 352–55, 360–61
mut'ah, 192, 193

Nadira Banu, 175, 429
Nagarchain (City of Rest), 102
Naim, C. M., xxxvii, 315
Nala, 290
Nand, 349
Nanha, 351, 429
Naqib Khan, 203, 291
naqqara drums, 128, 287
naqqar khana, 153, 178, 287, 352, 472
Naqshbandi order, 193, 372
Naqshbandi Sufi Khwaja, 129
Narayan, 95, 349, 417
Narwar, 66, 100, 105, 106, 439
Nasir Khan Afghan, 388
Nasir ul-mulk, 44
Naskh calligraphy, 165

nata marriages, 131
Nauroz festival, 395, 399
Nihani of Agra, 302
Nimat-khana (Book of Pleasures), 102
Nirguna Bhakti tradition, 276, 281, 383
Nizami, 339, 404
Nizam Shahi dynasty, xvi
Nizamuddin Ahmad (Chronicler), 19, 25, 48, 95
Nizamuddin Auliya (Chishti Shaikh), 7, 58, 81, 85, 121, 376, 425
nizam ul-mulk, 408
Noor Jahan, 211, 335
Nuqtavi thinker, 210

O'Hanlon, Rosalind, 111, 380
opium usage, 237, 329, 403, 442,
  as a soporific drug, 237
  messengers, 88
  Salim's dependence, 427, 444, 445, 449, 452, 466
Orchha (fort-palace), xvi, 295, 368, 408, 439, 440, 441, 463
Ottomans, xxviii, 222, 249, 251

Padmasundara, 135
Padshah-e Ghulam, 301
Padshah Ghazi of Hindustan, xx, xxxv
Padshah-i Islam, viii, xxii, 225, 227
Pakhli Route, 323
Panchatantra, 171, 175, 225
Panch Mahal, 266, 472
Panipat, Battle of
  First (Babur's forces and the Lodis), 7, 8, 39, 41, 70, 162
  Second (Akbar's forces with Rana Pratap), 186, 202, 205, 206–09
pardeh-giyan, 132, 304
Pari Khanim, 210
Parodi, Laura E., 24, 472
patka, 87, 232, 273
Persian language
  evolution, 366,
  Persian scholars, 366, 391, 394, 404, 434
  uses in court, 364, 367, 368, 436, 437, 441, 445, 455, 457, 468
Peshawar, 262
peshkash, 185, 331, 375, 442, 443, 452
Pietro Della Valle, 141
Pilau/pilaus, 23, 24, 161
Pir Panjal Pass, 354
Portuguese colonization of Goa,

Portuguese missionary, 104, 239, 218, 454-55
  Manrique, Father Sebastian, 10
Pravin Ray, 295
Prayag, 178, 179
Prithviraj Chauhan, 75
Prophet Muhammad, 27, 73, 214, 239, 240, 269, 274, 313, 341, 346, 437, 464
polo, 103, 298

qaba, 31, 87, 235, 254, 314
Qara Bahadur Khan, 101
Qasim-i Kahi, 284
Qasim Khan Mir Bahr, 324
Qazi Muhammad Yazdi, 241
Qazi Musa (popular Sunni leader), 324
qissa-khwan, 90, 101, 171
qit'a, 339
Queen Elizabeth I, 212, 221, 317, 454
Qulij Khan, 197
qumargha, xxxii, 108, 109, 121, 147, 215, 350, 359
qumargha (ring hunt), xxxii, 108, 109, 121, 147, 215, 350, 359
Qutb Chela, 349
Qutbuddin Bakhtiyar Kaki, 7, 81
Qutlugh Nigar Khanum, 6

Rafiuddin Shirazi, 53, 78, 272, 313
Rai Ram Das, 176
Rai Rayan, 120, 439
Rai Singh Mahotsav, 327
Raja Ali Khan, 422, 425
Raja Bhagwant Das, xiv, 118, 122, 123, 148, 149, 151, 178, 201, 202, 283, 296, 303, 316, 323, 325, 331, 353, 358, 360, 444
Raja Bharmal, xiii, xiv, xxi, xxix, 41, 75, 76, 77, 105, 139, 143, 148
Raja Birbal, xxxvii, 84, 94, 134, 138, 149, 151, 165, 178, 214, 229, 255, 269, 270, 284, 285, 294, 296, 309, 314–20, 360, 361
  composing in Braj/Hindi, 368
  death, 413
Raja Hemchandra Vikramaditya or Hemu, 36, 37, 39, 40, 41, 43, 57, 68
  death of Hemu, 40
  defeat of Hemu, 36–38
Raja Indrajit of Orchha, 295
Raja Loonkaran of Sambhar, 302
Raja of Kumaon, 386
Raja Ramachandra of Baghela, 84
Rajasthan, vii, xxviii, xxxvi, 41, 56, 59, 67, 76, 93, 114–15, 121, 130, 137, 149, 158, 185,

186, 189, 202, 207, 268, 296, 450, 463
Raja Suraj Singh, 439
Rajatarangini, 171, 290, 356
Raja Todar Mal, xv, xxiii, xxx, 101, 117, 121, 136, 147, 148, 153, 181, 188, 189, 198, 202, 212, 242–44, 246, 269, 283, 299, 332, 345, 353, 357, 359, 361
Raja Udai Singh of Mewar, xix, xxiii, 115, 185, 202, 302, 327, 328, 331
Raj Kanwar, 129
Rajkumari Nathi Bai, 129
Rajput clans,
    Mughal-Rajput alliance, 76, 209
Rajput jauhar, 96, 118, 202, 209, 236
Ramayan, xv, 290, 340–41, 450
Rana Prasad of Umerkot, xx, 17
Rana Sangha, 8, 114, 121, 208
Rani Durgavati, vii, xvi, xxxix, 95–96, 112, 175, 361
Rani Roopmati, xvi, 63, 64
Ranthambore, xxi, xxxvi, 77, 121, 122
Rao Kalyanmal, xxi, 129
Rathores, xxi, xxiii, 75, 118, 122, 327
Ratnabhavani, 368
Ratnasena, 368
Ravi River, 14, 34, 109, 337, 377, 386, 396, 397
Rawat Durga Das of Deogarhi, 131
Razmnama (The Book of War), xxiii, xxxi, 291, 292, 404
Rezavi, Syed Ali Nadeem, xxxvi, 162, 167, 190, 240
Richards, John F., 86, 191
Rogers, J. M., 22
Rumi's *Masnavi*, 282
Ruqaiya Begum, 28, 29, 44, 374, 388, 451, 461

Sadiq Khan, 181
Sa'di's Gulistan, 300
Safavids, xxviii, 222, 416
Salcette, 305
Salim's elephant,
    Giranbar, 459
Salima Sultan Begum, xii, xiii, 46, 59, 93, 158, 175, 196, 433, 442, 451
Salimi, 198
Salimuddin Chishti (Salim Chishti), 55, 123, 127, 147, 157, 158, 165, 266, 364, 467
Salt Range, 81, 244, 333
Samarkand, xxxiv, 3, 4, 5, 6, 7
Samkhya philosophy, 308
Sanganer, 75, 138, 139

Sanskrit, xv, 11, 13, 122, 135, 158, 170, 171, 172, 182, 221, 225, 242, 289, 290, 291, 295, 306, 327, 341, 356, 364, 366, 367, 370
sant tradition, 295
Sarangpur, 65
Satabadhana, 291
sati, xxxiii, xxxvii, 209, 236, 237, 302, 303, 327
Sayyid Beg, 78
Sayyid Mahmud of Baraha, 294
Sayyid Mir Quraish, 332
Schimmel, Annemarie, 35, 339
Sen, Geeti, 351
Seyller, John, 338, 432
Shah Abbas of Persia, 301
Shahabuddin Ahmad Khan, 55
Shahbaz Khan, 178, 207, 229, 285
Shah Fathullah Shirazi, 359
Shahi Qila, 336, 337
Shah Jahan (Khurram), xiii, xviii, xix, 208, 374, 388, 415, 416, 450, 452, 458, 460, 461, 463, 466
Shah Mansur, 210, 212, 256, 257
Shahpur, 181, 414
Shah Tahmasp of Persia, 19, 22, 78, 89, 90, 194, 210, 456
Shaibani Khan Uzbek, 6
Shaikh Abdullah Sultanpuri, 73, 311
Shaikh Abd un-Nabi (sadr us-sudoor), xvii, 73, 113, 121, 159, 190, 193, 215
Shaikh Ahmad Sirhindi, 193, 214, 313, 381, 467
shaikh al-Islam, 73
Shaikh Bhavan, 291
Shaikh Ghawth, 13
Shaikh Jamaluddin, 228
Shaikh Mubarak, xiv, xv, 54, 55, 146, 147, 170, 218, 227, 228, 229, 237, 276, 284, 297, 315, 348
Shaikh Mubarak Nagauri, 54
Shaikh Muhammad Ghaus, 444
Shaikh Phul, 13
Shaikh Rukn ud-din Rohilla, 372
Shaikh Salim, 127, 134, 147, 157, 158, 159, 165, 230, 427, 467
Shaikh Zada Gosala, 284
shaikhzadas, xxx, 8, 67, 74, 85, 121, 154, 205, 389
Shaitanpurah, 311
Shakr un-Nisa Begum, 326, 387
Shalimar Gardens (City of Gardens), 337
Shamsuddaulah Shah Nawaz Khan, 348
Shamsuddin Ataka Khan Ghaznavi, xii, 34,

43, 45, 49, 51, 53, 66, 67, 68, 74, 80, 81, 158, 425
Shankar, 349
Sharma, Sunil, 300, 356
Shattari Sufis, 13
Sher Khan, 13
Sher Shah Sur, xi, xx, xxvi, xxx, 13, 16, 21, 30, 31, 33, 57, 63, 70, 99, 101, 472
Shia Safavids, 416
Shihab al-Din Suhrawardi Maqtul, 276
shikhar khana, 53
Shiv Dutt Brahman, 388
Shivram, Balkrishan, 42
Siddhichandra, 308
sijda, 227, 350, 463
Sikandar Shah Sur, 32, 35, 36
Sindhi Begum, 377
Singhasan Battisi, 182, 225
Singh, Kavita, 29, 32, 240, 339, 403, 430, 432, 475
Sirhind, xx, 39, 50, 57, 112, 192, 260, 261, 392
Sisodiyas, 8, 416, 467
slavery, xxi, 82, 85, 103, 440
Smith, Vincent, 244
Sreenivasan, Ramya, 363, 366
Subedar of Bengal, 394, 415, 417, 424, 459
Subrahmanyam, Sanjay, 10, 222, 376, 407
suchi khanas, 312
Sufi Ahmed, 284
Sulaiman Karrani Afghan, 107, 175, 183, 189
Suleiman the Magnificent, 251, 456
sulh kul, xiii, xiv, xxxii, 281, 282, 284, 290, 358, 382, 468, 470, 471
Sultanam Begum (wife of Askari), xx, 20, 195
Sultan Bahadur, 12
Sultan Ghiyath Shah, 102
Sultan Khusrau, 327
Sultan Khwaja, 284
Sultan Thanesari, 291
Sunni Mughals, 416
Surat Singh, 263
Surdas, 349
Suryasahasranama, 309

Tabaqat-i-Akbari, 48
Taj Bibi, xxiii, 328
Taj Khan Karrani (Indo-Afghan ruler of Bengal), 136, 175
takauchiya, 154
Talikota, battle of, 406
Tansen Kalavant Gwaliyari (known as Tansen), xiv, 84, 85, 232, 295, 297, 315, 352, 353, 355, 360, 361
Tapa Gaccha sect, 306
Tardi Beg, 16, 35, 37, 38, 39, 43, 49
Tarikh-i Alfi, 274
taswir khana, xxxvii, 32, 91, 93, 305, 349, 428, 432, 444, 445
Thanesar, battle of, 258, 259
Thatta, 377, 386
Tiflis, 4
Tillotson, 475
Timurid–Chaghatai royals, 8
Timurid Mughals, xxviii
Timur (or Timour or Tamarlane), xi, xxxiv, 3, 4, 5, 6, 7, 9, 15, 17, 31, 63, 105, 136, 142, 149, 164, 245, 268, 269, 365, 387
Tipati, 301
tobacco in Mughal court, 447, 448
Transoxiana, 111, 387
Truschke, Audrey, 135, 291, 306, 341
Tughlaq, 5, 31, 63, 65, 75
Turani clan, 129
Turanis, 8, 67, 99, 112, 154, 263, 283, 294
Turkestan, 336
Tusi, 282
Tutinama, 93
Two Fighting Camels, 349

ulema, xv, xxxi, xxxiv, xxxviii, 12, 55, 73, 86, 113, 146, 167, 168, 169, 170, 190, 191, 192, 213, 214, 218, 219, 227, 228, 238, 247, 275, 324, 348, 383
Umerkot, xx, 17, 18
Uzbeks,
  death of Abdullah Khan Uzbek, 333
  Malwa brought under control, 78
  Sikandar Khan Uzbek, 106

vernacular languages, 11
Vijayanagar, 12, 35, 406
Vijayasena, 307, 308
Virsimhdevcarit, 368, 369, 440
Vithal Rai, 361

Wahdat-al-Wujud, 276
wakil-e-saltanat, xi, 35, 37, 51
wakil-i mutlak, 38
wazirat-i-diwan-i-kul, 99
Welch, Stuart Cary, 91

Yakub Shah Chak, 323
yassa law, xxi, 85

Yog Vashisht, 310
Yusuf Shah Chak, xxiii, 247, 323
Yusufzai, xiv, xxiii, 318, 332
Yusufzai Disaster, xxiii, 318

Zafar Khan or Muzaffar Shah, 136
    flight to Gujarat, 110
Zain Khan Koka, 149, 318, 329, 375, 404

Zamana Beg, 328
zarbaft, 273
Zarrin Qalam (Golden Pen), 338
zat, 204, 396, 469
zenana deorhi or rawala, 78, 131, 133
Zinda-Fil, 15
zuban-i-qudrut, 226